Removing Peoples

Studies of the German Historical Institute London

GENERAL EDITOR: Andreas Gestrich

Political Languages in the Age of Extremes
Edited by Willibald Steinmetz

The Voice of the Citizen Consumer
A History of Market Research, Consumer Movements, and the Political Public Sphere
Edited by Kerstin Brückweh

The Holy Roman Empire 1495–1806
Edited by R. J. W. Evans, Michael Schaich, and Peter H. Wilson

Unemployment and Protest
New Perspectives on Two Centuries of Contention
Edited by Matthias Reiss and Matt Perry

Wilhelmine Germany and Edwardian Britain
Essays on Cultural Affinity
Edited by Dominik Geppert and Robert Gerwarth

The Diplomats' World
A Cultural History of Diplomacy, 1815–1914
Edited by Markus Mösslang and Torsten Riotte

European Aristocracies and the Radical Right 1918–1939
Edited by Karina Urbach

The Street as Stage
Protest Marches and Public Rallies since the Nineteenth Century
Edited by Matthias Reiss

Monarchy and Religion
The Transformation of Royal Culture in Eighteenth-Century Europe
Edited by Michael Schaich

Science across the European Empires, 1800–1950
Edited by Benedikt Stuchtey

The Postwar Challenge
Cultural, Social, and Political Change in Western Europe, 1945–1958
Edited by Dominik Geppert

Writing World History, 1800–2000
Edited by Benedikt Stuchtey and Eckhardt Fuchs

Britain and Germany in Europe, 1949–1990
Edited by Jeremy Noakes, Peter Wende, and Jonathan Wright

The Mechanics of Internationalism
Culture, Society, and Politics from the 1840s to the First World War
Edited by Martin H. Geyer and Johannes Paulmann

Private Law and Social Inequality in the Industrial Age
Comparing Legal Cultures in Britain, France, Germany, and the United States
Edited by Willibald Steinmetz

British and German Historiography, 1750–1950
Traditions, Perceptions, and Transfers
Edited by Benedikt Stuchtey and Peter Wende

Rethinking Leviathan
The Eighteenth-Century State in Britain and Germany
Edited by John Brewer and Eckhart Hellmuth

England and Germany in the High Middle Ages
Edited by Alfred Haverkamp and Hanna Vollrath

Removing Peoples
Forced Removal in the Modern World

EDITED BY

RICHARD BESSEL

AND

CLAUDIA B. HAAKE

GERMAN HISTORICAL INSTITUTE LONDON

OXFORD
UNIVERSITY PRESS

OXFORD
UNIVERSITY PRESS

Great Clarendon Street, Oxford OX2 6DP

Oxford University Press is a department of the University of Oxford.
It furthers the University's objective of excellence in research, scholarship,
and education by publishing worldwide in

Oxford New York

Auckland Cape Town Dar es Salaam Hong Kong Karachi
Kuala Lumpur Madrid Melbourne Mexico City Nairobi
New Delhi Shanghai Taipei Toronto

With offices in

Argentina Austria Brazil Chile Czech Republic France Greece
Guatemala Hungary Italy Japan Poland Portugal Singapore
South Korea Switzerland Thailand Turkey Ukraine Vietnam

Oxford is a registered trade mark of Oxford University Press
in the UK and in certain other countries

Published in the United States
by Oxford University Press Inc., New York

© The German Historical Institute London 2009

The moral rights of the authors have been asserted
Database right Oxford University Press (maker)

First published 2009
First published in paperback 2011

All rights reserved. No part of this publication may be reproduced,
stored in a retrieval system, or transmitted, in any form or by any means,
without the prior permission in writing of Oxford University Press,
or as expressly permitted by law, or under terms agreed with the appropriate
reprographics rights organization. Enquiries concerning reproduction
outside the scope of the above should be sent to the Rights Department,
Oxford University Press, at the address above

You must not circulate this book in any other binding or cover
and you must impose the same condition on any acquirer

British Library Cataloguing in Publication Data
Data available

Library of Congress Cataloging in Publication Data
Data available

Typeset by John Saunders Design & Production
Printed in Great Britain
on acid-free paper by
The MPG Books Group, Bodmin and King's Lynn

ISBN 978–0–19–956195–7 (Hbk)
ISBN 978–0–19–969872–1 (Pbk)

Editors' Foreword

This volume arises from the conference 'Removing Peoples: Forced Migration in the Modern World', which was held at York in April 2006. The conference would not have been possible without the help and generosity of many people and institutions, for which we are deeply grateful. We owe special thanks to the Thyssen Foundation for their especially generous support for the conference, together with the German Historical Institutes in London and Washington, and the Department of History at the University of York (UK).

The contributions of a number of people were crucial in the production of this volume. Without the commitment and help of Professor Hagen Schulze, then Director of the German Historical Institute in London, Dr Benedikt Stuchtey (Deputy Director), Dr Indra Sengupta, and Wolfgang Haack, we could not have got this project off the ground; and without the editorial work of Angela Davies this book would not have appeared. Professors Christof Mauch and Dirk Schumann, respectively Director and Deputy Director at the German Historical Institute in Washington, DC, at the time of the conference, were extremely supportive of the idea and helped us make it a reality. We also would have been unable to organize the conference without the help of a number of people at the University of York, in particular Professor Mark Ormrod (then Head of the History Department) and Johan de Jong, who served as conference administrator, ensured that everything ran smoothly, and even took participants to the gym.

We also want to thank all of those who attended the conference and enriched our discussions, including those participants who gave papers but who, for a variety of reasons (including giving birth), were unable to commit to the very tight publication schedule. And last but not least, we thank the two readers who consented to review the manuscript at short notice and who encouraged us with their praise and improved the volume through their critical suggestions.

Richard Bessel and Claudia B. Haake

York and Washington, DC
February 2008

Contents

List of Figures	ix
List of Maps	x
List of Tables	xi

Part I: Introductory Remarks

1. Introduction: Forced Removal in the Modern World   3
   RICHARD BESSEL AND CLAUDIA B. HAAKE

2. Explaining Forced Migration   13
   ALF LÜDTKE

Part II: Forced Removal and Indigenous Peoples

3. On the Trail of Tears: Daniel Butrick's Record of the
   Removal of the Cherokees   35
   TIM ALAN GARRISON

4. Breaking the Bonds of People and Land   79
   CLAUDIA B. HAAKE

5. The Federal Indian Relocation Programme of the
   1950s and the Urbanization of Indian Identity   107
   DONALD L. FIXICO

6. Calculating Lives: The Number and Narratives of
   Removals in Queensland, 1859–1972   131
   MARK COPLAND

7. The Slave Trade as Enforced Migration in the Central
   Sudan of West Africa   149
   PAUL E. LOVEJOY

Part III: Forced Removal and War

8. The Great Unweaving: The Removal of Peoples in
   Europe, 1875–1949   167
   DONALD BLOXHAM

viii CONTENTS

9. Explaining Genocide: The Fate of the Armenians in
the Late Ottoman Empire 209
RONALD GRIGOR SUNY

10. Trial Run: The Deportation of the Terek Cossacks
1920 255
SHANE O'ROURKE

11. National and International Planning of the 'Transfer'
of Germans from Czechoslovakia and Poland 281
DETLEF BRANDES

12. 'Nobody's People': The Dalits of Punjab in the
Forced Removal of 1947 297
GYANENDRA PANDEY

13. The 1947 Partition of India and Migration:
A Comparative Study of Punjab and Bengal 321
IAN TALBOT

14. Explaining Transfer: Zionist Thinking and the
Creation of the Palestinian Refugee Problem 349
BENNY MORRIS

Part IV: Forced Removal in Post-Colonial Times

15. Sustainable Violence: Mass Resettlement, Strategic
Villages, and Militias in Anti-Guerrilla Warfare 361
CHRISTIAN GERLACH

16. Coerced or Free? Considering Post-Colonial Returns 395
ANDREA SMITH

Part V: Concluding Thoughts

17. Comparing Forced Removals 417
JOANNA DE GROOT

Notes on Contributors 439
Index 445

List of Figures

6.1 Stated reasons for removal   138

6.2 Removals with health as a stated reason   138

List of Maps

4.1 Removal of the Delawares   83

4.2 Removal of the Yaquis   93

List of Tables

15.1 Resettlement and militias in anti-guerrilla warfare
since 1932   362–3

PART I
Introductory Remarks

1

Introduction:
Forced Removal in the Modern World

RICHARD BESSEL AND CLAUDIA B. HAAKE

One of the most terrible themes of modern history has been the forced removal of millions of human beings. During the past two centuries scarcely a corner of the world has been spared the violence of the forced removal of people from their homes for political, economic, 'racial', religious, or cultural reasons. Recent history is littered with examples, ranging from well-known cases such as the fate of the Palestinians, the peoples of former Yugoslavia, and the Maasai of Kenya—cases which have put this dreadful phenomenon squarely in the public gaze—to those much less prominent in popular consciousness and involving indigenous peoples in various places around the world. Of course, the forced removal of groups from their homes is hardly something novel or invented in the modern era. However, its occurrence across the world as a mass phenomenon is peculiarly modern.

This constitutes the subject of the present volume. During the nineteenth and twentieth centuries, a number of factors combined to make forced removal a global phenomenon on a massive scale. These include the use of extensive apparatuses of organization and of modern technology. The combination of the development of a global capitalist economy, the emergence of modern race thinking, the conduct of two world wars, and the triumph of popular and national sovereignty has given this dreadful phenomenon a quantitatively and qualitatively new character. At the same time, the failure of modern efforts to control population movement and migration by more civilized means has led states to consider forced removal.

'Modern' does not necessarily refer to something that is radically new, but often to an updated version of something old. Although the practice of forced removal undoubtedly changed

4   RICHARD BESSEL and CLAUDIA B. HAAKE

with the application of modern technology, for example, the practice cannot simply be regarded as its consequence. Rather, there is a two-way street: new technologies together with ideology have affected practice. When it became physically possible to remove human beings from their places of settlement on a mass scale, people began to consider doing just that—and especially so in times of crisis connected with war, colonization, and decolonization.

To date, forced removal as a modern phenomenon has been given relatively little attention by historians.[1] Studies of the phenomenon in various contexts do exist, but these tend to be limited to exploration of particular examples.[2] The few studies that have approached the topic from a broader perspective have considered it within the frame of regional history.[3] We still lack comparative investigations, although Dirk Hoerder has made some advance in this regard through his study of world migration, *Cultures in Contact*, which considers voluntary, coerced and forced migrations. The collection of essays *Coerced and Free Migration*, edited by David Eltis, also has a comparative element; however, while it focuses mainly on forced and free migration in the Atlantic world and establishes a clear link between the need for labour and (coerced) migration, it does not consider the mass and global occurrence of the phenomenon as the peculiarly modern one that we suggest it is.[4]

That the pervasiveness of mass forced removal in the modern world (shown in this volume by Donald Bloxham among others) has tended to be overlooked thus far may be due in part to the analytical framework applied. Many recent studies have focused on genocide or 'ethnic cleansing', concepts that are related to that of forced removal but are not identical to it. In the case of

[1] Dirk Hoerder has commented on this lack of scholarship. See *Cultures in Contact: World Migrations in the Second Millennium* (Durham, NC, 2002), 1 and 8.

[2] e.g. Gyanendra Pandey, *Remembering Partition: Violence, Nationalism and History in India* (Cambridge, 2001); Lotte Hughes, *Moving the Maasai: A Colonial Misadventure* (Basingstoke, 2006); Claudia B. Haake, *The State, Removal and Indigenous Peoples in the United States and Mexico, c.1620–2000* (New York, 2007).

[3] See Hoerder, *Cultures in Contact*, 8.

[4] David Eltis (ed.), *Coerced and Free Migration: Global Perspectives* (Stanford, Calif., 2002). For another investigation of the middle passage as forced migration within the context of the formation of the modern world, see Emma Christopher, Cassandra Pybus, and Marcus Rediker (eds.), *Many Middle Passages: Forced Migration and the Making of the Modern World* (Berkeley, 2007).

Introduction

genocide and 'ethnic cleansing', the focus is upon the attempt to destroy people and/or the actual achievement of this goal; in the case of forced removal, the focus is upon the displacement of people, something which may take many forms, only one of which is their physical destruction. Furthermore, the reasons for the removal of peoples more often than not have been no less multifaceted than those that have impelled genocide. Arguably, forced removal has also been a more widespread phenomenon than genocide, just as its consequences probably have been greater than those of genocide, if only because they are usually cross-generational and longer-lasting in nature. Studies framed by the concept of 'genocide' usually conclude when the attempted genocide either has been achieved or has failed; studies whose focus is 'forced removal' often are concerned more with the consequences of the event long after it has occurred. 'Forced removal' thus can perform descriptive and explanatory work of a kind that the frameworks offered by 'genocide' or 'ethnic cleansing' seldom attempt or cannot undertake.

Forced removal, as Alf Lüdtke and others point out here, can sometimes be part of a genocide and at other times can proceed or anticipate it. This suggests that forced removal and genocide, different though they may be, are often related and inter-connected phenomena. In contrast with the deadly intent of genocide, the focus with 'forced removal' is on removing or transplanting a group of people rather than killing them, though death often has been considered an unavoidable side-effect of the policy, an acceptable price to pay in order to achieve the under-lying aims of removal.

'Forced removal' is a framework which allows us to consider together practices that previously have been treated as distinct from one another, such as mass deportations like those of the Germans after the Second World War (discussed in this volume by Detlev Brandes) and the Yaquis in early twentieth-century Mexico (explored by Claudia Haake), expulsions from former colonies like that of the *pieds noirs* from Algeria (examined by Andrea Smith), and relocations like that of Native Americans in the United States of the 1950s (discussed by Donald Fixico). Yet, however useful we regard the concept of 'forced removal', we need to remain conscious that the term 'removal' is one created by the perpetrators of the policy and practices under consideration here. For example, it was employed during the 1830s by a United States government intent on clearing the lands east of the Mississippi of all Native Americans and was chosen for the specific purpose of making an aggressive and traumatic action sound tame and even benevolent.

We believe that 'forced removal' suggests more strongly than more customary terms, such as expulsion, deportation, or forced migration, that these very same processes have often been shaped by actors and agents other than just the state, and that in many of the cases discussed in this volume those actors or agents have proved crucial both for the occurrence of the phenomenon and for its outcomes. 'Forced removal' is also more suggestive of the push and pull factors that can shape the practice of removing peoples from their homes. That is not to say that (forced) removal is distinct from the other phenomena mentioned above, but rather that it can encompass them.

The need to look afresh at the causes of the forcible removal of so many millions of people from their homes over the past two centuries raises a number of questions, as we already have implied. To what extent can forced removal be explained with reference to the growth of race-thinking—of the idea that there is a 'racial' hierarchy of human worth? To what extent was it a consequence of the triumph of nationalism, of popular and national sovereignty, which presupposes defining who does *not* constitute the 'people' as a corollary of defining who does? Can the forced removal of so many people be attributed to a break-down of civilized values and patterns of behaviour as a consequence of war, and particularly of the wars of the twentieth century? Was forced removal necessarily the consequence of war, or of colonial endeavours and their unravelling? How was it facilitated by modern technological advances, which made such practices possible in new and comprehensive ways? These and related questions, focusing mostly on the causes of, but also on the responses to, forced removal are addressed by the contributors to this volume, which attempts to explain how it happened that in the past two centuries millions of human beings across the world were forced from their homes—with many being killed in the process—in attempts to transfer whole peoples from the lands in and on which they had settled.

While we might regard the cases of forced removal discussed

Introduction

in this volume as products of developments which characterize the modern age, the diversity of the removal experiences is striking, and the causes of forced removals have been complex. These causes have involved (but have not necessarily been limited to) economic and strategic considerations as well as issues of inclusion and exclusion (that is, of belonging to a people)—factors which in turn have often been shaped by cultural, religious, and ethnic/racial considerations, and the relationship of people to land.

Where forced removal has been initiated by states for political and strategic ends, the considerations involved frequently have been economic ones, focusing to a significant degree on land. Economic factors gained new force with the global expansion of capitalism in the nineteenth and twentieth centuries. Coveting land as a resource or a commodity was among the prime incentives for removing people from it. In some cases, as in the removal of the Cherokees and Delawares in the United States and the Yaquis in Mexico, land was sought as a commodity and consequently had to be 'freed' from its Indigenous owners. Similarly, in the case of the Armenians, land was coveted because of its increasing scarcity, and competition for land has figured prominently in the conflicts among Arabs and Jews in Israel/Palestine. In some instances, the control of land allowed the control and removal of people, while in others control and removal of people was necessary to achieve control of land. Thus in his contribution on slavery as enforced migration in the Sokoto Caliphate, Paul Lovejoy discusses how gaining power over a territory allowed control over a people who were viewed as a commodity, and thus enabled the reaping of benefits from their economic value as slaves.

States frequently regarded forced removal as a solution to a perceived problem. A case in point is the movement of population that accompanied the Partition of India, examined here (from differing perspectives) by Gyanendra Pandey and Ian Talbot. In another instance, discussed here by Ronald Suny, Turkish nationalists decided to take action against a perceived threat: as the crumbling Ottoman Empire struggled to cope with foreign threats, defensive efforts by the Armenians in Anatolia were misinterpreted as hostile acts and the decision was taken to eliminate what was seen as a long-standing enemy. The drastic steps taken by the Ottoman government were made yet worse by the actions of non-state actors on the ground, who saw themselves as the legitimate yet cheated providers of the benefits that the Empire had brought and who were eager to destroy a people they viewed as a competitor for land and other resources.

Considerations similar to those at the heart of the conflict in Anatolia were a significant element in the expulsion of Germans from Poland and Czechoslovakia after the Second World War, and form the subject of Detlef Brandes's contribution. There, forced removal took the shape of revenge and retaliation against what was seen as an 'eternal German foe'. At the same time, the removal of the German population had the strategic aim of preventing the recurrence in the future of problems similar to those which had arisen before and during the Second World War. Strategic considerations also appear to have driven the forced removal of the Cossacks in the 1920s, the first mass deportation during the Soviet period. In a context of ethnic conflict between Cossacks, Chechen, and Ingush, the Soviet government began to assert that identification with a particular ethnic group was a sign of political disloyalty and sought to address this perceived threat by adopting the simple but drastic method of removing the Cossacks. As Shane O'Rourke notes in his essay, this drew on contemporary European practices employed in the colonies and set a fateful precedent for future actions by the Soviet regime. Strategic concerns also influenced the forced resettlement of people into 'strategic hamlets' in countries across the globe—from Kenya and Algeria to Vietnam, Guatemala, and Peru—during the second half of the twentieth century. As Christian Gerlach points out in his essay, these 'hamlets' were supposed to protect not only national territories and borders, but also political ideologies and economic resources.

In some instances, removal was shaped by considerations that had little if anything to do with the people targeted for uprooting. In the case of the removal of the Cherokees in nineteenth-century America, the subject of Tim Garrison's contribution, the decision was influenced by a struggle over state and federal rights in the United States. The Southern states were fiercely protective of their rights, and they interpreted the insistence of the Federal Government on its jurisdiction over interaction with American Indian tribes as an intrusion into the affairs of the states. Such

Introduction

considerations, regardless of the real or perceived fears or goals they were meant to address, did not preclude the existence of double standards both within governments and among the citizenry. As Mark Copland demonstrates in his essay on the removal of Aboriginal people in Queensland, it appears that the rationales given for campaigns of removal were seldom real but often were subterfuges that masked the true motivations, which tended to be economic. On some occasions it was the labour of the deportees which was most important; on others it was the raising of money to defray administrative expenses; on yet others it was simply the quest for a cheaper way to 'store' troublesome Natives. Similarly, as Claudia Haake's comparison of Native removal in Mexico and the United States in the later nineteenth century demonstrates, the benevolence which ostensibly impelled the policy of removal in the United States was but one factor among many.

Usually, the state has been the main instrument of forced removal, but the role of people on the ground was also crucial, as a number of the studies in this volume illustrate. For example, as Alf Lüdtke argues, those who actually carry out the forced removal have often determined the sequence of events when people are forced from their homes. In other cases, bystanders played an important role. Nowhere is this more evident than with regard to the property that had belonged to the victims of campaigns of forced removal. For example, after the displacement of the Cherokees, white Southerners rushed to loot what had been left behind; the possessions of the Armenians were seized by former neighbours who had participated in the expulsions and even in the massacres; Chechen and Ingush peoples entered the vacated Cossack settlements to grab belongings that had been left behind; and the property abandoned by evacuees after the Partition of India was taken by new arrivals looking to make a home for themselves after they had been forced from their own homes. The active involvement of non-state actors should not be overlooked, not least as their motive for participating in campaigns of forced removal often diverged significantly from those of governments. Furthermore, in virtually all the cases examined here the targets of forced removal were not merely passive victims. Their behaviour could also shape the ways in which the practice was carried out.

In all the cases explored in this volume, the question of belonging lay at the heart of the matter. Whatever the factors driving forced removal—whether these were economic, strategic, ideological, or a mixture of all three; whether fuelled by fear or a craving for revenge and retaliation; whether animated by a desire to protect or to destroy; whether based on religious belief, cultural identification, or notions of race and ethnicity—carrying it out necessitated determining who belonged within an 'imagined community' and who did not.

The question of belonging, it should be noted moreover, did not necessarily disappear once removal had taken place. The impact of forced removal on its victims (and on its perpetrators) does not end with the deed itself, but has had long-term consequences. Thus, for example, the *pieds noirs*, the Dutch, and the Portuguese compelled to leave their homes after decolonization often found after their arrival in their so-called homelands that they were not deemed to belong; instead they were frequently regarded as outsiders or even intruders, and sometimes were not even granted citizenship rights. Yet some achieved acceptance more quickly and easily than others. Notions of 'race' or phenotype could play a role in this: the less different one appeared, the more easily one could be accepted.

All the cases described and analysed in this book are still remembered vividly today, whether they occurred in the nineteenth or in the twentieth century. They have a presence today, another thing that makes them distinctly modern. This may be because the problems that forced removals tried to resolve or eliminate persist in one form or another, or because people have come to regard the practice in a different light from earlier generations, or because we have become more aware of some of the long-term consequences of forced removals. It may be that we continue to debate the events discussed in this volume because their meaning still eludes us, or because the different narratives which are employed to explain instances of forced removal are too divergent to coexist peacefully. Indeed, part of the difficulty involved in talking about forced removal as a modern phenomenon may arise from the fact that we still are coming to grips with it and would rather relegate it to a past disconnected from our present. Issues of guilt, retribution, commemoration, and the presence of the past have all

Introduction

contributed to historical contestation. As Joanna de Groot remarks in her contribution, when power remains unequal in the wake of past removals, discussion about these events continues.

Thus many of the events discussed in this volume remain subjects of heated debate and controversy. The campaigns against Armenians, the treatment of Australian Aborigines, and the displacement of Palestinians, resonate and provoke dispute and strong opinion. This is reflected in Benny Morris's essay, which views the creation of many modern states as the result of population transfer and credits it with the 'pacification' of areas of Europe through the elimination of minority communities. The suggestion that forced removal, awful though it is for the people involved, may offer a solution to otherwise insoluable conflicts, is both controversial and challenging. And it goes to the heart of the difficulties involved in pursuing this subject.

While the contributions to this volume may help to answer some questions about forced removal as a modern phenomenon, they should also prompt the formulation of new ones. We hope this volume will make a contribution towards understanding the complex mechanisms of human domination and the causes and consequences of one of the major sources of human suffering in the modern world.

2

Explaining Forced Migration

ALF LÜDTKE

Practices: 'How did (s)he do it?'

The desire to find explanations for the 'doings' of historical actors apparently resonates with the 'extremes' that millions of people encountered during the twentieth century.[1] Such desire obviously sparks the continuous interest if not obsession both of the historical profession and the wider public in finding, for instance, 'the one and only' document that contains the order for exterminating European Jewry, signed by Hitler or one of his paladins. From here, so the internal logic seems to go, one could pursue the events down the 'line of command', not least the forced migration of the related deportations, and their fit to this man-made catastrophe. Yet most people would agree: any written declaration of intent to that effect may be a necessary but nevertheless not a sufficient element for understanding—or explaining—the Holocaust in general and the related forced migrations in particular.

Raul Hilberg pioneered the analysis of the political and, in particular, the administrative process of marking 'Jews' and others who were similarly labelled as 'racially unfit' (such as the people often referred to as 'Gypsies'), of excluding them and, in due course, of deporting and, finally, exterminating them.[2] The machinery of administration and its functionality for any purpose occupies the centre of Hilberg's explorations. Thus it is the bureaucratic persona that emerges from his scrupulous analyses. This self-'administered individual' (H. G. Adler) in many ways

---

[1] Eric Hobsbawm, *The Age of Extremes: The Short Twentieth Century, 1914–1991* (London, 1994).

[2] Raul Hilberg, *The Destruction of the European Jews* (rev. edn., New York, 1985); id., *The Politics of Memory* (New York, 1994). For the distant if not hostile stance of members of the Institut für Zeitgeschichte (Munich) in the late 1950s and 1960s towards the work of Joseph Wulf, effectively excluding him from professional exchange, see Nicolas Berg, *Der Holocaust und die westdeutschen Historiker: Erforschung und Erinnerung* (Göttingen, 2004).

resonated with the portrait Hannah Arendt drew of one of the vice-captains of annihilation, Adolf Eichmann. Her phrase, the 'banality of evil', applied to Eichmann and his co-perpetrators, stirred much protest. At the same time, however, this concept brilliantly captured one of the two dimensions of 'doing' mass killing: organizational routine and skilled paperwork. Others added their manual labour at the killing sites themselves.[3]

In his studies Raul Hilberg focused on perpetrators, but the main emphasis of his work has been on the institutional settings and administrative procedures that allowed for and routinized the practices of exclusion, demarcation, and deportation, and, finally, extermination of European Jewry. In Hilberg's research the actual practices of killing remained out of sight. Here, pioneering studies were authored in the 1960s by another outsider to established historiography, Joseph Wulf. In his research on the Łodz ghetto and Warsaw ghetto respectively he focused on the victims.[4]

Both Hilberg and Wulf neglected the themes that dominated academic research at that time: policy and ideology. What is more, their investigations did not gear towards the general picture, the annihilation of millions of people. Rather, in their studies they tried to scrutinize the actual processes of excluding those who were marked by the state authorities and ruling party as 'foes' or 'subhuman': how did perpetrators, and bystanders as well, do or support it, tracing and segregating ordinary citizens, even neighbours? And who segregated and denigrated, deported and killed these people (and how)?[5]

Only since the late 1980s have others elaborated on this topic, widening its scope and enriching its perspective.[6] These studies have not only made increasing use of court records but have also

[3] Cf. Hannah Arendt, *Eichmann in Jerusalem: A Report on the Banality of Evil* (London, 1963); see also H. G. Adler, *Der verwaltete Mensch: Studien zur Deportation der Juden aus Deutschland* (Tübingen, 1974).

[4] Joseph Wulf, *Vom Leben, Kampf und Tod im Ghetto Warschau* (Bonn, 1960); id., *Das letzte Ghetto auf polnischem Boden* (Bonn, 1962).

[5] Götz Aly, *'Endlösung': Völkerverschiebung und der Mord an den europäischen Juden* (Frankfurt am Main, 1995).

[6] In particular the work by Christopher Browning has alluded to concrete ways of 'doing' the killing. His zooming in on specific cases does not show any kind of 'standard' practice. Instead, his approach reveals ranges of (non-)participation, of doing or not doing things. See Christopher Browning, *Ordinary Men: Reserve Police Battalion 101 and the Final Solution in Poland* (New York, 1992).

Explaining Forced Migration

used accounts of survivors and recollections from bystanders. They reveal both myriad forms of suffering and of distancing or resisting—and they also show the manifold practices of cooperation within support for official policies. Not least, these narratives made clear that bystanders only rarely 'stood by'.[7] Many applauded, for instance, the degrading of people who were accused of *Rassenschande*.[8] Others nodded approvingly while the person standing next to them may have turned away or shaken his or her head; and the same people or others may have formed a human corridor as deportees were herded to the railway station for deportation. At any rate, many did more than simply 'stand by', even if they were not directly among those who regularly, or occasionally, actually perpetrated acts of forced removal and, hence, extermination.[9] These examples indicate the ranges and degrees of active participation or active support, even if many who acted in that way never wanted to or did remember.

From this angle it becomes even more obvious that the causal model has clear limits for explanation. It does not grasp the complexity and multiplicity of societal or, for that matter, historical practices and situations. Attempts to link X as 'causal' to Y— if X, then Y—do not work. (That, however, was implied by the Hempel/Nagel model that has been popular among social scientists since the 1950s: accordingly, under given circumstances the occurrence of X would result in Y.[10]) But it is neither just the big criminals nor the anonymous forces that drive people, even behind their backs. Instead, research ought to focus on everyone, on every setting or situation, whether 'on top' or 'on the ground', and on what individual people did. It must ask: *how did he or she do it?*

More concretely, how did German administrators and academics design plans for reshuffling 'peoples in the east', especially after the occupation of Poland in 1939? These were plans

---

[7] Raul Hilberg, *Perpetrators, Victims, Bystanders: The Jewish Catastrophe 1933–1945* (New York, 1993).

[8] Alexandra Przyrembel, *'Rassenschande': Reinheitsmythos und Vernichtungslegitimation im Nationalsozialismus* (Göttingen, 2003).

[9] Michael Wildt, 'Gewalt gegen Juden', *WerkstattGeschichte*, 6/18 (1997), 59–80.

[10] Carl Hempel, 'The Function of General Laws in History', in H. Feigl and W. Sellars (eds.), *Readings in Philosophical Analysis* (New York, 1949), 459–71; Ernest Nagel, *The Structure of Science* (London, 1961), 454–6, and esp. 558; see also Jürgen Habermas, *Zur Logik der Sozialwissenschaften*, Philosophische Rundschau 5 (Tübingen, 1967), 30–2.

that entailed the expulsion of Jews and non-Jewish Poles on a mass scale, in order to enable the 'resettling' of so-called 'native Germans' from the sites they had made their own for generations in south-eastern and eastern Europe. At the level of individual activity: *how* did the young Melita Maschmann perform in 1942–3 when she was in charge of a labour camp in occupied Poland, in the Warthegau, and became involved in the resettlement of 'native Germans'?[11] Or, *how* did 'resettled' people deal with their removal; how did Jewish and non-Jewish expellees go about it? Materials such as those preserved in the Ringelblum archive,[12] and the recollections of survivors, allow some answers about the perceptions and the ways of coping among people who were targeted by Nazi policies of removal and expulsion. Not least, what impact did experience or imaginations of colonization, in particular, of colonial violence, have? In what sense and to what degree did the resulting 'colonial fantasies' fuel the violent fervour for labelling, excluding, and expelling 'enemies' of the German Reich, the German *Volk*, or the 'Aryan race' after 1933?

How can one approach the grey zones of cooperation between the dominant and the dominated, the occupiers and the occupied? This mix did not simply 'occur', but was produced in people's everyday lives, whether in commercial or industrial firms, in administrations, or in the military—and among inmates of concentration camps. Thus such a mix was instrumentalized time and again by the camp guards and, consequently, served to promote ruthlessness among those targeted for exclusion if not extermination.[13]

Terms: Blind for Violence?

The term 'forced migration' was accepted by the fifteenth edition of the *Encyclopaedia Britannica* in the 1970s.[14] This is certainly

[11] Melita Maschmann, *Fazit: Kein Rechtfertigungsversuch* (Stuttgart, 1963).

[12] Ruta Sakowska, *Die zweite Etappe ist der Tod: NS-Ausrottungspolitik gegen die polnischen Juden, gesehen mit den Augen der Opfer* (Wrocław, 1986; Berlin, 1999).

[13] Cf. Christopher Browning, 'Jewish Workers and Survivor Memories: The Case of the Starachowice Labor Camp', in id., *Nazi Policy, Jewish Workers, German Killers* (Cambridge, 2000), 89–115; Primo Levi, *The Drowned and the Saved* (London, 1989).

[14] *The New Encyclopaedia Britannica, Macropaedia*, xii (Chicago, 1976), 186–7.

Explaining Forced Migration

indicative for the English-speaking world. In the German-speaking context, more precisely, in West Germany, the term which covered that area was 'expulsion' (*Vertreibung*). In East Germany the authorities banned this term. And it was precisely this effort which kept it present in public consciousness.[15]

Specific emphases and, thus, horizons of these terms refer to the particular contexts of their usages. During my childhood in 1950s West Germany, 'expulsion' or *Vertreibung* were treated as seemingly natural and given catastrophes that had hit people without any man-made impact. The rhetoric of politicians and of the mass media reverberated with such parlance, as it was dominant not only among people whom my parents knew and met with. At coffee tables and in pubs throughout the socio-political spectrum the term for 'it' was—expulsion. The issue was, of course, the forced removal or expulsion of 'ethnic Germans' from territories of what was then Poland and Czechoslovakia which many, at least at that time, still claimed as 'German'. Using this word meant simultaneously to mourn the expellees and to denounce those who had expelled them. Furthermore, this usage granted the expellees a position of innocent victimhood. The term reflects and reverberates with immediate action conveying some of the shocks or violence both at the centre of the practice of the perpetrators and of the experience of those targeted.

By contrast, the term 'forced migration' resonates with a view of society and history that emphasizes processes of a somewhat longer duration. After all, the main reference is migration. At least the term presents it as a process without any definite limit, going on for weeks and months if not years, and having a bearing for one's lifetime if not beyond. At the same time, and in contrast to 'expulsion', the emotional flavour of the term smacks of a certain optimism which even the adjective 'forced' does not totally erase. The term still rings with some of the brighter sides of history. Thus, even as 'forced migration', the modernizing appeal of processes of change that seem truly fundamental for the modern era seeps through. And, again in contrast to 'expulsion', the observers are looking from afar and from above. Yet it is not just the commanding heights that invite such a view (and

---

[15] See policies and terminology in, among others, Volker Ackermann, *Der 'echte' Flüchtling: Deutsche Vertriebene und Flüchtlinge aus der DDR 1945–1961* (Osnabrück, 1995).

18 ALF LÜDTKE

terminology). Such relative distance also seems implied when ethnographers try to look 'closely', aiming for 'thick description'.

The notion normalizes what people have encountered as removal. Even the adjective 'forced' covers up the sheer brute violence which is at the centre of all such removals. What is specifically missing is the emotional charge on both sides: the rage and revenge (if not pleasure) among those who did the expelling; the mixture of anger, desperation, and hatred among those who were expelled, hatred of those who inflicted (or seem to have inflicted) misery and grief on oneself. To be sure, the latter are the emotions of victims: expulsion emphasizes victimhood. Still, it also reflects the will or desire of the instigator, perhaps for vengeance, as in the 'wild expulsions' of Germans in 1945 in Poland and Czech areas, but also in the context of more orderly removals such as those in the same regions in 1946–7. At the same time, the term reverberates with the violence that is at the very centre of expulsion.

This violence was produced and encountered in interactions. Thus the study of face-to-face settings and configurations is central. This holds for the academics who, in German academic institutions and the centres of the SS establishment, since 1937 and 1938 had drawn up plans for the expulsion and resettlement of Jewish and non-Jewish Poles, and also of native Germans.[16] This similarly holds for various levels of the SS and ministerial bureaucracies: in particular, for subordinate administrative units, those who actually operated 'on the ground'. These low-level officials or police (or soldiers) had only rarely 'volunteered'. However, many did not just plod along grudgingly, but began to invest ambition and zeal if not pride in their task. The same holds, for instance, for the drivers of locomotives or the clerks who drafted lists in an office or on a railway platform. In sum, there was ample daily and, not least, nightly activity among the many who made 'it' work. Plans from 'Berlin' and orders from superiors turned into that very 'corporeality' which we historians face when considering the wide margin of self-guidance among those who actually handled things and people.

It is this field of forces that deserves much more scrutiny. Of

[16] On this see Michael Wildt (ed.), *Die Judenpolitik des SD 1935 bis 1938: Eine Dokumentation* (Munich, 1995); id., *Generation des Unbedingten: Das Führungskorps des Reichssicherheitshauptamtes* (Hamburg, 2002).

Explaining Forced Migration

course, local and regional studies and survivors' reports have touched on this issue of active, sometimes spontaneous participation in removing or expelling people: that is, in threatening or inflicting violence.

Forced Migration—'Ethnic Cleansing'—Genocide

The very term 'forced migration' implies that ordinary migration does not involve force. According to a widely established understanding both inside and outside academia, two 'factors' drive migration: push and pull. For instance, it may be the push of hunger or starvation that drives people to migrate. In a more abstract view, social deprivation and economic misery can make survival extremely hard if not unlikely unless one migrates. Letters or accounts by priests and administrators 'on the ground' testify abundantly to such drives among those who departed for the 'new world', for instance in sixteenth- and seventeenth-century Spain, in nineteenth-century Hesse or Swabia, in southern Italy, or in the 1870s or 1880s in the easternmost provinces of the German and Austro-Hungarian empires and in the western provinces of the Russian Empire. But it was precisely these migrants who vividly claimed the attraction (or 'pull') of this 'new world', promising relief, and perhaps joy and happiness, for themselves or their children.

Forced migration means something else.[17] It is not the 'push' of dire living conditions or waning job opportunities; nor is it the stern single-mindedness of semi-feudal lords or factory owners who gave no thought to 'just prices' or 'just wages'. 'Forced migration' refers to the very physical violence of police batons or the military's guns, to the violence executed in the name, if not by the consent, of state authorities.

In modern times such violence has become the 'productive force' of 'ethnic cleansing'. Notions of and aspirations for national identity were wide open to almost any attempts to draw distinctions between 'us' and 'them'. Others have shown that the 'biopolitical dispositive' (Michel Foucault) of 'pure blood' capitalized

---

[17] On the complex interrelationships of free and 'unfree labour' and, in turn, 'forced migration' see Paul E. Lovejoy and Nicholas Rogers (eds.), *Unfree Labour in the Development of the Atlantic World* (Ilford, 1994).

on the promise of scientific precision and truth and fuelled a vigorous dynamic of its own. In post-colonial histories this drive has not ceased to operate; the case of Rwanda from 1994 is mentioned often in this respect. But what is frequently overlooked, at least in Europe, is Partition in India and the expulsions undertaken for such 'cleansing'; Gyanendra Pandey gives a powerful account of this in his essay in this volume.

Across different historical cases the respective debates and activities revolved around images and notions of national identity, if not purity. They often triggered processes of erecting or solidifying national states. Efforts to mark border lines and purify those on the inside focused on, for instance, a national language, thus eradicating dialects or minority languages. A case in point in the early and mid nineteenth century is the rigorous measures of the French central state to ban the Norman-Celtic language in the north-west or Provençal in the south; similarly, dialects were stigmatized as outcast and administratively outlawed in public schools in the mid twentieth century in Germany.

Purification was demanded even more forcefully by the policies and practices of religious homogenization implemented in the German territories and states from the Reformation. Here, the 'father state' of early modern times forced his subjects into the strict discipline of either Protestant or Catholic rites and conduct. However, people 'on the ground' had multiple and inter-confessional ways of getting by, a practice that was by no means rare. Nevertheless, what justified such encroachments was the religious spell that the dominant felt or, at least, claimed. Thus they bore responsibility for the well-being of every 'subject', at least during his or her worldly pilgrimage. Still, why and how people took confessional rigidity as an agenda of their own is a matter for empirical study. Such investigations definitely show that acceptance did not exclude ways and means of deviating, disagreeing, or manoeuvring out from under the demands from above, of practising a different form or language, or of deciding when and how one might emigrate or choose exile.

'Ethnic cleansing' has been the common denominator of massacres and the resulting expulsions and refugees' movements in former Yugoslavia since 1991–2, a term used interchangeably both by those who did the expelling and those who observed. However, as the anthropologist Alexander Hinton noted, this is a 'vague

Explaining Forced Migration

term . . . which . . . exoticize[s]' that violence which is pivotal for the 'sweeping off' of people; importantly, 'cleansing . . . d[oes] not carry the legal imperative of intervention'.[18] For Hinton the term 'genocide' is preferable because it directly addresses the killing of 'a national, ethnical, racial or religious group, in whole or in part'.[19] Thus the term focuses explicitly on what is crucial but concealed in the term 'ethnic cleansing': the violence of killing or of mutilating.

It was the slaughter of almost one million people within a few months in the spring of 1994 in Rwanda and the killings of tens of thousands of people in former Yugoslavia from 1992—that is, it was the scale and simultaneity of these atrocities—that gave 'genocide' a special momentum, the stark differences between the two cases notwithstanding.

The renewed focus on 'genocide', that is, on actions that were or seemed to be characterized 'by the intention to annihilate "the other"',[20] triggered reassessments of massacres and past genocides, making one of them an issue of national politics in several central and western European countries (especially in France): the forced expulsions and massacres, the genocide of probably more than one million Armenians by Turkish authorities and soldiers during and after 1915. Whereas in this case forced expulsions seem to have led to massacres, in Rwanda and former Yugoslavia refugee movements and expulsions often seem to have resulted from massacres. By contrast, the mass scale and particular cruelty of mass killings as reported of the Khmer Rouge in Democratic Kampuchea in the mid-1970s did not trigger any comparable international reaction at that time.[21]

---

[18] Alexander L. Hinton, 'Introduction: The Dark Side of Modernity: Toward an Anthropology of Genocide', in id. (ed.), *Annihilating Difference: The Anthropology of Genocide* (Berkeley, 2002), 23. On the issue cf. also Eric Weitz, *A Century of Genocide: Utopias of Race and Nation* (Princeton, 2003) and Robert Gellately (ed.), *The Spectre of Genocide: Mass Murder in Historical Perspective* (Cambridge, 2003). Their differences notwithstanding both focus less on people's practices but explore macro-dimensions and emphasize stages of development towards genocidal killing.

[19] Hinton, 'The Dark Side of Modernity', 3, quoting from the 1948 Genocide Convention on the Prevention and the Punishment of Genocide. However, the Convention is lacking on several scores, as Hinton emphasizes. For instance, it remains silent about 'political groups' that might be targeted, persecuted, or killed by the mighty; and about pressures which the Soviet Union in particular exerted on these groups, as these clauses were dropped prior to the final version, according to Hinton.

[20] Hinton, 'The Dark Side of Modernity', 1–40, 6 quoting the Polish jurist Raphael Lemkin, who had coined the term 'genocide' in 1942.

[21] See, on further cases, Hinton (ed.), *Annihilating Difference*, 8–10, 23–5.

Shock, outrage, and, not least, efforts to get a closer view and to investigate causes, reasons, and, what is more, practices and trajectories of events in order to intervene—this emphasis is a very recent phenomenon.

Focus on Local Settings and Concrete Practices

The task, then, is not to fall prey to the attraction of seemingly clear-cut distinctions or bold definitions. Any effort to be ever more precise merely adds to the power of binaries pitting 'us' versus 'them'. What is needed is a more sensitive approach to the concrete actions and scenes of 'doing' the killing. Or, as Hinton has asked: how was it made and how did it start? Who did it and what practices served to 'prime' things? How, for instance, did the instigators in Rwanda employ pivotal symbols for the mass killings, such as those of the necessary 'flow' in human life and between humans?

How can we capture the dynamics of 'doing' violence? It is this micro-analytical approach that relates such deeds to claims that promised justification to perpetrators and to those consolations that granted relief if not glory to the victims or targets. The main issue, then, is to trace the concrete forms and activities that 'primed' things towards the actual violence of killing. It is in this vein that one should place the actual practices of pushing people and acting upon their bodies at the centre of attention, research, and description. Forced migration refers to force and violence as it does to expulsion. Both reverberate with the drive, among those doing the expelling, to act violently and with the shock that makes those who are expelled suffer at the time and possibly for years or even decades afterwards.

Accordingly, authors of studies on violence have shifted their emphasis from macro- to micro-perspectives when researching 'who did it'. The sociologist Jacques Semelin has observed the repercussions of the extreme violence of massacres:[22] massacres triggered forced removals even if they were not designed to 'force people out'. First, Semelin recommends that we consider the extent to which the perpetrators target not soldiers or guerrilla

---

[22] Jacques Semelin, 'Toward a Vocabulary of Massacre and Genocide', *Journal of Genocide Research*, 5 (2003).

Explaining Forced Migration

fighters but civilians of all ages, women as well as men. What is it that turns civilians into particularly fitting targets? Secondly, and even more disturbingly, those who actually expel people have often been their good neighbours for many years. Thus the proximity between those forcing people out and those being forced out seems only to stimulate that brutality to which many of those doing the expelling seem to have driven themselves.[23] Thirdly, perpetrators increasingly tend to be teenage boys and girls. Whether this is also a feature of removals and expulsions of previous conjunctures remains to be seen.[24]

Slavery

The disciplining of subjects is obviously one element in 'producing' citizens who could, and also did, function in and for modern societies and states. This process involves a specifically European *longue durée*. Therefore it is important to address another *longue durée* which is particularly significant in the field of migration or, as it were, forced migration: slavery.

This is not to address the ancient and ubiquitous institution that existed in most parts of the populated world. What I have in mind is the kind of slavery that became a pivot in and of the Atlantic triangle described and analysed so incisively by Sidney Mintz in his masterly analysis of both the direct interrelationships and the twisted resonances between 'power' and 'sweetness'.[25] Amongst its other accomplishments this study masterfully demonstrates a productive combination of perspectives. The author combines macro- and micro-analyses in his reconstructions of economic calculations and political incentives on the 'commanding heights' as well as among the practitioners 'on the ground' when they set out to hunt and hurt Africans, shipping them across the Atlantic in order to sell them to plantation owners in Brazil, the Caribbean, or North American colonies or states.

[23] Slavenka Drakulic, *They Would Never Hurt a Fly: War Criminals on Trial in The Hague* (London, 2004).
[24] Cf. for the 1990s especially Liberia.
[25] Sidney W. Mintz, *Sweetness and Power: The Place of Sugar in Modern History* (New York, 1985).

24   ALF LÜDTKE

Mintz never loses sight of the suffering and deaths of those being enslaved, and their efforts and strategies for surviving (including resistance and escape). What is more, in tracing the products and uses of slavery in England and on the European continent this study shows the dynamics of enslavement and forced migration and how they fed into the accumulation of capital and rigorous labour discipline. It is the specificity of the practices of historical actors in specific settings that reveals resonances and interrelationships, while never ignoring the material dimensions and the violence attributed and encountered time and again at almost all moments of these processes.

Numbers—and their Magic?

Narratives of removal, expulsion, and various forms of forced migration always contain or revolve around numbers. More precisely, debates and references employ enormous figures. Thus, it comes as no surprise that millions are mentioned time and again when the removals and expulsions between the late 1930s and late 1940s in eastern and central Europe are mentioned or analysed. A case in point is Philipp Ther's account of Europe.[26] He distinguishes three 'large waves of ethnic cleansing' for the twentieth century (1913–23 in south-eastern Europe; 1938–48 in eastern and central Europe; and the 1990s in the Balkans), which forced 30 million people to leave their homelands permanently. More specifically, for the Polish–German and Czech–German discussions the figure of about 12 million expellees covers both the 'wild' expulsions in 1945 and the more regulated and 'controlled' ones of 1946 and 1947.

The importance of large figures is also obvious when it comes to those forced migrations and expulsions that European debates and textbooks regularly overlook or forget: among them the refugee movements leading up to and in the wake of Indian Partition in 1946 and 1947. Here, half a million are counted as having perished and up to 12 million people as having been made homeless or forced to leave home and resettle. One may wonder

---

[26] Philipp Ther, 'A Century of Forced Migration: The Origins and Consequences of Ethnic Cleansing', in id. and Ana Siljak (eds.), *Redrawing Nations: Ethnic Cleansing in East-Central Europe, 1944–1948* (Lanham, Md., 2001), 43–73, 49–58.

Explaining Forced Migration

about the figures and their similarity (12 million here and 12 million there). In addition, in the European context another figure is at least as present: the 6 million murdered Jews who are usually attributed to 'Auschwitz' and the Holocaust/Shoah.[27] Such figures point at least indirectly to what one might call the monotony and, at the same time, the magic of large and 'simple' numbers.

For the Indian case Gyanendra Pandey has traced the issue in his own work. In minute detail he shows how figures such as the 'about 500,000 presumably killed between August 1946 and December 1947' have become 'standard in all accounts about the occurrences'. He himself acknowledges having accepted this figure as 'most likely in a previous contribution to debate'.[28]

Strong State—Weak State?

Accounts by historians emphasize the state as the driving or at least legitimizing force in removals, resettlements, and forced migration. Norman Naimark's comparative analysis of 'ethnic cleansing' in twentieth-century Europe is a case in point.[29] In this view, state and state agencies set the frame. They and their agents give licence as they provide plans and necessary material resources, from the means of transportation to weapons and manpower for actually pushing people 'out' or herding them towards their new destination.

Thus the state appears as a direct and particularly suitable product of man's devotion to perfecting him- or herself and, even more, others. In this view the state has been considered as 'gardener'. Zygmunt Bauman, who conspicuously employed this

[27] This figure is still prominent, although for more than two decades research has shown that it was somewhat smaller. Efforts to clarify the issue by the specialist Wolfgang Benz settle on the figure of about 5 million killed by the Nazi actions of deportation and expulsion (and for Auschwitz in particular a figure of about 1.1 million is now considered plausible). Cf. Wolfgang Benz (ed.), *Dimension des Völkermords: Die Zahl der jüdischen Opfer des Nationalsozialismus* (Munich, 1991).

[28] Gyanendra Pandey, 'Woman's Place in the No Man's Land of Violence: The Indian Subcontinent, 1947–48', in Alf Lüdtke and Bernd Weisbrod (eds.), *The No Man's Land of Violence: Extreme Wars in the Twentieth Century* (Göttingen, 2006), 153–82; and his contribution to this volume.

[29] Norman M. Naimark, *Fires of Hatred: Ethnic Cleansing in Twentieth-Century Europe* (Cambridge, Mass., 2001).

image, has found many followers, for instance James C. Scott in his *Seeing Like a State*.[30] The metaphor of 'gardening' reflects plans and practices of intervention in society. This drive was intensified and, in fact, emotionally charged consonant with the emergence of nation-states. Increasingly, 'we' seemed to need guarding against 'them'. Actual or possible enemies were to be found 'out there', beyond what controlling zeal had turned more and more into clear-cut boundaries and frontiers.[31] However, the gaze of suspicion not only looked outward but inadvertently turned back inward when detecting those who would undermine the established order of things 'from within'.

Notions and visions of gardening lent themselves to demands for engineering social relationships and, simultaneously, the shape and direction of institutions. Biopolitics and the furthering of demographic reproduction became imperative, at least in the late nineteenth century among socio-cultural and socio-political elites in central and western Europe and in North America.

Thus, gardening impinged upon people's hygiene and their diet; it concerned child-rearing and people's reproductive inclinations and abilities as well. The gardener begins with a natural site and aims to create an entirely designed space of botanical order. The organic dimension of the flora limits his or her possibilities; yet she or he has wide-ranging discretion in pruning and planting and weeding out plants that look like destroying or disturbing the intended order. Or to quote James Scott: 'What grows in the garden is always a small, consciously selected sample of what *might* be grown there. Similarly, social engineers consciously set out to design and maintain a more perfect social order.'[32]

More concretely, at issue are the people who envisaged and longed for the 'state'. These are the individuals and networks that designed, established, and ran 'well-ordered police states' from the eighteenth century on, at least in central and western Europe.[33] Its

[30] James C. Scott, *Seeing Like a State: How Ascertained Schemes to Approve the Human Condition Have Failed* (New Haven, 1998), 92–3.

[31] See, for this process of abandoning zones of mixture and simultaneity for the linear frontier, Peter Sahlins, *Boundaries: The Making of France and Spain at the Pyrenees* (Berkeley, 1989).

[32] Scott, *Seeing Like a State*, 92.

[33] See on this also Marc Raeff, 'The Well-Ordered Police State and the Development of Modernity in Seventeenth- and Eighteenth-Century Europe: An Attempt at a Comparative Approach', *American Historical Review*, 80/5 (Dec. 1975), 1221–43.

Explaining Forced Migration

commissars set out to homogenize the multitude of localities and the specific methods of domination and administration. These officials pursued not only the interest of the respective prince comprehensively to exploit the resources of the territory and the population ruled. This is because, in the societal field of forces, those who had claimed domination since ancient times also acted, as did the 'many', that is, that majority of people who stubbornly pursed their own goals, interests, and needs, thus often outflanking controls and demands 'from above'. For their own justification, officials who acted in this field emphasized the demands of the state, which they linked to the 'common weal'. By this token, however, one would also protect and support the respective sovereign. In this regard, most of the agents of the state showed devotion, if not love, not only for the prince but also for the state, not least when they aimed to weed out and remove those among its population who seemed 'unfit'.

Pre-modern or Modern?

In the wake of the Shoah, as of Stalinist deportations and killings, it was the imminent terror 'from above' as witnessed by survivors that inspired analyses of a new kind of devastating power being produced by particularly 'modern' or 'total' rule (Hannah Arendt).[34] This view invoked history's *longue durée*: interrelationships between societal modernization or its breakdown on the one hand and conjunctures of mass killing on the other became an issue of academic and, more generally, of public debate.

However, as the sociologists Tzvetan Todorov and Zygmunt Bauman have both argued,[35] manually killing and executing acts of cruelty on bodies of the 'other' in concentration camps was not a sudden re-emergence of pre-modern or 'primitive' attitudes. On

---

[34] Hannah Arendt, *Elemente und Ursprünge totaler Herrschaft* (Frankfurt am Main, 1955), which is the largely rewritten German edition of her *Origins of Totalitarianism* (New York, 1951). There she addresses especially imperialism and antisemitism as providing a lasting imprint. Others have argued that mass participation in politics as proclaimed by the French revolutionaries of 1789 had instilled in the 'masses' a sense of empowerment by implementing programmes of 'national' or other kinds of 'purity'. See Michael Hanagan, 'Gewalt und die Entstehung von Staaten', in Wilhelm Heitmeyer and John Hagan (eds.), *Internationales Handbuch der Gewaltforschung* (Wiesbaden, 2002), 153–76.

[35] Tzvetan Todorov, *The Conquest of America: The Question of the Other* (New York, 1992), 14; Zygmunt Bauman, *Modernity and the Holocaust* (Cambridge, 1989).

28 ALF LÜDTKE

the contrary, these mass killings rely on the combination of intensified fury with sober, rational calculation. This very blend has fuelled the murder of people and groups who were marked as foes (as Jews or Romani were under Nazism); this blend has informed and still does inform killing actions against whole peoples, and makes them cases in point of a particularly modern combination of intensified action, in emotional and cognitive terms alike.

Removal and Expulsion: 'Weapons of the Subaltern'?

The shocking ubiquity of relocations and removals leaves no doubt that such practices were popular, and not only in well-established states (states modelled on the European and, thus, colonial and colonizing paradigm). Expulsions and removals in republican Turkey and, consequently, in republican Greece from 1918 to 1921/3, and the violence of 'ethnic cleansing' from 1992 in former Yugoslavia (or in various African settings today), reflect not strong but non-existent or, at least, weak or faltering states. In fact, removals have almost become an ingredient of post-colonial states. Aspirations of subalterns to challenge those very states that have set the tone not only in Europe but worldwide since the late nineteenth century also turned to 'ethnic cleansing . . . as a weapon of the subaltern' (Michael Geyer), including not least the expulsions of Germans from Poland and Czechoslovakia during and after 1945.

If the oppressed or the 'subaltern' confronts the dominant, she or he employs or threatens violence. This very violence focuses on the actual or recalled pain inflicted previously by the 'prick' of the master's baton, whip, gun, or bayonet, and by the silent gestures of denigrating the subaltern. It is in their effort to (re)claim or (re)capture space or time (or both) that dominated people may embark on practices of violence. But what they may present as their last resort, the dominant can easily turn into an excuse for applying even more violence. The latter, in turn, can easily enhance confrontation and, in the end, instigate the removal and expulsion of those being attacked in the first place.

In this view, expulsions and removals do indeed change or, at least, suspend the top-down relationship that seems so characteristic of power and domination. However, Hannah Arendt has

Explaining Forced Migration

emphasized that totalitarian rule flattens out if not erases the distinction between the dominant and the dominated. Accordingly, self-mobilization imbues a sense of domination to those who actively participate in subjugating others. And it is physical violence that seems particularly 'fit' for this very job. If removal and expulsion are practices in and by which the dominated empower themselves, such a perspective is chilling, or at least unsettling.[36]

Afterthought: Emotions and their Multivalences

The emergence of standards of 'civilized' if not humane conduct appears as a long-term process in history. Several decades ago (in the wake of fascism) the historical sociologist Norbert Elias explored what he called the 'process of civilization' in people's everyday life. He emphasized not only the reduction of physical violence but also the simultaneous refinement of eating habits and table manners. More recently such wide-ranging tableaux have met with some scepticism. Nevertheless, only a few years ago Jürgen Osterhammel proposed to reflect on a similar long-term process: the formation of a 'western' or, as he put it, 'transatlantic and Euro-American consciousness of norms'. For him the outstanding example is the abolition of slavery.[37]

I am not so sure about the assumed 'normativity' of such norms, that is, the extent to which people's conduct and its changes are dictated by norms. This may be even more the case when the humane treatment of others is at stake. Certainly, Osterhammel is well aware of the multivalence of such norms. They were easily available for campaigns to abolish slavery as waged by the great powers for their own benefit, in fact, justifying the global intervention of these powers during the nineteenth century. Nevertheless, parallel to the cognitive statements, both their utterance and their performance dwelled on or openly displayed emotional charges that the arguments of both critics

---

[36] See Michael Geyer's review of Norman Naimark, *The Fires of Hatred*, in *Journal of Modern History*, 75 (2003), 935–8; Walter Benjamin, *Das Kunstwerk im Zeitalter seiner technischen Reproduzierbarkeit* (Frankfurt am Main, 1969).

[37] Jürgen Osterhammel, *Sklaverei und die Zivilisation des Westens* (Munich, 2000), 57–9, esp. 62–3.

and defendants of slavery were imbued with.[38] And these emotions that are invested in or were related to, or triggered by, normative speech and practice have been shed, or have gone rather unnoticed so far.

More concretely, when people sing 'Rule Britannia, Britannia rules the waves' (which at least in Britain considerable numbers of people sing emphatically at least once a year, on the last night of the Proms at the Royal Albert Hall in London), they also sing the line 'Britons never, never shall be slaves'. These lines date back to the early eighteenth century but they still reflect in most audible vigour at least two sets of feelings: on the one hand the terror of enslavement and deportation; on the other the joy of having beaten the actual danger of it becoming reality. Here terror and anxiety fiercely resonate with joy and longing—the longing for freedom. Or, as with the 'Britons' who are singing and whom the song also addresses: many take it as their ferocious claim to ever again seize that freedom. Thus one could take the longing for and the joy at the abolition as 'mirror emotions' of the very terror that shook people who were actually enslaved, but also the fear of those who later envisioned themselves facing 'barbarians' and their forces of evil.

Terror and joy do not easily match. They go together, although in rather asymmetrical ways. It is this interrelationship that is ignored in the debates and contestations about the universal usage and legitimacy of Euro-American concepts of forced migration, similar to Jürgen Osterhammel's argument about slavery (see above). Critiques of such 'western' modes, ideas, and forms of (intellectual or academic) conduct focus on what they consider the denial of respect or at least awareness of the specifics of those who never got beyond the threshold of being treated as 'the same but not quite' (Gayatri Spivak). However, such criticism tends to omit that notions and practices commonly labelled 'western' had and have multiple facets. Thus they could cover, for instance, both enslavement and abolition or freedom as well. Still, in its historical presence the universalizing claim of western notions in many parts of the world and for many generations meant experiences of being subdued, exploited, and dominated, often ruthlessly. Even more, processes of westernization lumped

[38] The latter is, of course, not to deny that enslavement as a process continues and has even spread in the most recent times.

Explaining Forced Migration

together multiple ways of encroaching upon people and making them receptive to 'western' ways of perceiving the world and of making do. One of its more recent slogans in people's everyday usage is consumerism. In other words, westernization denotes processes of hegemony and domination, with wide-ranging consequences as far as spatial mobility and migration are concerned, from 'induced' migration to violent enslavement and deportation.

To approach it from yet another angle: if subjugation, deportation, and slavery sparked emotions of pleasure but also dismay and horror among observers and witnesses, they also strengthened longings for pleasure among the profiteers and co-dominators and those related or tied to them; and horror and disgust among many others, most of them excluded from the heights of societal command.

What, then, does this mean for the interrelationship between the terrifying encounter of deportation (or slavery) on the one hand, and the longing to be 'free at last' on the other? In contrast to the brute violence of such forced removals, the forms of westernization may work differently. Obviously, in people's appropriation of 'western' ways of thinking and perceiving the world in which they find themselves, of doing things and of enjoying themselves, they do not encounter that 'prick' which persists from slavery. It was that 'prick' of violence that hurt the subjugated especially hard. However, this very same 'prick' occasionally galvanized individuals and helped to spark a broad movement to counter that very mode of subjugation and domination. Still, this would also mean that softer means of domination do not carry this very 'prick'. And precisely for this reason, these softer means appear more effective for establishing or sustaining domination than does solely physical violence and brute force. It is the lack of an emotional 'other' to which the dominated could or would aspire that makes it so effective for the dominant.

In that vein, to refrain from employing terms such as 'forced migration' for what was, on closer inspection, forced removal, deportation, or expulsion may be a first step towards more carefully tracing the emotional dynamics on both sides: among the people who were expelled and removed as well as among those who designed and actually did the expelling and deporting. This will not change violent practices, but it is an 'indispensable' analytical step (Dipesh Chakrabarty)[39] towards developing more adequate perceptions of what happened and how it did.

[39] Dipesh Chakrabarty, *Provincializing Europe: Postcolonial Thought and Historical Difference* (Princeton, 2000), 19: 'Categories and strategies we have learned from European thought (including the strategy of historicizing) are both indispensable and inadequate.' He is referring to the attempt to represent a 'particular case of a non-European modernity' by upper-caste Hindu Bengalis in the 1990s.

PART II

Forced Removal and
Indigenous Peoples

3

On the Trail of Tears: Daniel Butrick's Record of the Removal of the Cherokees

TIM ALAN GARRISON

Let us fancy the feeling of a dear sister, an aged father or mother, or a beloved wife or child, driven by strangers (of adamantine hearts) scorching with fever, under a burning sun, parching with thirst, rendered more tormenting by the heated dust filling the air, see this dear wife of our bosom, languishing, and almost ready to drop to the ground every step, and yet hanging to her friends, choosing rather to die in their arms, than be torn from them and thrown into a heated wagon, to be separated forever from all she held dear. See her last despairing look at her dear husband, as she sinks at his feet and falls in the road.

Now she is taken and thrown into a great wagon, covered with thick cloth, and all the air confined and wet by a burning sun. Here she has no cordial, no kind friend to wipe the cold sweat from her face.

As she awakes from a swoon, and calls for water to quench her thirst, no kind voice replies, no hand can minister to her relief. The wagoner is in all the noise of the crowd, and cannot hear her faint lispings, and when he does hear, cannot understand. Thus she must lie perhaps from morning till night parching with thirst, or in the most excruciating pains of body, thrown, as it were upon the rack, by every heavy jolt of the wagon, rolling over a rough road.

And thus from day to day till death kindly releases her departing spirit. And now where is the dear partner of her bosom, the children of her love, or the fond mother of her childhood? They are mingled in the crowd, and perhaps scarcely permitted to take even a parting view of the dear object of all their delight. The first they know, perhaps, some one accidentally remarks that such a person died and was left at such a place to be buried.

Let us imagine such scenes daily, and for a long time together; and then inquire why the dear Cherokees are doomed to such miseries; have they murdered their white friends? Have they robbed or

36   TIM ALAN GARRISON

plundered? Or have they done any wrong to the United States for
which that powerful nation is thus putting them to the torture?

(Daniel S. Butrick, 26 July 1838)[1]

In May and June of 1838, the United States seized at least 15,000
Cherokee Indians from their homes and marched them off to
concentration stockades. After holding most of them in the
rancid camps for several scorching summer months, the US
government forced the Cherokees to migrate through a brutal
winter to the Indian Territory (in what is now the state of
Oklahoma) over 800 miles from their homes. The relocation of
the Cherokees was an unmitigated human disaster. Scholars
have estimated that between 4,000 and 8,000 Cherokees died on
what is now known as the Trail of Tears. This represented a
catastrophic annihilation of at least one-quarter of the Cherokee
population.[2]

The Cherokee removal was the product of two primary forces.
First, the burgeoning profitability of cotton agriculture in the early
eighteenth century increased the demand for arable land in the
southern United States; and white planters, farmers, and speculators in the region called for the United States to seize the valuable
lands that the Native nations possessed and open them up for
cultivation. Second, many white Southerners had by this time
developed insidious feelings of prejudice against their Indigenous
neighbours; the loudest and most persistent demanded the
general expulsion of the Native population. By the late 1820s
Southern political leaders had developed a plan in which the
tribal nations in the eastern United States would cede all of their
territory and remove to new lands beyond the Mississippi river.

The Cherokees were long accustomed to demands for land
cessions. Before the arrival of non-Indians they had possessed a
vast territory that included what is now northern Georgia and
Alabama, eastern Tennessee, southern Kentucky, and the
western regions of North Carolina, South Carolina, and Virginia.

---

[1] Journal of Daniel Butrick, 26 July 1838, Records of the American Board of
Commissioners for Foreign Missions, Houghton Library, Harvard University,
Cambridge, Mass. I have used the dating adopted by Jess Bushyhead in his transcription
of a portion of Butrick's journal. See Trail of Tears Association, *The Journal of Rev. Daniel
S. Butrick, May 19, 1838–April 1, 1839* (Park Hill, Okla., 1998).

[2] Russell Thornton, 'Cherokee Losses during the Trail of Tears: A New Perspective
and a New Estimate', *Ethnohistory*, 31 (1984), 289–300.

On the Trail of Tears

Settlers of European ancestry began moving into the Cherokees' territory in the early eighteenth century; and from that point forward, the British colonial governments in the region had been securing cessions from the Indians. By the end of the American Revolutionary War (1781), the Cherokees had surrendered more than half of their original territory. The pressure on the Cherokees to cede their lands did not abate with the rise of the United States. Despite determined and well-publicized efforts to acculturate by many Cherokees, the white residents of the Southern states that abutted the Cherokee Nation refused to accept the Cherokee people as social equals and urged their political representatives to seize all Indian land. After the war of 1812, political leaders in the South, led by the governor and congressional delegation from Georgia, initiated a concerted effort to force the United States government to extinguish the land title of the Cherokees and the other southern tribal nations and expel them from the region.

The Cherokee leadership, however, maintained that their people constituted a sovereign nation independent of the American state and federal governments. They pointed out that their Treaty of Hopewell with American agents in 1785 had established national borders between the United States and the Cherokee Nation and made American settlers residing in Cherokee territory subject to Cherokee law. These provisions, Cherokee leaders argued, were acknowledgements by the United States that the Cherokee Nation retained fundamental sovereign powers. The Cherokee National Council advised the United States that it would refuse future cession requests and enacted a law prohibiting the sale of national land upon penalty of death. In 1827 the Cherokees adopted a written constitution, an act that further antagonized removal proponents in Georgia. In response to the Cherokee reaffirmation of its sovereignty, the Georgia legislature extended the state's jurisdiction over Cherokee territory, passed laws purporting to abolish the Cherokees' laws and government, and set in motion a process to seize and subdivide the Cherokees' land and sell it in parcels to white Georgians. At the national level, Andrew Jackson, long an advocate of expelling the southern tribal nations, was elected President of the United States in 1828. He immediately declared removal a national objective. By 1830 his allies in Congress had passed the Indian Removal Act, which authorized the President to negotiate removal treaties with the Indian tribes.[3]

With Jackson and the majority of Congress set on imposing removal on the tribes, the Cherokee Nation, led by its Principal Chief, John Ross, asked the US Supreme Court to intervene on its behalf and protect it from the trespasses of white squatters and the Georgia state government. In *Cherokee Nation v. Georgia* (1831), John Marshall, Chief Justice of the Court, determined that the Cherokees comprised a 'domestic dependent nation' that existed under the protection and tutelage of the United States. The Court, however, did not redress the Cherokees' grievances. A year later, in *Worcester v. Georgia*, the Supreme Court returned to the question. This time the Court declared that Georgia's statutory effort to extend its jurisdiction over Cherokee territory violated the Cherokee Nation's sovereignty and wrongfully intruded into its special treaty relationship with the United States. President Jackson, however, refused to enforce the decision and continued to pressure the Cherokees to remove.[4]

With their legal and political options foreclosed, the Cherokee Nation began to divide between a majority who wanted to continue their resistance against the removal programme and a minority Treaty Party that urged surrender and relocation. In December 1835 the latter group, led by Major Ridge, his son John Ridge, and Elias Boudinot, prominent Cherokee statesmen, signed a removal treaty at the Cherokee capital of New Echota. The Treaty of New Echota, negotiated without the authority of the Principal Chief and National Council, required the Cherokee Nation to exchange its national lands for a parcel in the Indian Territory set aside by Congress (in 1834) and to relocate there within two years. The federal government promised to pay five million dollars to the Cherokee Nation for the territory, to compensate individual Cherokees for their improvements and fixtures, and to pay the costs of relocation. The United States also promised to honour the title of the Cherokee Nation's new

---

[3] For general histories of Cherokee cessions and the Removal Crisis, see Thurman Wilkins, *Cherokee Tragedy: The Ridge Family and the Decimation of a People* (Norman, Okla., 1970); William G. McLoughlin, *Cherokee Renascence in the New Republic* (Princeton, 1986); and Tim Alan Garrison, *The Legal Ideology of Removal: The Southern Judiciary and the Sovereignty of Native American Nations* (Athens, Ga., 2002).

[4] For discussions of the Cherokee cases, see Garrison, *The Legal Ideology of Removal* and Jill Norgren, *The Cherokee Cases: The Confrontation of Law and Politics* (New York, 1995).

On the Trail of Tears

land, respect its political autonomy in the west, and protect its people from future trespasses. Even though it was completed by a dissident faction outside the sanction of the Cherokee national government, the US Senate ratified the treaty by a margin of one vote. In protest, the Cherokee government collected a petition, signed by more than 16,000 Cherokees, opposing the treaty. Ross and the Cherokee government continued to protest the legality of the treaty up to the point of their constituents' removal from their homeland.[5]

All but 1,000 of these Cherokees were ultimately exiled in the winter of 1838–9, and somewhere between 4,000 and 8,000 of them died as a direct consequence of their detention and relocation. These simple numbers, however, do not reflect the dehumanizing suffering the Cherokees experienced during their expulsion from the south. Only testimony and memory can provide insight into the despair the Cherokees felt as they walked away from their homes. Unfortunately the contemporary sources describing the Trail of Tears are limited.[6] We do have, however, one consistent eyewitness account of what happened to a large group of Cherokees during their apprehension, internment, and removal. Daniel Butrick, a Congregationalist minister living in the Cherokee Nation, maintained a journal during this critical period. Butrick remained in the Cherokee Nation until the last groups of detainees departed in early November 1838. He was therefore in a position to observe much of what happened as the United States Army and its allied state militias and volunteers rounded up the Cherokees and incarcerated them in concentration stockades. He continued to detail his observations as he accompanied a detachment of over 1,000 Cherokees on the long, circuitous route to the Indian Territory. His journal is the only daily diary maintained by a victim of the exile programme, and it reveals the physical and mental hardships suffered by the Cherokees during the ordeal.[7] This essay uses Butrick's journal

---

[5] For a history of the treaty, see Wilkins, *Cherokee Tragedy*, 264–90.

[6] For references to other eyewitness accounts of the removal, see Grant Foreman, *Indian Removal* (Norman, Okla., 1932), 230–312.

[7] Michael J. Murray, 'The Private Journal of Daniel S. Butrick: A New Interpretation of American Missionaries and Cherokee Removal' (MA thesis, University of New Hampshire, 1996), p. vii. Murray's thesis concentrates on Butrick's perception of the missionary role in the culmination of the removal policy. He devotes very little space to Butrick's account of the Trail of Tears.

to recount the experiences of the Cherokees who were captured, interned, and then removed. I should point out that although Butrick was writing for his eyes only, and not for the aggrandizement of the public or his mission board, many of his comments are grounded in hearsay and rumour. Butrick, however, made a conscious effort to distinguish what he saw or experienced from what he heard. I have retained that distinction in this summary.

Daniel Sabin Butrick was born in Windsor, Massachusetts, on 25 August 1789 and spent most of his youth in Richmond, New York. He attended the Cooperstown Academy and accepted the Christian faith at the age of 14. He then studied at the Andover Theological Seminary and was licensed to preach as a Congregationalist minister in 1811. He was formally ordained in Boston on 3 September 1817. That same year, the American Board of Commissioners for Foreign Missions, the Congregationalist missionary society in Boston, established plans to send its agents to the Cherokee Nation to convert the resident Indians. The board established a mission at Brainerd in the Cherokee Nation (located on the outskirts of present-day Chattanooga) and sent Butrick there, just a few weeks after his ordination, to minister to the Cherokees in the area. Along with serving at Brainerd, Butrick also ministered in Carmel, Willstown, and Hightower during his subsequent twenty years in the Cherokee Nation. He maintained his journal during two lengthy periods of that service (1819–25 and 1829–45).[8]

Butrick performed his duties in his own way and, at times, pursued a path rather independent of the board's wishes. According to a student of Butrick's journal, '[H]e spent more time than any other American board missionary ministering to the less acculturated, educated, and wealthy Cherokees who lived in the rural regions of the nation.' He was particularly interested in the Cherokees' language and believed that the missionaries would only be successful in spreading the gospel to Indians if they learned the Indigenous tongue. For that reason, Butrick was working on a system to write Cherokee at roughly the same

---

[8] Trail of Tears Association, *The Journal of Rev. Daniel S. Butrick*, unnumbered foreword; William G. McLoughlin, *Cherokees and Missionaries, 1789–1839* (Norman, Okla., 1995), 110, 126, 136; Robert Sparks Walker, *Torchlights to the Cherokees: The Brainerd Mission* (repr. Johnson City, Tenn., 1993), 43–4; Murray, 'The Private Journal of Daniel S. Butrick', 3, 15–16.

On the Trail of Tears

time that Sequoyah was perfecting his syllabary. Butrick even left the Brainerd mission for a time and moved in with a Cherokee family so that he could immerse himself in the language.[9]

Butrick adamantly opposed the removal of the Cherokees, and in 1831 he was elected chairman of a convocation of Congregationalist, Moravian, and Baptist ministers that issued a statement opposing the policy. It was not long after this that the state of Georgia, in an effort to quash missionary aid and advice to the recalcitrant Cherokee government, ordered white people living in the Cherokee Nation to either swear an oath of allegiance to the state or leave its borders. When the Georgia Guard arrested several missionaries in the attack that would be condemned by the US Supreme Court in *Worcester* v. *Georgia* (the decision in which the Court recognized the principle of Native tribal sovereignty), Butrick happened to be away on a preaching tour. By this time he had become disillusioned about the role the missionaries were taking in the Cherokee resistance movement, and he became suspicious of the motives of some of the missionary leaders of the removal opposition. He confided in his journal that he believed that some of his colleagues were abandoning their flock to wage their campaign and were, in some cases, intentionally provoking the state of Georgia. The political actions of such men, he thought, were hindering the true objective of leading the Cherokees to Christ. Butrick was also not afraid to challenge the positions of his superiors in Boston. When in the midst of the Removal Crisis the mission board asked the federal government to compensate it for the value of property it would have to abandon in the removal of the Cherokee Nation, Butrick criticized the action. This was 'blood money', he insisted, and he reminded the church leaders that they had promised in 1817 that the Church would never 'call on [the Cherokees] for land'.[10]

---

[9] Murray, 'The Private Journal of Daniel S. Butrick', 3; McLoughlin, *Cherokees and Missionaries*, 136–7, 346; William G. McLoughlin, *Champions of the Cherokees* (Princeton, 1990), 36, 39.

[10] *Missionary Herald*, 27 (Feb. 1831), 79–81; 27 (May 1831), 166; McLoughlin, *Cherokees and Missionaries*, 312–13; Murray, 'The Private Journal of Daniel S. Butrick', 46–50; Garrison, *The Legal Ideology of Removal*, 169–97.

42 TIM ALAN GARRISON

The Capture and Internment

In the spring of 1838, the US War Department appointed General Winfield Scott to implement the terms of the New Echota Treaty. At this point, most of the Cherokees continued to resist relocation in a peaceful manner or tried to live as if it might never unfold. As the date the United States had fixed for expulsion approached, only about 2,000 of the 17,000 Cherokees had left for the west. Scott arrived in Athens, Tennessee, on 8 May and took command of the troops in the region. Scott not only brought with him men, cavalry, and artillery, he also possessed the authority to request militia troops and volunteers from the governors of the south-east to supplement his regular troops. By the time Scott had marshalled his forces, he had some 7,000 men to round up a little more than twice that many Cherokees. On 10 May Scott announced that the Cherokees had one month to prepare for their departure. He declared that thousands of troops would soon arrive 'to render resistance and escape alike hopeless', and he made clear that he would use force, if necessary, to secure the Cherokees' cooperation. 'I am an old warrior, and I have been present at many a scene of slaughter,' Scott said, 'but spare me, I beseech you, the horror of witnessing the destruction of the Cherokees.' He ordered his address printed up as a handbill and had it distributed throughout the Cherokee Nation. Scott set up headquarters at New Echota and divided the Cherokee Nation into three districts for the purpose of organizing the round-up. He sent his troops throughout Cherokee territory and ordered them to bring the resident Indians into one of twenty-three hastily built stockades. From the stockades, the Cherokees were to be moved to embarkation depots at the Cherokee Agency on the Hiwassee river, and Ross's Landing (in present day Chattanooga) and Gunter's Landing (Guntersville, Alabama) on the Tennessee river.[11]

Butrick watched intently as federal soldiers rounded up the Cherokees; in fact, many of the captured groups passed by his house or stopped in his lane on their way to the concentration stockades. He described the process by which the troops collected

---

[11] Wilkins, *Cherokee Tragedy*, 319; James Mooney, *Myths of the Cherokees* (Washington, 1900), 129; Gary E. Moulton, *John Ross: Cherokee Chief* (Athens, Ga., 1978), 95; Grace Steele Woodward, *The Cherokees* (Norman, Okla., 1963), 205.

On the Trail of Tears

the Cherokees and forced them to their prisons: 'In driving them a platoon of soldiers walked before and behind, and a file of soldiers on each side, armed with all the common appalling instruments of death; while the soldiers, it is said would often use the same language as if driving hogs, and goad them forward with their bayonets.' Butrick heard that one man, tired of being prodded and seeing his children mistreated, 'picked up a stone and struck a soldier'. The soldiers inflicted one hundred lashes on the Cherokee father when they arrived at the stockade.[12]

The American soldiers did not discriminate; they ruthlessly drove the young and the old, the healthy and the infirm, to the stockades. Butrick personally identified individuals who were blind, sick, and pregnant among the Cherokees caught in the gathering. He reported that one of the captured Cherokee parties included an 'old lady, near a hundred years old'. Another group included a man 'considerably over one hundred years old' who had been abandoned and was sick with 'the flux'. The elderly gentleman became frightened and wandered off into the woods. He was later 'left by the soldiers, in his cabin, to the mercy of any who might providentially find him'. 'It is said', Butrick added, 'that he was almost starved when some white children found him, and carried him some food.' Butrick sent for the man, named Tik-i-kiski, and tried to nurse him back to health. Later, however, Tik-i-kiski walked off from his removal detachment and was never mentioned again in Butrick's account.[13]

---

[12] Butrick, *Journal*, 26 May 1838, 1 July 1838. A few witnesses other than Butrick recorded their observations of Scott's apprehension of the Cherokee population. John G. Burnett, a soldier who helped intern the Cherokees, wrote that: 'Men working in the fields were arrested and driven to the stockades. Women were dragged from their homes by soldiers whose language they could not understand. Children were often separated from their parents and driven into stockades with the sky for a blanket and the earth for a pillow. And often the old and infirm were prodded with bayonets to hasten them to the stockades.' John G. Burnett, 'The Cherokee Removal through the Eyes of a Private Soldier', *Journal of Cherokee Studies*, 3 (1978), 183.

[13] Butrick, *Journal*, 31 May, 3, 10, 22 June, 18 Aug. 1838. It could be that Butrick is repeating the same episode in an entry for 28 July 1838. In this passage he described an old man who had been left behind by his wife because he was 'too heavy and old to be handled without some inconvenience'. The old man, 'being unable to walk, came to the point of starvation, when some white children found him in the house and fed him.' This man was taken to one of the internment camps. Evan Jones wrote: 'Females, who have been habituated to comforts and comparative affluence, are driven on foot before the bayonets of brutal men.' Cited in Foreman, *Indian Removal*, 288, as 'Letter from the Rev. Evan Jones', in *Baptist Missionary Magazine*, 18: 236.

44 TIM ALAN GARRISON

Butrick heard a number of reports of Cherokees taking ill, fainting, and dying during the process. He personally witnessed several deaths. It is no wonder that so many took ill. 'From their first arrest', Butrick wrote, 'they were obliged to live very much like brute animals, and during their travels, were obliged at night to lie down on the naked ground, in the open air, exposed to wind and rain.' '[M]en, women and children', Butrick said, were herded together, 'like droves of hogs'. He lamented that many of the Cherokees were 'hastening to a premature grave'.[14]

At one point, a lieutenant in the US Army asked if he, his fellow officers, and a group of Cherokee internees could camp near Butrick's home. Butrick was subsequently surprised to discover that 'about two hundred Cherokees were driven into our lane'. It had been raining, Butrick recorded, and 'all men, women and children were dripping wet, with no change of clothing, and scarcely a blanket to cover them'. He noticed that some of the women possessed only the 'poorest dress' that they wore on their back, and he surmised that 'this of course was the amount of their clothing for a journey of about eight hundred miles'. Butrick and his wife tried to comfort the group. He wrote: 'As soon as permission was obtained from the officers, we opened every door to these poor sufferers. Mothers brought their dear little babes to our fire, and stripped off their only covering to dry. Oh how heart rending was the sight of those little sufferers, their little lips blue and trembling with cold.' The soldiers led the Cherokees to the mission meeting house, where a captain with the company told them that 'he had the power to destroy them',

[14] Butrick, *Journal*, 10 June, 26 May 1838. Long after the removal, James Mooney, a noted anthropologist from the Smithsonian Institution, interviewed Cherokee informants and penned what came to be an oft-quoted description of the capture and internment: 'Families at dinner were startled by the sudden gleam of bayonets in the doorway and rose up to be driven with blows and oaths along the weary miles of trail that led to the stockade. Men were seized in their fields or going along the road, women were taken from their wheels and children from their play. In many cases, on turning for one last look as they crossed the ridge, they saw their homes in flames, fired by the lawless rabble that followed on the heels of the soldiers to loot and pillage. So keen were these outlaws on the scent that in some instances they were driving off the cattle and other stock of the Indians almost before the soldiers had fairly started their owners in the other direction. Systematic hunts were made by the same men for Indian graves, to rob them of the silver pendants and other valuables deposited with the dead. A Georgia volunteer, afterward a colonel in the Confederate service, said: "I fought through the civil war and have seen men shot to pieces and slaughtered by thousands, but the Cherokee removal was the cruelest work I ever knew." ' Mooney, *Myths of the Cherokees*, 130.

On the Trail of Tears

and that he had orders to do so 'if they did not behave well'. The officer then ordered the Cherokees to remain in the meeting house until the next morning. When the captain's interpreter told him that some of the Cherokees had 'the dysentery' and might need to go outside, the captain responded that if that were the case, they had to obtain permission. Otherwise, he said, 'they would be in danger of being shot'. The next day the Cherokees were driven to a camp about '2½ miles' away, where, Butrick said, 'they wait to be sent down the river'. Butrick clearly did not expect these Cherokees to survive their ordeal: 'We wept and wept again, and still wept at the thought of that affecting scene. Our prayer is that these dear children, who must doubtless be soon ushered into eternity, may be taken into the arms of their dear Redeemer.'[15]

Butrick noted that Scott had ordered that the Cherokees were to be 'taken as they were found by the soldiers, without permission to stop either for friends or property'. The citizens of Georgia pressured Scott to move with even more expediency. On 26 May 1838 Butrick reported that 'a number of Georgia citizens near New Echota took sixteen Cherokees and drove them to the fort and then requested permission of General Scott to take them out and whip them, though in this they were not gratified'. The Georgians, Butrick speculated, wanted to send a message to Scott that 'no farther delay would be made with regard to collecting the Indians'. Despite this pressure, Butrick believed that Scott was attempting to complete his disagreeable task without embarrassing or injuring the Cherokees. Scott had ordered his troops to avoid 'acts of harshness and cruelty'. 'Every possible kindness', he declared, 'must, therefore, be shown by the troops.' He urged his officers to capture and bring to justice any soldier who violated his command. Scott also ordered the soldiers to refrain from firing at detainees who tried to escape. (Scott's order was ignored in at least one case. Butrick reported that he had heard that one man who could neither speak nor hear was surprised by the approach of soldiers arriving to take him away. With his affliction, he could not hear the orders of the soldiers; and when he began running away out of fear, he was 'shot dead on the spot'.) Scott also instructed his troopers to inform the

---

[15] Butrick, *Journal*, 31 May, 1 June 1838.

Cherokees that while they were called upon to disarm the men, they would return the confiscated weapons once they reached their destination. Butrick, who was appalled by profanity, was particularly pleased with another of Scott's commands. The general, he said, 'gave orders that no improper language should be used towards the Indians'.[16]

Butrick noted that Scott's efforts to ameliorate the indignity of the process were usually contingent on 'the disposition of the under officers, and soldiers'; in fact, Scott simply was unable to control some of the less scrupulous of his charges. Butrick recorded a number of inhumane acts committed by men under Scott's command. He heard reports that the soldiers assaulted and murdered victims during their apprehension. In one case, a 'Mr. Nave' told Butrick that he had witnessed a company of prisoners crossing a creek near his house. Nave told Butrick that he had heard a 'horseman' say that 'a certain old Creek woman had given out, and some wagons must stop and take her in'. Nave said that another soldier on foot subsequently came up and ordered the company forward. Nave told Butrick that he believed the soldier had killed the Creek woman. Butrick's confidant added that he and several others hunted for the woman 'but could find nothing of her'.[17]

The Cherokees were also terrorized and beaten by the white civilians who were moving onto their lands. In one case, Butrick saw three drunken white men chasing a group of Cherokees near his home. The thugs had beaten a Cherokee named Young Turkey. When Young Turkey struck one of his assailants in the face and ran away with his colleagues, the gang gave chase. The white men were 'running their horses with all speed, swearing that they would kill one of those Indians' when Butrick spotted them. The Cherokees escaped by running into Butrick's 'door yard'. Butrick refused to let their pursuers enter; eventually, one of his acquaintances persuaded the assailants to leave.[18]

Butrick's diary also reveals that the lawless situation fostered by the round-up left many Cherokee women subject to harassment and molestation. Alcohol was often a factor in these assaults. Butrick reported an incident where some 'poor Cherokees' in

---

[16] Ibid. 26 May 1838; Moulton, *John Ross*, 95; Woodward, *The Cherokees*, 204.

[17] Butrick, *Journal*, 26 May, 28 June 1838.

[18] Ibid. 2 Aug. 1838.

On the Trail of Tears

Cassville 'were enticed to drink, and when drunk, one of the women was taken out into the public street, and her clothes pulled up, and tied over her head.' She was 'thus left to the gaze of the multitudes passing by'. In the same town, he had heard, two men had attacked a Cherokee woman and her granddaughter and grandson. One assailant held the woman and her grandson at bay with a knife while the other 'abus[ed] [the granddaughter] in the most shameful manner'. He continued: 'After abusing her in this manner as long as they wished, they took her to a vacant house near by and frightened her friends away, and it was not, I believe, till the next day, that she was permitted to wander, in shame, to her home.'[19]

Butrick recorded disturbing hearsay accounts of how the removal soldiers treated pregnant women. He heard that one Cherokee woman in 'the pains of childbirth' asked her military captors to 'retire' from the march. The informant told Butrick that '[T]his was absolutely forbidden, and she was obliged to fall in the road amidst a company of soldiers, and pass through the pains of a traveling woman.' Butrick wrote that he had heard that 'six children were born in like circumstances'. Butrick reported an even more shocking story: 'We also learn that when the last company were taken over the river at Ross's landing, a woman, in the pains of childbirth, stood and walked as long as possible, and then fell on the bank of the river. A soldier coming up, stabbed her with his bayonet, which, together with other pains, soon caused her death.' Butrick noted the story of another Cherokee woman who had 'lately died on the bank of the river, opposite the agency'. He described her death: 'She had been driven, with many other from the Valley Towns, and on the way, was delivered of a child. She needed, at least, a little rest, but even this was denied by the officer, and she was thrown into a wagon, and hauled on over a rough road, with the company and lived till she reached the bank of the river, and then expired.'[20]

The round-up tore families apart. Butrick noted that one man had killed a deer and 'was taking it home to meet the joyful salutations of his family, when at once he was surprised & taken prisoner to a fort'. He continued: 'Women absent from their families on visits, or for other purposes, were seized, and men far from

[19] Ibid. 18 July 1838.
[20] Ibid. 12 July, 20 Aug. 1838.

their wives and children, were not allowed to return.' Children, Butrick wrote, were 'forced from home' and 'dragged off among strangers'. One woman 'between 80 and 100 years old came to me and wept like a child'. The woman was concerned about her daughter, who had gone into hiding in the woods to escape the round-up. The missing daughter 'had long been afflicted with swelling in her limbs'; her mother, according to Butrick, supposed that 'her sick daughter was in the woods, in danger of starving and of being devoured by beasts'. Although the families were eventually reunited, the daughter who had caused the woman so much concern soon died from her affliction.[21]

Butrick was at his most distressed when reporting on how Cherokee children had been treated in the round-up: 'Dear little infants; O how distressing to see their feeble little hands holding to their mothers bosoms, and pulling back to life, while ruthless monsters snatched them away, and drove them lonely to the grave.' He wrote that when infants took sick, 'they were taken from their mothers' arms and thrown into wagons, and driven on over a rough road'. To make matters worse, the 'mothers were denied the privilege of being with them, but were driven on like beasts of prey'. 'There in that torturing wagon,' Butrick wrote, 'the suffering infant must lie, and die, unnurtured, and at night, be taken out and put away in a lonely tomb.' One wagon master who had returned from accompanying a group of Cherokees told Butrick that he had witnessed 'two infants' suffer this fate.

---

[21] Ibid. 26 May, 18 June 1838. John G. Burnett recalled a poignant scene in his account: 'In another home was a frail Mother, apparently a widow and three small children, one just a baby. When told that she must go the Mother gathered the children at her feet, prayed an humble prayer in her native tongue, patted the old family dog on the head, told the faithful creature good-bye, with a baby strapped on her back and leading a child with each hand started on her exile. But the task was too great for that frail Mother. A stroke of heart failure relieved her sufferings. She sunk and died with her baby on her back, and her other two children clinging to her hands.' The children, we must presume, were hustled to the nearest stockade. Burnett, 'The Cherokee Removal through the Eyes of a Private Soldier', 183. On 16 June 1838, Evan Jones, a Baptist missionary, corroborated Butrick's observations: 'The Cherokees are nearly all prisoners. They have been dragged from their houses, and encamped at the forts and military posts, all over the nation. In Georgia, especially, multitudes were allowed no time to take any thing with them, except the clothes they had on. Well-furnished houses were left a prey to plunderers, who, like hungry wolves, follow in the train of the captors. These wretches rifle the houses, and strip the helpless, unoffending owners of all they have on earth. Females, who have been habituated to comforts and comparative affluence, are driven on foot before the bayonets of brutal men. Their feelings are mortified by vulgar and profane vociferations.' Evan Jones letter, 16 June 1838, repr. in McLoughlin, *Champions of the Cherokees*, 174.

On the Trail of Tears

Butrick wrote that in another case two young children ran away from their mother and into the woods when they saw soldiers approaching their home. The woman begged the soldiers to allow her either to find her children or wait for them to return. She promised to catch up with the group when she found them. The soldiers, however, forced the mother to leave without her children. The youngsters were left on their own for two days in the forest before the despairing woman could obtain permission for one of her friends to go back and find them. The deaths of two other children sent Butrick into despair: '[T]he poor little children are almost all dying off. . . . O how distressing to the Cherokees who think so much of the graves of their friends, to be now called to leave so many of their dear little babes in this land of enemies, where they can never hope even to drop a tear on their graves again.'[22]

Butrick reported that the Cherokees were regularly robbed of their material possessions during the gathering. They were not allowed to take their property with them when they were abducted, and they left behind 'cattle, horses, hogs, household furniture, clothing, and money', among other items. Once they were brought into the stockades, the Cherokees' horses were sold at auction to the highest bidder. The minister complained that after being seized by the troops, Harriet Newel, a Cherokee who had studied at Brainerd, had gone back to her home to retrieve her bed. She discovered, however, that 'the whites had taken every thing from the house and thus stripped them naked'. Butrick said that 'the white inhabitants around, stood with open arms to seize whatever property they could put their hands on'. '[T]he coffers of some of their rich oppressors', he added, 'have been crowded to overflowing.' Soldiers systematically partici- pated in the larceny, according to Butrick: 'We understand that when the soldiers were taking the Cherokees, a woman would sometimes spread a blanket to put beddings etc. in, and the soldiers would snatch it away saying there are others appointed to take care of property.' All of this disappointed and depressed

---

[22] Butrick, *Journal*, 26 May, 8 Aug., 3 Sept. 1838. John G. Burnett described one particularly cruel episode: 'In one home death had come during the night, a little sad faced child had died and was lying on a bear skin couch and some women were preparing the little body for burial. All were arrested and driven out leaving the child in the cabin. I don't know who buried the body.' Burnett, 'The Cherokee Removal through the Eyes of a Private Soldier', 183.

Butrick. He described how the expropriation affected his feelings as he made his regular rides to minister at Candy's Creek. 'For a year or two past', he wrote, 'I was frequently led to keep my eyes directly before me to avoid seeing stolen fields and houses in the hands of intruding robbers.' Now, he said, 'I was tempted to keep my eyes in the road to avoid seeing the desolating judgments of heaven. Corn driven to the roots, some large fields appear as if they would scarcely produce one good ear of corn. The sins of these unfeeling robbers will be sure to find them out.'[23]

According to Winfield Scott's reports, by 30 May his forces had rounded up 2,500 Cherokees. By 4 June, 4,000 had been removed to the concentration stockades. By the end of June almost all the Cherokees, except for approximately 1,000 who had escaped capture or remained hidden in the mountains, were locked up. While his numbers did not correlate with those of Scott, the reverend agreed that the general's forces had worked expeditiously. In a matter of just 'two or three days', Butrick wrote, 'about 8,000 people, many of whom were in good circumstances, and some rich, were rendered homeless, houseless and penniless, and exposed to all the ills of captivity'. Butrick wrote that the work of Scott's men would 'doubtless long eclipse the glory of the United States'. The troubles for these Cherokees were just beginning.[24]

The Concentration Stockades

In a disastrous coincidence of unusual weather, federal disorganization and confusion, and contemporary communications, most of the Cherokees were forced to linger in the concentration stock-

---

[23] Butrick, *Journal*, 26 May, 17 June, 23 July, 10 Oct. 1838. 'It is a painful sight', Evan Jones wrote. 'The property of many has been taken, and sold before their eyes for almost nothing—the sellers and buyers, in many cases, being combined to cheat the poor Indians.' Jones added: 'These things are done at the instant of arrest and consternation; the soldiers standing by, with their arms in hand, impatient to go on with their work, could give little time to transact business.' In the end, 'the poor captive, in a state of distressing agitation, his weeping wife almost frantic with terror, surrounded by a group of crying terrified children, without a friend to speak a consoling word, is in a poor condition to make a good disposition of his property and is in most cases stripped of the whole, at one blow.' Evan Jones letter, 16 June 1838, repr. in McLoughlin, *Champions of the Cherokees*, 174.

[24] New American State Papers, 10: 127–30; Mooney, *Myths of the Cherokees*, 131; Butrick, *Journal*, 26 May 1838. For a history of those Cherokees who avoided removal see John R. Finger, *The Eastern Band of Cherokees, 1819–1900* (Knoxville, Tenn., 1984).

On the Trail of Tears 51

ades for many more weeks than the government had planned. Secretary of War Joel Poinsett sent a letter instructing General Scott to refrain from rounding up the Cherokees until days before they were to depart for the Indian Territory. Unfortunately, Poinsett's instructions arrived after most of the Cherokees had already been captured and placed in the stockades. When the reports of how disease and hot weather, including a persistent drought, were afflicting the first emigrants, who had departed in June, Scott determined to wait until the autumn to order the departure of the remainder of the Cherokees. While this meant that they avoided travelling during the hottest weeks of the summer, it consigned the Cherokees to a long and extremely unhealthy detention in the stockades. The Cherokees who removed with Butrick were thus locked up in the filthy stockades until August, and then moved to unsheltered assembly camps near the embarkation points for several more weeks. To make matters worse, postponing their departure resulted in another calamity: the Cherokees were forced to march hundreds of miles during one of the worst winters in contemporary memories.[25]

Butrick reported on the conditions in the concentration stockades, one of which he noted to be 'within a few rods' of his home. Most of the stockades were constructed by Tennessee volunteers. According to one source, the volunteers 'built rows of log pens, each approximately sixteen feet square and crudely roofed' for the Cherokee captives in the stockades. The summer heat was unbearable for the Cherokees trapped in these cramped holding pens. The overcrowded camps also lacked clean water and safe waste disposal arrangements. Butrick was appalled that Cherokee men and women were required to live under the constant surveillance of the soldiers and suffered the most invasive intrusions into their bodily privacy. Butrick visited one camp and reported that 'The Cherokees had been kept on a small spot, surrounded by a strong guard, under such circumstances that it would seem impossible for male or female to secrete themselves from the gaze of multitudes for any purpose whatever, unless by hanging up some cloth in their tents, and there they had no vessel for private use.'[26]

---

[25] Butrick, *Journal*, 8 Aug. 1838; Moulton, *John Ross*, 95–6.

[26] Butrick, *Journal*, 10 June, 16 July, 8 Aug. 1838; Woodward, *The Cherokees*, 194, citing Gilbert E. Govan and James W. Livingood, *The Chattanooga Country, 1540–1951* (New York, 1951).

It did not take long for contagious diseases to pass through the stockades. On 11 June Butrick reported that 'many of the Cherokees are sick'. On 1 July Butrick wrote that 'the fever and dysentery are now desolating the camps'. He also noted that others were inflicted with and dying of 'the Ague and fever'. During the internment Butrick also witnessed or heard of cases of whooping cough, influenza, measles, pleurisy, 'bilious fevers', 'bowel complaint', and consumption spreading among the detainees. The minister witnessed women fainting in the camps from disease and exposure. He saw one woman 'lying senseless' on the ground. 'Being unwell,' Butrick wrote, 'she was not able to endure the sight of some friends she saw in the camps, and immediately on seeing them, she fainted and fell to the ground.'[27]

Butrick's journal reveals a summer of death for the Cherokees. In early June he noted that he heard that 'four to ten die in a day' at the camp at Calhoun and that 'half the infants six months or a year and all the aged over sixty had been killed directly'. On 22 July he reported: 'We understand that from ten to twenty die daily at the Agency.' A week later he noted that 'deaths at the agency among the Cherokees, are 20 daily'. According to one source, perhaps as many as 2,000 to 2,500 died in the stockades and camps alone. Butrick would be called upon over and over again to perform services for Cherokees who died as a consequence of the round-up, internment, and removal. Although he witnessed many of these deaths, recorded reports of dozens of others, and wrote that 'we are becoming almost familiar with death', he still expressed surprise that more Cherokees had not died as a consequence of the conditions in the stockades.[28]

Butrick expressed serious concern about the treatment of the aged in the stockades. He saw 'a very old man, near the point of death' who had been suffering 'some time with the dysentery'. The man 'had a small piece of an old blanket under him, and nothing over his body except a handkerchief drawn about his middle, and no shelter, but a few bushes and a piece of bark

[27] Butrick, *Journal*, 10, 11 June, 1, 19 July, 5 Sept., 7, 10, 29 Oct. 1838; R. Palmer Howard, 'Cherokee History to 1840: A Medical View', *Oklahoma State Medical Association Journal*, 63 (1970), 77.

[28] Butrick, *Journal*, 10, 11, 17, 18 June, 22, 30 July, 14 Aug. 1838; McLoughlin, *Champions of the Cherokees*, 173. For reports of deaths by illness in the stockades and camps, see Butrick, journal entries for 17, 18 June, 1, 2, 11, 12, 13, 22, 23, 26, 29, 30 July, 8, 11, 14, 19, 22, 24, 25 Aug., 6 Sept., 13, 17, 18, 29 Oct. 1838.

On the Trail of Tears

three or four feet long'. Butrick was able to procure medicine for the man, but he could not find a doctor capable of administering the proper dosage. He reported that during this episode he discovered that the only doctor in the stockade was 'merely a dentist'. At one stockade, there were three doctors available to treat some 4,000 Cherokees. Butrick understood, however, that the problem was the quality rather than the quantity of the medical practitioners. He had been told that 'a man who favored the administration could obtain any employment, qualified or not'. Medical care was so poor, he added, that a rumour had spread among the Cherokees that 'one of the physicians at the camps, was killing the people'.[29]

Conditions in the camps, of course, demoralized the internees. Butrick described visiting a 'poor old sick woman'. When she heard some of the removal wagons passing by, she issued 'an involuntary sigh from her heaving bosom [that] led me to consider how dreadful that sound was to her ears'. Butrick continued: 'Such carriages brought her from her peaceful house, from her aged husband, from her children, and grandchildren, and also racked her aged and withering frame, and hurried her away, far away from all the scenes of her childhood, to cruel camps, where she was guarded as a prisoner of war, denied that kind of food congenial to her feeble stomach, almost unable to rise, and yet torn from all those on whose kind arms she had been accustomed to lean for support.' The next day, Butrick went to visit the old woman again. He found, however, that 'she had just expired'. Some became so desperate that they committed suicide. Butrick wrote of one man who swore that 'he would never go to the Arkansaw'. The reverend then described the distraught man's demise: '[H]e joined Mr. Bushyhead's detachment, I think, and started towards the place of encampment. At length he stopped and remarked that he had gone as far toward the Arkansaw as he should ever go. He loaded his rifle, lay down at the foot of a tree, with his rifle by his side, the muzzle toward his head, and by means of his toe, discharged his gun, and thus put an end to his existence.' Butrick also reported that several Cherokees were murdered while they were being detained. On 21 September, for instance, he wrote: 'We learn that three

---

[29] Howard, 'Cherokee History to 1840', 77; Butrick, *Journal*, 19 July 1838.

54 TIM ALAN GARRISON

murders have been committed by the Cherokees at the agency since Ben Harris stabbed his fellow in the bowels. Previous to that there had been five on five Saturday nights successively.'[30]

Cherokee women were harassed and molested in the camps. Butrick reported that Moses, a Cherokee Methodist preacher, had informed him that 'the volunteers go about the camps at night, endeavoring to find Cherokee women and girls'. When one group of women saw them coming, Moses said, they cried for help. Having been revealed by the calls, the men 'went out cursing' and 'calling them liars'. Butrick also complained that federal soldiers stood by and watched Cherokee women as they bathed in a nearby creek. He heard from a fellow missionary, Brother Vail, that he had seen 'six soldiers about two Cherokee women'. 'The women stood by a tree,' Vail told Butrick, 'and the soldiers with a bottle of liquor were endeavoring to entice them to drink.' The soldiers' commander did nothing when Vail complained; the missionary later heard that 'those soldiers had the two women out with them all night'. Butrick also heard that soldiers captured a 'young married woman, a member of the Methodist society', and 'dragged her about'. The soldiers then, 'through fear or other causes', 'induced [her] to drink, and yield to their seduction'. The young woman was 'now an outcast, even in the view of her own relatives'. 'How many of the poor captive women are thus debauched,' Butrick concluded, 'that eye which never sleeps alone can tell.'[31]

Several hundred Cherokees avoided the brutal summer incarceration in the stockades. They, however, endured their own miseries. Three detachments, totalling 2,800 Cherokees, departed on a water route on 6, 13, and 17 June.[32] When it was time for a detachment to leave, they were moved to one of the embarkation points. Butrick had 'the painful pleasure' of seeing a group of 'about fifteen hundred' as they were 'marched down to the river' in preparation for their removal: 'They were driven to the bank of the river, and there guarded all night, to lie down like so many animals on the naked ground.' Those who refused to

[30] Ibid. 28 July, 21 Sept. 1838.

[31] Ibid. 7 June, 1 July 1838. According to one scholar, the Cherokees' 'imprisonment in rude stockades by Scott's troops were accompanied by rape, robbery, murder, and acts of bestiality on the part of some of the soldiers'. Woodward, *The Cherokees*, 205.

[32] McLoughlin, *Champions of the Cherokees*, 172. For a broader description of the conditions on the removal boats, see Foreman, *Indian Removal*, 273–8, 284–5, 291–3.

leave were threatened. When one man told the soldiers that he could not depart because his little boy had been left behind, 'the soldier immediately leveled his gun at him, and compelled him immediately to go'. 'O that the Lord would be his defense,' Butrick moaned in his journal, 'and save him and his dear family from all the dangers to which they are exposed.'[33]

Butrick watched as the Cherokees who had spent the evening at his house were forced onto the boats. 'Those dear trembling doves who spent a night at our house', he wrote, were 'literally crammed into the boat'. He wrote that the vessel was 'a flat bottom boat, 100 feet long, 20 feet wide, and two stories high, fastened to an old steam boat'. The boat was so full, he added, 'that the timbers began to crack and give way, and the boat itself was on the point of sinking'. '[I]t is said,' he wrote, that 1,200 Cherokees 'were hurried off' in this manner at one time'. 'Who would think of crowding men, women and children, sick and well, into a boat together, with little, if any more room or accommodations than would be allowed to swine taken to market.' Butrick talked to a man who had been on a boat carrying a number of Cherokee men, women, and children to the Indian Territory. The man told Butrick that a 'great sickness was prevailing' among the Cherokees on the boat and that 'thirty had died'.[34]

On 25 July Butrick reported that there were 'about eight thousand Cherokees in camps waiting the first of September, then to be sent off to the West'. At the time, he apparently was not planning to depart with his spiritual charges; discussions on that issue were taking place with his mission board and the Cherokee leadership. At this point, therefore, Butrick continued to consider himself an observer of rather than a participant in the relocation. What Butrick heard over the summer about the fate of the first detachments to remove frightened and angered him. He heard, for example, a terrifying report that sick emigrants were being abandoned along the way. He also learned that some Cherokees

---

[33] Butrick, *Journal*, 10, 29 June 1838. According to a national newspaper, when individuals or groups of Cherokees refused to board the boats, 'The agent then struck a line through the camp;—the soldiers rushed in and drove the devoted victims into the boats, regardless of the cries and agonies of the poor helpless sufferers. In this cruel work, the most painful separations of families occurred.—Children were sent off and parents left, and so of other relations.' *Niles' National Register*, 18 Aug. 1838.

[34] Butrick, *Journal*, 10, 11 June 1838.

56 TIM ALAN GARRISON

were escaping and heading into the mountains, 'saying they never will go to the Arkansas'. Several thousand Cherokees migrated to the Arkansas river valley between 1780 and 1820, and some Cherokees in the east apparently believed that they were being forced to the same location. In fact, the appointed destination for the 1838 relocation was west of Arkansas in what is now Oklahoma.[35]

Butrick also received disturbing news from a group of about twenty Cherokees who had escaped one of the removal parties as it was being ushered to its embarkation point. The fugitives had been travelling among a group of about 1,100 Cherokees. They told Butrick that 'the whole company almost famished,—that for two days together they had nothing to eat, and the rest of the time but very little'. They also told him that as they were starting to cross a river one day that one woman was 'very sick' and 'unable to sit up, and lay on the ground'. One of the soldiers appeared, they told Butrick, and 'kicked her in the side and drove her into the boat'. They saw no other sign of the woman after the crossing, they said, and assumed that she had died. 'Six individuals', they added, 'had died before they left the company.' Butrick also heard 'by a person from Arkansas, that the last company of eight or ten hundred, are dying very fast'. He added: 'If three fourths of the three thousand hurried off as prisoners should be in eternity in six months, we should have no cause of surprise.'[36]

On 4 August Butrick was told that one company of Cherokees had missed their steamboat and returned to wait at Waterloo, Alabama, for another boat. Many of the 200 in the group were ill, and according to the report Butrick received, 'sometimes ten died in a day'. He listened to reports of catastrophic numbers of deaths: 'We also understand that a letter has been received from a physician at Waterloo, saying that one thousand of those who were sent in the fore part of summer to the West, are dead.'[37]

[35] Ibid. 25 July, 5 Sept. 1838. His sister, who visited him at the end of June, told him that a Creek woman, sick and near the point of death, had been abandoned by the army escorting the Creeks to the Indian Territory. '[H]er friends wished permission to stop and take care of her,' Butrick's sister told him; 'this however, was denied, and the poor woman was left alone to die in the dreary desert and be devoured by wild beasts.' Ibid. 27 June 1838.

[36] Ibid. 28 June, 23 July 1838.

[37] Ibid. 4, 7 Aug. 1838.

On the Trail of Tears

Butrick began to perceive a malicious intent behind the mounting casualty reports he was receiving. 'The question occurs', he wrote, 'whether these thousand deaths may not be viewed in the light of deliberate murder.' After describing the reports of the conditions on the boats, he wrote: 'This was known to the United States government. It was known to the agents engaged in getting the Indians to the West. It was told by Cherokees resident in Arkansas, and favorable to emigration, that it would be almost certain death to take the people there in the hot season of the year.' Butrick wrote that Isaac Bushyhead, a prominent Cherokee, had asked that the Cherokees not be sent by water on the crowded, disease-ridden steamboats to the west. 'Yet,' Butrick wrote, 'the removing agent, N. Smith, with the cruelty of a Nero, forced them into boats, into poisoned air, and hurried them away to a land of darkness, and the shadow of death, where they must sicken and die.' Butrick questioned the motivations of the officials superintending the schedule: 'Driving them under such circumstances, and then forcing them into filthy boats, to overflowing in this hot season, landing them at Little Rock, a most sickly place, to wait other means of conveyance 200 miles up the Arkansas river, is only a most expensive and painful way of putting the poor people to death.' Butrick predicted that 'Of the whole number sent this summer, the probability is that but very few comparatively will be alive one year from the time they started.'[38]

Butrick witnessed mismanagement of the provision procurement process that led to deaths from malnutrition, starvation, and intestinal diseases. He surmised, correctly it turns out, that many of the removal agents were enriching themselves and their colleagues in the procurement business. He saw valuable flour and corn being left to rot, food that could have been used to feed those going to hunger on the removal trails. 'O what liberality in the work of death,' he wrote, 'in getting the poor Cherokees to the West, how many thousand the United States will hasten into eternity.' He added, 'And these are mostly women and children and helpless old people.' The New Echota Treaty had 'placed both the lives and the entire possessions of the nation in the hands of strangers', Butrick said, and the United States knew at the time that 'the probability one hundred to one was that the

[38] Ibid. 4, 7 Aug., 10 June 1838.

58   TIM ALAN GARRISON

business would fall into the hands of merciless speculators'. Not only that, Butrick wrote, the US government understood that the removal was grounded upon a fraudulent treaty. He wrote: 'But here it is said, the country has been purchased by treaty. But who says this? The President evidently knows there has been no treaty made with the nation. The secretary of war knows it. Both houses of congress know it. And does not every governor, and every other officer of high standing in the whole union know it? Do they not all know that the nation, have continually and almost unanimously protested against that fraudulent instrument, purporting to be a treaty?'[39]

Butrick was enraged by what he saw: 'As I write, the poor Cherokees are passing by, carrying their loads from one place to another, beneath a most melting heat, vainly hoping to find some place of repose. The heat, together with their journeyings and distress, is overpowering them, and bringing them, and bringing them swiftly, to the grave.' He was furious with his own nation: 'Now, in view of the whole scene, how does the United States government appease a great nation, laying aside her dignity and with thousands of soldiers, and all her great men, and all her mighty men, and all her powerful generals, with all her civil and military force, chasing a little trembling hare in the wilderness, merely to take its skin, and send it off to broil in the scorching deserts of the West. O how Noble! How magnanimous! How warlike the achievement! O what a conquest! What booty! How becoming the glory and grandeur of the United States!'[40]

The Trail of Tears

After the calamities experienced by the detachments that had departed in the early summer, the Cherokee government had

---

[39] Ibid. 7, 8 Aug. 1838. Butrick also complained about how the removals were being treated in the newspapers: '[A]ll this removal of the Indians is represented by Editors of newspapers as being conducted with the utmost kindness, and without suffering, and I am sorry to say that the *Boston Recorder* gives a perfectly incorrect view of this subject by publishing only such extract from Southern papers, as keep the sufferings of the Indians entirely out of view.' Even his home paper, the *Missionary Herald*, he added, provided misleading information about the Treaty of New Echota that had called for the Cherokees' removal. Ibid. 23 July 1838.

[40] Ibid. 7, 8 Aug. 1838.

On the Trail of Tears

persuaded General Winfield Scott to allow it to manage the relocation of the remaining detachments. Scott had conceded, and the Cherokee leaders had agreed to recommence the departures on 1 September. The Cherokees were thus freed from the close supervision of the federal army and reacquired some freedom of movement. In late August, most of the Cherokees in the stockades near Butrick's home were moved to camps where they were organized into detachments of approximately 1,000 individuals. At the time, Butrick remained unsure as to whether he and his wife would remove with the Cherokees. Their Cherokee congregation wanted and expected the Butricks to accompany them to the west. On 2 August Butrick had written to Stephen Foreman, the Cherokee minister and leader, and asked him to 'bring the case of our going to the West before the council, as we concluded not to go unless the chiefs favour it'. 'Other difficulties in the West', he added, 'will be sufficient without opposition from the council.' By difficulties, Butrick was referring to the 'gambling, frolicking, drinking, fighting, adultery, and every species of vice [that] prevail there to an alarming extent, without opposition from the present chiefs'. He had also heard that Fort Gibson in the Indian Territory was a 'source of moral corruption to the Cherokees', and that the New Echota Treaty had created factions among the Cherokees and the missionaries in the west.[41] Butrick was, however, willing to follow a calling: 'In the face of so many difficulties, we would not urge our way to the West, but when our duty is clear, all objections vanish. Should the Lord direct, we will cheerfully go with our dear Cherokee friends wherever they may be obliged to go.' On 21 August Butrick wrote again for advice 'with regard to going to the west'. By 27 August Butrick had his decision. He wrote in his diary that Richard Taylor, who was to lead one of the removal companies, told him that John Ross had decided that Butrick and his wife

---

[41] The Treaty of New Echota not only created divisions in Cherokee society, but misinformation about its contents had created confusion among those waiting to depart. According to the treaty, the United States was to pay individual Cherokees for their homes and improvements. Over the summer, the false rumour spread that those who accepted money from the US government for their property would have to depart for the west, while those who refused to accept compensation could remain in their homes. Those who believed these rumours 'went off in the night', Butrick reported. 'Probably they will be sent for again,' he wrote, 'and hunted up by the soldiers, and driven on as prisoners to the west.' Ibid. 2, 26 Aug., 12 Sept. 1838.

could 'go in any detachment we please and draw our rations by the way, the same as if a Cherokee family'. 'This', Butrick said, 'is all we could desire.' Butrick secured permission to travel with Taylor's detachment. Butrick contemplated how he would travel to the Indian Territory and what he might do with his possessions at Brainerd. After receiving an offer for his 'occupant right' to his home, he wrote: '[T]he thought occurred that I might perhaps obtain 8 or 1000 dollars, purchase a decent carriage and go in good style to the west.' After randomly coming across a pertinent passage from *Pilgrim's Progress*, Butrick recognized that he would be profiting from the Cherokees' plight and 'concluded to let the occupant right, and every other method of getting money wrongfully, alone. And may God help me to keep my resolutions.'[42]

On 1 September, the date scheduled for a mass departure, the Cherokee leadership again delayed the embarkation date. Butrick explained that 'the drought is such that they cannot travel in large companies without great suffering for want of water'. 'The Chickamauga Creek,' he added, 'is probably lower than it has ever been known to be by the oldest persons living.' The removal managers decided to again postpone the departures until autumn rains replenished the creeks and rivers. Several thousand Cherokees were therefore required to sit in the embarkation camps for many more weeks.[43]

On 4 October Butrick and his wife left their home in Brainerd for the assembly camp 'near Mr. Vanns'. 'Thus we leave this place,' he wrote, 'perhaps never to return.' He continued to feel a powerful sense of ambivalence about going to the west. He wrote: 'O what scenes of distress we have experienced here for two years past. Yet the Lord has been kind, and delivered us out of all our distresses, so that the water floods have not overflowed us. And I set out for the Arkansaw bound in spirit, feeling that afflictions await us.' As the Cherokees waited to embark, the Butricks, living in a tent, continued to hold services and visit the ill. Butrick's work and sleep were often interrupted by drunks who were procuring whiskey from a white man who was operating a tavern near the camp. Butrick complained that 'At night the woods around us seem filled with drunkards, who went about

---

[42] Ibid. 2, 21, 27 Aug., 21 Sept. 1838.
[43] Ibid. 1 Sept. 1838; Woodward, *The Cherokees*, 214; Foreman, *Indian Removal*, 299–300.

On the Trail of Tears

yelling like dogs all night long, so that we could not sleep till the latter part of the night.' The card-playing and blasphemies of the drunks, some Cherokee and some white, frustrated Butrick and the devout Cherokees. Predatory malingerers also annoyed Butrick: 'White men flocked in from every quarter, some to collect debts, some to sell cabbages, or other things, and some simply to walk about, seeking whom they might devour, leading the unwary Indians down to death. . . . The white men in this country generally, seem devoid of moral principles.'[44]

Alcohol and gambling were sore issues for Butrick. He pointed to the habits as the source of the Cherokees' ills, and he believed that the United States and the Southern state governments had intentionally fostered the chaotic situation that had developed in the Cherokee Nation. 'For ten years,' Butrick wrote at one point, 'the power, the wisdom, and the funds of the whole union have been employed for the temporal and eternal ruin of this little handful of Indians.' He provided his own interpretation of the series of events that had led to the Cherokees' removal:

They were rendered lawless, and it was made a penitentiary crime for any of their rulers to execute or attempt to execute their laws. Thus all the laws which the council had wisely enacted respecting liquor and gambling, were at once annulled, and every one left to follow his own inclination. The country was soon filled with liquor to overflowing; and stores of liquor and cards were set up to induce gambling, while white gamblers were strolling through the country, seeking whom they could destroy. Many of the white men who established little stores to induce drinking and gambling go in with some Cherokees, who thus became engaged with them in carrying the plans of government into effort, thus gambling spread like wild fire through the country with none to check it.

As a consequence, the young people of the Cherokee Nation had come to 'disregard their own chiefs' and 'despise their parents and teachers'. Butrick believed that these spiritual indiscretions had brought about the Cherokees' demise: 'Their almost universal Saturday night frolics, carried through the Holy Sabbath, had already drawn down Divine wrath upon them.'[45]

As they lingered in the embarkation camp during much of October, the weather began to change. Concerns about the

[44] Butrick, *Journal*, 4, 5, 17, 20, 21, 22 Oct. 1838.
[45] Ibid. 1 July 1838.

damp and the cold began to creep into Butrick's diary. He worried, for instance, that many Cherokees had refused to accept the clothing provided by the government on the grounds that it would signify their acceptance of the removal. To make matters worse, rumours were unsettling the Cherokees as they awaited their departure. They had heard that 'most of those sent from Ross's landing last summer are dead, and those not dead are mostly sick'.[46]

The Cherokees remained determined to overcome these challenges. A number of them assembled at Rattlesnake Springs, near what is now Charleston, Tennessee, and agreed to abide by their national constitution and laws once they reached the Indian Territory. Hearing that their time for departure was nearing, the members of the Brainerd and Haweis churches met to organize plans for how they would carry on as a congregation on the removal trail. They passed resolutions stating that they would continue to observe the Sabbath while on the road 'as far as practicable' and that they would take their spiritual interests into account in deciding where and how to settle once in the Indian Territory. Butrick personally vowed to honour the Sabbath and spend it in worship while on the trail. In accordance with these resolutions, Butrick held services on almost every Sunday as they travelled and hosted prayer meetings many other nights after they encamped at the end of the day. He was often forced to ride ahead of the detachment on Saturday evenings or catch up with it on Mondays to fulfil his promise regarding the Sabbath commandment.[47]

One of the resolutions of the congregation demonstrated how the removal had divided the Cherokees. The congregants agreed that 'they would not unite in Christian fellowship with those who made, signed or executed the New Echota treaty, without a confession on their part'. The treaty signatories had not just committed a political crime against the Cherokee people, the congregation declared; they had committed a sin and needed to seek forgiveness from their fellow Cherokees. The congregations also resolved that they would not recognize the Revd John F. Schermerhorn, the agent who had arranged the treaty, as a minister, 'or even as a common Christian'. According to Butrick,

[46] Ibid. 15, 16, 18 Oct. 1838.
[47] Ibid. 31 Oct., 4, 11, 18 Nov. 1838.

the resolutions were passed with assent of all present but one. Butrick suggested that the dissenter, Johnson Reece, was reluctant to agree because he was 'doubtless influenced by his father & brothers, who evidently favour the treaty, and have moved to the west agreeable to its requisitions'. Butrick connoted those sympathetic to the Treaty of New Echota with those involved in 'unchristian practices'. After suggesting that one of Reece's brothers had engaged in 'criminal intercourse with a young woman', Butrick wrote: 'I fear there is not one who has favoured this treaty who has any true love to God.' He pointed out that Elias Boudinot, the former editor of the *Cherokee Phoenix* and one of the leading members of the Treaty Party, 'went to a ball play on the sabbath' and refused to 'acknowledge his fault before the church'. Boudinot, of course, had worked extensively with the missionary Samuel A. Worcester to translate spiritual materials into the Cherokee language. Butrick's specific criticism of Boudinot is another indication of how the divisions over removal had spread from the Cherokee polity into their attendant clergy. Butrick's anger towards Boudinot and the other Cherokees who had signed the Treaty of New Echota continued throughout the journey. Butrick fretted that Samuel Worcester would 'excuse Mr. Boudinot in the course he has taken'. The board, he complained, had already named Boudinot an assistant missionary in the west. 'They doubtless look over his conduct in making the treaty', he wrote. Butrick called for a full investigation into the circumstances surrounding the signing of the Treaty of New Echota in front of 'his Brainerd brethren' when they reached their destination.[48] The treaty had also created divisions between some Cherokees and the missionaries. Butrick discovered over the summer of 1838 that many Cherokees were reluctant to shake his hand. When he asked why, he was told that there was 'an idea in circulation' among the Cherokees that Worcester and Elizur Butler had conspired to bring about the Treaty of New Echota and that all of the missionaries were suspect.[49]

On 11 October the remaining Cherokees who were sympathetic to the Treaty Party departed under the leadership of John

---

[48] Ibid. 31 Oct. 1838; McLoughlin, *Champions of the Cherokees*, 179–80. For a discussion of Boudinot and his motives, see Theda Perdue (ed.), *Cherokee Editor: The Writings of Elias Boudinot* (Knoxville, Tenn., 1983), 23–33.

[49] Butrick, *Journal*, 18 June 1838.

A. Bell. Eight more detachments of approximately 1,000 each followed in October. Unlike the first emigrants, who set out in June on steam and flat boats, the detachments that removed in October travelled overland to the west. By the autumn, the Tennessee and Arkansas rivers were still so low from the summer drought that they were not navigable, and there was a real concern that the detachments might not have access to regular supplies of drinking water for themselves and their stock. With boat transport out of the question, most the Cherokees had to travel by foot. Butrick's contingent did not leave until the morning of 1 November 1838. Four other detachments left the same week, all from Ross's Landing, with the final party pushing off on 4 November. Ross remained behind at the Cherokee agency in Calhoun, Tennessee to oversee the departures. The chief, his family, and a large number of ill and infirm Cherokees followed their countrymen on a predominantly water route on 4 December 1838.[50]

Butrick's detachment usually arose long before daybreak and was on the road by early morning. A detachment typically carried with it several hundred wagons and drove before it thousands of head of stock. Most of the wagons were required to carry provisions for the Cherokees and the horses, swine, and oxen; little room was reserved in the wagons for the exiles. While many Cherokees were forced to walk the entire way, the Butricks were fortunate to travel in a wagon for most of the journey. Butrick, it should be noted, was not unaccustomed to arduous travel. According to a report he filed with the mission board early in his career, he held 171 meetings in a one-year period in the Cherokee Nation, a chore that had required him to ride 3,400 miles. Perhaps this explains why Butrick often complained about the weather conditions and the morality of the towns they passed along the way, but never bemoaned the travel required in the relocation.[51] Butrick's detachment followed the same general

---

[50] Ross's wife Quattie caught sick and passed away on the journey. According to a soldier who accompanied the Cherokees: 'This noble hearted woman died a martyr to childhood. Giving her only Blanket for the protection of a sick child she rode thinly clad through a blinding sleet and snow storm developed Pneumonia and died in the still Hours of a bleak winter night.' She was buried near Little Rock. Moulton, *John Ross*, 99.

[51] Butrick, *Journal*, 24, 25 Dec. 1838, 19 Mar. 1839; Daniel Butrick to Jeremiah Evarts, 3 Sept. 1824, in McLoughlin, *Cherokee Renascence in the New Republic*, 382–3; Foreman, *Indian Removal*, 302, 310–12.

On the Trail of Tears

path trodden by the earlier companies that moved overland: from Ross's Landing they crossed the Tennessee river at Blythe's Ferry at the junction of the Hiwassee river. They then marched on through Pikesville, McMinnville, and Nashville, Tennessee. At Nashville, Lewis Ross, the chief's brother, met the detachments and provided them with supplies, including clothing for the coming winter. After a brief respite in Nashville, Butrick's detachment crossed the Cumberland river. After travelling in a north-west direction, they turned due west at Marion, Kentucky, and crossed the Ohio at Golconda, Illinois. From there they travelled west across southern Illinois and crossed the Mississippi at Cape Girardeau, Missouri. The Cherokees then passed through Farmington, Rolla, Lebanon, and Springfield, Missouri, travelled north of Fayetteville, Arkansas, and entered the north-eastern corner of the Indian Territory.[52]

The Taylor detachment ran into problems as soon as it set out. One of the wagons almost sank in a river crossing. Soon thereafter, they came to a spot on the trail where the white property-owner had built a fence across the road, forcing the wagons to push through a space on a dangerous side hill barely wide enough to pass. One wagon ran off down a hill; another turned over. During the early part of their journey the rain continued for several days, and the wagons became mired in mud.[53]

Though they were now beyond the control of the soldiers, they were still not free from harassment. On the first several nights of their journey, 'whites' met the detachment with barrels of whiskey and enticed some in the group to drink. Butrick complained that the drunks kept the detachment up each night fighting and swearing. One Cherokee, drunk from the whiskey, fell asleep next to a campfire and caught fire. He succumbed to his injuries a month later. Further along in their journey, an elderly man suffered the same horrible death. Drinking remained a problem the entire time the Cherokees were travelling to the west. Perhaps indulging in some hyperbole, Butrick described the case of a young Cherokee man who drank himself into oblivion: 'Soon after we crossed the Tennessee River this young man was taken sick. The physician being called, bled him, and it was said that the blood was so impregnated with whiskey as to emit a

---

[52] Moulton, *John Ross*, 100; Butrick, *Journal*, 1 Nov.–1 Apr. 1838.
[53] Ibid. 12–14 Nov. 1838, 14 Jan. 1839.

strong smell of it, as it flew from his vein. He had been intoxicated, it was said, for a number of weeks.' The young man eventually died in Missouri. The Cherokees were not without means to deal with these disruptions. The detachments maintained police and legal institutions along the trail to deal with the unrest. In some cases, the Cherokee Lighthorse Guard, the nation's police unit, captured the drunks and tied them up until they were sober. The guard turned the troublemakers over to a council of the Cherokees, who levied fines for their misbehaviour.[54]

White malingerers, liquor pedlars, and vagrants plagued the Cherokee caravan all the way across Tennessee. A few days out on the trail, the Cherokees camped overnight in a spot known as the Vale of Sodom. 'Here', Butrick wrote, 'the people were wicked exceedingly, and gathered in from every quarter.' The detachment was accosted by a group of drunken whites, who disturbed Butrick's prayer meeting and kept the Cherokees up for much of the night. Butrick wrote: 'All night long they wandered about among the camps seeking whom they might destroy, and seemed intent on filling the air about our fire with their horrid oaths.' He added that '[T]he poor Cherokees seemed to stand astonished at the exceeding wickedness of the whites, and kept very sober during the night.' 'Just as day broke,' he concluded, 'these evening wolves raised their howl and retreated to their thickets.' White locals also came begging for money. Near Stone's River in Tennessee, Butrick wrote: 'Soon after we had pitched our tents, a great company of white people came in, as eager, apparently, for money, as ever birds of prey were for a dead carcass. Some appeared civil, but others were awfully profane.'[55]

The weather began to turn worse as they traversed the hills and mountains of eastern Tennessee. Butrick's detachment often had to camp in the rain, wind, and snow. Many of the Cherokees did not possess a tent and were forced to sleep 'soaking wet, lying on the wet ground'. On 6 November, as they moved over a mountain near Warren County, Tennessee, Butrick described

[54] Ibid. 1, 3, 4, 5, 6, 11, 16 Nov., 1, 13, 17 Dec. 1838, 17, 18 Jan., 4 Mar. 1839.

[55] Ibid. 6, 15 Nov. 1838. Butrick occasionally met beneficent whites. Near Nashville, 'a gentleman by the name of Bryant, his wife & two other ladies' visited Butrick at the Cherokee encampment and offered clothing to those in need. A minister in the town provided Butrick's wife with 'a valuable cloak, bonnet, shawl, and a pair of shoes'. Ibid. 21, 26 Nov. 1838.

On the Trail of Tears

the inclement weather: 'Soon after dark it commenced raining, and the wind drove the water into our carryall so that our bed and clothes became quite wet on one side. The weather also became very cold, and our blankets over the wagon were covered with snow when we arose.' By morning the steep road down the mountain was frozen and treacherous.[56]

By the time they reached Kentucky in early December, the Taylor detachment was encountering heavy snow and frozen rain at frequent intervals. Despite the weather, they were now progressing toward their destination at ten to twelve miles a day. By late December, the Cherokees were experiencing what Butrick called 'piercing cold'. On 23 December Butrick gave thanks 'for the preservation of the last night'. He and his wife had survived a bitter winter storm: 'The wind blew a gale nearly the whole night, and seemed to threaten almost certain calamity, both by scattering the fire through the leaves and tents, and also by throwing limbs, trees etc. upon our heads. But those eyes which never slumber watched over us, and preserved us in safety, though we had but little sleep.'[57]

The Cherokees continued to be afflicted with a variety of ailments along the way. When they took ill, the sick had to continue walking or riding, or be left behind. 'The poor sick Cherokees cannot stop, when sick & be refreshed by kind friends,' Butrick wrote, 'but must be exposed and die.' Butrick's detachment passed acquaintances who had become ill and been left behind by their own groups. On 13 December, near the Ohio river in Kentucky, Butrick saw Isaac Bushyhead and two other men who had fallen back from their detachment. Butrick spent the evening in conversation with the men, who told him that 'sixty persons had died out of their detachment previous to their arrival at that place'. In at least one case, near the end of the march, an old Cherokee man, sick from some unstated affliction, fell behind and was left for dead. He apparently walked all night in an effort to catch up with his own group. Butrick heard about the situation and sent the man's brother back with a horse to find him. 'Had it been a common time,' Butrick wrote, 'I should have seen more about it, but today we had to perform two days travel, & were obliged to hasten on as

---

[56] Ibid. 4, 6 Nov. 1838.
[57] Ibid. 3, 23 Dec. 1838.

the road was hard.' The next day, Butrick found time to meet with the man, who was 'very sick'.[58]

Butrick himself took ill on several occasions on the trip. On the morning of 14 November he complained that he 'puked up my breakfast, and felt that I must soon yield to sickness and disease'. On 18 December he complained of a high fever. When he took an emetic, he 'was seized with a severe pain in my right side'. A bleeding by a physician, and an application of a mustard seed poultice on his side, relieved the pain. Although the Butricks preferred assistance from white doctors, at times they accepted Cherokee medicine. For example, at one point Butrick noted that 'War Club, our old friend, gave us some slippery elm bark to use for the bowel complaint.' Butrick's wife was also ill for much of the journey. Their afflictions often ran concurrently, and they had difficulty taking care of each other. On 5 January he recorded that 'My dear wife is now unwell, afflicted with a ague. Her strength has been declining a number of days.' On the same day Butrick wrote that 'I am also scarcely able to walk.' On 21 January Butrick again complained about the couple's health: 'My dear wife and myself are both troubled with a diarrhea. I have also been troubled with a swelling I feared would become dangerous.'[59]

Despite these troubles, Butrick and his spouse survived the long march to the west. Many of their Cherokee friends and acquaintances, however, did not. Butrick often recorded deaths along the way, and his journal was replete with the passings of his cohorts. He listed deaths on at least twenty-two days of his journal during the five-month march.[60] On 14 December Butrick noted in his diary that a 'child about 12 months old' had died. 'This is the 15th death', he wrote, 'since we crossed the Tennessee River.' Most died from illness, malnutrition, and exposure, but some were injured in accidents. One woman was killed when a wagon, traversing a side hill, flipped over on top of her. Another woman died and two others were wounded when a tree fell on them as they slept. One of the wagons ran over the neck and head of a 'little boy'. 'The physicians were called,'

---

[58] Ibid. 18 Nov., 2 Dec. 1838, 16, 17 Mar. 1839.

[59] Ibid. 14 Nov., 18, 28, 29 Dec. 1838, 2, 3, 5, 9, 10, 12, 21 Jan. 1839.

[60] Ibid. 5, 10, 16, 18 Nov., 1, 13, 20, 22 Dec. 1838, 1, 7, 22, 24 Jan., 12 Feb., 1, 3, 4, 6, 8, 11, 16, 17, 20 Mar. 1839.

On the Trail of Tears

Butrick reported, 'but supposing he would certainly die, did nothing for him.'[61]

Some died in Butrick's presence: 'Just before meeting, I visited a family, in which was a boy ten or twelve years old, sick with the bowel complaint. He extended his emaciated hand to take mine, & then pointed to the place of his extreme pain. Before our meeting closed, he was a corpse.' Most of the deceased were simply buried along the side of the road, and Butrick presided at several of their funerals. The sides of the trail, in fact, became dotted with makeshift cemeteries for the Cherokee dead. On 13 December Butrick described the death and burial of a woman who had recently given birth:

During the night a Cherokee woman died in the camps. Though she had given birth to a child but a few days before, yet last evening she was up, & no danger was apprehended, but in the morning she was found dead, with the infant in her arms. As the man living near was not willing to have her buried there, and as no plank could be obtained for a coffin, the corpse was carried all day in the wagon, and at night a coffin was made, and the next morning she was buried near the graves of some other Cherokees who had died in a detachment that had preceded us.[62]

The caravan did enjoy a few brief respites from the difficult journey. After one calm evening, Butrick wrote: 'Here we had a pleasant night. The elements were still & quiet, and the stars sparkled with peculiar luster.' In many spots along the way, the Butricks were met by local religious leaders and brought in out of the weather. For example, Butrick was pleased and impressed with the reception when they paused for a few days to resupply in Nashville: 'This is a beautiful city. I have seen no such place in my view since I left Boston.' Butrick spent a day 'delightfully' with the Bryants, a Christian family who lived in the town. While in Nashville, Butrick arranged to have two local ministers conduct services on Saturday and Sunday. With the weather cold, a local Baptist elder invited the Cherokee Christians to hold their services at his home—'a large brick house, well finished, and furnished with two stoves'. Butrick wrote that 'The whole was delightful, & will not soon be forgotten by us. O how kind was our Heavenly Father in providing for us such a meeting

---

[61] Ibid. 5 Nov., 14 Dec. 1838, 22 Jan., 22, 23 Mar. 1839.
[62] Ibid. 13 Dec. 1838, 17 Mar. 1839.

house, & such kind friends, just at the time they were so much needed.' In most cases, however, the hospitality was dispensed to only the missionary and his wife. The Cherokees were usually left to spend their evenings along the road. Only a few Cherokees received acts of kindness from the whites they passed along the way. One was of a particularly patronizing character. Near the Red river in Kentucky, a woman 'gave the little Cherokee boy with us, a Dollar, wishing him to take the sir name of Usher'.[63]

The detachment also had its moments of joy. Butrick performed a wedding during the trip. Fifteen children were born along the way. These moments, however, were always overshadowed by subsequent grief in Butrick's journal. For example, on 1 December Butrick noted: 'On Wednesday night of this week, sister Ooskoone gave birth to a son, and on Thursday two children, one a daughter of our dear sister Ashhopper, were called into eternity.'[64]

In mid December, the Taylor detachment moved briefly into Illinois; and Butrick was surprised and disappointed to discover that Northerners were just as vulgar and just as antagonistic towards the Cherokees as Southerners. On 15 December he wrote about their ferry crossing over the Ohio river: 'As we were passing out of a slave state into a free, we reflected on the pleasure of landing where all were in a measure equal and free. But we had scarcely landed when we were met with volleys of oaths from every quarter.' He complained about the 'awful profaneness' of the men near the landing. Even the 'little boys in the streets had already learned to lisp the infernal language'. Some of the white residents of southern Illinois, moreover, refused to allow the Cherokees to cut wood or camp on their land. The Illinois locals, Butrick wrote, 'come to sell & get gain, but not to invite any to a friendly roof'. At one point, 'a very aged Cherokee' man from the detachment in front of Butrick's wandered back to the latter's group. After a few days, the 'old man' wandered away and died. 'The citizens near the river' discovered the man's body, tied it to a chain, and used a team of oxen to pull it along the road to a burial site. This group then tried to force George Hicks, one of the Cherokee detachment leaders, to pay for the 'cost' of burying the man. When Hicks

[63] Ibid. 25 Nov., 2 Dec. 1838, 21 Jan., 23, 24 Feb., 3, 23 Mar. 1839.
[64] Ibid. 1, 13 Dec. 1838, 8 Jan. 1839; Foreman, *Indian Removal*, 311.

On the Trail of Tears

refused, claiming that the deceased belonged to another detachment, 'the citizens' secured a warrant for Hicks's arrest. 'The man who was the principal in this prosecution', Butrick wrote, 'is suspected of having killed the old man himself.' Hicks was acquitted and released. 'The citizens of this state', Butrick concluded, 'seem thus far to display a more mean & niggardly disposition than I have ever found in any other part of the union.' This was quite a statement, considering the ruffians he had encountered in Georgia and Tennessee.[65]

Butrick and the Cherokees spent Christmas in the state they found so inhospitable. On Christmas eve, the wagon Butrick and his wife were riding in lost a linchpin out of one axle and the wheel came off. They walked six miles until they reached the home of a wagon-maker, where they spent the night. These residents of Illinois failed to impress Butrick: 'The workman, the man of the house, came home a little before night in a high state of intoxication, & almost every word was accompanied by an oath.' The woman told Butrick that this was not uncommon for those parts; even 'their preacher himself sometimes gets drunk'. Butrick left the wagon-maker's home, and the state, with this impression: 'Thus far the citizens of Illinois appear more & more pitiable. They seem not only low in all their manners, but ignorant, poor, and ill humoured. They have no slaves . . . and because they cannot have slaves, let their work go undone.'[66]

The coming end of the year put Butrick in a reflective mood. He was disappointed at his own spiritual fallibility: 'Previous to starting on this journey, I determined to let it be a journey of prayer, and to devote much time every day to that sacred duty, but instead of this, I have strangely neglected prayer.' He complained that his mornings were taken up in preparing for departure: 'taking our bed etc. from the little wagon in which we sleep, to the large wagon which carries it, replacing the seat, getting water, cooking breakfast, putting up things, harnessing, etc. Soon we are hurried on by the wagons we accompany to the next encampment. Here we have to undo what we did in the morning, put up our tent, get wood, and water, prepare supper, fix our bed, etc.' By the time all was completed, Butrick said, he was too tired to conduct his prayers. The rationalizations

---

[65] Butrick, *Journal*, 15 Dec. 1838, 1, 14 Jan. 1839.
[66] Ibid. 24, 25 Dec. 1838.

bedevilled Butrick: 'I know that all this cannot justify a neglect of prayer. I think my own heart is more peculiarly depraved, especially as respects impatient & angry feelings.' At the time his health was also making him despondent. '[I]t is very doubtful whether I live to reach that place', he wrote.[67]

As their detachment neared the Mississippi river, Butrick heard reports that the companies in front of him were impeded from crossing by 'floating ice'. The Ohio to the north, he heard, was also similarly obstructed. By now, the weather was so difficult that Butrick's group made camp for a week. 'Here,' he wrote, 'the snow increased to three or four inches, and the weather was excessively cold.' In the following entry, he described the progress and condition of the detachments that had departed in late October and early November:

It is distressing to reflect on the situation of the [Cherokee] nation. One detachment stopped at the Ohio River, two at the Mississippi, one four miles this side, one 16 miles this side, one 18 miles, and one 3 miles behind us. [At this point, Butrick's detachment was approximately 25 miles from the Mississippi.] In all these detachments, comprising about 8,000 souls, there is now a vast amount of sickness, and many deaths. Six have died within a short time in Maj. Brown's company, and in this detachment. Of Mr. Taylor's there are more or less affected with sickness in almost every tent; and yet all are houseless & homeless in a strange land, and in a cold region exposed to weather almost unknown in their native country.

James Mooney reported decades later that he had interviewed men and women at Tahlequah and 'found that the lapse of over half a century had not sufficed to wipe out the memory of the miseries of that halt beside the frozen river, with hundreds of sick and dying penned up in wagons or stretched upon the ground, with only a blanket overhead'.[68]

On 31 December Butrick again angrily reflected on the recent course of events. This time he directed his attention to the architects of the removal policy:

O what a year it has been! O what a sweeping wind has gone over, and carried its thousands into the grave; while thousands of others have been tortured and scarcely survive, and the whole nation comparatively

---

[67] Ibid. 20, 22 Dec. 1838.
[68] Ibid. 26, 27, 28, 29 Dec. 1838; Mooney, *Myths of the Cherokees*, 133.

On the Trail of Tears

thrown out of house & home during this most dreary winter. And why? As coming from God, we know it is just. But what have they done to the U. States? Have they violated any treaty? Or any intercourse law; or abused any of the agents or officers of the U. States? Or have they refused to accommodate U. States citizens when passing through their country? No such thing is pretended. For what crime then was this whole nation doomed to this perpetual death? This almost unheard of suffering?

He closed with a self-indictment: 'The year past has been a year of spiritual darkness. We have had but few happy seasons, and as for myself, I have by no means been faithful to my trust. I have wanted faith & love & zeal. A great part of my time my heart has been grieved to hear the awful profanements and see the scenes of wickedness which have been brought before us.'[69]

Butrick's anger at the end of the year was replaced by gratitude in the new year that opened the following morning: 'O how kind the Lord is in providing all things to keep us from suffering. . . . Though we have been distressed on every side, yet we have not been destroyed.' He was appreciative of 'the dear Board that supports me, & the poor Cherokees, who still bear with me', and 'thankful for the health and love of his wife'. '[T]hrough the whole summer and fall, her labours have been peculiarly trying,' Butrick wrote, 'and since we have been on this journey, for three long months, she has slept in a wagon or a tent, & been exposed to cold & wet, and at present has to go forward again, and take care of me in my ill health, yet she has not sunk under her burdens.' 'The Lord has sustained, & blessed be His Name,' Butrick completed his thanksgiving for his wife: 'O that her health, spiritual & temporal, may be still preserved.' With the coming of the new year, Butrick could now look back at the miserable things that had occurred and realize that they could have been worse:

O what unspeakable gratitude is due for his mercies past. And O how kindly has he dealt with us since we set out on this journey. During the three months we have been thus in the wilderness, no tempest has been let loose to throw down the many trees hanging over, and no flashing lightning to frighten the timid. And very seldom have we experienced any special inconvenience from rain. Though some have been sick, & fallen on the way, yet many still survive, in circumstances calling for gratitude.

[69] Butrick, *Journal*, 31 Dec. 1838.

74 TIM ALAN GARRISON

Thus concluded what was a rare spasm of optimism for Butrick, who had endured with his company the most challenging of circumstances.[70]

They reached the Mississippi river, 'one of the wonders of creation', on 25 January. Butrick and his wife were transfixed by the sight of 'a large, beautiful & grand steam boat'. 'Neither my dear wife, nor myself,' he wrote, 'had ever seen one before.' Butrick described the crossing procedure near Camp Girardeau: 'At this place a sand bar in the middle extends probably half across the bed of the river, leaving two sluices of about an equal width on each side. Therefore it is like two rivers, crossed by two ferries, that is, two sets of boats, one conveying passengers to the bar, and the other from it.' Sighting the river set off another episode of emotion. Butrick noted that 'We have long been looking forward to this river; and numbers who crossed the Ohio with us have not lived to arrive at this. O how kind our dear heavenly Father has been to us. Though some affliction has fallen to our lot, yet O how light & with what peculiar kindness it has been laid upon us.'[71]

Butrick's detachment crossed the next day: 'Through Divine goodness, we were conveyed safely over the great river, though we had to wait some hours on the sandbar when the wind blew almost a gale.' A storm was apparently approaching, and the next two days after the crossing were marked by wind and cold rain and snow. Ice began to form again in the river. The Cherokees who had not crossed with Butrick were left stranded on the eastern side, and it took them another two weeks to cross that great divide. Butrick's group remained for three weeks near the Mississippi, waiting for the ice to thaw so that the remainder of the detachment could cross and catch up. For unknown reasons, Butrick wrote very little during this hiatus. While he had recorded at least a sentence or two almost every day of the preceding several months, in February he left comments on only six days. He did note that five of the sojourners, 'one old Cherokee woman, one black man, & three Cherokee children', had died during their delay along the river. In all, Butrick determined that twenty-six members of their entourage had died since they crossed the Tennessee river a few weeks before.[72]

[70] Ibid. 1 Jan. 1839.   [71] Ibid. 25 Jan. 1839.
[72] Ibid. 26, 28 Jan., 12 Feb. 1839.

On the Trail of Tears

By 21 February the Cherokees were 'eleven miles west of Farmington (Missouri) & 80 miles from the Mississippi River'. In his entry for 26–8 February Butrick reported that the directors of his detachment had consulted with John Ross at Jonesborough. Ross told them that 'considering the unexpected delays and expenses of the journey', the detachment needed to 'press forward as fast as practicable'. He noted that the assistant director of the detachment, Judge Adair, had urged them to travel on the Sabbath. 'I reminded our Cherokee friends however,' Butrick wrote, 'that the Lord is here and requires the same observance of the Holy Sabbath as when we are at home.'[73]

When the calendar turned to March, Butrick was back to his old voluble self in his diary, recording entries on twenty-seven days of the month. Optimistically, he believed for a short time that the worst had passed. Just as he thought the weather was moderating, his detachment was struck by a late winter storm. On 8 March he wrote:

The day was beautiful, and warm as May, so that we began to talk of Summer clothes. In the night on hearing it thunder and rain as we supposed, I sprang up to secure some things exposed to the weather, when I found our summer had changed to winter; and instead of rain we were beset with hard round snow. Soon, however, the snow fell in flakes and covered the ground about ankle deep. I kindled a fire, but the wind kept whirling in almost every direction so that I could scarcely stand by the fire, without being enveloped in smoke. We soon found ourselves encountering a southern winter, and could not secure ourselves from the piercing cold. I told my dear wife that it seemed almost as if we must perish. We, however, succeeded in getting breakfast, and with the company of poor suffering Cherokees started on our journey, and proceeded seven miles. On the way we suffered exceedingly with the cold; and after passing through a long piece of woods, we arrived at a house which gave us great joy.

When Butrick approached the house seeking warmth and shelter for his party, he was told 'by an unseen voice, we could not warm by the fire, as the house was full, though I believe there were but few persons by the fire'. Butrick's company was forced to spend the frigid evening camped beside the Little Piney river.[74]

By the middle of March, Butrick's group was approaching the

---

[73] Ibid. 21, 26, 27, 28 Feb. 1839.
[74] Ibid. 8 Mar. 1839.

Arkansas river valley, or 'that land of spiritual darkness', as he called it. As the Cherokees approached their destination, Butrick despaired that he might not have the faith to continue his ministry: 'I fear I am becoming more & more unfit for the holy warfare.' By this time the fickle southern spring was beginning to impress itself upon Butrick's commentary. He noted another particularly vicious March cold front:

The weather was almost uncomfortably warm, and the clouds seemed charged with electricity, and about sunset we heard low thunder. Soon after dark the wind arose almost to a tempest. We retired to rest as usual in our little carryall, but were awakened in the night by a severe storm. The wind drove with such violence, that a part of our tent was thrown down, and the rain beat in between the curtains of our carryall & wet our bed. We arose and partly dressed us, but could not think of going entirely into the open air, and therefore again wrapped ourselves in our bed clothes and fell asleep. A little before day, the rain was changed to snow, the cold seemed very severe.

By the next morning Butrick, his wife, and most of the Cherokees were wet and terribly cold. One little girl, who had been sick, died during the stormy night.[75]

On 30 March 1839 the Butricks and what remained of the Taylor detachment finally arrived at their destination at the property of a Mr Woodhall. Under the arrangements negotiated months before, the detachment was to be met by federal officers, who would provide the Cherokees with one year's worth of provisions. The next day, the officers arrived from Fort Gibson; and they held a meeting with the Cherokees. 'Thus by means of the U. States officers,' Butrick complained, 'the first Sabbath in the country must be profaned by almost every individual in the detachment.' Butrick wrote that, before they all split up, he tried once more to warn his Cherokee friends of the 'dangers & temptations' that awaited them.[76]

On 1 April, after an arduous, deadly journey of over 800 miles, Butrick's contingent finally separated. According to the report filed by Richard Taylor upon their arrival, fifty-five of the detachment had died along the route. Butrick made his last entry for the trip on that day: 'We made arrangements to send Jonas, the little boy who came with us, to his father; gave our tent to an

[75] Ibid. 16, 19, 20 Mar. 1839.
[76] Ibid. 30, 31 Mar. 1839.

On the Trail of Tears

old Cherokee woman, who had none, & took our leave of the dear detachment, with whom we had been wandering these five months past.'[77]

From that point forward, the Butricks settled in and returned to their mission work with the Cherokees. They built a home, a mission, and a school. They continued to preach and teach in the Cherokee Nation as long as their health allowed. Butrick continued his journal until 1845, and it remains a valuable record of the civil conflict that occurred among the Cherokees during the post-removal period. Remarkably, the Cherokees who survived the removal, and the subsequent civil war between the 'Ross' and 'Treaty' parties, quickly re-established their nation, developed a vibrant economy, and recast their social, legal, and political institutions in the Indian Territory. Having witnessed the nadir of Cherokee history, Butrick lived long enough, until 1851, to witness that resurrection. Over time, the Trail of Tears became the defining moment for the Cherokee Nation; and we should acknowledge that it was the Cherokees' characteristic courage, resilience, and capacity to accommodate that prevented the removal from developing into a de facto genocide. In August, Butrick recalled the departure of the first detachments and offered a conclusion that would become a prescient counterfactual prediction for the Cherokees who migrated over the brutal winter of 1838–9. If General Winfield Scott had not relented and allowed the Cherokees to manage their own migration, he surmised, 'the probability is, that even the few who might survive the torture would be thrown beggars into a sickly wilderness'. Indeed, one can only shudder at the thought of what might have happened on the trail if the Cherokees had been left subject to the same treatment and contempt they had experienced in the round-up and internment at the hands of the United States agents.[78]

Still, we should remember that Butrick's journal reveals only a glimpse of the pain inflicted upon the Cherokees. During the brutal summer of internment, Butrick only reported on information that he observed or heard about in his own particular corner of the Cherokee Nation; and when he travelled the removal path,

---

[77] Ibid. 1 Apr. 1839; Foreman, *Indian Removal*, 311.

[78] Butrick, *Journal*, 7 Aug. 1838; McLoughlin, *Champions of the Cherokees*, 206; Trail of Tears Association, *The Journal of Daniel S. Butrick*, unnumbered foreword.

he was among a detachment of approximately 1,000 out of the 15,000 who were interned and exiled. What Butrick saw or heard about represented only a fragment of the atrocities and indecencies imposed upon the Cherokees. He only saw a few dozen pass from this life in the stockades and in the camps and on the trail; they were only a portion of the 4,000 or more who died as a consequence of the removal. While it is certainly not a complete record of the removal by any means, Butrick's journal does frankly illuminate the deep misery that resides behind the poetic phrase 'The Trail of Tears'.

4

Breaking the Bonds of People and Land

Claudia B. Haake

In the late Vine Deloria's judgement, even if 'the United States has rarely fulfilled the spirit of the law, it has nevertheless done better by its native people than other countries'.[1] These 'other countries' would include its often overshadowed neighbour to the south, Mexico, and opinions such as Deloria's, largely based on legal texts, have led to the belief that the United States has a comparatively good record in its dealings with Native Americans while Mexico, supposedly, has done much worse. Looking specifically at the problem of removal, the admittedly rare scholarship considering both of these countries has concluded that removal in Mexico was intended to break up tribes, while in the United States it was meant to preserve them.[2] This essay considers the removal of two Native American tribes, the Mexican-based Yaquis and the United States Delawares, in order to challenge this verdict.[3]

This erroneous judgement has masked the fact that, as the Delaware case study shows, United States Indian policy in the era of removal was pursuing two potentially conflicting aims. Officially, the policy based on the 1830 Indian Removal Act sought to preserve Natives by removing them from detrimental white influences and thus giving them more time to adjust. This idealistic goal rallied many well-meaning reformers to the policy. However, the 'covert' or unofficial yet dominant agenda backed by often less than well-intentioned people was one of land acquisition. As these

---

[1] Vine Deloria, Jr., 'Congress in its Wisdom: The Course of Indian Legislation', in Sandra L. Cadwalader and Vine Deloria, Jr. (eds.), *The Aggressions of Civilization: Federal Indian Policy since the 1880s* (Philadelphia, 1984), 108.

[2] See Christian F. Feest, 'Die Indianerpolitik Mexikos und der USA, 1830–1930', in Friedrich Edelmayer, Bernd Hausberger, and Hans Werner Tobler (eds.), *Die vielen Amerikas: Die neue Welt zwischen 1800 und 1930* (Frankfurt, 2000), 104.

[3] The essay draws on various chapters of Claudia B. Haake, *The State, Removal and Indigenous Peoples in the United States and Mexico, c.1620–2000* (New York, 2007).

goals were to an extent contradictory, this, as well as Indigenous resistance and various other factors, ultimately foiled the complete acquisition of Indian land. Moreover, by removing entire tribes, the policy served to maintain rather than undermine tribal organization. In the long run this led to the survival of landholding tribes to the present day.

In the case of the Yaquis in Mexico, in contrast, the goals of removal were the clearing of fertile lands, the so-called pacification of the rebellious Yaqui tribe, and the exploitation of their labour force. There was no covert agenda. Here, the ruthless practice of removal had the potential to have a more devastating impact on the Indigenous people since it worked to undermine their communities. As it happened, this did not occur because of the outbreak of the Mexican Revolution, which resulted in the discontinuation of the policy of removal.

These two case studies indicate that, ultimately, both countries pursued very similar goals through Indigenous removal, and foremost among them was the acquisition of Native lands.

The Era of Removal

The term removal originates in the 1830 Indian Removal Act in the United States. This law, passed largely on the initiative of President Andrew Jackson, arranged for a so-called 'exchange' of lands, whereby Native tribes were relocated from the east to the west of the Mississippi. This allegedly took place on a voluntary basis but the practice was much more varied than the rhetoric suggested. Similarly, the supporters of the Act threw their weight behind it for different reasons.[4] Some genuinely seem to have had the Indians' best interests at heart but thought that removing them from detrimental white influences would benefit them in the long run, allow them to get civilized in their own time, and save the race. Others must have seen the flaw in this argument, which claimed to protect and civilize Native Americans by putting distance between them and what passed as civilization. It was less assimilation and more land that constituted the main driving force behind the Act. In my view, land appropriation was

[4] See Jeremiah Evarts (ed.), *Speeches on the Passage of the Bill for the Removal of the Indians, Delivered in the Congress of the United States, April and May 1830* (Boston, 1830).

Breaking the Bonds of People and Land 81

the 'covert' and unofficial yet dominant agenda of removal, albeit one masked very effectively by the rhetoric of benevolence used to justify the passage of the Act. This agenda, moreover, was by no means a new one. Indians had been removed since the beginning of encounters between Natives and whites. Yet even though this was not the first time a line was to be drawn between Indians and Euro-Americans, it can be viewed as the first organized attempt at the mass removal of Native Americans.[5]

'Removal' officially lasted from 1830 to 1887. However, the latter date marked the passage of the Dawes or Allotment Act which, in my view, was not the end point but rather a continuation of removal, although in a slightly different manner. The policy of allotment further reduced Indian landholdings and displaced many Natives once again. Therefore it cannot be interpreted as having terminated removal. Even in the twentieth century the policy of removal did not end as, for instance, the termination era demonstrates. In fact, in my view the history of Native–white relations is essentially one in which removal has been *the* central theme. What is generally termed the removal era formed merely the most organized and open attempt at forced migration of masses of Native Americans.

In spite of uniform legislation, removal in the United States was different for different tribes. Some had to be removed by military force, while others, such as the Delawares, simply packed up and left when they were told to do so.[6] But removal as a practice was not confined to the United States. Mexico, for instance, used it against the Maya and, at various later dates, against the Yaquis.[7] In Mexico, however, the policy was not nationwide and thus lacked the legal framework and the treaty process that marked it in the United States.

---

[5] A colonial forerunner of such an exercise in line-drawing was the British Proclamation of 1767. However, while Indians had been crowded out, pushed away, and had seen their land acquired by dubious means, there had been no coordinated attempt at mass removal on a national scale before.

[6] Some refused until starvation forced them to comply. See Haake, *The State, Removal and Indigenous Peoples*, ch. 4.

[7] Some Maya were deported to Cuba during the so-called Caste War. See Luis González y González, 'Liberals and the Land', in Gilbert M. Joseph and Timothy J. Henderson (eds.), *The Mexico Reader: History, Culture, Politics* (Durham, NC, 2002), 243.

Removal in the United States: The Delawares

The Delawares, also known as Lenape, the first tribe ever to sign a treaty with the United States and one of the last to be removed under the 1830 Act, originally lived along the banks of the Delaware river and its tributaries, but today are based in Oklahoma.[8] Their history is essentially one of almost continuous removals, as even before 1830 they were repeatedly displaced. Sometimes they were simply pushed back and crowded out by force; at other times this was done by means of treaty. This process saw them leaving their original homes along the Delaware river to go to Ohio, Indiana, Missouri, and Kansas. Their last removal, which falls within the official removal era, took place in the late 1860s and saw the tribe being transplanted from Kansas to the newly created Indian Territory, now Oklahoma, where they had to settle among the Cherokees (see Map 4.1).

Four treaties between 1854 and 1866, the last one signed on 4 July 1866, removed the Delawares to Indian Territory/Oklahoma. The Lenape had repeatedly looked at lands available to them, and had eventually decided to relocate to within the boundaries of the Cherokee reservation. This was not an easy decision and also not a truly voluntary one, but rather born out of necessity as the situation in Kansas had become intolerable. Their agent reported that the entire tribe had discussed the issue of moving in a number of council meetings and had concluded that 'they would remain no longer in this country if they could find elsewhere, a country anything as good as this'.[9] The effects of the Kansas–Nebraska Act of 1854 affected the tribe deeply, and white harassment had increased to unbearable levels. The Superintendent was informed that 'the white people around them are continually annoying them with threats, telling them that they cannot nor shall not long own so much land here among them'.[10] But the tribe

---

[8] This was the Treaty of Fort Pitt, concluded in Sept. 1778.

[9] Letter from Indian Agent Thomas Sykes to Commissioner of Indian Affairs Alfred B. Greenwood, 12 Mar. 1860, National Archives (of the USA), M234, roll 275. Sykes deemed this to be a 'happy result of the council'. References to these councils can be found in a number of documents on this roll. They appear to have been going on at least since February. The exact dates are hard to determine as the tribe seems to have attempted to keep their agent in the dark about these meetings.

[10] Letter from Agent Thomas Sykes to Superintendent B. F. Robinson, dated 10 Feb. 1860, National Archives, M234, roll 275.

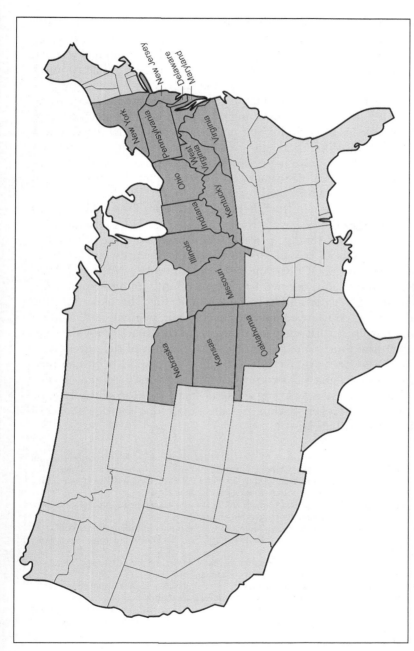

MAP 4.1 *Removal of the Delawares (the shading indicates areas of relevance)*

was long divided over where they should go, some favouring the west where they hoped to be able to maintain their traditional lifestyle, and others feeling more inclined to Indian Territory where they hoped to modernize their way of life.[11] The ruptures introduced by this difficult decision aggravated seemingly pre-existing problems between these groupings which might tentatively be referred to as modernists and traditionalists, although they were by no means uniform in their opinion and their membership was not fixed.[12] While both groups sought to preserve the tribe, the latter saw their only chance of doing so in insisting on their traditional ways, while the former group favoured the adoption of more modern and 'white' ways.[13]

A treaty between the Cherokee Nation and the USA, signed shortly after the Delaware treaty, allowed the USA to settle 'civilized Indians friendly with the Cherokees' on their territory.[14] But in order to be able to do so, the Delawares had to make another compact, this time with the Cherokee Nation.[15] After much discussion, the two tribes entered into an agreement on 8 April 1867. According to this document, the Cherokees sold the Delawares 160 acres of land for every man, woman, and child on the enrolment list their agent drew up for their removal.[16] Yet when the time came to sign the final version of the agreement, the Delawares discovered that a few terms had been changed from the version the two parties had previously agreed on. For instance, the new wording spoke of incorporation of the Lenape into the Cherokee Nation, possibly suggesting the dissolution of Delaware tribal ties.

[11] See William W. Newcomb, Jr., *The Culture and Acculturation of the Delaware Indians* (Ann Arbor, 1956), 101. See also Claudia B. Haake, 'Identity, Sovereignty and Power: The Cherokee–Delaware Agreement of 1867, Past and Present', *American Indian Quarterly*, 26/3 (2002), 418–35, and ead., *The State, Removal and Indigenous Peoples*.

[12] Charles Journeycake and Captain Fall Leaf were among the most vocal spokespeople of these two informal and unorganized groupings.

[13] See Charles Journeycake and others to Commissioner of Indian Affairs William P. Dole [1861], National Archives, M234, roll 275. See also Haake, 'Identity, Sovereignty and Power'.

[14] Treaty between the USA and the Cherokee Nation, 1866. See Charles J. Kappler, *Indian Affairs, Laws and Treaties*, 3 vols. (Washington, 1904), 947.

[15] While this was not a singular occurrence (the Shawnees signed a similar agreement with the Cherokees), it differentiated this removal from that of most other tribes.

[16] See Cherokee–Delaware Agreement, 8 Apr. 1867, in Richard C. Adams, *Legends of the Delaware Indians and Picture Writing*, ed. with an introd. Deborah Nichols (New York, 1997), 55.

Breaking the Bonds of People and Land 85

The Delaware delegates sent to sign the agreement did so in spite of it having been modified from the agreed-upon version, and probably at least partly in response to pressure from the government officials present.[17] They had been authorized to sign the Articles of Agreement and, presumably, also to accept or refuse any changes, as was customary. Yet that written authorization was based on a bona fide agreement between the delegates and their tribe, on an unwritten premiss that the former would act in the best interest of the tribe and not consent to any changes that would be unacceptable to the community. The authorization document itself was probably considered just one of the many strange 'white' things that the government officials insisted on, and which were customarily accommodated to by the tribe. No one in this society still largely based on consensus decisions thought they would have to approve something other than what had been previously agreed, and especially not in an area of such importance to the tribe.

From the very beginning of the negotiations the Lenape had expressed their firm 'wish to remain Indians, and to preserve our nation, it was a nation from the earliest times', as Captain Fall Leaf put it in a letter to the Commissioner of Indian Affairs.[18] Members of the tribe furthermore impressed upon the United States that 'before the Government of the United States was formed, we were a nation, and for time to come, so far as human mind can conceive, we wish to be a nation'.[19] Clearly, they were not inclined to compromise on this central issue. After all, everyone who had chosen to remove had done so specifically in order to preserve tribal ties, instead of accepting the treaty option to stay on in Kansas as United States citizens, which only very few Delawares elected to do.

Yet after the 1867 agreement had been signed there was no way out of it, in spite of some obvious legal problems with the document. The wording in the new document was highly ambiguous. It conflated both options contained in Article 15 of the Cherokee treaty, which described ways to surrender and to

[17] Clinton A. Weslager, *The Delaware Indians: A History* (New Brunswick, NJ, 1996), 425.
[18] Letter from Captain Fall Leaf and J. W. Armstrong to the Commissioner of Indian Affairs, dated 3 Feb. 1864, National Archives, M234, roll 276.
[19] Letter dated 3 Feb. 1864, addressed to the Department of the Interior, and signed by various Delawares (though not all chiefs). National Archives, M234, roll 276.

86 CLAUDIA B. HAAKE

maintain a separate tribal organization. It is not clear how these new terms entered the agreement, or who exactly was responsible for them. On the one hand, it may have been the result of another attempt by the Cherokees to keep as much control as possible. It was only natural for the Cherokees to feel resentful of the Delawares, as the latter were being used by the United States government to punish the Cherokees for the role some of them had played in the Civil War. On the other hand, representatives of the federal government might have been responsible. They may simply have been confused or misinformed about the terms and conditions mentioned in the Delaware and Cherokee treaties of 1866. Among several of the officials involved, a genuine confusion about the terms of the two treaties seems to have reigned.[20] Frequent changes of Commissioner of Indian Affairs (July 1865, November 1866, and March 1867) and of the Secretary of the Interior (May 1865 and July 1866) during this period may also have contributed to the confusion of the lower-ranking officials on the ground and led to misunderstandings.[21]

The officials also may have been reluctant to admit making a mistake with regard to the modified terms and thereby cause themselves additional work remedying that error. This would also have delayed the signing process and thus have caused additional problems for them. It was probably deemed easier to pressure the Delawares into signing than it would have been to

[20] See various letters, primarily M234, roll 279. A specific example of this is the 'east–west' question—the common misconception that tribal organization could not be kept east of the 96th meridian. It probably stemmed from the fact that Art. 15 of the Cherokee treaty of 1866 provided for ways in which to settle tribes east of the 96th meridian, while Art. 16 did so for ways in which to settle them west of this. Among those suffering from this confusion were Agent Pratt, Superintendent Murphy, and Fall Leaf. See e.g. Fall Leaf and others to General James Blunt (autumn 1869), and Superintendent Thomas Murphy to Commissioner of Indian Affairs Ely S. Parker, 11 Nov. 1869, National Archives, M234, roll 280. See also Superintendent Thomas Murphy to Acting Commissioner of Indian Affairs Charles Mix, 6 June 1868, and Fall Leaf and others to the Commissioner of Indian Affairs, National Archives, M234, roll 279. See Commissioner of Indian Affairs Nathaniel G. Taylor to Superintendent Thomas Murphy, 4 May 1867, National Archives, M21, roll 68.

[21] This problem of frequently changing office-holders was hinted at in a letter from James Secondine of the Lenape to Commissioner of Indian Affairs James W. Denver (dated 15 Aug. 1857), in which Secondine says he had been informed 'that the commissioner had just come into office and consequently knew nothing about our business affairs'. National Archives, M234, roll 274. The situation became even worse thereafter. These changes may also be the reason why several letters from the Delawares to the Commissioner of Indian Affairs were sent without including the name of the addressee.

Breaking the Bonds of People and Land 87

renegotiate with the numerically larger Cherokee Nation already established on the lands in question. The officials may also have believed that in the future it would be easier to deal with one tribe instead of two (though this is unlikely given that the United States kept up a government-to-government relationship with the Delawares for some years to come). The government officials probably regarded this agreement as a necessary evil or a nuisance they had to tolerate. Ordinarily, removal would have been arranged through treaties with the United States government only. However, since no lands had been ceded by the Cherokees at the time the Delaware treaty of 1866 was concluded, the United States government could not at the time provide for the Lenape's removal to a specific section of the Cherokee lands.[22] Thus an additional agreement had to be entered into by the two tribes, causing the agents and others additional work.

Whatever the reasons for the agreement's new terms, it seems likely that the United States officials wanted to have this already drawn-out and unusually complicated matter settled as quickly as possible and the Delawares removed from Kansas to Cherokee lands in Indian Territory. They were not overly concerned about the terms, or about the Lenape, as long as the latter signed the agreement and vacated their lands. Thus the ambiguous terms of the agreement most likely stemmed from a mixture of factors, including local misinterpretations of official United States Indian policy, in particular, a genuine confusion about the terms, as well as the clash of interests between the Delawares and the Cherokees. But still the United States government appeared determined to hold the tribes to the terms and especially to remove the Delawares as quickly as possible, in spite of all their protests.

And the majority of the Lenape immediately protested against 'incorporation' and 'consolidation'. They specifically pointed to their 1866 treaty in which there was no mention of having to give up their tribal organization. There was little they could do apart from petitioning and protesting, however. The so-called traditionalists among them were especially reluctant to remove under

---

[22] For a different explanation of the haste with which the negotiations were conducted see Gina Carrigan and Clayton Chambers, 'A Lesson in Administrative Termination: An Analysis of the Legal Status of the Delaware Tribe of Indians', unpublished manuscript (1994), 9.

88 CLAUDIA B. HAAKE

the modified terms of the Cherokee–Delaware Agreement. As General James Blunt, an official involved in the matter, reported in February 1868, three-quarters of the Delawares, whom he called 'full bloods', were 'averse to locating among the Cherokees'.[23] He realized that their 'nationality is dearer to them than all else'.[24] Superintendent Thomas Murphy, who was in charge of the Delawares' removal, was probably correct when he mentioned later that fear of the loss of 'national organization, name and power' was the principal reason for the Delawares delaying their removal.[25] And 712 tribal members, about two-thirds of the Delawares, signed a petition stating that in council and with a majority of the tribe present, 'it was agreed unanimously that the Delawares will never give up their nationality and become merged in the Cherokee Nation'.[26] Furthermore, the Lenape reminded the Commissioner of the treaty of 1866, which had specified that they were to 'go in a body to a distinct reservation', and of the USA's duty as a guardian.[27] But all protests and petitions were to no avail.

The movement to Oklahoma began in December of 1867 and continued during the spring and summer of 1868, thirty-five years after the removal of the Choctaws, who had been the first to suffer removal on the basis of the 1830 Indian Removal Act. Each family had to make its own preparations and arrangements, though sometimes several families travelled together. They had to cover a distance of 180 to 200 miles before they arrived in Indian Territory. They were not accompanied or supervised by

[23] General James Blunt to Commissioner of Indian Affairs Nathaniel G. Taylor, 27 Feb. 1868, National Archives, M234, roll 279.

[24] Ibid.

[25] Superintendent Thomas Murphy to Acting Commissioner of Indian Affairs Charles Mix, 6 June 1868, National Archives, M234, roll 279.

[26] Petition by Captain Anderson Sarcoxie and others to the Commissioner of Indian Affairs Nathaniel G. Taylor, 13 June 1867, National Archives, M345, roll 278. The sheriffs, Jacob Easy and John Buffalo, went around collecting the signatures, but apparently no one really kept track of who had contacted whom. Thus a few people signed twice or even three times, unaware of what kind of an impact this would have on them. This gave various government officials, among them Agent John Pratt, the opportunity to discard the document as invalid. See Agent John Pratt to Superintendent Thomas Murphy, 6 Feb. 1868, National Archives, M234, roll 279.

[27] Ibid. Agent Pratt did not forward the petition until he was specifically ordered to do so by the Commissioner of Indian Affairs. When no response arrived, Sarcoxie wrote to the Commissioner directly to enquire if he had received the letters. See letter from Chief Anderson Sarcoxie to Commissioner of Indian Affairs Nathaniel G. Taylor, 8 July 1867, National Archives, M234, roll 278.

Breaking the Bonds of People and Land   89

the military. Unlike with several of the Five Tribes (then still known as the Five Civilized Tribes), no force was necessary to remove the Delawares from what had been their home for close to thirty-eight years. There was obviously no need for that. After all, probably only a little over a thousand Lenape were left, and they had for a long time attempted to live peacefully with the Europeans.

There was no particular reason for this removal except a general desire to 'colonize', land hunger, and a tendency to favour the railways, the main beneficiaries of two of the four treaties leading up to the Delawares' removal.[28] Unlike many other tribes, the Lenape had given the federal government no reason to remove them. They had stayed loyal to the Union during the Civil War and a very large percentage of them had served in the Union forces.[29] Yet the land itself provided sufficient incentive for their removal.

Removal in Mexico: The Yaquis

Land was also the driving force behind the removal of the Yaquis from Sonora to Yucatán around the turn of the century. This ever-troublesome tribe, which had managed to retain large portions of its ancestral lands throughout Spanish and Mexican rule, had been involved in what was essentially a defensive war against the Mexican government. This kept intruding upon their fertile lands, which it sought in order to settle white colonists on them. The Yaquis, who refer to themselves as Yoeme, were so successful in their struggle that after recurring bouts of warfare, the government turned to a policy of deportation finally to undermine and eliminate the resistance.

This policy of physical removal was new to the Yaquis. Before the mass deportations started in 1902, there had been occasional

[28] These were the treaties of Sarcoxieville (30 May 1860) and of 2 July 1861, at Fort Leavenworth.

[29] See Laurence Hauptmann, *Between Two Fires: American Indians in the Civil War* (New York, 1995), 22; Clinton A. Weslager, *The Delaware Indian Westward Migration: With Texts of Two Manuscripts, 1821–22, Responding to General Lewis Cass's Inquiries about Lanape Culture and Language* (Wallingford, Pa., 1978), 224. See also a Memorial compiled by Richard C. Adams for a Hearing of the Committee of Public Lands, House of Representatives, 'To Compensate the Delaware Indians for Services Rendered by them to the United States in Various Wars', 1909, 2 (United States National Archives).

90 CLAUDIA B. HAAKE

relocations, but only on an individual basis and for active rebels. The removal of 1902 was directed at the entire tribe: at men, women, and children. The Díaz government tried to drain the rebellion by taking away the peaceful people who clandestinely supported it, especially since the line between the *broncos* and *pacíficos* had become increasingly hazy, making it difficult if not impossible to deport only active rebels, as sooner or later most male Yoeme could be counted among that group.[30] The excuse for the unrestrained adoption of this measure was the guerrilla warfare that the Yoeme quite successfully conducted against the Mexicans. To eliminate the social base seemed to be a way of putting an end to the guerrilla movement. After all, earlier measures such as drawing up registers and designating special camps for the *pacífico* population had not had the desired effects. The government had not been able to prevent an active interchange between *broncos* and *pacíficos*. There was also the growing interest of outsiders—Mexicans and Americans—in the fertile lands of the Yaqui valley and in Sonora in general, partly because of its proximity to Arizona. It was to an extent the commercial interest from the United States that inspired the Mexican government finally to rid itself of the 'Yaqui nuisance' and to open the way for the commercial agricultural development of the area, while at the same time helping out the Yucatecan plantation owners who wanted to obtain cheap labour for their plantations.

Like the Delawares, the Yoeme suffered from technological innovations, and especially from the advance of the railways. Unlike the Delawares, who were viewed as being in the way of the planned lines, the Yoeme were at first convenient for this development, providing cheap labour for the mines, railways, industries, and most of all for expanding agriculture. But, coincidentally, at about the same time an almost insatiable market for workers arose on the henequen (sisal) plantations in Yucatán, counteracting the need for Yaqui labour in Sonora. Previously, the government had largely agreed to tolerate Yaqui activities in order not to lose their labour. But now it could have both; it was able to deport the Yaquis while at the same time satisfying labour needs. At this point, there was nothing they could do to avoid removal. Even the option of joining Mexican society was by that time closed to them.

---

[30] There was an active exchange between rebels and workers, the former switching places with the latter when they needed time to rest and recharge.

Breaking the Bonds of People and Land   91

After 1902 the government forces increasingly put Yoeme men, women, and children in jail, where they had to await their fate. Although the official policy at the start was only to deport hard-core rebels, this was not always followed. Instead, removal was arbitrary. Consequently, most of the captured men, and some women and children, were removed by this means, although some were punished in other ways, for instance, by hanging. Yet in 1904, after two years of deportations and in spite of the draconian measures generally employed against the Yoeme, the government had to acknowledge that some Yaquis were still somehow managing to carry on their resistance. This made President Díaz encourage the state government to renew its efforts and, as a result, sealed the fate of the entire Yaqui population. He also sent some federal troops to help the Sonoran government out, a somewhat unusual measure since normally these matters were largely left to the state governments.[31] From then on, in many cases no distinction at all was made between *pacíficos* and rebels.

While the Yaquis still maintained their resistance, these measures were taking a toll on them. In a letter of 25 April 1904 to the Sonoran State Governor Rafael Izábal, the Nueve Capitanes, nine Yaqui captains, stated that the rebellion was taking place only at the river and not in the countryside, presumably to persuade the army to spare the *pacíficos* who were so crucial to the rebellion.[32] They generally expressed concern for the Yoeme working outside the *Yaquimi*. Apparently many of them feared relentless persecution by governmental forces, and hanging in particular. The men who referred to themselves as the Nine Captains also expressed their concern for the Sonoran harvest, which they claimed would be lost without Yaqui labour. This argument was also used in a letter to the *vecinos*, Mexican citizens, on the same day, probably echoing and feeding fears the *hacendados* had anyway, while at the same time proving the Yaquis' awareness of their main advantage.[33] In this letter the Yoeme insisted they did not know what they had done wrong and that

---

[31] See Shelley Bowen Hatfield, *Chasing Shadows: Indians along the United States–Mexico Border, 1876–1911* (Albuquerque, N. Mex., 1998), p. xii.

[32] In response, Izábal had a statement published in *El Imparcial* saying he considered the Yaquis 'útil' and during the war had treated them humanely but had also been forced to castigate them severely. See Archivo Histórica General del Estado de Sonora (AHGES), tomo 1881 (1904).

[33] Ibid.

they had always kept their word.[34] They asked for Santa Paz, holy peace, and hence implored the recipients of the letter to 'do them the favor' with 'El Señor Precidente'.[35] Yet their pleas were to no avail and the campaign against them continued.

By 1907 even haciendas, mines, and railways were instructed no longer to employ Yaquis. At that time the government also dropped its attempts to disguise the war against the tribe, and openly tried to clear all Yoeme from Sonora. It attempted to pass off and justify removal as a benevolent act because it permitted the Yaquis to live instead of being killed outright to solve the problem they posed. They were rounded up and thrown into jail before being deported to Yucatán by ship and on foot, and their belongings were confiscated (Map 4.2).[36]

The apprehended Yaquis were intensely interrogated, even tortured, to make them disclose information about the rebels and their whereabouts. As a result the Yoeme came to be known for their resilience under torture.[37] But when threatened with removal some did talk, hinting at the terror this possibility carried for them. Yet even under duress many Yaquis claimed not to know where their *parientes*, their fellow Yaquis, had gone. Their weapons had been 'lost' or stolen just before their arrest. They told on Yaquis long dead, thus rendering the denunciation ineffective. Furthermore, they gave incomplete names, or claimed not to know them at all, dead-ending government efforts in yet another way. Some admitted to having fed the rebels, claiming to have done this out of fear, or saying that everybody did it. But others also denounced neighbours, friends, or even family members. Only very few of the Yoeme admitted freely to their own direct and intentional involvement in the rebellion, while others refused to say anything at all. Indeed, after interrogating the Yaqui Miguel León, his captors stated: 'No quizo decir nada, que mejor quiere morir.'[38] This Yoeme would have chosen to die rather than talk. Yet even those who

---

[34] They also claim never to have harmed any passengers, presumably meaning travellers. Ibid.

[35] Ibid.

[36] A few were also sent to Oaxaca.

[37] See Evelyn Hu-DeHart, *Yaqui Resistance and Survival: The Struggle for Land and Autonomy, 1821–1910* (Madison, 1984), 167–8.

[38] 'He did not want to say anything and preferred to die' (trans. Claudia Haake). AHGES, tomo 2314 (1908).

Breaking the Bonds of People and Land

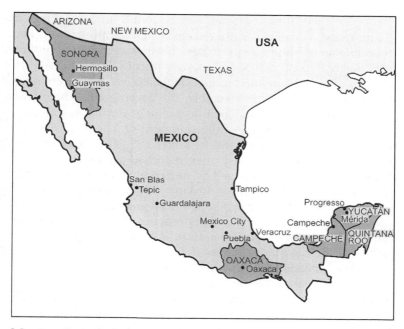

MAP 4.2 *Removal of the Yaquis (the shading indicates areas of relevance)*

talked did not necessarily escape removal.[39] Still the rebels gave no sign of surrender.

In view of the rebels' success in eluding apprehension and castigation or removal, the government's step of adopting removal as the official policy by 1907 becomes almost logical and even understandable from the official point of view.[40] It was a measure in part born out of desperation, but also a cunning business decision. It is not evident from the sources available who was behind this decision, or even the idea behind the programme. Evelyn Hu-DeHart speaks of the 'ruling elites of Sonora and Yucatán'.[41]

---

[39] See AHGES, tomo 1881 (1904). And even those who stayed were often kept specifically to work.

[40] See Hu-DeHart, *Yaqui Resistance*, 180. Many officials, for instance, Secretary Alberto Cubillas, were of the opinion that only the Yaquis' elimination from Sonora could bring peace to the state. See Centro de Estudios de Historia Mexicana (CONDUMEX), Colección Ramón Corral, Carpeta 1/3, Legajo 30 (letter from Alberto Cubillas to Ramón Corral, Sept. 1908).

[41] Hu-DeHart, *Yaqui Resistance*, 180. She is referring to Olegario Molina, Ramón

94 CLAUDIA B. HAAKE

However, the information that can be found in the archives in Sonora and Yucatán is rather sketchy. The apprehension and rounding up of Yaquis seems to have been among the responsibilities assigned to various Sonoran government officials such as the prefects. Troops were used to guard the captives, who were often kept in prisons, buildings owned by the government. The official correspondence also points to a degree of governmental involvement in the organization of the shipment of Yaquis, at least to their first stopover on their way to Yucatán.[42] (They were shipped down part of the west coast, then marched across the width of Mexico, only to be transported by ship again in order to reach the Yucatán peninsula.) What is striking is that some areas of the project are so well documented in official governmental and military correspondence, while others remain almost entirely in the dark. This may be because certain government officials were (ab)using their positions for some kind of semi-private business enterprise, making money by providing labourers for Yucatán.

To the federal government, the officials could justify removal as a necessary clean-up programme in response to the Yaqui rebellion, while at the same time they themselves stood to benefit financially from sending the Yaquis to a Yucatán starved for labour. These men may have received money for their efforts and might also at times have benefited from the sale of the Indians' belongings.[43] Money changing hands like this would have contributed to the rumours of the Yaquis being sold outright into slavery.[44] And the Sonorans in charge of the deportations would not have suffered from them in the same way as others from the same area. They would not have deprived themselves of Yaqui labour as they did others. There is evidence that as late as 1905 there was no shortage of Yaqui labour on the hacienda of Rafael

Corral, Luis Torres, and Rafael Izábal. See also Raquel Padilla Ramos, *Yucatán: fin del sueño yaqui* (Hermosillo, 1995), 105. Similarly, Gilbert Joseph points to Olegario Molina's business connections. See Gilbert M. Joseph, 'Rethinking Mexican Revolutionary Mobilization: Yucatán's Seasons of Upheaval, 1909–1915', in id. and Daniel Nugent (eds.), *Everyday Forms of State Formation: Revolution and the Negotiation of Rule in Modern Mexico* (Durham, NC, 1994), 140–1. Yet this does not explain why a few Yaquis were sent to Oaxaca rather than to Yucatán.

[42] See AHGES, tomos 2319 (1908), 2077/78 (1906), 2193 (1907).

[43] I have found one case in which the officials ask who is to receive the money coming out of a cattle sale. The original owner had been deported and his wife along with him. No answer is on file.

[44] See John Kenneth Turner, *Barbarous Mexico* (repr. Austin, Tex., 1969), 38.

Breaking the Bonds of People and Land 95

Izábal, one of the key figures in the removal venture, and that he may even have received new contingents of Yaquis.[45] And in general, as the export-oriented henequen industry on Yucatán was booming, it was considered to be more important than the Sonoran economy. Yet it is doubtful whether this programme would ever have been undertaken if the men in charge had only been government officials and not also private businessmen with a knack for advancing their own fortunes.[46] Individuals involved could profit handsomely through the deportations. Greed and private profit seem to have been crucial in the semi-commercial enterprise that was deportation.

Yet while individuals may have profited from the venture, this was not necessarily so for the Mexican state, at least not in purely financial terms. However, for the government this may have been an acceptable price to pay in order to clear the so-called Yaqui nuisance from Sonora and supply Yucatán with much-needed labour. The Sonoran sources reveal next to nothing about the costs of 'project removal'. But costs were incurred all along the way, for instance, when it came to guarding the Yoeme. The Secretary of State authorized funds for this purpose, 'a efecto de vigilar á los indios yaquis prisioneros de guerra'.[47] Various ships were supposed to take the Yaquis part of the way to Yucatán, their final destination. At least one of the vessels mentioned was a warship, which might have made this part of the transport free as far as the Sonoran government was concerned.[48] In 1907 Luis Torres, who at that time was serving as governor of the Yaqui town Tórin, asked the Secretary of War for a 'buque de guerra', a warship, so that 200 Yaquis of both sexes could be deported.[49]

---

[45] See AHGES, tomo 1984 (1905), esp. a letter dated 31 Oct.

[46] Raquel Padilla concurs. See Padilla, *Fin*, 65.

[47] 'For the purpose of guarding the Yaqui Indian prisoners of war' (trans. Claudia Haake). AHGES, tomo 1881 (1904). This happened in response to a request by the prefect of Guaymas.

[48] See AHGES, tomo 2077/78 (1906). The warship in question was the *canonero Tampico* and it was supposed to return for another shipment of Yaquis once this trip had been concluded. Two non-military ships were also mentioned as taking contingents of Yoeme. See also Jane Holden Kelley, *Yaqui Women: Contemporary Life Histories* (Lincoln, Nebr., 1978). The memories of Chepa Moreno (126–53) talk about a small boat taking them the first part of the voyage.

[49] AHGES, tomo 2193 (1907). Other mentions of ships of that type can be found in AHGES, tomo 2319 (1908). If the first leg of the voyage was usually conducted by means of a warship, that would explain why Yucatecan Yaquis entertained the hope that a warship would return them to their home.

96 CLAUDIA B. HAAKE

This form of transportation would have created further expenses for the army and the federal government. But since this was only part of the trip to Yucatán, at some point further costs must have arisen through the enforcement of removal, even though it seems that shipments of Yoeme were sent out only once enough of them had become available for removal, 'suficientes para completar el viaje de un buque'.[50] This is even more probable since there is no evidence that the second leg of the shipment was also undertaken by warships. However, it remains unclear who paid for this part of the journey. When, after the Mexican Revolution, removals were resumed under a new government, some cotton-growers asked for a contingent of Yaquis and offered to arrange part of the transport.[51] It is possible that this suggestion was made with knowledge of the arrangements that had been customary the first time around.

Some captives were also hired out to work on haciendas in Sonora.[52] Presumably at least part the money they earned went to the state. The passage of the Yaquis to their Sonoran employers was paid for by the latter, possibly as they stood to benefit most from this arrangement. The practice in these instances was for the state government to pay up front and to be reimbursed later.[53] Again, the procedure may have been similar when it came to the deportees to Yucatán. As contemporary witnesses spoke of an outright sale of Yaquis to Yucatán, the money to cover the cost of transport may have come from those who received the Yaquis.[54] The money that did change hands, whether as a fee or a sale price, may have been used to cover such costs. Or perhaps the Yucatecan employers specifically paid for at least part of the passage. And to the government, defraying the costs of the first part of the Yoeme's voyage may have seemed like an investment, an acceptable price to pay for the elimination of the Yaquis from Sonora.

The massive shipments of Yaquis stopped abruptly at the end

[50] 'Sufficient to complete/fill one boat trip' (trans. Claudia Haake). AHGES, tomo 2316 (1908). For more on the expenses, see Hu-DeHart, *Yaqui Resistance*, 112.

[51] See AHGES, tomo 3253 (1918). This application was turned down as the Yaquis in question were already spoken for.

[52] These working captives earned between 11 and 25 centavos on the haciendas. See AHGES, tomo 2314 (1908).

[53] See AHGES, tomo 2077/78 (1906).

[54] See Turner, *Barbarous Mexico*, 38.

Breaking the Bonds of People and Land   97

of July 1908, but smaller numbers continued to be deported. This was probably at least partly because of a slump in the henequen market, which made removal less lucrative. Yet the government still had a price on the heads of Yaquis and, to avoid more attacks by the few remaining rebels, threats were made that each would be avenged by more deportations. The exact numbers of Yaquis deported remain unknown, but estimates for the period between 1902 and 1908 run as high as 15,000. Raquel Padilla, as a preliminary estimate, suggests that more than 6,000 Yaquis were deported to Yucatán alone.[55] Even assuming a population of 30,000 Yaquis on the eve of removal, which is probably too high, that would still mean that the tribe lost between one-quarter and one-half of its entire Sonoran population. And these calculations do not even include the Yoeme who escaped over the border into the United States, or the ones who were killed.

When, after several failed attempts, most, but not all, of the Yaquis finally agreed to make peace with the Mexican government in 1909 it was under harsh conditions. The government would attend to and sustain all those who surrendered, and all but sixty would be disarmed. The Yaquis were permitted to occupy vacant lands on the Yaqui river, but were not to resettle the original eight pueblos. Instead, they were to spread out. They would be provided with work in other parts of the state and transport to their new location would be provided. In spite of many requests by the Yoeme, the deportees to Yucatán were not mentioned.

Once in Yucatán, the Yoeme worked on the henequen plantations and seem largely to have stopped their famed resistance there, although it continued among those who managed to avoid removal and remained in their traditional territory in Sonora. Those who carried on the fight in Sonora demanded the return of their traditional territory and of the deportees. Only the Mexican Revolution alleviated the pressure on the last remaining

---

[55] Padilla, *Fin*, 130. The total number of deportees from the Yaqui tribe has never been officially tabulated. Estimates for the period between 1902 and 1908 range from 8,000 to about 15,000, amounting to one-quarter or even one-half of the entire population when estimating the total number of Yaquis as 30,000 on the eve of the deportations, which is probably an optimistic figure. It is also next to impossible to estimate the total number of Yaquis on the eve of the deportations because of wide dispersal, wars, and generally high mobility. Contemporary estimates put their number at about 30,000. See Hu-DeHart, *Yaqui Resistance*, ch. 6, for a more detailed discussion of these figures.

98 CLAUDIA B. HAAKE

rebels, set the deported Yaquis free, and enabled at least some of them to return to their homeland.[56]

The Consequences of Removal

Mexico and the United States did not remove Indians because they were Indians but because they were Indians, 'Others', holding precious economic resources—mainly their lands. At times, outside society would temporarily and to a certain extent let the Indigenous communities be. This was the case when the Indians had been pushed away far enough not to 'disturb' the aims of the state and generally only if the Natives did not control any resources considered valuable by the state. Yet this constituted indifference more than tolerance. And should some unfortunate tribes find themselves quite literally in the way, they were soon being treated accordingly, as both the Delawares and the Yaquis discovered.

The nation-state determined who belonged and what had to be done in order to belong, as well as who would control the resources within its borders. Anything outside that mould could generally not be tolerated, especially since, during the periods in question, both Mexico and the United States found themselves in difficult political situations that required all their strength.[57] Even those individuals who were willing to conform had no guarantee of acceptance, especially if they held valuable resources desired

[56] There is little evidence about how many made it back to Sonora, or how they did this. I have found only one reference to Yaquis returning from their Yucatecan exile. In 1912 a group of forty Yaquis—men, women, and children—went back to Sonora via Mazatlan on the steamship *Pesqueira*. They were at first furnished with the barest necessities and then told to find work to finance themselves. It is unclear who paid for their passage home. See various correspondence in June 1912, mainly by Governor Maytorena, in AHGES, tomo 2782 (1912). Other evidence suggests that Yaquis returned on foot. See Juan Silverio Jaime León, *Testimonios de una mujer yaqui* (Mexico City, 1988), 11–13. Padilla found a group of 500 being sent to Veracruz on a warship. See Raquel Padilla Ramos, *Progreso y libertad: los Yaquis en la víspera de la repatriación* (Mérida, tesis de maestría, 2002), 90. For the unresolved mysteries of the Yaquis' return, see ibid. 92 and 94. The stories found in Jane Holden Kelley's book are rather vague but nonetheless indicate that it was possible and probably not uncommon to return to Sonora. See Kelley, *Yaqui Women*, 126–53 and 154–96.

[57] At the time, the United States was going through, or just emerging from, the Civil War and had to cope with the problems inherent in Reconstruction. Mexico under the so-called Porfiriato, the government of Porfirio Diaz, was engaged in nation-building and in efforts to modernize.

Breaking the Bonds of People and Land 99

by other members of the nation-state. Particularly in such cases, there was a reluctance to work out alternative ways to incorporate Native societies unless they had something valuable to offer in return and could thus make it worth the effort. The Delawares could never really make such an offer and the Yaquis were only in a position to do so for a while, until their sought-after labour could be put to better use in Yucatán than in Sonora.[58]

Yet removal also had some surprising and less predictable consequences, especially in the case of the Delawares. In spite of their apparent fragmentation over removal and especially the Articles of Agreement with the Cherokees, the Lenape did not lose their sense of identity. And these internal conflicts arose specifically over different plans and ideas of how best to preserve tribal unity and separateness, thereby confirming a continued sense of tribal identity in spite of internal disagreements. After all, these are a normal occurrence in any group or society, even where a basic consensus exists on matters of importance. There were also many indications that the outside world—especially US officials and the Cherokees—still considered the Lenape a distinct group. The frequent clashes with Cherokees certainly proved that that tribe was not really inclined to have the Delawares merge with them. Thus what at least some of the officials in charge of the Lenape's removal may have been hoping for—the disappearance of the tribe by consolidation with the Cherokees—never happened.

The determination to keep their tribal ties alive displayed early did not simply ebb away later, and so in the years following their removal, the Lenape did not just vanish from view as might have been expected. On the contrary, they continued to fight the Articles of Agreement and what they feared might be the consequences thereof. They were quite articulate, especially the dissenters who were most ardently opposed to the terms included in the document. Over time, and especially when the negative consequences of this forced removal and resulting cohabitation with the Cherokees became apparent even to those who had originally been disposed to accept the terms of the agreement, the tribe was united in opposing the conditions they found themselves in. In fact, it seems that the Delawares became more articulate

---

[58] After the end of the fur trade, Natives in the United States were considered to be of little economic value.

over time, learning to use what d'Arcy McNickle has called the white man's weapons, taking their grievances and claims to the officials and the courts.[59] And partly through their fight against adverse conditions, the tribe came together again.

For the Yaquis, on the other hand, a more optimistic situation presented itself initially and on the outbreak of the Mexican Revolution. Deportees were given the chance to leave the plantations and make their way back to their native Sonora, where the merciless campaign against the tribe was finally discontinued. But many parties were involved in this revolution, and the Yaquis, listening to promises made by various of these groups, sometimes found themselves fighting on opposite sides. And keeping the Yoeme occupied in this way had the added benefit that they would be less likely to revolt while a large number of their fighters was occupied elsewhere.[60] Yet even though many Yaquis had supposedly joined the revolution to achieve benefits for the tribes, they found that these promises were hardly ever kept once the Yaquis—after all the 'Mexicans' with the most fighting experience—were no longer needed any more after the fighting had largely ceased, at least temporarily. Thus participation in the revolution may mainly have served to introduce friction. Ironically, the same seems to have been true for the Yoeme returning from Yucatán. After all, this was what the Sonoran Yaquis had repeatedly asked for before the revolution. Yet their return after many years of enforced exile and without any contact to the Sonoran homeland was not unproblematic for the deportees or those who had managed to remain in Sonora during the period of removal.[61] Therefore the immediate post-removal period may have been as disruptive and challenging for the tribe as removal itself had been. Still, the Yaquis were one of

[59] Perhaps cases like the one won by Milton S. Turner in 1888 for the Cherokee Freedmen and, along with them, for the Delawares and the Shawnees encouraged the Delawares to use this option for themselves. Turner won for his clients, the Cherokee Freedmen, a pro rata share of some of the Cherokees' land proceeds. Others to profit from this decision were the Shawnees and Delawares incorporated in the Cherokee Nation. See National Archives, M574, roll 81.

[60] The Sonoran governor in a letter to General Salvador Alvarado (13 Aug. 1913) states that it would be very convenient to incorporate the Yaquis into their forces, 'pues de esa manera se logrará no solo aumentar nuestro efectivo de combate sino tambien evitar que sigan dando guerra en los Pueblos del Rio'. See AHGES, tomo 2950 (1913).

[61] See Kelley, *Yaqui Women*, the memories of Chepa Moreno and Dominga Ramírez, 126–53 and 154–96.

Breaking the Bonds of People and Land

the few groups to participate in the revolution on the basis of their ethnic identity, hoping to achieve something for the tribe of the Yoeme by joining the struggle.[62]

Yet somehow, both tribes had survived the event of removal. They were neither unharmed nor unchanged, but they were still alive. The saviour of the Yaquis was the Mexican Revolution, although this soon proved to create more difficulties for them. The Delawares as a tribe survived removal damaged, but with the goal of tribal unity unchanged.

If we follow the history of the two tribes further, we discover that it was the destruction of their home, their territorial base, by modern agriculture that affected the Yaquis and their sense of community most seriously. With the advent of modern technology, the Yaquis were no longer needed as labourers, and the intricacies of financing agricultural enterprises along with the conditions imposed upon them by the banks saw the tribe increasingly surrender control over their lands.[63]

The Delawares, on the other hand, in Indian Territory/ Oklahoma, after a hard period of adjustment to life among the Cherokees, were given a chance to rediscover and also to reconstruct their identity, and grew stronger in the process. Perhaps living in a quasi doubly hostile environment, with both US and Cherokee society largely against them, made the Lenape even more aware of how precious their tribal identity was to them. This later enabled them to fight the revoking of their federal recognition.[64] In this respect, the increased outside oppression

---

[62] See Ingrid Kummels, 'Von "Indianern" und "indigenen Völkern": Episoden aus der Geschichte Mexikos', in Ellen Schriek and Hans-Walter Schmuhl (eds.), *Das andere Mexiko: Indigene Völker von Chiapas bis Chihuahua* (Gießen, 1997), 22.

[63] For instance, the Yaquis once again clearly voiced their demands in the context of the campaigns for the elections of 2000. They stated that they wanted the territorial problem solved, their water rights and their autonomy respected, to preserve the union among the Yaqui communities, and that the political and economic interests of the state were not to be confused with those of the Yaquis. They made it clear that while they wanted help they were not looking for any paternalistic attitudes. They only wanted their young people to be able to work the land, work that, they say, they were meant for.

[64] In 1975, the Cherokee Nation had received administrative approval for its reorganization after almost sixty-five years without a tribal government. In 1977, Cherokee Chief Ross Swimmer, an attorney and banker, suddenly declared that the Delaware Tribe had ceased to exist in 1867, with the signing of the Cherokee–Delaware Agreement. Consequently any monies connected to the Delawares would have to be turned over to the newly reorganized Cherokee Nation. Significantly, the Delawares had just been given a large amount of money when Swimmer decided to take them over in this manner. And by increasing their numbers the Delawares also supplemented the Cherokees' federal

created by removal and cohabitation with the Cherokees may ultimately have served to help ensure the survival of Delaware tribal identity.

Removal: A Success Story?

If we accept US government rhetoric that removal as a policy was intended to give Native Americans more time gradually to assimilate with society, then removal did not succeed and would have to be considered a failure as a policy. Removal did not erase Native tribal and ethnic identity, and did not turn Indians into Americans. On the contrary, by transplanting entire tribes, many of the attributes which the rhetoric claimed needed to be destroyed were actually maintained.[65] For example, US Indian policy in general built up an administrative apparatus to organize Indians, usually as tribes, and therefore reinforced tribal boundaries and thus their sense of themselves as members of a tribal group. In the case of the Delawares, removal—while doubtlessly a stressful and traumatic event for the tribe—eventually served to overcome the internal differences it had previously aggravated. In other words, instead of destroying tribal ties and identities in accordance with its supposed agenda, among the Lenape removal ended up strengthening those very ties and identities. After a hard period of adjustment, this enabled the Delawares to meet most of the challenges posed by future policies and by life among the Cherokees. Their tribal unity even survived the diffi-

monies. At the time the Cherokees had only some 10,000 members, while the Delawares numbered about 7,000. Two years later, in 1979, the Delawares were informed by the Bureau of Indian Affairs that they did not exist, and had not existed since 1867, except for claims purposes. In September of 1996, the Lenape's efforts to fight this decision were finally crowned by success and the Delawares finally regained federal recognition. The 1996 decision clarified the government-to-government relationship between the United States and the Delawares, which was understood to have existed before the 1979 determination. With this ruling, the Delawares once again held the same legal rights and responsibilities as other tribes and were returned to the Department of the Interior's list of federally recognized tribes. The decision was repeatedly challenged by the Cherokee Nation, which claimed that the Cherokees had a treaty right perpetually to govern the Delawares. The case was heard by several courts over the following years, with various outcomes. In 2005 a decision against the Delawares was passed but the Lenape show no signs of surrender even in the face of this, and conflict is ongoing.

[65] Bernhard W. Sheehan, *Seeds of Extinction: Jeffersonian Philanthropy and the American Indian* (Chapel Hill, NC, 1973), 270.

Breaking the Bonds of People and Land 103

cult first period of lost federal recognition. However, I will argue that removal in the United States was at least initially a success when it came to its 'covert' agenda of economic gains for the nation-state and its white citizens.

For the Yaquis in Mexico, matters presented themselves somewhat differently. The Díaz government had wanted to clear Yaqui lands without losing Yaqui labour and it was well on the way to achieving this aim when the revolution put a stop to the programme. It had sought assimilation only to the extent that it wanted the Yoeme deportees to become subservient workers on Yucatán; removal as such was not intended to turn them into Mexicans.

Instead, as I have suggested, their removal had been born out of something like desperation, a means the government had resorted to because all other attempts to deal with the so-called Yaqui menace had failed. Much less reflection, either ethical or legal, was put into planning the removal of the Yaqui tribe than had been invested in removal in the United States. Unlike in the USA, removal of the Yaquis was geared to achieve maximum economic exploitation and was specifically tailored to them. It was probably the way in which the tribe was broken up by the deportations, as well as the forced exile, that made removal such a destructive force for the Yoeme. It was not the tribe that was transplanted, but individual workers. Because its agenda was clear cut and overt, and its policy tailored to the specific situation, Mexico came much closer to achieving the goals of removal than did the United States.

Removal and Covert Agendas

Yet I believe that what I have termed the 'covert' agenda of land appropriation—which was not all that covert—was the true driving force behind removal in the United States. And in this respect the USA was much more successful than in the policy's overt aim, which was assimilation. While it was no secret that Indians would lose lands through the application of the policy, this fact was at most portrayed as a side effect. This agenda of land acquisition contributed considerably to the failure of the policy's apparent goal, assimilation. The United States openly proclaimed its intent to destroy tribal communities and to assimilate Indians into American society as individuals. Removal, it claimed, would give Natives more time to assimilate, something that was considered beneficial for them. Yet, as Reginald Horsman has so convincingly shown, removal as a policy failed truly to pursue its stated objectives and to meet its own moral standards.[66]

In the United States, the aforementioned mix of intentions permitted the 'covert' agenda of land acquisition to dominate the official one of assimilation, and was probably the main reason why attempts to assimilate the Indians were half-hearted, incomplete, or abortive. Thus, while the policy at the time was very successful economically for the settler society, it enabled tribal survival. This ultimately foiled both its goals—assimilation and land acquisition—as the survival of tribal structures to this day stands in the way of the complete achievement of the covert agenda. The desire to maintain an air of benevolence and legality while taking the Natives' lands ultimately helped to enable those Natives to keep some of their lands.

Matters were both easier and more complicated in Mexico. As removal was not a nationwide programme that was supposed to apply to all Indians, but a measure applied just to the Yaquis (although it had been used before), the state did not perceive a need for the sweeping rhetoric and legal framework that was used in the United States. Only part of the way through the campaign, the removal was passed off as benevolent treatment for the tribe. The government wanted to control the Yaquis' lands and to open them up to white settlers. It also aimed to destroy the Yoeme's community, which was held responsible for the continued resistance that the tribe kept up in the face of attempts to take their lands.

While initially the Yaquis had been temporarily encouraged—albeit in a not very pronounced way—to become something like subservient Mexicans, the option blending with society was closed to them as soon as the deportations started, suggesting that land ranked higher on the government's agenda than assimilation. However, in contrast to the situation in the United States, in Mexico another factor entered the equation. This was the

---

[66] See Reginald Horsman, *The Origins of Indian Removal, 1815–1824* (East Lansing, Mich., 1969), 18.

Breaking the Bonds of People and Land

exploitation of Native labour, which was especially significant in the case of the Yaquis, who were very highly valued as labourers. While for a long time this had been a factor staving off removal (and thus helping the Yaquis to hold on to their land), it eventually turned into a disadvantage when their labour could more usefully be exploited on Yucatán. This also meant that the Yaquis' lands in Sonora would become available. I believe the fact that the exploitation of Native labour ranked high on the government's agenda next to land acquisition is largely accountable for how close Mexico came also to achieving a lesser goal, namely, the breaking up of the tribal community. Instead of transplanting the entire tribe, as was the case with the Delawares and others in the United States, the Sonoran state government, with federal help and in something like a semi-private business venture, exported groups of workers who ended up in isolated communities in forced exile, thereby seriously affecting the ties that had made them so successful in matters of survival before removal. Because Mexico was not torn over its reasons for pursuing removal, it was more successful in achieving the goals of this policy.

To sum up the crucial points, the investigation of these two cases and of the more general policies of the two nations reveals a number of conclusions:

1. The ways in which the policies of removal were decided and carried out in Mexico and the United States were, at times, very dissimilar. For instance, in Mexico removal was not a nationwide policy, but paired with the economic exploitation of the deportees. Yet still the basic intention behind those policies was the same in both countries; both nation-states aimed at breaking up the Native American societies within their borders.
2. Especially in Mexico, the removal programme came close to achieving its destructive goal as it left the Yaquis and the deportees in particular very few practical options. The United States, where the avenue of joining the outside society was still nominally available to the Natives and where the official agenda of benevolence conflicted with the dominant agenda of land acquisition, left the Delawares more room to manoeuvre.

3. The impact which removal from tribal lands had on the identity of these indigenous peoples was of the gravest nature. In Mexico, where the state's power was applied and removal was, furthermore, paired with the exploitation of the Natives' labour, the Yaquis' tribal identity came close to being eradicated. In the United States, the Delawares, finding themselves in a doubly hostile environment after having been forced to live among the Cherokees, were able to overcome the divisions introduced or aggravated by removal as they were left in relative peace for a few years after the event. (Even so, their recent loss of federal recognition can be counted among the long-term consequences of removal.)

These examples suggest that it was primarily (though not exclusively) greed and land hunger that was at the bottom of indigenous forced migration in the United States and Mexico. This fact has been somewhat disguised by some variations in method and circumstances, such as, for instance, legal differences, as the Delaware tribe was/is a so-called domestic dependent nation, while the Yaquis were at least nominally Mexican citizens. Yet in both cases forced migration was a product of colonialism and affected Indigenous peoples, as the original proprietors of the lands were forced from their homelands. Equally, the rise of the nation-state and, especially, periods of nation-building or rebuilding seem to have been instrumental in bringing about removal in both countries. And at the time of the removal of the Yaquis and Delawares both Mexico and the United States were advancing technologically, and the improvement in communications and transport contributed to the successful removal of the two tribes in a number of different ways. However, from the investigation of these two cases, it would seem to me that an increasing awareness that land was becoming scarcer was perhaps the determining factor in bringing about forced migration.

Undoubtedly, the bonds between people and land were affected by forced migration, as can be seen especially in later days, but the main driving force behind the policy and the attack on these bonds was a means to an end.

5

The Federal Indian Relocation Programme of the 1950s and the Urbanization of Indian Identity

DONALD L. FIXICO

Following the Second World War, the world changed and altered the minds of bureaucrats about American Indians. This new view reintroduced the idea of assimilating Native peoples into the American mainstream. Government officials wanted Indians integrated into urban areas, forcing them to move from their reservations and rural homes to cities. Once again, as under the notorious Indian Removal Act of 1830, Indian people felt the firm hand of federal paternalism changing their lives for what was supposed to be a better one. Instead, numerous problems occurred during the transition from reservation living in a traditional culture to an urban mainstream culture. Even more, a hidden agenda involved the securing of tribal lands. While the following pages address the problems of forced removal for Native peoples to cities in America, they also raise questions for analysis in a larger context. With the displacement of Indians from their tribal homelands on reservations to urban areas, who stood to benefit the most: American Indians in new urban homes with unstable jobs, or non-Indians who saw capitalist profit in the natural resources of reservations, which consisted of only 2 per cent of the land in the United States. Indians became victims in the relocation programme of removal, but motive is in question while reasons can be provided for enacting the urbanization of Indian Americans. This story is about the relocation of Indian people to urban areas and their experiences, but there is more to it than that.

Generally, the relocation experience frustrated many Indians moved to urban areas during the 1950s, 1960s, and extending into the early 1970s. This essay is an analysis of the multiple experiences of Native people who went on relocation and became quasi-assimilated to form a new identity called the 'urban Indian'. Some of these memories are the experiences of my own relatives. This cultural transition of reservation to urban was one of socio-cultural adaptation. Living 'off-reservation' represented a means of survival after relocation officials persuaded many individual Indians to leave dilapidated home-lands for a presumed better life in cities.

The United States government introduced 'Relocation' as a federal programme offered to all American Indians from 1952 to 1973. This innovative programme had two goals: to help American Indians find jobs and housing in cities, mainly in the western half of the United States; and, more importantly, to convince them to leave their homes, their reservations, and the traditional areas that they had come to love. Simultaneously, the federal government enacted the termination policy under House Concurrent Resolution 108 passed by the 83rd Congress. This new Indian policy ended the federal trust relationship with many tribes, communities, and individuals. In all, there were 109 cases of termination, with the Menominee tribe being the first case that finally occurred in 1961. Termination removed all federal protective measures from Indian lands, including individuals, and this dreadful policy finally ended almost at the same time as relocation in 1973. Until then, bureaucrats in the Bureau of Indian Affairs (BIA) and congressmen argued that both relocation and termination liberated Native peoples to enjoy full citizenship and all the privileges like everyone else.[1]

Relocation officers processed Indians like numbers through an experimental system of moving them from rural areas that nobody initially wanted, to cities where nobody cared about Indians.[2] During these years, American Indians became another group in cities, just like European immigrants and others who went to America and were exploited—Irish, Chinese, Polish—different peoples who were taken advantage of and cheated by American capitalism. As a result, American Indians became the

[1] See Donald L. Fixico, *Termination and Relocation: Federal Indian Policy, 1945–1960* (Albuquerque, N. Mex., 1986).

[2] William Willard, 'Outing, Relocation, and Employment Assistance: The Impact of Federal Indian Population Dispersal Programs in the Bay Area', *Wicazo Sa Review*, 12 (Spring 1997), 29–46 and Donald L. Fixico, *The Urban Indian Experience in America* (Albuquerque, N. Mex., 2000).

The Federal Indian Relocation Programme 109

unwritten chapter in the fictitious saga *The Jungle*, by Upton Sinclair. They had been cheated in the previous 100 years, and the century before that.

Former Cherokee Principal Chief Wilma Mankiller described going on relocation as a child with her family. In rural Oklahoma, she said,

I never like the idea of moving away. I can still remember hiding in a bedroom in our house of rough-hewn lumber, listening while my father, mother, and oldest brother talked in the adjoining room about the benefits and drawbacks of relocating our family. We younger children tried to listen through the door. We were terrified. They were talking about possible destinations. They spoke of places we had barely heard of—Chicago, New York, Detroit, Oakland, and San Francisco.[3]

The Mankillers, a family of nine, took a train from the backwoods of north-east Oklahoma to Kansas City and transferred to another train to San Francisco. Mankiller described:

My folks had the vouchers the BIA officials had given them for groceries and rent. But when we arrived, we found that an apartment was not available, so we were put up for two weeks in an old hotel in a notorious district of San Francisco called the Tenderloin. During the night, the neighborhood sparkled with lots of neon lights, flashily dressed prostitutes, and laughter in the streets. But in the morning we saw broken glass on the streets, people sleeping in doorways, and hard-faced men wandering around. The hotel was not much better than the streets. The noises of the city, especially at night, were bewildering. We had left behind the sounds of roosters, dogs, coyotes, bobcats, owls, crickets, and other animals moving through the woods. We knew the sounds of nature. Now we heard traffic and other noises that were foreign. The police and ambulance sirens were the worst. That very first night in the big city, we were all huddled under covers, and we heard sirens outside in the streets. We had never heard sirens before. I thought it was some sort of wild creature screaming. The sirens reminded me of wolves.[4]

For Indians, the new life in cities proved to be confusing and harmful. An article in the *Christian Science Monitor* described the reality of a Native family relocating to a city. The story itself depicted a true picture of what relocation was probably like for a Native family in an unfamiliar situation.

---

[3] Wilma Mankiller and Michael Wallis, *Mankiller a Chief and Her People* (New York, 1993), 69.

[4] Ibid. 71.

Tony and Martha Big Bear and their family had just arrived in Los Angeles from the reservation. Everything was new to Martha and she never said a word and scarcely raised her eyes while holding the children during the bus ride to the relocation office. The first thing the relocation officer did was to advise Tony about spending money wisely. A $50 check was drawn up for Tony and he was told how to open a bank account. The Big Bears were then temporarily lodged in a nearby hotel.

Although Tony wanted to be a commercial artist, he settled for a job in an aircraft plant. The Indian Bureau placement officer persuaded Tony to accept this job first and then he could check into the art field later after he became familiar with Los Angeles and when his family had a more permanent place to live. Everything was moving too fast for the Big Bears. The field office helped Tony find an apartment—a 'slum,' according to most people, but it was better than anything Martha was accustomed to.[5]

The experience of the Big Bears could have been more difficult. For many families, it was. Sometimes factories closed down and welfare agencies had to aid relocated families. Promised jobs fell through. Nearly all relocatees experienced difficulties of one kind or another. A writer for the *Atlantic Monthly* magazine described an incident of an Indian family of seven, struggling in the city. The situation involved Little Light, her husband, Leonard Bear, and their five children. From a Muscogee Creek community in Oklahoma, they found city life harsh. 'Today they are slum dwellers in Los Angeles, without land or home or culture or peace.' The author described meeting Little Light and her children

in the chairless kitchen-dining-living room of a small shanty on the outskirts of Los Angeles. Five children, black eyes round with wonder in their apricot faces, sheltered against her skirt. The walls were unpainted, the floor a patchwork of linoleum. Through an archway, another room was visible where three beds crowded together. A two-burner stove stood on a box, and on the only other piece of furniture in the room—a battered table—rested the remains of a dinner; some white, grease-soaked bags which had contained hamburgers and fried potatoes prepared by the restaurant a few blocks away.

In response to the interviewer's questions, Little Light spoke of how her husband went out drinking every night, of people in

---

[5] Kimmis Henderick, 'U.S. Helps Indians Move', *Christian Science Monitor* (Boston), 6 Mar. 1956.

The Federal Indian Relocation Programme

stores laughing at her, and about the need for a doctor for her sick child. She wanted to return to Oklahoma, but there was not enough money to go back. The woman stared solemnly, and her face became distorted as she lamented: 'They did not tell us it would be like this.'

The federal government introduced the relocation programme by offering its services to all qualified American Indians. The qualifications were not strict. This was an experimental project that started with the Navajo because of a severe blizzard that occurred during the winter of 1947–8 in the Four Corners area. The Navajo and Hopi were starving and their livestock were dying, compelling the federal government to move them to Denver, Salt Lake City, and Los Angeles. Housing and jobs awaited them with assistance from relocation officials. The Navajo had served admirably during the Second World War, especially as code talkers in the US Marine Corps, starting with twenty-eight of them. In all, an estimated 25,000 Indian men and several hundred Indian women served in the Second World War. Another 10,000 Native Americans served in Korea and an estimated 43,000 served in the Vietnam War when relocation ended in the early 1970s.

At this time, President Harry Truman appointed Dillon S. Meyer as the new Commissioner of Indian Affairs to start both the relocation programme and the new Indian policy of termination. Meyer, a conservative Republican from Ohio, had recently left the directorship of the War Relocation Authority that involved relocating Japanese-Americans from the west coast to hinterland camps during the war. His new appointment as Indian Commissioner was not probably to be a friend to American Indians, but rather to get a difficult job done. While Meyer served as Indian Commissioner when termination and relocation began, newly elected President Dwight Eisenhower appointed a former banker from New Mexico, Glenn Emmons, as the new head of the BIA in 1952.

In the beginning, most Indians did not know what relocation was about. Indian activist Russell Means lived in California at the time and said: 'What the hell was relocation? Eventually, I learned that the [Dwight] Eisenhower administration had come up with yet another plan to depopulate Indian reservations. The idea was to integrate Indians into urban ghettoes so that in a few generations we would intermarry and disappear into the underclass. Then the government could take the rest of our land and there would be no one left to object.'[6]

The BIA made relocation services initially available in Oklahoma, New Mexico, California, Arizona, Utah, Colorado, and Chicago, with the first official relocatees arriving in Chicago in early 1952. The small numbers of Indians relocating in the 1950s grew enormously by the mid-1960s. In all, from 1952 to 1973 an estimated 100,000 Native Americans relocated to metropolitan areas, and later in plains states, to Oklahoma City, Tulsa in Oklahoma, and Wichita in Kansas.[7] Western cities and those on the west coast proved to be popular, making Los Angeles the urban Indian capital of Indian Country. Russell Means wrote that 'relocation applicants ostensibly were limited to three preferences among seven cities—Los Angeles, San Francisco, Denver, Chicago, Saint Louis, Dallas, and Cleveland. . . . In general, most people were lucky if they ended up with their third choice, unless they were willing to wait—sometimes years until the quota for a particular city opened up.'[8]

It did not take much to qualify for the relocation programme. Because the government wanted it to succeed, the criteria were not hard. A person had to be between 18 and about 45 years old, and in good health. The applicant had to be capable of working and learning a job skill. Any prior job experience in the mainstream proved to be helpful, although it did not guarantee being placed in a job that was found by relocation officials.

In my own home community around Shawnee, Oklahoma, relatives and friends moved to Wichita, Kansas, to work in the aeroplane industry for Boeing Aircraft. Other Indians and friends of my family went on relocation mostly to Dallas, and my grandfather ended up in southern California. Many Indians from Oklahoma went to California, to Los Angeles and the San Francisco Bay area. Many relocatees returned home to reservations broke and filled with stories about the big city. Some accounts were adventurous. Daunted by urban frustration, they felt compelled to try relocation again and this time went to visit

[6] Russell Means with Marvin J. Wolf, *Where White Men Fear to Tread: The Autobiography of Russell Means* (New York, 1995), 68.

[7] Kenneth R. Philp, 'Stride toward Freedom: The Relocation of Indians to Cities, 1952–1960', *Western Historical Quarterly*, 16 (Apr. 1985), 175–90.

[8] Means, *Where White Men Fear to Tread*, 77.

The Federal Indian Relocation Programme 113

other cities. Many stayed permanently and many found that the big city life was not meant for them.

In the early years of the relocation programme, 54 per cent or more than half of the relocatees came from Indian agencies at Aberdeen, South Dakota; Billings, Montana; and Minneapolis, Minnesota. Another 46 per cent, including my relatives, came from the south and south-west, from Anadarko and Muskogee, Oklahoma; Gallup, New Mexico; and Phoenix, Arizona. The heavy migration of Indians to cities occurred from 1954 to 1961.[9] These first relocated Indians caused a major demographic shift of the Native American population from reservations and rural areas historically known as Indian Country.

The first relocatees felt cultural shock as they soon learned about elevators, stop lights, subways, and electrical implements that they had never seen before. The constant crowds of urbanization made the relocated Indians apprehensive about what they were doing and what might happen to them next. In such a foreign reality, they were on their own with little prior experience of living off their reservations, except for the Indian veterans. The relocatees felt abandoned by relocation workers and they needed help on a daily basis for the first couple of months. In addition, they soon learned about prejudice, racism, and street-life ways in the cities. Forced into new lives, Native Americans found that the federal government exercised increasing control over them in its plan to make Indians invisible via assimilation, and they would eventually lose their native identity.

Finding life hard in southern California with little job experience and almost no education, one angry Indian called relocation an 'extermination program' and said that President Eisenhower believed 'the Indians would be integrated by taking all the youngsters off the reservation, the old would die off, the young would be integrated, and the land would become free for public domain, and all the people could grab it'.[10]

Other new urban Indians found modern institutions, such as buying on credit, too overwhelming, and their inability to make instalment payments caused indebtedness, and possibly

---

[9] Fixico, *Termination and Relocation*, 138.

[10] Joseph C. Vasquez, interview by Floyd O'Neil, 27 Jan. 1971, Los Angeles, California, Interview no. 1009, box 53, acc. no. 24, Doris Duke Indian Oral History Collection, Special Collections, Marriott Library, University of Utah, Salt Lake City.

DONALD L. FIXICO

bankruptcy.[11] This was learning things the hard way, by experience. It was unfortunate for relocatees that the school of experience gave tests first, before one could study for them.

Realizing that Native Americans needed job training, Congress passed the Indian Vocational Training Act in 1956,[12] and the government offered loans and assistance to companies that would move or establish factories near the estimated 250 reservations. American Indians received on-the-job training, pretraining for certain occupations, and job placements. After 1957 relocation became known as the Indian Employment Assistance programme until it ended in 1973. In the early 1970s the federal government funded urban counselling centres and sites with opportunities to serve Native Americans as central points for socialization and community life. Such centres emerged with others funded independently in Oklahoma City and Tulsa in Oklahoma; two sites in Dallas-Fort Worth, Texas; the Lincoln Indian Center in Lincoln, Nebraska; three Indian centres in Rapid City and one in Sioux Falls, South Dakota; and the Mid-America Indian Center in Wichita, Kansas.

Working with Indians arriving in Minneapolis, a social services director at the Minneapolis Native American Center witnessed the frustrations and hopelessness of Indian people. The director lamented the disillusionment of relocation goals and hopes, saying, 'I think everybody who comes to the city has a dream—a dream of making it, a dream about improving their lives. But then prejudice slaps them right in the face and they're worse off. Call it culture shock. When your bubble is burst, there's nothing left but to go back home and start dreaming again.'[13]

Tragedy struck the lives of urban Indians as the pressure of socio-cultural alienation became too great to handle. One young Indian woman received bad news about her brother, and her roommate managed to save her from ending her own life. The

[11] L. Madigan, 'American Indian Relocation Program', 17; James O. Palmer, 'A Geographical Investigation of the Effects of the Bureau of Indian Affairs' Employment Assistance Program upon the Relocation of Oklahoma Indians, 1967–1971' (Ph.D. thesis, University of Oklahoma, 1975), 104; and US Congress, Senate, discussion on the success of the Relocation Program, 85th Cong., 1st sess., 14 Mar. 1957, Congressional Record 103: 3643.

[12] 'Adult Indian Vocational Training Act', PL 959, 3 Aug. 1956, US Statutes at Large, 70: 986.

[13] Howell Rains, 'American Indians: Struggling for Power and Identity', *New York Times Magazine*, 11 Feb. 1979, section VI, 28.

The Federal Indian Relocation Programme

roommate recalled the 'Queen of Angeles Hospital being nearby because my roommate tried to commit suicide and we had to rush her over to the hospital. . . . She was Blackfeet . . . from Montana . . . her brother got killed in Vietnam and when she got the news she kind of freaked out. And she stayed drunk for about three days and locked herself in the bathroom.'[14] She wanted to commit suicide, one of the leading causes of death for American Indians as the number of Indian suicides continued to increase in the 1980s.

Self-destruction in many cases involved alcoholism. The urbanizing effect of relocation robbed many American Indians of their confidence and self-esteem. They had nowhere to turn, except to each other. A common occurrence was for relocatees to gather and talk about their frustrations and problems. Many times local bars in the various cities became meeting places on a regular basis. These Indian bars became infamous over the years, with some not staying in business very long. Columbine in Los Angeles, Red Race in Oklahoma City, and other bars were popular hangouts. Franklin Avenue in the twin cities was lined with bars for Indians to frequent, and they did. A bar culture among relocated Indians developed in cities, much like among the Irish in Boston, Samoans in Seattle, and other ethnic groups who had their favourite places. It is there that they talked about their families, concerns, and problems.

In July 1968, in response to police brutality, Clyde Bellecourt and other concerned Indians met with attorney Gus Hall at 1111 Plymouth Avenue in Minneapolis to found an organization which came to be known as the American Indian Movement (AIM). Several noted individuals, such as Dennis Banks (Ojibwa), Clyde Bellecourt (Ojibwa), Eddie Benton Benai (Ojibwa), Mary Jane Wilson (Ojibwa), and George Mitchell (Ojibwa), were instrumental in the early formation of the movement. 'I was constantly frustrated when I was trying to be a white man', said George Mitchell, a full-blood Ojibwa and co-founder of the American Indian Movement. 'I am proud of my Indian dress. I'd rather see this country become a rainbow culture. I'd like for us to be able to see different peoples and their different ways.'[15]

---

[14] Ned Blackhawk, 'I can Carry on from Here: The Relocation of American Indians to Los Angeles', *Wicazo Sa Review*, 11/2 (Fall 1995), 21.

[15] Elizabeth Wheeler, 'Indians have Found a Mecca in Minneapolis', *Rocky Mountain News* (Denver), 13 Sept. 1976.

Indian patrols were organized to scrutinize police, and started to locate drunk Indians before the police found them. The patrols carried citizens' band radios to intercept police calls, so that they could witness police arrests and make sure that the arrested Indians were not abused. Some carried Polaroid cameras. Patrol members began wearing red jackets. Later, a black thunderbird emblem was added and the Indian Patrol was referred to as 'shock troops'.

At this time the coalition became a structured organization, a non-profit corporation with an Indian board and staff. Some people say Indian women of the new organization renamed it the American Indian Movement. Vernon Bellecourt stated: 'AIM members were going to call the organization the Concerned Indian Americans, CIA. They couldn't use that! So a couple of older, respected women said, "Well you keep saying that you *aim* to do this, you *aim* to do that. Why don't you call it AIM, the American Indian Movement?" That's how we got our name.'[16]

AIM fought back in the twin cities, fighting the police who brutalized Indians caught in or near bars, mainly along Franklin Avenue. One strategy used by the police was to open the doors of a paddy wagon, back it up to the front door of a bar, and herd everyone into the wagon. There was no chance to escape, except by fighting the police. AIM organized itself into patrols with radios to intercept police reports about where the next raid was going to occur. Taking cameras with them, the AIM patrols photographed the police arresting Indians as evidence and a means of stopping the beating of Indians.

One relocatee described the whole situation as problems with change, saying,

It [confusion] really starts when we are born on a reservation, because while we are there, we are geared to a lifestyle that is not very comfortable to take along with us into the city. When we get there, we don't know really what do we leave and what do we pick up to develop a healthy personality and to develop some character out here, because we really haven't the kind of discipline and the kind of character built in and the kind of responsibility on the reservation that we need out here [in the city]. . . . I look at the self image, the self respect, the personal

---

[16] Vernon Bellecourt interview in Peter Nabokov (ed.), *Native American Testimony: A Chronicle of Indian–White Relations from Prophecy to the Present, 1492–2000* (New York, 1991), 375.

The Federal Indian Relocation Programme 117

worth, this kind of thing, and I don't know what it was like before the reservation got here. This is one of the things that has done a lot to harm the Indian person.[17]

Humiliation and frustration drove many Indians back to their reservations and rural communities. This returning experience has been called 'returning to the blanket' in a pejorative reference that Indians had failed in adopting white ways and wanted to remain in the secure confines of the reservation with dependence on the federal government for assistance. But it was much more than this. Close to their traditions and values of the old ways, Indians continued to see things and understand life in their Native cultures. They thought in circularity with a perspective of connecting all things, human and non-human. Their ethos held respect for all things in a kind of 'natural democracy' based on respect and acknowledging all relationships, human and non-human. This Native ethos involved a tandem reality of the physical and metaphysical reality, understanding all relations as they were a part of this scheme of life.

This so-called 'Indian problem' of relocation and urbanization had to be understood by Indians themselves and solved by them. They had to gain information, knowledge about urban life, and courage to stick it out in the cities. Betsy Kellas, a Hopi, grew up in Arizona and lived in southern California during the 1960s and 1970s. She was educated in the public school system and recalled feeling alone as an Indian person. After graduating from California State University at Northridge, she worked as a counsellor at Urban Indian Center in Los Angeles. She described the urban Indian youth experiencing personal problems of being Indian. Betsy said,

It is exciting to work in the Center because most of these [young] people have problems. Many of the parents work, and the children only have a mother. They have to work just to keep going. They are examples of the society, of persons shut out by society. They have not been given a chance. They need to be themselves, and they need more than skills. They need to have opportunities to express themselves. The children are

[17] Richard Woods and Arthur M. Harkins, 'An Examination of the 1968–1969 Urban Indian Hearings Held by the National Council on Indian Opportunity Part V: Multiple Problems of Adaptation', Training Center for Community Programs in coordination with Office of Community Programs, Center for Urban and Region Affairs, University of Minnesota, Minneapolis, October 1971, 28.

so quiet. They cannot come up and tell you what is bothering them. They just hold it inside. They need people who will listen, and find out how they feel. The Indians need to find out how to express how they feel [about] themselves, and let it be known. . . . The Indian people need a chance to see what the world is about. They will know where they are at. They will know they are at the bottom, and how much they have to work to get up where they want to be.[18]

A former director of the American Indian Center in Chicago, John Walker (Sioux-Ottawa), described the second generation of urban Indians in the big city. And their urban struggle was no easier. 'All of a sudden, we were left in a vacuum', said Walker, who was born and raised in Chicago. He found it difficult to establish credibility in the Indian community whose elders were from reservations.[19] Unsure what to do, the urban Indian was left abandoned to find his or her own way of survival in the big city. George Scott, Education Director of the Chicago American Indian Center, stated: 'Indians don't know how to deal with the cities. They need some basic orientation.' Furthermore, Scott felt that some Indians were fulfilling stereotypes and the expectations of others, since they had no guidance.[20]

It was not all right to be Indian, since racism and prejudice towards 'Indian-looking' Indians still occurred, especially in border towns off the reservation. These were the roughest places for Indians, even more than the cities. Sometimes the biggest racists against Indians were Indians (mixed-bloods) themselves, who could pass as whites. One Native person described a woman who was mean to her while they grew up. The Indian woman said that after a workshop years later for the Eureka City Schools, the offender, now a schoolteacher, came up to her and blurted out an apology while crying. The Indian woman described: 'She had big alligator tears, and she said, "You know, I'm half Hupa and our folks were so ashamed of being Indian that we destroyed everything. Baskets, everything." They were burned because they didn't

---

[18] Roger W. Axford (ed.), *Native Americans: Twenty-Three Indian Biographies* (Indiana, Pa., 1980), 37.

[19] Allan Parachini, 'Chicago's Indian Ghetto Where Hopes Slowly Die', *Chicago Sun-Times*, 2 May 1976, Folder Indian News Clippings 5, Box 35, Theodore Marrs Papers, Gerald R. Ford Presidential Library, Ann Arbor.

[20] Minutes of First Meeting of the Task Force on Racially-Isolated Urban Indians, December 12 and 13, 1969, Box 114, Folder Urban Indians 4 of 4, White House Central Files, Leonard Garment Papers, Richard Nixon Materials Project, National Archives, DC.

The Federal Indian Relocation Programme   119

want anybody to know that they were Indian. I understand now that that's just the characteristic of people. If you want to cover something up you make fun of somebody else.'[21]

Surviving urbanization in the big city was intimidating. Many relocatees failed, but the struggle went on since the reservations' economies offered much less. With few jobs on the reservations, many American Indians had no choice, but to try a new life in the big city. The first point of survival was to understand the situation of Indian cultures being alien to other people in big cities. This cultural alienation would always be there so that the relocatees had to find a comfort zone of taking on and adjusting to the urban mainstream and its ways. This was a constant struggle and an individual battle for everyone to wage. Learning to be like a white man in the city was new, but not for those with previous urban experiences. Russell Means described the humiliation of being shown the simplest things when asked if he had bought an alarm clock to get up in time for work. He said:

> Yes, sure. Then a huge fat woman came into the [relocation] office to teach me how to live in Los Angeles. She began with a telephone. She grabbed my right hand and shoved my index finger into the dial of a rotary phone and 'taught' me how to dial. She told me about prefixes and made me practice dialing. I was thinking that those had to be the stupidest people I had ever met, but that was my first experience with government bureaucrats. While the fat lady was gripping my hand and showing me how to dial, I looked at her and the counselor. With all the sincerity I could muster, I said, 'What will they think of next?'[22]

Such individuality was not a part of Indian life and Indian people found themselves at an acute disadvantage. Their communal ways did not work in the urban mainstream that stressed individual desires and individual goals. Urban Indians had to make quick adjustments in their thinking and form new goals that mirrored those of mainstream America. Feeling estranged from the other peoples in the cities, urban Indians began to realize that they had to socialize with other individuals. As they made the effort, they often found themselves rejected by people living in cities. This was disheartening. In addition to this new socialization process, they had to take on new attitudes, values with a different

---

[21] Judith Anne Antell, 'American Indian Women Activists' (unpublished Ph.D. thesis, Department of Ethnic Studies, University of California, Berkeley, 1990), 24.
[22] Means, *Where White Men Fear to Tread*, 82.

outlook on life, if they were going to survive in cities. In urban areas, they had no land to call their own. They rented apartments and houses. Seeking lower rents and finding other Indians, they began to form Indian neighbourhoods in the poorer parts of cities, the ghettos. Their new neighbourhoods represented a new kind of home space without land. This was a new kind of tribalism or re-tribalization that formed new groups such as Chicago Indians, Los Angeles Indians, Bay area Indians, and Seattle Indians. This newly formed identity was one that transformed tribalism on reservations into Indianness in cities.

Racism and discrimination proved to be serious problems for Native Americans. While it proved difficult enough to make the switch to urbanization, other Americans often rejected Indian people. Racial differences were an enormous problem during the 1960s in America and for the following decade of the 1970s. African Americans, Mexican Americans, Asian Americans, and Native Americans suffered from racism.

Having little or no familiarity with American Indians, the urban mainstream believed old stereotypes. Because Indians looked different and their skin was darker, they were rejected by the urban mainstream. Wilma Mankiller described her child-hood years in schools following relocation and moving to Daly City, California. She said:

In Daly City, I was getting ready to enter the seventh grade. The thought of that depressed me a great deal. That meant having to meet more new kids. Not only did I speak differently than they did, but I had an unfamiliar name that the others ridiculed. We were teased unmerci-fully about our Oklahoma accents. My sister Linda and I still read out loud to each other every night to lose our accents. Like most young people everywhere, we wanted to belong. Also, there were changes going on inside me that I could not account for, and that troubled me very much. I was experiencing all the problems girls face when approaching the beginning of womanhood. I was afraid and did not know what to do. Besides having to deal with the internal changes, I was also growing like a weed and had almost reached my full adult height. People thought I was much older than twelve. I hated what was happening. I hated my body. I hated school. I hated the teachers. I hated the other students. Most of all, I hated the city.[23]

---

[23] Mankiller and Wallis, *Mankiller a Chief and Her People*, 103.

The Federal Indian Relocation Programme   121

American Indians found themselves and their tribes involved in the red tape of '389 treaties, 51,000 statutes, 2,000 federal court decisions, 500 attorney general opinions, 141 tribal constitutions and 112 tribal charters'.[24] Jack Haikey, editor of the Los Angeles Indian Center's publication *Talking Leaf,* believed that the Indians' special legal relationship with the United States had helped to isolate Indians and caused them to be misunderstood by the mainstream.[25]

In the mid-1970s, anthropologist Garrick Bailey of the University of Tulsa conducted a study of urban Indians in Oklahoma, and he found a number of public myths about American Indians. 'The average non-Indian Oklahoman believes the Bureau of Indian Affairs spends vast sums of money on the Indian', reported Bailey's study. 'They believe the bureau takes care of every need of the Indians and even gives them a monthly allowance check. The general consensus is that the Indian receives far too many benefits from the government and there is a great deal of resentment against Indians because of these alleged benefits. This resentment is strongest among the poor whites and other minorities', concluded the report. In sum, 'The urban Indian is one of America's forgotten people. To the Bureau of Indian Affairs, to the Indian Health Service, and all too frequently to his own tribal leaders, he no longer exists.'[26] Bailey debunked the public belief that the government took care of Native Americans. In fact, the opposite was and remains closer to the truth. The Bureau of Indian Affairs proved to be ineffective, stifling tribal communities with rules and regulations. Where the BIA found itself limited in its supervision of Indian affairs, tribes one by one found resources to take care of their own people by the mid-1980s.

[24] Georgia Anne Geyer, 'Indians Have Trouble Raising Family in City', *Chicago Tribune, c.*1963, Box 282, Folder 28, Fred Harris Papers, Carl Albert Congressional Research and Studies Center, Congressional Archives, University of Oklahoma, Norman.
[25] Ronald Ham, 'Urban Indians Misunderstood', *Northwest Leader* (Los Angeles), 20 Nov. 1975, Box 35, Folder Indian News Clippings (3), Theodore Marrs Papers.
[26] In his study, Professor Garrick Bailey obtained his information from the Senior Workers Action Program of Oklahoma County, Nutrition Program for the Elderly, Area Development Education Placement and Training Program, Head Start, Youth Development Program, and Oklahoma City Housing Authority. See Bill Sampson, 'Urban Indians "Forgotten" ', *Tulsa Tribune,* 22 Sept. 1976, Box 4, Folder, News Clippings (3), Brad Patterson Papers, Gerald R. Ford Presidential Library, Ann Arbor.

The federal relocation programme initiated the creation of a new subculture when Indians took buses or trains or drove their cars to big cities. This 'off-reservation' experience occurred over and over again, with each Indian person leaving his or her home in rural areas. Arriving in an unfamiliar urban environment meant establishing a new home space and learning the ways of a new culture. Parallel to the travels of their warriors of the previous centuries, these urban pathfinders represented the first generation of a new modern culture in American Indian history.

The gathering of urban Indians represented another parallel to the past, such as 'making camp' to establish a new community. Although the relocation officials sought to desegregate Indians by sending them on various job assignments and finding individual housing for them, native people looked for each other. As Indians found Indians, members of various tribes met other Indians. This Indian to Indian gathering began to dissolve tribal barriers and initiated a pan-Indian effect. The growing movement of relocated Indians in cities began demographically to affect the population of native people. With each year of relocation, the residential presence shifted to urban regions. Ultimately the number of urban Indians was greater than the reservation population. Even more, the second generation of urban Indians began to identify with cities as their homes instead of the reservations that their parents came from.

By the 1970s, the typical dichotomy of reservation and urban Indians had changed. With the dual identity of reservation Indians and urban Indians, the federal government found itself involved in a trichotomy in Indian affairs. This situation added to the complexity of federal supervision of Native Americans. At the same time, the federal government under Jimmy Carter, and especially under Ronald Reagan in the 1980s, promoted privatization of industry and entrepreneurship.

The attention of the federal government shifted from reservation tribes to the urban scene. Urban Indian frustration with inadequate housing such as unliveable apartments, low-paying jobs, and bad working conditions led to Indian protests. Interestingly, such protests happened as early as 1964 in the Pacific north-west over tribal fishing rights, and they led to others. The American Indian Movement emerged in the summer of 1968, voicing concerns about urban conditions. The Alcatraz

The Federal Indian Relocation Programme   123

takeover in the following year captured more national headlines. As more urban Indians voiced their concerns, the American Indian Movement became the source of a national Indian voice, forcing the federal government to listen through its protests and occupations in the late 1960s and early 1970s.

A new leadership established itself that rivalled the tribal leaders on the reservations. Now the federal government had various sets of Indian leaders to deal with. In fact, the protests and takeovers took attention and federal concern from the reservations and tribal leaders. AIM leadership consisted of young men and women who had attended boarding schools. Some even had some years of a college education, such as Leighman Brightman in California and Clyde Warrior in Oklahoma. Dennis Banks, Clyde Bellecourt, Anna Mae Aquash, and most others had gone to Haskell, Chilocco, and other boarding schools.

The modern Indian leadership could be profiled as youth oriented, boarding-school educated, some with a college education, outspoken, and angry. Modern urban leaders knew of past injustices committed against their peoples, possessed knowledge of treaties, and were willing to risk harm to themselves against police, sheriffs, federal agents, and even the US Army.

Relocation had a profound effect on Native Americans. By the 1980s more than half of the Indian population lived in cities. Critics, especially many relocated Indians, blamed the government for inadequate urban housing, and low-paying jobs that were seasonal or temporary. Furthermore, cultural alienation proved to be a major problem. Living off the reservation for the first time and learning to cope with the urban mainstream proved too hard for many relocatees who returned to reservation life. Although critics called relocation a form of Indian removal, the relocated Indians eventually survived the city life and began to develop urban Indian communities throughout the western cities and in other urban areas. The relocation plan had failed to integrate Indians into urban communities, thereby colonizing the Indian identity. The population shift of the majority of Indians from reservations to urban areas finally resulted in about two-thirds of the total American Indian population living in cities. Largely, urban Indians lived in western cities such as the twin cities area, Denver, San Francisco, Seattle, Dallas, Albuquerque, Phoenix, and Los Angeles, the largest urban Indian concentration.

The effects of relocation caused a gathering of Indians in certain neighbourhoods. In Minneapolis and St Paul, urban Indians met socially and lived near Franklin Avenue. Tribal barriers began to dissolve such that Indians of different tribes began to form Indian neighbourhoods. The native neighbourhood in the mission district in San Francisco was called the Reservation. Uptown became identified as the Indian area in Chicago's northside. As Indians identified with cities such as Chicago, Dallas, and the Bay area, a new urban tribalism manifested itself. The common ground became the city as young Native men and women married people from different tribes and races. Tribal traditions became mixed and cultural knowledge decreased. Unfortunately, tribal languages became lost with each generation of relocated Indians. By the end of relocation, fewer than one-third of Native Americans spoke their languages. Using English every day made them forget their languages.

As urban Indians began to succeed in relocation, they became frustrated for other reasons that were justified. As Indian children attended schools, they felt that they were studying a foreign culture which was the mainstream. The history of the United States did not include them in the textbooks used in classrooms. Values of the urban mainstream were different. Racism and discrimination against Indians and other minorities became obvious. As a response, Indian neighbourhoods began to experiment with forming alternative schools. Milwaukee and its Native people of Ojibwa, Menominee, Oneida, Potawatomi, and other tribes formed the Milwaukee Indian Community School. In the twin cities, concerned Indians and AIM organized the Heart of the Earth School in 1972. In Chicago, Little Bighorn High School was founded. Also in Chicago, the first urban Indian college was founded in Native American Education Services, Inc., known as NAES College, in 1974.[27]

The forming of alternative schools showed that Indians in cities wanted to invest in their children's future. They wanted to offer a curriculum in their own schools that would help prepare their children and offer courses that would help to teach their cultures and histories to their youth. These were mixed tribal schools, furthering the pan-Indian development in cities.

[27] Donald L. Fixico, *The Urban Indian Experience in America* (Albuquerque, N. Mex., 2000), 135–60.

The Federal Indian Relocation Programme 125

By the end of the twentieth century, an estimated four generations of Indians had been urbanized. At least five generations had attended boarding schools. Ironically, boarding schools used to be institutions that American Indians dreaded. Threatened and mistreated, even abused in these school institutions, now urban Indians created school institutions of their own. Now, American Indians altered institutions and created them to suit their own needs.

The survival of three generations of Indians in cities had created an urban Indian identity. By the end of the 1970s, Indians were more in control of their lives. Many graduated from college and worked as teachers and in other professional areas. By the 1980s, an Indian middle class had emerged. Professional Indian teachers, lawyers, doctors, and others formed a small core that associated with others who wanted a better life for their families. By the end of the twentieth century, the numbers of Indians in professional areas increased, but they were still small.

The results of the relocation of native people produced an urban Indian identity. As a part of urban families, city Indians became increasingly individualized. They learned to adapt to urban life, but also surrendered much of their cultures, tribal values, and languages in the process. This provoked the question: what kind of new Indian had they become? Had they become more like the mainstream person? How did they survive the domination of federal paternalism? Urban Indians had forged a new identity of their own.

For each urban Indian who experienced relocation, moving to the city for the first time was never forgotten. Memories would haunt them of being lost, not knowing where to go, and depending on strangers for help. From tribal cultures based on communalism, urban Indian identity was based more on individuality. Urban Indians found themselves among non-Indians on a daily basis. They experienced themselves as minorities, different by culture, values, logic, and in appearance. They had to adapt to new surroundings. For some urban Indians, they felt 'Indian' no more.

The worst situation involved those Indians who could not adapt. Many Indians could not make the adjustment to urban living. The pressures proved to be too great as social and cultural alienation presented insurmountable obstacles. In the end, many

American Indians could not deal with these problems compounded by discrimination, prejudice, and racism. Feeling overwhelmed, many urban Indians with these feelings took their own lives. Committing suicide was their escape from urban pressures and feelings of rejection and not fitting into the urban mainstream.

One researcher discovered that in Minnesota in 1969, in more than 700 foster homes that had Indian children, only two had an Indian parent. Furthermore, a survey of placements of Indian children in Washington State in 1974 revealed that 114 of 159 children were placed in non-Indian homes.[28] In a statement in early April 1974, former Senator James Abourezk of South Dakota and chairman of the Oversight Hearing on the Welfare of Indian Children noted that

25 percent of all Indian children are either in adoptive homes, foster homes, or boarding school. In Minnesota one out of every four Indian children were removed from their home to foster care; in Montana, the rate was 13 times that for non-Indian children; 16 times high in South Dakota; and in the State of Washington, 19 times higher. In Wisconsin, it was 16 times more likely for an Indian child to be removed in comparison to non-Indian families.[29]

As Indians came into contact with other people on a regular basis, mixed marriages occurred. An Indian person working in a factory, for example, was glad to see another Indian, but more often it was a person from a different tribe. Mixed-tribal marriages happened, thus resulting in children of more than one tribal affiliation.

Mixed marriages also began to occur with people of other races—Mexican-American, African-American, and especially Anglo-American. Since white Americans dominated the urban mainstream, many young Indian men and women married whites, resulting in bi-racial children, often with bi-cultural problems. The most important concern was social acceptance of the mixed marriage and the mixed-blood children. While Indian blood diminished, Indian identity continued. Many Indians

---

[28] Minutes of First Meeting of the Task Force on Racially-Isolated Urban Indians, 12–13 Dec. 1969, Box 114, Folder Urban Indians 4 of 4, White House Central Files, Leonard Garment Papers, Richard Nixon Materials Project, National Archives, DC.

[29] 'Senate Probes Child Welfare Crises', 'Indian Family Defense', *Bulletin of the Association on American Indian Affairs, Inc.*, 2 (Summer 1974), 1.

The Federal Indian Relocation Programme 127

suffered identity crises and felt tormented by mainstream pressures.

One Indian mother living in the San Francisco Bay area said that other Indians said she did not act like an Indian. She had married a white American man and did not feel close or obligated to her Indian relatives. She had arrived in the city when she was 11 years old and was brought up in the white world and 'could handle it'. She felt assimilated and voluntarily rejected her Indian family and cultural background.[30]

Of the Indians in the San Francisco area, among Indian mothers with a high school education or above, 71 per cent preferred their children to marry Indians, and of the mothers with less than a high school diploma, 59 per cent said the same.[31] This preference has been carried out, but the percentage of non-Indian spouses is high. One-quarter of the Indian youth in the San Francisco area are mixed-bloods whose fathers are non-Indian. This means that they will face problems of identity, self-recognition, and heritage at an early age. Children seem confused, as one parent might teach Indian values and cultural practices such as the language, while the other parent uses the English language. Overall, children who can handle such a situation are usually well adjusted.[32]

One Navajo person in Gallup wondered, 'what is in store for us in the future? Because we have lost most of our traditional values which bonded us together in the past, we must find new ways, new values and new customs that will restore the stability and the respect in our relationship. Otherwise chaos will continue to rule, destroying the fiber of our society, leading the moral decline and eventually to the disappearance of us as a people and a nation.'[33] Pat Locke, a Chippewa-Sioux, and Director of Planning Resources in Minority Education for the Western Interstate Commission for Higher Education (WICHE), stated in 1976 that 'Today's Indians must learn to walk both the white path and the red path. Both are important for survival.'[34]

Indian Americans have sometimes experienced a form of schizophrenia about their Indian identity and newly acquired

[30] Ibid. 36.   [31] Ibid. 68.   [32] Ibid. 72.

[33] 'Navajos Need New Values', *Gallup Independent*, 30 Jan. 1976, Box 35, Folder Indian News Clippings 3, Theodore Marrs Papers.

[34] Josephine Robertson, 'Pat Locke: Liaison between Two Cultures', *Christian Science Monitor* (Boston), 2 Feb. 1976.

mainstream identity. This is an individual experience that affects family members differently. For the majority of urban Indians, it becomes a continuous effort of making adjustments and changes while retaining connection to traditional ways. The perpetual internal question asked is 'how much Indianness have I lost?' Some urban Indians found it easier than others, while some preferred life on reservations or in cities living like everyone else. This torment between urban and reservation explains why many relocated Indians returned to the blanket of preference. They desired the former ways on the reservations rather than individualization as urban Indians in cities and making efforts to form urban Indian organizations and communities.

The next generation of urban arrivals helped to build urban Indian communities. The population of American Indians and urban Indians has rapidly increased, especially during the last two decades. In 1960 the Indian population was 551,669 and in 1970 it was 827,091.[35] In the 1970s, the Indian population grew three and a half times faster than the mainstream population.

As American Indians made the adjustment to urbanization, the third generation of urban Indians found life hard, but less harsh than the previous one and much less than the original relocatees who went to various cities such as Denver, Chicago, and others. They worked in various jobs, mostly those that nobody else wanted, especially dangerous ones in high steel as Mohawk iron workers.

Relocation following the Second World War was much like the removal of Indian people from their Native homelands from the east and other parts of Indian Country to Indian Territory and other designated areas that became reservations and also felt like prisoner-of-war encampments. Indians fell victim again, as they had in the mid-1800s, when many tribes had experienced forced removal to lands in the west in a government effort to clear their lands east of the Mississippi to open them for white settlement. They felt abandoned and forgotten by government officials who had made many promises. In the end, the relocation programme created a brain-drain effect, with the promising future Indian leadership going to the cities. With a less effective leadership on reservations, tribal lands became increasingly

---

[35] Task Force Eight, Final Report, 11.

The Federal Indian Relocation Programme 129

vulnerable to mining companies and timber companies who desired coal, oil, uranium, gas, and timber on Indian lands that had little protection until twenty-five tribes themselves formed the Council of Energy Resource Tribes (CERT) in 1975. CERT sought to identify natural resources on tribal lands and to force the federal government to release tribes from long-term leases with energy companies. This common situation raised important questions about the true intention of the relocation programme, particularly whether this was a deliberate attempt to seize certain desired tribal lands and reap the natural resources from them in the form of land leases. By the late 1970s at least twenty-five companies were mining natural resources in the Black Hills, timberlands were lost on the Klamath Reservations in Oregon and on the Menominee Reservations in Wisconsin, while the Four Corners area on the Navajo Reservation became the largest strip-mining site in the world.

Overall, an estimated one-third of the coal west of the Mississippi river lay beneath tribal lands on reservations. Tribal lands in twelve states possessed large oil reserves below ground. One-third to one-half or more of the estimated reserves of uranium in the United States existed in the Four Corners area.[36] Ironically, reservation lands possessed enormous amounts of coal, oil, gas, uranium, and water, which was the most precious resource of all.

On the local scale, relocated Indians suffered in the cities in a strange urban environment. As tears of adjustment ran dry and when hope was almost gone, the irony—and another resemblance with the removal policy—was that Indians survived as communities, not as individuals. In the worst of times for relocated Indians, many found strength and learned to laugh at themselves as they became strong, starting new homes and working new jobs in strange lands called urban Indian America. Surrounded by non-Indians who were in control of almost everything and frequently experiencing feelings of powerlessness, many Indians in cities thought to themselves: 'they didn't tell us it would be like this.'

---

[36] Philip Reno, *Mother Earth, Father Sky, and Economic Development: Navajo Resources and their Use* (Albuquerque, N. Mex., 1981), 133.

6

Calculating Lives:
The Number and Narratives of
Removals in Queensland,
1859–1972

MARK COPLAND

Removal from Cape York

Before daylight on the morning of 24 December 1932,[1] an Aboriginal man of about 50 years of age awoke in his camp and emerged lighting his pipe. Constable Alex Thies from Coen struck him on the back with a doubled whip. He was handcuffed to two other men and forced to march towards the river. Thies struck the men severely to hurry them along towards their destination. Upon arriving at the river, the men were repeatedly questioned as to where their wives had gone. The men refused to cooperate and were threatened with removal to Palm Island, an island in Northern Queensland established as a type of penal institution where Aboriginal people were sent from the 1920s through to the 1970s. After this, they told Thies they would find them 'by and by' and were further frightened with a revolver.[2] Unable to locate any women with these men, Constable Thies later released them. The police constables continued to cause havoc in the camp—destroying vegetable patches, Aboriginal dwellings, spears, and hunting equipment.

This was not the first act of police brutality meted out in this location. Earlier in 1932, Erick Brenning, a returned soldier and local miner, nursed an Aboriginal man who had received a beating from the Coen police for allegedly deserting his place of

---

[1] This is the date given in evidence to an inquiry held by DCPA. Photographs and notes taken by anthropologist Donald Thomson suggest this removal might have taken place around 13 Dec. Both sources document the removal as occurring in December of 1932.

[2] Evidence taken before J. W. Bleakley, CPA, 22 Oct. 1933, QSA A/58802.

132   MARK COPLAND

employment. The man was found to be suffering from a broken
rib, split lower lip, contusions to the jaw, contused scalp, wounds,
abrasions, and large bruises all over his body.[3] Brenning also
reported the destruction of gardens, humpies, and shelters. The
police had done this, as they wished to force the Aboriginal
people to congregate in one camp rather than several. Brenning
reported:

I can honestly say that I have never seen more wanton and brutal
cruelty inflicted on natives in this, or any other country, and I was a
resident in Iquitos, Upper Amazon, Peru, during and before the inquiry
into the Peruvian Rubber atrocities.[4]

These early morning attacks on camps of Aborigines had many
echoes of police and white vigilante violence on the nineteenth-
century frontier. The rushing of camps before dawn and the
destruction of Aboriginal weapons and property similarly
occurred on the Queensland frontier.[5] This wanton destruction
of Aboriginal homes and property also occurred in the removals
from a community named Mapoon in 1963.[6] The common
thread in these attacks is that they were largely made upon
unarmed, defenceless people who posed no real threat to the
safety and security of the police or vigilantes involved.

                        The Long March to Laura

Following the raid of 24 December four women and one child
were captured and started on a long march to Laura from where
they would be taken to Cooktown, Cairns, Townsville, and then
Palm Island. The journey to Laura was 232 kilometres, which
was walked in twenty days in oppressive wet season conditions.
One of the women described how the journey began:

  [3] Ibid.
  [4] Ibid. Statement from Erik Brenning, Batavia, 8 Apr. 1933.
  [5] Two examples: destruction of a camp at Breakfast Creek, Brisbane in 1860—Police
Magistrate, Brisbane Report on destruction of Blacks Camp, Breakfast Creek, COL A/7
60/1952; Destruction of camp on Umbercollie Station in Southern Queensland—
Maitland Circuit Court Depositions *Regina* v. *Richard Knight, Stephen Holden, John Reardon,
Martin Cummins, 'Billy' Aboriginal*: standing trial for the murder of an Aboriginal 'Bootha'
Mar./Apr. 1849 NSW Archives (9/6354).
  [6] See G. Wharton, 'The Day They Burned Mapoon' (BA thesis, University of
Queensland, 1996).

Calculating Lives

The native trooper, Tommy Hamilton put a chain around my neck and chained me to Judy. Then they brought Nancy Graham, with her little baby and chained her to Judy. Then they brought us to Thompson's store. We stayed in Thompson's saddle room. That was on Sunday, Christmas Day. We had Christmas dinner at Thompson's with chains on our necks and legs. That night we were chained to posts by our legs and the chains were still on our necks.[7]

One of the men asked if he could accompany his wife and use some of his horses for her to ride on. He was told by Constable Thies to 'Let her walk'.[8] Constable Thies repeatedly flogged men and women for walking too slowly. One of these women was six months pregnant:

After we left Mein Constable Thies flogged me with a stockwhip round the legs. I still have the scars on my legs from it. He flogged me because I would not walk quick enough. The sun was very hot and the ground was slippery and I got sick and could not walk fast.[9]

This same woman went for long periods of time without water and later had a fit near Yarraden Station.

A number of other Aboriginal people were captured and removed along the way to Laura. Freddy, removed from Coen for disciplinary reasons, described the dehumanizing tactics employed by the police during the same removal:

Constable Thies took my belt off and gave me a hiding with it. He put a chain around my neck and made it fast to a tree. He made me lie down on the ground. I was lying on my side. He then started to belt me with the strap, saying, 'Do you feel it?' I did not speak for a long time and he kept flogging me. Then I sang out, as my shoulder where he was hitting me was very sore. I did not get up for some time after he flogged me. Constable Thies did not hit me any more after that.[10]

Another man who was removed for 'probable insanity—for his own protection' spent a large amount of the journey un-clothed. He was repeatedly beaten to the point of blood running from his legs.[11] The above descriptions of brutal treatment received whilst being removed are but a few incidents from evidence given to Queensland's Chief Protector of Aborigines. Included in this evidence was an allegation that Constable Thies

---

[7] Statement given to Cornelius O'Leary, DCPA, 31 Mar. 1933, QSA A/69470.
[8] Ibid. [9] Ibid. [10] Ibid. [11] Ibid.

134 MARK COPLAND

had forced an Aboriginal woman to have sex with him. This woman was not removed from Batavia river.[12]

One of the remarkable things about this removal is that part of it was captured on film. Anthropologist Donald Thomson described the scene that he captured as people were taken from the church-run Aurukun mission to Palm Island.

> Terrible though this picture is, it gives no idea of the misery of the scene, with the relatives of the prisoners wailing and weeping and screaming good bye to their kin—who they know from long experience they will never see again. Nor of the widows and orphans that are left at the Mission.[13]

This instance of removal is one of close to 13,000 which occurred in the colony and later state of Queensland between 1859 and 1972. Along with instances of cruelty and brutality there are incredible stories of resistance where people travelled thousands of kilometres to return to their own country. It is important to note that in a small number of instances white Aboriginal Protectors (policemen) and other community members aided and abetted acts of resistance. One of the things to take from this incident is that Aboriginal removals in Queensland were largely a police operation. A very small bureaucracy or Aboriginal department existed, but it appointed individual police officers as protectors and enforcers of so-called protective legislation.

Removal

In 1997 a national inquiry into the separation of Aboriginal and Torres Strait Islander children from their families took place. The published report entitled *Bringing Them Home* made a number of recommendations. One of these recommendations was that archival institutions make efforts to link Indigenous Australians with records relating to the breaking apart of their families. As part of this recommendation a project was initiated by Griffith University and the Queensland Government Department of Aboriginal and Torres Strait Islander Policy (DATSIP). As the

[12] Ibid.
[13] Donald Thomson, unpublished notes, Dec. 1932, Donald Thomson Collection on loan to Museum Victoria.

Calculating Lives

principal researcher for this project I spent the equivalent of three years in the Queensland State Archives producing a computer database. This database makes it possible for descendants of Aboriginal people to identify where their ancestors were removed from, removed to, and to locate archival references to these removals. The systematic gathering of the data also provided an opportunity to conduct an analysis of the nature of removals in Queensland. While the project dealt with the phenomenon of child removal it also focused on all forced removals of Aboriginal people in the nineteenth and twentieth centuries. In Queensland this included adults, children, and, in some cases, whole communities.

From the mid to late nineteenth century removals were largely conducted on an ad hoc basis. Survivors of frontier violence might be 'given' to white settlers as domestic servants. A number of experimental mission stations were established where local Indigenous people were gathered together. In a small number of cases, Aboriginal people were taken overseas. These involved informal adoptions of children and engagements as domestic servants.[14] In August of 1900, an Aboriginal girl was returned from London to Queensland. She had originally been taken from Hughenden but a Mrs Christison found that the English weather was making her ill.[15] Upon her return, the girl was placed in the Aboriginal Girls' Home in South Brisbane and then removed to Fraser Island.[16] Possibly the highest-profile case of child removal overseas occurred in 1899 with the proposed taking of a pair of children from Fraser Island to London by Lady Lamington and her husband, the governor of Queensland.[17]

In terms of the removal of children, from 1865 a child could be deemed to be 'neglected' under Child Welfare policy if he or she was born of an Aboriginal mother. The recorded instances of this, it must be said, are relatively few. The reason for this was

---

[14] Police Magistrate at Herberton requesting permission for Mr Beckley to take an Aboriginal boy named Snowball to England, 7 Feb. 1887, QSA Col/A489 87/1268; telegram from J. H. Bond in Normanton requesting permission for his wife to take a young Aboriginal girl to England for about twelve months. She is required to look after their baby. A second telegram in the file states, 'No objection', QSA Col/A572 89/1813.

[15] Mary Christison to Horace Tozer, Hampstead Heath, 19 July 1900, QSA COL/145 00/14806 Microfilm frame numbers 64–80.

[16] Ibid.

[17] *Queenslander*, 15 Apr. 1899.

that the cost of the state supporting an Indigenous child was deemed to be unnecessary and in those cases where it did happen the money spent on Aboriginal children was substantially less then that spent on their white equivalents. Between 1859 and 1972 an estimated 16.9 per cent, or one in six Aboriginal people, were affected by this policy of child removal or separation from family.

The introduction of the 1897 Aboriginal Protection and Restriction of the Sale of Opium Act brought about the beginning of an extensive system of removal. The requests for removal, removal orders, and entries in the removal registers were all written exclusively by white men. Naturally these men all had their own ideas as to what constituted proper behaviour and when the removal of Aboriginal people from a location might be deemed to be necessary. While the Chief Protector of Aborigines (CPA; later the Department of Native Affairs) made the official request for authorization to remove an Aboriginal person, he usually relied on the advice and recommendations of local police officers to inform his decision. Superintendents of reserves and missions and other officials could also be appointed 'Protectors of Aboriginals', but the majority of removals were recommended by police officers appointed as local 'Protectors of Aboriginals'.

These individual officers did not act in a uniform way with regard to removals. Some energetically sought to clear camps of Aborigines not 'usefully employed' while others tried to ensure that Aboriginal people could remain in their country. The CPA and local protectors did not make decisions regarding removal from within a power vacuum. As soon as the 1897 Act was passed, white farmers and townspeople began to call on the state to exercise its new power to have unwanted Aboriginal people removed.

The Database

Three removals' registers form the backbone of the database.[18] For a removal to appear in the register there would have been a relay of letters and memoranda from local Aboriginal Protectors

[18] The registers of removal were created and maintained by the Office of the Chief Protector of Aboriginals and are currently held at the Queensland State Archives.

Calculating Lives
137

(in the majority of cases, policemen) to the office of the CPA. Upon deciding to have an Aboriginal person removed, the CPA would then seek the signature or approval of the government minister responsible for Aboriginal affairs. The majority of these 'official removals' emanated from country towns and centres throughout the state.

A database personal card was created for each individual. A removal card was then attached to this. In this way a person's multiple removals could be viewed at once. By filling in reason for removal, age, gender, and so on, the data could be viewed through other lenses. Factors such as gender, age, and geographical location could all be analysed across the entire number of recorded removals. What emerged was that a range of factors brought about a fluctuation in the number of removals. In some locations this could be attributed to zealous Police Protectors. During some periods of time this could be the result of policy direction and legislative changes. What emerged from the analysis of removals in Queensland was that a grand narrative needed to be constructed. For the removals to take place the wider population needed to believe that there was intrinsic logic involved in the removals project. The population needed to be convinced that the removal of Indigenous people was inevitable. It was portrayed as a part of progress and in the best interests of the removees.

A detailed analysis of these statements for removal revealed that the stated reasons used for removal had very little to do with the actual reasons. Along with the need to construct a narrative to justify removals, there was also a need to 'mark' those who were to be removed. These markings were often descriptions which portrayed the removee as a threat to the health or well-being of the wider community. One of the reasons used for the introduction of the 1897 protective legislation was to prevent the use of opium amongst the Aboriginal population. When the reasons used for removal are analysed, it can be seen that only 2 per cent of all removals involved the use of opium. The largest reason cited for removal was discipline at 36 per cent (see Fig. 6.1).

Similarly, when removals involving health as a reason are analysed it becomes clear that there *was* no explosion of poor health in the mid-1930s and during the years of the Second World War. This increase in removals had far more to do with

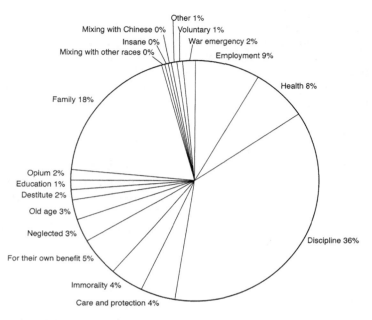

FIG. 6.1. *Stated reasons for removal*
Source: Compiled by the author from his own research.

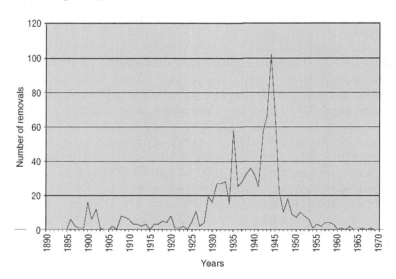

FIG. 6.2. *Removals with health as a stated reason*
Source: Compiled by the author from his own research.

Calculating Lives

the effects of the depression and economic downturn in the 1930s and also an obsession with sexually transmitted diseases during the Second World War (see Fig. 6.2).

'Mixing of races', 'immorality', and 'destitution' were reasons used for removal which linked quite closely to those initiated ostensibly for issues of health. The influence of Dr Raphael Cilento, a senior government health officer in the development of the 1934 Amendment Act and the increase in removals during the 1930s, was quite pronounced. Cilento was Director of Tropical Hygiene in the Commonwealth Health Department from 1928 to 1933 and was appointed Director of Health and Medical Services in Queensland in 1934.[19]

In November of 1932 Cilento conducted a survey of Aboriginal people in North Queensland. He used the survey to compare residents of Palm Island with what he termed a 'coloured' population living with 'minimal restrictions' in North Queensland.[20] He described Aboriginal people living in North Queensland as 'hanger-ons' living on the fringes of white settlements and part of a rapidly declining tribal remnant.[21] Venereal disease was believed by Cilento to be widely carried by the 'non-white' population of North Queensland:

It is almost impossible for any aboriginal woman to escape venereal infection in the neighbourhood of (say) Cairns or Innisfail, and among the large foreign and sometimes coloured populations that exist in these localities. Promiscuity is encouraged by circumstances almost impossible of governmental control.[22]

Cilento's 'intermediate coloured persons' were South Sea Islanders and other non-Aboriginal people of non-European descent. In the view of Cilento, they were carriers of not only venereal diseases but also others such as hookworm, filariasis, and malaria. The solution for Cilento was clear: all non-whites had to be brought under stricter governmental control.

It is emphatically my opinion that the coloured groups, both aboriginal and other, in the neighbourhood of towns, should be eliminated, either by absorption of the better elements into the general community, or by

[19] Ros Kidd, 'Regulating Bodies: Administrations and Aborigines in Queensland 1840–1988' (unpublished thesis, 1994), 371.

[20] Raphael Cilento, *Report of a Partial Survey of Aboriginal Natives of North Queensland*, Oct.–Nov. 1932, NAA A 1928/1 4/5 SECT 1 Survey of Aboriginals.

[21] Ibid.   [22] Ibid.

the transfer of the aboriginals to Aboriginal Settlements. Coloured persons living as natives might be given their choice of transfer to Aboriginal Reserves or Settlements, passing thus voluntarily under the control of the Chief Protector, or otherwise dealt with in accordancy with the laws relating to vagrancy and so forth.

If the mainland natives are to remain in their present locations, it will be necessary to provide them with a much more liberal food issue, and one that is not only received by them, but eaten, and not disposed of for tobacco or other luxuries. It is difficult, from the experience of other countries, to see how this could be effected without transferring the natives to compounds, but without it, they are merely doomed to extinction, in a way that reflects little credit upon the community.[23]

Part of the motivation for Cilento's policy recommendations was the threat posed to Queensland's population by 'non-whites' or the 'coloured' people. Cilento's proposal went far beyond health—rather it proposed a total 'solution'. He concluded his 1932 survey:

I would venture to suggest that the whole aboriginal problem from the point of view of Settlements, be regarded as an indenture system, with the State as protector. The aboriginal is sufficiently low in the scale of economic progress to respond to a modified and temporary programme of paternalism, unadapted as such a system may be to people educated in the consciousness and independence of thought and action.[24]

The idea was that once Natives had reached an 'adequate stature of development' they were to be returned to the white community:

If it be suggested that this converts Palm Island into no more than a clearing station for the health of natives, it may be pointed out that, in effect, the care of the native is essentially a matter of constant medical supervision—a supervision that goes all the way from actual disease control to the control of adequate food supplies and suitable working supplies and suitable working conditions, and methods of recreations and educational improvement.[25]

The peak of removals with health as a stated reason occurred in 1944, with 102 recorded cases. This surge in numbers can be attributed directly to concerns over the spread of venereal disease during the years of the Second World War. Ninety-eight (96 per cent) of these were to Palm Island.

[23] Ibid.   [24] Ibid.   [25] Ibid.

Calculating Lives

Rationales for Removal: Fiction

There was a perceived threat of Aboriginal people on Cape York collaborating with the Japanese during the first half of the 1940s. Presbyterian and Church of England mission authorities were investigated by the Deputy Director of Security for Queensland and found to be of minimal risk in terms of collaborating with the Japanese.[26] Aboriginal people on Cape York were, however, also perceived to be a potential health threat to Australian and US army personnel stationed in the area.

In November 1942 Colonel Wills of the Australian Army suggested that 'for reasons other than operational, transfer should be effected of certain female natives from Missions in Cape York Peninsula, situated in close proximity to Military encampments'.[27] The major reason for this suggestion was that it was believed that US and Australian troops were at risk of contracting venereal disease from local Aboriginal women. Wills voiced a concern that 'white control is deteriorating due to natives associating with AMF and Negro troops in the Peninsula'.[28]

Michael McKernan describes a climate in which the spread of venereal disease was viewed as an increasing menace in Australian society during the Second World War.[29] Women were viewed as the carriers of the disease and the Australian and Allied military forces worked with civilian health and police departments to detect and detain women suspected to be infecting soldiers.[30]

There was little evidence of venereal disease amongst Aboriginal people living in the church-run missions on Cape York. Nevertheless, the Department of Native Affairs (DNA) agreed to a request from the military that Aboriginal women who came into contact with troops periodically be examined and that if they were found to be suffering from venereal disease,

---

[26] R. F. B. Wake, Deputy Director of Security for Queensland to Commanding Officer Security Section, Brisbane, 11 Feb. 1943, NAA A373/1 3950 Transfer of Natives—Cape York Peninsula.

[27] Ibid. L. H. Lemaire, Lt.-Col. Inspector Administration to Chief Inspector of Army LHQ, 18 Nov. 1942.

[28] Ibid.

[29] Michael McKernan, *All In! Fighting the War at Home* (St Leonards, 1995), 255.

[30] Kay Saunders, *War on the Homefront: State Intervention in Queensland* (St Lucia, Queensland, 1993), 91.

removal from the area would take place. Because of the inability of the DNA to implement such a strategy, it was agreed that the examinations would be conducted by military medical officers.[31]

Once again, the perceived threat to the white population was weighed against the benefit of Aboriginal labour. Discussions on removal of Aboriginal people from the Cape York district highlighted the value of Aboriginal labour. It was decided that those suffering from venereal disease be removed whilst ensuring that there was sufficient Aboriginal labour to supply fresh fruit and vegetables to the army personnel on Cape York. The provision of fresh fruit and vegetables was seen to be of the utmost importance to the health of the troops in the district.[32]

Even if the reasons for removal were as stated, it is important to look at how people were dealt with when they arrived in their enclosed institutions. The majority of people suspected to be suffering from venereal disease were sent to Palm Island or a Lock Hospital at the nearby Fantome Island. In 1932 the Director of Queensland Health visited the Fantome Island Lock Hospital and observed one man treating 160 patients. He stated that many would never leave the island.

But health was not the only subterfuge used to justify removal of Aboriginals. Education was another reason. Those removed for education in some instances were taken from a situation where they attended a local mainstream school and sent to a settlement where they were taught by an unqualified teacher. It was not until the mid-1960s that children on Aboriginal settlements would receive more than a year four education. Supposed concerns about Aboriginal education, like health, were just one of the many 'narratives of the lie', a useful fiction to justify removal.

Rationales for Removal: Fact

When we look at the destination of those people removed with mental health or insanity as a reason we find that only 20 per cent were removed to a mainstream mental health institution. The reason for this was very clear. In the early 1900s it cost the

[31] Ibid. Brigadier i/c Administration HQ to Allied Land Forces HQ.
[32] Ibid. Major General S. R. Burton, Minute Paper to Adjutant-General 1 Dec. 1942.

Calculating Lives

state £25 to care for a patient per year and £2 to incarcerate an Aboriginal person deemed to be insane.

The cost and benefit to the state of removals was always a factor. The need for a cheap and useful labour force saw the number of removals peak during the First World War. Removals were the cornerstone of Indigenous policy in Queensland. They could be used as a disciplinary tool, as a way of crushing resistance, and in many cases to enforce exploitative labour relationships. Removal orders were also used as a way of quelling complaints about employment conditions. Ten per cent of removals involved employment as a stated reason (taking into account family removals). This means Aboriginal people were faced with a stark choice—engage in an employment agreement or be removed to a government-run settlement. The historian Dawn May rightly asserts that one of the reasons that there was never a strike amongst pastoral cattle workers in Queensland (whereas there was in Western Australia and the Northern Territory) was that perceived agitators could be sent to Palm Island. Removal was used as a threat to keep Aboriginal workers in line.

For much of the period between 1897 and 1972 many Aboriginal Queenslanders only received 30 per cent of their wages. The remainder of what they had earned was the money that ran the Queensland Aboriginal bureaucracy, but was also dipped into by the government for other purposes. Involuntarily, however, Aboriginals helped carry the cost of their own removals. Between 1901 and 1947 there were 9,562 documented removals. During the same period there were also 165,638 recorded employment agreements. The policy and practice of removals helped to make this possible.

Removals can also be analysed along gender lines. Seventy-two per cent of males were removed for disciplinary reasons while 25 per cent of those removed for disciplinary reasons were females. Sixty-nine per cent of removals with immorality as a stated reason were females while 25 per cent were males. (In 6 per cent of cases, gender was not recorded.) In many ways the removal orders and registers tell us more about the assumptions made by Police Protectors and white administrators than they do about the removees.

When removals are analysed over time a pattern emerges. The peak of all removals occurred in 1915. This peak was the result not of an outbreak of 'ill discipline' amongst the Aboriginal population of Queensland, but of the dearth of white labour. Young white men moving from the land to enlist or be conscripted into the army to fight in the First World War meant that labourers were needed to keep the pastoral and agricultural industries functioning in Queensland. Forced removals of Aboriginal people helped to fill this gap, and 'ill discipline' and health, among other things, helped to justify Aboriginal removal.

Periods of intervention with a relatively high number of removals alternated with periods of less activity in which the number of removals was comparatively low. Economic factors, racial thought, policy direction, and the personal influence of local protectors and the Chief Protector of Aboriginals all played a part in the fluctuation in the number of removals over time. What remained consistent throughout the period of time studied is the power that removals had over the lives of Aboriginal Queenslanders.

An Enduring Solution

Removals such as the one from the Batavia goldfields to Palm Island during December 1932 were not rare numerically. More than 250 Aboriginal peoples were removed from the Coen Police District to missions and reserves through to the early 1970s.[33] Nor were they rare in terms of brutality; the 1932 removal was not unique. In 1950 a policeman from Coen tracked twelve Aboriginal people and surprised them at gunpoint. They were marched for twenty hours non-stop to Coen. Amongst those people captured were four children and one heavily pregnant woman.[34] This woman gave birth to a child shortly after the removal.

In 1936, the CPA approached the Bishop of Carpentaria regarding the removal of more people from the Coen district. The Bishop agreed to co-operate and steps began to be taken in the 'drafting of the old and incapable natives of the Coen, Moreton and Batavia Districts into the Lockhart River Mission'.[35]

[33] RD.

[34] Commissioner of Police to Under Secretary, Dept. of Health and Home Affairs, 19 May 1950, QSA A/58862.

[35] CPA to Under Secretary, Dept. of Health and Home Affairs, 15 June 1936 QSA A/3842.

Calculating Lives

Whilst the Queensland government used the term 'Aboriginal protectors' the Chief of these protectors, J. W. Bleakley, spoke of 'absorbing' populations into missions and reserves and local Police Protectors spoke of 'cleaning districts of native problems'. Aboriginal people were not all passive victims of these policies. The response of white officials to the policy of removal also varied. In 1940 the Police Protector of Coen, in stark contrast to his counterpart of 1933, pleaded with the DNA not to remove people from Coen:

> Your suggestion to send these old people is unthinkable. If you send them there they will only walk back to their own native country. Coen is their home, their native land, and at least they might be happy in the knowledge that they might die in the place where they first saw the light of day. They speak of Lockhart in terms of fever and starvation, whether true or untrue, they tremble when spoken to of Lockhart. They have been here before and came away. If you decide not to build for them, please leave the old people in their native land and surroundings. The expense in sending these poor old people to Lockhart is not justified, be it ever so small, for so sure as the sun rises they will return immediately, or if unable to return, will die of fever. I would much prefer to leave them in their present condition than to send them to Lockhart. Their present homes, be they ever so humble, are vastly preferable to sending them to Lockhart to be unhappy.[36]

This was, however, just a small brake on the removals process; sixty-two people were recorded as being removed from Coen after 1940.[37] For the removals project to succeed, it required the cooperation and support of local police constables and sergeants—those hundreds of men acting as protectors of Aboriginals.

Aboriginal people responded to removals such as this in a range of ways. Some of the people living on Cape York fled the whips and pistols of the patrolling police and missionaries. Others took on the uniform of authority and 'played the game'. One of the most interesting aspects of this event is the degree to which those forced to march from Batavia river to Laura engaged in an inquiry process later held at Palm Island. Those most affected by the violence of the removal gave great quantities of oral evidence to the Office of the CPA. Just as the violence of

---

[36] PA, Coen to DNA, 17 Dec. 1940, Tape Transcript of document held by Professor Bruce Rigsby, University of Queensland.

[37] RD, DATSIP, Queensland Government, 2001.

146 MARK COPLAND

the initial removal established a pattern of race relations between those with power and those with diminished power, so did the inquiry.

Over the past seventy years numerous inquiries into violence and brutality have taken place on the community of Palm Island, along with other Queensland reserves and missions. Generations of white officials and Indigenous community members have grappled with the reality of a truth that recognizes the original violence but cannot seem to redress the original shift in personal power.

Conclusions

The removal of Aboriginal people in Queensland was part of a response to that age-old colonial question: 'Once you take the land what do you do with the people?' This analysis shows that the truth can be found in what Aboriginal administrators and protectors did, rather than what they said.

This study of removals assists in unravelling some of the 'narratives of the lie'. The first and most basic of these lies emerged during the frontier period of history. This narrative held that Aboriginal people had no real ties with the country. They could be moved from location to location enduring little if any hardship. The second of these lies was that Aboriginal people had little connection with each other. Children could be taken from parents; women and men could be taken from families and wider kinship groups. On occasions it was a colonial 'nicety' that people be returned from where they were taken, but this was not considered an absolute necessity.

The construction of a database of removals has provided a basis on which to interrogate the rhetoric used to justify policies of enforced removal. Persons removed for insanity were not taken to asylums; persons removed for health reasons were not provided with health care. In a number of cases children were removed from situations in which they enjoyed a comparatively high level of education to government settlements where the quality of education was sub-standard. Furthermore, interrogation of the official record has revealed that in many cases the underlying causes that influenced removals were not recorded on

Calculating Lives

the removal order. Indeed, the official justification provided for many removals was misleading and in some cases deliberately so. The fluctuations in the range of official explanations provided over time to removals demonstrate that the needs and demands of the dominant society drove many of those orders. Although removals were authorized under legislation which was supposed to protect Aboriginal people, the peaks and troughs in the rate at which removals were enacted bears little relation to fluctuations in the social and economic conditions actually experienced by Aboriginal people in Queensland.

The lies that Aboriginal people were 'bad', 'mad', and 'carried disease' underpinned many removals. The results of this study severely call into question the validity of individual reasons used for removals. It cannot be believed that there was an outbreak of 'discipline' problems for Aboriginal people when the number of related removals jumped from 30.6 per cent in 1914 to 50.7 per cent in 1915. Similarly, there is no evidence to suggest that there was an Aboriginal health crisis which meant that the number of health-related removed jumped from 16.6 per cent in 1941 to 42.7 per cent in 1944. Very few people were recorded as 'voluntary' removals and the level of choice open to those who did move to missions and reserves was very minimal.

When we look at removals on a geographical basis we observe huge dislocation. In many cases, removals took Aboriginal people thousands of kilometres from their original locations. There appears to be no pattern of removal in terms of geography. Many of the descendants of those people removed from the Batavia river area (described at the beginning of this essay) never came back to Cape York. They, along with people from numerous language groups from around the state, were incarcerated on an island designed for control and punishment rather than care and support. The disastrous results of this forced dislocation are still being experienced by Queensland people at present living in Aboriginal communities.[38]

---

[38] In Nov. 2004 reaction to the death of an Aboriginal man in custody led to a riot on Palm Island. A number of reports on the incident mentioned the lack of stability in the community as the legacy of removals (Tony Koch, *Australian*, 29 Nov. 2004).

7

The Slave Trade as Enforced Migration in the Central Sudan of West Africa

PAUL E. LOVEJOY

The slave trade was a specific mechanism of enforced migration. Although the slave trade has sometimes been likened to the Holocaust, a more appropriate analogy would be to the uncertainties and terror of refugees who are forced to move. In the case of the slave trade, the process of enslavement created conditions that produced refugees, as well as the enslaved victims who were forcibly removed. Such an approach to the slave trade highlights the extent to which enslavement and the movement of individuals through the slave trade were consciously pursued as reflected in government policy and political and religious ideology. In order to consider the slave trade from this perspective, this essay focuses on that dimension of the slave trade in Africa specific to the Muslim regions of West Africa centred on what today is Nigeria and which in the nineteenth century was the Islamic state known as the Sokoto Caliphate. This focus allows a consideration of the policies of a major African state towards the slave trade and towards the use of enslavement as a mechanism of enforced migration and social engineering.

The Sokoto Caliphate was the largest independent state in Africa in the nineteenth century, and had an enslaved population of several million people at the time of the colonial conquest (1897–1903).[1] As is argued here, the Caliphate consciously pursued a policy of enslavement as a means of consolidating political control, economic development, religious conversion, and social planning. Although the process of enslavement entailed risks to the enslavers and untold hardship and suffering for targeted populations, religious and political ideology justified this form of

---

[1] Paul E. Lovejoy, *Slavery, Commerce and Production in West Africa: Slave Society in the Sokoto Caliphate* (Trenton, NJ, 2005).

enforced migration through the call for jihad against unbelievers. The fact that implementation resulted in considerable loss of life and the destruction of property was an inefficiency that may have been troubling to some, but was tolerated in the interests of the Muslim community.

The essay first considers the relationship between enforced migration as a phenomenon and slavery as a means of enforcement. It is argued that this migration was reflected in the degree of urbanization in Muslim areas of West Africa, and especially in the Sokoto Caliphate, which is reflected in surviving biographies.[2] Although it is not often recognized, there were many towns and cities in the nineteenth century. This urbanization demonstrates two aspects of slavery as enforced migration: namely, the necessity of congregating in walled towns for defence in the face of the insecurities of slave raiding and war, on the one hand, and the fact that much of the congregated population was enslaved and brought from elsewhere as a means of economic and political consolidation. People were moved around and they were enticed to gather in defensible locations behind walls. People generally moved to farming communities and plantations outside the towns, according to season and safety. The purpose of slavery in Islamic West Africa then had to do with demographic planning, however brutal in its implementation. The impact of enforced migration in this setting, it is argued, was softened through various institutions and practices that were intended to ease the introduction of the enslaved into the state. The official and religious policies of assimilation included practices of *murgu*, in which slaves were allowed to work on their own account in exchange for a payment, and various methods of achieving emancipation. Such ameliorative practices stand in stark contrast to the brutality of enslavement, the callousness of the slave market, and the tribute payments in human bodies.

Ethnicity was an important factor in considerations of enslavement and enforced migration, which is examined below as a means of understanding the relationships among peoples who were involved in enslavement, opposition and resistance, and demographic and cultural transformation. Identification according to ethnicity and origins was a dynamic factor in a political

---

[2] Id., 'The Urban Background of Enslaved Muslims in the Americas', *Slavery and Abolition*, 26/3 (2006), 347–72.

The Slave Trade as Enforced Migration   151

economy in which enslavement and enforced demographic change were state policies. In this study, the Sokoto Caliphate is the focus because its policy towards enslavement was a major reason that a jihad was consolidated into a confederation of thirty emirates and many sub-emirates that stretched from Burkina Faso through Niger and Nigeria to Cameroon and the Central African Republic. As the reference to 'caliphate' indicates, this was a state whose foundation in jihad was a factor in succession to leadership, with each 'caliph' a direct relative of the founder, 'Uthman dan Fodio (d. 1817). The state emerged during a series of campaigns between 1804 and 1808 that swept aside the governments of the main walled towns in the central Sudan, and state policy subsequently extended the initial successes through expansionist wars and slave raids that effectively lasted until European conquest by a combined assault from Britain, France, and Germany, culminating in complete colonial occupation in 1903. The focus here is on the nineteenth century and the policies of this Islamic state with respect to demographic restructuring, a process that lasted until the colonial era and, indeed, set the demographic landscape of the northern region of Nigeria today.

Slavery and Demography

The process of enslavement implies a demographic model in which areas that are attacked lose population and the aggressors force people to return to their own centres. The slave trade involved enforced migration, and hence resulted in the removal of populations, but we are faced with a number of anomalies. The slave trade is usually considered a conscious commerce, in which individuals are commoditized. People are moved as goods, appropriate for the extraction of labour, their sexuality, productive and reproductive capacities, and valued according to the market for specific needs and services, including sacrifice at funerals or employment in high government office. What happens to individuals where they end up can be called the 'arrival factor'. This essay is not only concerned with the phenomenon of removal itself, but also the impact of enforced migration through slavery in terms of demographic change.

Enslavement forced people to move, and those who resisted were killed or otherwise dispersed. Forced migration by walking in fetters, sometimes carrying loads, having to survive injuries, hunger, disease, and sexual abuse, under conditions in which mortality was high—this was not an efficient means of reallocating human resources across geography. The only market that operated was the treatment of humans as commodities, which is far from an efficient means of reallocating labour and, in fact, precludes other forms of marketing arrangements. The inefficiency of this mechanism of demographic 'planning' offers insights into the imperfections in planned demographic change, which in the case of slavery have their own specific political, ecological, and economic implications.

The model of slavery as a form of enforced migration and population removal requires an understanding of what has been called the 'enslaving frontier', which has variously been defined on the basis of religion, ethnicity, and politics. Implicitly, the concept implies population removal and dispersal.[3] Movement characterized the displacement of enslavement in which distance was a factor that reduced the risks of resistance and escape. In the enforced removal of people through slavery, inevitably, individuals were distanced from their natal homes, which were often left in a mangled condition in the consequences of the enslavement of its people. The idea of a 'frontier' also reflects the fact that people abandoned territory that was raided, if they were not captured or killed. Consequently, there was often a buffer zone, largely uninhabited, between states.

The context of slave raiding and warfare raises questions of who moves and why, and the degree of consciousness in defining those who could be enslaved. On the most superficial level, this requires an understanding of specific historical circumstances and the interplay between politics, ecology, and economy. The

[3] See e.g. P. Burnham, 'Raiders and Traders in Adamawa: Slavery as a Regional System', in J. L. Watson (ed.), *Asian and African Systems of Slavery* (Oxford, 1980), 43–72; J. S. Hogendorn, 'Slave Acquisition and Delivery in Precolonial Hausaland', in B. K. Schwartz and Raymond E. Dumett (eds.), *West African Culture Dynamics: Archaeological and Historical Perspectives* (The Hague, 1980), 477–93; Paul E. Lovejoy (ed.), *Slavery on the Frontiers of Islam* (Princeton, 2004); Michael Mason, 'Population Density and "Slave Raiding": The Case of the Middle Belt of Nigeria', *Journal of African History*, 10/4 (1969), 551–64; Joseph P. Smaldone, *Warfare in the Sokoto Caliphate* (Cambridge, 1977); Femi James Kolapo, 'Military Turbulence, Population Displacement and Commerce on a Trading Frontier of the Sokoto Caliphate: Nupe *c*.1810–1857' (Ph.D. thesis, York University, 1999).

The Slave Trade as Enforced Migration 153

resort to enslavement was a viable and common political action in West Africa. Inevitably, the prevalence of slavery meant that the subject was hotly debated in Islamic areas of West Africa, as demonstrated in the written literature in Arabic, court records, and diplomatic correspondence. The issue of slavery and specifically complaints that free-born Muslims were regularly enslaved and thereby not protected by political authorities was one of the causes of the jihad that established the Sokoto Caliphate. Moreover, the diplomatic correspondence between the jihad leadership and the Muslim government of neighbouring Borno demonstrates that the subject of who could be enslaved was a contested subject among Muslims.[4]

The legitimacy of enslavement was also fundamental to the practice of ransoming, which was common in Muslim areas. Free-born often had to pay twice the market price of slaves to obtain their redemption. This practice provided some protection for Muslims in a situation in which slavery was endemic, thereby limiting the unrestricted movement of people. Whenever environmental or political factors forced people to evacuate their homes there was grave risk of enslavement, but these same conditions sometimes enabled people to escape, and if they claimed to be Muslims, it was difficult to dispute their status at birth. Therefore, warfare was both a mechanism for enslavement but also an opportunity for those who were enslaved to escape or otherwise alter their conditions. Inevitably, the discussion of who could be enslaved and resistance to enslavement were factors in the discourse of forced removal. While it has sometimes been alleged that the victims of slavery were passive and experienced a form of 'social death', to quote Orlando Patterson, the reality in West Africa shows that this approach is deceptive.[5] Instead, the extent of strategizing in terms of resistance and the public debate about legitimacy demonstrate that people were actively involved in the reality of enslavement. To avoid slavery, people stored food in caves, retreated to defensible hills, grew cactus fences, dug trenches, used divination, amulets, rituals and counter-rituals, and manipulated kinship, age, and gender relationships.

[4] Paul E. Lovejoy, 'The Bello–Clapperton Exchange: The Sokoto Jihad and the Transatlantic Slave Trade', in Christopher Wise (ed.), *The Desert Shore: Literatures of the Sahel* (Boulder, Colo., 2001).

[5] Orlando Patterson, *Slavery and Social Death: A Comparative Study* (Cambridge, Mass., 1982).

154   PAUL E. LOVEJOY

These were features of life and society in areas on the frontiers of Muslim slaving. Many enslaved boys died from castration, which was performed in frontier areas because of the high demand for eunuchs, which was a further incentive to resist.

Although moving enslaved people considerable distances was a feature of slavery, slaves sometimes came from places not so distant, as demonstrated in the origins of concubines in the Sokoto Caliphate. Court records from Kano, Zaria, and other emirates reveal that many concubines came from areas within 150 km of their place of enslavement.[6] Moreover, women were less likely than men to return to their homes because of the difficulties of escaping in areas dominated by Muslim men—it was impossible to join caravans, while children also limited the mobility of women. Hence age and gender were important factors in the movement of population. Women and children were targeted because of the relative difficulty of their escaping. This policy was further encouraged because it was thought that women and children were easier to assimilate and indoctrinate into the cultural norms of society than men. There was a conscious effort at assimilation, even if full incorporation was regulated and the reliance on enslaved labour entailed the continued settlement of newly enslaved. Although children were born into slavery, their numbers were not sufficient to sustain the slave population, which required steady replenishment from the frontiers.

Urbanization and Population Displacement

Muslim society in West Africa was urban, and the concentration of population through settlement of captives taken in raiding and warfare was a common strategy of state. The enslaved population was settled in agricultural districts near walled towns, and hence there was a process of movement from frontiers where people were enslaved to urban centres and their surrounding villages. In the nineteenth century there were hundreds of towns

---

[6] Paul E. Lovejoy, 'Concubinage and the Status of Women Slaves in Early Colonial Northern Nigeria', *Journal of African History*, 26/2 (1988), 245–66; and Lovejoy and J. S. Hogendorn, *Slow Death for Slavery: The Course of Abolition in Northern Nigeria, 1897–1936* (Cambridge, 1993).

The Slave Trade as Enforced Migration 155

in West Africa, and at least 200 in the Sokoto Caliphate, with populations of at least several thousand people, and identified because they were walled, with market places, central mosques, schools, cemeteries, and government buildings.[7] The walls of Kano were enormous, with thirteen gates and defensive trenches. The capitals of the thirty emirates and numerous sub-emirates in the Caliphate were towns, and although less pretentious they were nonetheless each surrounded by satellite settlements, many of which were plantations.[8]

For defensive reasons, the jihad encouraged urbanization and the construction of fortified settlements, *ribat*, that were intended to be focal points of demographic concentration. In the Islamic context, the establishment of *ribat* played a major role in the consolidation of empire. Such fortified settlements provided security for nucleated populations and in some cases served as outposts from which to launch slave raids and war. These fortified settlements became focal points for newly enslaved people who had effectively been removed from one part of the central Sudan to another. Hence population removal to a great extent involved the forced transfer of people from hill retreats and distant places to the towns and surrounding agricultural settlements of the jihad states, the largest of which was the Sokoto Caliphate, but which was also characteristic of other Muslim states in West Africa.

By the middle of the nineteenth century, the Sokoto Caliphate had a considerable slave population, certainly on the same order

[7] In the British census of 1911, Sokoto Province alone had thirteen towns with populations over 6,000, the largest being Sokoto with 21,624, Isa with 18,919, and Kaura-Namoda with 13,067, while Bongudu, Gwandu, Moriki, Wurno, Gusau, Jega, Talata Mafara, Gummi, Argungu, and Birnin Kebbi had populations from 6,000 to 10,000. See Garba Nadama, 'Urbanization in the Sokoto Caliphate: A Case Study of Gusau and Kaura-Namoda', in Y. B. Usman (ed.), *Studies in the History of the Sokoto Caliphate: The Sokoto Seminar Papers* (Lagos, 1979), 140–62. These estimates did not include dependent villages and plantations surrounding the towns that were integral to the urban landscape. For a discussion of the underlying official concern with urbanization as a strategy in planning, see Besim S. Hakim and Zubair Ahmed, 'Rules for the Built Environment in Nineteenth-Century Northern Nigeria', *Journal of Architectural and Planning Research*, 23/1 (2006), 1–26.

[8] In Adamawa alone there were forty walled towns, including Cheboa, Tibati, Ngaundere, Banyo, Malabu, Rai-Buba, Song, Zummo, Gola, Holma, Pakorgel, Marwa, Bogo, Kobotshi, Laro, Belel, Daware, Mayo-Farang, Sorau, Madagali, Gider, Michika, Moda, Mubi, Uba, Mindif, Binder, Ridadu, Bibemi, Kalfu, Be, Demsa (Cisiga), Vokna, Tola, Agorma, Pette, Wuro Mayo-Najarendi, Mbere, Garwa, and Balala, besides the capital at Yola. For a discussion, see Lovejoy, *Slavery, Commerce and Production*, ch. 1 and the sources cited therein.

as the United States and Brazil and much larger than Cuba. The number of slaves may have approached two to three million by the 1860s, which was at least a quarter of the total population and perhaps as much as half. A considerable proportion of this population had been enslaved. In short, there was a substantial population displacement for at least fifty to sixty years after the jihad and, in fact, annual campaigns to enslave were conducted for the rest of the century. In addition to the enslaved population that was forcibly resettled within the Sokoto Caliphate, there were many slaves who were exported both across the Sahara and to the Americas. Perhaps 200,000 people were sent to Brazil, most of them before the middle of the 1830s, while unknown numbers, but certainly in the thousands, went to Cuba. Another 400,000 people were sent into the Sahara or to North Africa during the course of the nineteenth century, and unlike the trade to the Atlantic, which ended by the 1850s, the trade across the Sahara lasted until the colonial conquest, although abolition in the various Ottoman domains inhibited the trade after the 1840s.

As in the Americas, a substantial proportion of the population of the Muslim areas of West Africa was enslaved, which involved population displacement on a scale comparable to the transatlantic slave trade at its height. The estimated population of enslaved people indicates major population shifts through slavery, not only across the Atlantic and the Sahara, but within West Africa. The relatively high incidence of emancipation and the fact that the children of concubines were considered to be free-born, following their fathers, tended to limit the growth of the enslaved population. Certainly the number of slaves would have been much greater if slave-owners had been less willing to allow slaves to purchase their freedom and if the children of concubines had inherited the status of their mothers, as in the Americas, rather than the status of their fathers. The incidence of emancipation and claims of paternity over the children of concubines are indicators of assimilation, which mirrored the political and religious ideology. Enforced population displacement that began with enslavement was supposed to strengthen the Islamic state, which was achieved through demographic concentration.

The leadership of the Sokoto Caliphate actively promoted population concentration through the construction of a system of walled towns as a defensive system. The establishment of fortified

The Slave Trade as Enforced Migration 157

settlements is associated specifically with the policies of Muhammad Bello, the son and close adviser of Shehu Uthman dan Fodio, who not only was a leading officer of the jihad, but also founded the capital at Sokoto. In *Jawab shafi' wa-khitab minna kafin ila Muhammad al-Jaylani*, a treatise written in 1815, Muhammad Bello advised the Tuareg leader Muhammad al-Jaylani how to manage a Muslim community among nomads in the wake of the jihad.[9] For Bello, the issue was how to settle the nomads. In *Kitab al-ribat wa al-hirasa*, Bello elaborated on the merits of working and living in defensive settlements, and such *ribat* were interpreted in the context of Islamic tradition and history.[10] Bello's influence was enormous, both while his father was alive and when he became the first caliph of the empire upon his father's death in 1817. He reigned until 1837, was responsible for the construction of numerous settlements, and inspired the emirs of the various provinces to do likewise. According to Murray Last,

The establishment of *ribats* was a part of the policy of stabilising the frontiers and providing strongholds round which settlement could flourish despite the raids of the Kebbawa, the Tuareg, the Gobirawa and their allies in Zamfara. Likewise Bello encouraged the building within the frontiers of walled towns where mosques and schools could be opened and trade and workshops started: with scholars appointed to those towns as Imams, judges, *muhtasib*s (legal inspectors), and teachers, Bello hoped to maintain both the practice of Islam and the military control of the area.[11]

Muhammad Bello always lived in *ribats*. After founding Sokoto, he established himself at Karindaye, then Magaria, and finally Wurno. Bello established dozens of other *ribat* in the Sokoto area. In some places, existing towns were reinforced, so that every walled town effectively became a *ribat*, but Bello encouraged the foundation of new communities away from the pre-jihad towns. Some of these *ribats* became major settlements, which in turn became focal points of smaller *ribats*. Eventually,

[9] The *Jawab shafi' wa-khitab minna kafin ila Muhammad al-Jaylani* was 'a complete and adequate response to Muhammad al-Jaylani', MS dated 1230/1815, according to John Hunwick, *Arabic Literature of Africa*, ii: *The Writings of Central Sudanic Africa* (Leiden, 1995), 121, item 30.

[10] Cited ibid. 123, item 44. Also see Hakim and Ahmed, 'Rules for the Built Environment', 2–3.

[11] Murray Last, *The Sokoto Caliphate* (London, 1967), 79–80; and id., 'An Aspect of the Caliph Muhammad Bello's Social Policy', *Kano Studies*, 1 (1966), 56–9.

whole areas were consolidated in this fashion, as, for example, in the countryside between Sokoto and Wurno, which became densely inhabited, second only to the closely settled zone around Kano city.[12] Kano, with its forty walled towns, was even more pronounced in the extent of urbanization, with each town surrounded by a belt of dependent villages and plantations. Free merchants and craftsmen were encouraged to settle, and they bought slaves, so that the concentration of population was achieved through the settlement of slaves on the lands of the aristocracy and their clients. The acquisition of land sufficient to employ slaves depended upon patronage. In this context, political factors governed the incorporation of captives. Who was retained, who was sold, who was killed, and who escaped were decisions affecting every slave raid and military campaign.

In following Bello's lead in founding settlements, the governments of the various emirates pursued a militant military policy of conducting annual raids and reinforcing each other in combined military action against the pockets of resistance that formed in the central Sudan. These campaigns were conceived as part of a conscious economic policy of settlement and population management. The focus was not only on slaves but also on the nomadic population of Fulani cattle herders and Tuareg transporters. Incentives were extended to these people, often in the form of low taxes and proximity to walled towns, so that besides a forced migration of the enslaved population there was free immigration and settlement. Nonetheless, the largest immigration was the subjugated population, which involved the dispersal of communities and the removal of people from homelands to nucleated areas within the Caliphate.

The demand for slaves encouraged enslavement, and therefore government decisions to target particular populations. There was a desire for women because Muslim societies sanctioned marriage to four free women and the subjection of enslaved women as concubines in whatever number could be afforded. There was also the need for manual labour, also performed by concubines.

---

[12] John Edward Philips, 'Slavery on Two Ribat in Kano and Sokoto', in Lovejoy (ed.), *Slavery on the Frontiers of Islam*, 111–24; Ibrahim Muhammad Jumare, 'Land Tenure in the Sokoto Sultanate of Nigeria' (Ph.D. thesis, York University, 1996); Mohammed Salau, 'Growth of the Plantation Economy in the Sokoto Caliphate: Fanisau, 1819–1903' (Ph.D. thesis, York University, 2005).

The Slave Trade as Enforced Migration   159

The distribution of people was commoditized on the basis of skill, attraction, and perceived need, both economic and social, and indeed sexual. Slaves were employed extensively in government and the military. Hence what happened to individuals upon settlement was intentional integration. In the urban context of Muslim society, assimilated slaves with skills could work on their own account through arrangements known as *murgu*, in which slaves paid their owners regular and set fees but otherwise were on their own, even being allowed to set aside money to purchase their own freedom. In effect, removal was further commoditized through a form of alienation that is parallel to the alienation of labour through capital formations of production. State policy promoted the 'individualization' of slave labour in a market economy in which wages were a means of reimbursement that slaves could obtain but wage labour was not a preferred mechanism of income. People sold their services, they collected things from the common for sale, and otherwise worked for money, if they had to, and this usually applied to slaves who were working on their own. In effect, slaves were forced into wage employment, a further dimension of 'removal' that had begun with their seizure. In some ways, the results were similar to the enclosure of land that forced the resettlement of people and the reallocation of labour in Britain. Hence removal did not only result in shipment to the Americas to work on sugar plantations, but was an integral feature of developing Islamic urban society in West Africa. Individuals who were enslaved faced the extremes of plantation labour in the Americas and religious subjugation in Islamic areas of Africa. The employment of slaves for wages through *murgu* and the commissions that could be acquired through petty trade and agency provided income for slave-owners and incentives for slaves. Hence, once removed, slaves did not necessarily want to return to their homes, which they might suspect had been destroyed anyway.

Ethnicity and Enforced Demographic Change

There was a strong correlation between ethnicity and slavery, and efforts to protect identity and therefore safeguard against enslavement included the use of facial and body scarification.

Free-born Muslims marked their children with distinct patterns that were recognizable and could be distinguished from those used by groups targeted for slavery. Scarification was a specific badge of identity that was visual and could not be altered. People could learn new languages, but not change their scarification. Children born into slavery, by contrast, were given markings of their master or more general markings indicating where they were born, whether in Kano, Katsina, Sokoto, and so forth.

In the Sokoto Caliphate, slaves came from many different ethnic backgrounds, but they were grouped broadly into categories that continued to have currency because new arrivals kept coming. In Kano, slaves of the same ethnic background had often been enslaved under similar conditions, such as those identified as Warjawa and Gwari. The Warjawa and other people inhabited the Ningi hills to the south-east of Kano, which served as a retreat for political and religious dissidents who raided Kano as well as suffering invasion. The Gwari lived in scattered villages south of the Hausa cities in the Kaduna river region. The removal of people from these areas into slavery, therefore, did not necessarily entail loss of contact with others of the same culture and language, although Hausa was the language of communication in the Sokoto Caliphate. The political elite, which was mostly Fulani, also spoke Fulfulde. Some were even fluent in Arabic and many people could read at least some Arabic. Thus the use of language and ethnic identification were complicated and reflected the interactions among peoples.

An expansive state like that of Sokoto, which based its demographic growth on enslavement and the integration of the descendants of slaves, pursued an ongoing and annual campaign to obtain new captives, as if there was a 'slaving frontier' that separated the nucleated regions of the state from the peripheral areas that were not Muslim. Because of the necessity of retreating to defensible locations, the hills where people lived were densely inhabited, such as those of Ningi, already mentioned, and the region of the Jos Plateau, the Tangale hills, Tula, and other places in distant Adamawa. In addition, slaves came from the wars of expansion and consolidation, including the foundation of several emirates in Nupe, the destruction of the Oyo Empire, the resulting wars that led to a massive population displacement among the Yoruba, including the shipment of a million Yoruba

The Slave Trade as Enforced Migration 161

to the Americas between 1817 and 1840, the abandonment of the capital district of Oyo, and the incorporation of Ilorin as an emirate within the Sokoto Caliphate.

Muslims in the Sokoto Caliphate debated the efficacy of the 'slaving frontier' in ethnic terms. The discourse on the subject arose within the literary tradition of Islamic Africa. One of the most distinguished scholars of the subject was Ahmad Bābā (1556–1627) of Timbuktu.[13] Ahmad Bābā was one of the most learned and respected scholars associated with the Sankore mosque, then part of the Songhay Empire of which Timbuktu was the most important city. A Moroccan expedition from Marrakesh crossed the Sahara in 1591 in a brazen attempt to conquer Songhay and extend a Muslim Sharifian empire into the heart of Africa. Ahmad Bābā was taken into captivity as a consequence of this invasion. Many Songhay citizens were enslaved, and even more Songhay slaves were effectively re-enslaved and taken to southern Morocco to work the sugar plantations that had been established there. Distinguished individuals such as Ahmad Bābā were held to ransom, enslavement befalling them should ransom not be forthcoming. In fact, he eventually returned to Timbuktu, where he wrote his famous treatise, *Mi'raj al-su'ud—The Ladder of Ascent Towards Grasping the Law Concerning Transported Blacks*, which was based on his experience and extensive knowledge of Islamic law. In his treatise, Ahmad Bābā engaged the historic Islamic literature on the subject of enslavement, in effect developing the concept of enslaving frontier with respect to Muslim regions.

Who is removed and why, and when. There was a sharp distinction between war between Muslim states, such as between Sokoto and Borno, and systematically attacking non-Muslim populations with the purpose of enslavement. In the case of the war and continued hostilities between Sokoto and Borno, the

---

[13] For a discussion of Ahmad Bābā, and the debate within Muslim circles about who could be enslaved and who should not be, see my 'The Context of Enslavement in West Africa: Ahmad Bābā and the Ethics of Slavery', in Jane Landers (ed.), *Slaves, Subjects, and Subversives: Blacks in Colonial Latin America* (Albuquerque, N. Mex., 2005); Mahmoud A. Zouber, *Ahmad Baba de Tombouctou (1556–1627)* (Paris, 1977); and John Hunwick and Fatima Harrak, *Mi'raj al-su'ud: Ahmad Bābā's Replies on Slavery* (Rabat, 2000). Excerpts are also to be found in John Hunwick and Eve Troutt Powell (eds.), *The African Diaspora in the Mediterranean Lands of Islam* (Princeton, 2002). Also see J. O. Hunwick, 'Ahmad Baba and the Moroccan Invasion of the Sudan (1591)', *Journal of the Historical Society of Nigeria*, 2/3 (1962), 311–26; J. O. Hunwick, 'Further Light on Ahmad Baba al-Tinbukti', *Research Bulletin, Centre of Arabic Documentation*, 2/2 (1966), 19–31.

problem of slavery was exacerbated by the destruction of the capital district and dispersal of its population, in which case the population, at least the free population, was clearly Muslim. Yet many free Muslims were enslaved. In a region of enslavement, with a frontier exposed to Muslim encroachment, it was important that there was a system of ransoming which effectively enabled those who could afford it to achieve their redemption should they be unlucky and have been enslaved. Ransoming was a form of redemption which was allowed and encouraged under Islamic law, often involving third parties. This form of achieving or re-establishing free-born status was an alternative means of social ordering that affected the distribution of the population that was enslaved. In terms of transaction costs, the ability to ransom captives, usually at a higher price than the sale price, affected the market for slaves and served as a constraint on population dispersal. Ransoming was the brake on removal.

The proponents of jihad particularly targeted those associated with other religious beliefs, such as *bori* in the central Sudan and *orisa* priests among the Yoruba. In both cases, those considered 'deviant' were effectively deported as slaves. The *bori* practitioners were sent to North Africa, where they were able to reconstitute religious and social communities in Tunisia and elsewhere.[14] The rebellion of Muslims at Ilorin in 1817 and the subsequent prosecution of the jihad in Oyo, with Ilorin receiving recognition as an emirate in 1823, led to an attack on the *orisa* cult of *shango*, which was associated with the Oyo government. *Shango*, the god of thunder, required specific ceremonies and rituals, which included the use of *bàtá* drums, and therefore these adherents were targeted. Hence, the presence of *bàtá* drums establishes that Oyo Yoruba, and, specifically, adherents of *shango*, were sent into enslavement. The purge of religious opponents in Oyo was similar to the dispersal of *bori* adepts in the Hausa emirates, although the Yoruba were sent to the Americas, as is confirmed by the presence of *bàtá* drummers in Cuba and Brazil.[15] The *bàtá*

[14] Ismael Musah Montana, 'Slavery and its Abolition in the North African Regency of Tunis, 1730–1846' (Ph.D. thesis, York University, 2007); and id., 'Ahmad ibn al-Qādi al-Timbuktāwī on the *Bori* Ceremonies of Tunis', in Lovejoy (ed.), *Slavery on the Frontiers of Islam*, 173–98.

[15] Henry Lovejoy, 'Drums of Retention: *Bàtá* Drums and the Symbolic Reestablishment of the Oyo Empire in Colonial Cuba, 1817–1867', Major Research Paper, York University, 2006.

The Slave Trade as Enforced Migration 163

drummers are evidence that the politics of deportation resulted in the symbolic re-creation of Oyo in Cuba. Hence jihad involved enslavement, and in the process the war spelled the collapse of Oyo. This is recounted in numerous biographies, a degree of specificity that documents displacement and chronicles the consciousness of the removal.[16] The results, which had parallels in the western Sudan, resulted in the extension of Islam, the displacement of non-Muslims, such as the *orisa* practitioners, and the re-creation of new communities both in North Africa and the Americas.

The community of Islam was a constantly changing construction that involved complex interactions in this setting. The perpetration of jihad was used to justify enslavement that had as its intention the formation of a community on a national scale that would protect its own citizens from enslavement. The protection of Muslims included the institutionalization of ransoming, so that those who were 'wrongfully' enslaved might regain their freedom. However, persecution and the threat of alienation resulted in ethnic ordering. Through reference to local Islamic practice and legal tradition, individuals and communities were defined as insiders or outsiders, and as 'good' Muslims, apostates, or 'pagans'. The debate between Muhammad Bello and Sheikh al-Kanemi and political confrontation between Sokoto and Borno focused on the significance of identity, dependence, and mechanisms of insurance against enslavement and oppression. The debate was cast in terms of Islam, but the problem was that there was no guarantee against enslavement. Despite the possibility of ransom and redemption for the enslaved, the removal of many opponents of jihad to the Americas and North Africa undermined these flimsy safeguards.

As the case of the central Sudan demonstrates, removal inevitably required acculturation to a new setting, a process which can be considered a form of 'creolization' or even a process of cultural 'hybridization' through social interaction in a new society. However, removal through enslavement involved violence that shaped the structures of the new social formations that were created. The scale and intensity of the enslaved migration in the

---

[16] Paul E. Lovejoy, 'Biographies of Enslaved Muslims from the Central Sudan in the Nineteenth Century', in H. Bobboyi and A. M. Yakubu (eds.), *The Sokoto Caliphate: History and Legacies, 1804–2004* (Kaduna, 2006), i. 187–216.

central Sudan influenced the extent and pace of incorporation, while the legacy of slavery had various influences on cultural survivals, identity reformulation, and mechanisms for interpreting subjugation. As in other migrations, the extent of coercion or degree of incentive involved affected the survival and reinterpretation of culture, often expressed through religion and ritual.

On the basis of an analysis of the central Sudan, it is possible to conclude that there was no 'normal' or 'typical' pattern of forced removal and exploitation through enslavement in Africa. Muslim regions have to be distinguished from other parts of Africa. But in virtually all cases, the impact was devastating, although localized, time and place specific. The enforced nature of transatlantic slavery allows comparison with other migrations, serving as a test of the impact of migration on population when geographically separated from homelands. This study distinguishes between the impact of enforced migration within Africa and external deportation. The impact on the consolidation of a particular religion demonstrates religious change and patterns of ethnic identification. An appreciation of the cultural manifestations of identity can be gleaned from music, language, and religious expression. The examination of enslavement and the slave trade in the central Sudan reveals a form of forced removal that targeted specific populations, in which jihad was used as a justification for enslavement of both those who were not Muslims and those who resisted the imposition of Islamic government as defined by the jihad governments. From this perspective enslavement was politically motivated and therefore comparable to other situations of enforced exodus, with the qualification that the conditions of forced migration through slavery varied greatly. The legacy of this violent past is clearly evident in the political problems that have faced Nigeria into the twenty-first century.

PART III
Forced Removal and War

8

The Great Unweaving:
The Removal of Peoples in Europe,
1875–1949

DONALD BLOXHAM

Charles de Gaulle, Ernst Nolte, and Enzo Traverso called it the 'European civil war'. Others have dubbed it 'Europe's second thirty years war', or 'the era of total war'. These epithets, which enjoy varying intellectual currency, have all been deployed in an attempt to capture the essence of the period of ideological and geopolitical conflict framed by the two world wars. The years *c.*1914–45 indeed provide a convenient temporal frame for the emergence of the tripartite battle of fascism, Communism, and liberal democracy as they each sought to address issues of industrialization, political representation, social welfare, and intensified international competition.[1] The study of population removal, at least in two of its major guises, genocide and ethnic cleansing, has been no exception to this general rule.[2]

There is merit to the periodization. As the time of 'total war' created conditions for the far-reaching reconstitution of the political and moral economies of the European states, it likewise

I thank Pertti Ahonen and Michael Gelb for their comments on drafts of this essay.

[1] Ernst Nolte, *Der europäische Bürgerkrieg, 1917–1945* (Frankfurt am Main, 1987); Enzo Traverso, *À feu et à sang: de la guerre civile européenne 1914–1945. Un ordre d'idées* (Paris, 2007); and see also K. M. Pannikar, *Asia and Western Dominance, 1498–1945* (London, 1959); Ian Kershaw, 'Europe's Second Thirty Years War: The Twentieth-Century World and Beyond', *History Today*, 55/9 (2005), 10–17; William R. Keylor, *An International History since 1900* (Oxford, 2005), pt. 1: 'The Thirty Years' War (1914–1945)'; Volker R. Berghahn and Martin Kitchen (eds.), *Germany in the Age of Total War* (London, 1981); Arthur Marwick (ed.), *Total War and Social Change* (Basingstoke, 1988).

[2] If, on occasion, some scholars have pushed the chronological parameters somewhat forward or backwards. Eugene M. Kulischer, *Europe on the Move: War and Population Changes, 1917–47* (New York, 1948); Terry Martin, 'The Origins of Soviet Ethnic Cleansing', *Journal of Modern History*, 70 (1998), 813–61; Robert Gellately and Ben Kiernan (eds.), *The Specter of Genocide: Mass Murder in Historical Perspective* (Cambridge, 2003), pt. 3: 'The Era of the Two World Wars'; Norman M. Naimark, *Fires of Hatred: Ethnic Cleansing in Twentieth-Century Europe* (Cambridge, Mass., 2001).

168   DONALD BLOXHAM

created propitious circumstances for the forced removal of peoples that in quantitative terms was unique in modern European history. If much of this movement was based on ethnic, national, racial, or religious affiliation—the four determinants of identity stipulated in the 1948 UN Convention on the Prevention and Punishment of Genocide—then the upheaval of prolonged, costly, 'existential' war also permitted and stimulated deportations for labour-related reasons or based on political affiliations that were often broadly and curiously defined. This essay, however, extends its first chronological parameter back into the nineteenth century, considering the period 1875 to 1949 as a continuum in European history, and taking a broad definition of Europe, stretching to and including the Eurasian rimlands.

Actors and Concepts

Ethnic cleansing and genocide above all concern this essay. For the purposes of this discussion they are considered to be on a continuum. Both contain significant commonalities of rationale, though the ethical dimensions may differ. Both entail eradication of a group; and while the former is the quest for eradication from a particular political and geographical space, and accordingly accommodates simple expulsion as well as, and sometimes instead of, murder, and is, thus, strictly separate from genocidal killing as commonly understood (spatial removal versus existential removal, as it were), this neat distinction is in practice often blurred.

Many full genocides, including the 'final solution', have sprung from an initial desire to get the victim group out of a particular territory—the Nazis forcing Jewish emigration from Germany in the first instance, and considering other 'territorial solutions'[3] subsequently—and so have an intrinsically spatial character. The Armenian genocide exemplifies the blending of a policy of ethnic cleansing and ethnic murder, with the latter pursuant to the former. Like the mass crimes committed during the break-up of the former Yugoslavia, the Armenian episode is in this sense a more common historical form of genocidal massacre than the

---

[3] Uwe Dietrich Adam, *Judenpolitik im Dritten Reich* (Düsseldorf, 1972), 303–13.

The Great Unweaving 169

sort of total killing into which the 'final solution' developed. Thus while ethnic cleansing may appear to be a policy alternative to genocide, not only are the two not mutually exclusive in reality, but the terms in which the 'choice' between them is made are tightly circumscribed by the prior build-up of stigmatization and violence, and by the continuous jettisoning of other policy options of a much more humane nature than either of the final two. In other words, the choice is made between two divergent forks at the end of a long downhill path littered with disregarded crossroads. Both forks lead to removal of a very literal kind.

Removal of ethnically defined collectives by 'population transfer' is understood here as a variant of ethnic cleansing, despite the fact that it is externally sanctioned in the form of bilaterally or internationally mandated treaties. If the end result of removal is similar, however, the idea of sanctioned transfer is, in theory, the lesser of two evils, the process in theory less violent than unilateral expulsion. We shall see later on to what extent these theoretical differences have been sustained in historical practice.

The story begins with the 'eastern crisis' of 1875–8, in which most of the remaining Ottoman domains in Europe were torn away. The eastern crisis is the first, and smallest, of three major bursts of forced mass movement of peoples, the others being the First World War era, stretching from the Balkan Wars of 1912–13 to the military and diplomatic conclusion to the Greco-Turkish War of 1921–2, and the Second World War era, c.1936–49. There was also a fourth burst that is not covered here, for while the greatest ruptures of the unweaving were over by the middle of the twentieth century, the end of the Cold War freeze saw considerable aftershocks in areas of ethnic contention in the Caucasus, as the Soviet Empire in turn collapsed, and in what swiftly became the former Yugoslavia. The period from 1875 to 1999 might qualify for entirely grim reasons for the epithet 'the long twentieth century'.

The eastern crisis is chosen as a starting point even though it is a shorter time period than the later two bursts and the numbers of people removed are correspondingly smaller, both because of its intrinsic significance and because of the way that it prefigures, in a nineteenth-century Ottoman context, so many of the issues of population policy traditionally associated with the 'second thirty years war'. As to the eras of the two world wars, it should be obvious that these do not refer to some neatly defined times-pan of military and economic war mobilization spanning precisely the years 1914–18 and 1939–45—a pair of spans that might ultimately only be applicable together to the British and German experience of those wars.

The most problematic of the three periods is the Second World War era. The starting point of 1936 is only approximate, and is only partly based on Paul Preston's variation on the European civil war idea, which places that conflict's supposed opening with the Spanish civil war.[4] The Spanish civil war did not feature extensive, targeted, permanent, or semi-permanent population removal. This contrasts, for instance, with the later Greek civil war, which had distinctly ethnicized aspects, notably the forced displacement of Macedonians as part of Greece's ongoing attempt to subsume that population. The other part of the justification is that in the late 1930s, but before the outbreak of the Second World War, far-reaching reorganization of the Soviet body politic had begun, and this entailed both the tempo-rary and permanent removal of many people and peoples.[5] The 'closing' year of 1949 marked simultaneously the end of the Greek civil war, and the last chapters in the expulsion of the ethnic Germans from east-central Europe. By that time, too, the major deportations of subject nations in the USSR had been completed, though smaller parts of some population groups would continue to be deported until Stalin's death in 1953.

The overarching historical context is the disintegration of the European dynastic empires and the establishment—sometimes only temporarily—in their stead of polities organized according to new ideas about inclusive and exclusive group identities, and the relationship of 'loyal' citizen to sovereign state. The situation was exacerbated by the intrusion of two new imperial forms into the continent-in-flux. The Soviet empire expanded to fill the space left by its tsarist predecessor, and, pursuant to policies of political penetration, 'security', and 're-education', or any mixture thereof, predicated on a sometimes inconsistent understanding of the

---

[4] Paul Preston and Ann L. Mackenzie (eds.), *The Republic Besieged: Civil War in Spain 1936–1939* (Edinburgh, 1997).

[5] Amir Weiner, *Making Sense of War: The Second World War and the Fate of the Bolshevik Revolution* (Princeton, 2001); id., 'Nature, Nurture, and Memory in a Socialist Utopia: Delineating the Soviet Socio-ethnic Body in the Age of Socialism', *American Historical Review*, 104/4 (2000), 1–65.

The Great Unweaving

relationship between socio-economic status or political disposition and heredity (nurture and nature), relied heavily on deportation of targeted individuals and groups. The Nazi empire, less troubled by matters of doctrinal consistency on imperialism and subject peoples, tried to introduce into the central and eastern European political spaces vacated by the earlier great powers the principles of ethnic homogenization and stratification that had hitherto only been employed within the borders of self-confessed nation-states.

The greatest individual social engineers in the period were the two 'totalitarian' regimes, so some justification is required for the greater focus that this essay has upon the Nazi case of the two, and for the extensive focus on other states and regimes besides. The first consideration is that authoritarian and more liberal states were entirely complicit, if with varying motivations, in mass removal of peoples. Indeed, the largest single removal under discussion, the expulsion of 12 to 13 million ethnic Germans at the close of the Second World War, was agreed upon between the 'totalitarian' USSR, the democratic UK and USA, and a variety of Polish, Czech, Hungarian, Yugoslavian, and Romanian Communists, ethno-nationalists, and 'liberal' nationalists. This is one reason why the terminology of ethno-nationalism is absolutely not deployed here to sustain a comforting distinction between civilized, western, liberal-civic nationalism and barbaric eastern nationalism. In general, these variants are understood not as different *types* so much as different *phases* of nationalism, in concurrence with Anthony Marx's observation that the few European states that developed more liberal forms of nationalism by the nineteenth century could do so precisely because they had initiated processes of more-or-less coercive cultural or ethno-religious homogenization in the early modern period.[6] More importantly, in the modern period actions by 'liberal' states in the non-European colonies from the seventeenth century onwards showed the 'racial' limits of their conceptions of fraternity, while the crises of the twentieth century would also force these older, liberal nationalisms into more draconian, statist, and generally right-wing mindsets.

---

[6] Anthony Marx, *Faith in Nation: The Exclusionary Origins of Nationalism* (Oxford, 2003). Of course, much work remained to be done in, for instance, rendering 'peasants into Frenchmen', on which see Eugen Weber, *Peasants into Frenchmen: The Modernization of Rural France, 1870–1914* (Stanford, Calif., 1976).

Another reason to be wary of overly sharp distinctions between types of state and state ideology[7] is that elites of the older dynastic regimes sometimes showed themselves capable of responding in just as collectively violent an idiom as anyone to threats confronting their order. This was true whether those putative threats were primarily internal, as with Ottoman Armenians and with Poles, Jews, or ethnic Germans in imperial Russian territory, or primarily external, as with Austria-Hungary and the Serbs, approximately 10 per cent of whom were vengefully deported for labour purposes by the Hapsburgs at war. This was partly because these elites historically had always had to balance the use of coercion with incentive in the management of their domains, but partly also, in the Ottoman case at least, because the states these elites led were 'nationalising states',[8] seeking to transform their heterogeneous order into something more homogeneous. Conversely, new or would-be nation-states were not simply that. They were also capable of acting, in the words of Ronald Suny, like the 'imperial nations' at the nationalizing core of the dynastic empires,[9] hungry for the acquisition of overseas territory or, more often, if they were 'lesser powers', neighbouring territory coveted or owned by other nearby states.

A third consideration works from a materialist international relations perspective. The former imperial peripheries of east-central, eastern, and south-eastern Europe, which were the areas most affected by removal in the period in question, would probably have become the focus of demographic and other forms of turmoil irrespective of the precise ideological convictions of the larger states surrounding them, or of would-be elites native to them, just as they were certainly the subject of economic competition from well before the advent of Nazism.[10] From the defeat of Napoleon, it seemed that Russia might expand significantly westward and south-westward, while the emergence of Germany created a colossus that would press its interests from the other

[7] Something of which e.g. Niall Ferguson's *War of the World: History's Age of Hatred* (London, 2006) is guilty.

[8] Marx, *Faith in Nation*, 19; also p. ix.

[9] Ronald Grigor Suny, 'Nationalities in the Russian Empire', *Russian Review*, 59 (2000), 487–92.

[10] Paul N. Hehn, *A Low, Dishonest Decade: The Great Powers, Eastern Europe and the Economic Origins of World War II, 1930–1941* (London, 2002); Miklós Lojkó, *Meddling in Middle Europe: Britain and the 'Lands Between' 1919–1925* (Budapest, 2006).

The Great Unweaving

direction, first by economic and cultural penetration, but, after Bismarck, and particularly from 1912–13 and even more so from 1917, and again from 1933, by expansion. The experience of the North Caucasus from the mid nineteenth century illustrates that the Romanovs were happy to use expulsion of natives and settler-colonialism to consolidate imperial rule on the peripheries, while Wilhelmine plans for the establishment of an eastern empire during the First World War had great ramifications for local demographics.[11] Any lands either state expanded into were unlikely to be left as they were, but equally the geo-political arrangements enforced by other great powers to limit Russian or German influence in the region, as in the terms of the Versailles peace settlement, had great demographic ramifications too.

On the other hand, if the basic matter of power politics over the *longue durée* should not be ignored, the different rationales employed in this period for lifting up populations, or large numbers of individuals, and dumping them elsewhere are not simply matters of intellectual nuance. These rationales influenced the duration of removal and often the treatment of the removed. One basic distinction is between removal based on economic or power-political considerations on one hand and ethnicity or 'race' on the other. Though the distinctions are not always absolutely clear, the former categories were mostly selective among individual population groups and often impermanent.

The Soviet political purges of the late 1930s, with their more than 800,000 executions, were the most extensive direct killing actions of the regime. The 'dekulakization' campaign of the early 1930s featured relatively few executions, and the majority of the approximately 3 million deportees were moved only within their own region or *raion*. Nevertheless, death tolls also run into the lower hundreds of thousands for kulaks ('rich peasants') who were sent to labour camps or deported with their families for 'special settlement' in central Asia, the Urals, Siberia, and elsewhere. ('Dekulakization' also contributed to the up to 6 million deaths during the Soviet famine of 1931–3.) Both 'dekulakization' and the

---

[11] On Germany, Vejas Gabriel Liulevicius, *War Land on the Eastern Front* (Cambridge, 2002). On Russia, Peter Holquist, 'To Count, to Extract, and to Exterminate: Population Statistics and Population Politics in Late Imperial and Soviet Russia', in Ronald Grigor Suny and Terry Martin (eds.), *A State of Nations: Empire and Nation-Making in the Age of Lenin and Stalin* (Oxford, 2001), 111–44.

purges had some ethnicized aspects, particularly as far as they concerned 'diaspora peoples', who would continue to be objects of suspicion into the Second World War itself—Germans, Finns, and Poles, for instance.[12] The famine itself also had distinctly anti-Ukrainian aspects. Yet while the Soviet regime was happy on occasion to label national peoples pejoratively, this did not necessarily mean that those peoples would be targeted 'as such'—as in the Genocide Convention—or in their entirety. Thus the deportation of up to 1,300,000 Poles and members of other nationalities from within the former eastern Poland in 1939–45 was not an attempt at 'de-polonization' of Poland, being instead a means of removing potential political and 'socio-economic' opposition in order to smooth the path for Communist rule. Deportations from the expanding Soviet border territories of Moldavia and the Baltic states also remained in principle assaults on 'class' and 'social' enemies, and were thus selective if quite large in scale.[13]

The USSR did engage in ethnic cleansing, but not outright mass murder of targeted groups, albeit that the Terek and Don Cossacks could testify to the vengeful murderousness of the Bolshevik regime in times of crisis, as during the Russian civil war,[14] and that at least scores of thousands of members of the subject nationalities deported during the Second World War perished because of the conditions of their transit and at their destinations (again, central Asia, the Urals, and Siberia), while there were also some massacres as they were rounded-up for deportation. The major motivation for ethnic cleansing was not some enduring Great Russian chauvinism, though this was exploited by Stalin at times. On the one hand, the USSR remained committed to 'managing difference' within its borders, and at points put great effort into accommodating and promoting the national traditions and aspirations of some, at least, of its subject peoples. On the other hand, when cultures suffered under

[12] Martin, 'The Origins of Soviet Ethnic Cleansing'; Nicolas Werth, 'Repenser la Grande Terreur', Le Débat, 122 (Nov.–Dec. 2002), 118–39; Michael Gelb, 'The Western Finnic Minorities and the Origins of the Stalinist Nationalities Deportations', Nationalities Papers, 24/2 (1996), 237–68.

[13] On Poland, Günther Häufele, 'Zwangsumsiedlungen in Polen 1939–1941', in Dittmar Dahlmann and Gerhard Hirschfeld (eds.), Lager, Zwangsarbeit, Vertreibung und Deportation (Essen, 1999), 515–33.

[14] Peter Holquist, Making War, Forging Revolution: Russia's Continuum of Crisis, 1914–1921 (Cambridge, Mass., 2002).

The Great Unweaving

Soviet rule, Russian culture suffered as much as most. The culprit in Soviet ethnic cleansing was rather what Terry Martin calls 'Soviet xenophobia', meaning a profound suspicion of external capitalist regimes and of their putative—and, in some cases, real—influence among Soviet subject populations. In accordance with the complexity of Soviet nationalities policy, ethnic cleansing simply sought to remove select populations from particular areas to others while often allowing the groups to retain their cultural institutions, and this without a desire ethnically to homogenize the areas cleared in the process.[15]

Explicitly ethnically based internal Soviet deportations from 1937 onwards affected around 3 million people by recent estimates.[16] The largest target group in absolute terms was the ethnic German populations ('Volga Germans' and others), with around 750,000 deportees, while the greatest victims in relative terms were the smaller nationalities deported in their entirety after the German retreat in 1943–4 from the Caucasus and the Crimea and thereabouts: the Crimean Tatars, the Kalmyks, the Chechens and Ingush, and the Balkar, Karachai, and Meskhetian Turk populations.[17] Other groups were deported in part. Overall, however, while the Soviet regime conducted social engineering on a huge scale, murdering hundreds of thousands of people and promoting economic policies that resulted in the deaths of millions more, in terms of removal of peoples as ethnically or nationally defined, the quantitative ramifications of its deportations unfortunately are not remarkable in the context of the removal of peoples in the Europe that this essay considers. Finally, as political circumstances changed—wars ended, central control was entrenched, and, most importantly, with the advent of 'de-Stalinization'—deportations could be reversed, as was the case with the repatriation of about half of the deported Poles and the surviving members of most of the deported nations of the Second World War era, though

---

[15] Martin, 'The Origins of Soviet Ethnic Cleansing'; Naimark, *Fires of Hatred*, ch. 3; Weiner, 'Nature, Nurture, and Memory'.

[16] Nikolai Bougai (ed.), *The Deportation of Peoples in the Soviet Union* (Hauppauge, NY, 1996); Pavel Polian, *Against their Will: The History and Geography of Forced Migrations in the USSR* (New York, 2004); J. Otto Pohl, *Ethnic Cleansing in the USSR, 1937–1949* (Westport, Conn., 1999).

[17] Generally on these deportations, see the works cited in the previous notes, plus Aleksandr M. Nekrich, *The Punished Peoples: The Deportation and Fate of Soviet Minorities at the End of the Second World War* (New York, 1978).

notably not the Crimean Tatars, Volga Germans, or Meskhetian Turks.

If some of the deportation policies of Stalinism were in principle selective and reversible, they found rough approximation in some of the economic deportation policies of the Nazi regime. For this, we can read the forced labour programmes of the Second World War, though not the use of Jewish slave labour or that of other concentration camp inmates.[18] While not overlooking the obviously racist aspect of the corralling of eastern European labourers by the Nazi regime, these and similar labour policies in western Europe targeted individuals rather than groups as such, albeit individuals in numbers running to 12 million. These labourers could and often did have the opportunity to return home after their period of work.[19]

When population removal was determined by racists and ethno-nationalists according to their long-term social engineering goals, however, nowhere was it supposed to be anything other than permanent. Regimes run according to these tenets were more interested in 'annihilating difference'[20] than managing it, more interested in creating demographic *faits accomplis* than negotiating futures of coexistence. Exceptions to this rule did occur, as within the Nazi eastern empire, because the size of the imperium and the ambitions of the imperialists required more manpower than their 'racial' base could provide. Here, difference was preserved in the interests of divide and rule, and insofar as the different ('inferior') could be transformed into helots. But the concession to necessity was reconciled by the violence with which legal boundaries between groups were policed.

This essay does not seek to account for every single instance of forced group removal in the period. Instead, it seeks to examine broad patterns of and motivations for such removal, while focusing upon instances that highlight general issues. Two major qualifications need to be made at the outset, however. Each affected the extent, timing, and nature of forced population movement, and both together mean that it is facile simply to ascribe the

[18] Donald Bloxham, 'Jewish Slave Labour and its Relationship to the "Final Solution"', in John K. Roth and Elisabeth Maxwell (eds.), *Remembering for the Future: The Holocaust in an Age of Genocide*, 3 vols. (New York, 2001), ii. 163–86.

[19] Ulrich Herbert, *Hitler's Foreign Workers* (Cambridge, 1997).

[20] Alexander L. Hinton, *Annihilating Difference: The Anthropology of Genocide* (Berkeley, 2002).

The Great Unweaving

phenomenon of coercive displacement to the development of ethno-nationalism, or racism, or political utopianism, or whatever ideological meta-motivation might be forwarded in any given case. The first factor is 'simply' the impact of shorter-term historical contingency on policy-making and events.

It should go without saying that nothing is foreordained. This includes the opening phase of our narrative: the downfall of the dynastic empires. Each empire reformed its internal structures over the nineteenth century in order to adjust to the forces accelerated by the French Revolution and the British industrial revolution, namely, the external challenges of western European technological and economic advances, and the internal challenges of the nationalism of subject peoples. While it is true that some of the economic, infrastructural, and educational changes involved in imperial modernization themselves inadvertently contributed to the furthering of subject nationalisms,[21] it is equally true that fortuitous circumstances were still required for nationalisms to succeed. Alone of the empires, it is questionable to what extent the Ottoman polity could have survived the nineteenth century without British and then German support. The First World War was at least as important in radicalizing subject nationalisms in the Hapsburg Empire as in providing an opportunity for national liberation,[22] and it is distinctly possible that, with wiser leadership than prevailed in the crisis culminating in the First World War, the Hapsburg imperium would have endured in some form for a considerable time but for that conflict. As to Russia, Lenin was correct in saying war was the mother of revolution: without the First World War, the 1917 revolutions would have been unthinkable. The element of contingency was also vital in population removal, and the fact that the major catalysts for expulsions or deportations came with or around warfare leads on to the broader question of the role of political crisis situations in precipitating the selection of particular policy options.

The second factor bridges considerations of shorter-term contingency and those of a longer-term, structural nature. It also

---

[21] See e.g. Ernst Gellner, *Nations and Nationalism* (Oxford, 1983).

[22] Robert A. Kann, Béla K. Király, and Paula S. Fichtner (eds.), *The Habsburg Empire in World War I: Essays on the Intellectual, Military, Political, and Economic Aspects of the Habsburg War Effort* (New York, 1977).

178 DONALD BLOXHAM

lends further overall coherence to the chosen periodization. It is what might be called the 'international management' of European affairs. From the 1878 Treaty of Berlin to the Versailles settlement and the Potsdam conference, a combination of hegemonic powers, with Britain the constant, adjudicated on borders and minority issues and set the parameters for reconciling the distribution of peoples with new political realities in the interest of principles of both international stability and self-interest. Accordingly, even in the age of the nation-state we must pay attention to the role of the 'great powers' as arbiters of population removal.

Ideology and Practice: From the Eastern Crisis to the Second World War Era

The 'eastern crisis' of 1875–8 tends to receive little serious consideration in the history of political violence in modern Europe. Where it looms in the consciousness of 'western' historians it has traditionally been addressed first in terms of the high diplomacy of the 'eastern question' and secondly as just another episode of Ottoman-Muslim atrocities against Christians, in this case, Bulgarians and Bosnians.[23] This perspective perpetuates the stereotypes of 'brutal Turks' and the unruly Balkans, and very decidedly places the events outside the developmental trajectory of a more civilized, 'mainstream' Europe. Less well known is that during the eastern crisis and in the years up to the First World War, Muslims were the primary victims of violence in the region by state and sub-state Christian actors working in the name of nationalist liberation and self-determination for their ethno-religious group. As Serbia, Montenegro, Romania, and part of Bulgaria achieved independence from the rule of Istanbul, and Bosnia, Herzegovina, and the rest of Bulgaria gained extensive autonomy, hundreds of thousands of Muslims were expelled from these former Ottoman domains, with others murdered or perishing along the way. To their numbers may be added millions more Muslims from the Caucasus, expelled or fleeing from there in the face of Russian policy. The stream from the Caucasus grew to a

---

[23] For an expansion of this point, see the introduction to Donald Bloxham, *Genocide and the World Wars: The Unweaving of Europe* (London, 2008).

The Great Unweaving

flood around the time of the Crimean War (1854–6), but was further augmented during the 1877–8 Ottoman–Russian War as Russia gained new border territory at Ottoman expense.[24]

In Turkish ethnic memory the suffering and dislocation experienced at the time of the eastern crisis is known as the *sökümü*, the disaster or 'unweaving'.[25] The fate of these Muslims signified the unravelling of centuries of some form of coexistence between different ethnic groups, however stratified it was and however rough it could frequently be, as the prevailing socio-political order changed irreversibly with the decline of the Ottoman Empire.

The unweaving: in the meaning of that poignant term lies the key to much of the tragedy of greater Europe in the twentieth century. For if the process of what Rogers Brubaker calls the 'unmixing' of peoples[26] began in earnest in central and eastern Europe around the First World War as the Austro-Hungarian Empire collapsed and the Russian Empire receded prior to its re-emergence in Soviet form, the unweaving was actually already well under way by that time in the former Ottoman Balkan domains. The eastern crisis marks the high point of the unravelling of the Ottoman Empire in the nineteenth century, and with its own very modern form of violence—ethnic cleansing—it provided an ominous portent of what was to come with subsequent imperial collapses.

Other problems that would characterize European inter-war politics were also prefigured in the aftermath of the eastern crisis. These included: the creation of aggressively insecure new states that were prey to each other but also to the agendas of greater powers (all of the states 'liberated' from Ottoman rule); 'minorities treaties' in the remaining Ottoman state and some of its successors that served less to guarantee the security of the minorities in question than to make them the objects of still greater suspicion by the dominant ethnic group (Armenians in the

[24] Izzet Aydemir, *Muhaceretteki Çerkes Aydınları* (Ankara, 1991), 43; Justin McCarthy, *Death and Exile: The Ethnic Cleansing of Ottoman Muslims, 1821–1922* (Princeton, 1995); Stephen D. Shenfield, 'The Circassians: A Forgotten Genocide?', in Mark Levene and Penny Roberts (eds.), *The Massacre in History* (Oxford, 1999), 149–62.

[25] Kemal Karpat, 'The Transformation of the Ottoman State, 1789–1908', *International Journal of Middle East Studies*, 3 (1972), 243–81, at 272.

[26] Rogers Brubaker, *Nationalism Reframed: Nationhood and the National Question in the New Europe* (Cambridge, 1996).

Ottoman Empire, Jews in Romania); secessionist terrorism copying the model of the Balkan nationalists who had emerged triumphant in 1878 and aimed at attracting the support of external powers (Armenians, Macedonians, Cretans); and, in consequence, increased state repression up to and including measures of massacre and forced emigration. For the great powers, the final stage of the 'eastern question' that the 'eastern crisis' introduced foretold the prolonged management of the collapse of the Hapsburg Empire from the end of the First World War to the conclusion of the expulsion of the ethnic Germans.

In the decades prior to the First World War central and eastern Europe itself had seen perhaps 5 million Christian refugees, including Slovenes, Slovaks, Croats, and Germans, leaving the mixed lands of their birth, in light of geo-political and ideological shifts. Their numbers were augmented by nearly 3 million Jews fleeing tsarist Russia from the 1870s, not a few of whom came to embrace Zionism in the quest for a safe domicile. The deeper causes of their flight were the changing socio-economic conditions of the Russian Empire, but it was greatly accelerated by the pogroms following the assassination of Alexander II in 1881, for which the Jews were often blamed. There were still more than enough 'problem minorities', however, and ethnic or national 'questions' dominated the population politics of many a central and eastern European state from the late nineteenth century onwards, gaining in prominence with the establishment of a raft of new, unstable, and competing nation-states from 1918, as a result of which some 10 million more refugees were created.[27]

Some of the most vivid examples of the 'solutions' to population 'problems' actually occurred on the eve of the First World War, in the 1912–13 Balkan Wars when ethnic groups on the 'wrong' side of any border were used alternately as recruiting grounds for irregular warfare and targets for collective reprisals, and 'alien' populations in lands coveted and conquered by the participants were subjected to ethnic cleansing, terrorization, or forced assimilation. Muslims again were the primary victims, with as many as 40,000 dead and hundreds of thousands more fleeing to the Ottoman Empire.[28]

[27] Statistics from Michael Mann, 'The Darkside of Democracy: The Modern Tradition of Ethnic and Political Cleansing', *New Left Review*, 235 (1999), 18–45, at 30.

[28] Carnegie Endowment for International Peace, *Other Balkan Wars: A 1913 Carnegie Endowment Inquiry in Retrospect* (Washington, 2003); McCarthy, *Death and Exile*.

The Great Unweaving

These wars were conducted 'at the high noon of mass ethnic nationalism, undertaken by states bent on shaping their territories in accordance with maximalist—and often fantastically exaggerated—claims of ethnic demography and committed to moulding their heterogeneous populations into relatively homogeneous national wholes'.[29] In the aftermath of the Balkan Wars, a new practice was introduced into European diplomacy and population politics: a population exchange as agreed between erstwhile combatants with the aim of creating ethnically homogeneous territory. This was mandated by the Ottoman Empire and Bulgaria as a continuation of the ethnic cleansing that began with the eastern crisis, and accelerated from 1912, but it now accommodated the new post-1913 boundaries that marked the expulsion of the Ottomans from all of Europe bar a sliver of Thrace. In actuality, it was merely a retrospective legitimization of a *fait accompli*.[30]

It was a well-established paranoia that concentrated minority populations could serve as the basis for separatist movements manipulated externally, and irredentism was frequently used as a weapon in struggles for national expansion. The fear of ethnically defined fifth columns found expression in the tsarist wartime deportation of Jewish, Polish, German, Latvian, and Lithuanian groups as well as Chinese and Koreans, and of Muslims in the Caucasus (and central Asia).[31] The most famous case of forced population movement from the First World War occurred to the south-west of the Caucasus, when the ruling Ottoman 'Committee of Union and Progress' (CUP) perpetrated the genocide by deportation and massacre of some one million Armenians under the influence of an explosive mixture of late Ottoman Muslim chauvinism and half-digested ideological imports from the west, radicalized by the prospect of the imminent collapse of the empire as heralded by the Balkan Wars.[32] The genocide was part of a larger exercise in population engineering in the pursuit

[29] Brubaker, *Nationalism Reframed*, 154.

[30] Stephen P. Ladas, *The Exchange of Minorities: Bulgaria, Greece and Turkey* (New York, 1932), 18–20.

[31] Eric Lohr, *Nationalizing the Russian Empire: The Campaign against Enemy Aliens during World War I* (Cambridge, Mass., 2003).

[32] On Young Turk ideology, Feroz Ahmad, *The Young Turks: The Committee of Union and Progress in Turkish Politics 1908–1914* (Oxford, 1969); Mehmet Sükrü Hanioğlu, *Preparation for a Revolution: The Young Turks, 1902–1908* (Oxford, 2001). On the genocide, Donald Bloxham, *The Great Game of Genocide: Imperialism, Nationalism, and the Destruction of the Ottoman Armenians* (Oxford, 2005).

of Turkic-Muslim population homogeneity, and owing to wartime upheaval, as in and around the First World War, approximately one-third of the pre-war Anatolian population of more than 17 million people migrated internally or were subject to 'relocation'. Recent research on the CUP's genocidal attacks on the Assyrians/Syriacs (Süryani and Asuri) suggests very close parallels with the Armenian fate.[33] Circassians, Albanian, Bosnian, and Georgian Muslims, Kurds, 'Gypsies', and some Arab and Jewish groups were also moved around the empire in and around the war period for purposes of assimilation and, in some cases, punishment, though none were so comprehensively dislocated as the Armenians, and none subject to quite the same level of murder.[34] Only as CUP doctrine was replaced by the more purely secular beliefs of Mustafa Kemal's nationalists would the ground be prepared for the extensive internal deportation and forced assimilation of the eastern Anatolian Kurds.[35]

The nationalist's concern with security of borders and 'territorial integrity' coincided dangerously with the ethnic-essentialist's obsession with population homogeneity and the social Darwinist's belief in inter-group struggle to produce a panoply of explosive and paranoid chauvinisms in east-central and south-eastern Europe and the Near East, and all of these developments were complemented by a general move in the direction of heavier state intervention in the regulation of human affairs.[36] If, like anti-semitism, general racist thought had gained a respectable pedigree amongst European elites over the previous decades, then organicist nationalisms could shade into outright racism. It may, in fact, be appropriate to talk of a general 'racialization' of European nationalism since the late nineteenth century, and even earlier.[37] And while internalizing a bastardized version of

[33] David Gaunt, *Massacres, Resistance, Protectors: Muslim–Christian Relations in Eastern Anatolia during World War I* (Piscataway, NJ, 2006).

[34] Fuat Dündar, *Ittihat ve Terakki'nin Müslümanları Iskân Politikası (1913–1918)* (Istanbul, 2001).

[35] Erik Jan Zürcher, 'Young Turks, Ottoman Muslims and Turkish Nationalists: Identity Politics 1908–1838', in Kemal H. Karpat (ed.), *Ottoman Past and Today's Turkey* (Leiden, 2000), 150–79; Martin van Bruinessen, 'Genocide in Kurdistan?', in George J. Andreopoulos (ed.), *Genocide: Conceptual and Historical Dimensions* (Philadelphia, 1994), 141–70.

[36] On statism, Mann, 'The Darkside of Democracy'.

[37] Paul Gilroy, *Between Camps: Nations, Cultures and the Allure of Race* (London, 2000); Eric Hobsbawm, *Nations and Nationalism since 1780* (Cambridge, 1990), 106–10; Eric Weitz, *A Century of Genocide: Utopias of Race and Nation* (Princeton, 2003).

The Great Unweaving 183

Darwin's theories, or, like the CUP, adopting a fashionable socio-logical positivism,[38] the idea that human affairs were governed by scientific laws and were appropriate for scientific solutions, with the state as scientist, did not require a fully fledged racial theory. The potentially malign influence of such trends is nonetheless clear, especially where the very meaning of the key concept of assimilation into the majority ethnic group was open to varying interpretations.[39]

This is not to suggest that every state was intolerant to the same degree. Poland, Romania, and Yugoslavia were instantly and correspondingly as resentful of the Versailles minorities treaties as they were of certain minorities; Czechoslovakia initially much less so. Yet while Czechoslovakia, like Yugoslavia, embodied a limited multi-ethnicity in its very name, this name did not indicate the reality that there were more Germans than Slovaks in the state. Those Germans, while not subjected to the same threats and abuse as elsewhere in east-central Europe, were very decidedly second-class citizens, though even then the 'ethnic German question' in the Sudetenland and beyond still had to be heavily manipulated by internal and external German national-ists to bring it to the boil. (The explosion of Yugoslavian violence from 1941 can partly be traced to manipulated Croatian fears of Serbian ethnic dominance in the early decades of the Yugoslav state.)

In the immediate aftermath of the First World War the great-est inter-ethnic violence occurred predictably in those areas where the European armistice meant nothing: civil war Russia and Anatolia and its border regions. The states of Transcaucasia took advantage of their brief period of independence between the end of tsarist dominion and the imposition of Soviet rule to fight each other over border territory and to evict members of other ethno-religious groups, with Armenia and Azerbaijan particu-larly culpable. In the middle of this conflict Britain held some tenuous influence in the region, and the commander of the British expeditionary force abortively mooted another episode of what was to become a favoured method of confliction resolution:

[38] Ahmad, *The Young Turks*.

[39] Hans Lemberg, 'Das Konzept der ethnischen Säuberung im 20. Jahrhundert', in Dahlmann and Hirschfeld (eds.), *Lager, Zwangsarbeit, Vertreibung und Deportation*, 485–92, at 486–7.

184　　DONALD BLOXHAM

an Armenian–Azeri population exchange over the contested regions in and around Mountainous Karabagh.[40]

After their own vicious war in Anatolia, in which civilians were targeted alongside soldiers, Greece and Turkey built on the concrete pre-war Ottoman–Bulgarian precedent of exchange. This was now an internationally mandated affair, however. The formalized exchange agreement, approved by all of the signatories to the Lausanne Peace Treaty, was partly just a recognition of the reality on the ground from the time of Kemal's ascendancy in the Greco-Turkish War, yet the refugee movement continued until around 1926 and until some 1.25 million Ottoman subjects of the Orthodox faith and 356,000 Greek Muslims had traded countries.

Partly because the 'transfer' had its roots in a demographic *fait accompli*, partly because of the height of inter-ethnic tension between Greece and Turkey, partly because of the appalling conditions in which so many made their transit either way across the Aegean, and partly because of the lack of resources to cater for the refugees' arrival 'home', the exercise bore little relationship to the controlled thing it was supposed to be. As in the later near-simultaneous population unweavings involving the ethnic Germans and across what was to become the India–Pakistan border, a large number of deaths ensued, and a host of other atrocities were inflicted besides.[41]

The suffering and penury of 'Greeks' and 'Turks' predictably did not feature in British advocacy of population exchange during the Second World War, nor did that of the approximately 280,000 people exchanged at the same time by Greece and Bulgaria. On the contrary, the Lausanne solution was presented as a model diplomatic resolution to an explosive situation. The idea served as a precedent of massive population engineering not only for Winston Churchill as he later advocated a 'clean sweep' of the minorities issues that had plagued inter-war nationalists and international relations, but also for future nationalist leaders such as Edvard Beneš and David Ben-Gurion, and, indeed, for

[40] Bloxham, *The Great Game*, 103–5, 160.

[41] René Hirschon (ed.), *Crossing the Aegean: An Appraisal of the 1923 Compulsory Population Exchange between Greece and Turkey* (New York, 2003); on the ethnic Germans, Philipp Ther and Ana Siljak (eds.), *Redrawing Nations: Ethnic Cleansing in East-Central Europe, 1944–1948* (Lanham, Md., 2001), pts. 1 and 2; Naimark, *Fires of Hatred*, ch. 4; Detlef Brandes, *Der Weg zur Vertreibung 1938–1945* (Munich, 2002).

The Great Unweaving

Italian fascists and the demographers of the Nazi state.[42] The rhetoric of troublesome minorities who had, perforce, to be dealt with also gave sustenance to the ethnic designs of a later generation of Greek nationalists who, during the civil war, justified their assault on Macedonians by labelling them 'Sudetens of the Balkans'.[43]

One factor that might have served ethical differentiation between different forms of removal—especially between 'exchange' and ethnic cleansing, since outright total murder was at least one step beyond both—was the theoretical possibility in organized transfer of rendering it as peaceful and as controlled as possible. Yet the Lausanne death toll and that of the ethnic Germans, at least 500,000 of whom perished during the expulsion alone (excluding military-related deaths, as broadly defined),[44] substantially reduces the distinction. And while 'transfers' were not officially internationally condoned everywhere at the close of the Second World War, in the spirit of the times expulsions-by-terrorization were tolerated, as in Israel–Palestine from 1947,[45] and as Italians were evicted from Fiume, Dalmatia, and Istria. (The Finnish inhabitants of Karelia did not wait to be kicked out, or deported eastwards: more than 400,000 of them simply fled in advance of the arrival of Soviet forces at war's end.[46]) Further, the initial, murderous, 'wild' anti-German actions at a local level by Poles and Czechs from before the conclusion of the war clearly served the larger design of expulsion. They were also structurally important to the nascent Allied design for 'transfer', irrespective of the Potsdam conference stipulation that the eviction be 'orderly and humane', since they instilled the urgency of fear in their targets. After all, the

[42] MacGregor Knox, 'Das faschistische Italien und die "Endlösung"', *Vierteljahreshefte für Zeitgeschichte*, 55/1 (2007), 53–92, at 73; Manfred Kittel and Horst Möller, 'Die Benes-Dekrete und die Vertreibung der Deutschen im europäischen Vergleich', *Vierteljahreshefte für Zeitgeschichte*, 54/4 (2006), 541–81; Götz Aly and Suzanne Heim, *Vordenker der Vernichtung: Auschwitz und die deutschen Pläne für eine neue europäischen Ordnung* (Frankfurt am Main, 1993), ch. 13; Mark Levene, 'The Limits of Tolerance: Nation-State Building and What it Means for Minority Groups', *Patterns of Prejudice*, 34/2 (2000), 19–40; Brandes, *Der Weg zur Vertreibung*.

[43] <http://www.makedonija.info/aegean3.html>, accessed 14 Apr. 2008.

[44] Rüdiger Overmans, *Deutsche militärische Verluste im Zweiten Weltkrieg* (Munich, 2000).

[45] Ilan Pappe, *The Ethnic Cleansing of Palestine* (London, 2006); Benny Morris, *The Birth of the Palestinian Refugee Problem, 1947–1949* (Cambridge, 1987).

[46] Pertti Ahonen, 'Taming the Expellee Threat in Post-1945 Europe: Lessons from the Two Germanies and Finland', *Contemporary European History*, 14/1 (2005), 1–21.

Versailles boundary-makers had stipulated that minority inhabitants of the post-1918 states should leave their new state within a year if they were unhappy, yet many both remained in place and remained unhappy. In a slightly different context, a number of South Tyrolean ethnic Germans had decided that they preferred to remain *in situ* rather than join Hitler's 'Heim ins Reich' programme, suggesting that many ordinary people had priorities other than 'racial homogenization'.

It is a delicate issue to insert full-scale Nazi genocide—the identification and systematic deportation and/or murder of up to 6.2 million Jews from across the near continent-wide sphere of Nazi interest—at least partially into a continuum of ethnic cleansing and ethnic homogenization in eastern and central Europe and the Eurasian rimlands. The process of comparative analysis has been made unnecessarily harder by the insistence on a phenomenological approach to the Holocaust that is concerned more with its difference and 'uniqueness' than its immediate historical contexts beyond the one context of racialized anti-semitism.[47] It has been made harder still by the fact, as Robert M. Hayden points out with reference to the expulsion of the ethnic Germans, that 'the crimes of the Holocaust provide a rhetorical structure that lends itself to justifying the process that it professes to abhor: the destruction, in whole or in part, of national, ethnic, or religious . . . groups as such'.[48]

Germany itself is a case of a great power temporarily reduced to second-rank status in 1918 by its victorious competitors, partly through the stripping of its extra-European territories, and seeking in the Second World War era to compensate itself territorially within Europe instead of beyond the continent. It imported to eastern Europe the settler-colonialist practices and racial arrogance that marked white rule in non-white places,[49] but its attitudes to German-populated territories immediately beyond its own borders were similar to those of other intra-European

---

[47] On 'uniqueness' see Gavriel D. Rosenfeld, 'The Politics of Uniqueness: Reflections on the Recent Polemical Turn in Holocaust and Genocide Scholarship', *Holocaust and Genocide Studies*, 13/1 (1999), 28–61.

[48] Robert M. Hayden, 'Schindler's Fate: Genocide, Ethnic Cleansing, and Population Transfers', *Slavic Review*, 55/4 (1996), 727–48, at 730.

[49] Woodruff D. Smith, *The Ideological Origins of Nazi Imperialism* (New York, 1986); Jürgen Zimmerer, *Deutsche Herrschaft über Afrikaner: Staatlicher Machtanspruch und Wirklichkeit im kolonialen Namibia* (Münster, 2001).

The Great Unweaving

irredentist ethno-nationalisms. Other European states, whether victims or accomplices of Nazi imperialism, also acted according to their own nationalist imperatives, though this was influenced to varying degrees by the nature of their interaction with the Nazi state.

The expulsions of the ethnic Germans were demonstrably stimulated in part by fear of future German manipulation of the minority question and revenge for German occupation. Nevertheless, they were also pursuant to the logic that had been actively present since before the Second World War about the necessity of population homogeneity for national stability. The eviction of more than 200,000 ethnic Germans from Hungary from 1945, conducted by many of the same Hungarian personnel as had helped deport Jews in 1944, had been tacitly envisaged by the then regent, Admiral Miklos Horthy, as part of a reciprocal exchange as early as 1934, and had been discussed with the Nazis during the war.[50] (The end of the Second World War also saw an abortive Hungarian–Slovak population exchange at the behest of the re-formed Czechoslovak state, and a more successful 'voluntary' population exchange of peoples with the USSR in light of the latter's annexation of Carpatho-Ukraine.) In this sense, Nazi policies and Nazi rule were a precipitant for removal of ethnic Germans just as war had been a precipitant in, say, the Armenian genocide, but it would be as absurd in the former case as in the latter to focus on the short-term political context to the exclusion of the longer-term ideological context.

Pursuant to the point of comparison with the Armenian genocide, the simple existence of some sort of socio-political dynamic prior to removal—the idea, bluntly put, that nationalist elements of minority populations may have played some role in bringing their fate down upon their collective—does not constitute a blanket *mea culpa* for the removers. The few historians who seriously try to justify the extirpation of the Armenian national group with reference to an exaggerated revolutionary threat do so from a strongly pro-Turkish nationalist perspective. Yet we need not go as far as debating outright genocide to expose the weakness of many simplistic apologias for mass removal: the Soviet deportation of the Chechens-Ingush in 1944 has, for

---

[50] Christian Gerlach and Götz Aly, *Das letzte Kapitel: Der Mord an den ungarischen Juden* (Stuttgart, 2002), 425–33.

instance, sometimes been associated with anti-state action by Chechen insurgents, yet these were few in number and their actions limited in scope. The deportation of the Chechens, like that of the Volga Germans, reflects less a substantial threat to the Soviet state than the paranoia of a state constantly on the lookout for counter-revolutionary elements and fifth columns, as that paranoia was enhanced during the defining crisis of the Second World War.[51] What is common to the Armenian, Chechen, and ethnic German removals is that each was directed at a stigmatized collective rather than culpable individuals within the collective, and that removal was a lowest-common-denominator solution to the complex problem of inter-group coexistence.

Further to the matter of the socio-political dynamic, it is in any case true that most instances of removal during this period and others have arisen out of some sort of socio-political dynamic, albeit one often greatly exaggerated and propagandized by partisan elites: Hutu and Tutsi; Serb and Croat; Pole and Ukrainian (see below). We may allow for a continuum of such dynamics, with more and less interactive cases which were correspondingly more and less genuinely threatening to state territorial integrity or the agenda of the majority group, but it should be clear that the very implementation of removal suggests quite how unequal power relations actually were in most cases. Arguably the only murderous dynamic that did not have any basis in fact was the German–Jewish dynamic that existed in Hitler's head. But this is not to say that various eastern European states complicit in the Holocaust could not point to some ethno-religious divisions of labour in which Jews were disproportionately represented in particular areas (generally because of their value to former imperial elites and traditional religious dispensations shaping their socio-economic situation) to the chagrin of the ethnic majorities. Moreover, Hitler was far from alone in harbouring the antisemitic fantasy that the Bolshevik revolution was a Jewish revolution. And it should be allowed that, however unjustified, the idea of minority protection from 1878 came to be seen by many European ethno-nationalists as a medium for intervention in their internal affairs by international forces with Jewish interests at heart, just as externally influenced minority protection

[51] On the particular effect of the Second World War on Soviet policy, Weiner, *Making Sense of War*.

The Great Unweaving

189

'guarantees' in the Ottoman Empire had convinced successive Ottoman elites that they were the victim of a conspiracy of internal and external Christians.[52] In other words, the perceptions of political elites were as important as 'reality'. Indeed, as has been written of the French revolutionary terror, but in a way that might be applicable to many other instances of state violence too, there is a dialectic 'in which the imaginary and the actual work to radicalise the state of siege'.[53]

Moving from the psycho-historical level to the geo-political, the case of Poland in the Second World War era illustrates some of the conceptual connections between Nazi and non-Nazi demographic engineering. Poland is particularly interesting because this 'illegitimate' state, this 'monstrous bastard of Versailles', as the Soviet Foreign Minister Molotov described it, was so despised that the Nazis did not even allow it to provide any political collaborationist movements. During the Second World War itself, Poland was the primary state victim of Nazi population policy, not only the epicentre of the Holocaust but also the laboratory where fantasies of reordering 'race and space' were realized to a greater extent than elsewhere (the small mercy of the period being the fact that the even more stupendous design of the *Generalplan Ost* for the territories further east was never properly implemented[54]). Social, political, and cultural elites were systematically annihilated as part of the up to 2 million Polish victims of Nazism; Poles were systematically expelled from the western territories annexed to the Reich, and their dwellings allocated to ethnic Germans from elsewhere in Poland and eastern Europe, including some 128,000 transferred in agreement with the USSR in 1940.[55] In the years at the beginning and the end of the war the Soviet occupiers also conducted their aforementioned deportations of up to 1,300,000 Poles and others. Yet when the focus is expanded from pure Nazi and Soviet policy

[52] On Europe and its Jews, Carole Fink, *Defending the Rights of Others: The Great Powers, the Jews, and International Minority Protection, 1878–1938* (New York, 2004); on the Ottomans and their Christians, Bloxham, *The Great Game*, ch. 1.

[53] Erik Landis, reviewing Arno J. Mayer, *The Furies: Violence and Terror in the French and Russian Revolutions* (Princeton, 2000), in *Kritica*, 3 (2002), 152–63, at 155.

[54] On the *Generalplan Ost*, Czeslaw Madajczyk, *Vom Generalplan Ost zum Generalsiedlungsplan* (Munich, 1994).

[55] Martin Dean, *Collaboration in the Holocaust* (New York, 2000), 4–6. More generally Jan T. Gross, *Revolution from Abroad: The Soviet Conquest of Poland's Western Ukraine and Western Byelorussia* (Princeton, 1988); Martin Broszat, *Nationalsozialistische Polenpolitik: 1939–1945* (Stuttgart, 1960).

to the demographic changes wrought in Poland from 1939 to 1949 as a whole, the result was a remarkable homogenization of the Polish state, for the eviction of millions of ethnic Germans after the loss of 3 million Jews and the severing of areas of heavy Ukrainian, Lithuanian, and Belorussian population from 1945 meant that the population of the Polish state became almost entirely ethnically Polish.

Many of these excisions chimed in some way with aspirations of ethno-nationalists, though very few would have endorsed the extremity of Nazi methods. Thus, first, we might consider the pre-war Polish nationalist contemplations about reducing the 'excess' Jewish population by deportation—possibly to Madagascar, the island temporarily entertained by the Nazis as a destination for all of Europe's Jews—in the interests of economic advancement in an 'overpopulated' region.[56] Arguing to the longer term, one might contend that the 'cleansing' of Germans from Poland was only the final chapter in a larger battle to establish ethnic primacy in what were now Poland's western borderlands. In imperial Germany before the First World War, Germans had been exported as colonizers and had tried to 'Germanize' local Poles, thereby precipitating the creation of nationalist organizations that would later be instrumental in the eviction of the Germans.[57] After the First World War, power relations were reversed, and involved coercive emigration as well as forced assimilation of Germans. In those inter-war years, German protests against the treatment of the very large, embattled German minority in Poland were based on real grievances, with conflicts over the disposition of Upper Silesia a prime source of ill will.[58] As to the Polish–Ukrainian dynamic, from 1942 a 'homogenization' process was conducted on the changing Polish–Ukrainian borders by local actors at first, though with heavy Soviet involvement at the war's end. Poles were the chief victims in the first instance (though according to the perception of Ukrainians many Poles had acted as imperialists during pre-1939 Polish rule over regions of the western Ukraine), as with the

[56] Magnus Brechtken, 'Madagaskar für die Juden': Antisemitische Idee und politische Praxis 1885–1945 (Munich, 1997), 81–91; Aly and Heim, Vordenker der Vernichtung, passim.

[57] T. David Curp, A Clean Sweep? The Politics of Ethnic Cleansing in Western Poland, 1945–1960 (Rochester, NY, 2006), 14–17.

[58] Richard Blanke, Orphans of Versailles: The Germans in Western Poland, 1918–1939 (Lexington, Ky., 1993).

The Great Unweaving

murder of some 40,000 Volhynian Poles in 1943–4;[59] from the close of the Second World War, mutual violence brought up to 100,000 deaths to both communities and hundreds of thousands expelled from each.[60] The post-war Communist Warsaw regime would use internal deportation westward as its means of dispersing the remnant of Ukrainians, the easier to assimilate them.

Further evidence of the, again interactive, link between Nazi population policy and other instances of forced 'homogenization', including 'transfer', is provided by the wartime actions of countries allied to or ruled indirectly by Germany. One of the basic principles of German rule in the east was to divide the ethnic elements of a country against each other if, indeed, encouragement was needed. But Germany was not always immediately successful with the strategy amongst its collaborators. Hitler had to cajole Slovak leaders out of their initial reticence to secede from the Czechoslovak state in the late 1930s. Even the introduction of antisemitic measures, Germany's foremost racial priority, was not always satisfactory to the Reich authorities. Bulgaria, Romania, and Hungary acted at their own paces with the enactment of antisemitic legislation. Then they proceeded, like France, to deport (or kill) Jews (or not) in accordance with their own priorities, whether related to the citizenship status of particular groups of Jews or to the repercussions for their economies of mass removal. Also significant was where precisely within changing borders Jews lived: if they lived in contested territory in the lands of Germany's south-eastern allies, they were much more likely to be killed outright or passed into German hands. All of this only serves to underline Jan T. Gross's recommendation to comprehend 'a society's experiences of war [as of] occupation as if they were endogenous' rather than the result simply of 'external, imposed circumstances'.[61]

Each country had its own dynamics, both ethnic and political,

---

[59] Tadeusz Piotrowski (ed.), *Genocide and Rescue in Wolyn: Recollections of the Ukrainian Nationalist Ethnic Cleansing Campaign against the Poles during World War II* (London, 2000); id., *Poland's Holocaust* (London, 1998).

[60] Pt. 1 of Ther and Siljak (eds.), *Redrawing Nations*; Timothy Snyder, ' "To Resolve the Ukrainian Problem Once and for All": The Ethnic Cleansing of Ukrainians in Poland, 1943–1947', *Journal of Cold War Studies*, 1 (1999), 86–120.

[61] Jan T. Gross, 'Themes for a Social History of War Experience and Collaboration', in István Deák, Jan T. Gross, and Tony Judt (eds.), *The Politics of Retribution in Europe: World War II and its Aftermath* (Princeton, 2000), 15–35, at 15.

and its own pattern of interaction with Germany.[62] Like Italy, Hungary went down its path of alliance with Germany in good part because of bitter disappointment at the territorial terms of the 1918–20 treaties, while Bulgaria had as one of its motivations the attainment, at Greek and Serbian expense, of what it had failed to attain in Macedonia in 1878 and again in 1912–13. Romania would also join Axis ranks in order to regain some of what it lost to the USSR as a result of the Nazi–Soviet pact of 1939. The war for each country was a means of expansion or re-expansion, but predictably also of homogenization, as in the 1940 'exchange' of 100,000 Romanians and 61,000 Bulgarians in the Dobruja. Some 150,000 Muslims ('Pomaks') were ushered out of Bulgaria at the end of the war as well. In Hungary, the swingeing territorial losses of 1918–19 left the large Jewish minority exposed in the rump of what had previously been a multinational polity, subject to radicalized Magyar opinion. Prevailing Hungarian antisemitism was not inherently genocidal, as the comparative security of Hungarian Jews up until the German occupation in 1944 showed, though non-Hungarian Jews within the kingdom's borders were killed and deported from 1941 onwards. It did, however, demand at least the economic marginalization of Jews to the end of ethnic Magyar control.[63] Like some Polish nationalists, pre-war Romanian nationalists, too, seriously entertained thoughts of deportation of Jews.[64] And each programme echoed aspects of Ottoman policy up to and during the First World War and Republican Turkish policy at points from the 1920s to the 1950s, as Greeks and Armenians were targeted for expropriation (often as part of the process of forcefully 'encouraging' them to leave) in the interests of creating a Turkish 'national economy'.[65] Each episode in turn provides a vital contextualization for Nazi policies of 'Aryanization', another point at which economic and ideological calculations intersect.[66]

[62] Generally on eastern Europe, Christoph Dieckmann, Christian Gerlach, and Wolf Gruner (eds.), *Kooperation und Verbrechen: Formen der Kollaboration im östlichen Europa 1939–1945* (Göttingen, 2003).

[63] Gerlach and Aly, *Das letzte Kapitel*, chs. 2 and 4.

[64] Ibid. 422 on Romania.

[65] Zafer Toprak, *Türkey'de 'Milli Iktisat' (1908–1918)* (Ankara, 1982).

[66] As Hans Safrian shows, the establishment of the 'Vienna model' in 1938, so influential in the way that 'Aryanization' was conducted in Germany itself, gained much of its impetus from indigenous Austrian measures of expropriation of Jews: 'Expediting Expropriation and Expulsion: The Impact of the "Vienna Model" on Anti-Jewish Policies

The Great Unweaving

Elsewhere, the threads of inter-war society swiftly unravelled just as comprehensively, and no more obviously than in Yugoslavia. The Croatian Ustashe who murdered Jews also murdered Serbs; in fact they killed more Serbs than Jews. And Serbian right-wing royalist partisans, the Chetniks, carried out revenge massacres, as well as killing some Jews. And both Serbs and Croats killed Yugoslavian Muslims, who themselves were not passive, as illustrated by a group of Bosnian Muslims who formed their own regiment in the Waffen-SS. In terms of absolute numbers, Muslims suffered fewer deaths than either Serbs or Croats.[67] The Second World War and the wilfully immoral and violent nature of Nazi rule only served to exaggerate and give free rein to the most extreme pre-existing nationalist, irredentist, and secessionist tendencies.

Little of this was clear cut in terms of allegiance to the Axis cause, just as the large number of volunteers of different nationalities who joined the Waffen-SS did so in furtherance of their own political and ideological ambitions.[68] The Organization of Ukrainian Nationalists that was the main organ of Ukrainian collaboration with Germany and the chief political supporter of the murder and ethnic cleansing of Poles sided with the power which appeared (falsely) most likely to pave the way to independent Ukrainian statehood and liberation from Soviet rule. Even in the ostensibly more stable, long-established nation-state of France, defeat and occupation brought massive internal tensions to the fore, between population groups to a degree, but primarily between different visions of what sort of country France should be. The political influence that manifested itself as the Vichy government was the right wing that inherited the mantle of the anti-revolutionary tradition and of the persecution of Alfred Dreyfus in the 1890s. It clearly partook of antisemitism, yet of a form different from that of the Nazis. The deportation of many foreign and some French Jews to the extermination camps was not so much an expression of French antisemitism as of

---

in Nazi Germany, 1938', *Holocaust and Genocide Studies*, 14 (2000), 390–414. On other policies of ethnic expropriation, see Martin Dean, Constantin Goschler, and Philipp Ther (eds.), *Robbery and Restitution: The Conflict over Jewish Property in Europe* (New York, 2007).

[67] Hayden, 'Schindler's Fate', 746.

[68] Hans Werner Neulen, *Eurofaschismus und der Zweite Weltkrieg: Europas verratene Söhne* (Munich, 1980).

194   DONALD BLOXHAM

straightforward French collaboration. The infamous anti-Jewish legislation, the *statuts*, derived, on the other hand, from their conservative, religious tradition.[69]

As well as being a coercive presence, Nazism was thus a facilitating force for older, broader, and more diverse exclusionary tendencies across the continent. Indeed, Nazism itself would not have been conceivable without the history of generally right-wing European nationalisms obsessed with national 'space' and borders and with 'alien' minorities, and prepared to wage war in each connection. And though the peculiar history of Europe's relationship to its Jews renders the nature of the 'Jewish question' in turn somewhat anomalous in this comparative context, the idea of violent 'solutions' to population problems was by no means novel, and was applied by Germany to Jews and many other groups besides.

As indicated above, the simple presence of ideologies of exclusion, cannot, however, be the whole story in explaining mass removal. If there was a general political crisis of identity, security, and 'national viability' in the European continent and to its southeast in the decades either side of the turn of the century, manifestly not every state or people opted for the most violent of means to achieve its aims, and, equally self-evidently, there were times when violence was not expressed by those who at other times would deploy it. The immediate context in which some reached for the gun was vital, and while the potential range of circumstances is simply too broad to be considered on a case-by-case basis, two aspects of wide applicability will be considered: the relationship between removal (ethnic cleansing and genocide) and *war*; and the relationship between removal ('transfer') and international power structures in the attempt to create the conditions for *peace*.

Catalysts and Opportunities: Ethnic War

It is nothing new to seize upon the relationship between war and radical population policy.[70] Societies at war are bound more

---

[69] Robert Paxton, *Vichy France* (New York, 1982).

[70] Martin Shaw, *War and Genocide: Organised Killing in Modern Society* (Cambridge, 2003); Omer Bartov, *Hitler's Army: Soldiers, Nazis and War in the Third Reich* (Oxford, 1992); Robert Melson, *Revolution and Genocide: On the Armenian Genocide and the Holocaust* (Chicago, 1992).

The Great Unweaving

tightly together than in peacetime, but simultaneously pre-existing societal fault-lines can be more exposed, as G. F. Hegel noted. Established suspicions of particular social or ethnic groups tend to harden under pressure, leading to a stronger bifurcation between 'loyal in-groups' and 'disloyal out-groups'. This is obviously the case in civil wars cast along ethnic lines, but also true when external enemies can be identified with internal 'out-groups'. States at war strengthen and expand their internal means of surveillance and coercion in the interests of national security; this extends their ability to identify and act against 'problem elements'. The violence of war itself tends to barbarize, making more acceptable more radical measures that are not themselves actually part of the war. War enhances a sense of crisis, making radical measures seem more immediately necessary, justifiable, and, therefore, rational. Populations acquired through the conquest of territory are particularly at risk because they do not enjoy the same constitutional protections as the domestic population of the conquering state.

Yet it would be unwise to see war as just an external factor, one acting on but nevertheless extrinsic to some separate, long-standing perpetrator 'character' or 'intention'. War does not fall simply into the second half of a straightforward dichotomy of long-term ideological cause versus short-term circumstantial precipitant. That would constitute a rudimentary and unrealistic model of policy-making, as recent scholarship transcending the old 'intentionalist–functionalist' debate on the genesis of the 'final solution of the Jewish question' has shown.[71] There is actually an intimate interrelationship between 'intention' and 'contingency', and the choice for war is often an expression of a paranoid or crisis mentality as well as a radicalizing moment in itself.

In regimes of every colour war remained the ultimate testing ground of the political order. Preparation for war, whether conducted in fear or anticipation, entailed streamlining of the state machinery and 'pre-emptive' assaults on potential internal obstacles and fifth column individuals and groups. These measures were most marked in the 'totalitarian' regimes, which additionally, by means of purge and/or quasi-legal 'coordination' in the 1930s, placed more committed or pliable individuals in key

---

[71] Peter Longerich, *Politik der Vernichtung: Eine Gesamtdarstellung der nationalsozialistischen Judenverfolgung* (Munich, 1998).

military and administrative positions at the expense of 'racial' or 'political' enemies. In the Ottoman Empire, which entered war less expectedly and thus in a state of lesser preparation, and with the ruling faction enjoying a more precarious hold on power, the penetration of the state by Committee of Union and Progress agents actually had to take place during the conflict itself.[72] Moreover, as far as many nationalist elites were concerned, a wartime process of identity-hardening was only an extension of the pre-existing state ideology where representing the popular will seemed to presuppose population homogeneity, and where the most important form of homogeneity was deemed to be ethnic. (And who is to say that these elites miscalculated, given the failure of class-based internationalism in the era of the world wars?)

The very nature of the wars embarked upon by, for instance, Bulgaria in 1912, the Ottoman Empire in 1914, and Nazi Germany from 1939, contained the seeds of radicalism, irrespective of their very different circumstances. These were not only wars fought over traditional material, diplomatic, and territorial issues, they were also ethnic wars or, in Foucauldian terms, 'biopolitical' wars, with any resulting territorial aggrandizement or change in sovereignty likely to result in a demographic reordering of the *status quo ante*.[73] Though the precise nature of decision-making among, say, Ottoman or German political elites is still a matter for debate, the ideological inclinations of the regimes in question affected the way that these elites interpreted developments in the conflicts they entered into, even when those developments were unplanned or counter to their original plans.

Wartime frustrations and military defeats were liable to be given an ethnic or racial inflection, interpreted, possibly, as grounds for 'revenge' against groups thought likely to profit from them or thought to be implicated in their advent. This was demonstrably the case in the Ottoman Empire in the First World War, when anti-Armenian policy intensified with every Entente military advance or success. The pattern held following initial

---

[72] Donald Bloxham, 'Organised Mass Murder: Structure, Participation and Motivation in Comparative Perspective', *Holocaust and Genocide Studies*, 22/2 (2008), 203–45.

[73] For references to Foucault and an application of 'biopolitics' to the context of genocide, see Michael Wildt, 'Biopolitik, ethnische Säuberungen und Volkssouveränität: Eine Skizze', *Mittelweg 36*, 6 (2006), 87–105.

The Great Unweaving

small-scale Russian incursions into Ottoman territory in November 1914, the famous Ottoman defeat at the turn of 1914–15 at the battle of Sarikamish in the Caucasus, the initial Anglo-French assaults on the outer forts of the Dardanelles in March 1915, the near simultaneous Russian successes in Persia, the Gallipoli landings immediately prior to 24 April 1915 (the day commemorated as the beginning of the genocide), and, finally, the Russian advance into the Anatolian interior throughout May and June 1915.[74]

Military victory, meanwhile, could equally well radicalize in accordance with ideological precepts but in the absence of concrete planning. In the Nazi context we might consider the actions of the SS's *Sicherheitsdienst* (SD). After the conquest of Poland the SD was presented with 'racial security problems' and dilemmas of demographic restructuring whose scale and logistical complexity they were not fully prepared for. Nevertheless, their prior training in thinking proactively about the 'solutions' to such problems, invariably involving ever more radical measures, and their self-conception as an ideological vanguard, meant that they took full advantage of expanding conceptions of the possible and the permissible in the experimental chamber that was the Polish colony. In the absence of concrete blueprints, policy was shaped by action, as well as vice versa.[75] Many of these high-ranking officers then went on in 1941 to lead *Einsatzgruppen* killing squads in the invasion of the Soviet Union, where their experience in using their own initiative to interpret instructions according to local conditions and 'in the spirit of the order' was vital in the swift expansion of mass murder from Jewish men in certain categories to all men, women, and children.[76] As Christopher Browning has recently written, in the contexts of war and imperialism in eastern Europe, genocide was there to be discovered as a possibility,[77] but the officers of the SD were the ideal men to do the discovering.

The nature of the conflicts in question as ethnic wars is at least

---

[74] Bloxham, *The Great Game*, ch. 2.

[75] Michael Wildt (ed.), *Nachrichtendienst, politische Elite und Mordeinheit: Der Sicherheitsdienst des Reichsführers SS* (Hamburg, 2003), 24–5, 33–7.

[76] Id., *Generation des Unbedingten: Das Führungskorps des Reichssicherheitshauptamtes* (Hamburg, 2003).

[77] Christopher R. Browning, *The Origins of the Final Solution: The Evolution of Nazi Jewish Policy, September 1939–March 1942* (Lincoln, Nebr., 2004).

as important as the nature of the world wars as 'total wars' (a notoriously slippery term in any case). This may run against the grain of a body of socio-cultural, political, and military history privileging the significance of total war in the radicalization of the participant states: in terms of one of the most obvious historical 'moments' in Europe's twentieth century, a vast historiography illustrates the role of the First World War in traumatizing the continent, shaping more radical forms of politics and new communities based on the romanticization of the front, and spawning revolution, the fear of revolution, revanchism, and expansionist territorial revisionism. Insofar as the emphasis in this strand of scholarship is also placed on the industrialization and dehumanizing effects of trench warfare, its ramifications extend to Auschwitz. Each of these insights is very important, and yet examination of the European continent and its border regions suggests that the lineage of violence they depict can and should be complemented by another such lineage.

It is a fair generalization that the most influential historians of the First World War have taken on some of the perspectives of those western European countries in which they are primarily interested. These historians tend themselves to be working in western European or American milieux, and generally focus upon the historical cases of France, Britain, and Germany—the more modern, industrialized, literate, urbanized nation-states of the early twentieth century.[78] After the Franco-Prussian War and the unification of Germany, four decades of peace in western and central Europe inevitably meant that 1914 would appear to be *the* watershed. Yet if we look to the experience of the Balkans and the eastern Mediterranean, in the litany of conflicts in this period, the First World War was but one of many, and depending on the state in question, not necessarily even the most devastating.[79] The 'second eastern crisis' of 1885–8, the Greco-Turkish

---

[78] Though the following influential books sometimes reach very different conclusions, they are all western-centric in their concerns: Modris Eksteins, *Rites of Spring: The Great War and the Birth of the Modern Age* (London, 1990); Paul Fussell, *The Great War and Modern Memory* (London, 1975); Jay Winter, *Sites of Memory, Sites of Mourning: The Great War in European Cultural History* (Cambridge, 1995); Stéphane Audoin-Rouzeau and Annette Becker, *1914–1918: Understanding the Great War* (London, 2002); Omer Bartov, *Mirrors of Destruction: War, Genocide, and Modern Identity* (Oxford, 2000). On the generational impact of the war, see Wildt, *Generation des Unbedingten*.

[79] As Mark Biondich has pointed out.

The Great Unweaving

War of 1897, the Macedonian Ilinden Uprising of 1903, and particularly the Balkan Wars were all accompanied by coercive population movement as well as great violence directed at civilians as well as soldiers. (In Serbia the First World War was sometimes referred to as the third Balkan war.) These were all ethnic wars, and their lineage of ethnicized violence was perpetuated into the First World War and beyond, and provides a continuum upon which the civil conflicts unleashed by Nazi rule in eastern Europe are best viewed. Further, like tsarist atrocities against Jews during the First World War or the Ukrainian and White Russian Army's murder of perhaps 50,000 Jews in the Russian civil war,[80] the crimes of the unweaving of the Ottoman, Hapsburg, and (the western parts of the) Romanov empires, some of which, as we have seen, were also an intrinsic part of the aggregate crime we now call the Holocaust, bear little relationship to 'industrial warfare' or 'bureaucratic killing'.

Managing Peace: Great Power Politics and Population Exchanges

If war was part opportunity, part catalyst, then the conclusion of war provided an imperative and an opportunity for the victors, along with other arbiters of the international system (if these were not one and the same), to lock a new, favourable status quo in place. In the quest for a new stability, the disposition of minority populations was central, for, as should by now be apparent, sizeable minorities were viewed as sources of instability, not just by ethno-nationalists but also by the great continental and world powers.

Discontented minorities could either be a focal point in themselves for the interventionist or irredentist goals of neighbouring states with some ethnic or religious affinity, or a cause of internal disturbance which might, if severe enough, again trigger external intervention. Either eventuality might lead to inter-state warfare, the avoidance of which was the main concern of statesmen interested in regional stability, particularly insofar as this entailed areas of the globe important to the commerce flows and capital

---

[80] See respectively Lohr, *Nationalizing the Russian Empire*; and Henry Abramson, *A Prayer for the Government: Ukrainians and Jews in Revolutionary Times, 1917–1920* (Cambridge, Mass., 1999).

investment of the world economy. The desire to defuse the minority issue brought forth the two measures of choice adopted successively by the managers of the European system: internationally guaranteed minority protection (the minorities treaties) and internationally sanctioned minority eviction (exchange or transfer). Each of these solutions corresponded approximately to the nature of the European and Eurasian peace settlements after the world wars.

It has been said that after the First World War the attempt was made to reconcile state boundaries with national groups by drawing borders as closely as possible around areas of contiguous ethnic majority, while after the Second World War this unsuccessful measure was reversed: peoples were made, by removal, to correspond to borders.[81] Despite major exceptions to each side of the juxtaposition—most obviously after the First World War the Greek–Turkish exchange and after the Second World War the westward movement of Poland's boundaries—the generalization holds. It should be stressed, however, that neither demographic measure was primarily concerned with the well-being of minorities. Both worked from the principle of the minority as the problem. In that sense, the progression from the apparently more benign protection to the more coercive transfer was not really a reversal of principle.

If the treaties were in the medium term to provide a measure of cultural self-determination for minorities in states dominated by 'different' ethnic groups, ultimately they were only a transitional measure. The final result of their application was supposed to be the peaceful absorption of the minorities into majority culture, towards the wider end of ensuring the stability of the post-war territorial settlement. In effect, as empires collapsed, those ethnies which, for whatever reason, were not gifted independent statehood were expected first to sideline their nationalist aspirations by accepting their status as minorities, and then to conceal the fact that they had ever had nationalist aspirations by forgetting their very minority identity. Since the treaties were a means to an end, fractures of their terms were treated with a certain tolerance, and the more so as it appeared, with the passing of the early post-war years, that minorities were showing

---

[81] See Tony Judt, *Postwar: A History of Europe since 1945* (London, 2005).

The Great Unweaving

no sign of assimilating of their own accord.[82] Indeed, from well before 1918, considerable latitude had been allowed for governmental violence against minorities provided that did not appear set to trigger inter-state conflict. Sometimes such violence was positively supported in the interests of quickly suppressing any 'local discontent', as when, for instance, in the 1860s the British ambassador to Constantinople—prioritizing the bolstering of the Ottoman Empire against Russian advances over the concern for Ottoman Christians enshrined in the post-Crimean War Paris Peace Treaty—recommended to the Porte the settlement of Muslim Circassians from the Caucasus in Bulgaria as a way of intimidating the locals into compliance with Ottoman rule.[83]

The aftermath of the eastern crisis might have alerted observers to the idea that international guarantees for minorities were unlikely to be enforced because of lack of will, interest, or agreement among the supposed international enforcers. If there were few repercussions for Romania for disregarding its responsibilities after 1878, neither were there for the Ottoman Empire, even as it massacred 80,000–100,000 Armenians in 1894–6.[84] It was not, however, the continuing abuse of minorities that discredited the minorities treaties in the eyes of the victorious First World War Entente powers, but rather the abuse of the treaties pursuant to territorial revisionism by a major power with the will and means to follow through on its demands. 'Munich' sounded the death-knell of minority 'protection'.

The demographic distribution of the 1918 settlement meant that Germany became an upholder of the Versailles minority protection clauses, manipulating the 'minority question' in the inter-war period, by protesting to the League of Nations on behalf of ethnic Germans in Czechoslovakia or Poland pursuant to a covetousness of the territories on which these minorities dwelt.[85]

---

[82] Levene, 'The Limits of Tolerance', 28–30; Patrick Finney, '"An Evil for All Concerned": Great Britain and Minority Protection after 1919', *Journal of Contemporary History*, 30 (1995), 533–51; cf. Jacob Robinson, *Were the Minorities Treaties a Failure?* (New York, 1943), 244.

[83] Richard Thomas Shannon, *Gladstone and the Bulgarian Agitation 1876* (Hassocks, 1975), 16–19.

[84] Jelle Verheij, 'Die armenischen Massaker von 1894–1896: Anatomie und Hintergründe einer Krise', in Hans-Lukas Kieser (ed.), *Die armenische Frage und die Schweiz (1896–1923)* (Zurich, 1999), 69–129.

[85] Carole Fink, ' "Defender of Minorities": Germany in the League of Nations, 1926–1933', *Central European History*, 5 (1972), 330–57.

When, on the back of rearmament, Hitler was able to exploit the situation to bring about the partition of Czechoslovakia, the Versailles order was fatally undermined. It would take the Nazi invasion of Poland, the other great central European bulwark erected in 1918 against Germany, to precipitate all-out war, but 1938 was the year to which Beneš and, more importantly, Churchill would later refer in justification of the expulsion of the ethnic Germans.[86]

One reason why population transfer had only hitherto been considered for the eastern Mediterranean may be summed up in a word: racism. What was thought acceptable in 1913–23 for Turks and Balkan dwellers, in a region in which the powers had long instrumentalized populations for their own geo-political games, was not thought acceptable for more civilized Germans.[87] With the vengeful passions aroused by 'total war' between 1939 and 1945, the unacceptable became wholly desirable. But this brutal new 'realism' was also predicated upon the recognition that bodily removing ethnic Germans was the best way to reduce German influence in east-central Europe and, therefore, in the continental power balance as a whole.

The pre-Second World War European management of minority protection illustrates a truth that is equally applicable to the management of transfer. It is that there was no pure and consistently applicable principle of demographic organization, no objective guide to who should be moved and when. The power-political interests of the arbiters of the international system shaped these issues as much as did actual population distribution.

In 1918 boundary decisions were not simply determined on the basis of national self-determination according to ethnic majoritarianism. The principle was qualified by the requisites of stability as understood by the First World War victors, namely, stability slanted towards their interests. This entailed the containment of both (Soviet) Russia and Germany in the 'lands between'[88] the two by the creation of a row of hopefully capitalistic buffer nation-states from north to south, which necessitated consideration of the 'viability' of each state in terms of resources,

---

[86] Brandes, *Der Weg zur Vertreibung.*

[87] Lemberg, 'Das Konzept', 487.

[88] As adopted from Alan Palmer's *The Lands Between: A History of East-Central Europe since the Congress of Vienna* (London, 1970).

defence, and communications. Where viability and majoritarianism conflicted, as in the 'Danzig corridor', or where ethnic ownership was simply contested, adjudications over sovereignty tended predictably to go against the defeated states; yet this simultaneously left open the potential for 'Munichs'. At the close of the Second World War, the Allies were unanimous that more radical and permanent measures had to be taken to curtail German strength. The expulsions were an intrinsic part of the successful attempt to reduce Germany in status to one below the major world players in military and foreign-political terms. Where western and eastern Allies differed, of course, was in their aspirations for the political alignment of post-war Germany. As any resurrection of the east-central European buffer state design of the 1918 victors became impossible in light of predominant Soviet influence in the region, the chastened western Germany itself became part of a more westerly, capitalist bulwark against the USSR.

At the end of the Second World War Germany could be treated with the severity that befitted a state forced into unconditional surrender and the temporary surrender of its sovereignty. When the boot had been on the other foot in 1939, Britain had still been prepared to countenance population transfer, but this time to appease Germany, as when immediately prior to the invasion of Poland the Foreign Office supported a population exchange for Danzig, West Prussia, or Upper Silesia to ease tensions.[89] The British 'offer' was ignored, yet nevertheless confirms the differing possible strategic purposes of 'transfer' in international relations. A retreat to the years 1920–3 brings us to a second pair of transfer scenarios, where again an actual population exchange may be contrasted with a potential one that never came to pass. The actual event, and precedent for the Second World War era transfers, is of course the Lausanne exchange; the stillborn transfer, or rather set of transfers, is that implicit in the terms of the Sèvres peace settlement for the Near East that the Lausanne Treaty superseded.

Between 1920 and 1923, Kemal's remarkable nationalist resurgence, culminating in the defeat of the Greek occupying forces, meant that Lausanne was negotiated from a position of relative

[89] Lemberg, 'Das Konzept', 488.

Turkish strength. As far as the Ottoman Empire/Turkey is concerned, Sèvres was a much closer approximation to the 1945 settlement for Germany, since it was handed down with a minimum of negotiation to a defeated state. The draconian Sèvres terms allowed for the creation in huge areas of eastern Anatolia of an independent Armenia and Kurdistan, and in western Anatolia an extension of the Balkan Greek state. With the exception of parts of the Kurdistan award, none of these terms made much demographic sense, but they decidedly did embody a hubristic Allied determination, with British regional aspirations paramount, to make the demographic facts fit the proposed new map.

By the terms of the treaty the port city of Izmir/Smyrna and its hinterland and the majority of eastern Thrace were allocated to Greece, with a plebiscite to be held in five years' time in Izmir to determine ownership in the long term. Yet while the pre-war population of Izmir was approximately half Greek, the surrounding province of Aidin as a whole had a Muslim majority over the Christians in a ratio of around three to two.[90] Greece's claim was based on the theory that most Anatolian Greeks outside the Greek zone would migrate into it, and Greek virility would ensure the successful consolidation of the state. The Greek Prime Minister Venizelos revived a pre-war scheme for mutual Greek–Turkish intermigration between Aidin and eastern Thrace by suggesting that the peace treaty should encourage voluntary exchange across the new national boundary.[91] Quite how voluntary this process would have been is, however, open to question, given the Greek need to gain a positive result in the plebiscite and the fact that any residual minority on either side of the border would have been seen as suspect.

As for the four large provinces of eastern Anatolia allocated by Woodrow Wilson to Armenia (these to be consolidated with the territory of formerly 'Russian Armenia'), whatever the reluctance of more sensitive diplomats to concede the *fait accompli* of the genocide by redrawing the Near Eastern map on the basis of post-war ethnic distribution, even the pre-war situation would not have provided a legitimate Armenian claim for separatism

---

[90] Richard Clogg, *A Short History of Modern Greece* (Cambridge, 1986), 111–13; Michael Llewellyn Smith, *Ionian Vision: Greece in Asia Minor 1919–1922* (London, 1973), 29.

[91] Llewellyn Smith, *Ionian Vision*, 32–4, 71–3; Clogg, *Modern Greece*, 111–16.

based on ethnic majoritarianism. In the post-genocidal state, given the destruction of the Armenian population, substantial Armenian territory in eastern Anatolia would have been impossible to justify on demographic grounds alone. Nevertheless, the boundary award gave many regions with strong Muslim majorities to Armenia in the interests of defensibility, communications, and resources. The idea was that the state would become a focus of immigration for Armenians elsewhere in the region and the diaspora. The much denser Armenian population of the Transcaucasian republic would assure an Armenian-Muslim plurality in the combined Armenian territories as a whole, that strong minority hopefully increasing in succeeding months and years to an overall majority.[92] Another part of the solution, however, was Wilson's effective approval for the eviction of Turks from the proposed territory, and he did not dissent from the Allied plan to allow Greek forces forcibly to remove any recalcitrant Muslims.[93]

These demographic designs were ultimately academic given the Kemalist revival, but they do illustrate the role of the great powers in exacerbating ethnic dynamics to the point where internationally sponsored ethnic cleansing may have been the only viable alternative to genocide. Kemal's nationalist resistance was catalysed by the landing of British-backed Greek forces in Anatolia in 1919, and given further impetus when the Sèvres terms were announced. The subsequent Greco-Turkish War was originally encouraged by a Britain seeking to use Greek force to repress the nationalist resistance in order to stamp British imperial designs on Anatolia. The Lausanne exchange itself was, therefore, amongst other things, a convenient way for Britain, as the hegemonic regional power at the time, to cut its losses and wash its hands of a problem partly of its own making, particularly as it was starting to think of moving back towards a position of friendship with Turkey as a regional bulwark against Bolshevism. (As Britain had also been involved both by omission and commission in agitating the 'Armenian question' in the late Ottoman Empire, its responsibility for the murderous

[92] Bloxham, *The Great Game*, 156–8.
[93] Laurence Evans, *United States Policy and the Partition of Turkey, 1914–1924* (Baltimore, Oh., 1965), 279–80; *Papers Relating to the Foreign Relations of the United States* (Washington, 1920), ii. 750–3.

disintegration of that polity across the whole First World War era is great indeed.[94])

From the perspective of international relations, the Greco-Turkish exchange undoubtedly 'worked', as did the expulsion of the ethnic Germans, for both ultimately eased tensions between the states involved (though many other factors reduced Germany's revisionist abilities after 1945). As has previously been implied, however, the diplomat's view does not encompass the misery and suffering of the expelled, nor the want of proper protection for them en route. What also becomes clear from studying the sociology of these events is the nonsense of the idea of simple co-identification of ethnic groups across borders. Cultural differences were evident in the interaction of ethnic German immigrants with the wider population, but these variations were probably less significant than those dividing, respectively, some 'mainland' from Anatolian 'Greeks' and Greek from Anatolian Muslims. For a start, the guiding criterion of the Lausanne exchange was religion rather than 'ethnicity' as it might now be understood; language, culture, and level of religious conviction did not come into the question, and often refugees had to be 'assimilated' into what was supposedly their culture, whether they wanted it or not.[95]

The convenient myth of homogeneity also allowed Ankara to begin increasingly repressive campaigns of enforced assimilation of the Kurds who, as a Muslim minority, were not even considered at Lausanne. The great powers were, to all intents and purposes, happy to go along for decades with the fiction of Kurds as 'mountain Turks', and thus to permit the Turkish state to act as it liked towards its own.[96] Repression, here, again served the goal of regional stability (and Britain particularly had Iraqi stability in mind) just as intermigration served it in Greco-Turkish relations. This matter is but one illustration of the way that the politics of the international system continued to shape the destinies of weaker states and minorities and could channel in different ways what many at the time thought of as the inevitable force of nationalism. Unfortunately the idea of population

[94] Bloxham, *The Great Game*, ch. 1.
[95] Hirschon (ed.), *Crossing the Aegean*.
[96] Mesut Yeğen, 'The Kurdish Question in Turkish State Discourse', *Journal of Contemporary History*, 34 (1999), 555–68.

The Great Unweaving

exchange as a diplomatic solution of last resort also encouraged later nationalists who wished it as a point of ethnic principle. It served as a precedent for what such people could hope to achieve at the negotiating table if they were sufficiently brutal or intransigent as to make it seem the only remaining option.

9

Explaining Genocide:
The Fate of the Armenians in
the Late Ottoman Empire

RONALD GRIGOR SUNY

In late February to early March 1915, the Young Turk government of the Ottoman Empire ordered the deportation and eventually the massacre of hundreds of thousands of its Armenian subjects. The first victims were soldiers, who were demobilized, forced to dig their own graves, and killed; when some Armenians resisted the encroaching massacres in the city of Van, the Committee of Union and Progress had the leading intellectuals and politicians in Istanbul, several of them deputies to the Ottoman parliament, arrested and sent from the city. Most of them perished in the next few months. Women, children, and old men were systematically forced to leave their homes at short notice, to gather what they could carry or transport, and to march through the valleys and mountains of eastern Anatolia. The survivors reached the deserts of Syria where new massacres occurred. Ninety per cent of the Armenians of Anatolia were gone by 1922; it is estimated conservatively that between 600,000 and 1,000,000 were slaughtered or died on the marches. Other tens of thousands fled to the north, to the relative safety of the Russian Caucasus.

Much of the public debate about the events of 1915 has foundered on the question of whether or not there was a genocide in Ottoman Anatolia during the First World War. Does the term, invented some decades later, apply to these mass killings? Were the deportations and mass murder of a designated ethnoreligious group planned, initiated, and carried out by the Young Turk authorities? These debates, as heartfelt as they are for some and as cynically manipulated by others, have not advanced the understanding of the motives of the perpetrators. The research of most scholars interested in these events has produced overwhelming evidence that would lead any serious investigator to conclude that, by any conventional definition, genocide had occurred. The principal question remains, however, 'why genocide?' In this essay I will review the existing interpretations—those of the denialists who claim that no genocide occurred, as well as those who argue for genocide but differ as to why it happened. I will then suggest my own analysis that brings together ideological/political factors, social/environmental context, and emotions as keys to the framing of the ultimate decision to commit mass murder.[1]

The Denialist Position

Surprisingly, much of the existing literature has either avoided explanations of the causes of the genocide or implied an explanation even while not systematically or explicitly elaborating one. For deniers of genocide there is simply no need to explain an event that did not occur as stipulated by those who claim it did. What did occur, in their view, was a reasonable and understandable response of a government to a rebellious and seditious population in a time of war and mortal danger to the state's survival. *Raison d'état* justified the suppression of rebellion, and mass killing is explained as the unfortunate residue ('collateral damage' in the now fashionable vocabulary) of legitimate efforts at establishing order behind the lines. The denialist viewpoint might be summarized as: there was no genocide, and the Armenians are to blame for it! They were rebellious, seditious subjects who presented a danger to the empire and got what they deserved. But there was no intention or effort by the Young Turk regime to eliminate the Armenians as a people.

Even though the denialist account fails both empirically and morally, its outrageous claims have shaped the debate and led many investigators to play on their field. Many historians sympathetic to the Armenians have shied away from explanations that

---

[1] For my version of a social environmental analysis, see Ronald Grigor Suny, 'Rethinking the Unthinkable: Toward an Understanding of the Armenian Genocide', in id., *Looking Toward Ararat: Armenia in Modern History* (Bloomington, Ind., 1983), 94–115. For my version of a strategic political explanation, see 'Religion, Ethnicity, and Nationalism: Armenians, Turks, and the End of the Ottoman Empire', in Omer Bartov and Phyllis Mack (eds.), *In God's Name: Genocide and Religion in the Twentieth Century* (New York, 2001), 23–61.

Explaining Genocide

might place any blame at all on the victims of Turkish policies. Because a nuanced account of the background and causes of the genocide seems to some to concede ground to the deniers, Armenian scholars in particular have been reluctant to see any rationale in the acts of the Young Turks. Explanation, it is claimed, is rationalization, and rationalization in turn leads to the denialist position of justification.

The denialist argument proposes the following theses:

1. that Armenians and Turks lived in relative harmony for many centuries, and that that peaceful coexistence was undermined by noxious outside influences—American missionaries, Russian diplomats, Armenian revolutionaries from the Caucasus—who worked to undermine the territorial integrity and political system of the Ottoman Empire;
2. that the response of the government to Armenian rebellion was measured and justified;
3. that Armenians, therefore, brought on their own destruction, launching a civil war against the government.

The first fundamental criticism to be made of the idea that 'outside agitators' disrupted the relatively peaceful relationship that had long existed between the *millet i-sadika* ('the loyal *millet*') and the ruling Turks is that such an imagined past, rather than being based in 'reality', was the cultural construction of the dominant nationality, its ideologues and rulers, and was not shared by the subordinate peoples of the empire who lived in a limbo of legally enforced inferiority. The Armenians, like the other non-Muslim peoples of the empire, were not only an ethnic and religious minority in a country dominated demographically and politically by Muslims, but, given an ideology of inherent Muslim superiority and the segregation of minorities, the Armenians were also an underclass. They were subjects who, however high they might rise in trade, commerce, or even governmental service, were never to be considered equal to the ruling Muslims. They would always remain *gavur*, infidels inferior to the Muslims. For centuries Armenians lived in a political and social order in which their testimony was not accepted in Muslim courts, where they were subject to discriminatory laws (for example, they were forced to wear distinctive clothes to identify themselves), where they were not allowed to bear arms when most Muslims were armed, and where their property and person were subject to the arbitrary and unchecked power of Muslim officials.

Most Armenians most of the time tried to improve their situation through the institutions of the empire. Beginning in the late 1870s and through the following decade the Armenians of the provinces began to petition in ever larger numbers to their leaders in Istanbul and to the European consuls stationed in eastern Anatolia. Hundreds of complaints were filed; few were dealt with. Together they make up an extraordinary record of misgovernment, of arbitrary treatment of a defenceless population, and a clear picture of the lack of legal recourse.[2] Although the most brutal treatment of Armenians was at the hands of Kurdish tribesmen, the Armenians found the Ottoman state officials either absent, unreliable, or just one more source of oppression. It was hard to say which was worse—the presence of Turkish authorities or the absence in many areas of any palpable political authority. Corruption was rampant. Even after the 'bloody Sultan', Abdul Hamid II (1876–1909), abrogated the Ottoman constitution, the Armenian religious leaders and the middle class preferred to petition the government or appeal to the western powers for redress.

When Armenians resisted the extortionist demands of the Kurds, either individually or collectively, the response from the Turkish Army was often excessive. Massacres were reported from all parts of eastern Anatolia, particularly after the formation in the early 1890s of the officially sanctioned Kurdish military units known as the Hamidiye. Against this background of growing Kurdish aggressiveness, western and Russian indifference, and the collapse of the *Tanzimat* reform movement, a small number of Armenians turned to a revolutionary strategy. Armenian revolutionaries attempted to protect Armenians but in general were few in number (though the Turks exaggerated their strength, organization, and effect). More importantly, they were allies of the Young Turks, who were themselves active opponents of the Sultan's regime, and after 1908, when the Young Turks

---

[2] Great Britain, *Parliamentary Papers: Accounts and Papers. Turkey*, for the years 1877–81; A. O. Sarkissian, *History of the Armenian Question to 1885* (Urbana, Ill., 1938). Sarkissian used the thirty volumes of records of the Armenian National Assembly in Istanbul, 'a true mine of information on Armenian affairs in Turkey', *Adenakerutiunk Azkayin Zhoghovoi, 1870–1914* (Constantinople, 1870–1914).

Explaining Genocide

came to power, the leading Armenian party, the *Dashnaktsutiun,* collaborated with the Young Turk Committee of Union and Progress (CUP) and gave up revolutionary struggle. The party called for autonomy within Turkey, not separation or break-up of the empire.

The revolutionaries were aware that their activities would result in Turkish reprisals, but they believed that it was no longer possible to remain hostage to those fears. If they did not act soon, it was feared, Armenians as a distinct people would disappear. Undeniably the radicals raised the banner of resistance, but those historians who see their rebellion, isolated and intermittent as it was, as a rationale for the horrendous massacres of 300,000 Armenians in the years 1894–6 excuse the government that carried out those massacres as its preferred method of keeping order in the empire. Armenian revolutionaries set aside rebellion as a strategy after the triumph of the Young Turk revolution of 1908. The major party allied with those forces intending to reform the empire. Therefore, imputed Armenian subversion is even less justification for mass killing after 1908 than it might have seemed to some before.

The Arguments from Religion and Nationalism

Confronted by the denialist construction of the Ottoman past, some authors avoid any explanation for why the Young Turks embarked on their destructive (even self-destructive) policy. Avoiding explanation that may be seen as justification, a number of writers have relied on essentialized notions of how Turks customarily act. No further explanation is required. An unfortunate consequence of the essentialist argument—that massacres, even genocide, are intimately connected to the nature of the Turks, their culture, and fundamental political practices—is the tendency of some writers to collapse quite distinct historical events into a single organic narrative. Thus the Hamidian massacres of 1894–6, the Adana killings of 1909, and the genocide of 1915 (and even the Kemalist battles of 1920) are all parts of a consistent pattern of Turkish violence aimed at elimination of the Armenians and Turkification of Anatolia. The differences between regimes and their various objectives, the different contexts of the violence, as well as the perpetrators, are simply erased. Abdul Hamid's efforts to restore through exemplary repression a traditional status quo by punishing 'rebellious' subjects ought to be distinguished from the urban riot of 1909 which, at least initially, was directed against the Young Turks, and the genocidal deportations and massacres by the Young Turks in 1915, which aimed at the effective elimination of a whole people from Anatolia.

Neither denial of such extensively documented events nor avoidance of causal explanation is acceptable for historical scholarship. Briefly, I will survey some of the major interpretations that have emerged in western writing on the genocide and then offer an alternative explanation. Two principal questions need to be answered. Why did the Young Turks embark on a programme of mass deportation and murder of their Armenian subjects? And why did ordinary people—Turks, Kurds, Circassians, and other Muslims (though not Arabs)—participate in these genocidal events?

Arguments for the genocide have generally circled around two poles, nationalism and religion, sometimes combining the two. Those who argue that the motivations were basically religious argue that:

- the genocide was a religious war, Muslim against Christian, a jihad, and was part of a long and traditional hostility against Ottoman Christians.
- As Islamic rulers the Ottomans were tolerant of non-Muslims as long as they recognized their inferiority and remained loyal. Religion contributed to conflict when European powers intervened in the empire's affairs in defence of oppressed Christians; the effect was to raise the political hopes of non-Muslims and the resentment of Turks. Turkish motives stem primarily from their religious conviction of inherent and deserved Muslim Turkish superiority.
- Islam could not tolerate the reforms that Turkish bureaucrats and European powers attempted to implement in the nineteenth century that would have created more egalitarian relations with the non-Turkish peoples of the empire. The theocratic dogmas of Islam denied that the *gavur* could be equal to the Muslim, and permanent disabilities and inequities were

Explaining Genocide

imposed on non-Muslims by the Ottoman state. Vahakn Dadrian writes: 'The reforms were a repudiation of fundamental socio-religious traditions deeply enmeshed in the Turkish psyche, and institutionalized throughout the empire. . . . The Ottoman Empire, for most of its history, was and remained a theocracy which, by definition and fact, cannot be secularized; laws that are predicated upon permanently fixed and intractable religious precepts cannot be modified, much less reformed.'[3]

- The Ottoman rulers could not tolerate religious heterogeneity and sought to Islamicize their empire as much as possible.

A major limitation of the 'religious argument' is that it removes all agency from the Armenians, who are presented only as passive victims, rather than as active Ottoman subjects with their own political aspirations and organizations. In general Turks acted, Armenians reacted. Secondly, its characterization, indeed reification, of Islam assumes an unchanging doctrine, a consistent and coherent dogma from which rules of behaviour and attitudes may be deduced. The relationship of Muslims to the doctrine is also consistent and predictable. Yet Islam does not in all cases preclude political reform. While certain precepts of Islam may thwart egalitarian reform, some Muslims, like westernizing Ottoman bureaucrats, pushed for reform in a European direction at the same time that conservative clergy and army officers opposed the reforms. At the same time, non-Muslims in the empire resisted ending their privileges and distinctions inherent in the *millet* system, even though they desired certain aspects of equality.

Thirdly, it is not true that a theocracy by definition and fact cannot be secularized; indeed, this is precisely what happened in Europe in the transition from medieval to modern times, and to some degree in Turkey in the nineteenth and (even more so) twentieth centuries. Religious orthodoxy was certainly a powerful inhibitor to effective reform both in Europe and the Ottoman Empire, but it was not an insurmountable barrier, as reforming Ottoman bureaucrats, Young Ottomans, Young Turks, and Kemalists would seek to demonstrate. Fourthly, the argument

---

[3] Vahakn Dadrian, *Warrant for Genocide: Key Elements of Turko-Armenian Conflict* (New Brunswick, NJ, 1999), 20.

that the Ottoman Empire could not tolerate heterogeneity also fails before five centuries of imperial rule. Empire, indeed, may be defined by its preservation, even enforcement, of heterogeneity. Distinction and discrimination, separation and inequality were hallmarks of Ottoman imperial rule (and, indeed, of all empires). That heterogeneity was marked in the *millet* system, an imperial structure through which the Islamic state managed other religious communities. The argument also fails empirically, for the Young Turks who seized control of the empire in 1908 were not religious fanatics but secular modernizers devoted to bringing technology, science, and greater rationality and efficiency to their country. Suspicious, even hostile, to conservative clerics who blocked reform, they were, however, willing to deploy Islamic rhetoric when it served their strategic ends.

If the genocide was not carried out primarily for religious motives, and if religion did not prevent other outcomes such as coexistence or reform, perhaps the source of violence was nationalism, the all-purpose explanans for modern mass killing. The argument that two nationalisms—even two competing nations—faced each other in a deadly struggle for the same land has been made repeatedly in the literature. Consider the words of the eminent scholar of Islam, Bernard Lewis, which can be read as an implied rationale for the Turkish massacres of Armenians:

> For the Turks, the Armenian movement was the deadliest of all threats. From the conquered lands of the Serbs, Bulgars, Albanians, and Greeks, they could, however, reluctantly, withdraw, abandoning distant provinces and bringing the Imperial frontier nearer home. But the Armenians, stretching across Turkey-in-Asia from the Caucasian frontier to the Mediterranean coast, lay in the very heart of the Turkish homeland—and to renounce these lands would have meant not the truncation, but the dissolution of the Turkish state. Turkish and Armenian villages, inextricably mixed, had for centuries lived in neighborly association. Now a desperate struggle between them began—a struggle between two nations for the possession of a single homeland, that ended with the terrible holocaust of 1915, when a million and a half Armenians perished.[4]

In what appears to be a cool and balanced understanding of why their Ottoman rulers would have used mass violence against a perceived Armenian danger, Lewis places the Armenians

---

[4] Bernard Lewis, *The Emergence of Modern Turkey* (Oxford, 1961; 2nd edn. 1968), 356.

Explaining Genocide 217

'nearer [the Turkish] home' and 'in the very heart of the Turkish homeland', employing language that already assumes the legitimacy and actuality of a nation-state. In this transparent paragraph Lewis subtly rewrites the history of Anatolia from a land in which Armenians were the earlier inhabitants into one in which they become an obstacle to the national aspirations of the Turks, who now can claim Anatolia, rather than central Asia, as their homeland. His language employs the logic of nationalism as if it has a kind of universal relevance, even in political structures that evolved out of and still worked within a contradictory logic of empire. In 1915 the Ottoman Empire was still an imperial state, albeit already long existing within an international system of powerful nation-states and an increasingly hegemonic western conviction that the nation, however defined, was the principal source of political legitimacy. The nature of that system and its self-justifications were changing, but Lewis's reading of a notion of ethnic homogeneity as the basis for a national republic of the Kemalist type, which lay in the future, into the moment of Armenian annihilation is ahistorical and anachronistic.

Such a scenario, that the Armenian genocide was primarily a struggle between two contending nationalisms, one of which destroyed the other, presupposes that two well-formed and articulated nationalisms already existed in the early years of the war. Among Armenians, divided though they were among a number of political and cultural orientations, identification with an Armenian nation had gained a broad resonance. Yet Turkish identity was not clearly focused on the 'nation'. The term 'Turk' was in the early twentieth century still infrequently used except as a pejorative for country people. Turkish nationalists were beginning to exploit the concept of Turk, which was based on the linguistic affiliations of a group of languages, in a more positive way, but Turkish identification was still weak, confused, and mixed in with Islamic and Ottoman identities. As he is well aware, in the last years of the empire conflicting and contradictory ideas of Turkish nationalism, some deeply racist, vied with pan-Turanism, pan-Islamism, and various strains of Ottomanism in an ideological contest for new ways of reformulating the state.

The Young Turk CUP was not so much engaged in creating a homogeneous ethnic nation as it was searching, unsuccessfully flailing around, to find ways to maintain its empire. Deporting and killing Armenians was a major, deliberate effort to that end. Rather than primarily aiming at creating a homeland for an ethnically homogeneous Turkish nation, something that in the next decade would become the hallmark of the Kemalist republic, the Young Turks sought to preserve their multi-ethnic, polyglot empire. The imperial mission of the CUP still involved ruling over Kurds and Arabs, as well as Jews, Greeks, and even Armenian survivors, in what would essentially still be a multinational Ottoman Empire. In the vision of some, like Enver Pasha, that vision was now greatly expanded to include the Turkic peoples of the Caucasus and possibly central Asia. Even as some thinkers, notably 'Turks' from the Russian Empire, advocated an empire in the more ecumenical civic sense of the Ottomanist liberals of the nineteenth and early twentieth centuries, the policies of the Young Turks never were purely Turkish nationalist, but remained Ottoman in fundamental conception. In a word, they were primarily state imperialists, empire preservers, rather than ethno-nationalists.

It should be noted, however, that neither religion nor nationalism was wholly absent in the political discourse of the time. Religion was important as a marker of difference, the premodern equivalent of ethnicity. The key difference in early Ottoman society was religion, rather than ethnicity or language, which took on relevance only later. The *millets*, the various communities headed by religious leaders that were systematized only in the nineteenth century, were based on religion, rather than some idea of primal origin, language, or culture. The state ruled over the *millets* indirectly and interfered little, delegating much authority to the religious head of the *millet*. Certainly no effort was made to break down the boundaries of these communities and homogenize the population of the empire, or even Anatolia, around a single identity. There was no state project of 'making Ottomans' or turning 'peasants into Turks' in the Ottoman Empire, at least not before 1908, as there was to a degree in the absolute monarchies of western Europe or the French state after the revolution of 1789. There was also no idea until the *Tanzimat* reforms of the mid nineteenth century of equality under the law, a notion of equal citizenship for all members of Ottoman society. From the eighteenth century the term *reaya* was applied only to non-Muslims, underlining their

Explaining Genocide

inferior status.[5] The Ottomans, particularly in the early modern period but even during the nineteenth century, were not engaged in any kind of nation-building project but in an imperial state-building effort that sought at one and the same time to maintain the distinctions of hierarchy between rulers and ruled, Muslim and non-Muslim, without integrating a disparate society into a single, homogeneous whole. Unity in the empire came from the person of the sultan-caliph to whom all peoples regardless of religion or ethnicity owed allegiance.

As for Turkish nationalism, the Young Turks increasingly over time gravitated away from the liberal Ottomanism from which they had sprung and perceived that the security and unity of the empire required it to become more Turkic. Key leaders perceived Turks and Muslims to be more trustworthy and dependable allies in the imperial mission than Christians, with their ties to Europe, Greece, and Russia. Ottoman Turkey was to become an imperial nation, with Turks as the *Herrenvolk* ruling over subordinate nationalities and religious communities, rather than a multinational state of distinct nations with institutionalized privileges. At a certain point, early in the war, the Armenians were seen as a deadly threat to this conception and the continuance of the empire.

Emotional Dispositions and Strategic Imperatives

Arguments from neither religion nor nationalism adequately explain the genocide, though both provide hints as to the general disposition of the Young Turk leaders and many ordinary Turks and Kurds that would contribute to mass murder. The question 'why genocide?', after all, is primarily about a mental world that permitted, even encouraged, the Turkish government to carry out the extermination of their Armenian subjects, and ordinary Turks and Kurds to participate in that extermination of their neighbours. My argument is that the genocide occurred when

[5] Roderic Davison, 'Nationalism as an Ottoman Problem and the Ottoman Response', in William W. Haddad and William Ochsenwald (eds.), *Nationalism in a Non-National State: The Dissolution of the Ottoman Empire* (Columbus, Oh., 1977), 36; Stepan Astourian, 'Testing World-Systems Theory, Cilicia (1830s–1890s): Armenian–Turkish Polarization and the Ideology of Modern Ottoman Historiography' (Ph.D. thesis, University of California at Los Angeles, 1996), 367.

state authorities decided to remove the Armenians from eastern Anatolia in order to realize a number of strategic goals—the elimination of a perceived Armenian threat to the war against Russia, punishment of the Armenians for activities which the Turkish authorities believed to be rebellious and detrimental to the survival of the Ottoman state, and possibly the realization of grandiose ambitions to create a pan-Turkic empire that would extend from Anatolia through the Caucasus to central Asia. Rather than resulting primarily from Turkish racial or religious hatred of the Armenians, which existed in many and was available for exploitation, or long-term planning by militant nationalists, the genocide was a rather contingent event that was initiated at a moment of near imperial collapse when the Young Turks made a final, desperate effort at revival and expansion of the empire that they had reconceived as more Turkic and Islamic, shifting the meaning of what had been Ottoman. The year 1915, then, can be understood as the moment of imperial decline, when a fundamental reconceptualization of the nature of the state along more Turkic, Islamic, and pan-Turkic lines took place, and Young Turk policies became increasingly radical in the fierce context of the First World War.

Rather than arguing that the genocide was planned long in advance and was continuous with the earlier policies of conservative restoration through massacre, I contend that the brutal policies of killing and deportation (*surgun*) that earlier regimes used to keep order or change the demographic composition of towns and borderlands must be distinguished from the massive expulsions of 1915, the very scale of which, as well as their intended effects, to rid eastern Anatolia of a whole people, made the genocide a far more radical, indeed revolutionary, transformation of the imperial set-up. As in earlier and later massacres of Armenians, victims and victimizers were of different religions, but these mass killings were not primarily driven by religious distinctions or convictions. Rather than spontaneously generated from religion or even ethnicity, the motivations for murder arose from decades of hostile perceptions of the 'other' exacerbated by a sense of loss of status, insecurity in the face of perceived dangers, and the positive support and encouragement of state authorities for the most lawless and inhumane behaviour. In order to understand the mentality and motivations of the Young Turk leaders as well

Explaining Genocide

as ordinary people to engage in mass murder, it is necessary to explore the affective disposition of these state actors and of ordinary perpetrators, the fear, resentment, and hatred that shaped their understandings and led to their strategic calculations to eliminate what they perceived to be an existential threat to the empire and to the Turks.

What I seek to understand is the aetiology and evolution of that emotional disposition, the affective universe within which things were understood and in which decisions were made. A cascade of social, political, and international destabilizations battered older ways of thinking, feeling, and acting and generated a particularly pathological interpretation of the Armenians. Rather than religion or nationalism in isolation being catalysts to genocide, a toxic mix of past experiences, conflicts over land and status, and anxiety over their future all contributed to the disposition of the Young Turks that led them to genocide. At a moment when the Ottoman Empire was in danger—its very existence was at stake—and the Russians on one front and the British on another launched attacks, the Young Turks acted on the fears and resentments that had been generated over time. They directed their efforts to resolve their anxieties by dealing with those they perceived as threatening their survival: not with their external enemies, but an internal enemy they saw as allied to the Entente—the Armenians. What to denialists and their sympathizers appears to be a rational and justified strategic choice to eliminate a rebellious and seditious population, in this view is seen as the outcome of a pathological construction of the Armenian enemy, a mental picture shaped by deep emotions and perceptions of the Ottoman world whose origins and costs must be examined. The actions decided upon were based on an emotional disposition that led to distorted interpretations of social reality and exaggerated estimations of threats.[6]

The Armenians of Anatolia were a conquered people, an ethno-religious community that had lost both political and

---

[6] For interpretations of the genocide that are compatible with my own analysis see e.g. the thoughtful essay by Stepan Astourian, 'The Armenian Genocide: An Interpretation', *History Teacher*, 23/2 (Feb. 1990), 111–60; Michael Mann, *The Dark Side of Democracy: Explaining Ethnic Cleansing* (Cambridge, 2005); Mark Levene, *Genocide in the Age of the Nation State*, 2 vols. (London, 2005); Benjamin A. Valentino, *Final Solutions: Mass Killing and Genocide in the Twentieth Century* (Ithaca, NY, 2005); Donald Bloxham, *The Great Game of Genocide: Imperialism, Nationalism, and the Destruction of the Ottoman Armenians* (Oxford, 2005).

demographic hegemony over its own historical homeland between the fall of the last Armenian kingdom in 1375 and the national 'awakening' of the early nineteenth century. Their survival through those five centuries can, in part, be attributed to the religious and linguistic tenacity of many Armenians (those who did not convert or emigrate), to the continued efforts of clerics and intellectuals to maintain the Armenian literary tradition, but also must be credited to the remarkable system of indirect rule through religious communities (the *millet* system) that the Ottoman government eventually sanctioned. Whatever discrimination, abuses, and inferiority the Armenians were forced to endure must be weighed alongside the considerable benefits that this cultural and political autonomy provided. The Church remained at the head of the nation; Armenians with commercial and industrial skills were able to climb to the very pinnacle of the Ottoman economic order; and a variety of educational, charitable, and social institutions were permitted to flourish. Without exaggerating the harmony of Turkish–Armenian relations between 1453 and 1878 or neglecting the considerable burdens imposed on non-Muslims, particularly Anatolian peasants, we can safely, nevertheless, characterize this long period in which the Armenians came to be known as the 'loyal *millet*' as one of 'benign symbiosis'.

Linked primarily by religion and the Church, which nurtured a sense of a lost glorious past and ancient statehood, Armenians before the nineteenth century made up a diffuse ethno-religious community whose people were dispersed among three contiguous empires and scattered even further abroad by their mercantile interests and the oppressive conditions in eastern Anatolia. Armenians were much more divided than united, separated by politics, distance, dialects, and class differences. Yet the clerical elite worked to create a collective identity for Armenians, a notion of their distinction from their neighbours of different linguistic and religious communities. Though we know very little about the identifications of ordinary Ottoman Armenians, many of whom spoke Turkish rather than Armenian, the Armenian clerical and merchant leadership in the Ottoman Empire maintained a sense of Armenian distinctiveness, marked by a particular form of Christianity, and a memory of past glory. At the same time they preached deference to the rulers that God had imposed

Explaining Genocide

upon them. Religious distinction was foundational to culture and identity, but local identities, a sense of place and where one came from, seem to have been extremely important to Armenians. The historiographical and literary tradition, family, place of origin, occupation, and religion, as well as recognition of the power of the state and its authorities, all played parts in the construction of Armenian identity. And that identity was institutionalized in the *millets*, the official communities recognized by the Sultan as the instruments of his rule over his subjects.[7] The lines of distinction between Muslims and non-Muslims drew people of one religion together with their fellow-religionists and distanced them from those of different religions. Yet *millets* did not correspond exactly to ethno-linguistic lines. The *Ermeni millet*, for instance, included not only the Armenians of the national ('apostolic') Church, but also Copts, Chaldeans, Ethiopians, Syrian Jacobites, and others, while Armenian Catholics and Protestants gained their own *millet*s in the early nineteenth century. Even as, over time, Armenians borrowed the idioms of the nation, blending them with their own religious distinctions, religion remained the principal official marker of difference.

The turn from a primary identification with an ethno-religious community to an ethno-national identity was gradual and prolonged. The genesis of Armenian nationalism occurred in the diaspora, in far-removed places such as Madras, where the first Armenian newspaper was published at the end of the eighteenth century, and Venice, where the Catholic Mekhitarist fathers revived the medieval histories of the Armenians and commissioned new ones. The literary and cultural revivalists of the late eighteenth and early nineteenth centuries, particularly the Mekhitarist monks, saw themselves as cultivating the national spirit through promotion of the language.[8] But even as they promoted enlightenment and borrowed the idiom of the nation from the west, the generation of religious teachers rejected the

---

[7] Minorities had to obey restrictions in the way they dressed and interacted in society. These restrictions prevented them from developing social ties with Muslims through marriage, inheritance, or attending the same places of worship and bathhouses. Instead, they developed social ties with other non-Muslims, who were either members of other Ottoman minorities or foreign residents of the empire, who were often connected to European embassies. Fatma Müge Göçek, *Rise of the Bourgeoisie, Demise of Empire: Ottoman Westernization and Social Change* (New York, 1996), 35.

[8] For an appreciative treatment of the Mekhitarists, see Kevork B. Bardakjian, *The Mekhitarist Contributions to Armenian Culture and Scholarship* (Cambridge, Mass., 1976).

more radical and democratic aspects of western and eastern European nationalism that they observed. The precise connection (or disconnection) between religion and nationality became the ground upon which clerics and secular intellectuals would contest the nature of being Armenian.

The new images of community generated in Europe and by diaspora activists fitted well with the new forms and institutions of Armenian life emerging in Ottoman cities, particularly Istanbul. As capitalist production and exchange penetrated the empire, different *millets* (and even segments within *millets*) benefited (and suffered) unevenly from the new economic opportunities. With the Greeks suspect as rebels (and after 1821 possessing their own independent state), the Ottomans favoured the Armenians as the 'loyal *millet*' (*millet-i sadika*). In the late eighteenth and first half of the nineteenth centuries urban Armenians profited enormously from their association with the Porte. The *amiras* and *sarafs*, the wealthy money-lenders and bankers who financed the tax-farming system, along with the less affluent *esnafs*, the craftsmen and artisans of the towns, accumulated wealth with which they subsidized schools, hospitals, and philanthropic organizations.[9] Though highly placed, the *amiras* were always vulnerable to the arbitrary power of the Sultan, and when reforming officials progressively eliminated the tax-farming system, the wealthy *sarafs* suffered financially. When social tensions between the rich and the not-so-rich tore at the Armenian community and threatened the peace of the Ottoman capital, the Sultan responded to the pleas of leading Armenians and reluctantly granted a 'constitution' to regulate the Armenian *millet*. Community identity and self-sufficiency solidified, as well-to-do Armenians settled in Galata and other discrete sections, adopted European styles, and established close ties with and even came under the formal protection of foreign states. They published the first newspapers in the empire, sent their children abroad for specialized and higher education, and became visibly distant from the demographically and politically dominant Muslims. Armenians ran the imperial mint; an Armenian was chief architect to the Sultan; and Armenians ran the government's Foreign Correspondence Office. But for all their success and visibility, Ottoman Armenians were

---

[9] Hagop Barsoumian, 'Economic Role of the Armenian Amira Class in the Ottoman Empire', *Armenian Review*, 31/3–123 (Mar. 1979), 310–16.

Explaining Genocide

also the victims of unequal treatment and 'other doubts and suspicions that emerged increasingly as faith in the viability of the Ottomanist synthesis of nationalities—a synthesis to which the official commitment to egalitarianism was directly linked—began to erode'.[10]

The 'nationalization' of Armenians occurred not in isolation or primarily from within, but in synergy with and in response to the developing discourses of liberalism and the nation in Europe and the nationalisms of other peoples, most notably the French and the Greeks. Nationalist movements of the Ottoman peoples of the Balkans, along with the western imperialist incursions into and defeat of the Ottoman Empire, contributed to a general sense of Ottoman decline that stimulated westernizing bureaucrats to attempt to reform the empire and Europeanized Christians to consider either separating from the empire or, in the case of the Armenians, to petition for internal reform along more liberal lines. In a vision shared by many in power and those they ruled, the Ottoman Empire was 'backward', 'sick', and was expected to collapse, for it was an unfit pre-industrial power in an age of ruthless international competition, an imperial victim of western imperialism.

Appropriately for a dispersed people faced by three imperial authorities, the nationalism of many Armenian thinkers was not primarily territorial. Neither the clergy nor the powerful conservatives in the capital, who benefited from their privileged positions within Ottoman society and close to the state, were interested in creating a territorial nation. Armenians were dispersed throughout the empire, and Istanbul Armenians were a distinct community living both geographically and mentally distant from the Anatolian peasants of historic Armenia to the east. Armenian leaders in Turkey hoped for reform from above and spoke of their 'benevolent government'. Until the end of the 1870s, Ottoman Armenians conceived of themselves as a religious community that needed to work within the context of the empire to improve its difficult position. Encouraged by the *Tanzimat* reformers and the theorists of Ottomanism, liberal

---

[10] Carter V. Findley, 'The Acid Test of Ottomanism: The Acceptance of Non-Muslims in the Late Ottoman Bureaucracy', in Benjamin Braude and Bernard Lewis (eds.), *Christians and Jews in the Ottoman Empire: The Functioning of a Plural Society*, i: *The Central Lands* (New York, 1982), 363–4.

226   RONALD GRIGOR SUNY

Armenians petitioned and pressured the Porte and tried occasionally to enlist foreign support for reform.[11]

The Hamidian Empire

The horizons for Armenians changed radically with the coming to power of Abdul Hamid II (1876–1909), the Russo-Turkish War of 1877–8, his abrogation of the Ottoman constitution in 1877, and the turn towards a pan-Islamic policy that involved repression of the Armenians in the 1890s. As an Armenian national discourse took shape, the more liberal and radical elements focused on the eastern provinces and the poverty and oppression suffered by the Armenian peasantry. A sense of a 'fatherland' (*hairenik*) developed among Armenian writers, and a distinction was drawn between *azgasirutiun* (love of nation), which heightened the sense of a cultural nation beyond a specific territory, and *hairenasirutiun* (love of fatherland), with emphasis on the people in Armenia (*haiastantsiner*). Imbued with a deeply populist nationalism, centred on the peasants of eastern Anatolia, Armenian intellectuals travelled as teachers to the east in an effort characterized as *depi Haiastan* (to Armenia). The government responded by removing prominent teachers, such as Mkrtich Portukalian in Van and Martiros Sareyan in Mush, from their home provinces and exiling the patriotic priest Khrimian to Jerusalem.

Though most Armenian leaders wished to work within the Ottoman system, on a number of discrete occasions they made overtures to the Russians and the British. In 1872 merchants in Van requested that the Russian government send a consul to their city to guarantee 'the safety of trade routes and protection of religion, lives, and goods of the down-trodden Christian people of Vaspurakan'.[12] Six years later, in the aftermath of the war with Russia, the Patriarch Nerses Varjabedian made contact with the Russians at San Stefano and sent Khrimian to Berlin to plead the

---

[11] The classic work on the reform period known as *Tanzimat* is Roderic Davison, *Reform in the Ottoman Empire, 1856–76* (Princeton, 1963). See, also, his very useful essay 'Millets as Agents of Change in Nineteenth-Century Ottoman Empire', in Braude and Lewis (eds.), *Christians and Jews*, i. 319–37.

[12] Gerard Libaridian, 'The Ideology of Armenian Liberation: The Development of Armenian Political Movement before the Revolutionary Movement (1639–1885)' (Ph.D. thesis, University of California at Los Angeles, 1987), 145–6.

Explaining Genocide

Armenian case before the great powers. When the Russians were forced by Europe to retreat from their demands on Turkey, the Patriarch attempted to interpret the new role taken by Britain as the principal protector of the Ottoman state in the most positive light. These overtures to the great powers, along with the western styles affected by some wealthy Armenians, conspired to create in the minds of many Turks an image of an alien population within an Islamic empire. Armenians in eastern Anatolia and Cilicia competed with Muslims for the most desired and scarce resource, land.

From the middle of the nineteenth century through to the First World War, Muslims migrated into and were deported and settled in regions where Armenian peasants worked the land. When tsarist Russia defeated the Cherkess (Circassians) in the North Caucasus, thousands chose to move to Anatolia, where the government welcomed Muslim settlers. For the next century, as the Ottomans lost territories in the Balkans, Muslims left Europe for the hinterlands of the east. In some areas Armenians fell victim to Muslims favoured by local officials and courts. In others, not only were Armenians prominent in urban trades and crafts, finance, and international commerce, but their superior economic position allowed them to buy up large landholdings, for example, in Cilicia from the 1870s on.[13] Once the Sultan permitted non-Muslims and foreigners to buy Muslim lands (1856), Armenians and Greeks began purchasing properties that Muslim debtors could no longer pay for. Armenian emigrants to America and Europe sent home their savings and on their return brought new machines and technology to their farms. At the same time Muslim refugees from the Caucasus and the Balkans, displaced by the Russian victory in the North Caucasus and the independence of the Balkan states, migrated to Anatolia, and an intense competition for land developed. Petitions to the government and the Armenian Patriarchate enumerate hundreds of cases of Muslim usurpation of Armenian lands. The state most often supported Muslim claimants, and many Armenians reluctantly moved to the towns. Only after the 1908 revolution were they able to renew efforts to return to their lands.

[13] Astourian, 'Testing World-Systems Theory', 552–63. See also Donald Quataert, 'The Commercialization of Agriculture in Ottoman Turkey, 1800–1914', *International Journal of Turkish Studies*, 1/2 (Autumn 1980), 38–55.

While Armenian clerics taught submission and deference and often allied with state authorities to persecute those modernizing intellectuals who attempted to bring western enlightenment to young Armenians, Abdul Hamid II brought the reform period of the *Tanzimat* to an end and eliminated moderate and liberal alternatives within the system. The Sultan created a system of personal, autocratic rule and centralized power within the palace. Both Christians and Turks who opposed the 'bloody Sultan' saw the restoration of the 1876 constitution as a principal political goal. By the 1880s a significant minority of Armenians, many of them from Russian Transcaucasia, conceived of revolution as the only means to protect and promote the Armenians. A new idea of the Armenian nation as secular, cultural, and based on language as well as shared history challenged the older clerical understanding of Armenians as an ethno-religious community centred on faith and membership in the Armenian Apostolic Church. Faced by what they saw as the imminent danger of national disintegration, the Armenian radicals turned towards 'self-defence', the formation of revolutionary political parties, and political actions that would encourage western or Russian intervention in Ottoman affairs. For the young nationalists, revolution was the 'logical conclusion' of the impossibility of significant reforms coming from the state.[14]

With the failure of reform—the end of *Tanzimat*, the withdrawal of the constitution in 1878, the steady replacement of Ottomanism with policies preferential to Muslims—and in the face of European lack of interest in the fate of the Armenians through the 1880s, the situation of the Ottoman Armenians began to deteriorate rapidly. At the same time the Armenians had themselves changed dramatically in the four middle decades of the nineteenth century. The increase in social communication among Armenians had fostered a powerful sense of secular nationality among many Armenians. Influenced by western ideas, Armenian intellectuals had developed a new interest in the Armenian past, and instead of conceiving themselves solely as part of a religious community, more and more Armenians began to acquire a western sense of nationality, a feeling of kinship with Christian Europe, and a growing alienation from the Muslim

---

[14] 'Logical conclusion' comes from Libaridian.

Explaining Genocide

229

peoples among whom they lived. The depth or spread of this new nationalism should not be exaggerated. Certainly more potent in the larger cities and in localities where Armenian or missionary schools helped to shape new ways of thinking, Armenian nationalist ideas spread slowly into eastern Anatolia. Equally if not more influential in shaping Armenian attitudes in the late nineteenth century than the positive images created by Armenian and foreign intellectuals was the negative experience of poor Armenians at the hands of their Muslim overlords.

The former equilibrium between the *millets* was rapidly disappearing by the last decades of the century. And nowhere was this more brutally evident than in the Armenian provinces. The rise in tension in eastern Anatolia and the resultant resistance and massacre must be understood not only as the product of the failure of the traditional Ottoman political structure to adapt to the new requirements of the non-Muslim peoples, but also as the result of fundamental social changes in eastern Anatolia itself. The mountainous plateau of historic Armenia was an area in which the central government had only intermittent authority. An intense four-sided struggle for power, position, and survival pitted the agents of the Ottoman government, the Kurdish nomadic leaders, the semi-autonomous Turkish notables of the towns, and the Armenians against one another. Local Turkish officials ran the towns with little regard to central authority, and Kurdish beys held much of the countryside under their sway. Often the only way Istanbul could make its will felt was by sending in the army.

Diplomatic reports and eyewitness accounts by travellers and missionaries testify to the 'great severity' with which the Ottoman government suppressed any effort by Armenians to defend themselves. A series of massacres began with clashes in Sassun. In the summer of 1893 Kurdish tribes entered the *kaza* of Sassun and attacked the Armenian village of Talori. The Turkish *mutessarif* of Guendj arrived with his troops, arrested several Armenians, but no Kurds. The soldiers then plundered the Armenians, and the *mutessarif* told the authorities at Bitlis that the Armenians were in revolt. The villagers retreated into the mountains for several months, returning only the next spring. They refused to pay taxes because of the state's failure to protect them from the Kurds. This led to a second visit by the army, along with Hamidiye troops.[15] Abdul Hamid decided to deal with the Armenian Question 'not by reform but by blood'.[16] This violence would later be read by Armenians as the first stage of a series of massacres that would culminate in the genocide of 1915. But unlike the genocide, these massacres in eastern Anatolia in 1894–6, which were largely carried out by Kurdish tribes and local lords, were part of an effort by the state to restore the old equilibrium in inter-ethnic relations, in which the subject peoples accepted with little overt questioning the dominance of the Ottoman Muslim elite. That equilibrium, however had already been upset by the Sultan's own policies of centralization and bureaucratization, as well as his strategic alliance with Muslim Kurds against Christian Armenians. This pan-Islamic policy, which was institutionalized in the formation of irregular Hamidiye units of armed Kurds, helped to undermine the customary system of imperial rule as much as did the emerging revisioning of nationality borrowed from the west.[17] When British consuls in eastern Anatolia complained to the Sultan about the excessive force used against the Armenians, Abdul Hamid replied to the British ambassador:

The Armenians, who for their own purposes invent these stories against the Govt., and finding that they receive encouragement from British officials, are emboldened to proceed to open acts of rebellion, which the Govt. is perfectly justified in suppressing by every means in its power. . . . His Imperial Majesty treated the Armenians with justice and moderation, and, as long as they behaved properly, all toleration would be shown to them, but he had given orders that when they took to revolt or to brigandage the authorities were to deal with them as they dealt with the authorities.[18]

[15] Letter of Sir Currie to the Earl of Kimberley, Great Britain, Foreign Office, *Turkey, no. 1 (1895), (Part I) Correspondence Relating to the Asiatic Provinces of Turkey, Part I. Events at Sassoon, and Commission of Inquiry at Moush* (London, 1895), 8–10.

[16] The words are those of the Sultan as conveyed by Grand Vizier Said Pasha when he fled to the British embassy in December 1895. Quoted in Astourian, 'Testing World-Systems Theory', 606.

[17] On state reform, inter-ethnic relations, and economic developments in Abdul Hamid's reign, see Carter Vaughn Findley, *Bureaucratic Reform in the Ottoman Empire: The Sublime Porte, 1789–1922* (Princeton, 1980); and Stephen Duguid, 'The Politics of Unity: Hamidian Policy in Eastern Anatolia', *Middle Eastern Studies*, 9/2 (May 1973), 139–55; Donald Quataert, *Social Disintegration and Popular Resistance in the Ottoman Empire, 1881–1908* (New York, 1983).

[18] Quataert, *Social Disintegration,* 20–1.

Explaining Genocide

This policy of massacre, which crested in the killings of 1894–6, was a means of maintaining the decaying status quo as the preferred alternative to reform and concessions to the Armenians.[19] Encouraging the anti-Armenian hostility of the Muslims, the state created an Armenian scapegoat on which the defeats and failures of the Ottoman government could be blamed. The social system in eastern Anatolia was sanctioned by violence, now state violence, and the claims of the Armenians for a more just relationship were rejected. No right of popular resistance was recognized, and all acts of rebellion were seen as the result of the artificial intervention of outside agitators.[20]

The Sultan's language would be repeated by other officials and would echo in the justifications of the Young Turks and the apologist historians who would later attempt to reconceive state-initiated massacres as 'necessary', figments of Armenian imagination, or a Muslim–Christian civil war. Yet the continuity in the rhetoric about these events should not obscure the difference between Abdul Hamid's essentially conservative and restorationist policy towards unruly subjects and the Young Turks' far more revolutionary attempt surgically to remove a major irritant.

The revolutionary nationalism of the Armenian committees and parties was exaggerated both by the revolutionaries themselves and by their opponents. While they struggled to convince villagers of the 'Armenian cause' and threatened businessmen who refused to contribute to their movement, the Armenian nationalists were forced to rely on a handful of activists, many from Persia and Russia. They engaged in a number of spectacular activities, culminating in the seizure of the Imperial Ottoman Bank in August 1896, but this revolutionary act was followed by riots and

---

[19] Robert Melson, 'A Theoretical Inquiry into the Armenian Massacres of 1894–1895', *Comparative Studies in Society and History*, 24/3 (July 1982), 503, 509.

[20] Less understandable than the Sultan's justifications of his actions is the defence of those policies by western historians. William Langer, for example, writes: 'Whether Abdul Hamid deserves the black reputation that has been pinned to him is a matter of debate. If he was "the bloody assassin" and the "red Sultan" to most people, he was the hard-working, conscientious, much harassed but personally charming ruler to others. Those who have spoken for him have pointed out that the Sultan felt his Empire threatened by the Armenians, who, he knew, or at least believed were in league with the Young Turks, the Greeks, Macedonians, etc. They believe that Abdul Hamid was the victim of what we moderns call a persecution complex.' William Leonard Langer, *The Diplomacy of Imperialism, 1890–1902*, 2 vols. (New York, 1935), i. 159. Langer does not ask if what Abdul Hamid 'felt', 'knew', and 'believed' was accurate, or a fantasy, or self-delusion.

massacres in the city that left 6,000 Armenians dead. The number of militants remained small and divided, but the nationalist framing of the Armenians' plight gained followers. In the period after 1908 the Armenians elected socialists, liberals, and nationalists to the Ottoman parliament, where they collaborated (and competed) with the Young Turks. Resented by the more conservative clerical and merchant leaders in Constantinople whom they displaced over time, the revolutionary nationalists became the de facto leaders of a nation that they had helped to create through their teaching, writing, and sacrifice. The leading party, the *Dashnaktsutiun*, made it clear in its ten-point 'Platform' (December 1908) that it was in favour of 'Turkish Armenia [as] an inalienable part of the empire, reorganized in accordance with the principle of decentralization'.[21] Their commitment to the territorial integrity of the empire, however, did not prevent the Armenians from accusations of separatism and subversion, particularly when the Young Turks developed a quite different idea of what their empire should look like.

Social differentiation among *millets* and the resultant tensions existed throughout the nineteenth century, but the frames in which they were given meaning changed. Ottoman westernizers recognized that the Muslims were the least prepared of the *millets* to adopt western ways and would require the state to assist their progress. To religious Muslims, the visibility of better-off Armenians in the capital and towns appeared as an intolerable reversal of the traditional Muslim–*dhimmi* hierarchy that, in turn, generated resentments towards Christians. The inferior status of Muslims in the industrial and commercial world only intensified the sense of exploitation at the hands of Armenians and foreigners. After 1877, Turkish patriots constructed Armenians as disloyal subjects suspiciously sympathetic to Europeans. Anxiety about status, xenophobia, and general insecurity about the impersonal transformations of modern life combined to create resentments towards and anxieties about the Armenians.[22]

---

[21] Anahide Ter Minassian, 'The Role of the Armenian Community in the Foundation and Development of the Socialist Movement in the Ottoman Empire and Turkey, 1876–1923', in Mete Tunçay and Erik J. Zürcher (eds.), *Socialism and Nationalism in the Ottoman Empire, 1876–1923* (London, 1994), 140.

[22] For a particularly telling reading of Turkish attitudes towards the *gavur* (unbeliever) and Armenians, see Stepan Astourian's analysis of Turkish proverbs in Astourian, 'Testing World-Systems Theory', 409–31.

Explaining Genocide

233

Social grievances in towns, along with the population pressure and competition for resources in agriculture, were part of a toxic mix of social and political elements that provided the environment for growing hostility towards the Armenians. Whatever resentments the poor peasant population of eastern Anatolia may have felt towards the people in towns—the places where they received low prices for their produce, where they felt their social inferiority most acutely, where they were alien to and unwanted by the better-dressed people—were easily transferred to the Armenians. The catalyst for killing, however, was not spontaneously generated out of the tinder of social and cultural tensions. It came from the state itself, from officials and conservative clergy who had for decades perceived Armenians as alien to the Turkish empire, dangerous revolutionaries and separatists who threatened the integrity of the state. Armenians were seen as responsible for the troubles of the empire, allies of the anti-Turkish European powers, and the source of politically radical ideas, including trade unionism and socialism, entering the empire.[23]

Under Abdul Hamid, ethnic differences, hostilities, and even conflict did not become genocidal. That would require a major strategic decision by the elites in power. Though Abdul Hamid used violence to keep his Armenian subjects in line, as he and his predecessors had done against other non-Muslims, he did not consider the use of mass deportation to change radically the demographic composition of Anatolia. He remained a traditional imperial monarch prepared to use persecution when persuasion failed to maintain the unity as well as the multiplicity and diversity of his empire. More fundamental ideological shifts took place before the images of Armenians as subversive and alien appeared absolutely incompatible with the empire as it was being reconceived.

The Young Turks and the 'Modernizing' Empire

In the second half of the nineteenth century Turkic intellectuals, both in the Ottoman and Russian empires, stimulated interest in a new conception of a Turkish nation. Responding to the works

---

[23] The Union of Employees of the Anatolian Railroad, which briefly flourished in 1908 before the Minister of the Interior outlawed unions and prohibited strikes, was largely a non-Muslim affair.

of European Orientalists who discussed an original Turkic or Turanian race, men such as Ismail Gasprinskii in Crimea, Mirza Fethali Akhundov in Transcaucasia, and Huseynizade Ali Bey from Baku attempted to teach pride in being Turkish and speaking a Turkic language. Identification with a supranational community of Turks distinguished the 'race' or 'nation' of the Turks from the multinational Ottoman state. Yet inherent in that identity with the Turkic was a confusion about the boundaries of the nation and the location and limits of the fatherland (*vatan*). Was the homeland of the Turks Anatolia or the somewhat mystical Turan of central Asia?

Several scholars have traced the roots of Kemalist Turkish nationalism back into the late Ottoman period. Their discussion has focused exclusively on intellectuals and has revealed little about a popular response to nationalist or pan-Turanian ideas. In a population in which multiple identifications competed, such as religion, ethnicity, empire, or subnational communities, such as tribes, clans, or regions, an ambiguity about what constitutes the nation thwarts (or at least delays) the development of a strong and coherent nationalism. In the late Ottoman Empire allegiance to the 'nation' of Turks was quite weak. The word 'Turk', which referred to the lower classes of rural Anatolia, was in the nineteenth century contrasted to 'Ottoman', a term usually reserved for the ruling elite, and Islam probably had a far more positive valence among ordinary Turks than identity with being Turkish. There were signs of change, however, in the latter part of the century, and the shift came from the top down. The Ottoman constitution of 1876 established Turkish as the official state language and required members of government and parliament to know Turkish. At the turn of the century Young Turk nationalists, such as Ahmed Riza, began to substitute the word Turk for Ottoman.[24] Though Ottomanist views remained dominant among the first generation of Young Turk intellectuals, rival visions of the future led to tensions between the dominant Turks and the non-Turkish *millets* and reduced the commitment to Ottomanism.

The Turkish revolutionary elite at the turn of the century, including those who emerged from the Young Turk committees

[24] M. Şukru Hanioglu, *The Young Turks in Opposition* (New York, 1995), 216. This occurred around 1902 at the time of the Congress of Ottoman Oppositionists in Paris.

Explaining Genocide

to lead the Kemalist movement, grew out of an intellectual milieu that exalted science, rejected religion, and borrowed freely from western sociology. Influenced by the ideas of Charles Darwin, Claude Bernard, Ludwig Buchner, even the phrenology of Gustave Le Bon (who 'proved' that intellectuals have larger craniums by doing research in Parisian millinery shops), 'the Young Turk ideology was originally "scientific," materialist, social Darwinist, elitist, and vehemently antireligious; it did not favor representative government'.[25] Neither liberals nor constitutionalists, the Young Turks were étatists who saw themselves as continuing the work of the *Tanzimat* reformers—Mustafa Reshid Pasha, Mustafa Fazil Pasha, Midhat Pasha—and the work of the Young Ottomans. According to Şukru Hanioglu, the historian of its early years: 'The Young Turk movement was unquestionably a link in the chain of the Ottoman modernization movement as well as representing the modernist wing of the Ottoman bureaucracy.'[26] Earlier, Ottoman westernizers had hoped to secure western technology without succumbing to western culture, somehow to preserve Islam but make the empire technologically and militarily competitive with the west. Reform had always come from above, from westernizing statesmen and bureaucrats, a response to a sense that the empire had to change or collapse. The Young Turks shared those values, but steadily they added new elements of nationalism to their imperial étatism.

The first generation of Turkish revolutionaries was divided in their attitudes towards working with Armenians in a common struggle. After Damad Mahmud Pasha, brother-in-law of Abdul Hamid, fled to Europe with his two sons, he made an agreement with the *Dashnaks* and published an open letter urging joint action. The *Dashnak* newspaper, *Droshak*, wrote: '*Dashnaktsutiun* would not accept the re-establishment of the Constitution of Midhat as a solution of the Turkish problem, but look to a democratic federative policy as the way out.' The Armenian party 'would fortify the Young Turks if first it received a guarantee that the situation of the peoples would be bettered'.[27] The more liberal Young Turks believed that an alliance with the Armenians would reap a favourable response in western Europe. But the dual issue of an alliance with the Armenians and inviting

---

[25] Ibid. 32.   [26] Ibid. 17.   [27] Ibid. 150.

European intervention to secure the end of autocracy in the empire exposed the ultimately unresolved tension among Young Turk activists between their ecumenical Ottomanist impulses and the growing influence of an exclusivist Turkish nationalism.

On 4 February 1902, the First Congress of the Ottoman Opposition opened in Paris. The nationalist minority at the Congress, led by Ahmed Riza, categorically rejected foreign intervention and special arrangements for the Armenians in the six eastern Anatolian vilayets, while the majority, led by Sabahaddin Bey, favoured such concessions as a basis for an Armenian–Turkish alliance. When the majority came out in favour of mediation by the great powers to implement the treaties that the absolutist regime refused to execute, the minority essentially broke with the rest of the movement. Efforts by the majority to appease the minority failed. The Armenian delegates submitted a declaration that the Armenian committees were ready to collaborate with the Ottoman liberals to transform the present regime; that outside of common action, the committees would continue their own efforts with the understanding that their actions were directed against the present regime and not against 'the unity and the organic existence of Turkey'; and that their particular actions would be directed towards implementation of Article 61 of the Treaty of Berlin and the Memorandum of 11 May 1895 and its annexe.[28]

Mutual suspicions were high between the Armenians and the Turkish opposition, and the Armenian activists could conceive of collaboration only with the implementation of special reforms in the east guaranteed by Europe. For many Turks this was an outrageous demand. As Ismail Kemal, a member of the majority, put it: 'I recognize you not as an independent element but as Ottomans. You have rights as Ottomans. [However,] you do not have the right to bargain with us and make offers as if you were [representatives of a] state.'[29] In response to this statement, the

[28] Ibid. 193. 'This text', writes Hanioglu, 'reveals how antithetical the vantage point of the members of the Armenian committees was to the rest of the movement and how they had divorced themselves from the notion of "liberaux Ottomans" by emphasizing their willingness to work with them' (p. 193). In my own reading, this Armenian declaration makes a clarification, which Sabahaddin Bey then declared had been accepted by the majority, that the clauses of the treaties signed by the Sublime Porte must be implemented.

[29] Ibid. 195.

Explaining Genocide 237

Armenians walked out of the congress. Only later, after the Armenians sent a letter to Sabahaddin stating that they 'were ready to participate in all efforts to overthrow the present regime' and that 'they did not oppose the establishment of a constitutional central administration that would execute' special reforms for the six provinces, was a compromise reached between the majority and the Armenians.[30] The Young Turks even agreed that an Armenian was to sit on their central committee. Ominously for the Armenians, however, it was the minority at the Congress, not the majority, that actually represented the more powerful, even dominant, tendency in most of the Young Turk committees and newspapers.

Most analysts agree that in the first decade of the twentieth century there was a significant shift among the Young Turks from an Ottomanist orientation, in which emphasis was on equality among the *millet*s within a multinational society that continued to recognize difference, to a more nationalist position in which the superiority of the ethnic Turks (already implicit in Ottomanism itself) and their privileged position within the state was more explicitly underlined.[31] In the years after the Paris Congress a Turkish nationalism based on linguistic ties among Turkic peoples and notions of a common race spread among Turkic intellectuals, like Yusuf Akcura, outside the Ottoman Empire and influenced those within. After the 1908 coup that brought the Young Turks to power, a number of small nationalist organizations were formed that put out occasional newspapers or journals—*Türk Dernegi*, *Genç Kalemler*, *Türk Yurdu*, and *Turk Ocagi*—in which the conception of a Turkish nation extended far beyond the Ottoman Turks or Anatolian Turks to a pan-Turkic ideal celebrating the ties between all the Turkic peoples stretching from Anatolia through the Caucasus to central Asia. This was expressed most vividly in Ziya Gokalp's famous poem *Turan*: 'The fatherland for Turks is not Turkey, nor yet Turkestan, | The fatherland is a vast and eternal land: Turan!' Many of the Turanists argued for a purified Ottoman Turkish language, freed of Arabic and Persian words, that would serve as the language of

---

[30] Ibid. 197.

[31] See e.g. Ernest Edmondson Ramsaur, Jr., *The Young Turks: Prelude to the Revolution of 1908* (Princeton, 1957); and Feroz Ahmad, *The Young Turks: The Committee of Union and Progress in Turkish Politics, 1908–1914* (Oxford, 1969).

this Turkic nation and also as the official language for the non-Turkic peoples of the empire, those that made up the Ottoman *millets*. The Young Turk government passed resolutions reaffirming Turkish as the official language of the empire, requiring all state correspondence to be carried on in Turkish, and establishing Turkish as the language for teaching in elementary and higher education, with local languages to be taught in secondary schools. Not surprisingly, the Young Turk promotion of Turkish was seen by non-Turks as a deliberate programme of Turkification.[32] Not only Greeks and Armenians, but Arabs as well, resisted some of the modernizing programmes of the CUP that at one and the same time attempted to universalize rules and obligations for all peoples of the empire and threatened to undermine the traditional privileges and autonomies enjoyed under the *millet* system.

Turkish nationalism, pan-Turanism, pan-Islam, and Ottomanism were all part of a complex, confusing discussion among Turkish intellectuals about the future of the Ottoman state and the 'nation'. Uncomfortable with the supranational ideal of Ottomanism, the Turkish nationalists criticized the thrust of the

---

[32] Hasan Kayali, *Arabs and Young Turks: Ottomanism, Arabism, and Islamism in the Ottoman Empire, 1908–1918* (Berkeley, 1997) argues that the Young Turks 'subscribed to the supranational ideal of Ottomanism' rather than to 'a Turkish nationalist cultural or political program' (p. 14). 'The Young Turks did not turn to Turkish nationalism but rather to Islamism as the ideological underpinning that would safeguard the unity and continuity of what was left of the empire. Islam became the pillar of the supranational ideology of Ottomanism, with religion imparting a new sense of homogeneity and solidarity' (p. 15). Therefore, the perception of Turkification on the part of non-Turks, he claims, was incorrect. My own understanding is that rather than being primarily dedicated to a pan-Islamic policy, as Kayali argues, the Young Turks adopted different orientations towards different constituencies and that there was no overriding consensus, let alone unanimity, among the Young Turks on ideology. He seems closer to the mark when he writes: 'The Young Turks envisaged the creation of a civic-territorial, indeed revolutionary-democratic, Ottoman political community by promoting an identification with the state and country through the Sultan and instituting representative government. Though they remained committed to the monarchy within the constitutional framework, they conceived of an Ottoman state and society akin to the French example in which religion and ethnicity would be supplanted by "state-based patriotism" ' (p. 9). The difficulty of assessing the weight of nationalism and Ottomanism among the Young Turks is reflected in the work of Nyazi Berkes, *The Development of Secularism in Turkey* (Montreal, 1964). Writing about the period just before the First World War, Berkes argues: 'When, later, rival parties became harbingers of anti-Ottoman nationalisms, Turkish nationalism gained some influence in the Society, but never replaced Ottomanism' (p. 329). Much of his book is concerned with three competing schools of thought among the Young Turks from 1908 to 1918: the westernist, the Islamist, and the Turkist.

Explaining Genocide

universalism of the *Tanzimat* reforms. Gokalp tried to clarify the differences:

If the aim of Ottomanism (*Osmanlilik*) was a *state*, all the subjects would actually be members of this state. But if the aim was to construct a new *nation* whose language was the Ottoman language (*Osmanlica*), the new nation would be a Turkish nation, since the Ottoman language was no other than Turkish.[33]

Four choices were possible for the empire after 1908: either to remain an empire dominated by Turks, subordinating the non-Turks, and perhaps expanding eastward to integrate other Turkic peoples into a Turanian empire; to transform the empire along pan-Islamic lines, allying Turks with Kurds and Arabs; to adopt the programme of the Ottomanists and become an egalitarian multinational state with the different religious and ethno-national communities within it constituting a single civil nation of Ottomans; or, finally, to cease to be an empire altogether and become an ethno-national state of the Turks. This last option was not yet clearly envisioned, for it would require both the dismemberment of the empire state, the loss of the Arab territories, and the physical removal from Anatolia or assimilation of millions of Armenians, Greeks, and Kurds. Though the Ottomanist option remained part of the official rhetoric up to the First World War, many of the leading Young Turk theorists and activists gradually abandoned the liberal, multicultural approach for more intensive Turkification. After the coup of 1913 the CUP, though never completely in full agreement on a clear ideological orientation, moved away from liberal Ottomanism and towards Turkism, the pan-Turanian form of Turkish nationalism, and pan-Islam.[34]

The pan-Turanian form of Turkic nationalism seemed to key leaders to offer the most effective alternative for preserving the empire and the political hegemony of the Turks. This steady shift towards Turkism and pan-Turanism presented the Armenian

---

[33] Cited in Masami Arai, *Turkish Nationalism in the Young Turk Era* (Leiden, 1992), 61.

[34] This position is reflected in Jemal Pasha's statement: 'Speaking for myself, I am primarily an Ottoman, but I do not forget that I am a Turk, and nothing can shake my belief that the Turkish Race is the foundation stone of the Ottoman empire . . . In its origins the Ottoman empire is a Turkish creation.' Djemal Pasha, *Memories of a Turkish Statesman, 1913–1919* (London, n.d. [1922]), 251–2; quoted in Jacob Landau, *Pan-Turkism in Turkey: A Study of Irredentism* (London, 1981), 50.

political leadership with an extraordinarily difficult choice—remaining in alliance with the increasingly nationalist Young Turks or breaking decisively with the government. The Armenian Revolutionary Federation (*Dashnaktsutiun*) decided to continue working with the Young Turks, while the Armenian Church leaders and the liberal Ramkavar party distanced themselves from the government party. Even when the Marxist *Hnchaks* denounced the Young Turks for their steady move away from Ottomanism towards Turkism and their failure to carry out agricultural and administrative reforms, the *Dashnaks* maintained their electoral alliance with the CUP.

From Massacre to Genocide

Ottoman Armenians and other minorities joyfully greeted the 1908 revolution that brought the Young Turks to power. They hoped that the restoration of the liberal constitution would provide a political mechanism for peaceful development within the framework of a representative parliamentary system. Armenians favoured the promised reforms of the Ottomanists, but many conservative elements in the empire feared loss of status to the upwardly mobile Christians or loss of property to the wealthy Armenians. Armenians were now able to bear arms, and some defiant clergymen boldly proclaimed that their people would never be massacred again without defending themselves.[35]

The initially liberal programme of the Young Turks met opposition from the leaders of the non-Muslim *millets*, who were fearful that a civil order without ethnic distinctions would cost them their privileged status. Powerful Greek and Armenian clergy opposed the laws that would have eliminated the separate (and usually superior) educational institutions and the exemption from the draft of non-Muslims. The goal of the Young Turks to restore full sovereignty to the Ottoman state, thus ending the privileges of foreign powers within the empire, also challenged the advantages that the non-Muslims had gained from their association with the European states.

[35] Aram Arkun, 'Les Relations arméno-turques et les massacres de Cilicie de 1909', in Hrayr Henry Ayvazian et al. (eds.), *L'Actualité du genocide des arméniens: actes du colloque organisé par le Comité de Défense de la Cause Arménienne à Paris-Sorbonne les 16, 17 et 18 avril 1998* (Paris, 1999), 60.

Explaining Genocide

The social tensions arising from competition for land and work, the new freedom felt by the Armenians, and the accumulating resentments and fears of Muslims erupted in a massacre of Armenians in the eastern Mediterranean region of Cilicia. When supporters of the Hamidian regime revolted against the CUP government in Istanbul on 12–13 April 1909, anti-reform and anti-Armenian groups in the city of Adana turned on the Armenians. Within a few days the CUP was restored to power in the capital, but before order could be re-established in Cilicia some 20,000 Armenians and 2,000 Muslims were dead. Not only crowds of ordinary people took part in the massacres, but also the police and army.[36]

As Europe drifted through the last decade before the First World War, the Ottoman government experienced a series of political and military defeats: the annexation of Bosnia-Herzegovina by Austria-Hungary in 1908, the subsequent declaration of independence by Bulgaria, the merger of Crete with Greece, revolts in Albania in 1910–12, losses to Italy in Libya (1911), and in the course of two Balkan wars (1912–13) the diminution of Ottoman territory in Europe and the forced migration of Turks from Europe into Anatolia. As their liberal strategies failed to unify and strengthen the empire, the Young Turk leaders gradually shifted away from their original Ottomanist views of a multinational empire based on guarantees of civil and minority rights to a more Turkish nationalist ideology that emphasized the dominant role of Turks. In desperation a group of Young Turk officers, led by Enver Pasha, seized the government in a *coup d'état* in January 1913, and for the next five years, years fateful for all Armenians, a triumvirate of Enver, Jemal, and Talaat ruled the empire. Their regime marked the triumph of Turkish nationalism within the government itself.

Less tolerant of the non-Turks in the empire, the triumvirate scuttled the liberal Ottomanism of earlier years and amalgamated the views of pan-Islam and Turanist nationalism. 'Pan-Turanism, like Pan-Islam', writes Feroz Ahmad, 'was an expansionist ideology which suited the mood of the Young Turks, then in full retreat at the opposite front [in Europe]. . . . Turkish nationalism, centered around the Turks in Anatolia, was

[36] Ibid. 62–3.

in the process of development in 1914. It was to emerge out of the defeats in World War I, only after Pan-Turanism and Pan-Islam had proved to be mere dreams.'[37]

This shift towards Turkism and pan-Turanian expansionism left the Armenian political leadership in an impossible position. Torn between continuing to cooperate with the Young Turks in the hope that some gains might be won for the Armenians, and breaking with their undependable political allies and going over to the opposition, the *Dashnaktsutiun* decided to maintain its alliance with the ruling party. Other Armenian cultural and political leaders, however, most notably the *Hnchak* party and the Armenian Patriarchate, opposed further collaboration with the government. As Turkey entered the First World War, the *Dashnaks* agreed that all Ottoman Armenians should support the empire's war effort, but they rejected the request from the Young Turks that they agitate among Russia's Armenians to oppose the Tsar. Even as Armenian soldiers joined the Ottoman Army to fight against the enemies of their government, the situation grew extremely ominous for the Armenians. They were dangerously exposed. The bulk of their population lived in the mountainous plateau that lay between the two belligerents, Turkey and Russia. Everywhere in their historic homeland, except for an occasional town or cluster of villages, they were a minority living among Turks and Kurds, and the Muslim perception of Armenians as a disloyal, treacherous people, one that favoured the Christian government of the tsars over that of the Turks, seemed to be reinforced by the events of the First World War.

Anxious to fight the Russians in 1914, the Turkish government instigated the war by attacking Russian ships in the Black Sea. Enver led a huge army against tsarist forces on the eastern front late in the year, and at first he was dramatically victorious. Kars was cut off and Sarikamish surrounded. But the Turkish troops were not prepared for the harsh winter in the Armenian highlands, and early in 1915 the Russians, accompanied by Armenian volunteer units from the Caucasus, pushed the Turkish Army back. A disastrous defeat followed in which Enver lost three-quarters of his army, perhaps as many as 78,000 men killed and 12,000 taken prisoner. Ottoman Armenians fled to the areas

---

[37] Feroz Ahmad, *The Young Turks: The Committee of Union and Progress in Turkish Politics, 1908–1914* (Oxford, 1969), 154–5.

Explaining Genocide

occupied by the Russians, confirming in Turkish minds the treachery that marked the Christian minorities.

Enver's defeat on the Caucasian front was the prelude to the 'final solution' of the Armenian Question. The Russians posed a real danger to the Turks, just at the moment that Allied forces were attacking at Gallipoli in the west. In this moment of defeat and desperation, the triumvirate in Istanbul decided to demobilize the Armenian soldiers in the Ottoman Army and to deport Armenians from eastern Anatolia. What might have been rationalized as a military necessity, given the imperial ambitions and distorted perceptions of the Ottoman leaders, quickly metamorphosed into a massive attack on their Armenian subjects, a systematic programme of murder and pillage. An act of panic and vengeance metastasized monstrously into an opportunity to rid Anatolia once and for all of the one people now blamed for Enver's defeat.

With the defeat at Sarikamish and the approach of the British towards the Turkish capital, a general panic gripped Istanbul. It was feared that the city would fall to the Bulgarians who might join the war on the side of the Entente or to the British who were rumoured to be about to break through the Dardanelles. The American ambassador to the Porte, Henry Morgenthau, reported that Talaat 'was the picture of desolation and defeat' in January 1915 as the thunder of the British guns at the straits seemed 'to spell doom'.[38] There was fear of revolution in the city, and posters denounced Talaat. The Prefect of Police, Bedri Bey, rounded up unemployed young men and expelled them from the capital. Towards the end of the month Enver returned from the front, unsure of his reception by the public, after the devastating defeat at Sarikamish. The Young Turk leaders planned to burn down the city if the British broke through, a wanton act that shocked Morgenthau. 'There are not six men in the Committee of Union and Progress', Talaat told him, 'who care for anything that is old. We all like new things.'[39]

The mood in Istanbul in early 1915 needs to be carefully assessed, for many historians believe that it was precisely in this atmosphere that the Committee of Union and Progress took the decision to deal with the Armenians. As a friend of the Young

---

[38] Henry Morgenthau, *Ambassador Morgenthau's Story* (Detroit, 2003), 135.
[39] Ibid. 138.

244 RONALD GRIGOR SUNY

Turk leaders, Ambassador Morgenthau's account of the atmosphere in the government and the mentalities of Talaat and Enver is an essential source. He reports that the authority of the CUP at this time 'throughout the empire was exceedingly tenuous'. At the moment when the Allied fleet attacked the Dardanelles on 18 March, the Ottoman state 'was on the brink of dissolution'. Among the subject races the spirit of revolt was rapidly spreading. The Greeks and the Armenians would also have welcomed an opportunity to strengthen the hands of the Allies.[40] But the Allies did not break through; the Germans and Turks held them off, and the fleet pulled back. A month later the Allies landed troops at Gallipoli in another futile campaign. The Turks responded by rounding up foreigners to use as hostages placed among the Muslim villages in the Gallipoli region.[41]

Morgenthau elaborates a number of causes for the deportations and massacres of the Armenians, many of which have been foundational for western and Armenian historiography of the genocide. He begins with the nationalist perspective that the Young Turks were committed to a Turkified empire and adopted the policy of Abdul Hamid. 'Their passion for Turkifying the nation seemed to demand logically the extermination of all Christians—Greeks, Syrians, and Armenians.'[42] The error of past Muslim conquerors had been that they had not obliterated the Christians, 'a fatal error of statesmanship' that 'explained all the woes from which Turkey has suffered in modern times'.[43] The war presented an opportunity, for Russia, France, and Britain could no longer stand in the way as they had during Abdul Hamid's reign. 'Thus, for the first time in two centuries the Turks, in 1915, had their Christian populations utterly at their mercy. The time had finally come to make Turkey exclusively the country of the Turks.'[44]

The Armenians, in Morgenthau's account, are innocent. While the fact 'that the Armenians all over Turkey sympathized with the Entente was no secret', the Armenians acted with restraint. Their leaders urged them not to be provoked.[45] Rather than being primarily a matter of religious difference or conflict, the decision to carry out the deportations and massacres was a strategic choice. 'Undoubtedly religious fanaticism was an impelling motive with the Turkish and Kurdish rabble who slew

[40] Ibid. 158.   [41] Ibid. 176, 190–1.   [42] Ibid. 200.   [43] Ibid.
[44] Ibid. 201.   [45] Ibid. 203–4.

Explaining Genocide

Armenians as a service to Allah, but the men who really conceived the crime had no such motive. Practically all of them were atheists, with no more respect for Mohammedanism than for Christianity, and with them the one motive was cold-blooded, calculating state policy.'[46]

Already in January and February 1915, 'fragmentary reports began to filter in' to the American embassy of killings of Armenians, 'but the tendency was at first to regard these activities as mere manifestations of the disorders that had prevailed in the Armenian provinces for many years'.[47] Talaat and Enver dismissed such reports 'as wild exaggerations'.[48] What the Armenians would later call 'the defense of Van' was declared by officials 'a mob uprising that they would soon have under control'.[49] When prominent Armenians in the capital were arrested on 24 April, Morgenthau brought the issue up to Talaat, but the Young Turk leader argued that the government was acting in self-defence, that the Armenians in Van 'had already shown their abilities as revolutionists', and that Armenian leaders in Istanbul 'were corresponding with the Russians, and he had every reason to fear that they would start an insurrection against the Central Government'.[50]

Yet inseparable from their cool strategic calculation was the emotionally generated preference for the ends anticipated and the appropriate means to be used to achieve them. Talaat explained to Morgenthau his reasoning for the Young Turks' treatment of the Armenians: 'These people . . . refused to disarm when we told them to. They opposed us at Van and at Zeitoun, and they helped the Russians. There is only one way in which we can defend ourselves against them in the future, and that is just to deport them.'[51] When Morgenthau protested that that was not a reason for 'destroying a whole race' or 'making innocent women and children suffer', Talaat simply added: 'Those things are inevitable.'[52] In a later, extended conversation—this one without Morgenthau's Armenian dragoman present—Talaat spoke most frankly:

I have asked you to come today. . . so that I can explain our position on the whole Armenian subject. We base our objections to the Armenians on three distinct grounds. In the first place, they have enriched themselves at the expense of the Turks. In the second place,

[46] Ibid. 221–2.   [47] Ibid. 224.   [48] Ibid.   [49] Ibid.   [50] Ibid.
[51] Ibid. 230.   [52] Ibid.

246   RONALD GRIGOR SUNY

they are determined to domineer over us and to establish a separate
state. In the third place, they have openly encouraged our enemies.
They have assisted the Russians in the Caucasus and our failure there
is largely explained by their actions. We have therefore come to the
irrevocable decision that we shall make them powerless before this war
is ended.[53]

When Morgenthau attempted point by point to refute Talaat's
argument, Talaat interrupted: 'It is no use for you to argue . . .
we have already disposed of three quarters of the Armenians;
there are none at all left in Bitlis, Van, and Erzeroum. The
hatred between the Turks and the Armenians is now so intense
that we have got to finish with them. If we don't, they will plan
their revenge.' He told Morgenthau that he had 'asked you to
come here so as to let you know that our Armenian policy is
absolutely fixed and that nothing can change it. We will not have
the Armenians anywhere in Anatolia. They can live in the desert
but nowhere else.'[54] In despair, Morgenthau told Talaat: 'You
are making a terrible mistake', and repeated that three times.
'Yes, we may make mistakes', he replied, 'but—and he firmly
closed his lips and shook his head—"we never regret".'[55] Later
he told Morgenthau: 'No Armenian . . . can be our friend after
what we have done to them.'[56] On 3 August 1915 Morgenthau
wrote in his diary of his meeting with Talaat: 'He gave me the
impression that Talaat is the one who desires to crush the poor
Armenians.'[57] Talaat reportedly told friends with pride: 'I have
accomplished more toward solving the Armenian problem in
three months than Abdul Hamid accomplished in thirty years.'[58]

As more and more evidence came into the American embassy
that Armenians were being deported and murdered, Morgenthau
requested a meeting with Enver, who was extraordinarily frank
about what was happening.

The Armenians had a fair warning . . . of what would happen to them
in case they joined our enemies. Three months ago I sent for the
Armenian Patriarch and I told him that if the Armenians attempted to
start a revolution or to assist the Russians, I would be unable to prevent
mischief from happening to them. My warning produced no effect and
the Armenians started a revolution and helped the Russians. You know
what happened at Van. They obtained control of the city, used bombs

---

[53] Ibid. 231.   [54] Ibid. 232.   [55] Ibid.   [56] Ibid. 233.   [57] Ibid. 229.
[58] Ibid. 234.

Explaining Genocide

against government buildings, and killed a large number of Moslems. We knew that they were planning uprisings in other places. You must understand that we are now fighting for our lives at the Dardanelles and that we are sacrificing thousands of men. While we are engaged in such a struggle as this, we cannot permit people in our own country to attack us in the back. We have got to prevent this no matter what means we have to resort to. It is absolutely true that I am not opposed to the Armenians as a people. I have the greatest admiration for their intelligence and industry, and I would like nothing better than to see them become a real part of our nation. But if they ally themselves with our enemies, as they did in the Van district, they will have to be destroyed. I have taken pains to see that no injustice is done.[59]

Enver argued that European sympathy only encouraged the Armenians:

I am sure that if these outside countries did not encourage them, they would give up their efforts to oppose the present government and become law-abiding citizens. We now have this country in our absolute control and we can easily revenge ourselves on any revolutionists. . . . The great trouble with the Armenians is that they are separatists. They are determined to have a kingdom of their own, and they have allowed themselves to be fooled by the Russians. . . . You must remember that when we started this revolution in Turkey there were only two hundred of us. . . . It is our experience with revolutions which makes us fear the Armenians. If two hundred Turks could overturn the Government, then a few hundred bright, educated Armenians could do the same thing. We have therefore deliberately adopted the plan of scattering them so that they can do us no harm.[60]

Morgenthau went on:

In another talk with Enver I began by suggesting that the Central Government was probably not to blame for the massacres. I thought this would not be displeasing to him.

'Of course. I know that the Cabinet would never order such terrible things as have taken place,' I said. 'You and Talaat and the rest of the Committee can hardly be held responsible. Undoubtedly your subordinates have gone much further than you have ever intended. I realize that it is not always easy to control your underlings.'

Enver straightened up at once. I saw that my remarks, far from smoothing the way to a quiet and friendly discussion, had greatly offended him. I had intimated that things could happen in Turkey for which he and his associates were not responsible.

---

[59] Ibid. 236.   [60] Ibid. 236–8.

248 RONALD GRIGOR SUNY

'You are greatly mistaken,' he said. 'We have this country absolutely under our control. I have no desire to shift the blame on to our underlings and I am entirely willing to accept the responsibility myself for everything that has taken place. The Cabinet itself has ordered the deportations. I am convinced that we are completely justified in doing this owing to the hostile attitude of the Armenians toward the Ottoman Government, but we are the real rulers of Turkey, and no underling would dare proceed in a matter of this kind without our orders.'[61]

Morgenthau noted differences between Talaat and Enver. 'Enver always asserted that he wished to treat the Armenians with justice—in this his attitude to me was quite different from that of Talaat, who openly acknowledged his determination to deport them.'[62] He reported a conversation with the German naval attaché, Humann, who told the ambassador of Enver's hesitance about the deportation of the Armenians: 'At first Enver wanted to treat the Armenians with the utmost moderation, and four months ago he insisted that they be given another opportunity to demonstrate their loyalty. But after what they did at Van, he had to yield to the army, which had been insisting all along that it should protect its rear. The Committee decided upon the deportations and Enver reluctantly agreed.'[63] But even with these differences, the attitudes towards the Armenians of most of the Young Turk leaders were quite similar. Foreign Minister Halil Bey 'regarded the elimination of this race with utmost good humour', and defended the analysis of Enver.[64]

Morgenthau's account gives a compelling interpretation of the motivations of the principal Young Turk leaders. Fear was the driving emotion, insecurity compounded by the defeats in the winter of 1915 and the threats from Allied forces. Armenians were seen as an internal subversive force allied to the Russians. The war presented a unique opportunity to eliminate a long-term existential threat to the empire and the plans of the Young Turks for a more Turkified empire. Reason, strategic advantage, and emotion—fear, a sense of future danger, humiliation at the hands of Armenians, and a sense of betrayal—conspired together to generate plans for mass deportation and massacre.

Morgenthau's account is corroborated by Talaat in his posthumously published memoirs, where he revealed the thinking of the state authorities at the moment of decision and how the

[61] Ibid. 240–1. [62] Ibid. 240. [63] Ibid. 258. [64] Ibid. 246.

Explaining Genocide 249

deportations escalated into mass killing that involved ordinary civilians. Although he attempts to apologize for unintended excesses, he tells more about the motivations for mass killing than more recent apologists have.

The Porte, acting under the same obligation, and wishing to secure the safety of its army and its citizens, took energetic measures to check these uprisings. The deportation of the Armenians was one of these preventive measures.

I admit also that the deportation was not carried out lawfully everywhere. In some places unlawful acts were committed. The already existing hatred among the Armenians and Mohammedans, intensified by the barbarous activities of the former, had created many tragic consequences. Some of the officials abused their authority, and in many places people took preventive measures into their own hands and innocent people were molested. I confess it. I confess, also, that the duty of the Government was to prevent these abuses and atrocities, or at least to hunt down and punish their perpetrators severely. In many places, where the property and goods of the deported people were looted, and the Armenians molested, we did arrest those who were responsible and punished them according to the law. I confess, however, that we ought to have acted more sternly, opened up a general investigation for the purpose of finding out all the promoters and looters and punished them severely. . . .

The Turkish elements here referred to were shortsighted, fanatical, and yet sincere in their belief. The public encouraged them, and they had the general approval behind them. They were numerous and strong. . . .

Their open and immediate punishment would have aroused great discontent among the people, who favored their acts. An endeavor to arrest and to punish all those promoters would have created anarchy in Anatolia at a time when we greatly needed unity. It would have been dangerous to divide the nation into two camps, when we needed strength to fight outside enemies.[65]

Both Talaat and Morgenthau affirm that the murder of Armenians was not motivated primarily by religious fanaticism, though distinctions based on religion played a role. While most victims of the massacres were condemned to deportation or worse because of their ethno-religious identification, there were many cases in which people were saved from death or deportation when

---

[65] Talaat Pasha, 'Posthumous Memoirs of Talaat Pasha', *Current History*, 15/1 (Oct. 1921), 295.

250 RONALD GRIGOR SUNY

they converted to Islam.[66] The identity of Armenians for the Turks was not as indelibly fixed as the identity of Jews would be in the racist imagination of the Nazis. Still, the collective stereotypes of Armenians as grasping and mercenary, subversive and disloyal, turned them into a alien and unsympathetic category that then had to be eliminated.

In yet another memoir of a Turkish leader, this one written after his trial and conviction for crimes committed during the massacres and just before his suicide, the Young Turk governor of Diarbekir in 1915, Reşid Bey, draws a vivid picture of the chaos that accompanied the deportations.[67] As the Russians approached and order in the city disintegrated, Armenians, encouraged by the revolutionary committees, refused to be drafted. By this point the events at Van had already occurred, and Armenians were preparing for the worst. Muslims expected vengeful attacks by Armenians. The governor sent troops into Armenian homes and discovered caches of arms. At this point, he writes, he received the 'temporary law' (*Muvakkat Kanuni*) of 27 May 1915 that ordered deportation of the Armenians. He complained that there were not instructions on how to carry out the expulsions, which Armenians to deport. At first he deported only the men but then was ordered to send all Armenians into exile. With inadequate troops, no planning or provisions, the governor relied on Circassian gendarmes, decommissioned soldiers from the Balkan Wars, and local recruits from the peasantry and *esnaf* class. Thousands of Armenians deported from Bitlis, Kharput, and Trabizond passed through Diarbakir province. Looters and pillagers set upon them, following the Armenians for days to pick up what they could. Like Talaat, Reşid Bey claims that an orderly deportation was impossible, particularly in the face of frightened Muslims. Reşid Bey turned the homes of exiled Armenians over to Muslims, who then destroyed the houses in a mad search for hidden wealth. What is most vivid in this somewhat apologetic and self-serving account is the weakness and disorganization of the state authorities and the

[66] See Ara Sarafian, 'The Absorption of Armenian Women and Children into Muslim Households as a Structural Component of the Armenian Genocide', in Bartov and Mack (eds.), *In God's Name*, 209–21.

[67] Ahmet Mehmetefendioglu (ed.), *Dr. Reçid Bey'in Hatiralari, 'Sürgünden Intihara'* (Istanbul, 1992), esp. 43–76. My thanks to Fatma Müge Göçek for translating the relevant passages.

Explaining Genocide

251

massive participation of ordinary people in the looting and killing.

The Armenian genocide was the central event in the last stages of the dissolution of the Ottoman Empire. The traditional imperial paradigm that had reigned in the Ottoman Empire was steadily undermined by a number of factors: the revolutionary changes in the west that rendered the Ottoman Empire a backward and vulnerable society; the attempt to modernize along western lines by the *Tanzimat* reformers; the differentially successful adaptations to modern life by different *millets*, with the Christians and Jews ahead of the Muslims; and the discourse of the nation that created new sources of political legitimization and undermined the traditional imperial ones. After centuries of governing the Armenians as a separate ethno-religious community, the *Ermeni millet*, and conceiving of them as the 'loyal *millet*', the Ottoman state authorities and Turkish political elites, including the Young Turks, began to see Armenians as an alien people, as disloyal, subversive, 'separatist', and a threat to the unity of the empire, which now required greater homogenization. This perception was compounded more broadly by anxiety about the relative economic success of Armenian businessmen and craftsmen, the competition for the limited economic resources, particularly land, between Kurds, Turks, and Armenians in eastern Anatolia, and a sense that Armenian progress was reversing the traditional imperial status hierarchy with Muslims above the *dhimmi*. A hostile disposition towards the Armenians made Turks more likely to see their actions not as defensive but rebellious, not as loyal but treacherous, and allowed Turks to take vengeful action against these traitors.

When in the first year of the First World War the Young Turks suffered a series of defeats in the east, their sense of an imminent Armenian danger became acute, and they decided to carry out a vicious policy of deportation and massacre to clear the region of Armenians. Initiated by the state in the brutalizing context of war, the removal of the Armenians soon became a massive campaign of murder. Social hostilities between Armenians and Turks, Kurds and Armenians, fed the mass killings, which the state encouraged (or at least did little to discourage). More than any other instance of *surgun*, the genocide came to be seen as an opportunity to rid the empire of the Armenian problem, which had been used as a wedge by Russians and other Europeans to interfere in the Ottoman Empire. While fear and resentment, anger and hatred contributed to the disposition of the leaders who ordered the deportations, so did a perverse sense of justice and revenge against an internal threat.

Social science, at least political science and economics, has in the last decades moved away from affective explanations towards a model of human action directed by rational assessment of costs and benefits. Yet emotions are central to human beliefs, values, actions, group formation, and social relationships, and therefore must be incorporated into explanations of ethnic and national identification, ethnic, religious, and national conflict, and violence. Among the most salient political emotions related to ethnic identification and conflict, national identity, and nationalism are fear, anger, hatred, and resentment, but also, on the positive side, empathy, compassion, love, and pride. In his reports on the Young Turk leaders, Morgenthau saw fear as prevalent. The Armenians' role in Ottoman society, their successes at the expense of Turks, their lack of gratitude, and, in general, the reversal of traditional status relationships in which Muslims were meant to be on top and Christians below, all contributed to a generalized resentment of Turks towards Armenians. Anger and fear were also expressed—anger at rebellion and fear produced by the perceived Armenian threat to the war effort given their relationship with the Russians. But anger is an emotion directed at what someone has done to you, while hatred is an even more powerful and destructive emotion directed at someone for what they are. For the Young Turks anger had turned into hatred of a group that was now conceived as an existential threat to their empire and their rulership.

The Armenian genocide had its origins in the minds of a small group of Turkish politicians associated with the Committee of Union and Progress (Young Turks). Fear and anger, resentment and hatred are all found in the affective disposition of Enver and Talaat as related by Ambassador Morgenthau. Given their strategic aim to preserve the empire, and their conceptualization of the Armenians as internal traitors threatening its existence, Young Turk anger metastasized into hatred and made possible the choice to deport and murder the Armenians. Here was an ethnic cleansing combined with mass annihilation carried out not

Explaining Genocide

by a nation-state, but by a decaying empire determined to save itself. That salvation required, in the minds of the Young Turks and many of their German allies, the elimination of the Armenians. Both the radicalization of their intentions and the final implementation of their plans occurred in the context of a deepening political and military crisis and the near destruction of the Ottoman state at the hands of external enemies—a crisis that consolidated a hostile affective disposition that biased the Young Turks to suspect that Armenians presented a mortal danger to the empire.

But these attitudes, seemingly confirmed by isolated instances of Armenian behaviour, were self-deceptive; they were pathological and led to a misrepresentation of the actual political and social environment in the Ottoman Empire. Armenians served in the Ottoman Army; they were productive citizens; most were not disloyal or interested in separatism. The very actions taken by the Young Turks pushed Armenians to act in ways that conformed to the CUP's image of treacherous Armenians. Defence became rebellion. Turkish state violence against Armenians then put the empire in greater danger and helped to bring about its defeat. In one aspect genocide was instrumentally irrational, based on incorrect beliefs, self-deception, driven by a distorted emotional disposition and web of beliefs that constructed an Armenian enemy—the same Armenian enemy that the current Turkish deniers and their pseudo-scientific allies claim actually existed and was engaged in a civil war against the empire. Yet in another, retrospective perspective, ethnic cleansing and mass murder appear more rational—the founding crime on which the succeeding regime, the Republic of Turkey, a relatively homogeneous nation-state, was built.

10

Trial Run: The Deportation of the Terek Cossacks 1920

SHANE O'ROURKE

We have definitely decided to expel eighteen *stanitsas* along this side of the Terek with a population of 60,000 to Stavropol' *guberniia*. How can we do this? No government whatsoever can simply drive them away. In fact we have done this in relation to three *stanitsas*, but we had to suppress a revolt there. (Now this matter has been resolved and places have been fixed for their resettlement.)

(G. K. (Sergo) Ordzhonikidze)[1]

Sergo Ordzhonikidze's speech to a congress of the Don and Caucasus party organizations in Vladikavkaz on 29 October 1920 was one of the very few public references at the time and, indeed, throughout the existence of the Soviet regime to a momentous operation that had been under way fitfully since the spring of 1920, but had expanded dramatically in the autumn. It was the only precise reference, overt or veiled, to the intended scale of the deportations, involving almost a quarter of the entire Terek Cossack population.[2] The deportations began in April 1920 and ended prematurely in January 1921. By the end of the operation all the inhabitants of nine *stanitsas*, approximately 30,000 people, had been expelled.[3] The first mass deportation in Soviet history was followed almost immediately by similar operations in Kazakhstan and Turkmenistan and the following year in Tambov province.[4] Deportation, which was to become

---

[1] G. K. Ordzhonikidze, *Izbrannye Stat'i i Rechi* (Grozny, 1962), 104.

[2] In 1914 the Terek Cossacks numbered 234,692 out of a total population of 1,235,223. R. Kh. Gugov, *Sovmestnaia Bor'ba Narodov Tereka za Sovetskuiu Vlast'* (Hal'chik, 1975), 26–7.

[3] *Rossüskii Gosudarstvennyi Arkhiv Sotsial'no-Politicheskoi Istorrii* (hereafter RGASPI), f. 64, op. 1, d. 247, ll. 105–6. (Given the situation at the time these population figures and subsequent must be treated with some caution. My sense is that they are broadly accurate if not exact. The total of 30,677 in this file is an underestimation since it did not include Assinovskaia, the last *stanitsa* to be deported.)

[4] Terry Martin, *The Affirmative Action Empire: Nations and Nationalism in the Soviet Union, 1923–1939* (New York, 2001), 59–61; N. F. Bugai, *Kazachestvo Rossii, Ottorzhenie, Priznanie, Bozrozhdenie (1917–90 gody)* (Moscow, 2000), 42.

emblematic of the Stalin years, was already a routine policy tool by 1921.

The fact of the deportations has long been known, but little investigated. In Soviet times it was hardly ever mentioned, but since the end of the Soviet Union reference to the Terek deportations has appeared in many works in Russia and abroad.[5] A small selection of the documents relating to the deportation was published in Russia in 2004.[6] None of these, however, provides a comprehensive account of the deportations. Figures vary as to the number of *stanitsas* deported, the number of people involved, and even more the scope of the operation. There is virtually nothing about the precise circumstances in which the deportations were initiated and carried out, nor has the key role of Sergo Ordzhonikidze been appreciated. The significance of the deportations in the short and long term extends far beyond the relatively small numbers of people involved and this, too, needs to be articulated.

The Significance of the Deportations

The deportation of a quarter of the Terek Cossack population was an attempt by the Soviet state to produce an immediate and permanent solution to the strife racking the former Terek Voisko or, as it became known from 1920, the Autonomous Mountain Republic. At the core of this strife was a savage ethnic war between the Terek Cossacks on one side and the Chechen and Ingush people on the other. Revolution and civil war had only made an already intractable problem even more irreconcilable as both communities actively sought the expulsion and preferably destruction of the other and the aid of the Soviet state in doing so. The new Soviet state, however, had its own interests and priorities in the region that sometimes coincided with the interests of one community, sometimes with the other, and often with neither. These priorities were not stable and were subject to abrupt changes with potentially catastrophic consequences for both communities.

[5] See e.g. N. F. Bugai and A. M. Gonov, *Kavkaz, Narody v Eshelonakh (20–60-e gody)* (Moscow, 1998), 81–8; Bugai, *Kazachestvo Rossii*, 25–36; V. D. Dzidoev, *Belyi i Krasnyi Terror na Severnom Kavkaze v 1917–1918 godakh* (Vladikavkaz, 2000), 123–4; Martin, *Affirmative Action Empire*, 60–1.

[6] *Shpion*, 1 (1994), 47–54.

Trial Run

Important as the Terek deportations were to the communities and territories where they took place, their significance extended beyond those concerned. They illuminate important facets of the early Soviet regime. They clarify continuities and discontinuities with tsarist policies, particularly in a colonial setting;[7] the deportations connect Soviet policy to the mainstream of European colonial practices less than three years after the October Revolution;[8] they reflect the total mobilization of societies during the First World War and continued, in the Russian case, during the civil war.[9]

However, the deportations have in addition a peculiarly Soviet context. On a practical level they were part of a tradition already established in the civil war of radical policies launched without preparation or planning, demanding that Soviet officials improvise solutions on the spot.[10] They were indicative that mass violence against the civilian population was not just a response to military emergency, but had become a permanent part of Soviet political culture. The deportations emphasized, in addition, the critical importance of individuals situated strategically in the Soviet power structure in formulating and carrying out policy.[11]

At a deeper level the deportations reflected the conflation of ethnic identity and political loyalty that had developed under the tsarist government during the war and which the Soviet state had began to draw close to, particularly in regard to the Cossacks.[12] But the Terek deportations marked a significant intensification of these tendencies which admitted no exceptions whatsoever. Finally, the deportations sprang from the millenarian strand in

---

[7] Austin Jersild, *Orientalism and Empire: North Caucasus Mountain Peoples and the Georgian Frontier, 1845–1917* (Montreal, 2002), 22–32; Andreas Kappeler, *The Russian Empire: A Multiethnic History* (London, 2001), 179–85.

[8] Peter Holquist, 'To Count, to Extract and to Exterminate: Population Statistics and Population Politics in Late Imperial and Soviet Russia', in Ronald Grigor Suny and Terry Martin (eds.), *A State of Nations: Empire and Nation-Making in the Age of Lenin and Stalin* (Oxford, 2001), 111–44.

[9] Ibid. 124–6; Eric Lohr, *Nationalizing the Russian Empire: The Campaign against Enemy Aliens during World War I* (Cambridge, Mass., 2003), esp. ch. 5, 121–65.

[10] See e.g. Julie Hessler, *A Social History of Soviet Trade: Trade Policy, Retail Practices, and Consumption, 1917–1953* (Princeton, 2004), 4–9.

[11] A. V. Kvashonkin, 'Sovetizatsiia Zakavkaz'ia v Perepiske Bol'shevistskogo Rukovodstva 1920–22', *Cahiers du monde russe*, 38 (1997), 164–5; Gerald Easter, *Reconstructing the State: Personal Networks and Elite Identity in Soviet Russia* (Cambridge, 2000), 13–16.

[12] Peter Holquist, *Making War, Forging Revolution: Russia's Continuum of Crisis, 1914–1921* (Cambridge, Mass., 2002), 174–9.

258   SHANE O'ROURKE

Bolshevik ideology which constantly sought to reduce highly complex problems to binary opposites, allowing for an equally simple but drastic solution.[13]

In the midst of the great themes of colonialism, wartime mobilization, and ideology we should not lose sight of the two subordinate populations at the core of the Terek tragedy. They, too, had their own interests and agendas behind which they hoped to enlist the support of the powerful new state. They did not passively wait for their fates to be decided by the new overarching imperial power, but through their desires, actions, and reactions helped shape Soviet policy, although not always in the way they wanted.

Tsarist Policy in the North Caucasus

Until the mid nineteenth century tsarist policy half-heartedly attempted to assimilate the population of the North Caucasus by demonstrating the manifest superiority of the Russian culture. Their chosen instrument for this was the Terek Cossacks, but far from acting as a conduit for Russian influence the Cossacks appeared much more receptive to the indigenous cultures of the North Caucasus.[14] In the early nineteenth century the government began to abandon assimilation and to experiment with expulsion.[15] This was not fully articulated until the second half of the nineteenth century, but it marked an important change in tsarist policies towards colonial peoples. The campaign launched between 1863 and 1864 in the Western Caucasus had as its primary goal not the conquest and occupation of the territory, but the expulsion of the population. By the time it was over almost 500,000 people had been expelled from their homes.[16]

Government policy shifted from assimilation to expulsion in the light of heightened concern over its ability to defend the empire's borders in the aftermath of the Crimean War and fears of new

---

[13] Igal Halfin, *From Darkness to Light: Class, Consciousness, and Salvation in Revolutionary Russia* (Pittsburgh, 2000), 78–84.

[14] Thomas M. Barrett, *At the Edge of Empire: The Terek Cossacks and the North Caucasus Frontier, 1700–1860* (Boulder, Colo., 1999), 6.

[15] T. Kh. Kumykov (ed.), *Problemy Kavkazskoi Voiny i Vycelenie Cherkesov v Predely Osmanskoi Imperii (20–70-e gg XIX V)* (Hal'chik, 2001), 12–15.

[16] Ibid. 22.

Trial Run

European war. These fears were compounded by what was perceived as the irreversible hostility of the non-Russian population of the borderlands, particularly the Poles on the western borders and the Muslim peoples of the North Caucasus.[17] Russian practice in the North Caucasus drew on contemporary European practices which allowed colonial peoples to be expelled and deported although, as yet, they could not be applied in Europe.[18]

The Terek Voisko to 1914

The Terek Voisko had been reorganized in 1860 as part of the ongoing conquest of the North Caucasus. The mountainous terrain and the fierce opposition of the Chechen and Ingush people to the conquest convinced the government to expel the indigenous population rather than engage in a protracted and costly military occupation and pacification of the territory.[19] Tsar Alexander II's Chief Minister Loris-Melikov justified these policies on the grounds that they 'would once and for all free us from our onerous position in Chechnia'.[20] Over 20,000 Chechen families were forcibly driven into the Ottoman Empire in 1865.[21] Other Chechen and Ingush suffered expropriation and eviction from their homes, but contrived to remain within the Terek Voisko, living under a virtual military dictatorship.[22] The Cossacks were the prime beneficiaries of this policy, rewarded for their loyalty with the land and property of the expelled Chechens.[23] The Sunzhenskaia line, the focus of the Soviet deportations, was established on the lands vacated by the Chechen and Ingush.[24]

Contrary to the hopes of Loris-Melikov, the policy of expulsions and expropriations did not establish ethnic harmony. Far from the clean lines and ethnically compact areas envisaged by

---

[17] William C. Fuller, *Strategy and Power in Russia 1600–1914* (New York, 1992), 279–80.

[18] Holquist, 'To Count, to Extract, to Exterminate', 116.

[19] Kumykov (ed.), *Problemy Kavkazskoi Voiny*, 14–15.

[20] Ibid.

[21] Ibid. 21.

[22] Gugov, *Sovemestnaia Bor'ba Narodov Tereka*, 55.

[23] Kappeler, *The Russian Empire*, 184; Jersild, *Orientalism and Empire*, 23–4.

[24] Dzidoev, *Belyi i Krasnyi Terror*, 34.

Loris-Melikov, what emerged was, in fact, an even more variegated mosaic with Cossack *stanitsas* and Chechen and Ingush *auls* existing in close proximity to each other. Living in sight of the land that they or their fathers had owned only deepened the rage of the dispossessed. Nor did time reconcile them to their loss. In 1921 Chechen and Ingush representatives told a Soviet commission of inquiry into the situation in the Mountain Republic: 'There was a time when our forefathers had rich and fertile lands. But they were ripped from us by force of arms by black Tsarist generals and their stooges; and the mountain peoples were driven on to the bare and infertile slopes. . . . we say expand our territory, expel the Cossacks from their *stanitsas*.'[25] Tsarist policy had not achieved ethnic peace; nor had it enhanced internal and external security through the expulsions. In fact, it had achieved precisely the opposite. The fall of the tsarist regime bequeathed these goals unfulfilled to its successor. They were to remain as elusive to the Soviet regime as to the tsarist.

Revolution and Civil War

The October Revolution unleashed the long-suppressed conflict in the Terek Voisko. The civil war on the Terek followed its own intrinsic paths as well as merging with the wider conflict. The fighting in the territory was merciless from the very beginning. Tsarist legacies of expulsion, expropriation, and mass violence provided an example to both communities on how to conduct an ethnic conflict.[26] Neither community saw the solution to their problems in a redistribution of land, which became a secondary issue. For both communities the primary goal was the physical destruction of the other or, at the very least, its expulsion.[27] What made any compromise impossible was the torrent of violence unleashed by the civil war. In 1918 the Cossack elites offered to ally with the Soviet state if it would commit to an even more brutal colonial war against the Chechen and Ingush.[28] Equally, the Chechen and Ingush saw in the Soviet state the means to regain for themselves their ancestral lands. A delegation of

---

[25] *Gosudarstvennyi Arkhiv Rossiiskoi Federatsoi* (hereafter GARF), f. 1235, op. 95, d. 517, l. 174.
[26] Dzidoev, *Belyi i Krasnyi Terror*, 36.   [27] Ibid. 66.   [28] Ibid. 38.

Trial Run

Ingush to a Soviet commission in 1918 announced: 'We the Ingush of the village Ekadzhiev and almost all the Ingush people stand on a platform of Soviet power. We Ingush, not only of the village Ekadzhiev, but all the Ingush will defend Soviet power not only to the smallest child, but to the last drop of blood.'[29] Orzhonikidze himself acknowledged in a report to the Council of Ministers in 1919 that 'this recognition of Soviet power by both sides took place purely for tactical reasons'.[30]

The new Soviet government sought to orient itself between the different factions, trying to forge alliances and recruit soldiers for its cause. Ordzhonikidze expressed the instinctive sympathy of the party and government for the Chechens and Ingush in his analysis of the political situation to the Council of Ministers.

Here we have on the one hand the land-rich, wealthy Cossacks, enjoying all rights in the past—'peasant landlords' if we might express it so—on the other hand the *inogorodnie* (outsider) population and highlanders who were without lands and rights in the past. All the non-Cossack population in the past in the North Caucasus was in complete political subordination to the Cossacks and this in spite of the fact that the Cossacks consisted of not more than a fifth of the total population of the North Caucasus.[31]

This instinctive sympathy, however, had to be balanced with the need to keep open the possibility of attracting Cossacks to the Soviet side. Many Cossacks did, indeed, fight with the Red Army and Ordzhonikidze frequently singled them out for praise in his reports of the civil war in the North Caucasus.[32]

All sides conducted themselves in a particularly brutal manner from the beginning of the civil war. Attacks on the civilian population, the burning of settlements, and the expulsion of entire communities became standard practice. Between November 1917 and spring of 1918 three Cossack *stanitsas*, Fel'marshal'skaia, Khakhanovskaia, and Ilynskaia, were destroyed by the Ingush, forcing over 4,000 people to flee their homes.[33] The Cossacks likewise sought the physical removal of the indigenous population,

---

[29] RGASPI f. 64, op. 1, d. 247, ll. 3–4.

[30] Ordzhonikidze, *Izbrannye Stat'i i Rechi*, 65.

[31] Ibid. 60–1.

[32] e.g. on 7 Feb. 1919 he telegraphed Lenin that 'the Cossacks of the Sunzhenskaia Line under the command of c[omrade] D'iakov are standing firm for Soviet power, threatening with artillery counter-revolutionary *stanitsas*'. Ibid. 58.

[33] RGASPI f. 64, op. 1, d. 247, ll. 104–6.

consciously resorting to terror to achieve this.[34] After the fall of Grozny to the Volunteer Army in 1919, the victorious Whites hanged more than 2,000 people.[35] The indiscriminate mass violence of the civil war demolished any lingering barriers confining the war to combatants or even adult males. Women, children, and the aged were all targets whose destruction was as necessary and as legitimate as the destruction of opposing armies.

In the spring of 1920 the Red Army began the decisive reoccupation of the North Caucasus. Despite its near complete triumph over the White armies, the strategic situation of the regime remained perilous. Its armed forces were stretched thinly around the former empire. Conflict was already looming with the Transcaucasian states where the British and the Turks were actively working to consolidate their spheres of influence.[36] In April 1920 war broke out with Poland and in the summer of that year, the last White commander, General Wrangel, attempted to re-ignite the civil war in the North Caucasus by launching a seaborne attack across the Black Sea on the Taman peninsula, hoping to draw the Cossacks of the Kuban and Terek back into the struggle.[37] Internally, Soviet control outside the cities was tenuous at best. Surrounded by enemies from without and within, a constant sense of insecurity and threat pervaded the regime and its officials.

Soviet forces responsible for occupying the North Caucasus were under the command of Sergo Ordzhonikidze, compatriot and close ally of Stalin. Ordzhonikidze was appointed head of the Caucasian Buro of the Party or Kavbiuro, which had authority over all Soviet institutions and personnel in the North Caucasus.[38] In addition, Lenin had personally cabled Ordzhonikidze: 'concerning the land question you can act independently. Advise, however, any measures taken by you in this area.'[39] Answerable in theory to the Politburo, Ordzhonikidze was in effect a free agent in the North Caucasus enjoying exceptional latitude to formulate and implement his own policy in the territory. It was an opportunity ideally suited to a man of Ordzhonikidze's temperament.[40]

[34] Dzidoev, *Belyi i Krasnyi Terror*, 88.
[35] Gugov, *Sovetskaia Bor'ba Narodov Tereka*, 359.
[36] Kvashonkin, 'Sovetizatsiia Zakavkaz'ia', 165–6.
[37] Bugai, *Kazachestvo Rossii*, 88–9.   [38] Ibid. 75.   [39] Lenin, PS, T.51, 178.
[40] For a discussion of Ordzhonikidze's character see O. V. Khlevniuk, *In Stalin's Shadow: The Career of 'Sergo Ordzhonikidze'* (New York, 1995), 17–20 and Dzidoev, *Belyi i Krasnyi Terror*, 146.

Trial Run

263

The Revolt of the Sunzhenskaia Line

In September 1920 an armed revolt against Soviet power broke out among five Cossack *stanitsas* on the Sunzhenskaia line of the Terek. The Cossacks cut the main railway line, blew up bridges, and shot up some trains.[41] On one level this was no different from hundreds of other revolts against Soviet power that were taking place at the same time. Yet the authorities regarded the revolt as part of a seamless attack on the Soviet state orchestrated by its enemies.[42] A member of Ordzhonikidze's staff recalled: 'in the autumn of 1920 the English imperialists unified all the counter-revolutionary elements including the Terek and Sunzhenskoe White Cossacks against Soviet power.'[43] It is possible that Ordzhonikidze took the revolt as a personal insult since one of the trains attacked by the Cossacks had been carrying delegates from the Congress of the Peoples of the East which had just taken place in Baku. On the train were such national figures as Mikoian and international ones as Bela Kun and John Reed. Mikoian in his memoirs related how Ordzhonikidze sent his personal armoured train to ensure the further safe passage of the delegates.[44]

Whatever the causes, the fury with which Ordzhonikidze reacted still echoes almost ninety years later in the order issued on 23 October 1920:

Cossacks of the Terek district, the Terek and Sunzhenskaia lines have repeatedly organized rebellions against Soviet power. The traitors fell on separate units of the Red Army, shooting up a passenger train, sabotaging the railroad, bridges etc. Suppressing these rebellions with an armed fist, the representatives of Soviet power on the Terek were absolutely humanitarian, even in relation to the rebel *stanitsas*. The most recent events, the uprising of Kalinovskaia *stanitsa* on the Terek, of Ermolovskaia, of Zakan-Iurtskaia/Romanovskaia, Samashkinskaia, and Mikhailovskaia on the Sunzha, have overfilled the cup of the peace-loving, long-suffering Soviet power. Member of the Revolutionary Council of the Kavfront, Com Ordzhonikidze orders the following: first Kalinovskaia *stanitsa*—burn it. Second *stanitsas* Ermolovskaia, Zakan-Iurtovskaia/Romanovskaia, Samashkinskaia, and Mikhailovskaia to be

---

[41] RGASPI f. 85, op. 11, d. 131, l. 12.

[42] Bugai, *Kazachestvo Rossii*, 88–90.

[43] R. G. Seiraniat (ed.), *O Sergo Ordzhonikidze: Vospominaniia, Ocherki i Stat'I Sovremenikov* (Moscow, 1981), 103.

[44] A. I. Mikoian, *V Nachale Dvadtsatykh* (Moscow, 1985), 10.

given to the poorest, landless population and in the first place to the Chechen people who have always been devoted to Soviet power.[45]

Ordzhonikidze then spelt out what was to happen to the Cossack population of the *stanitsas*.

All the male population from 18–50 of the aforementioned *stanitsas* to be loaded on to special trains and sent under escort to the north for heavy forced labour. Old people, women, and children are to be evicted from the *stanitsa*, but are permitted to resettle in *stanitsas* and *khutora* in the north. Horses, sheep, and other livestock and any property suitable for the army to be given to the Kavtrudarmy and its corresponding organizations.[46]

Ordzhonikidze ended with a warning: 'All commanders and commissars are to declare to the entire Cossack population that in future for any infringement whatsoever against Soviet power and also for attempts at rebellion they will receive exactly the same punishment.' The men from Kalinovskaia were sent to Arkhangelsk in the far north while the men from the other *stanitsas* were sent to the mines of the Donbass as slave labourers.[47]

The Process of Deportation

The order from Ordzhonikidze created a commission in each *stanitsa* to carry out the evictions and deportations under the overall command of one of Ordzhonikidze's trusted subordinates, Vrachev. Vrachev was responsible for organizing the deportation of approximately 22,000 people: the entire population of the five *stanitsas*.[48] The priority was to remove the adult males and this appears to have been done swiftly. At the first meeting of Vrachev's commission in late October, he reported 'the evictions of the men have began and without particular obstacles should be completed within a very few days'.[49] After the men had gone, there still remained over 14,000 women, children, and elderly.[50] Removing these, however, turned out to be much more complicated.

[45] RGASPI f. 85, op. 11, d. 131, ll. 12–13.
[46] Ibid.
[47] GARF f. 1235, op. 95, d. 517, l. 210; RGASPI f. 85, op. 11, d. 131, l. 1.
[48] RGASPI f. 64, op. 1, d. 247, ll. 104–6.
[49] *Rossiiskii Gosudarstvennyi Voennyi Arkhiv* (hereafter RGVA), f. 217, op. 5, d. 1, l. 1.
[50] RGASPI f. 64, op. 1, d. 247, l. 107.

Trial Run

The order from Ordzhonikidze stipulated that the Cossacks were to be stripped of their property, evicted from their homes, and deported, but provided no details on how any of this was to be done. Officials carrying out the deportation had to improvise the operation even as it was under way. Not surprisingly, things began to go awry almost immediately. Lines of communication between the different branches and layers of the bureaucracy broke down, leaving Ordzhonikidze's immediate subordinates Kirov, Kvirikeliia, and Kosior completely in the dark as to what was going on. A conversation by direct wire between Kvirikeliia and Kosior on 3 November 1920 clarified only the degree of chaos engulfing the operation.

C. Kvirikeliia: For the last few days we have had no information whatsoever about the course of the evictions. I and Kirov request you to inform us in more detail if possible how the business of deporting the Cossacks is progressing.

C. Kosior: . . . please make clear the following matter. From the Oblast *Ispolkom* we have not received any information relating to the resettlement of the expelled and the commission which has as its task the eviction of the five *stanitsas*, finds itself in complete ignorance of where to resettle the evicted, who is to be responsible for them, and who to give orders to. If the commission resettles the Cossacks on its own responsibility, then it is unavoidable that the work will be chaotic and possibly it will be necessary to do it again.[51]

Characteristically, the solution to the problem was to insert another layer of bureaucracy into the operation in the form of a new commission. This commission, which began work on 3 November 1920, had some strategic sense of what was necessary and took a much more robust attitude to coordinating the different branches of the bureaucracy. Even so, it was shocked to find that Vrachev's commission had not bothered to count the number of deportees and, in some cases, had simply loaded them onto trains without the least idea of where they were being taken.[52] Nor did it prove easy to impose its will on the plethora of organizations involved in the deportation. For example, the Kavtrudarmy which controlled the movement of trains promised to inform the new commission in advance whenever trains were

---

[51] RGVA f. 217, op. 5, d. 2, l. 42.
[52] RGASPI f. 64, op. 1, d. 247, l. 15.

being dispatched, but the very next day sent a train without informing it and the day after unilaterally announced that it was suspending any further shipments, much to the commission's fury.[53]

What in other circumstances might have been a black farce had desperate consequences for the deportees. Delays in moving the expelled Cossacks exposed them to the fury of the surrounding population. The crushing of the rising and the overt support of the Soviet state for mass expulsions allowed the indigenous communities to take their revenge for the decades of their own suffering, particularly when it became clear that Vrachev, far from trying to prevent the attacks, was encouraging them. The commission set up on 3 November to take control of the operation sarcastically asked Vrachev who had given permission for the robberies to take place.[54] Large gangs of Chechens, Ingush, and Ossetians descended on the now defenceless *stanitsas* to rob, kidnap, and kill. Officials appointed to assist in the deportations were horrified at what they witnessed. M. V. Dergachev, the head of the Terek land survey team, reported at the end of November 1920: 'From all sides information is coming in that in all the *stanitsas*, both among those who have been expelled and among those still subject to resettlement, robbery and murder reigns. Peaceful inhabitants are terrorized.'[55] Kvirikeliia acknowledged the collusion of Vrachev's officials in this violence and simply responded that 'members of the commission are themselves robbing', although he did add that 'it was necessary to apply the rod to the backs of these people'.[56]

The spiral of violence set in motion by the deportations was now so great that Kosior, in his capacity as commander of the Kavtrudarmy, warned that the state was losing control of the Mountain Republic. 'Hundreds of Chechens are attacking the evicted *stanitsas* every day and if these *stanitsas* are not given to the Chechens as a matter of urgency a real war will flare up. I urgently request that you send trains.'[57] Thousands of defenceless people waiting helplessly for transport with their property up for grabs acted as mobilizing agent for the Chechen and Ingush populations, who saw it as an opportunity for a final reckoning with their hated enemies. The suffering of the Cossacks was

---

[53] Ibid.   [54] Ibid., l. 16.   [55] GARF f. 1235, op. 95, d. 517, l. 200.
[56] Ibid.   [57] RGVA f. 217, op. 5, d. 2, l. 12.

Trial Run

immaterial to the Soviet state, but the mass theft of state property and the collapse of Soviet authority were matters of the deepest concern.

The trains that did trickle through to the *stanitsas* were too few in number to move the thousands of people waiting to be deported. But this was of little concern to the organizers of the deportations. Vrachev's priority was to remove the Cossacks as fast as possible. He reported simply that 2,211 families were put onto 537 cattle trucks.[58] Other officials, however, were more forthcoming.

Dear Comrades I am reporting for your information that the resettlement is a terrible and horrible nightmare. People are forced into wagons with lightning speed. They have sent wagons in such numbers that those being resettled have no possibility of taking even the barest minimum with them. This is a fact. For carrying 200 families only 25–30 wagons have been sent. Heaps of items have been abandoned to the mercy of fate.[59]

The process of deportation was starting to take on parallels with the Armenian deportations of 1915 on the other side of the Caucasus mountain range: the disarming and removal of the adult male population; the repeated attacks on those waiting for deportation or in the process of deportation by the surrounding population; and, finally, the clear encouragement to such attacks by officials on the ground. What was lacking and, in the end, critical to stopping the attacks before they reached Armenian levels was the absence of an explicitly murderous intent on the part of the central government.[60] Officials from the centre repeatedly condemned the attacks on the Cossacks and the collusion of local officials, most notably in the inquiry set up by the government under the chairmanship of the veteran Bolshevik Nevksii in January 1921 to review the situation in the Mountain Republic.

Deportations and the Soviet State

The deportations of October 1920 were an immediate response to an unforeseen act. The rebellion caught the Soviet authorities

---

[58] Ibid., l. 57.   [59] Ibid., d. 1, l. 18.
[60] For this critical factor see Norman M. Naimark, *Fires of Hatred: Ethnic Cleansing in Twentieth-Century Europe* (Cambridge, Mass., 2001), 98–9; Eric D. Weitz, *A Century of Genocide: Utopias of Race and Nation* (Princeton, 2003), 12–13.

268

SHANE O'ROURKE

by surprise and the furious reaction of Ordzhonikidze was entirely genuine. The deportation order was explicitly punitive, serving not only to punish the rebellious *stanitsas*, but also to serve as a warning to the rest of the Cossack population. Ordzhonikidze boasted to a party conference in Tiflis that 'the expulsion of five *stanitsas* of the Sunzhenskoe line has had a stunning impact on the Cossacks'.[61] No other community had as yet been punished in this manner. Nevertheless the policy was neither unpremeditated nor a spur of the moment decision of local officials, but was something the Soviet state had been working towards since the October Revolution. Nor was it a coincidence that the Cossacks were the first people to be subjected to such a policy.

The regime had already experimented with extremely radical methods of dealing with the Cossacks earlier in the civil war. In January 1919 it had issued instructions to local officials in the Don Cossack territory that arguably amounted to an order for genocide.[62] Among the supplementary measures to extermination contained in the order were policies that plainly envisaged mass expulsions and deportations. Point three of the circular decreed that it was necessary 'to take all measures assisting the resettlement of newly arrived poor, organizing this settlement where possible', and it ended with an instruction to the Ministry of Agriculture to work out quickly practical measures concerning the mass resettlement of the poor on Cossack land to be carried out through corresponding Soviet institutions.[63]

Local officials, encouraged by the explicit instructions to interpret the decree in the harshest possible manner, amplified the points relating to deportation. The party organization on the Don resolved 'to take all measures for the expulsion of the Cossacks with the exception of Red Cossacks from a 50 km strip on both sides of the railway and to colonize it with armed supporters of Soviet power'.[64] Point eleven of this resolution approved the 'resettlement of families of counter-revolutionary Cossacks and the confiscation of all property', while another

[61] Ordzhonikidze, *Izbrannye Stat'i i Rechi*, 12.

[62] For a discussion of this see Peter Holquist, ' "Conduct Merciless Mass Terror": Decossackization on the Don, 1919', *Cahiers du monde russe*, 38 (1997), 127–62.

[63] RGASPI f. 17, op. 65, d. 5, l. 216.

[64] Ibid., d. 35, l. 215.

point resolved that 'Cossacks over 45 who do not have sons in the Red Army and where there is information suggesting that they might support the counter-revolutionary movement are to be deported'.[65]

In the ebb and flow of the fighting on the Don in 1919 none of these deportations could be implemented. The absence of a single authoritative figure capable of imposing his will on the different Soviet agencies operating in the Don also probably impeded the implementation of any deportation. Yet the drift towards mass deportation was clearly evident, as were the widening categories of people liable for deportation. Central and local organizations interacted to radicalize further an already radical policy. Once this process of cumulative radicalism had started it was extremely difficult to stop.

Similar processes were at work on the Terek, but with the addition of intense pressure from the indigenous population to expel the Cossacks. When Soviet power was re-established in the Terek district in the spring of 1920, rumours swept the Cossack *stanitsas* that there was going to be a mass expulsion of Cossacks. Ordzhonikidze, far from denying the rumours, stated that 'in order to regulate mutual relations between the Russian population and the indigenous one, it is necessary to remove intermingling by resettling all the *stanitsas* which are territorially attached to the indigenous population'.[66]

This was no idle threat from Ordzhonikidze. In April 1920 three *stanitsas* numbering almost 9,000 were expelled, deported, and their land given over to the Ingush.[67] The little information that there is on this deportation suggests that it was the regional authorities who took the lead in carrying it out, not the Kavbiuro, yet Ordzhonikidze had clearly signalled his approval for resettlement and did nothing to prevent it. These deportations set the pattern of robbery, violence, and murder that accompanied all the subsequent ones. The commission of inquiry under Nevskii wrote of them:

For example from st[anitsa] Tarskaia 6 t[housand] were expelled. Land was given to them in Piatigorsk district. They had no possessions—everything had been robbed from them during the eviction. Piatigorsk

[65] Ibid.
[66] GARF f. 1235, op. 95, d. 517, l. 249.
[67] RGASPI f. 64, op. 1, d. 247, ll. 104–6. (The exact number was 8,871.)

270 SHANE O'ROURKE

is a barren place. There are no houses, children are dying like flies not to speak of the fact that 57 men and 11 women were murdered by the Ingush.[68]

The violence and chaos that accompanied the April deportations had no discernible impact on Soviet policy. In fact, it seemed to suggest that deportation was a feasible solution to the problems facing the Soviet regime in the former Cossack Voisko. Authoritative voices began to call for a more far-reaching policy. In a major report on the situation in the North Caucasus in the summer of 1920 Mikoian added to the chorus of calls demanding the expropriation of the Cossacks in favour of the highlanders.[69] In early September the Kavbiuro issued a decree initiating the expropriation and expulsion of the Cossacks, which was confirmed by a Politburo meeting on 17 September 1920. 'Resolved: to confirm the decree of the Kavbiuro cc, concerning the allotment of land to the Chechens at the expense of the Cossack *stanitsas* and to recognize the necessity of introducing the most decisive measures for the free activity of the mountain peoples.'[70]

The Politburo signalled its determination to solve the problems of the Mountain Republic by the most radical means by resolving 'to send c. Stalin to the Caucasus for overseeing the decisions in all their details of our policy in the Caucasus in general and towards the highlanders in particular'.[71] The same dynamic of cumulative radicalism that had been operating on the Don a year earlier now appeared on the Terek. However, unlike the previous year, the Soviet state was now much more powerful and in the Caucasus there were two men possessing the power and the will to mobilize the disparate Soviet agencies to carry out the deportations. All that was lacking was a convenient pretext to begin operations.

It was in this perilous atmosphere that the rebellion of the five *stanitsas* of the Sunzhenskaia line took place in September 1920, providing the perfect excuse to carry out the deportations. Ironically, the Nevskii commission looking into the revolt found

[68] GARF f. 1235, op. 95, d. 517, l. 249.
[69] Ibid., d. 150, l. 173: 'Soviet power must carry out the old policy of a redistribution of land [in favour of] the landless and landed mountain peoples at the expense of the Cossacks.'
[70] RGASPI f. 17, op. 112, d. 93, l. 30.
[71] Ibid.

Trial Run

that its main cause was the fear of the Cossacks that they were about to be deported, just like the three *stanitsas* in the spring.[72] But the five *stanitsas* were only the beginning. Stalin cabled Lenin on 26 October that 'several Cossack *stanitsas* had been punished in an exemplary manner', and that 'the question of the land and administrative arrangements of the highlanders and also of the Terek Cossacks will be resolved in the very near future'.[73] Three days later Ordzhonikidze's speech to party organizations in Vladikavkaz stated that a total of eighteen *stanitsas* were to be deported.[74] The following day Vrachev dropped a heavy hint to a delegation of Chechen and Ingush representatives that a much larger operation was going on than the removal of five rebellious *stanitsas*. 'I do not know all the tasks which the central government had charged itself with in the future for satisfying the needs of the poorest, labouring people, but I think that the present measure is only a beginning and that in future a lot more will be done to improve the life of the labouring people.'[75]

At the end of November Stalin sent another cable to Lenin informing him of the progress of the operation: 'First five *stanitsas* have been resettled in military fashion. The recent rebellion provided an appropriate cause and eased the eviction. The land is at the disposal of the Chechens. The position in the North Caucasus is undoubtedly more stable.'[76] His second point, however, suggested that the goal of removing eighteen *stanitsas* outlined by Ordzhonikidze a month earlier had now been superseded by an altogether more ambitious aim. 'Second: all the mass of materials gathered indicate that it is necessary to assign the Cossacks from the Terek Oblast to a separate *guberniia* since the cohabitation of the Cossacks and of the highlanders in one administrative unity is harmful and dangerous. . . . There is no doubt that this change had decisively cleansed the atmosphere in the North Caucasus.'[77] Stalin's words unconsciously echoed those of Loris-Melikov sixty years earlier. It seemed an opportune moment to settle the problems of the Terek Voisko once and for all. The only difference, of course, was that the victors and victims of tsarist times had been reversed.

Five more *stanitsas* were earmarked for eviction: Sleptsovskaia,

---

[72] GARF f. 1235, op. 95, d. 517, l. 248.　　[73] RGASPI f. 17, op. 112, d. 93, l. 31.
[74] Ordzhonikidze, *Izbrannye Stat'i i Rechi*, 104.　　[75] RGVA f. 217, op. 5, d. 1, l. 5.
[76] RGASPI f. 17, op. 112, d. 93, l. 33.　　[77] Ibid.

Assinovskaia, Nesterovskaia, Troitskaia, and Karabulakskaia.[78] Several of these had been singled out for praise by Ordzhonikidze for their contribution to the Soviet side during the civil war.[79] On 31 November Stalin and Ordzhonikidze issued an order to begin the deportation of Assinovskaia. 'You are ordered to carry out as a matter of urgency the resettlement of Assinovskaia beyond the River Terek. Member of RVC of the Republic. Stalin. Member of the RVC of the Kavfront. Ordzhonikidze.'[80]

Assinovskaia had taken no part in the September rebellion and the deportation was not a reprisal, but the beginning of the much more ambitious plan to remove at least the eighteen *stanitsas* mentioned by Ordzhonikidze, and possibly all the Terek Cossacks, from the Mountain Republic. The 'non-punitive' nature of this eviction was explained in a note attached to the deportation order by Kosior: 'Absolutely nothing of the property from those being resettled is to be confiscated or requisitioned apart from clear counter-revolutionaries.'[81] Dergachev, who witnessed the expulsion of Assinovskaia, was told by a military official that 'The eviction of Assinovskaia *stanitsa* does not have the nature of a repressive measure and therefore the inhabitants of the said *stanitsa* are to be permitted in the course of the eviction to take as much property as they can physically carry.'[82] However, since there were no trains available to carry the Cossacks from Assinovskaia, they lost nearly all their property regardless of the non-punitive nature of the deportation. Dergachev pointed out that moving thousands of people on foot in winter would have catastrophic results.[83] This was ignored.

Unlike the mooted deportations from the Don in 1919, those of the Terek had been carried out. A key difference from 1919 was the commanding figure of Sergo Ordzhonikidze. He drove the policy of deportations from the time of his arrival in the North Caucasus in the spring of 1920. His personal determination and ruthlessness was matched by the formal powers at his disposal

---

[78] RGASPI f. 64, op. 1, d. 247, l. 17.

[79] See e.g. the telegram sent to Lenin on 17 Sept. 1918. Ordzhonikidze, *Izbrannye Stat'i i Rechi*, 19.

[80] RGVA f. 217, op. 5, d. 2, l. 39.

[81] GARF f. 1235, op. 95, d. 517, l. 204.

[82] Ibid., l. 200.

[83] Ibid.

Trial Run

and the informal client–patron network of which he was the nodal point. Beneath him he had loyal and able clients, beginning with Mikoian and Kirov and including Kosior, Kvirikeliia, and Vrachev, who occupied key positions in institutions representing the centre and those representing the local organizations.[84] Ordzhonikidze, in his speech to the Council of Ministers in July 1919, emphasized the importance of personal connections if anything was to be done.

It was a very difficult time particularly for us comrades from the centre. On the one hand there was the so-called Soviet power on the spot and on the other there was an unfortunate assortment of every possible extraordinary commissars and plenipotentiaries, often simply swindlers and thieves who incited provincial comrades against those arriving from the centre. I myself experienced a few bitter moments of distrust, but the old link with many comrades from the underground period and joint work saw me through. And for the whole of my time in the South with a single exception, I hardly met with any opposition from local comrades.[85]

Ordzhonikidze's connections extended upwards. He could count on the unstinting support of Stalin and even Lenin until just before the latter's death.[86] Finally, Ordzhonikidze was the type of man to use his powers to the utmost. He frequently exceeded even the tremendous latitude he was given, most notably when he engineered the invasion of Georgia in 1921 in spite of explicit orders to the contrary.[87] Willing and able to take advantage of any opportunity to further his plans, the revolt of the five *stanitsas* in September was perfect for Ordzhonikidze.

With the deportation of Assinovskaia, Soviet policy was entering uncharted waters. Even as the operation unfolded it seemed as if the ambition of its architects, Ordzhonikidze and Stalin, was growing. The millenarian strain in Bolshevism came more and more to the fore as the operation proceeded. The multi-layered and complex ethnic and land problems in the Terek Voisko had been reduced to binary opposites of good and evil, light and dark. The desire to create a permanent and irreversible solution regardless of the human cost was a product of the same thinking.

---

[84] Kvashonkin, 'Sovetizatsiia Zakavkaz'iia', 165. Easter, *Reconstructing the State*, 82–4.
[85] Ordzhonikidze, *Izbrannye Stat'i i Rechi*, 60.
[86] Khlevniuk, *In Stalin's Shadow*, 14–15.
[87] Kvashonkin, 'Sovetizatsiia Zakavkaz'iia', 167–8.

274　　　　　　　　　　SHANE O'ROURKE

In such a solution there could be no exceptions based on individual attitudes or behaviour. Even those families with husbands and sons fighting in the Red Army were to be deported. Out of 2,211 deported families on which there was information, at least 898 were identified as supporters of Soviet power.[88] Nor was this something of which the authorities only belatedly became aware. As Ordzhonikidze knew well from his personal experience, many thousands of Cossacks were fighting loyally for Soviet armies. Indeed, just a few days before the revolt a 'week of action' had produced over 1,000 volunteers for the Soviet–Polish War from the Cossacks of the Sunzhenskoe line.[89] Such inconvenient facts, however, cluttered the stark simplicity of millenarian thinking and had to be discarded. Ordzhonikidze had declared all Cossacks traitors and Stalin's second telegram had announced that it was impossible for Cossacks and highlanders to live together. Presented in such terms the solution was simple: remove the Cossacks. Friends were rewarded, enemies punished; a historical wrong was righted; and stability and security were introduced into a strife-torn area. Vrachev's commission carrying out the deportations implemented this policy ruthlessly, although expelling wives, mothers, and children of men fighting in the Red Army did raise a few qualms. But these were easily stifled after a brief discussion.

Difficulties are only encountered with the eviction of the women, children, and families of Red Army and Soviet workers. Property is not to be confiscated from the families of Red Army and Soviet workers with the exception of surpluses on a common basis with all citizens. During the expulsions we must offer them the utmost help, giving them the possibility of resettling in neighbouring *stanitsas* or where they wish.[90]

Little now appeared to stand in the way of deporting thousands more Terek Cossacks.

The Ending of the Deportations

But on 21 January 1921 the central authorities abruptly halted the deportations. 'The Praesidium of the CEC [Central Executive

[88] RGVA f. 217, op. 5, d. 2, l. 57.
[89] Gugov, *Sovmestnaia Bor'ba Narodov*, 483–4.
[90] RGVA f. 217, op. 5. d. 1, l. 1.

Trial Run

Committee] decrees the immediate suspension of the expulsion of the Cossacks from the Mountain Republic.'[91] The moratorium came too late for Assinovskaia, but it stopped the deportations of any other *stanitsas*. The CEC then set up a commission under the veteran Bolshevik Nevskii to carry out an urgent review of the situation in the Mountain Republic and report back within two months. Included in the mandate to Nevskii was a specific instruction to report on whether it was necessary 'to consolidate or expel the Cossacks / about what number of Cossacks it will be necessary to evict if it is recognizable as unavoidable'.[92] This instruction offered further confirmation that something much broader than the eviction of five rebellious *stanitsas* was under way.

The report that Nevskii delivered at the end of March to the CEC was critical to ending the policy of expulsions. Nevskii damned the theoretical underpinnings of the operation, the way it was carried out, and its consequences. He argued that the deportations were unnecessary as there was more than enough land in the Mountain Republic for highlanders and Cossacks, and he demanded an immediate end to the expulsions.[93] Nevskii delivered a direct rebuke to Ordzhonikidze and an indirect one to Stalin for their conception of the problem. He reprinted Ordzhonikidze's original order deporting the five *stanitsas* and then commented: 'These lines speak for themselves. However difficult were the circumstances in which Soviet power had to struggle, *it is impossible to accept the thought that all Cossacks without exception are counter-revolutionaries*.'[94] Just in case the CEC might miss the point he underlined it.

As a Marxist, Nevskii rejected the theoretical basis on which the deportations were based, but he was equally concerned about the disastrous consequences that had ensued as a result. On his way to the Mountain Republic Nevskii had passed through Rostov-na-Donu where senior officials expressed their opposition to the policy of expulsions. Members of the food supply commission told Nevskii that the expulsions of the Cossacks were, from their point of view, 'a mistake'.[95] The food supply was absolutely fundamental to the survival of the regime by the end of 1920. As the civil war finally ended, getting sufficient food for the hungry

---

[91] GARF f. 1235, op. 95, d. 517, l. 37.   [92] Ibid.   [93] Ibid., l. 254.
[94] Ibid., l. 248.   [95] Ibid., l. 234.

276 SHANE O'ROURKE

cities of the north took priority over every other goal. Nevskii made much of this in his report. He visited the *stanitsas* which had been deported and saw only ruined farmsteads and abandoned fields with the remnants of the previous year's crops rotting away. None of them had been reoccupied by the Chechen and Ingush, although everything of value had been removed. It was the Cossack lands that had been the only source of food surpluses in the Mountain Republic and these had disappeared along with the Cossacks. 'Who will feed the army and the workers?' was Nevskii's tart rhetorical question.[96] The local party organization in Grozny supported Nevskii, characterizing the expulsion of the remaining *stanitsas* as 'inexpedient'.[97]

The expulsions were flawed from the point of view of another concern which was central to the regime throughout its existence: security. Stalin claimed that the expulsions had cleansed the atmosphere and created a much more stable situation in the republic. This was a blatant lie, as Nevskii discovered even before he arrived in Grozny. Report after report emphasized the lawlessness that now engulfed the republic. One official in Rostov-na-Donu told him that 'the only correct policy for the North Caucasus in general and the Mountain Republic in particular is the occupation of these regions by Soviet armies'.[98] Nevskii found that party and state organizations of the Mountain Republic were working hand in glove with the numerous bandit elements operating on the territory. 'The brazenness of the raids had reached such a degree that in Vladikavkaz a whole street was robbed and in Grozny they made off with horses from the *Ispolkom*. The second reason for these horrific manifestations is the protection which the bandits have from the authorities in the Mountain Republic.'[99] Soviet authority in the republic had broken down completely as a result of the deportations. The local party organizations were now operating virtually independently of Moscow, which was anathema to everything Bolshevism stood for.

On 14 April 1921 a Politburo meeting discussed Nevskii's report and accepted his recommendations. 'To receive com. Nevskii's report for information. Cossack *stanitsas* are not to be evicted. The land needs of the highlanders to be satisfied by

[96] Ibid., l. 251.   [97] Ibid., l. 189.   [98] Ibid., l. 233.   [99] Ibid., l. 252.

Trial Run

means of consolidation of Cossack *stanitsas* through agreement between the Cossack *Ispolkom* and the *Ispolkoms* of the Ingush, Chechen and Ossetians.'[100]

The Politburo decision brought an end to the support of the centre for any further deportations. This did not immediately end attacks on Cossack *stanitsas* or attempts to expel them. The republican authorities continued to demand the expulsion of Cossacks in every forum open to them. The Fourth Conference of Ossetian Soviets, for example, warned in April 1921 that 'any delay in the expulsion of the Cossack *stanitsas* would *unavoidably lead to bloody war between the different sections of the population*'.[101] But without the support of the central authorities, the necessary will and apparatus were no longer available. By this time Ordzhonikidze and Stalin had both moved on and were preoccupied with the ongoing invasion of Georgia; neither had much time to spare for the Mountain Republic. The conflict between the Cossacks and the highlanders reverted to traditional raiding and the rather less traditional imposing of punitive requisitioning quotas on the Cossack population.[102]

Conclusion

The deportation of the Terek Cossacks in 1920 was a small affair compared to later deportations. Deporting 30,000 people would literally be all in a day's work for the NKVD in the 1930s and 1940s.[103] But the Terek deportations were a vital link in the chain connecting Soviet practices to those of the western colonial powers in general and the tsarist regime in particular. The same desire to settle an intractable problem once and for all by drastic methods preoccupied the Soviet leadership as much as the tsarist one. The issues of security and stability were central to both regimes, and both came to the conclusion that the wholesale removal of a 'disloyal' population would provide a permanent solution to these concerns. That both attempts actually worsened

[100] RGASPI f. 64, op. 1, d. 247, l. 7.
[101] Ibid., l. 23.
[102] Ibid., d. 246, l. 21.
[103] The deportation of the Chechen people in 1944 was a case in point. N. L. Pobol' and P. M. Polian (eds.), *Stalinskie Deportatsii 1928–1953* (Moscow, 2005), 455.

the problems they had been designed to solve was of little concern to those implementing them.

In the Soviet case pragmatic decisions based on security issues were not the only operative ones. The millenarian strain that underlay Bolshevik ideology made it particularly inclined to seek total solutions to problems rather than partial ones based on compromise or negotiation. The reduction of a historically complex situation in the Mountain Republic to a pantomime cast of good and evil was an essential part of this process. It required that the leadership, especially Orzdzhonikidze and Stalin, display exceptional degrees of cynicism and the ability to lie on an epic scale, secure in the knowledge that in the long run the ends would justify any means.

The Soviet leaders were already experienced practitioners of these arts by the end of the civil war. Even so, there were still sufficient checks within the system to call a halt to policies that were manifestly failing. Yet what augured particularly ill for the future was that much of the core of the Stalinist leadership of the late 1920s and early 1930s had already assembled and was working together to carry out the deportations. These had driven the schemes for a total solution and the impulse to check had come from outside this core group. By the end of the 1920s all such checks had been removed.

Beneath the great issues of ideology and state policy were thousands of human victims. In this particular case it was the Cossacks. These were merely the first of a long list of peoples to experience the unlimited violence of the Soviet state on the basis that they belonged to a particular group defined as hostile to the Soviet state by virtue of being a member of that group. A year after the deportations, surviving Cossacks petitioned for permission to return to their homes.

Already soon it will be a year since we have suffered a terrible punishment for a crime of which only a very few are guilty. Our children are returning home from serving in the Red Army, but they will find neither their houses nor their families and those that do find them will see that their fathers, mothers, and sisters are dying of hunger. It is too cruel for all of us to suffer punishment for the actions of a very few and this only because we and they are called Cossacks.[104]

[104] RGASPI f. 64, op. 1, d. 247, l. 40.

Trial Run

The Cossacks had discovered that no service to the Soviet state was sufficient to override this stigma and exempt them from loss of property, home, and, for many thousands, loss of life. Millions of other people would discover this shortly.

11

National and International Planning of the 'Transfer' of Germans from Czechoslovakia and Poland

DETLEF BRANDES

The Effects of National Socialist Policy

The conflicts between Germans, Poles, and Czechs have a long history. In Prussia's eastern provinces national conflicts between Poles and Germans had existed at least since the partitions of Poland at the end of the eighteenth century. In the Bohemian lands national quarrels between Czechs and Germans had gradually exacerbated other, mainly social, differences only since 1848.

After the establishment of national states on the eastern borders of Germany, these conflicts became a problem of foreign relations. About half of the German minority in Poland emigrated to Germany, partly voluntarily and partly reacting to numerous oppressive measures introduced by the new authorities in the years following the foundation of the new Polish Republic in 1918. The national associations of the Germans remaining in Poland were supported by the Weimar Republic; after 1933 they declared themselves for the National Socialist regime. Of the Sudeten Germans, although they protested against their incorporation into the Czechoslovak Republic, only a few emigrated to Austria or Germany. Those German political parties which were prepared to collaborate actively with the Czechoslovak government still managed to attract three-quarters of the German votes in 1929. This changed after 1933.

At the next parliamentary elections, in 1935, the newly founded nationalistic and anti-liberal Sudeten German Party was supported by two-thirds of the Germans. In November 1937 its leader, Konrad Henlein, secretly placed his party at Hitler's disposal for the smashing of Czechoslovakia. His public demands

DETLEF BRANDES

for territorial autonomy were calculated in such a way that the government would not be able to meet them. In March 1938 the *Anschluss* of Austria to the German Reich weakened the strategic position of Czechoslovakia, as the belt of fortifications, still under construction, only went through the hinterland of the border with Germany and not along the border with Austria. In the communal elections in May and June 1938 the Sudeten German Party won a startling nine-tenths of the German vote, though in the meantime it had openly professed itself to National Socialism. When the government, contrary to all expectations, offered to form a German federal entity within Czechoslovakia with far-reaching competences, Henlein broke off the negotiations under a pretext and proclaimed: 'We want home into the Reich.' ('Wir wollen heim ins Reich.') From these developments not only the Poles and Czechs, but also the governments of the great powers and their advisers, concluded that they could not count on enduring loyalty of the German minorities to the Czechoslovak and Polish republics at any time in the future. Moreover, it was a prevalent opinion that the stipulations for the protection of minorities adopted at the Paris Peace Conference had not only proved a failure, but had also disturbed the integration of the national minorities into the successor states.[1]

The Czechoslovak crisis was solved by the agreement of Britain, France, and Italy to the German annexation of the Sudeten areas at the conference in Munich. As a result of the Agreement of 29 September 1938 the strategic position of the Czechoslovak Republic became so completely hopeless that a truncated Czechoslovakia was unable to offer resistance to its dismemberment, to the German occupation of the western part of the republic in March 1939, and to the establishment of the Protectorate of Bohemia and Moravia.

For the Polish Republic, facing a German semicircle extending from East Prussia to Upper Silesia after the last post-war Polish–German territorial quarrel had been settled in 1921 had already been difficult enough. With the German occupation of the western part of Czechoslovakia, Poland's military position

---

[1] Detlef Brandes, *Der Weg zur Vertreibung 1938–1945: Pläne und Entscheidungen zum 'Transfer' der Deutschen aus der Tschechoslowakei und aus Polen* (2nd edn., Munich, 2005). As the contents of my monograph are easily accessible by subject, name, and place indexes, footnotes here will be kept to a minimum.

Planning of the 'Transfer' of Germans   283

became untenable. Following the surprisingly quick defeat of September 1939, the question of a revision of the boundaries in the west and north naturally came to play a much greater role in Polish thinking than had been the case in the inter-war period, when political discussions focused on the Polish mission in the east. The wartime Czechoslovak resistance at home and abroad likewise looked for guarantees against a repetition of the *Anschluss* and the German annexation of the border areas.

Economic exploitation, cultural suppression, forced labour, hostage-taking, executions as reprisals for acts of resistance, and the mass murder of the Jews were common features of the German policy towards Poland and Czechoslovakia. The long-term objectives included the assimilation of those Poles and Czechs considered racially suitable to be Germanized and the deportation of the rest to the east. In terms of the policy actually carried out, however, the differences were significant. In Poland one million people—more than one and a half million when we add the inhabitants of Warsaw evacuated after the uprising of autumn 1944—lost their homes by displacement, and more than 400,000 so-called 'ethnic Germans' from the Baltic states, Bessarabia, and eastern Poland were settled in the 'incorporated territories' of western Poland. Almost three million Poles from these incorporated areas and the General Government were compelled to perform forced labour.[2] With minor exceptions, the Czechs were spared displacement from their homes and the settling of 'ethnic Germans' in their place. Because of the importance of the heavy industry of the so-called Protectorate of Bohemia and Moravia, German policy towards the Czechs was generally more moderate throughout the war.[3]

Nevertheless, shortly after his accession as acting Reichs-protector, Reinhard Heydrich, the chief of the Security Police and the SS, had more than 400 people shot.[4] The Foreign Press and Research Service, a team of scholarly advisers to the British Foreign Office, wrote in February 1942: 'If the Heydrich policy is continued in the "Protectorate" it may become true, as it is

---

[2] Czesław Madajczyk, *Die Okkupationspolitik Nazideutschlands in Polen 1939–1945* (Berlin, 1987).

[3] Detlef Brandes, *Die Tschechen unter deutschem Protektorat 1939–1945*, 2 vols. (Munich, 1969, 1975).

[4] Ibid. 207–12.

284   DETLEF BRANDES

certainly true for Poland, that the life and security of any
German left in an area restored to Czechoslovakia will be in such
danger that facilities for departure would be the best service
which could be rendered to the Germans themselves.'[5] After the
assassination of Heydrich, another 1,700 people were murdered,
among them the men and children from the village of Lidice,
while the women were deported to a concentration camp. Even
greater in its impact on the Czech hatred of the Germans was the
rumour spread by the occupation authorities that every tenth
Czech was to be shot if the assassins were not handed over.[6]

Plans and Decisions on the 'Transfer'

Beginning in October 1939, when the Polish Foreign Minister
raised the question of the annexation of East Prussia with the
British, the Polish government was always a few steps ahead of its
Czechoslovak counterpart with its requests for frontier rectifications and expulsion of the Germans. Under the influence of the
battle of Britain, the inclination to favour radical anti-German
solutions increased, not only among the British population in
general but also among the officials of the British Foreign Office.
Encouraged by this atmosphere, the Polish government submitted a memorandum to the Foreign Office detailing its demands
for the annexation of East Prussia, Danzig, and Upper Silesia, a
shortening of the Polish western frontier, and the transfer of the
German population out of the old and new Polish territories. In
alliance with Czechoslovakia, it argued, Poland would replace
France as Great Britain's most important partner in maintaining
security on the Continent. Hence its economic and strategic position needed to be strengthened. For its part, the Polish government considered Beneš's plans for the solution of the Sudeten
German problem to be too moderate.

As early as September 1938 Edvard Beneš had reacted to the
'home into the Reich' slogan of the Sudeten German Party,
whose groups were trying to seize power in Sudeten German
villages and towns at that time, by submitting a secret proposal to

---

[5] National Archive, FO 371/30930, C 2167/241/18, Memorandum of the Foreign
Research and Press Service (Arnold J. Toynbee) to Foreign Office (Ronald), 12 Feb. 1942.
[6] Brandes, *Die Tschechen unter deutschem Protektorat*, 254–67.

Planning of the 'Transfer' of Germans 285

the French government: Czechoslovakia could get rid of one-third of the Sudeten Germans by ceding certain border regions; another third should be expatriated; and the last third, especially the 'Democrats, Socialists, and Jews', could stay in Czechoslovakia. The Germans, who would leave the ceded territories to escape from the Nazi terror, could be replaced by members of the Sudeten German Party from territories that were to be kept by Czechoslovakia. Beneš, who dominated Czech policy in exile, adhered to that plan throughout the war. In May 1941 he for the first time publicly advocated 'organized population transfers' intended to prevent the German misuse of national minorities for pan-German goals and to render the postwar states as nationally homogeneous as possible. At that time the territories which Beneš was prepared to abandon still comprised three relatively broad border districts.[7] Their size shrank step by step, however, because the Czech resistance movement and exile army protested against the cession of any pre-war Czechoslovakian territory. The only element of Beneš's plan which remained in February 1945 was the willingness to exchange some densely settled for other thinly populated slices at the border, with a difference of 300,000 people.[8] About 800,000 Germans were to be allowed to stay in the Czechoslovak Republic. These remaining Germans were to merge gradually with the Czechs and Slovaks 'into a political and cultural unity'. Rump Germany should be forced to accept all transferred Germans as its own citizens. Thus in its memorandum of November 1944 the Czechoslovak government wrote to the European Advisory Commission that 'once and for all a very troublesome and dangerous problem' would be settled.[9]

Eden's visit to Moscow in December 1941 had produced a turn in British policy towards the nationality questions in east-central Europe. The Foreign Minister had several conversations with Stalin, who demanded British recognition of the Soviet annexations carried out in collusion with Nazi Germany. Poland was affected by Stalin's demand for the annexation of the Baltic states including Lithuania and of all territories up to the Curzon line.

---

[7] Columbia University Library, Lockhart Papers, Bruce Lockhart to Eden, 22 May 1941.

[8] National Archive, FO 371/47085, N 1402/207/12, Nichols to Eden on his conversation with Beneš, 13 Feb. 1945.

[9] National Archive, FO 371/38946, C 16563/1347/12, Memorandum of the Czechoslovak government, 23 Nov. 1944.

Poland was to be compensated by East Prussia and additional areas up to the Oder. Stalin also called for the return of the Sudetenland to Czechoslovakia and the handing over of Istria and Venezia Giulia to Yugoslavia. After his return to London, Eden asked the Foreign Office Research and Press Service to draw up special studies on the question of the German–Polish, the German–Czechoslovak, and the Austrian–Italian–Yugoslav boundaries, giving only secondary attention to ethnic factors. If its conclusions suggested the need for population transfers, the Service was to submit a second paper on the Turkish–Greek precedent and the resettlement of the Baltic Germans by Hitler.

On 21 January 1942 Eden met with the Czechoslovak President to acquaint himself in greater detail with the latter's views on the Sudeten German question. Beneš, however, declared that until the British government had revoked the Munich Agreement, he could neither enter into any agreements with the Poles nor engage in any official discussion about the boundaries and minorities of post-war Czechoslovakia. According to his plan the number of Germans should be reduced from three million to one million. At the end of June, Eden placed the Czechoslovak question on the War Cabinet's agenda. In a memorandum of 2 July 1942 he pointed to the wave of terror that had engulfed the Protectorate following Heydrich's assassination and proposed the adoption of the following declaration: 'As Germany has deliberately destroyed the arrangements concerning Czechoslovakia reached in 1938 . . . His Majesty's Government regard themselves as free from any engagements in this respect. . . . At the final settlement of the Czechoslovak frontiers to be reached at the end of the war, His Majesty's government will not be influenced by any changes effected in and since 1938.' Hitler himself, Eden continued, had carried out huge population transfers, and it was only natural to expect that after the war many countries, Poland and Czechoslovakia in particular, would be eager to expel their German minorities, which would affect somewhere between 3 and 6.8 million people. Eden requested the approval of the War Cabinet 'for the general principle of the transfer to Germany of German minorities in central and south-eastern Europe after the war where this seems necessary and desirable, and authority to let this decision be known in appropriate cases'. The War Cabinet endorsed not only the

Planning of the 'Transfer' of Germans 287

public declaration on the Munich Agreement but also the secret resolution on the principle of the transfer of German minorities to Germany. A few days later Eden informed Beneš and Jaksch about the resolution.[10]

At the beginning of the war under British pressure, and later only to safeguard the pre-war borders of Czechoslovakia should there be a military or revolutionary takeover in Germany which could lead to a compromise peace, Beneš had negotiated with Wenzel Jaksch, the exiled leader of the Sudeten German Social Democrats. Several times the Czech resistance groups at home and the army abroad had protested against these discussions and had cautioned against any concessions. After the repudiation of the Munich Agreement, Beneš resumed his conversations with Jaksch. The Sudeten German leader accepted Beneš's proposal to expel a section of the Germans on the basis of their collaboration with the occupiers. However, the British ambassador informed Beneš that his government rejected the application of such a guilt principle. The Sudeten German question had contributed to the outbreak of the war and should be resolved accordingly. He regarded the restoration of Czechoslovakia within its pre-war frontiers as unimaginable without a transfer of populations. The Central Department of the Foreign Office argued that it would be difficult to find reasonable criteria for establishing 'guilt'; it feared that this process might become confused with the projected punishment of war criminals. More crucial, however, was Cadogan's and Eden's warning that the introduction of the 'guilt' principle might actually make it impossible to expel as many Germans as desirable from Czechoslovakia. Beneš was informed of the British misgivings. The British had thereby destroyed a possible basis for a compromise with Jaksch, and on 1 December 1942 the Czechoslovak President broke off negotiations with him.

In May 1943 Beneš travelled to the United States, where he sought consent for his transfer plans. In the meantime, William Strang had informed the State Department of the British War Cabinet's general approval of the transfer of German populations and about his country's misgivings

[10] National Archive, CAB 66/26, WP (42) 280, Eden's memorandum 'Anglo-Czechoslovak Relations' of 2 July 1942; CAB 65/27, War Cabinet Conclusions of 6 July 1942.

288   DETLEF BRANDES

regarding the application of the 'guilt' principle. In his discussions with Roosevelt, Beneš proceeded very craftily. Already at their first meeting he strove to obtain American consent to his transfer plans, pretending that he had already received Soviet approval. After the conversations he telegraphed to the Czechoslovak government that Roosevelt favoured the greatest possible reduction of the German minority in Czechoslovakia and the assignment of East Prussia to Poland. Thereupon the Czechoslovak Foreign Minister and his deputy hurried to tell the Soviet ambassador in London that the Czechoslovak government no longer regarded as sufficient the earlier Soviet declarations that the Sudeten German question was a domestic Czechoslovak affair. In response, the Soviet ambassador notified the Czechoslovak minister that the Soviet government assented to the idea of the transfer of the Germans. In his second conversation with Roosevelt, Beneš could thus point 'once more' to Soviet support for his plan. He wired London that Roosevelt had spoken in favour of the 'transfer of the minority population from East Prussia, Transylvania, and from us'.[11]

After the Tehran conference, Stalin found time to receive the Czechoslovak President. Beneš submitted several memoranda to the Soviet government. In one of them, 'Population Transfers in the Czechoslovak Republic', he was so opportunistic as to describe the transfer as part of a 'political, economic, and social Five Year Plan'. He told Molotov and Stalin that he would prefer the expulsion of all Germans, but was also prepared to compromise and retain one million of them. His Soviet interlocutors promised support for the transfer, especially as Beneš declared that the property of the Germans would not be distributed, but nationalized, and that the Czech takeover of German property would be followed by the nationalization of Czech property. Thus the transfer would be the beginning of 'a great social upheaval'.[12] Five days later Beneš informed the Communists about his plans and Stalin's consent and agreed with them on common propaganda in favour of the transfer. From Moscow Beneš returned with the outlines of the Polish

[11] Edvard Beneš, *Paměti: Od Mnichova k nové válce a k novému vítězství* (Prague, 1947), 288–90.
[12] Vojtěch Mastný, 'Benesovy rozhovory se Stalinem a Molotovem', *Svědectví*, 12/47 (1974), 467–98.

Planning of the 'Transfer' of Germans

post-war territory that Stalin had put on the map during one of the conversations.

In the Polish case, plans for annexations and expulsion had become gradually more extreme. After the German attack on the Soviet Union, the National Party, the Peasant Party, and the Sanacja—the former followers of Marshal Piłsudski and his successors—demanded that the Polish frontier in the west be moved to the Oder and Lausitzer Neisse, while the Party of Labour claimed the whole Baltic coast from Stettin to Memel. The government, on the other hand, strove for a more modest expansion to a line extending from Kolberg to Crossen through Lower Pomerania and from there along the Oder and the Glatzer Neisse. The Polish army was to occupy East Prussia, Danzig, and German Upper Silesia and expel the Germans, thereby creating a *fait accompli*. In October 1942, the Polish government rejected suggestions for Polish acquisitions up to the Lausitzer Neisse or Bober as 'fantastic'. In a memorandum outlining its war aims in December 1942, it differentiated between territories it hoped to acquire and a Polish zone of occupation extending up to the Lausitzer Neisse; at the same time, it added Lower Pomerania (excluding Stettin) to the area to be annexed. The government assumed that part of the German population in the newly incorporated territories would flee and that another part could be 're-Slavicized', but that the rest would have to be forcibly expelled. In July 1943 this concept was endorsed by the Political Representation of the Country, consisting of the four main underground parties. The government stuck to that concept, and rejected the more extreme demands from some resistance and exile groups, since such a solution would force Poland into a permanent anti-German position and would make the defence of the pre-war eastern border against Soviet claims more difficult. In December 1942, Prime Minister Władysław Sikorski travelled to the United States to seek support for the Polish war aims. His hope of obtaining an official letter from the American President approving the territorial extension of Poland to the north and west, and the maintenance of the pre-war eastern frontier, was disappointed. The meagre result of his visit was a letter from Sumner Welles. The Under-Secretary of State wrote that, as Sikorski was already aware, Roosevelt did not consider the old 'Corridor' solution as compatible with a strong and independent Poland.

In the Foreign Office, the Polish memorandum met with a positive reception. The Central Department regarded the chapters on the transfer of the German population as 'satisfactory', as the British government had committed itself to the principle of forced population transfers anyhow. Britain should attempt to compensate Poland for its probable losses in the east and should generally seek to strengthen the industrial and strategic position of the Slavic countries against a possible renewal of Germany's power. In his endeavours to induce the Polish government to accept the Soviet territorial demands and to facilitate its return to Poland, Churchill offered the Polish Prime Minister, Stanisław Mikołajczyk, an ever larger part of Germany, in October 1944 even a border at the Oder and including Breslau and Stettin. When Mikołajczyk finally proposed to agree to a new post-war Poland between the Oder and the Curzon line, he was overthrown.

Since 1941 the Soviet leadership had demanded the extension of its territory up to the Curzon line, which the British Foreign Minister, trying to delineate the regions with a Polish majority from those with a Ukrainian and White Russian one, had suggested in 1919 as the provisional Polish border in the east. But at the time when Mikołajczyk was replaced by a new Prime Minister, the liberated Polish districts were already governed by the Lublin Committee, a puppet government installed by Moscow. At the beginning of 1945 Moscow recognized that Committee as the provisional Polish government which, with Soviet consent, took possession of all lands not only up to the Oder river, but also to the Western Neisse.

As it became apparent that the Warsaw government, supported by the Red Army and the NKVD, would prevail over the London-based government-in-exile, the British government no longer saw any reason why it should back an excessive extension of Poland to the west, for the Soviet puppets had accepted the Curzon line anyhow. At the conferences in Yalta and Potsdam the British and Americans therefore quarrelled with the Soviets over whether Poland should extend to the Oder and the Western Neisse or only to the Oder and the Eastern Neisse. Churchill now argued that Poland would not need so much territory up to the Oder and Neisse, from which 8 to 9 million Germans had to be expelled, in order to accommodate 2 to 3 million Poles from pre-war Poland east of the Curzon line.

Planning of the 'Transfer' of Germans

Supported by Stalin, however, the Polish government stubbornly stuck to the demand for the Oder–Western Neisse line. It was a package deal that offered a way out of the dead end in which the Potsdam conference found itself because of the conflict about the Oder–Neisse line. The British and Americans acquiesced in that line and in the transfer of the Germans from Poland, Czechoslovakia, and, in addition, Hungary, while the Soviets made concessions on the questions of reparations from Germany and the affiliation of Italy to the United Nations.

At the Potsdam conference Stalin argued that most of the Germans had already left Poland and Czechoslovakia. And, indeed, about half of the former German population of the pre-war and new Polish territories had been evacuated by the Nazi authorities to the west, or had fled before the arrival of the Soviet army, though in the case of Czechoslovakia the Germans of Slovakia and eastern Silesia had been transferred only to western Bohemia. In the period between the end of hostilities and the Potsdam conference, both the Polish and Czechoslovak governments endeavoured to create *faits accomplis* by expelling another about 400,000 Germans from Poland and about 560,000 from Czechoslovakia.

National Processes of Decision-Making

The Polish government set up a separate body, the Ministry of (peace) Conference Works, to plan the territorial shape of the post-war republic and the treatment of the national minorities, while the Czechoslovak government concentrated that task in a study group of the Ministry of Foreign Affairs. Both governments-in-exile faced pressure from resistance movements at home to demand additional territories and the wholesale expulsion of the Germans. The Foreign Office relied on the expertise of a body of distinguished scholars, at first brought together in the Foreign Office Research and Press Service and later transformed into the Foreign Office Research Department. These experts had a much greater influence on British decisions than did their colleagues in the United States within the Advisory Committee on Problems on Foreign Relations and its successors. While the British experts advocated more radical solutions to the minority problems in eastern Europe than did the Foreign Office up to 1942, the American experts revisited the measures discussed after the First World War: minor frontier rectifications; and exchange of territories. The documents on the post-war planning process within the Soviet Union demonstrate that the Soviet experts hesitated to make any suggestions before Stalin had committed himself to a certain course. Before the conference at Tehran, the British government established an Interdepartmental Committee on the Transfer of German Populations which studied the effects of the Polish and Czechoslovak border proposals and in May 1944 made a series of recommendations which were discussed by the War Cabinet during the following months. At the same time its Soviet counterpart pleaded for the return of the Sudeten areas to Czechoslovakia and the deportation of its German population, but still linked the annexation of East Prussia and Upper Silesia to the political orientation of the future Polish government. Evidently the Soviet experts were not informed of Stalin's commitments to Eden in December 1941 or to Beneš in December 1943. In the United States President Roosevelt in several cases overruled the scruples of the experts and the State Department and agreed to the more radical solutions of the territorial problems of eastern Europe proposed by the leaders of the other major or lesser allies.

Motives: Social Engineering, Retaliation, and the Ethnically Homogeneous State

Both the Polish government-in-exile and the Lublin Committee announced that a Land Office would be established to distribute the confiscated German holdings to peasants in need of, and hungry for, additional land.[13] Poland should use the unique opportunity to improve the agrarian structure in the pre-war Polish regions. This argument was also used in a memorandum from the Czechoslovak government to the major Allied powers of November 1944, which said that the expulsion of the Germans would enable it to solve the problem of surplus agricultural population in the eastern parts of the republic.[14]

[13] Michael G. Esch, *'Gesunde Verhältnisse': Deutsche und polnische Bevölkerungspolitik in Ostmitteleuropa 1939–1950* (Marburg, 1998), 128–225.

[14] National Archive, FO 371/38946, C 16563/1347/12, Memorandum of the Czechoslovak Government, 23 Nov. 1944.

Planning of the 'Transfer' of Germans   293

The main motives, however, were the desire for revenge and retaliation and the quest for an ethnically homogeneous state. During and after the war anti-German radicalism had gripped practically all strata of the Czech and Polish populations. In the first weeks after the liberation the politicians even stirred up the desire for retaliation. In April 1945 the Czechoslovak government appealed to the population to take revenge for all acts of brutality and to have no pity for the German enemies.[15] Three days after the German capitulation President Beneš announced in Brno: 'We said to ourselves that we have to liquidate the German problem in the Republic.' After the experiences of the terrible war the Czechs could not negotiate with the Germans once more and then risk another war after ten or twenty years of German recovery. At the anniversary of the annihilation of Lidice he declared 'the whole German nation responsible for National Socialism and all its crimes', and asserted that the 'main perpetrators, collaborators, and executive organs of the crime were Bohemian Germans'.[16] When the President opened the parliamentary session on 28 October 1945, he justified the transfer of the Germans by pointing to the failure of the negotiations in 1938. He said: 'Today it is clear that the majority of our Germans had since 1934 prepared the disruption of our state in full agreement with Hitler and with full responsibility. . . . Because of their actions all bridges between them and us are broken off; a further shared life with them is impossible. Therefore they have to leave, since there is no other solution on behalf of the calm and peace in Europe.'[17] The Nuremberg trials and the many local trials against leading figures of the occupation apparatus and concentration camp guards had powerful repercussions in both Poland and Czechoslovakia. The experiences which the population had had and the resuscitation of memories by the judicial hearings led to slogans such as 'That is like the Germans', or 'Höss [the commander of Auschwitz] is a typical representative of the

---

[15] Detlef Brandes, 'Die Vertreibung und Aussiedlung der Deutschen aus Polen und der Tschechoslowakei: Pläne, Entscheidungen, Durchführung 1938–1947', in Ulf Brunnbauer, Michael G. Esch, and Holm Sundhaussen (eds.), *Definitionsmacht, Utopie, Vergeltung: 'Ethnische Säuberungen' im östlichen Europa des 20. Jahrhunderts* (Münster, 2006), 77–95.

[16] Edvard Beneš, *Odsun Němců z Československa: Výbor zu Paměti, projevů a dokumentů 1940–1947* (Prague, 1996), 143.

[17] Brandes, 'Die Vertreibung und Aussiedlung der Deutschen', 92.

German nation.'[18] The illegal newspaper of the Polish Underground Army had already announced in July 1944 that the Germans would 'come to know what the principle of collective guilt means'. And the commander in chief of the Second Polish Army instructed his soldiers to deal with the Germans 'as they have dealt with us', so that 'the Germans flee on their own and thank God that they have saved their lives'. From March 1945, however, the Polish Supreme Command tried to restrain the acts of lynch law and the brutal and cruel treatment of prisoners-of-war and civilians.[19] Nevertheless, especially during the first months the Germans both in Poland and Czechoslovakia were treated as outlaws. Their property was confiscated or looted, and some of them were transported to camps, where after their arrival they were brutally treated by guards. Many lost their lives as a result of exhaustion or torture. Others had to work for the new owners of their farms or businesses. Almost all reports on the mood of the Germans waiting for the expulsion agree that they were anxious and timid. Cut off from all media, even those who were allowed to stay in their homes for the time being often did not know what was happening around them, sometimes even in the next street. Their property having been looted once again by the guards who accompanied them to the assembly places for their transport, they greeted their arrival in rump Germany with relief.

The propaganda of the first post-war months also points to the second main motive for the expulsion. Only a few days after the end of the war the Czechoslovak Prime Minister characterized the purge of the Germans as the solution to a problem which had 'weighed upon our people for a thousand years'. The Communist Party chief, Klement Gottwald, declared in a radio address: 'The new Republic will be a Slavic state, a republic of the Czechs and Slovaks.' And even before the end of the war the Polish Prime Minister demanded: 'In the first place we have to contribute to the smashing of our eternal German foe, to take away from him the lands in the north and west which he has stolen from us at different periods of history.' The Polish Deputy Minister for Public Administration declared at the time of the

[18] Edmund Dmitrów, *Niemcy i okupacja hitlerowska w oczach Polaków: Poglądy i opinie z lat 1945–1948* (Warsaw, 1987), 265.
[19] Ibid. 218–20.

Potsdam conference: 'We will have no ethnic minorities. We have switched over to the conception of a national state under the assumption that ethnic minorities ultimately will become a fifth column in the country. Therefore we push the Germans beyond our borders. . . . It is important to get rid of them now, and nobody knows whether we would be able to do that tomorrow too.'[20] That concept was based on the nationalistic ideology of the pre-war period and the cruel experiences of the Second World War.

To standing ovations the Czechoslovak Prime Minister, Gottwald, informed parliament on 16 October that the last transport with Sudeten German expellees to the US Occupation Zone would leave the country on 27 October and to the Soviet Zone two days later. During a rally on the occasion of the anniversary of the foundation of the First Republic on 28 October, President Beneš declared at St Wenzel's Square in Prague that from now on the Republic was a national state of the Czechs and Slovaks only. On the same occasion Gottwald spoke of the victorious accomplishment of the 'purging of the foreign element and deadly enemy of the nation from the Republic'.[21]

While the Germans were being expelled from Poland, Czechoslovakia, and Hungary, Slovaks were allowed to move from Hungary into Czechoslovakia and Magyars forced to leave Czechoslovakia for Hungary. Ukrainians, White Russians, and Poles passed the new border between Soviet Russia and Poland in opposite directions, and in the Soviet Union whole nations, such as the Chechen–Ingush, Kalmyks, and Crimean Tatars, were deported to the east because of alleged collaboration with the Germans. At the same time Marshal Tito was building a new Yugoslavia. The Sudeten German Social Democrat Wenzel Jaksch pointed to its federal character as a possible model for Czechoslovakia,[22] though the Yugoslav Germans were expelled and brutally treated, and many of them were killed, while the Italians from Dalmatia and Istria left Yugoslavia mainly because of their opposition to Communism. In September 1946, however, the South Tyroleans, who had opted for settlement in the so-called Great German Reich, were allowed to return to their

---

[20] Ibid. 94.   [21] Ibid.
[22] National Archives (Prague), Literary Bequest of Vladimír Klecanda, file 213, 5–8, Report of the Czechoslovak Ministry of Foreign Affairs (Fischl), 28 Dec. 1944.

homes in Italy. These developments indicate that even shortly after the war in some countries alternative solutions to the nationality conflicts were possible. In Poland and Czechoslovakia the expulsion of the Germans played a role in the power struggle between the Communist and anti-Communist forces. Both sides tried to outdo each other in national radicalism and to limit the number of the remaining Germans who were subjected to a verification of their 'loyalty' or their anti-fascist behaviour under Nazi rule.

The expulsion and transfer of the Germans from Poland, the newly acquired Polish territories, Czechoslovakia, Hungary, and Yugoslavia are part of the fourth wave of 'ethnic cleansing' in the twentieth century. The first wave had affected mainly Greeks and Turks following the failure of the Greek expedition into Anatolia. Within the Soviet Union, Stalin started the transfer of nationalities such as Poles, Germans, and Koreans from the border areas to Siberia and central Asia in the mid 1930s, fearing the potential activities of 'fifth columns'. The Soviet deportations reached their first climax after the German attack in 1941 and ended following the reconquest of the Baltic states, the Caucasus, and the Ukraine in 1943 and 1944. Another wave was initiated by Hitler in 1939 in western Poland and spread over other areas in eastern Europe supported by such politicians as Ante Pavelić, the leader of the Croat Ustashe movement. And, finally, the principle of 'ethnic cleansing' returned to south-eastern Europe in the 1990s. The main difference between the first four waves and the last expulsions on former Yugoslav soil, however, is that the international community attempted to stop some of the expulsions and to bring people back to their homes.

12

'Nobody's People':
The Dalits of Punjab in the
Forced Removal of 1947

GYANENDRA PANDEY

One aspect of the history of 'forced removals' that has not received as much attention as it should is the struggle that commonly takes place *within* a population that has been forced out over how the 'community', now uprooted, is to be reconstituted. Yet the very fact of forced removal disrupts customary structures, privileges, and power. Sometimes it also opens up an opportunity for the underprivileged to renegotiate the terms of participation in the community that is to be established in another place. It is one instance of this kind of struggle that I examine in this essay.

The example I take is the 'village community' of Punjab in the north-western part of the Indian subcontinent, famed as a province of peasant proprietors, village brotherhoods, and the extensive mixing of Muslim, Hindu, and Sikh populations.[1] My proposition about strains within an uprooted population allows me to approach the question of forced removal and its consequences through a somewhat unusual lens. Instead of asking what Partition does to relations between the recognized religious communities, which are seen as being the most obviously affected by the violence of Partition and the establishment of the two new states of India and Pakistan in 1947, I focus in this essay on the experience of the Dalits, whose part in the Punjabi village community is barely acknowledged in the literature, and who are supposed not to have been affected very much at all by the violence of the time.

The Dalits account for a good part of what are sometimes

---

[1] Cf. Malcolm Darling, *The Punjab Peasant in Prosperity and Debt* (new edn., New Delhi, 1977); C. J. Dewey, 'Images of the Village Community: A Study in Anglo-Indian Ideology', *Modern Asian Studies*, 6/3 (1975).

described as 'village servants' in accounts of the Punjab country-side. These were menial and artisanal groups of the lowest caste status, classified as untouchables and referred to in contemporary records by the official designations of Depressed Classes or Scheduled Castes, or as Harijans in Gandhi's favoured term.[2] Through an analysis of the contest over 'traditional' power arrangements, privileges, and disabilities in which the Dalits of rural Punjab come to be involved in 1947–8, I seek to re-examine the question of the uprooting of this rural community, and the attempted constitution of a more egalitarian village society in its place.

Neither Hindus nor Muslims

The title for this essay comes from Gandhi's reported exchange with Justice G. D. Khosla about the appropriate destination for Delhi's Muslims who had been herded into refugee camps in the city by the violence of Partition.

Khosla: 'The Muslims in the Old Fort camp have no wish to stay in this country. They told me, when I visited them, that they would like to go to Pakistan as soon as possible. Our own people are without houses or shelter. It breaks my heart to see them suffering like this, exposed to the elements . . . what should I do?'

Gandhi: 'When I go there, they [the Muslims] do not say they want to go to Pakistan. . . . They are also our people. You should bring them back and protect them.'[3]

No such luck for the Dalits in the course of the debates during Partition or in its recent historiography. The Dalit challenge to their classification as Hindus, which gathered strength from the second or third decade of the twentieth century, has led histori-ans to suggest that they were largely unaffected by Partition.[4] In

[2] Scheduled Castes and Tribes became the recognized official designation when a 'schedule' of 'untouchable' castes and tribes was drawn up for purposes of allocation of constituencies in the constitutional arrangements of 1935 and 1950. 'Harijans' or 'children of God' is the term Gandhi coined for the 'untouchable' castes in the 1930s. 'Dalits', meaning downtrodden or oppressed, is the name that militant ex-untouchables have adopted for themselves.

[3] G. D. Khosla, *Memory's Gay Chariot: An Autobiographical Narrative* (Delhi, 1985), 175–6.

[4] The single major exception to the neglect I am talking about is found in Sekhar Bandhopadhyay's work on the Namasudras of Bengal, who for a variety of reasons

'Nobody's People'

a chapter of her book *The Other Side of Silence* entitled 'Margins', Urvashi Butalia tells the story of a sweeper woman, Maya Rani, and her recollection of the abandon with which she and other Dalit children in Dinanagar (Batala) had moved around in the midst of the violence in 1947, entering deserted houses to loot bits of food and supplies, utensils, and other things they could use. 'The fighting was between Muslims and Hindus', Butalia quotes her as saying. 'We didn't fight with the Muslims, it had nothing to do with us.'[5]

Maya Rani's statement is in line with a joke told about the behaviour of Chuhra sweepers of Lahore in the midst of the violence which had Hindus fleeing in one direction and Muslims in the other. The story has the Chuhras declaring grandly, 'We don't need to escape to another place and nobody is going to touch us', as they continue to sweep the now empty streets of the city.[6] Aside from the implication of lower-class stupidity, the inference is meant to be this: the Scheduled Castes (or Dalits) were neither Hindu nor Muslim, and therefore quite unconcerned with the matter of Partition.[7]

Dalit groups make a miserably brief appearance in my book on Partition, in a paragraph where I refer to the many Hindus and Muslims who had been uprooted by violence from the villages around Delhi. Hindu and Sikh refugees from Pakistan

---

having to do with their numbers and the success of their social and political mobilization over the preceding decades have managed to form a distinct identity and hence a place for themselves in the detailed history of Partition and Independence; cf. Sekhar Bandhopadhyay, 'Transfer of Power and the Crisis of Dalit Politics in India, 1945–47', *Modern Asian Studies*, 34/4 (2000); and id., *Caste, Protest and Identity in Colonial India: The Namasudras of Bengal, 1872–1947* (London, 1997). Other scholars who have dealt with the question of Dalits and Partition include Ramnarayan S. Rawat, 'A Social History of "Chamars" in Uttar Pradesh, 1881–1956' (Ph.D. thesis, University of Delhi, 2004); and, more directly relevant to the concerns of the present essay, Ravinder Kaur, *Since 1947: Partition Narratives among Punjabi Migrants of Delhi* (Delhi, 2007); id., 'Narratives of Resettlement: Past, Present and Politics among the 1947 Punjabi Migrants in Delhi' (Ph.D. thesis, Roskilde University, 2004).

[5] Urvashi Butalia, *The Other Side of Silence* (Delhi, 1998), 254.

[6] Cited in Kaur, *Since 1947*, 164.

[7] See in this context (India Office Records, hereafter IOR) Photo Eur 425, photocopy of article, 'Partition of India 1947. The Memoirs & Experiences of a Sapper Subaltern with 2nd Indian Airborne Division', by Brig. D. A. Barker-Wyatt, CBE (n.d.), which reports the evidence of a Belgian missionary at Pasrur, south of Sialkot. 'Like some other Christian communities caught up in the communal conflicts his flock wore crosses sewn to their shirts or dhotis.' Apart from a few threats of circumcision, the Sapper did not hear of any attacks on them. 'Perhaps it helped that they didn't own much.'

300   GYANENDRA PANDEY

occupied many of the lands thus deserted, and conflicts subsequently arose between them and local Hindus and Muslims seeking to return to their villages. Dalit cultivators who had been among the chief tenants of local Muslims 'especially suffered', I wrote in that paragraph, 'since the immigrants—themselves cultivators—had no need of tenants on their newly occupied lands'.[8] Anees Qidwai's memoir, from which I derived this information, noted that the official Relief Committee in Delhi had been instructed to look after Hindu and Sikh refugees from Pakistan. An official Department of Relief and Rehabilitation had also been established. Unofficial peace committees had appeared in August–September 1948 to try to take care of the growing number of local Muslim refugees. However, there was no one to look after the 'local Hindus', which in this instance refers to Dalits. 'No Department had been opened for them', Qidwai observed.[9]

The Deportation of Dalits

The fact that no official department or peace committees had been established to look after the Dalits of Delhi and the northwest and north-east of British India more generally says more about the discourse of Partition than about the character of the social groups affected. For the available evidence makes it clear that Partition and Independence hardly left the Dalits untouched, even in the matter of being uprooted and exiled. Dalit migration was probably greatest among some of the low castes of Bengal, such as the Namasudras, but it was hardly negligible elsewhere.

According to the best estimates we have, some 6–7 per cent of the Hindus and Sikhs who migrated from West to East Punjab were from the Scheduled Castes. This would add up to the bulk of the Dalit population of the western districts.[10] As far we can tell, the majority of the Dalits of West Punjab migrated to the East in 1947–8: those who remained are today found chiefly in

[8] Gyanendra Pandey, *Remembering Partition: Violence, Nationalism and History in India* (Cambridge, 2001), 140.

[9] Anees Qidwai, *Azadi ki chhaon mein* (Delhi, 1990), 275.

[10] See Kirpal Singh, *The Partition of the Punjab* (Patiala, 1989), 188. For a discussion of Dalit caste numbers in West Punjab before Partition see Kaur, *Since 1947*, 160–2.

'Nobody's People'

the southern Punjab districts bordering Sindh.[11] In May 1948 some 250,000 Dalit refugees were said to be lying in refugee camps in East Punjab.[12] There were later attempts at migration from other parts of the new Pakistan territory, districts such as Bahawalpur in southern Punjab and the province of Sindh, moves that led the government of Sindh to pass an Essential Services Maintenance Ordinance. This was to prevent menial, agricultural, and artisanal workers who made up the Dalit population—people who kept the roads clean, cleared garbage and carcasses, performed essential repairs to implements, and carried out other menial tasks—from leaving the country. Again, we know that separate colonies were set up for Dalit refugees in India's capital city of Delhi, in Lajpat Nagar, Rehgarpura, and elsewhere.

The familiar version of the effects of Partition in Punjab is as follows.

The partition of the country brought with it misery, sufferings, grief and sorrow to millions on both sides. Most affected was . . . Punjab. . . . Millions of people had to leave their ancestral hearths and homes and migrate to the other side as refugees leaving behind everything they owned and possessed. But fortunate were those who could save their lives and the honour of their women-folk. Countless people could not escape the carnage and butchery. Innumerable persons were maimed and crippled, and an unknown number . . . were abducted, particularly young girls. Just think of those people who left behind their daughters and children and other relatives—killed or abducted!

I take this statement from the autobiography of Ishwar Das Pawar, the first Dalit to be appointed to the Punjab Judicial Service and one of the few Dalits to leave behind a first-person account of the events of the period. There is nothing surprising in the author's recollections of Partition in the extract cited above.

---

[11] See Pirbhu Lal Satyani, *Hame bhi jeene do: Pakistan mein Acchut logon ki surat-e-haal* (ASR Resource Centre, Lahore, 2005). One contemporary report noted that 'While a considerable percentage of Indian Christians [*sic*] continued to live in West Punjab, the non-muslim population of [West Punjab], Bahawalpur and N.W.F. and a proportion also from Sind poured into East Punjab' (IOR) MSS Eur F152/178, note on 'Economic Rehabilitation of Rural Refugees' (n.d., but written soon after Oct. 1948).

[12] National Archives of India (hereafter NAI), Rajendra Prasad Papers, File 5-R/48, col. 3, Report from Rameshwari Nehru, Head of Harijan Section, Ministry of Relief and Rehabilitation, no. 977, dated New Delhi, 3 May 1948 (hereafter Rameshwari Nehru, 'Report', 3 May 1948).

302 GYANENDRA PANDEY

What Pawar goes on to write immediately afterwards is rather more unusual: 'These sufferings were not confined to any particular group or community,' he notes. 'The Harijans shared the tragedy in no small measure. They suffered in life, honour and property as others did.'[13]

A contemporary report on the needs of rural refugees who had found their way from West to East Punjab provides the following description of the kind of groups that migrated. There were the well-publicized yeomen farmers, including many (we are told) whose families had migrated to the canal colonies of West Punjab two or three generations earlier. Next, there were numerous non-cultivating landlords, especially from the Rawalpindi and Multan Divisions, who held a certain amount of land cultivated largely by Muslim tenants, but whose primary income was derived from village trading and money-lending. There was also a not insignificant category of larger landholders in the Multan Division, the canal colonies, and a couple of other districts. Finally, as this summary statement has it, 'mention may be made of sections of [the] non-Muslim population who lived either by labour or by tenant-farming . . . or by devious pursuits such as those of Bazigars [sic!].' This last group is specifically identified as consisting of Harijans, Raidasi Sikhs, and Bazigars—all Dalit groups.[14]

In a census taken in February/March 1948, 386,581 of 823,671, practically 47 per cent, of the refugees found living in East Punjab towns claimed to have come from rural areas in West Punjab. Out of 375,170 refugees in rural camps, 294,183 (or over 78 per cent) belonged to the rural areas.[15] We do not know how many of these refugees were Dalits. One report, already cited, suggests as many as 250,000.[16] Several reports generated by the Military Evacuee Organization, the Fact Finding Committee, the East Punjab Liaison Agency, and other departments concerned with

[13] Ishwar Das Pawar, *My Struggle in Life* (Chandigarh, 1982; 3rd edn. 1993), 84–5.
[14] (IOR) MSS Eur F152/178, F. L. Brayne, 'Economic Rehabilitation of Rural Refugees'.
[15] Ibid.
[16] Rameshwari Nehru, 'Report', 3 May 1948. I need hardly add that statistics computed during times of war and other calamities are notoriously unreliable, and these figures need to be treated with caution. Nonetheless, quantitative as well as qualitative evidence points to the very large-scale migration of Dalit groups, along with that of caste Hindus and Sikhs, from West Punjab.

'Nobody's People'

the evacuation and resettlement of refugees in 1947–8 make only passing mention of the Dalits of West Punjab. Some speak of thousands of lower-caste converts, who were treated as 'suspects' by many Muslims and who apparently expressed their willingness to be evacuated to India as soon as some guarantee of safety appeared.

A report of work done in Montgomery district, dealing with the question of Hindus and Sikhs who wished to be evacuated, illustrates the point very well indeed:

Traders from Montgomery and Okara tehsils and peasants from Pakpattan were approached and a large number of them showed willingness to be evacuated. . . . Harijans from the Chichawatni Sub Tehsil also desired to be evacuated. A large number of Harijans, Oads, Rajputs and Bazigars were evacuated from the interior of the district during the following days. The last foot convoy who crossed the Indian border through Head Sulemanki [in early May 1948] consisted of *bazigars*. . . . Most of the Harijans became converts to Christianity for fear of life but when the Liaison Officer approached them they showed readiness to be evacuated and came out in large numbers.[17]

From Gujrat, where the 80,222 Scheduled Castes accounted for roughly 7.3 per cent of the population according to the 1941 census, it was reported at the end of November 1947, when the Indian Liaison Officer finally left, that perhaps 30,000 forcibly converted people still remained in the district. 'Most of the Harijans were . . . anxious to be evacuated but remained stranded as the Agency could not effectively operate in the district.'[18]

An April 1948 estimate of those awaiting evacuation from West Punjab noted that the vast majority of them had been nominally 'converted'. The breakdown it provided of roughly 25,350 persons still to be evacuated was as follows:

---

[17] 'Report of Work in Montgomery District', LAR File No. LIX/2, in Kirpal Singh (ed.), *Select Documents on Partition of Punjab—1947* (Delhi, 1991), 648–9. The original files of the Fact Finding Committees' investigations have unfortunately not been made available to historians. G. D. Khosla and Kirpal Singh were given access to them in the years immediately following Partition and Independence. Khosla used them for the production of his semi-official report, *Stern Reckoning: A Survey of the Events Leading up to and Following the Partition of India* (1949; repr. Delhi, 1989).

[18] 'Report of Work in Gujrat District', LAR File No. LIX/9, in Kirpal Singh, *Select Documents*, 637.

Dera Ghazi Khan	30 (almost all converts)
Muzaffargarh	398 (328 converts)
Multan	1,200 (1,100 converts)
Montgomery	5,000 (almost all converted Bazigars)
Sheikhupura	1,900 (all converts; 1,300 Bazigars)
Sargodha	300 (all converts)
Mianwali	900
Lyallpur	10,000 (all converts, mostly Bazigars)
Jhang	1,623 (all converts; 660 Bazigars)
Gujranwala	2,000 (all converts)
Lahore	2,000 (all converts)

The report noted that these figures were very likely to be an underestimate: 'a large number of people who have [so far] refused to get out of West Punjab are likely to apply for evacuation when they find . . . people converted like themselves going away.'[19]

The needs and aspirations of these different evacuees—'converts' and non-converts, landholders and the labouring poor—were hardly the same. It is clear from contemporary records that those who had held land and property in West Punjab wanted compensation and a restoration of rights in property. For others, however, who had had few privileges in the earlier situation, the uprooting of the traditional rural establishment provided an opportunity to search for changed social and economic conditions, new occupations, and an increased level of economic security and independence. As Pawar puts it: 'With the change of the entire structure of life of the people due to the upheaval their [the Dalits'] outlook on life underwent a radical change. They were . . . not inclined to go to villages in the capacity of slaves and *Kamins* [menials] of the village proprietary body. They wanted to lead an independent life as free citizens of some status.'[20]

The issue I take up for investigation here is the clash between these different aspirations. Received accounts say little about how groups that were distinctly different and had long maintained a careful distance in their social interactions came to be classified as *one* religious minority at this time. What was it that

[19] Chief Liaison Officer (India) to Chief Secretary, East Punjab, BRF 218-ER-48C, ibid. 613–14.

[20] Pawar, *My Struggle in Life*, 85–6.

'Nobody's People' 305

made Dalits and non-Dalits, menial and landowning castes, join the procession of people fleeing from one area to another? How were the refugees classified when they reached what would be their places of resettlement? And how did the renegotiation of relations and conditions of life and work play out?

The Making of Refugees

Many Dalits in Punjab and the north-western region more generally identified themselves as part of the Hindu or Sikh community on account of the fact that that was the position daily allotted to them, and a position that was perhaps reinforced by the Hindu social and religious reform efforts of the later nineteenth and early twentieth centuries.[21] In part they will have moved from their ancestral homes because their patrons were forced to move, or because the entire village was uprooted, and there was no knowing what was in store for them if they stayed on. Surely, too, part of the pressure to move came from the widespread seizure of land in which even small bits of agricultural, pasture, and homestead land held by the lowest castes and classes became the object of loot, appropriation, and aggrandizement.

Although it is widely noted and commented upon in studies of 'riots' in independent India, the importance of the question of land, livelihood, and profits, which took the form of a pervasive land-grab at Partition, has been somewhat underplayed in historical research on Partition. Perhaps this is because scholars have felt the need to underline the ways in which class and cultural distinctions were often disregarded when it came to the targeting of minority populations. It is clear that moments of violence and rupture such as this have tended to flatten popular perceptions of communities and peoples, and thus to homogenize and hollow out whole populations.[22] Nevertheless, struggles over land and

---

[21] In her study of Dalit refugees in Delhi, Ravinder Kaur emphasizes the importance of Arya Samaj activities and influence in determining the social position and fate of these groups who came, she suggests, from a largely urban, artisanal, or labouring background. However, if this was true for Dalit communities in Lahore and other urban areas of Punjab, it seems to me less likely to have affected the rural areas of Punjab and other provinces from where a majority of the Dalit refugees came; Kaur, *Since 1947*, 174 and *passim*.

[22] For an elaboration of this point, see my *Remembering Partition*, 39, 165, 198, and *passim*.

property clearly contributed to the widespread attacks and eviction of populations in 1947.

Let me illustrate this point by citing the example of Dalits who were forced out of their village homes in the vicinity of Delhi, not in this instance because of their association with Hindus or Sikhs, but because of a fortuitous link with a Muslim landowner. Here is the story as it is recounted in Anees Qidwai's detailed account of the Delhi region in the immediate aftermath of Partition and Independence.[23]

In October 1947, after more than a month of extreme violence in Delhi had uprooted the majority of local Muslims from their homes and forced them into refugee camps (and in many cases onto the road or railway to Pakistan), Qidwai and her colleagues saw that 'an entirely new kind of refugee'—well-dressed, well-fed, and confident-looking men, women, and children, with bags of grain, bedsteads, pots and pans, and the like, laden on bullock carts, trucks, and other vehicles—had arrived in the Muslim refugee camps, apparently on their way to Pakistan.

It transpired that they were from the village of Tihar, a few miles west of what were then Delhi's city limits. The Delhi administration had taken over the village, which was the property of a landowner named Badr-i-Alam, exchanged it officially for a very large property that he was to receive in Pakistan, and allotted the local lands to refugees from Pakistan. The population of the village was 7,000: 5,000 Muslims and 2,000 Harijans (or Dalits). The former had arrived in Delhi's Muslim refugee camps, the latter were camping in the open outside the village.

Qidwai makes the point that the pattern of polarization and eviction was roughly similar in both halves of Punjab and in Delhi. On both sides, 'Hindu' and 'Muslim' rule was proclaimed. 'The police and other local officials took full part in this propaganda . . . And whatever was done was done in the name of the [respective] governments.' People were told that it was the desire of 'both the Indian and the Pakistani Government' that the minorities be sent away; and panic-stricken individuals and families belonging to these minorities were forced to evacuate their villages and localities and to assemble in so-called 'safe' areas or camps.[24]

---

[23] I have put together this account from the scattered references found in Qidwai, *Azadi ki chhaon mein*, 26 and n., 80–6, 121–2, and *passim*.

[24] Ibid. 184–5.

'Nobody's People'

It was in this way that the 5,000 Muslim residents lost their homes and lands in Tihar. The Muslim refugees told social workers of how 40 per cent of their number were in government service. Their names had been removed from the rolls without explanation. Three months earlier they had also been deprived of their arms licences. Only one Muslim had been allowed to keep his licence and that, too, was taken away on 21 October. To top it all, the villagers of the surrounding areas had organized a social boycott of the Muslims. What option did they have, then, except to depart?[25]

The 2,000 Dalit cultivators, who had been among the chief tenants of the local Muslims, were turned out along with them. It was assumed that incoming Sikh and Hindu refugees, themselves cultivators, would have no need of Dalit tenants. If they wanted additional labour, that was for them to decide.

Gandhi and Jawaharlal Nehru, among others, strenuously opposed the wholesale expulsion of Muslims, but by themselves and from their elevated (and consequently distant) positions, they were unable to control the behaviour of local officials. 'Two parallel governments were at work—one in the hands of people bent on dividing [all of the property and people], the other in the hallowed hands of Gandhi.'[26] In the careful narrative provided by the Muslim refugees from Tihar, the interventions and directions of the *sarkar* loom large.[27] On 11 October, an officer visited their village, warned them of impending threats, and suggested they leave. On 16 October, an even more senior official came and repeated the same advice. A police official came to repeat this instruction on 21 October; and finally a high-ranking official of the province sent trucks and had them shifted to the camp.

---

[25] Ibid. 121. Qidwai also reports a more humane story, that of the Muslim employees of the Delhi Cloth Mills who were transferred by the management after two of them had been killed just outside the factory gates. Seeing the signs, the management arranged to transport them with their families to the DCM mill in Lyallpur, Pakistan, and brought the Hindu employees of Lyallpur to Delhi in their place (pp. 122–3). For other evidence regarding arbitrary dismissals and confiscations from the minorities, see my *Remembering Partition*.

[26] Qidwai, *Azadi ki chhaon mein*, 85; cf. 125.

[27] The dates in Qidwai's recounting are not always consistent. The arrival of Tihar's Muslim refugees in the camp is given as December 1947, but appears from other entries to have been in October. However, the refugees' account of different dates on which particular officers came to convey particular messages or demands simply points to a particular pattern of events, and a collective belief in how these had occurred.

'The truth was weak, and falsehood powerful,' concludes Qidwai.

At a loss, Qidwai and her colleagues sought the advice of Gandhi, Nehru, and other sympathetic leaders. As expected, the latter said these proceedings were entirely against government's policy and the local workers should do whatever they could to rehabilitate the local Muslims and Dalits in their homes. Emboldened by this, Subhadra Joshi, Qidwai, and others sought to persuade the villagers of Tihar to return, assuring them that there was no official order calling for their eviction. They succeeded in reinstalling the Dalit villagers along with their animals and meagre belongings, taking advantage of the absence of the police picket at night and appointing one or two volunteers to visit the village daily; but failed in the attempt to persuade Muslim refugees to return.

Just when the Muslims in the camp began to consider the possibility of returning to their homes with some guarantee of safety, Qidwai tells us, with their Dalit co-residents also urging the social workers to 'bring our Muslim brothers home', the Deputy Commissioner of Delhi visited their camp and gave them advice that worked to produce the opposite effect: 'As an official I would say that there is no fear, you should go back, because this is the desire of the government at this time. But as a friend, I cannot give you this advice; conditions are not good at present.'[28]

The question of who should live on the lands occupied by one major Muslim landowner in a village near Delhi provides the context for the transformation of thousands of Dalits (along with thousands of local Muslims who still preferred not to make the journey to a distant Pakistan) into what I have called refugees-at-home.[29] The Dalit refugees who fled from West to East Punjab were in a somewhat different position, yet affected by many of the same battles over land, property, and local influence.

Across Punjab, the official drive to partition everything into Hindu, Muslim, and Sikh (as well as Christian, as something of a residual category) had two consequences. First, it led to a classification of the entire population into Muslim and non-Muslim,

[28] Qidwai, *Azadi ki chhaon mein*, 122. The comments of Dalit villagers pleading for the return of the local Muslims are given on p. 86.
[29] See Pandey, *Remembering Partition*, 124, 151, and *passim*.

'Nobody's People'

309

with the question of which lands were to go to India and which to Pakistan being decided primarily on the basis of the distribution of population calculated in these terms. It also led, once the mass migration of populations had begun in both directions and come to be officially sanctioned, to sustained efforts on the part of many local officials and activists, especially on the Indian side, to get 'all our people' out.

A report of evacuation work done in Gujrat district stated that local Pakistani officials had been unsympathetic and even obstructive in their response. The workers of the Indian liaison agency had been attacked: and while the Liaison Officer escaped, many of his staff had been captured, beaten, and humiliated.[30] A report from Gujranwala declared: 'Cases were known in which the Harijans who had embraced Islam only to save their skin did not like [__?] and consequently exhibited a desire to migrate to the East Punjab. Most of them had embraced Islam as a matter of expediency, to save their skins and property. . . . On [over?] the whole area every people genuinely wanted to come out to the East.'[31]

The concerted efforts of Indian officials to get all Hindus and Sikhs out of West Pakistan stemmed in part from genuine concern over the fate of the relatively small sections of 'non-Muslims' who might be left behind. It flowed as well from an official belief that what they believed to be true *was* true, that these marginalized castes and communities classified as Hindu and Sikh were, in fact, Hindu and Sikh, and as such out of place in independent Pakistan. What followed from this was the argument that all of these people wished to escape from Pakistan and find a new home in India. Hence the repeated assertions in the reports cited above that low-caste converts to Islam or Christianity wanted no part of such conversion, and that they expressed their desire to migrate as soon as Indian officials appeared.

Yet there are at least stray references which suggest that the situation on the ground was rather more untidy. There were clearly some factors that went against the sweep to get the minorities out. Among these was the maintenance of economic production and perhaps some stability in rural existence.

[30] LAR File No. LIX/9, in Kirpal Singh, *Select Documents*, 636–7.
[31] 'Report of work in Gujranwala District', LAR File No. LIX/12, ibid. 632.

Consider Anees Qidwai's report that, while Hindu villagers were quite willing to see the backs of Muslim landowners and tenants, and indeed drove them out from many of the villages neighbouring Delhi, they were very keen to retain the services of Muslim artisans such as carpenters, ironsmiths, and oil-pressers, without whom the village economy would grind to a halt: many of these Muslims were forced to 'convert', at least temporarily.[32] Similar efforts to prevent the migration of non-Muslims were noted in contemporary reports from Pakistan. As the Fact Finding Officer for Gujranwala had it:

In the beginning the evacuation was in full swing . . . thereafter the task became difficult. A stage came when the Muslim[s] began to obstruct the evacuation of the non-Muslims who had by now become converted to Islam.

After some time . . . yet another change in the attitude of the public and the authorities was noted. They became anxious to get rid of the land-holders so that they could divide their land amongst the Muslim refugees. At the same time, they became averse to the migration of *Kamins* [menial labourers] and the Harijan non-Muslims for they could be useful slaves of the community.[33]

The widely reported efforts of Raja Ghazanfar Ali Khan, Minister for Refugees and Rehabilitation in Pakistan, to prevent an exodus of non-Muslims, and the attempt to use the police for the 'control of essential services' under the Sindh Maintenance of Public Safety Ordinance, 1947,[34] may well be seen as being part of the same concern.

As in the case of the Muslim and Dalit villagers of Tihar, there are indications in contemporary reports on refugees from West Pakistan that the non-Muslim evacuees were themselves not always so keen to migrate as the Liaison Officers sometimes suggested. The Gujrat report quoted above that spoke of the difficulties of evacuation work in the district and of 30,000 'forcibly converted persons' remaining stranded there, also noted that 'the Harijans accepted Islam more readily than the non-Muslims [*sic*]':[35] not altogether surprising since they had gained little, and

---

[32] Qidwai, *Azadi ki chhaon mein*, 174.

[33] LAR File No. LIX/12, in Kirpal Singh, *Select Documents*, 632.

[34] See Vazira Fazila-Yacoobali Zamindar, *The Long Partition and the Making of Modern South Asia: Refugees, Boundaries, Histories* (New York, 2007), 52.

[35] LAR File No. LIX/9, in Kirpal Singh, *Select Documents*, 634.

'Nobody's People'

now perhaps had even less to gain, from a nominal adherence to Hinduism. The report from Campbellpore that referred to Raja Ghazanfar Ali Khan's efforts to prevent the wholesale departure of Hindus and Sikhs similarly noted that the minister's campaign had had some effect. 'Influenced by this propaganda [*sic*] organized by the Raja and Col. Rab Nawab of 15th Punjab [Regiment] then stationed at Kahour, District Campbellpore a good number of refugees left Wah Camp for their respective homes. . . . The Sikhs of Chumtara were over confident after the speeches and assurances given by the Raja until . . . four of them were murdered in broad day light in the bazaar and the remaining were given shelter in the Police Station.'[36]

Those killings apparently turned the tide for the 'non-Muslims' of Campbellpore. The story parallels that of the Tihar Muslims, local peasants evicted under duress, uncertain of their future, and still willing to consider a return to their villages until a leading officer of the Delhi administration warns them of the dire consequences this might entail. One might return, in this context, to the reported exchange between Gandhi and Khosla that I cited at the beginning of this paper: 'when I go to see them, that is not what they say'; or recall the remark made to the Indian Prime Minister, Jawaharlal Nehru, by an old Muslim peasant in a village near Delhi: 'Have you ever heard of a peasant who wanted to leave his land?'[37]

The 'Village Community' and the Resettlement of Refugees

There is considerable evidence, then, of bitter and sometimes extended struggle over land and property in the course of efforts to evict 'Muslims' and 'non-Muslims' during Partition. This pattern of conflict was resumed when it came to the matter of the official resettlement and rehabilitation of refugees. The contest between local refugees and refugees coming in from distant districts, and between refugees and more stable and privileged (or lucky) groups, affected the Dalits as it affected other sections of the populace.

[36] 'Report of work in Campbellpore District', LAR File No. LIX/6, ibid. 626.
[37] (IOR) MSS Eur F200/53, Emergency Committee of the Cabinet, meeting of 17 Oct. 1947.

Enlightened social and political workers as well as many Dalits saw in 1947 an opportunity to right past wrongs. With the departure of Muslim artisans and the wider choice of occupations for Dalit workers, caste, some felt, would no longer be quite as tenable as a hereditary basis for occupation.[38] 'The Harijans, who generally comprise landless labourers and village artisans, have become fully conscious of their rights as citizens,' M. S. Randhawa, an ICS official responsible for rural rehabilitation in East Punjab, wrote in the early 1950s. 'There is considerable urge among them to acquire the respectable status of landowners, as ownership of land, however small in area, confers dignity and status.' Leather-workers began abandoning the degrading occupation of shoemaking and tanning of hides, even when it was more lucrative, 'simply to acquire respectability', thus causing what Randhawa calls 'a great national loss'.[39]

On the other hand, landholding and property-owning groups among the refugees demanded 'full compensation', and not just 'resettlement'. They saw no justice in the argument that their 'displacement offer[ed] the first convenient opportunity for economic reform', to be followed 'when political circumstances allow[ed]' by similar action in other quarters.[40] These groups were supported by influential elements in the administration who wanted to see the maintenance of the 'village community' and, with it, rural order. Hence Randhawa's comment: 'The village economy represented a co-operative enterprise in which the small peasant proprietors and the Harijan farm labourers were partners; and it is unfortunate that their relations have been disturbed and disharmony has resulted.'[41]

The balancing of the interests of different castes and classes among the refugees was never going to be easy. While the number of Muslims fleeing from East Punjab, and of Sikhs and Hindus coming into the province, was roughly comparable, the land and property they left behind was not. Officials estimated that while the economically better-off Sikh and Hindu refugees had left behind some 60 lakh acres of land in West Punjab, the

---

[38] MSS Eur F152/178, 'Economic Rehabilitation of Rural Refugees'.

[39] M. S. Randhawa, *Out of the Ashes: An Account of the Rehabilitation of Refugees from West Pakistan in Rural Areas of East Punjab* (Bombay, n.d.; preface dated 25 Oct. 1954), 213–14.

[40] MSS Eur F152/178, 'Economic Rehabilitation of Rural Refugees'.

[41] Randhawa, *Out of the Ashes*, 214.

'Nobody's People' 313

Muslim evacuees from East Punjab and adjacent princely states had left only 45 lakh acres.[42]

According to the policy initially laid down by the government of East Punjab, these 45 lakh acres would be allotted to landowners among the incoming refugees, 'as distinguishable from mere tillers of the soil [such] as Harijans'.[43] As Chaudhri Chotu Ram, the leader of the Punjab *zamindars* and erstwhile minister in the Unionist government, put it, the low and menial castes could not be included in the list of statutory agriculturists as this would adversely affect the protection given to 'agricultural castes' under the Punjab Alienation of Land Act.[44]

Quite where this left Dalits and other lower-class groups in the matter of resettlement is not clear. There was bitter controversy and much agitation over the fifty-year-old Land Alienation Act, which barred the bulk of the Dalit population and other 'non-agricultural' groups from acquiring land. The Dalit leader B. R. Ambedkar, independent India's first Law Minister, urged its repeal; and the Act was repealed in 1951 by presidential decree 'as it denied giving effect to the Fundamental Rights conferred by the Constitution on every citizen to acquire, hold and dispose of property'.[45]

There are conflicting reports on how much was done for the Dalits in the rehabilitation programme, an important arena in the new nationalist desire for 'scientific' planning of the economy. A scheme of temporary allotment of evacuee lands was inaugurated in September 1947 to provide some place of refuge and work for the huge influx of refugees. Many of the larger landholders, non-cultivating landlords as well as the bigger farmers, refused to accept these temporary measures. On the other hand, numerous landless groups, including Dalits, appear to have taken advantage of the scheme. 'It will be a problem of considerable size', an official report noted in 1948, 'to settle 42,000 families of non-land-holders who are at present holding temporary allotments.'[46] More

---

[42] A 'lakh' equals 100,000.

[43] NAI, Rajendra Prasad Papers, File 5-R/48, col. 3, letter no. 977, Ministry of Relief and Rehabilitation, Harijan section, Rameshwari Nehru to Rajendra Prasad, Congress President, 3 May 1948.

[44] Pawar, *My Struggle in Life*, 51.

[45] (IOR) MSS Eur F158/641B, Indiagram 11 Apr. 1951.

[46] MSS Eur F152/178, 'Economic Rehabilitation of Rural Refugees'. See also Tai Yong Tan and Gyanesh Kudaisya, *The Aftermath of Partition in South Asia* (London, 2000), 129.

generally, says a survey of 1952, officials were instructed to pay special attention to the needs of Dalits, including rural artisans and village servants, in the matter of jobs, loans, establishment of cooperative societies, and allotment of houses in the countryside. 'These instructions have been carefully enforced, with substantial consequent benefit to Harijans.'[47]

As against these reports, however, we have a detailed analysis from May 1948 that speaks of 250,000 Dalit refugees in East Punjab, 90 per cent of them agriculturists, 'living a life of misery and idleness' in makeshift camps and depending on the 'free but inadequate rations' supplied by the government.[48] In the early months of that year, with the sympathy and democratic aspirations generated by the first flush of freedom, and energized further perhaps by Gandhi's martyrdom, Gandhians like Rameshwari Nehru, Vinoba Bhave, and Rajendra Prasad turned up the pressure on the East Punjab government to take some concrete action, albeit one step at a time, to rehabilitate the Dalit refugees as 'citizens'.

The May 1948 statement, prepared by a team led by Rameshwari Nehru, noted that the Bikaner State had allotted roughly one lakh (100,000) acres of land vacated by Muslim refugees in Ganganagar colony to the actual tillers of the soil. Among these were 1,200 Dalit families, allotted 16 acres each along with other low-caste agriculturists. The same principle needed to be extended to East Punjab and the Punjab princely states. If a mere 5 lakh acres of the 45 lakh left by Muslim evacuees from the province could be reserved for the Dalits, the report noted, the latter would be able to live like citizens rather than serfs in independent India. There were 50,000 Dalit refugee families. 'Each Harijan family could thus be assigned 10 acres of land with occupancy rights and it should be possible to introduce cooperative farming among them to ensure increased production.'[49]

---

[47] Rameshwari Nehru Papers, Subject File no. 1(a), Pt. III, 'Harijan Welfare in Punjab', published by the Public Relations Department, Punjab (n.d.; information and statistics cover the period to Dec. 1952). The report notes e.g. that by December 1952 there were 24 cooperative societies for shoemaking, weaving, basket work, and so on: these had been granted loans adding up to a total of Rs. 84,200.

[48] Rajendra Prasad Papers, File 5-R/48, col. 3, letter no. 977, Ministry of Relief and Rehabilitation, Harijan Section, Rameshwari Nehru to Rajendra Prasad, Congress President, 3 May 1948.

[49] Ibid.

'Nobody's People'

The all-India Congress President Rajendra Prasad and the renowned social worker Vinoba Bhave pressed Gopichand Bhargava, the Premier of East Punjab, to give the 50,000 Dalit families still in refugee camps some land of their own to cultivate. 'This should be possible seeing that you have settled hundreds of thousands of people. . . . If you include these people also in the group which will be given the minimum quantity of land it would not very much affect the position of those higher in grade who get larger quantity.'[50]

At an informal conference with East Punjab ministers that he convened in June 1948, Rajendra Prasad reiterated the demand that the 50,000 Dalit families from West Punjab be allotted 5 lakh acres of land in East Punjab. 'If no land was allotted to the landless Harijans they would once again be relegated to the status of Kammies [kamins].' Gopichand Bhargava, the East Punjab Premier, reported that 65,000 acres of land had already been 'allotted on temporary basis' to about 6,000 families of Dalit refugees. About 8 lakh acres was still available and it had been decided that 'in making temporary allotments for cultivation for the next two crops, Harijan cultivators would be given preference in . . . land left over after allotment of land to owners [sic]'. Pressed further on this, Bhargava said that of the 8 lakh acres still with the government, 5 would have to be allotted to landowners: the 'remaining 2½ to 3 lac acres' could be allotted to Harijan refugees. He went on to say that 'all Harijans were not agriculturists'. Many were artisans, and should be absorbed in industrial channels. A good number worked as day labourers, and 'they could not legitimately be allotted land'.[51] Evidently, the political balance lay on the side of the landowning classes.

In August 1948, the East Punjab government was still dragging its feet. The government had agreed to allot some land to the Dalits on a temporary basis, after meeting the initial demands of the landowners from West Punjab, the Rehabilitation Minister Partap Singh now wrote. But it had come up against several obstacles. He lists among these the difficulties faced by the Dalits

---

[50] Rajendra Prasad Papers, File 1-C/48, col. 1, Rajendra Prasad to Gopichand Bhargava, 7 May 1948.

[51] Rajendra Prasad Papers, File 1-C/48, col. 1, Minutes of informal conference convened by Dr Rajendra Prasad on 25 June 1948 at his residence in New Delhi (signed Rameshwari Nehru, Head of Harijan Section).

in acquiring oxen and the basic implements required for cultivation, and mentions in passing that the landowners coming from West Punjab were dissatisfied with the compensation offered to them in the form of reduced lands (following a system of 'graded' cuts, to take account of the smaller amount of land available in the East). He goes on to say that the non-Muslim proprietors of East Punjab possess some 2 lakh acres of cultivable waste. With financial aid from the central government and the Harijan committee, the Punjab government could use its influence to acquire this land at reasonable rates and help develop it for purposes of cultivation. Meanwhile, 'if the Harijan [refugees] wish to have land on temporary cultivation basis, the land is still with us and it will be given to them up to, say, 75,000 acres for the present'[52]—a far cry from the 500,000 acres asked for by the Harijan Department, and a substantial climb-down from the 250,000 to 300,000 acres for temporary allotment offered by the Punjab Premier in the June conference.

Indeed, the actions of the landowning castes, refugee and local, to appropriate as much of the land as possible, and the consequent denial of even small plots of land for the 'non-agriculturist' Dalits, went further. There was a concerted effort throughout the districts of East Punjab and the princely states of the region to partition common lands (*abadi* and *shamilat zamin*). Fearing that these areas would be entrusted to newly constituted village *panchayats*, or democratic councils of local self-government, proprietors in many districts quickly partitioned such lands, thus whittling away the rights of Dalits and other village workers. Pawar visited several villages in Sonepat subdivision in connection with cases that had been brought before him, and found that 'Harijans had lost all the small plots of land already in their possession from long generations. . . . In some cases, for example, of weavers and rope-makers, they had no place to carry on their professions as they needed sufficiently long stretches of land to serve as rope-walks.'[53]

[52] Rajendra Prasad Papers, File 5-R/48, col. 5, Partap Singh, Rehabilitation Minister, East Punjab, to Rajendra Prasad, Congress President, 23 Aug. 1948. See also DO no. 3517, GOI, Ministry of Relief and Rehabilitation, Harijan Section, New Delhi, 29 Sept. 1948, for expression of disappointment and concern by Jagjivan Ram, Vinoba Bhave, Jairamdas Daulatram, Rameshwari Nehru, and others, over the Punjab government's failure to fulfil its promises.

[53] Pawar, *My Struggle in Life*, 91.

'Nobody's People' 317

A resolution passed at a Harijan Conference in September 1950 points to other aspects of the problem:

The house-fronts (Gitwaras) of non-zamindars are partitioned and sufficient land is not left for the growing population of Harijans. They [the Harijans] are forced to live in over-crowded small houses. . . . Where such partition is considered necessary, a law should be passed requiring the persons concerned to leave sufficient land for the expansion of the habitation of the growing population of the non-agriculturists . . . and sufficient land for the grazing of their animals in the jungle. Where the land in red cord [land reserved for dwellings] . . . is insufficient for the habitation of the growing population of the village within the Red Line . . . barren land outside the red cord may be granted to the Harijans so that they may set up their own colonies there.[54]

Another development that needs to be noted in this context was the attempt made to force several Dalit communities back into the status of Criminal Tribes. Ishwar Dass Pawar refers to the insidious consequences of the Punjab Criminal Tribes Act by which numerous Dalit castes and sub-castes, including Sansis, Bhangalis, Barars, Baurias, Nats, and Kuch-Bandhs, had been declared 'criminal tribes', with restrictions placed on their movement out of designated villages and settlements and members being required to report regularly at the local police posts when out of work or otherwise singled out by the administration. 'It is a matter of great shame', he writes in the 1982 autobiography, that 'in spite of the Government's plans [and] professions', little had been done for this group of marked and humiliated people. 'The only thing done so far is that the pernicious law has been repealed, and now they are termed as Vimukt-jatis, the "liberated castes",'[55] a designation that served only to perpetuate their segregation and mark them out for continued discrimination.

Alluding to the same issue, Rameshwari Nehru protested in September 1949 against an act of police firing in Jaipur State that resulted in a number of casualties from among the poor tribal group of Meenas. The government refused to institute an independent inquiry into the incident, apparently because the Meenas 'belonged to the so-called criminal tribes, their lives were supposed to be cheap and it was not considered necessary to

[54] NAI, Rameshwari Nehru Papers, Subject File no. 1(a), Pt. I, report of Haryana Harijan Conference held under Presidentship of Rameshwari Nehru on 26 Sept. 1950.
[55] Pawar, *My Struggle in Life*, 54.

318 GYANENDRA PANDEY

institute any inquiry'. Nehru noted that the Criminal Tribes Act was being repealed piecemeal: 'It is not understandable why this heinous Act is being repealed province-wise. An all-India measure to wipe out this blot is the urgent need of the day.'[56]

The situation appears indeed to have gone from bad to worse in some places. In the aftermath of Partition, some segments of the so-called Criminal Tribes who had earlier escaped such classification, or at least some of its worst consequences, appear to have been forced back into the category. Witness the following petition from the Dalit refugees who came from the agricultural settlement of Bauriya Criminal Tribes at Kot Khalsa in Tehsil Khanewal, District Multan. As many as 3,500 non-Muslims of the settlement were massacred in August 1947, the petition tells us.

There were 98 landholding hereditary Patedars tenants of the Government in the above mentioned Criminal Tribes settlement with agreements [that is, *pattis*, records of rights in land: hence *pattidars*] for 15 years.

About 91 of the total landholders had been murdered, only 7 of us the undersigned survived. . . .

Having suffered so much we come to understand that the Pakistan Authorities have not sent our Jamabandi Records [records relating to rent and revenue payment]. . . . We could not bring the patta deeds enacted with Government for 15 years as hereditary tenants to serve as documentary evidence.

Over and above all this, the Criminal Tribes Deptt. has imposed upon us restrictions of giving attendance every day and leaving station with Police permits which we or our parents and ancestors were absolutely exempted from.[57]

I do not know what came of this petition.

Their Own People

Many of the conflicts outlined above remained unresolved at the time of Partition and Independence. They have not been fully

---

[56] Rameshwari Nehru's letter to the *Hindustan Times*, 10 Sept. 1949.

[57] NAI, Rameshwari Nehru Papers, Subject File no. 1 (a) Pt I, petition of seven residents of village Qutbewal Arain, Tehsil, and District Ludhiana, through Shri A. S. Satyayarthi, Regional Working Secretary, Displaced Harijans Rehabilitation Board (Central Government Agency), Civil Secretariat, Jullunder (n.d., but apparently filed on 5 Aug. 1950).

'Nobody's People' 319

resolved since. I have suggested that the Dalits of Punjab were 'nobody's people' in 1947–8, in that neither of the new nations, India or Pakistan, spoke for them in the way in which they spoke for Hindus, Muslims, and Sikhs. From another point of view, they were nothing but other people's 'people', in the sense of being their dependants or charges: the 'people', and hence the responsibility, of the landowners, of the 'village community', of social reformers and Gandhians, and various other political groups.

As against this, the Dalit struggle might be described as being aimed precisely at becoming their own people: a people (or community) with self-respect and freedom, and the economic independence and political rights to have their say as citizens in an independent nation. The violence and forced removal of Partition, which provided unprecedented challenges as well as a modicum of new opportunities, may be seen as one moment in that struggle.

13

The 1947 Partition of India and Migration: A Comparative Study of Punjab and Bengal

IAN TALBOT

The 1947 massacres and migrations were for many years little more than footnotes in the study of the achievement of India's and Pakistan's Independence. Since the 1980s, however, historians have increasingly focused on them. The work of such scholars as Urvashi Butalia, Kamla Bhasin, and Ritu Menon enabled a gendered dimension to be brought to the Partition experience.[1] They have addressed the sensitive issues of the large-scale abduction of women and their recovery and, in some instances, forced repatriation. Accounts of the violence which sparked off the greatest refugee migration of the twentieth century have begun to see it as more than a 'temporary madness'. Anders Hansen, Paul Brass, and Ian Talbot have shown that it was organized, possessed a genocidal element, and was the result not merely of the collapse, but occasionally the involvement of local systems of civil and police administration.[2]

Work on the Punjab region of India has been at the forefront of the 'new history' of Partition. This reflects the fact that it was at the epicentre of violence. In less than three months, over 8 million Punjabis in chaotic and often brutalizing circumstances undertook a reverse migration across the new international boundary which divided the region. Accounts of this vast human

[1] Urvashi Butalia, *The Other Side of Silence: Voices from the Partition of India* (New Delhi, 1998); Ritu Menon and Kamla Bhasin, *Borders and Boundaries: Women in India's Partition* (New Delhi, 1998).

[2] Anders Bjorn Hansen, *Partition and Genocide: Manifestation of Violence in Punjab 1937–1947* (New Delhi, 2002); Paul Brass, 'The Partition of India and Retributive Genocide in the Punjab 1946–1947: Means, Methods and Purposes', *Journal of Genocide Research*, 5/1 (2003), 71–101; Ian Talbot, 'The 1947 Partition of the Punjab', in id. (ed.), *The Deadly Embrace: Religion, Violence and Politics in India and Pakistan* (Karachi, 2006).

tragedy have drawn on a variety of documentary accounts produced in the aftermath of Partition, on oral testimonies, and fictional representations. These together with the dramatic intensity of the migration experience have resulted in a Punjab-centred model of Partition emerging. The iconic images of the vast refugee columns, trains packed to the rooftop, and of bloody communal massacres have all been drawn from the Punjab. Such a standardized account ignores not only the variety of Partition experiences elsewhere in north India, but also homogenizes what was a highly differentiated pattern of violence, migration, and resettlement within the Punjab itself.

The paucity of comparative studies of Partition is a striking element in the evolving literature. The vastness of such a subject matter, and language and visa difficulties for Indian and Pakistani scholars have all been cited by way of explanation. Community and nation-building considerations have also obstructed such an enterprise. These tend to privilege the suffering, victimhood, and the ability to 'bounce back' of particular groups. Official histories trumpet the role of the state in dealing with the 'unprecedented refugee problem'. These types of historical discourse would not be served by a comparative approach.

This essay aims to examine migration in the two regions of the subcontinent, namely the Punjab and Bengal, that were most affected by Partition. The new international boundaries bisected both these Muslim-majority provinces of British India. The reasons why they were divided and the demarcation of their boundaries lie beyond the scope of this work, although they are addressed in an earlier comparative volume, *Region and Partition: Bengal, Punjab and the Partition of the Subcontinent*, which I edited in 1999 with Gurharpal Singh.[3] This essay possesses three main aims: first, to delineate the migratory processes in the Punjab and Bengal regions; secondly, to seek to explain them and to reveal how they affected the contrasting histories of resettlement and rehabilitation in the regions; and thirdly, to examine the different histories of migration constructed by Punjabi and Bengali migrants. Before turning to these themes, however, it is necessary to remind ourselves of the wider picture of Partition-related migration flows and to consider the variety of migration experience.

---

[3] Ian Talbot and Gurharpal Singh (eds.), *Region and Partition: Bengal, Punjab and the Partition of the Subcontinent* (Karachi, 1999).

The 1947 Partition of India

The 1947 Partition of India and Migration

British officials and Indian politicians were alike unprepared for the mass migrations that accompanied the division of the subcontinent. There had been warning signs from the Great Calcutta Killings of August 1946 that a new phase of communal violence had emerged which involved elements of ethnic cleansing. The outbreak of violence in the Punjab itself in March 1947, which started in Lahore and Amritsar but became known as the Rawalpindi Massacres after the region worst affected, rendered around 40,000 people homeless. Nevertheless, a transfer of population was unexpected in August 1947.

Politicians reassured minority populations that they would be safe and encouraged them to stay in their ancestral towns and villages. Within days of Independence, however, it became clear that a chaotic two-way flight was under way across the plains of the Punjab. This stemmed from outbreaks of violence that the impotent Punjab Boundary Force was unable to stem in the twelve districts in which it was deployed. The level of casualties remains controversial. Figures vary from the low estimate of 200,000 by the British civil servant Penderel Moon,[4] to that of 2 million. The Indian judge G. D. Khosla put the figure at 500,000 with an equal number of Muslim and non-Muslim casualties.[5] The MQM in its publications for reasons of community assertion maintains that as many as 2 million *mohajirs* (Muslim refugees from India) died. Such writers as Patrick French have adopted a median figure of a million casualties.[6] In the absence of verifiable figures, Gyanendra Pandey has correctly pointed out that the historical discourse on the killings 'continues to bear the stamp of rumour'.[7]

The tragedy unfolding in the Punjab dominated national and international headlines, but other regions were also affected. Muslims fled from UP, Delhi, Bihar, and Bombay to Pakistan. In Delhi, according to some unofficial estimates, violence in

---

[4] Penderel Moon, *Divide and Quit* (new edn., New Delhi, 1998), 293.

[5] Gopal Das Khosla, *Stern Reckoning: A Survey of Events Leading up to and Following the Partition of India* (2nd edn., New Delhi, 1999), 299.

[6] Patrick French, *Liberty or Death: India's Journey to Independence and Division* (London, 1998), 349.

[7] Gyanendra Pandey, *Remembering Partition: Violence, Nationalism and History in India* (Cambridge, 2001), 91.

324   IAN TALBOT

September claimed about 10,000 Muslim lives.[8] Muslims were driven to take sanctuary in refugee camps at Jama Masjid, Purana Qila, and Humayan's Tomb. The latter camp was still bulging with over 30,000 refugees in December 1947.[9] Shahid Ahmad, the publisher and progressive writer, has provided a harrowing account of its desperate conditions in his autobiographical work *Dilhi ki Bipta*.[10] Some 300,000 Muslims, two-thirds of the community's total population, eventually abandoned India's capital. A comparison of the 1941 and 1951 census reveals the dramatic demographic transformation. Muslims comprised 40.5 per cent of the population in 1941 with Hindus in a majority of 53.2 per cent. A decade later, Hindus made up 82.1 per cent of the population and Muslims a mere 6.6 per cent. Delhi's population increased by 1.1 million in the period 1941–51. This unprecedented growth of 106 per cent largely resulted from the influx of Partition migrants.[11] These were members of the Hindu Khatri and Arora commercial castes of the West Punjab. Most were drawn by the economic opportunities afforded by India's new capital. Some refugees already possessed professional, commercial, and kinship ties in the city which had a growing Punjabi community from the late nineteenth century.

Muslims also migrated from UP, Bihar, West Bengal, and Assam to the eastern wing of their new homeland. East Bengal/East Pakistan received around a million and a half refugees. Hindus and Sikhs left not only West Punjab for India, but also the West Pakistan province of Sindh and the North West Frontier Province. There was also, as we shall see later, an ongoing Hindu migration from East Bengal that continued for decades after the movement of population in Punjab had ceased.

The figures for migration are only slightly less haphazard and controversial than those for Partition-related deaths. They vary from 14 to 18 million. In either case, this eclipses violence-related migrations as a result of two world wars and the end of empire elsewhere in the twentieth century. There was no accurate accounting

[8] Ibid. 199.

[9] Report of A. S. Bhatnagar, Secretary to the Chief Commissioner Delhi, 4 Dec. 1947. MB1/D276, Mountbatten Papers, University of Southampton.

[10] Shahid Ahmad, 'Dilhi ki Bipta', in M. Shirin (ed.), *Zulmat-e-Neem Roze* (Karachi, 1990), 145–7.

[11] Ravinder Kaur, 'Narratives of Resettlement: Past, Present and Politics among the 1947 Punjabi Migrants in Delhi' (Ph.D. thesis, Roskilde University, 2004), 34–5.

The 1947 Partition of India

325

in the early period of flight in the Punjab. In West Bengal there was no enumeration of refugees between March 1958, when the government officially wound up its rehabilitation work, and 1 January 1964. After the latter date, refugees were termed 'new migrants' to differentiate them from Partition-related migrants. The most accurate figures are those provided by the Pakistan and Indian military organizations. They were established in response to the spiralling violence in the Punjab and oversaw what was a virtual exchange of population in the region.[12] According to the figures of the Pakistan Military Evacuation Organization, 4,715,919 Muslims were transported to West Punjab from East Punjab between 23 August 1947 and May 1948. Its Indian counterpart produced figures of 3,672,851 making the reverse journey. In both instances most refugees had moved by December 1947. This concentrated period of an organized exchange of population contrasted with the situation elsewhere in India.

Sarah Ansari's work on Sindh, for example, reveals a much longer timescale.[13] The province possessed a large Hindu and Sikh minority (a quarter of the population). Nevertheless, it remained calm in the immediate aftermath of Partition. The first serious outbreak of communal violence did not occur in Karachi until January 1948. This claimed around 200 lives and was accompanied by widespread looting in the city centre.[14] Following the disturbances, 10,000 Hindus crowded into refugee camps in the city, before their evacuation to India. The violence was linked with the flood of Muslim refugees into the city. The Sindh Prime Minister, Muhammad Ayub Khuhro, had been reluctant to accept refugees who could not be absorbed in West Punjab. This 'unco-operative stance angered the Centre and was to be a factor in his eventual downfall in April 1948'.[15] In August of that year, the Centre declared a state of emergency and reset-tled an additional 200,000 refugees in Sindh. The figure was even-tually to increase following the closure of the Punjab camps in October 1948.[16] There was a further influx of refugees from India

---

[12] For the work of the Indian Military Organization see Brigadier Rajendra Singh, *The Military Evacuation Organisation 1947–48* (New Delhi, 1962).

[13] See Sarah Ansari, *Life after Partition: Migration, Community and Strife in Sindh 1947–1962* (Karachi, 2005).

[14] Ibid. 56.

[15] See Ian Talbot, *Pakistan: A Modern History* (rev. edn., London, 2006).

[16] Ansari, *Life after Partition*, 66 and ff.

326   IAN TALBOT

following communal disturbances in Uttar Pradesh in 1950. By April, refugees were arriving at the rate of 3,000 to 4,000 a day.[17] Migration from India was to continue well into the 1950s. The inflow of 6,683 refugees was so high in July 1952 that the Pakistani authorities considered sealing the main border crossing into Sindh at Khokropar.[18] Eventually around 60 per cent of the refugees known as *mohajirs* from Uttar Pradesh resettled in Karachi, Hyderabad, and some of the smaller towns in the interior. By the time of the 1951 census, *mohajirs* numbered 616,906 and accounted for 58 per cent of Karachi's population.[19] The transplantation of an Urdu-speaking enclave into the sands of Sindh has possessed profound consequences for Pakistan's politics.[20]

The timing of refugee movements thus varied considerably between regions. There were also differences in experiences of migration. This has been obscured by the standardized portrayal drawn from an overly homogenized Punjab model. Recent scholarship has revealed a gendered dimension to Partition migration. Women were not only vulnerable to assault as symbolic upholders of community honour (*izzat*); they had to cope in unaccustomed roles as household heads following the slaughter of their menfolk and to adapt to close proximity to strangers on trains, in refugee camps, in queuing for rations, and in making claims for compensation. Work on Hindu female refugees from East Bengal has shown them not only as victims, but as undergoing processes of radicalization in the struggle for survival in Calcutta's post-Independence squatter communities.[21]

The outlines of a class-based differentiation in refugee experiences are also emerging from current research. The higher rank of government servants who had opted for service in the neighbouring country were guaranteed transportation, often by air, and had accommodation provided for them in their new postings. The British Overseas Airways Corporation transported 28,000 people from Pakistan and 18,000 from India in the period

---

[17] Ibid. 128.   [18] Ibid. 131.   [19] Ibid. 110.

[20] It should be noted that Karachi received not only Urdu-speaking refugees, but also Gujarati migrants from Bombay. They came largely from the Khoja and Memon trading communities.

[21] See Jhuma Sanyal, *Making of a New Space: Refugees in West Bengal* (Calcutta, 2003), 183–7; Nilanjana Chatterjee, 'The East Bengal Refugees: A Lesson in Survival', in Sukanta Chaudhuri (ed.), *Calcutta: The Living City*, 2 vols. (New Delhi, 1999), ii: *The Present and the Future*, 70–8.

The 1947 Partition of India

15 September to 7 December 1947. This was in addition to the twice daily service from Lahore to Amritsar and the daily service from Delhi to Rawalpindi run by Indian National Airways.[22] Such passengers could look down on the burning villages and antlike refugee columns traversing the Punjab's killing fields. On the rare occasions that the elite travellers were inconvenienced it could reach even Cabinet-level discussion. Nehru noted with displeasure, for example, an incident early in October when a flight direct from Peshawar to Delhi had to set down at Lahore because of slight engine trouble and its 'occupants had been stripped of all their belongings'.[23]

The business and political elites were also privileged migrants. Many had shifted female family members to hill stations and businesses to 'safe' areas well in advance of Partition. Huge sums of money flowed out of the future Pakistan areas of West Punjab and Sindh in the months leading up to Independence. The leading Muslim newspaper *Dawn* claimed that in the last days of June 1947 alone Rs. 6 crores (60 million) had been withdrawn from West Punjab.[24] New property-dealing businesses sprang up to exchange Muslim and Hindu properties. English-language newspapers advertised residences for sale or exchange in 'safe areas'. Similarly in East Bengal, it was the wealthiest individuals who migrated first. The *bhadralok* class was not only politically aware, but its members frequently had properties and social connections in Calcutta. Artisans such as drummers and idol-makers followed their wealthy religious patrons. Landless labourers were the last to leave and did so because of insecurity. They had no experience of migration, or connections to ease their plight on arrival in West Bengal.

Wealthy anticipatory migrants did not share in the dangers of the crossing to a new homeland that faced 'acute' migrants who were literally fleeing for their lives. Refugees also faced very different experiences on their arrival. On the whole, the ability to recover from the trauma of displacement was markedly improved if an individual possessed previous social and economic capital.

---

[22] Kaur, 'Narratives of Resettlement', 111 and ff.

[23] Extract from Emergency Committee 20th Meeting, 3 Oct. 1947 MB1/D275, University of Southampton.

[24] Raghuvendra Tanwar, *Reporting the Partition of the Punjab 1947: Press, Public and Other Opinions* (New Delhi, 2006), 227.

328   IAN TALBOT

From relief camps through to the construction of housing colonies, the Indian and Pakistan states differentiated between different classes of refugees. The ability to afford their own food rations, for example, determined whether refugees in Delhi would be directed to a life under canvas in the Edward and Outram Lines of the Kingsway camp, or be accommodated in concrete barracks at the Hudson and Reeds Lines.[25] Both Indian and Pakistani satellite towns and refugee housing colonies had varieties of house-plot sizes, streets, and availability of services to suit the different classes of refugee. 'The class differences visible during the population movement', Ravinder Kaur has appositely declared, 'became further entrenched when permanent housing projects were undertaken on such a basis. This ensured that refugees were reinvented in their old class of social stratification.'[26] Perhaps the clearest example of this was the Indian state's provision of separate colonies and camp accommodation for Untouchables.

The post-colonial state also upheld traditional gender roles in its treatment of refugees. Young female orphans were housed and trained in Lahore, for example, so that they would not become an economic burden. The state's guardianship role extended to their arranged early marriage. Like a family patriarch, it saw its role as to establish control over female sexuality. The social stigma attached to widowhood was reflected in the establishment in Delhi, for example, of a separate refugee colony for young widows. In Calcutta there was a similar Women's Camp.[27] But given the gender imbalance amongst East Bengal refugees, the conditions prevailing in the squatter colonies in Calcutta, and the dramatic changes in both caste-based and gender-based economic roles, traditional social mores and family roles were not as rigidly re-established.

The Punjab and Bengal Experiences of Migration

There are significant differences in both the intensity and the timescale of Partition-related migration between the Bengal and

[25] Kaur, 'Narratives of Resettlement', 143.
[26] Ibid. 166.
[27] Sanyal, *Making of a New Space*, 191.

The 1947 Partition of India

Punjab regions. Migration in Punjab was highly concentrated in the period immediately after the British departure. While more than 8 million Punjabis were uprooted between August and December 1947, the total number of refugees in Bengal at this time numbered only around half a million. The greatest migration in the Bengal region was in 1950, rather than at the time of Partition. According to official Pakistani sources, by the end of that March there were 400,000 refugees from West Bengal and Assam.[28] Within six weeks, the figure had leapt to 1.1 million.[29] The Hindu influx into West Bengal in 1950 peaked at 1.5 million. Migration in the Bengal region was to continue thereafter whenever there were periods of tension in Indo-Pakistan relations, or communal riots in the region or elsewhere in the subcontinent. The displacement of population continued after the West Bengal government officially wound up its rehabilitation work in March 1958. By 1981 the West Bengal Refugee Rehabilitation Committee put the number of refugees at around eight million, or one-sixth of the total population.[30] This was still not the level of concentration of refugees in Pakistan Punjab, which received 5.3 million refugees accounting for over 25 per cent of the population.[31] Nevertheless, because of its existing population density and weak regional economy West Bengal was much less able to cope with this burden. Partition had left it as the smallest (34,000 square miles) and most densely populated state in India. Most of the refugees from East Bengal/Pakistan settled in the Calcutta, Nadia, and twenty-four Parganas districts of West Bengal. Calcutta was favoured because of its hoped-for job opportunities. Migrants also clustered around the border areas of the Nadia district where there had been some exchange of population. These three areas were eventually to contain two-thirds of all the refugees from East Pakistan.

By July 1952 there were over 400,000 refugees in the Nadia district, where they constituted about 40 per cent of the

---

[28] *Civil and Military Gazette* (Lahore), 27 Mar. 1950.

[29] Ibid. 26 May 1950.

[30] Gyanesh Kudaisya, 'Divided Landscapes, Fragmented Identities: East Bengal Refugees and their Rehabilitation in India 1947–79', in D. A. Low and Howard Brasted (eds.), *Freedom, Trauma, Continuities: Northern India and Independence* (New Delhi, 1998), 111.

[31] Mohammad Waseem', 'Partition, Migration and Assimilation: A Comparative Study on Pakistani Punjab', in Ian Talbot and Gurharpal Singh (eds.), *Region and Partition: Bengal, Punjab and the Partition of the Subcontinent* (Karachi, 2000), 211.

population.[32] The 1951 census highlighted Calcutta's demographic transformation as a result of refugee migration. The city's population was nearly 20 per cent higher than it had been just five years earlier. By 1973, the number of refugees was just under 2 million and represented around two-thirds of West Bengal's urban refugee population and one-third of the state's total refugee numbers.[33] One in four of Calcutta's inhabitants was a refugee. Seven out of every ten migrants from East Pakistan had found their way there. The absence of arrangements over property exchange and of a population balance between Muslim evacuees and incomers meant that for all but the wealthy, accommodation was difficult to obtain in an already overcrowded city. The household deities in the possession of almost all East Bengal Hindu families had also become 'refugees', as there was no space for them. Some were anonymously abandoned in temples, others found their way to a 'camp' in Upper Chitpur Road Calcutta, where Swami Satyanand Tirth was deputed to perform puja (worship).[34]

In both the Punjab and Bengal, migration occurred in the context of outbreaks of violence. This differed from 'traditional' Hindu–Muslim conflict in that it contained dimensions of 'ethnic cleansing'. Communal riots previously had been about the 'renegotiation of local hierarchies of power'.[35] This is, in essence, what the common disputes over the routes of religious processions were about. The resulting clashes have been termed by some scholars 'consensual' in character.[36] The signs of 'ethnic cleansing' are first evident in the Great Calcutta Killings of 16–20 August 1946. Over 100,000 people were made homeless. They were also present in the wave of violence which rippled out from Calcutta to Bihar, where there were high Muslim casualty figures,[37] and to

[32] *Statesman Weekly* (Calcutta), 12 July 1952.

[33] Pranati Chaudhuri, 'Refugees in West Bengal: A Study of the Growth and Distribution of Refugee Settlements within the CMS', Occasional Papers 55, Centre for Studies in Social Sciences Calcutta (Mar. 1983), table 1, 38.

[34] *Civil and Military Gazette* (Lahore), 4 June 1950.

[35] See Veena Das and Ashis Nandy, 'Violence, Victimhood and the Language of Silence', in Veena Das (ed.), *The Word and the World: Fantasy, Symbol and Record* (New Delhi, 1983), 177–90.

[36] Shail Mayaram, 'Speech, Silence and the Making of Partition Violence in Mewat', in Shahid Amin and Dipesh Chakrabarty (eds.), *Subaltern Studies IX: Writings on South Asian History and Society* (New Delhi, 1996).

[37] See *Report on Disturbances in Bihar and UP* (Muslim Information Centre, 1946). P/T 3363, IOL.

The 1947 Partition of India

Noakhali, deep in the Ganges–Brahmaputra delta of East Bengal. With respect to the Noakhali riots, one British observer spoke of a 'determined and organised' Muslim effort to drive out all the Hindus, who accounted for around a fifth of the total population.[38] The Punjab counterpart to this transition in violence was the Rawalpindi Massacres of March 1947. The massacres paved the way for the later August violence in that they both created a Sikh desire for revenge and revealed the ease with which minority communities could be expelled in the absence of effective law enforcement. About 40,000 Sikhs had been left homeless. The August 1947 Punjab violence repeated this uprooting on a huge scale. The high levels of violence can be variously attributed to the militarization of the region's population which formed the sword-arm of India; the cycles of retributive genocide which began with the March 1947 Rawalpindi Massacres; the collapse or unreliability of the police and local administration; the existence of a Sikh Plan to 'ethnically cleanse' Muslims from East Punjab in order to carve out a Sikh state; and the involvement of the armed forces of such Sikh states as Patiala in attacks on minority populations. The princes themselves denied that they had contacts with the Sikh war bands (*jathas*), but high-ranking court, state, and military officers such as Bir Davinder Singh and Colonel Bhagwan Singh of Patiala along with the Chief Minister of Jind were widely believed to have connived at their activities.[39] The fact cannot be denied that troops from the princely states not only attacked their Muslim inhabitants and passing refugee trains, but joined in assaults on neighbouring districts of the former British-administered Punjab.

Bengal had witnessed horrific communal violence in 1946 in Calcutta and Noakhali. The figure of 4,000 deaths was officially quoted at the time of the Great Calcutta Killings. An English official maintained that this was 'a new order in communal rioting'. He described Calcutta as a 'cross between the worst of London air raids and the Great Plague'.[40] Around 10,000 people shifted out of the city. Seven weeks after the Great Calcutta Killings, violence spread to this south-eastern district of Bengal.

---

[38] Suranjan Das, *Communal Riots in Bengal 1905–1947* (Delhi, 1991), 199.

[39] Copland in fact cites evidence that the rulers of Kapurthala and Faridkot had direct contact with the *jathas*. Ian Copland, 'The Master and the Maharajas: The Sikh Princes and the East Punjab Massacres of 1947', *Modern Asian Studies*, 36/3 (2002), 639.

[40] Das, *Communal Riots*, 171.

332 IAN TALBOT

From Noakhali it fanned out to the Tippera district. In all, 350 villages were affected in the two districts. The disorders were only finally quelled by the deployment of around 2,500 troops and police. The minority Hindu populations living in inaccessible villages were the victims. Fifty thousand people took refuge in relief camps.

The cycle of violence had largely spent itself in Bengal by the time of Partition. Crucially, the region did not have the level of preparation for communal attacks that existed in the Punjab. Here weapons had been stockpiled and training given to paramilitary groups by ex-soldiers. Calcutta's relative quiescence has been attributed to Gandhi's moral influence. He stayed in a poor Muslim neighbourhood where he prayed and fasted for peace. Mountbatten dubbed him a 'one man boundary force'.

Official responses to the 1947 violence impacted on the patterns of migration in the two regions. As we have already noted, the violence in Punjab resulted in the two governments determining on a virtual exchange of population under the control of the Pakistan and Indian Military Evacuation Organizations.[41] Despite misgivings about this in both countries, fears for the security of minorities along with the need to utilize properties and land evacuated by them to accommodate refugees determined this policy. There were some hopes that Muslims who numbered 13.17 lakhs (100,000) could stay in the south-eastern Ambala division of the Indian Punjab. Eventually all the Muslims departed for Pakistan.

The Military Evacuation Organizations set up headquarters on both sides of the new international boundary which now bisected the Punjab. A joint civilian machinery was also established consisting of Liaison Officers. The two Chief Liaison Officers held the status of Deputy High Commissioners. There were also district officials who were provided with funds, escorts, and scarce supplies of petrol to facilitate their work on behalf of refugees. The Joint Evacuation Plan agreed on 20 October between the two Military Evacuation Organizations set a December target for the evacuation of 10 million refugees from both sides of the Punjab.[42] This elaborate machinery brought some order to the migration process, although not to the extent

[41] Singh, *The Military Evacuation Organisation*.
[42] Kaur, 'Narratives of Resettlement', 97.

The 1947 Partition of India

maintained in official histories.[43] Minority populations had no choice but to leave their ancestral homes, even when they were not in imminent threat of attack. The result was the denuding of Hindus and Sikhs from Pakistan Punjab who had numbered 33.99 lakhs before Partition and 53.85 lakhs Muslims from the Indian Punjab and surrounding Indian states. Further government control over the migration process was exerted by settling rural refugee populations together in assigned districts.[44] Both populations and land were, in effect, being exchanged.

The lower levels of violence in Bengal in 1947 encouraged a reverse policy. When migration did occur, it was seen as a temporary process. This meant that evacuee property was not freed up to house refugees. It led the right-wing Hindu leader, Shyama Prasad Mukherjee, to call for an exchange of populations or, alternatively, to demand that a third of the territory of East Pakistan should go to India to be utilized for refugee resettlement.[45]

Inter-dominion conferences were held to assure the minorities in East and West Bengal of their security. The rehabilitation ministers of India and Pakistan jointly declared in Calcutta in April 1948 that they were determined 'to take every possible step to discourage such exodus and to create such conditions as would check mass exodus in either direction'.[46] Partition left around 4 million Muslims in West Bengal (approximately 17 per cent of the population) and around 11.5 million (approximately 42 per cent) Hindus in East Pakistan. In contrast with the Punjab's dramatic demographic transformation, migration in the Bengal region occurred in a series of waves, rather than one tidal force.

The governments of both East and West Bengal sought to reassure minority populations. Upper-caste Hindus living in the eastern wing of Pakistan were, however, disturbed by status reversal, and were also sensitive to any threats to the honour (*maan*) of their female family members. In 1948 twice as many refugees left East Bengal (around 800,000) as at the time of Partition. The Muslim populations of West Bengal and Assam

---

[43] Ibid. 101–3.

[44] For details of this process with respect to Indian Punjab, see Kirpal Singh, *The Partition of the Punjab* (Patiala, 1989), 181–3.

[45] Sanyal, *Making of a New Space*, 133.

[46] Cited in Kudaisya, 'Divided Landscapes', 109.

334   IAN TALBOT

felt less insecure. The serious disturbances early in 1950, however, resulted in a peak of migration in both Bengals far greater than had occurred in 1947.

I visited Muladi . . . where I found skeletons of dead bodies at some places. I found dogs and vultures eating corpses on the riverside. I got the information there that after the wholesale killing of all adult males, all the young girls were distributed among the ringleaders of the miscreants.[47]

This was not Punjab in August 1947, but East Bengal in February 1950. The violence had started in Dacca, but spread within a few days to the Tippera, Noakhali, Syhlet, and Barisal districts. The coastal district of Barisal witnessed severe disturbances. Four villages were completely burned down. Muladi was one of its important riverine ports. Most of its Hindu victims died in the compound of the police station where they had taken shelter. The officer in charge was later found in possession of large amounts of looted property.[48] In the Syhlet district, over 200 villages were devastated and 800 Hindu temples desecrated.[49] In large areas, the repertoire familiar since 1946 was repeated: forced conversions, dishonouring of women, and attacks on trains.[50] The latter lasted from 11 to 14 February and claimed many victims on the Chittagong Mail. The bodies of at least a hundred Hindus were buried by the side of the railway line.[51]

Similar scenes of violence occurred in West Bengal. There were widespread disturbances in such Muslim localities of Calcutta as Bagmari, Beliaghatu, and Goolpara. Houses were looted and burned along with mosques. According to the *Civil and Military Gazette* newspaper, nearly 10,000 Muslims from Chinsurah, Paikpara, Goolpara, and Telnipara had to leave their homes and take shelter in open fields opposite the Victoria Jute Mills. Muslims were also attacked in Jalpaiguri town. Two

[47] This report was made by the Scheduled Caste former Minister for Law and Labour in the Pakistan government, Jogendra Nath Mandal. He resigned in the wake of the East Bengal killings. A. J. Kamra, *The Prolonged Partition and its Pogroms: Testimonies on Violence against Hindus in East Bengal 1946–64* (New Delhi, 2000), 173–4.

[48] Ibid. 63.

[49] Ibid. 76.

[50] The trains packed with up to 4,000 refugees had been easy targets in August 1947, despite the presence of armed escorts. Blood-splattered trains arrived in both India and Pakistan with whole compartments of butchered corpses.

[51] Kamra, *The Prolonged Partition*, 89.

The 1947 Partition of India

hundred shops were looted in the Muslim-controlled bazaar of Karimgunj in Assam.[52] Muslim refugees from Karimgunj and Hailakandi claimed that the police led the looters.[53] Certainly more resolute law enforcement would have cut short the disturbances. Their continuation sparked the largest wave of migration in the eastern Indian region since 1947.

The Indian and Pakistan Prime Ministers tried to restore some stability in the celebrated Nehru–Liaquat Pact in April 1950. It promised equality of citizenship for minority communities and stated that refugees who returned home by 31 December 1950 would be entitled to the restoration of their houses and land. This stemmed migration for a time and even led to around 12 lakhs of refugees returning to East Bengal.[54] Most were able to recover the houses they had abandoned, but the provincial government set aside a further Rs. 7 lakhs to cover the cost of their rehabilitation.[55] The returning Hindus together with Muslim refugees from West Bengal meant that the population of East Bengal increased by nearly 950,000 by the middle of 1951.[56] Thereafter, migration continued to fluctuate and depended on prevailing communal and Indo-Pakistan relations. It was West Bengal, however, that received the majority of migrants. The announcement at the beginning of October 1952 that a passport system would be introduced for cross-border travel encouraged another influx of Hindus amid fears that future migration would be more difficult.[57] Within a week, upwards of 2,000 people were daily arriving by train at the Indian border outposts of Bongaon and Ranaghat. The trains were 'dangerously overcrowded with passengers riding on footboards and hanging on to iron beams and rods beneath the carriages'.[58] The authorities opened an interception camp at Ambagaon less than half a mile from Bongaon railway station. Many of the 12,000 or so refugees preferred to sleep on the platform or under railway wagons. Eventually special trains had to be called in to dispatch them to Sealdah Station Calcutta which itself soon presented 'a scene of

---

[52] *Civil and Military Gazette* (Lahore), 22 Mar. 1950.
[53] Ibid.
[54] Chaudhuri, 'Refugees in West Bengal', 38.
[55] *Dawn* (Karachi), 18 June 1951.
[56] Ibid.
[57] India introduced passports on 15 Oct. 1952; Pakistan followed suit two days later.
[58] *Statesman Weekly* (Calcutta), 11 Oct. 1952.

indescribable confusion'. 'A fog of blue smoke' from countless cooking fires, a correspondent for the *Statesman* newspaper recorded, 'hangs over the listless grey brown mass of humanity.'[59] Many of the refugees were from poorer, lower-caste Namasudra, Mahisya, and Sadgop communities in the East Bengal hinterland. They were eventually dispersed to transit camps on the outskirts of the city or fended for themselves in the crowded and squalid squatter colonies which had sprung up in Calcutta. Their existence attested to refugee self-settlement in the absence of an adequate government response.

The squatter colonies literally sprang up overnight, when thatched huts were constructed under the cover of darkness on vacant land. Their *hogla* leaves became a refugee symbol. One of the earliest refugee self-settlements was at Bijoygarh, the site of American barracks during the Second World War. The pre-1950 developments were eventually to be regularized through the government's payment of compensation to landowners and the gifting of deeds to the occupiers. Even before their regularization, many colonies in such south-eastern areas as Tollygunj, Behala, and Javedpur were well managed by committees which raised subscriptions and labour for the construction of drains, roads, and water supplies. This was not the case, however, in the 'illegal' colonies that sprang up after 1950 on the west bank of the Hooghly river between Magra and Uluberia. Even worse off were the large numbers of agriculturalist refugees consigned to prolonged residence in refugee camps in Calcutta and elsewhere in West Bengal. In 1958 the camp population stood at 800,000. One-third of their inhabitants had spent anything from six to ten years living in these squalid conditions.[60]

Refugee camps in Punjab had been closed as early as 1948. In both Indian and Pakistan Punjab evacuee property had been supplemented by building refugee colonies in existing towns and creating new satellite towns such as Faridabad and Rajpura. The latter development on the GT Road, fifteen miles west of Ambala, was built at the cost of Rs. 20 million. It was termed 'one of the biggest experiments of the Government of India in building a well planned and simple yet dignified home for refugees'.[61]

[59] Ibid. 18 Oct. 1952.
[60] Chatterjee, 'The East Bengal Refugees', 74.
[61] *Statesman* (Calcutta), 28 May 1949.

The 1947 Partition of India

The sense that refugees from East Bengal were the main victims of Partition because of their neglect in contrast to their Punjabi counterparts is a central element in the Bengali historical discourse. It was an important factor in the support refugees gave to the Communist Party of India (CPI), especially in the wake of the threatened legislation in 1951 to evict 'Persons in Unauthorized Possession of Land'. The CPI portrayed the Congress administration of Bidhan Chandra Roy as being more concerned with the rights of landlords and property speculators than with the distress of the refugees. Before examining the problems surrounding the West Bengal government's rehabilitation programmes, we shall first consider the ways in which the characteristics of migration impacted on rehabilitation measures.

Refugee Rehabilitation in Punjab and Bengal

The circumstances of the Partition-related migration in East and West Punjab made it clear from the outset that violence had initiated a permanent demographic transformation. This was not the case in Bengal. Moreover, the scale of the Punjab crisis facing both the Indian and Pakistani governments inevitably prioritized rehabilitation efforts in the region. A number of Bengali writers have gone further and argued that the Punjab's greater proximity to the seats of power in India and Pakistan and the lobbying of powerful Punjabi bureaucratic and political elites resulted in a concentration of scarce resources in the region. This discourse will be examined in the final section of the essay. Suffice it to say here that oral testimonies from Punjabi refugees on both sides of the border, along with written complaints to newspapers and politicians, reveal a far less positive assessment of government rehabilitation efforts than some allegations of pro-Punjab bias would allow. Indeed, Raghuvendra Tanwar has declared that 'Attractive statements supported by huge statistics indicating the dimensions of the resettlement effort were routinely issued, sadly these statements concealed a whole body of corrupt decisions of injustice and unfairness. This trend increased as days and months passed for as long as the resettlement measures continued.'[62]

---

[62] Tanwar, *Reporting the Partition of the Punjab 1947*, 473.

Those without wealth or connections were at the mercy of corrupt and incompetent officials.

It is important to recognize here that there is no echo of Indian Bengali allegations of a pro-Punjabi bias in rehabilitation efforts amongst Muslim refugees who migrated to East Bengal. This in part reflects the fact that the refugee situation in East Bengal has been under-researched, for it cannot be deemed insignificant. Contemporary press reports in March 1950, for example, record that Dacca was 'overflowing with refugees'.[63] It may also be the result of a more efficient government response which was aided by the relatively greater availability of evacuee property.

The East Bengal government early in 1950 established refugee camps on the outskirts of Dacca and Chittagong to relieve congestion. Around 1,000 people were accommodated, for example, in specially constructed barracks at Samair in the Kurmitola area of Dacca.[64] About 8,000 refugees were rehabilitated in the Bogra district of East Bengal, where they were allotted between 3 and 6 acres of land.[65] Such short-term measures were accompanied by longer-term rehabilitation efforts. These were coordinated by a new East Bengal Relief Commissioner, N. M. Khan. He reported early in June 1950 that Rs. 50 lakhs had already been spent on such measures as the provision of stalls for shopkeepers, and the distribution of sewing machines and looms.[66] His Employment Bureau had placed 45,000 persons in various jobs by September 1950.[67] A month earlier, the Pakistan government had announced that it was advancing 12 million rupees to the East Bengal authorities for rehabilitation purposes. This enabled ambitious urban and rural rehabilitation schemes to be planned. The former involved the construction of five satellite townships near Dacca, Chittagong, Syhlet, Jessore, and Rangpur at the cost of Rs. 1 million. They were designed to house over 100,000 refugees. Three million rupees were set aside for a rural rehabilitation scheme. Families were to receive 5 acres of land along with a maintenance allowance of Rs. 50 per family until their first harvest.[68] In June 1951 the government finalized a scheme for a 10,000-acre refugee colony at Aflong in Sylhet.[69] It

---

[63] *Civil and Military Gazette* (Lahore), 18 Mar. 1950.   [64] Ibid. 5 Apr. 1950.
[65] Ibid. 20 Apr. 1950.   [66] Ibid. 7 June 1950.   [67] Ibid. 22 Sept. 1950.
[68] Ibid. 6 Aug. 1950.   [69] Ibid. 6 June 1951.

The 1947 Partition of India

simultaneously gave 250 houses free of charge to refugee families in the Mirpur colony, Dacca.[70]

The early rehabilitation effort of the Pakistan authorities in East Bengal appears both more planned and urgent than that of the West Bengal government. This was borne out by the latter's own Statistical Department figures published in February 1952. They revealed that 12 per cent of the 2.14 million refugees were living on land on which they had trespassed and 72 per cent were unemployed.[71] In addition to relying on grants from the Centre for rehabilitation purposes, the East Bengal provincial government from July 1952 levied a 'refugee tax' on the licences required for the export of raw jute. In contrast, the West Bengal state government only moved from ad hoc responses to the formulation of a comprehensive rehabilitation policy after the June 1953 report of a fact-finding committee.[72] Impressive as the East Bengal effort appears, it did not match that in West Punjab during the same period. In 1951, for example, the West Punjab government earmarked Rs. 17 million for different rehabilitation schemes in the latter province. They included the establishment of ten satellite towns, three of which were to girdle Lyllapur.[73] Why, then, is there no anti-Punjab discourse amongst Muslim Bengali refugees, unlike their Hindu counterparts?

Until there is further research, a definitive response cannot be given. It appears, however, that the funding was adequate, given the fact that the overall situation was more favourable for the Muslim refugees in East Bengal than their Hindu counterparts in West Bengal. This meant their lot was less intolerable than that of the highly articulate Hindu refugees who settled in Calcutta. There was a relative abundance of evacuee houses in the East Pakistan towns.[74] The Hindu population of Dacca, for example, declined from 58 per cent of the population on the eve of Independence to just 4.6 per cent.[75] According to a survey of

---

[70] *Dawn* (Karachi), 18 June 1951.

[71] *Statesman* (Calcutta), 16 Feb. 1952.

[72] Samir Kumar Das, 'Refugee Crisis: Responses of the Government of West Bengal', in Prudip Kumar Bose (ed.), *Refugees in West Bengal: Institutional Practices and Contested Identities* (Calcutta, 2000), 13.

[73] *Civil and Military Gazette* (Lahore), 23 Sept. 1951.

[74] Tai Yong Tan and Gyanesh Kudaisya, *The Aftermath of Partition in South Asia* (London, 2000), 169.

[75] Ibid.

Hindu neighbourhoods in December 1950, Muslims now controlled 6,255 out of 7,175 properties owned by Hindus in 1947.[76] Unlike in Calcutta the terms of trade in properties very much favoured the refugees. Although Dacca's population mushroomed by 53 per cent in the decade 1941–51, the housing demands of its migrants could be met. The East Pakistan countryside was also much better able to accommodate refugees than West Bengal's. The latter region was more overcrowded and its agriculture was both qualitatively and quantitatively inferior.[77]

Muslim refugees in West Punjab were also in more favoured circumstances than their counterparts in the Indian Punjab. Hindu and Sikh refugees vacated 9.6 million acres of land in Pakistan, while Muslims left behind 5.5 million acres of land in India.[78] While refugee Sikh farmers had to make do with unirrigated tracts of land and smaller holdings under the system of 'graded cuts', Muslim cultivators from the East Punjab took over the fertile tracts of land in the Canal Colony areas abandoned by Sikh farmers. Rural resettlement was nevertheless not all plain sailing in West Punjab. This was in part because Muslim owners of tenanted land abandoned by non-Muslim farmers still sought their share of the crop (*batai*) from refugees. There were also delays in making permanent allotments of land to refugees because of the time it took to exchange land settlement records. Some refugees were even ejected from land they had been semi-permanently allotted, in May 1952. Such organizations as the Muhajir League and the Jinnah Awami League lent their political support to the hunger strikes and public protests of the affected refugees.[79]

The East Punjab government attempted to ease the resettlement of West Punjab cultivators by establishing rural housing schemes. Model villages were constructed on the sites of evacuee villages which had been demolished during the violence. According to M. S. Randhawa's figures, there were some 1,800 East Punjab villages where 90 per cent of the houses were demolished.[80] Before refugees were permanently allotted land they

---

[76] Ibid. 168.   [77] Ibid. 144.

[78] See J. B. Schechtman, 'Evacuee Property in India and Pakistan', *Pacific Affairs*, 24 (1951), 411–12.

[79] *Statesmen Weekly* (Calcutta), 31 May 1952.

[80] M. S. Randhawa, *Out of the Ashes: An Account of the Rehabilitation of Refugees from Pakistan in Rural Areas of East Punjab* (Bombay, 1954), 153.

The 1947 Partition of India   341

were disbursed loans for food and for fodder. Large sums of money were set aside for the purchase of bullocks, seed, and the reconstruction of houses and wells. When land was permanently allotted in 1950, loans were provided for agricultural modernization such as water pumps, tractors, and tube-wells. Tractor loans, for example, amounted to Rs. 32 lakhs.[81] This laid the preconditions for the Green Revolution success story of the East Punjab. During the period September 1947 to March 1951, Rs. 4 and a half crores were disbursed to displaced cultivators.[82]

The state government in West Bengal, in contrast, did little more than provide basic immediate relief. It lacked sufficient funding to build large numbers of townships and houses. Its eventual solution to the refugee accommodation crisis was to try to disperse refugees to neighbouring states. This became politically controversial not only within the state, but in such places as Assam, which was reluctant to receive refugees. A large dispersal centre was established at Bettiah in the Champaran district of Bihar. The most ambitious and controversial settlement scheme involved the moving of over 25,000 families to the 270,000 cleared acres of forest at Dandakaranya in Orissa and Madhya Pradesh.[83] Many refugees saw this as deportation rather than rehabilitation. They were exiles in the 'dark forest' like Lord Rama in the *Ramayana*. By 1978 over 11,000 families had deserted the settlement.

Untouchable refugees from East Bengal were also resettled in the remote Sunderbans region of West Bengal at the beginning of the 1960s. The scheme was better thought through than that at Dandakaranya, in that the cultivators who were sent there originated from the Khulna and Barisal districts, so had some experience of roughly similar agricultural conditions. They were provided with 3 acres of land each and loans to build houses and purchase agricultural equipment. Nevertheless, a survey of the settlement a decade later found the bulk of the inhabitants mired in poverty. At least 25 per cent of the cultivators were living in distress and barely 58 per cent at subsistence level.[84] The government cash doles had ceased, while agricultural productivity

---

[81] Ibid. 167.   [82] Ibid. 162.

[83] See Kudaisya, 'Divided Landscapes', 115 and ff.

[84] S. L. De and A. K. Bhattacharjee, *The Refugee Settlement in the Sunderbans, West Bengal: A Socio-economic Study* (Calcutta, 1972), 47.

342   IAN TALBOT

remained low. The poor communications hindered economic
activity. The nearest market was 18 miles away, while a journey
by country boat of 35 miles was required to reach the nearest
railway station. As the investigators concluded in their findings,
much poverty was the result of the 'lack of far-sightedness of the
Government department responsible for planning the project'.[85]

The West Bengal government's limited response to the refugee
'problem' was in part the result of disputes with the Centre over
funding, and in part reflected the sense of the state's being over-
burdened because of its weak economy and high population
density. The refugee plight was further worsened by the decision
of the government of India not to extend evacuee legislation to
either West Bengal or Assam. This reflected the view that migration was not permanent and that further transfers of population
should be discouraged. Indeed, the latter waves of refugees were
seen as economic migrants rather than as victims of Partition. In
the Punjab region, the governments of East and West Punjab
agreed on a response to the problem of abandoned property as
early as September 1947. Arrangements were made for the
exchange of property and compensation for abandoned property. This, together with the official refusal to recognize the
illegal seizure of property, eased the rehabilitation of refugees. At
the same time, the East and West Punjab governments through
refugee taxes and disbursements from the Centre set aside large
sums for resettlement.

Punjabi and Bengali Refugee Discourses

The Indian government's account of refugee resettlement
focused around the Punjab 'success story'. This was reproduced
in official works such as *Millions on the Move* and in semi-official
studies such as M. S. Randhawa's carefully named study *Out of the
Ashes*. Such accounts reproduced the statistics of government
assistance interspersed with photographs of smiling refugees in
their new homes in East Punjab. There were even lapses into
Orientalist stereotypes of the 'sturdy' Punjabi Jat peasants with
their capacity for hard work and enterprise. These stereotypes
were later internalized. V. N. Datta's pioneering study of Punjabi

[85] Ibid. 50.

The 1947 Partition of India   343

refugees in Delhi extols their willingness to turn their hand to anything in order to make their way.[86]

First-hand accounts go even further and attribute the successful rebuilding of lives after the upheaval of Partition to self-help. Interviews in such cities as Lahore and Amritsar leave little room for government support for resettlement. We have seen above, however, that the governments of both East and West Punjab diverted large sums of money to 'the refugee problem'. Some refugees, for psychological reasons, may choose to forget the role government assistance played in their resettlement. They refer if at all to outside assistance coming from community and religious organizations. This may reflect the persisting influence of such organizations in their lives. It also is rooted in the fact that, as Raghuvendra Tanwar has noted, much government aid was mired in delays and corruption.

Official accounts often contrast Bengali dependency with Punjabi flexibility and entrepreneurial spirit. Aside from dealing in colonialist stereotypes, such understanding displaces blame from the government, for the more problematic resettlement process, to the refugees themselves. As we have seen, however, the emergence of the squatter communities in Calcutta displays just as much enterprise as that attributed to the Punjabi migrants.

Hindu *Purbo Bongiyo* (East Bengal) refugees argued that they were the principal victims of Partition because of the Indian government's half-hearted approach to their rehabilitation.[87] Salil Sen's 1950s play summed up this sense of victimhood in its title, *Natun Yehudi* (The New Jews). Such writers as Prafulla Chakrabarti have been at pains to highlight the greater government assistance to Punjabi than Bengali refugees.[88]

There was undoubtedly some truth in the claim made by the Rehabilitation Minister, A. P. Jain, in New Delhi on 18 June 1952 that 'it was unfair to compare official efforts to rehabilitate refugees (from East Pakistan with West Pakistan) for attention to

---

[86] V. N. Datta, 'Panjabi Refugees and the Urban Development of Greater Delhi', in R. E. Frykenberg (ed.), *Delhi through the Ages: Essays on Urban History, Culture and Society* (Delhi, 1986), 451, 453–5.

[87] For a discussion of these claims, see Joya Chatterji, 'Right or Charity? The Debate over Relief and Rehabilitation in West Bengal, 1947–50', in Suvir Kaul (ed.), *The Partitions of Memory: The Afterlife of the Division of India* (Delhi, 2001), 74–110.

[88] Prafulla Chakrabarti, *The Marginal Men: The Refugees and the Left Political Syndrome in West Bengal* (Calcutta, 1999), 250 and ff.

344 IAN TALBOT

evacuees from West Pakistan had been paid over a period of 5 years whereas the problem of refugees from East Pakistan had become a serious one over the past two years'.[89] Moreover, government assistance in West Bengal, although belated, was considerable. In response to the 1952 refugee influx, New Delhi allotted the West Bengal government Rs. 55 lakhs for relief and a further Rs. 25 lakhs for rehabilitation.[90] The following year, the West Bengal government received a sum of Rd. 2.7 crores for the task of refugee rehabilitation in the Burswan, Nadia, and 24 Parganas districts.[91] By the end of 1957, there were 83 government-sponsored refugee colonies with 21,500 families. Up to the previous June, Rs. 24.28 lakhs had been sanctioned to fifty-nine cooperative societies.[92] Loans were also advanced through the Refugee Businessmen's Rehabilitation Board and separately to lawyers and medical practitioners. Grants were also sanctioned for the opening of schools in refugee colonies.[93] Nevertheless, there was a clear difference in the amount and type of assistance that was on offer by the Indian authorities in the Punjab and Bengal regions. Moreover, delays in the flow of funds from the Centre to the West Bengal government hampered its rehabilitation programmes.[94] As much as a crore of rupees earmarked for relief in 1953–4 remained unspent.[95]

One similarity between the refugee experiences is that of nostalgia for the land left behind. Punjabi Hindus in Delhi look back to Lahore. This is reflected in the titles of such accounts as *Lahore: Portrait of a Lost City; Lahore: A Sentimental Journey; Lahore: Loved, Lost and Thereafter.*[96] East Bengal refugees look not to a city, but the villages they abandoned in 'Golden Bengal'. Accounts focus on memories of public holidays at the time of the major religious festivals, boat races, the abundance and beauty of the countryside, harmonious social relations, and the 'respect' for elders and women.[97] One of the Bengali words for refugee,

[89] *Statesman Weekly* (Calcutta), 21 June 1952. [90] Ibid. 25 Oct. 1952.
[91] Ibid. 17 Jan. 1953. [92] Das, 'Refugee Crisis', 20 and ff. [93] Ibid. 25.
[94] See *Statesman Weekly* (Calcutta), 20 Dec. 1952. [95] Ibid. 20 Feb. 1954.
[96] See Som Anand, *Lahore: Portrait of a Lost City* (Lahore, 1988); Pran Nevile, *Lahore: A Sentimental Journey* (New Delhi, 1993); Sahdev Vohra, *Lahore: Loved, Lost and Thereafter* (Delhi, 2004).
[97] See Sanyal, *Making of a New Space*, 163 and ff.; Dipesh Chakrabarty, 'Remembered Villages: Representations of Hindu-Bengali Memories in the Aftermath of Partition', in D. A. Low and Howard Brasted (eds.), *Freedom, Trauma, Continuities: Northern India and Independence* (New Delhi, 1998), 133–53.

The 1947 Partition of India

udvastu (outside of home), attested to this painful separation from ancestral roots. There is an elegiac quality about their memory of the idyllic villages of 'Golden Bengal', contained in such collections as *Chhere asha gram* (The Abandoned Village), just as *mohajirs* remember the small towns of eastern UP they have left for Sindh.[98] Punjabi and Bengali Hindu identification of Partition with loss, of course, sits more easily with the national historical discourse than does the similar sentiment of the migrant Uttar Pradesh elite within Pakistan.

Conclusion

The 'new history' of Partition reveals the extent to which it was a highly differentiated experience. This essay represents a modest contribution to this understanding. The waves of migration in Bengal contrast with the single flood of refugees in the immediate post-Partition period in Punjab. These differences reflected the varieties in the patterns of violence. The year 1950 was a far more significant date for East and West Bengal than 1947. Even when accounting for the propagandist element, it is clear that government responses were less focused and effective in the Bengal than the Punjab regions. A litany of reasons why rehabilitation was a more difficult task in West Bengal than East Punjab was provided by both state and Union-level ministers.[99] There was, however, differentiation in government responses within regions, as well as between them. The East Bengal government, for example, appears to have diverted greater energy to the rehabilitation task than its Indian counterpart. It allocated large sums of money from the Centre for both rural rehabilitation and the construction of satellite refugee towns and colonies. The East Pakistan authorities also raised their own funding by means of a 'refugee tax'.

---

[98] The latter is the setting for the famous Urdu writer Intizar Husain's short story *Akhri Mom Batti*, which explores the theme of Partition loss. See Ian Talbot, *Freedom's Cry: The Popular Dimension in the Pakistan Movement and Partition Experience in North-West India* (Karachi, 1996), 142–4. Nostalgia for East Bengal is seen in such poems as Taslima Nasreen's 'Broken Bengal', which has been translated into English by Subhoranjan Dasgupta, from the selection *Behula eka bhasiyechilo bhela*.

[99] See e.g. the press conference in Calcutta on 24 Dec. 1954 given by Mehr Chand Khanna, the Union Rehabilitation Minister. *Statesman Weekly* (Calcutta), 25 Dec. 1954.

As for the refugee experience, this was highly diverse. Even within the city of Calcutta, which underwent profound changes, differentiation in refugee experiences is visible. Despite their human suffering, the first wave of upper-caste refugees, whose memories and complaints fill the historical narrative, were better able to rebuild their lives than the later migrants from poorer agricultural backgrounds. Within Punjab, it was the poorer and less politically acute communities that were caught unawares and had to cross the killing fields in August 1947. Sections especially of the West Punjab Hindu elite had moved their money and families to places of safety well in advance of Independence. Wealth and connection impinged equally on refugee success in resettlement on both sides of the border.

At the same time, as a more detailed understanding of the Partition process is emerging it is clear that major gaps remain. Little, for example, has been written about the Untouchable community's experience of violence, migration, and resettlement. Just as the Punjab experience has been privileged in the general historical discourse of Partition, so the experience of the *bhadralok* refugees who settled in Calcutta has dominated writings on the population movement in eastern India. This excludes the movement to West Bengal of non-elite groups such as Santhals. There are also the untold stories of the migration of Bengalis to Tripura and of Muslim migrants from West Bengal, Assam, Tripura, Bihar, and Uttar Pradesh to what is now Bangladesh. Finally, work is required on the experiences of Muslims in West Bengal who did not migrate to what is now Bangladesh. Anecdotal evidence points to the fact that they faced displacement as Hindu refugees illegally occupied properties. There appears to have been a process in which former mixed localities in Calcutta were increasingly replaced by what were, in fact, Muslim ghettos. Rural Muslim populations also appear to have shown a tendency to migrate from south-west Bengal to concentrated Muslim areas in north Bengal, as well as clustering near the border in Nadia district, for example, over which they could flee in times of communal strife. Much more research is required on Muslim Partition-related migration within West Bengal.

Actual violence or its threat was a crucial factor in the migration processes in both Punjab and Bengal. Individuals were reluctant to leave their ancestral homes, not only because of the

The 1947 Partition of India 347

material loss this involved, but because their identity was vested in these localities. Uprootedness was to be avoided at all costs. The violence which demographically transformed vast swathes of north India was not spontaneous. While it possessed elements of retribution and opportunism, it was in many instances carefully planned and executed. Communal organizations sought forcibly to remove minority communities. The state afforded scant protection to all its citizens in situations of extreme polarization along community lines. In both Bengal and Punjab, local officials and policemen not only acquiesced, but participated, in communal violence. The dislocation was so severe in the Punjab that spontaneous mass migration gave way within a fortnight of Independence to a virtual exchange of population. Despite the continued violence and suffering which accompanied this process, it eased the Pakistan and Indian states' task of refugee resettlement in the region. In Bengal, the pattern of waves of migration occasioned by violence from non-state and sometimes state actors continued for years after Independence. The demographic transition was never as complete as in Punjab. The absence of evacuee property intensified the housing shortage, especially in Calcutta. The result was that refugees from East Pakistan termed themselves the 'New Jews' and principal victims of Partition. This discourse was created by the most privileged section of the refugee community. Their lower-caste counterparts were reduced to a miserable existence of pavement dwelling which etched Calcutta in both the national and international consciousness as the 'city of dreadful night'.

14

Explaining Transfer:
Zionist Thinking and the Creation of
the Palestinian Refugee Problem

BENNY MORRIS

The Palestinian refugee problem was born of the 1948 war, the first war between Israel and the Arabs. It was not the product of a preconceived master plan or, indeed, of a governmental policy decision or of a blanket, systematic implementation of a policy of expulsion. The overwhelming majority of the 700,000 Arabs who were displaced from their homes fled as a result of battle or encroaching battle. Most moved to other parts of Palestine (and, in this sense, they were not really refugees at all) rather than to neighbouring countries (the minority, some 300,000, reached and resettled in Lebanon, Syria, and Transjordan). They fled as the shells landed or, they feared, were about to land on their towns and villages. Many were driven by the economic privations of war—unemployment, soaring prices, and lack of food or fuel. Some left because their local leaders, military and political, urged or ordered them to leave, for military or political reasons. Many fled because of an accumulation of reasons. And some were expelled by advancing Israeli troops, primarily out of military calculation.

But these were the immediate causes of departure. Above and beyond them, there was a wider, general, explanatory metanarrative. Or, rather, two metanarratives. One metanarrative, traditionally trotted out in Zionist propaganda, is that the Arab leadership—the national Palestinian leadership and/or the leaders of the neighbouring Arab states—beyond the particulars of flight from each area or battle, advised or ordered the Palestinians to leave their homes and move out of actual or potential battle zones to clear the path for the invading or about-to-invade Arab armies and perhaps to affix the stigma of expulsion on the Israeli side, as a justification for their invasion (the

350   BENNY MORRIS

armies of Jordan, Egypt, Syria, and Iraq invaded Israel/Palestine on 15 May 1948). This narrative has been thoroughly discredited by historians because there is practically no basis for it in the contemporary documentation. The documentation contains no hint of a general Arab order of this sort and, indeed, for May 1948, contains a great deal of evidence from a contrary direction, showing that at least some Arab leaders (King Abdullah of Jordan and Fawzi al Qawuqji, the commander of the Arab Liberation Army, an Arab League volunteer force sent into Palestine to help the Arab militias even before the pan-Arab invasion) tried to persuade Palestinians to stay put or, if already displaced, to return to their homes.

The other metanarrative, that offered in traditional Arab historiography, is that the Zionists from the first, as part of their ideology and programme, sought to transfer or expel the native Arab population of Palestine, and during the first decades of Zionism, organized for it, prepared a master plan, and, in 1947–8, seized the opportunity and systematically implemented it and expelled the Arab inhabitants from the areas earmarked by the United Nations for Jewish statehood and the additional areas that became 'Jewish' in the course of the fighting.

I would like to focus on an element of this second metanarrative, that part dealing with Zionist aforethought and pre-planning, what can be termed 'transfer' thinking—that the Zionists, from the first, intended and planned to expel the Arabs of Palestine. It is certainly true that Zionist leaders, from the 1890s onwards, indeed, beginning with the Zionist movement's prophet and founder, Theodor Herzl, occasionally toyed with the idea of transferring some or all of the Arabs from the area of the Jewish-state-to-be to make way for massive Zionist immigration and settlement. (The movement's leaders anticipated massive waves of immigration as a result of the surge in eastern European anti-semitism, beginning with the pogroms of 1881–4 in the tsarist empire.) For example, in one passage in his diaries, Herzl wrote: 'We must expropriate gently. . . . We shall try to spirit the penniless population across the border by procuring employment for it in the transit countries [i.e. the countries of destination], while denying it employment in our country. . . . The removal of the poor must be carried out discretely and circumspectly.'[1]

---

[1] Theodor Herzl, *Complete Diaries*, 5 vols. (New York, 1960), i. 88, entry for 12 June 1895.

Explaining Transfer

351

But two points are worth making. First, generally, when speaking and writing about transfer, and they did so rarely, partly because the subject was sensitive, Zionist leaders such as Artur Ruppin and Leo Motzkin, and pro-Zionist writers such as Israel Zangwill, talked in terms of a voluntary agreed transfer of the Arabs out of Palestine, with compensation, rather than a coerced expulsion. Second, the idea of transfer was never adopted as part of the Zionist movement's platform, nor as part of the programme or platform of any of the main Zionist parties, not in the nineteenth century and not in the twentieth century. And, in general, the Zionist leaders looked to massive Jewish immigration, primarily from Russia and Europe, as the means of establishing and then assuring a Jewish majority in Palestine or whatever part of it was to be earmarked for Jewish statehood.

But around 1929 and, with even greater frequency, during the late 1930s and early 1940s, Zionist leaders began to talk, in ever-wider, less discreet forums, about the desirability and possibility of transferring Arabs or 'the Arabs'. Both of twentieth-century Zionism's main leaders, David Ben-Gurion, the head of the Yishuv (the Jewish community in Palestine) and Israel's founding Prime Minister, and Chaim Weizmann, the head of the World Zionist Organization and Israel's first President, repeatedly during these years referred approvingly to the idea. But, again, it is worth noting, this talk never translated into the co-option of the idea into official mainstream Zionist ideology or its advocacy in the movement's programme or in that of any of its chief component parties, the socialist Mapai, Hashomer Hatza'ir, and Ahdut Ha'avoda, the liberal General Zionists and Progressives, or the right-wing Revisionist Movement.

In August 1937 Ben-Gurion told an emergency meeting of the Zionist Congress, the movement's supreme decision-making body: 'We must look carefully at the question of whether transfer is possible, necessary, moral and useful. . . . Transfer of populations occurred previously, in the (Jezreel) Valley, in the Sharon and in other places [Ben-Gurion was referring to the small-scale removal of Arab tenant farmers from plots of land bought and settled by the Zionist movement during the previous decades]. . . . Now a transfer of a completely different scope will have to be carried out. In many parts of the country new settlement will not be possible without transferring the Arab peasantry. . . . [It] will make possible a comprehensive settlement program. Thankfully, the Arab people have vast empty areas. Jewish power, which grows steadily, will also increase our possibilities to carry out the transfer on a large scale.'[2]

Four years later, in 1941, at a meeting with Ivan Maiskii, the Soviet ambassador in London, Weizmann said 'that if half a million Arabs could be transferred, two million Jews (from Europe) could be put in their place. That, of course, would be a first instalment; what might happen afterwards was a matter for history.'[3]

The explanation for the increase in volume and intensity of pro-transfer pronouncements in the late 1930s and early 1940s is simple, and goes a long way to explaining the Zionist leadership's growing adoption of this idea in the first place. In 1929 the Palestine Arabs mounted their first major bout of violence against the Jewish community in Palestine. Altogether, some 130 Jews were killed—66 of them, incidentally, non- or anti-Zionist, ultra-orthodox yeshiva students and rabbis and their families, murdered by a Muslim mob brandishing clubs, hatchets, and knives in Hebron's Jewish quarter. In 1936 the Palestine Arabs launched a far more comprehensive campaign of violence directed at the British Mandate authorities and the Zionist settlers. The violence, dubbed by the Arabs the Great Arab Revolt, lasted until spring 1939, and claimed many hundreds of lives and entailed widespread destruction of property.

Apart from the ousting of British governance and the establishment of an independent Arab state in all of Palestine, the rebels demanded an immediate cessation of Jewish immigration to Palestine. And through this violence they succeeded in coercing the British—who faced the prospect of a three-front world war and were bent on appeasing the Arabs to achieve tranquillity in the Middle East, strategically vital because of land, sea, and air routes and oil deposits—severely to curtail Jewish immigration, a policy that was subsequently embodied in the government's White Paper of May 1939. The White Paper limited Jewish immigration to 75,000 over the following five years, with any

[2] Text of Ben-Gurion's speech, 7 Aug. 1937, Central Zionist Archive, S5-1543.

[3] 'Short Minutes of Meeting Held on Thursday, January 30th, 1941, at 77 Great Russell Street, London, WC 1', unsigned, Chaim Weizmann Archive, 2271; and 'Meeting: I. M. Maiskii-Ch. Weizmann', 3 Feb. 1941, in *Documents on Israeli-Soviet Relations, 1941–1953*, 2 vols. (London, 2000), i. 3–5.

Explaining Transfer

further intake of Jewish immigrants dependent on Arab agreement, and promised the country's inhabitants independence within ten years. Given the demographics of 1939, with about one million Arabs and 450,000 Jews, the British were endorsing the emergence of an Arab-majority state.

This British curtailment of Jewish immigration under Arab military duress, at a point when the Jews constituted about 30 per cent of Palestine's population, put paid to the possibility of the achievement of a Jewish majority through immigration. In the longer term, the problem, from the Jewish perspective, was to be compounded by the Holocaust, in which six million Jews were murdered and in which most of Zionism's potential pool of immigrants was annihilated. Thus Arab violence in the late 1930s coupled during the following years with the Holocaust nixed the possibility of the Jews achieving a majority in Palestine by way of immigration.

But this was in the medium term. In the short term, the Arab violence of 1929, and, even more so, of 1936–9, had a further effect: it put the Jewish community on notice that the Arabs would not countenance the emergence of a Jewish state in Palestine and would fight against it tooth and nail; and that an Arab minority included in that Jewish state, even if established only on a small part of Palestine, would be disloyal and rebellious and would destabilize or overthrow that state from within.

This was the conclusion of the British royal commission, headed by Lord Peel, that was established in late 1936 to investigate the causes of the Arab Revolt and to recommend a solution to the Palestine problem. In its thorough, 400-page report, published in July 1937, the commission made two major recommendations: the termination of the Mandate and the partition of the country into two areas, with a Jewish state to be established on less than 20 per cent of the land (the Galilee and the northern and central Coastal Plain) and an Arab state, to be conjoined to Transjordan, to be established on the bulk of the remainder of Palestine. (Some 5–10 per cent of the country, it further recommended, including Jerusalem, Bethlehem, and a corridor to the Mediterranean, should be retained by Britain.) The commission ruled that the Mandate could not continue and that the two peoples, the Arabs and the Jews, could not live in peace in one unitary state (either the Jews would dominate the Arabs or the

Arabs would dominate the Jews, and both possibilities were unthinkable). The commission further recommended the removal of most or all of the Arabs from the area of the Jewish-state-to-be (some 300,000 souls) and their transfer to the Arab part of Palestine or out of the country altogether. The transfer was to be achieved voluntarily, but, if that proved impossible, by coercion. The commission reasoned: 'The existence [of this minority inside the Jewish state] clearly constitutes the most serious hindrance to the smooth and successful operation of partition. . . . If the settlement is to be clean and final, the question of the minorities must be boldly faced and firmly dealt with.'[4] What the commission was saying was that a disloyal, discontented, and large Arab minority inside a future Jewish state, probably aided by the surrounding Arab world, would destabilize that state and, indeed, threaten the viability and longevity of the settlement itself. It was in the interest of the long-term prosperity of both peoples to separate them as completely as possible, determined the commission.

But the Peel Commission was driven to this conclusion not merely by the spectacle of Arab hatred for and violence against the Yishuv and the Arabs' stated unwillingness to live both inside and alongside a Jewish state in a partitioned Palestine. The commission had also been put on notice as regards the Palestinian Arabs' expulsionist mindset and programme. When the chairman of the Arab Higher Committee, Haj Muhammad Amin al Husseini, the cleric who headed the Palestinian national movement until 1948, testified before the Peel Commission, the members asked him: if Palestine is to become an independent, Arab-majority state—as Husseini, who flatly rejected any form of partition or Jewish statehood, was demanding—what would be the status of the 400,000 Jews already resident in the country? Husseini responded: those who were citizens of the Ottoman Palestine up to 1917— fewer than 60,000–70,000, all told—would receive Palestine citizenship. And what would be the fate of the remaining 330,000 Jews currently resident in the country, asked the commissioners. That would be for history to decide, he responded. The commissioners assumed that at the very least Husseini was consigning them to statelessness and, very possibly,

---

[4] Palestine Royal Commission Report, Cmd 5479 (London, July 1937), 389–91.

Explaining Transfer

to deportation. And, in their report, the commissioners hinted—alluding explicitly to the fate of the Assyrian Christian community in Iraq, hundreds of whom had recently been massacred by Muslims, despite Iraqi government assurances to the West—that the fate of Palestine's Jews under a Muslim Arab majority government might be much worse.

What Husseini implied before the Peel Commission, when he was at his diplomatic best, was what he usually said more explicitly elsewhere: the Jews who had arrived in Palestine after 1917, they and their children, would not be allowed to remain. And, of course, it was not just Husseini. The cry of 'idbah al yahud' (slaughter the Jews) had accompanied each of the bouts of violence, or anti-Jewish pogroms, unleashed by Palestine's Arabs in 1920, 1921, and 1929, and was echoed repeatedly by Arab mobs during the 1936–9 revolt. And it was in response to this violent and expulsionist mindset and ideology that the Zionist leadership increasingly turned to the idea of transfer as a solution to the Yishuv's 'Arab problem'. If this was the enemy and this is what they did and sought, no viable Jewish state could come into existence with a large Arab minority in its midst.

But events in Europe without doubt compounded the Zionist dilemma and further fuelled its new-found interest in transfer. From 1933 on, central and eastern Europe were in the throes of a violent antisemitic upsurge, leading to a progressive deterioration in the condition of European Jewry and a threat to its very existence. It was this that drove the urgency in the mid and late 1930s of the Zionist demand for a state that could serve as a haven for these threatened millions. And it was this that underlay the readiness both to compromise over territory—the Zionist movement had traditionally sought all of Palestine for its Jewish state, but by 1937 it was ready for partition and resigned itself to obtaining only a chunk of Palestine—and the demand that the small area allotted for Jewish statehood at least be clear of Arabs, so that there would be room to accommodate the needy millions and that they would not be threatened by violent, indeed murderous, neighbours within that state. The facts that the Palestinian Arabs, by their violence in 1936–9, had pushed the British into sealing off Palestine as a possible haven for Europe's persecuted Jews and that Husseini during the 1930s had repeatedly made friendly overtures towards the Nazi regime and, indeed, in 1941 had moved to Berlin and for the next four years worked for the Third Reich, recruiting Muslims for the *Wehrmacht* and calling for an anti-Allied jihad in the Middle East, only compounded the Yishuv's fears of Palestinian intentions and their animosity towards them. In short, Arab expulsionist and annihilationist, or perceived annihilationist, intentions towards Zion's Jews triggered expulsionist Yishuv attitudes towards Palestine's Arabs.

Without doubt, Zionist thinking about transfer in the late 1930s and early 1940s helped pave the way, at least on a psychological plain, for the massive transfer that occurred in 1948, resulting in the creation of the Palestinian refugee problem. But the process was also driven by the events of 1947–8 themselves, with what had occurred in the 1930s as a backdrop. Without doubt, the Holocaust played a part: the Holocaust had demonstrated that massive murderous intentions could and did translate into reality and that the world would not necessarily intervene to stymie the Arabs.

In November 1947 the Palestinian Arabs, followed by the Arab states, rejected the UN General Assembly partition plan (Resolution 181) and launched a war to prevent the emergence of a Jewish state. Indeed, by rejecting the succession of partition-based solutions—from Peel in 1937, and the United Nations in 1947—the Palestinians had turned the Palestine conflict into a zero-sum game. They had said and were saying, consistently, that it was all or nothing: they wanted all of Palestine, and not an inch for the Jews. In November–December 1947 Palestine's Arabs rose up to frustrate the implementation of the UN resolution. They failed. And in May 1948, the Arab states joined the fray, invading the country. Their radio broadcasts were explicit: the goal was to destroy the Yishuv. Or, as the Arab League's Secretary-General, Azzam Pasha, told the British minister in Amman, Alec Kirkbride, on the eve of the pan-Arab invasion: 'It does not matter how many [Jews] there are. We will sweep them into the sea.'[5] This was the message broadcast by the Arab 'street', which the Arab leaders held in awe, and this was the gist of the fatwas issued by the Muslim religious authorities in the Middle East. As the ulema, the council of theologians, of Cairo's al-Azhar University, perhaps the supreme authority in Sunni Islam, put it

---

[5] Avi Shlaim, *Collusion across the Jordan: King Abdullah, the Zionist Movement, and the Partition of Palestine* (New York, 1988), 228.

Explaining Transfer

in a fatwa on 26 April: 'The liberation of Palestine [is] a religious duty for all Muslims. . . . The Islamic and Arab governments should without delay take effective and radical measures.'[6] Jihad had been proclaimed and the infidel was to be put to the sword. Even Matiel Mughannam, the Lebanese Christian woman who headed the AHC-affiliated Arab Women's Organization in Palestine, told an interviewer (in January 1948): 'The UN decision has united all Arabs, as they have never been united before, not even against the Crusaders. . . . [A Jewish state] has no chance to survive now that the "holy war" has been declared. All the Jews will eventually be massacred.'[7]

Quite naturally, with the Holocaust still fresh in their minds, the Yishuv felt mortally threatened; as, indeed, it was. The Jews took the Arabs at their word; the talk of expulsion and worse lay heavily in the air. No decision was taken in 1947–8 by the Yishuv's leadership bodies—the Jewish Agency Executive, the People's Administration, the Provisional Government of Israel, the Haganah/IDF General Staff—to expel 'the Arabs'; expulsion was never adopted as policy (which is why, incidentally, the newborn Jewish state emerged from the 1948 war with almost a fifth of its citizens Arabs). But a mindset of transfer—not a policy but an unsystematic, inchoate will to be rid of the hostile, threatening Arab population in the area of the Jewish state—took hold in the Yishuv and helped propel the large-scale transfer that was reinforced and consolidated by the decision of the Israeli government, taken in summer 1948, not to allow the return of the refugees. Such a return, it was quite logically felt, would necessarily inject a potential large fifth column into the midst of the newborn state. It could not be countenanced. Continued Arab (including Palestinian Arab) hostility toward Israel made sure that Israel would never accept the refugees' 'right of return', as endorsed in UN General Assembly Resolution 194 in December 1948. At the same time, the Arab states refused properly to resettle the refugees in their midst. Together, these assured the persistence of the Palestinian refugee problem down to the present day.

---

[6] Campbell to Foreign Office, 1 May 1948 (no. 536), PRO FO 371-68371.
[7] Nadia Lourie, 'Interview with Mrs. Mogannam (Mughannam)', 10 Jan. 1948, Central Zionist Archives S25-9005.

PART IV
Forced Removal in Post-Colonial Times

15

Sustainable Violence:
Mass Resettlement, Strategic Villages, and Militias in Anti-Guerrilla Warfare

CHRISTIAN GERLACH

Introduction

The story told in this essay begins around 1950, about at the end of what some call the 'racial century'.[1] In scholarly discussion anti-partisan warfare has been relatively neglected, although it accounted for a large proportion of the victims of mass violence in the twentieth century.[2] Many of these victims resulted from resettlement, removal, and expulsion. Yet the events covered here have hardly played a part in debates about enforced population movements during the past decade or two, given that mass transfers of populations have increasingly been declared 'ethnic' in the course of what amounts to an ethnization of history due to post-1989 bourgeois triumphalism. While what is dealt with here for the most part hardly qualifies as 'ethnic cleansing', this essay looks at the removal of about 30 million people. At least 4 million died in the process (see Table 15.1).

In fighting protracted, brutal, anti-guerrilla wars in the countryside, a variety of regimes developed distinct systems of counter-insurgency involving mass removal plus the resettlement of some of the expelled in model villages. There they were promised economic advancement, while some of the men (sometimes

This essay draws heavily on a chapter of my forthcoming book *Extremely Violent Societies: Mass Violence in the Twentieth Century* (Cambridge University Press).

[1] A. Dirk Moses, 'Conceptual Blockages and Definitional Dilemmas in the "Racial Century": Genocides of Indigenous People and the Holocaust', *Patterns of Prejudice*, 36/4 (2002), 7–36, esp. 31–6.

[2] See Benjamin Valentino, *Final Solutions: Mass Killing and Genocide in the Twentieth Century* (Ithaca, NY, 2004), 81–4, lists at least 10 million deaths as a result. See also id. et al., '"Draining the Sea": Mass Killing and Guerrilla Warfare', *International Organization*, 58 (Spring 2004), 375–407.

TABLE 15.1. *Resettlement and militias in anti-guerrilla warfare since 1932* [a]

Country	Colonial/imperial power involved	Dates	Resettled in model villages (additionally regrouped)	Displaced: domestic/abroad	Militia membership (total auxiliaries)	Deaths
China	Japan	1932–45	>3,500,000		(200,000)	>2,300,000
Belarus	Germany	1943–4	20,000	>110,000	(100,000)	345,000
Greece	(British, US advice)	1945–9		830,000/100,000	<50,000	>100,000
Malaya	Britain	1948–60	570,000 (650,000)	(30,000)	300,000	>20,000
Vietnam	France	1952–4	3,000,000	?		?
Cambodia	France	1953–4	500,000	?		?
Kenya	Britain	1952–6	1,100,000	100,000	25,000 (50,000)	>100,000
Algeria	France	1954–62	2,350,000	1,000,000/ 300,000	60,000 (200,000)	500,000
South Vietnam	(USA) (British advice)	1959–65 (–1975)	8,700,000	3,500,000	3,000,000	1,000,000
Angola	Portugal	1962–74	>1,000,000 (500,000)		35,000	>52,000

Indonesia (Kalimantan)		1967–8		50,000		3,000
Mozambique	Portugal	1968–74	1,300,000		230,000 (?)	
Guinea Bissau	Portugal	1968–73	150,000	(60,000)	10,000 (18,000)	
Thailand	(US advice)	1968–73			170,000	
Rhodesia		1973–9	>750,000	400,000 (228,000)	20,000	>30,000
East Timor	Indonesia	1976–99	>300,000	400,000 (300,000)		100,000
Bangladesh		1976–		? (130,000)		>15,000
El Salvador	(US advice)	1981–93		750,000/ 1,000,000	11,000	75,000
Guatemala		1982–96	>60,000	1,000,000/ 200,000	900,000	150,000
Ethiopia		1984–90	700,000			>50,000
Turkey (Kurdistan)		from the 1980s		4,000,000	70,000	>23,000
Peru		1989–93	>56,000	600,000	300,000	25,000

[a] This list makes no claim to completeness. Counter-insurgency measures in the Philippines between 1946 and 1954 and in the 1970s came at least close to what is sketched here. The flight and resettlement of the Miskito in Nicaragua from 1981 to 1988 have been left out for reasons of scale. The same goes for Malaysian–British strategies employed in Sarawak and Sabah in the mid-1960s. For similar British measures in Oman in 1970 see Charles Allen, *The Savage Wars of Peace: Soldiers' Voices 1945–1989* (London, 1990), 184–5, 194, 198–201.
Source: Compiled by the author.

also women) were recruited for armed militias. Responding to political-military movements that profoundly challenged the existing socio-economic order, governments were essentially trying to compete with the guerrillas in offering rural dwellers social improvements and modernization. Some of the insurgencies combated in this way were Communist based on Mao Tse-tung's ideas, but others followed different Communist, somewhat leftist-nationalist, or anti-colonial, non-leftist concepts.[3]

In addition to long-term social consequences of dislocation per se, the special practices followed during these campaigns have actively involved substantial population groups in committing violence, and induced or aggravated deep conflicts within societies, transforming the latter profoundly. Despite some variations, the measures described were part of a comprehensive concept and are therefore to be considered as one distinct phenomenon. This essay portrays this interconnected set of practices, gathers basic facts about the main incidents, discusses variations and precursors, and offers a preliminary analysis of the violence generated, the role of the ethnic factor within anti-guerrilla warfare, and in particular the social changes that removal brought about.

The Phenomenon

My attention was first drawn to this topic during my research on German rule in Belarus, a stronghold of the European partisan movement in the Second World War. In brief, Nazi German anti-guerrilla tactics in the Soviet Union went through five phases, which may also serve a better understanding of similar strategies:

1. From the start in June 1941, they applied collective punishment and preventive measures of terror, including selective killings.

---

[3] The cases discussed below could be attributed to the Maoist approach (Malaya, Indo-China, Portuguese Africa, Indonesia/Kalimantan, Thailand, Guatemala, Peru), other Communist (Soviet Union, Greece), leftist nationalist (Algeria, Rhodesia, El Salvador, Turkish Kurdistan, Ethiopia, East Timor), and non-leftist nationalist or separatist currents (Manchuria, Kenya, Bangladesh). Counter-insurgency 'specialists' often attribute the occurrence of such movements to Maoism alone.

Sustainable Violence

2. In the autumn of 1941, the German military and then also the SS and police turned to mass raids against 'non-locals' and 'wanderers' as a security risk and a social burden.
3. From the spring of 1942 on, 'big operations' served to depopulate areas near partisan bases by means of mass murder, expulsion, and resettlement.
4. From 1943, larger 'dead zones' expanded the scale of such action, combined with intensified forced labour recruitment.
5. And from early 1944 on, the Germans established 'fortified villages' in Belarus where still reliable locals had to form militias under German supervision.[4]

It is important to understand that the 'fortified villages' (*Wehrdörfer*) were not a contradiction to depopulation, but rather a zonal supplement. Areas that could no longer be controlled and exploited were devastated, troops concentrated, and strategic villages declared in still relatively safe areas as a base from which German rule over the country was to be secured again step by step. The population in secured areas—especially fortified villages—was to receive improved social services such as schools and churches, land property titles, tax benefits, and consumer goods as economic incentives. The villages became the core of ongoing agricultural reform, transforming collective farms into cooperatives where peasant families could do a great deal of work separately. Groups of 'fortified villages' were formed and supervised by a German agricultural official rather than a military or SS and police officer. The Soviet army liberated Belarus before this experiment could affect more than 100 strategic villages with an estimated population of 20,000, and so its effects remained uncertain. Patchy evidence suggests that it was a moderate success, much more so than the parallel attempt to transplant armed pro-German groups of Caucasians, Cossacks, and Russians fighting on the German side to Belarus with their families.[5]

---

[4] Christian Gerlach, *Kalkulierte Morde: Die deutsche Wirtschafts- und Vernichtungspolitik in Weißrußland 1941 bis 1944* (Hamburg, 1999), 859–1054.

[5] Ibid. 1040–54.

366 CHRISTIAN GERLACH

Dimensions

As marginal as this episode may seem, such patterns have surfaced worldwide since the 1930s. They were either refined or independently developed in many other incidents of anti-guerrilla warfare. The names of the places for resettlement differed: from *new villages* in Malaya to *strategic hamlets* in Vietnam, *aldeamentos* in Angola, *aldeos modelo* in Guatemala, and *koykent* (attraction centres) in Turkish Kurdistan. The same goes for the militias, dubbed *patrullas de autodefensa civil* (civil self-defence patrols, Guatemala), *rondas campesinas* (peasant patrols, Peru), *Home Guard* (Malaya), *korucu* (village guards, Turkish Kurdistan), and so on. Still, the phenomenon was usually the same, comprising four elements:

1. large-scale depopulation of entire areas by resettlement, expulsion and, not infrequently, killings;
2. the creation of strategic villages;
3. plans for social improvements and economic 'development'; and
4. the arming of local rural populations in militias and/or military units.

The partisans were thereby supposedly denied supplies, recruitment, intelligence, and, above all, political support.

People were forced into such strategic villages not in some distant 'racial century', but from the 1940s to the 1990s. It happened from Guatemala to Thailand, from Peru to Rhodesia, from Vietnam to East Timor. These measures were taken by old colonial powers, by new twentieth-century empires, but also by post-colonial states, including socialist Ethiopia. Different empires applied this special sort of violence: the British in Malaya and Kenya (they played a crucial role in recommending similar measures in Greece and South Vietnam, together with the USA); the French in Vietnam, Cambodia, and Algeria; the Portuguese in Mozambique, Angola, and Guinea Bissau; and European settlers after unilateral independence in Rhodesia.

The number of people removed was often considerable: 3 million in French Algeria; 1 million each in Portuguese Angola and Mozambique, and in British Kenya; 500,000 in British Malaya; 700,000 during the Greek civil war; 4 million were

Sustainable Violence 367

resettled or expelled in South Vietnam; and an equal number in Turkish Kurdistan. Every tenth Malayan, Greek, and Angolan was displaced, as were 15 per cent of all Kenyans, a quarter of all South Vietnamese, every fourth Kurd in Turkey, every third Algerian and El Salvadorean, and about half of the population of East Timor under Indonesian rule.

Not always included in these figures are those who were 'regrouped', that is (in counter-insurgency-speak), resettled within walking distance of their old home, farm, or village, like another 600,000 inhabitants of Malaya and some of the inhabitants of South Vietnam's 'strategic hamlets'.[6] And people evaded persecution in prohibited zones or areas of terror by migrating to urban centres domestically (for instance, highland Mayas to Guatemala City), by emigrating to the colonial 'motherland' (such as 200,000 Algerians to France during the civil war), or by fleeing across heavily guarded borders abroad (for example, up to 200,000 Algerians to Tunisia and Morocco; 200,000 Guatemalans mostly first to Mexico, later to the USA; Angolans to Congo and Zambia; more than 1 million El Salvadoreans; and 60,000 Guineabés to Senegal).[7] This means that one-third of all Algerians had to leave their home—their houses were often destroyed—during the war of liberation, and about 40 per cent of all Mayas in Guatemala were displaced in the 1980s.

The methods involved were often locally reinvented but otherwise passed on, tailored, and refined by military academies and scholarship, or by the movement of commanders and troop units from one theatre to another—from Belarus to Greece, from

---

[6] In South Vietnam it was estimated that half of the strategic hamlets would only require minor regroupment (relocation of houses), 30% major regrouping (about half of the houses), 15% complete regroupment, and 5% a move to a completely new site. In addition, a distinction was made between more loosely organized 'strategic hamlets' and 'defended hamlets': Robert Thompson, *Defeating Communist Insurgency: The Lessons of Malaya and Vietnam* (New York, 1966), 121–2. However, in practice there were more complete relocations than initially planned.

[7] Richard Brace and Joan Brace, *Algerian Voices* (Princeton, 1965), 19 and 38; Liisa L. North and Alan B. Simmons, 'Fear and Hope: Return and Transformation in Historical Perspective', in eid. (eds.), *Journeys of Fear: Refugee Return and National Transformation in Guatemala* (Montreal, 1999), 3 and 17; Basil Davidson, 'Angola in the Tenth Year: A Report and an Analysis, May–July 1970', *African Affairs*, 70/278 (Jan. 1971), 47; Mustafa Dhada, 'The Liberation War in Guinea Bissau Reconsidered', *Journal of Military History*, 62/3 (1998), 580; Joan Gillespie, *Algeria: Rebellion and Revolution* (1st edn., London, 1960; Westport, Conn., 1976), 30; Hugh Byrne, *El Salvador's Civil War* (Boulder, Colo., 1996), 213; Mario Lungo Uclés, *El Salvador in the Eighties: Counterinsurgency and Revolution* (Philadelphia, 1996), 104–5.

Greece to Malaya, from Malaya to South Vietnam, from the Portuguese colonies to Rhodesia, and, oddly, from Algeria to Guatemala.[8] Different applications emerged, ranging from transplanting populations over hundreds of miles to locally resettling rural dwellers, or removing people from some areas while declaring fortified villages among populations that stayed put. Regimes could thus use strategic villages in secured areas as a starting point, with relative success, or have them in conflict zones, up to monstrous schemes to resettle almost the entire rural population, as in South Vietnam and East Timor.

In other cases, such as Greece in the 1940s and El Salvador in the 1980s, while displacement was systematic, the state gave it no direction. Expulsion and dispersal of populations to urban areas by far overshadowed any government attempts to create new rural settlements in target areas. Elsewhere, more systematic policies to resettle citizens in certain areas set in once refugees had become a major factor in national politics, as in Guatemala. The size of militias was another point of variation, ranging from comparatively small in some African colonies (Kenya, Rhodesia, and Angola) to mandatory membership in an attempt to use so-called self-defence units as a direct element of control over the male population, as in the highlands of Guatemala.

Precursors

Enforced resettlement and population concentration during combat and small-scale armed resistance are historically not new. It was an old colonial practice prior to the 1940s, employed, for instance, against the Indigenous population in the North American West. However, in the cases briefly discussed in the following section, either the population affected was not offered economic development organized in special settlements, and/or they were not armed in militias (plus offered political participation in state affairs). Both factors consequently limited the emergence of local elites, social differentiation, inner tensions within the group, and their loyalty to the rule of the resettling power. In other words, the measures described above are to be seen as one set that, if not applied together, did not have the same effects as otherwise.

[8] Because of limitations of space, I cannot elaborate on this point here; see Gerlach, *Extremely Violent Societies*.

Sustainable Violence 369

A classic champion of mass removal and resettlement for pacification was the Ottoman Empire. For centuries, the Porte shifted armed men with their families from one corner of their empire to the other, resettling them for defence purposes. Yet there was hardly any element of economic 'development' planning to this, nor to the forced resettlement or dispersion of Kurds in the 1920s and 1930s (when especially notables were banished). The idea of a capitalist penetration of Turkish Kurdistan only grew stronger through the ideas of a political current called 'Easterners' mainly in the 1960s.[9] Consequently social improvements did not become a part of counter-insurgency in Turkey before the 1980s.

Around the turn of the twentieth century, mass resettlement in small-scale warfare was practised in a number of places around the planet: by the Spanish in Cuba in 1898, causing 100,000 deaths; during the Boer War (1899–1902) by the British, who put between 120,000 and 150,000 people into concentration camps where more than 20,000 died; and by US troops after they occupied the Philippines (1899–1906). But only the latter case included a substantiated offer of 'development' and social improvements for those resettled or expelled, and hence involved an attempt to win over their sympathies, indeed their participation, for the existing or evolving system. Locals were recruited especially from the non-Tagalog-speaking groups for the Philippine Constabulary and village militias. Medical services, sanitation, schooling, limited food supplies, and public works projects were provided in resettlement areas after the US military forced locals to move out of forbidden areas with all their possessions. Nonetheless, 300,000 or more Filipinos died of deprivation.[10]

From 1933 to 1939, Japan expelled from remote rural areas, or herded into at least 10,000 strategic villages, between 3.5 million and 5.5 million people in Manchuria, plus an undetermined

---

[9] David McDowell, *A Modern History of the Kurds* (London, 1996), 402–9; Edgar O'Ballance, *The Kurdish Revolt: 1961–1970* (Hamden, Conn., 1973), 19–20.

[10] Anthony James Joes, *America and Guerrilla Warfare* (Lexington, Ky., 2000), 110–11; id., *Resisting Rebellion: The History and Politics of Counterinsurgency* (Lexington, Ky., 2004), 125; Valentino, *Final Solutions*, 203, 205; John J. McCuen, *The Art of Counter-Revolutionary Warfare* (London, 1966), 172, 211–13; John L. Tone, *War and Genocide in Cuba, 1895–1898* (Chapel Hill, NC, 2006). For population losses, see Eqbal Ahmad, 'Revolutionary Warfare and Counterinsurgency', in Gérard Chaliand (ed.), *Guerrilla Strategies: An Historical Anthology from the Long March to Afghanistan* (Berkeley, 1982), 256 n. 10.

370   CHRISTIAN GERLACH

number elsewhere in northern China. Kept behind palisades, mud walls, and barbed wire, with any homes outside the fortifications destroyed, all inhabitants were registered and provided with limited health services, credits, and famine relief by Japanese authorities.[11] Even though 9,000 places with 11 million inhabitants in north China had been declared Communication Protection Villages by 1942 (supervised by the North China Railway Company from 1940) and all this was combined with massive violence, it brought little success in putting down resistance.[12] However, in north China in particular, the Japanese hesitancy to arm the Chinese meant that—apart from a more symbolic army of 25,000, 63,000 male police, and 72,000 in the Internal Security Police—Chinese militias played little role in the Japanese security network.[13] As in all these early cases, there does not yet seem to have been any comprehensive system integrating resettlement, social policy, and militias.

Approach

In order to explain why I find this shift in anti-guerrilla warfare so important that it appears to be a new phenomenon, I shall briefly discuss my theoretical framework. By more effectively involving inhabitants, or citizens, in conflicts, examples of what I call 'extremely violent societies' were created. In extremely violent societies, *various* population groups become victims of massive physical violence, in which, along with state organs, large and diverse social groups participate for a multitude of reasons. Linked to the variety of motives, my approach is, above

[11] T. A. Bisson, 'Aikawa Asks for Fifty Millions', *Amerasia*, 2 (Mar. 1938), 9–10; Y. Nagano, 'Comments on Manchurian Protective Villages', *Amerasia*, 2 (Feb. 1939), 549–51; Ray C. Hillam, 'Counterinsurgency: Lessons from Early Chinese and Japanese Experience against the Communists', *Orbis*, 12/1 (1968), 237–41; Rana Mitter, *The Manchurian Myth: Nationalism, Resistance and Collaboration in Modern China* (Berkeley, 2000), 112–14, 122–3; Joes, *Resisting Rebellion*, 111.

[12] Lincoln Li, *The Japanese Army in North China 1937–1941: Problems of Political and Economic Control* (Tokyo, 1975), 86, 175–6, 189, 193–5, 201–4, and 208–11.

[13] A similar argument would appear to apply to population removals in the early Soviet Union from the 1920s to the 1940s (see the essay by Shane O'Rourke in this volume). While combining resettlement with chances for socio-economic advancement and modernization, they either did not include setting up armed militias or did not respond to armed insurgencies.

Sustainable Violence

all, designed to explain why participation is so widespread and why several groups become victims of violence.[14] Here I explore what population displacement and multi-polar mass participation in violence had to do with broader social transformations in these countries.

The phenomenon of extremely violent societies has, at best, been partially addressed by genocide studies so far. In practice and often also in theory, using the concept of 'genocide' has entailed a tendency to focus on the state—state crimes—and on one victim group, often with an emphasis on ethnic or racist motives, but in any case on one core motive. Despite efforts for change, this pattern automatically tends to stress centralized bureaucratic machineries, political systems, and the role of radical groups. More adaptive works use the concept of mobilization, still a top-down imagination. In other words, the Eurocentric model of totalitarianism has, explicitly or implicitly, retained some influence.

For the present short study, as in other cases, 'genocide' as a category does not seem functional chiefly because of the problems it poses for understanding the *origins* of violence. Leftist critics of anti-guerrilla warfare have analysed depopulation cum developmental village concentration as a one-sided, outrageous governmental strategy. Counter-insurgency experts have portrayed the phenomenon as a conflict between rulers and insurgents, observing a variety of outcomes in terms of power struggles. Both have a tendency to miss the role and complex motives of the crucial groups imperfectly called 'loyalists': how and why did they appropriate ideas of modernization? This way, one cannot fully address the broad local participation in violence on all sides, while at the same time failing to understand the longer-term societal consequences of setting up armed formations of rural citizens and mass resettlements. In order to write a social history of such conflicts, we need to understand how violence was very effectively induced, as well as usurped, or existing tensions intensified, in affected societies, and how, even more than before, conflicts were turned into civil wars.

---

[14] Cf. Christian Gerlach, 'Extremely Violent Societies: An Alternative to the Concept of Genocide', *Journal of Genocide Research*, 8/4 (2006), 455–71.

372 CHRISTIAN GERLACH

Analysis

Direct Violence and Indirect Death

Strategic resettlement directly implied enormous violence, most notoriously the Vietnam and Algerian wars. In Algeria, 150,000 inmates were said to have perished in resettlement camps or villages every year around 1960, according to data from the National Liberation Front (FLN).[15] The clearing of inhabitants from certain territories, the persistent shoot-on-sight pursuit of remaining inhabitants by patrols and aerial bombing, and the starving of those remaining by destroying houses and crops—by fire, manual destruction, and chemical defoliants—caused thousands of deaths. An estimated 100,000 to 150,000 people were killed in the Greek civil war from 1944 to 1949; about as many as in Guatemala between 1981 and 1983. Thousands of Angolans were killed during a wild Portuguese retaliation against an uprising in 1961.[16] But official deaths and more convincing numbers often differed greatly, as in Malaya, where the authorities put the blame for all 12,000 reported killings on the rebels.[17] In some campaigns, massacres were either infrequently publicized or accounted only for a fraction of actual deaths.[18]

The indirect victim toll was often at least as high, and for that, relocation was crucial. Apart from the deprivation of liberty, social uprooting, and humiliation, resettlement into strategic villages frequently entailed economic destitution, appalling hygienic conditions, lack of employment or medical treatment, and loss of social capital. As a result, for example, death rates in Algerian strategic settlements and for native minorities forced into the 'new villages' in British Malaya were considerable, especially among infants and children, as they were in Rhodesia, and even more in British Kenya and East Timor.[19] In Malaya, about

---

[15] Brace and Brace, *Algerian Voices*, 22 and 38.

[16] Amikam Nachmani, *International Intervention in the Greek Civil War: The United Nations Special Committee on the Balkans, 1947–1952* (New York, 1990), 23 (the official number of victims until March 1949, including missing Greek National Army soldiers, was 52,000); C. M. Woodhouse, *The Struggle for Greece 1941–1949* (1st edn. 1976; Chicago, 2002), 211, 286; Davidson, 'Angola in the Tenth Year', 41–2.

[17] Thompson, *Defeating Communist Insurgency*, 53 and 115.

[18] John Newsinger, 'Minimum Force, British Counter-Insurgency and the Mau Mau Rebellion', *Small Wars and Insurgencies*, 3/1 (1992), 51–4.

[19] Caroline Elkins, *Imperial Reckoning: The Untold Story of Britain's Gulag in Kenya* (New York, 2005), 242–65; Terrence Ranger, *Peasant Consciousness and Guerrilla War in Zimbabwe*

Sustainable Violence

8,000 Orang Asli (Indigenous people) died in resettlement areas between 1949 and 1952, with death rates as high as 8 to 12 per cent annually in some camps.[20] Apparently, as more and more Indigenous men fled back to the jungle, some of whom supported the Communists who increasingly retreated there, the British abandoned long-distance resettlement of the Orang Asli and replaced it with concentration within the jungle.[21] Possibly equally high were the numbers of victims of destitution among refugees and displaced people, for instance, in Guatemala and certainly in East Timor. A report by the Truth Commission in East Timor estimates that 83 per cent of fatalities resulted from hunger and deprivation.[22]

Executions of alleged insurgents after a more or less legal process generated few of the total population losses; yet numbers could still be considerable. In the Greek civil war, according to government figures, more than 1,500 people had been executed by May 1948, whereas a Communist publication stated that there were more than 3,000 executions between July 1946 and October 1949.[23] British authorities hanged no fewer than 1,015 Kenyans between 1952 and April 1956, including over 200 just for taking the Mau Mau oath.[24]

(London, 1985), esp. 263–8; 'Starvation Camps in East Timor', *Tapol*, 30 (Oct. 1978), 1; John G. Taylor, ' "Encirclement and Annihilation": The Indonesian Occupation of East Timor', in Robert Gellately and Ben Kiernan (eds.), *The Specter of Genocide: Mass Murder in Historical Perspective* (New York, 2003), 163–84, esp. 171–2.

[20] John D. Leary, *Violence and the Dream People: The Orang Asli in the Malayan Emergency 1948–1960* (Athens, OH, 1995), esp. 44–8, 217; Wade Markel, 'Draining the Swamp: The British Strategy of Population Control', *Parameters* (Spring 2006), 39; cf. Thompson, *Defeating Communist Insurgency*, 150–2.

[21] McCuen, *The Art of Counter-Revolutionary Warfare*, 93; Richard Clutterbuck, *Conflict and Violence in Singapore and Malaysia 1945–1983* (Boulder, Colo., 1985), 258; Leary, *Violence and the Dream People*, 66 and 96.

[22] Valentino, *Final Solutions*, 213–14; Taylor, 'Encirclement and Annihilation', 167–8; Benetech Human Rights Data Analysis Group of the Commission on Reception, Truth and Reconciliation of Timor-Leste (Romesh Silva and Patrick Ball), *The Profile of Human Rights Violations in Timor-Leste, 1974–1999*, 9 Feb. 2006, 1–2, <http://hrdag.org/resources/Benetech-Report-to-CAVR.pdf>, accessed 6 Dec. 2007; see Yehonatan Alsheh, 'What "De-facto state" is embodied in stating that: "There is no such thing as a Tim-Tim nation". Indonesian Defence Minister Benny Murdani speaking in Dili, Feb. 1990', paper delivered at the conference 'From Europe to Latin America and Beyond: The Continuity of Genocidal Social Practices', Buenos Aires, 22 Nov. 2007.

[23] Nachmani, *International Intervention in the Greek Civil War*, 95–6; Dominique Eudes, *The Kapetanios: Partisans and Civil War in Greece, 1943–1949* (London, 1972), 354; Woodhouse, *The Struggle for Greece*, 245.

[24] Newsinger, 'Minimum Force, British Counter-Insurgency and the Mau Mau

374 CHRISTIAN GERLACH

Numbers of mass arrests were much higher. Between 1947 and 1950, the number of left-wing prisoners and detained military suspects of left-wing persuasion in Greece oscillated between roughly 19,000 and 27,000, after 50,000 had been arrested in 1945 alone and 75,000 in twelve months in 1945–6.[25] In British Malaya 35,000 people were arrested under emergency regulations and 24,000 deported abroad, 90 per cent of them ethnic Chinese.[26] In Vietnam, French anti-guerrilla operations included routine searches with all able-bodied men routinely detained and questioned, and all non-locals arrested.[27]

Within twenty-five days after an 'emergency' was declared in Kenya on 20 October 1954, 8,000 people had been arrested. At one point almost all adult Kikuyu men in Kenya were either in detention camps (with 70,000 at their peak population and a total of at least 150,000 inmates) or held in fortified villages, according to Wade Markel (an author who comments that at some point mass detention may become necessary in US-occupied Iraq). At the end of April 1954, British authorities assembled 25,000 troops and police to conduct a systematic search of all Africans living in Nairobi; 15,000 Kikuyu were arrested and thousands more expelled, leaving only half of the earlier Kikuyu residents in the city.[28] This Operation Anvil resembled the German six-day search of Minsk (Belarus) during Operation Magic Flute in April 1943 (serving security reasons combined with labour recruitment and resulting in fewer arrests).[29] In Greece, Communists had to undergo a 'moral rehabilitation' process in special camps; in

Rebellion', 54; David Anderson, *Histories of the Hanged: The Dirty War in Kenya and the End of Empire* (New York, 2005).

[25] Polymeris Voglis, 'Becoming Communist: Political Prisoners as a Subject during the Greek Civil War', in Philip Carabott and Thanasis D. Sfikas (eds.), *The Greek Civil War* (Aldershot, 2004), 143, 147; Nachmani, *International Intervention in the Greek Civil War*, 96; Eudes, *The Kapetanios*, 260 (the left claimed 84,931 arrests from Feb. 1945 to Mar. 1946), 302.

[26] Charles Townshend, *Britain's Civil Wars: Counterinsurgency in the Twentieth Century* (London, 1986), 164–5; Kumar Ramakrishna, ' "Transmogrifying" Malaya: The Impact of Sir Gerald Templer (1952–1954)', *Journal of Southeast Asian Studies*, 32/1 (2001), 82, 87.

[27] Bernard Fall, 'Street without Joy', in Chaliand (ed.), *Guerrilla Strategies*, 124 and 129.

[28] Anderson, *Histories of the Hanged*, 5, 356; Charles Allen, *The Savage Wars of Peace: Soldiers' Voices 1945–1989* (London, 1990), 133; Frank Furedi, 'Britain's Colonial Emergencies and the Invisible Nationalists', *Journal of Historical Sociology*, 2/3 (1989), 257; Newsinger, 'Minimum Force, British Counter-Insurgency and the Mau Mau Rebellion', 48–9; Markel, 'Draining the Swamp', 42, 47.

[29] Gerlach, *Kalkulierte Morde*, 221, 288, 483.

Sustainable Violence

Algeria, the existence of ten re-indoctrination camps with 8,000 prisoners was admitted in 1962, but there were probably more.

In Kenya,

[o]nly a cathartic 'confession' of the secret oath could begin a reverse process or 'rehabilitation'. To this end an elaborate series of internment camps were established, the so-called 'pipeline' through which Mau Mau suspects were filtered back into society. The filters were loyalist Gikuyu, whose leaders determined the extent to which any individual could be accepted as rehabilitated. Suspects were graded from 'black' (irreconcilable) through 'grey' to 'white'—a revealing color spectrum— and the hardcore irreconcilables were gradually concentrated in remote security camps.[30]

Of course, the brutality of Nazi German military, SS, and police, who massacred large sections of the population of hundreds of villages in the Soviet Union, Yugoslavia, Greece, and other countries, was unmatched in most of these cases. Still, the systematic murder of refugees in restricted zones showed similarities. However, the hands-on massacres of yesteryear have been replaced by the ample use of airpower. Arguably, as many civilians died in the Vietnam War as in the course of Nazi German anti-guerrilla warfare across Europe. US counter-insurgency in the Philippines cost about as many lives of Filipinos—300,000— as German anti-partisan warfare in Belarus. The estimated death toll among Kenyans during the British repression of the Mau Mau uprising—100,000—was as high as that of German anti-partisan warfare in Greece, out of a population of seven million in each case. It has to be added that total population losses in German-occupied Greece and Belarus were higher than those in the course of anti-guerrilla warfare; most of the other victims were urbanites or POWs.[31]

Historical accounts that exclude mass expulsions and resettlement as well as destitution and undersupply of those resettled in

[30] Alexander Papagos, 'Guerrilla Warfare', in Franklin Mark Osanka (ed.), *Modern Guerrilla Warfare: Fighting Communist Guerrilla Movements, 1941–1961* (New York, 1962), 236, 240; Peter Paret, *French Revolutionary Warfare from Indochina to Algeria* (New York, 1964), 62–3; quotation: Townshend, *Britain's Civil Wars*, 205.

[31] Total losses among Greek civilians in the Second World War were close to 300,000, including about 100,000 victims of the 1941–2 famine and 70,000 murdered Jews; and in Belarus, a total of between 1.6 and 1.7 million non-combatants were killed by the Germans. Elkins, *Imperial Reckoning*, 346–7; Loukia Droulia and Hagen Fleischer (eds.), *Von Lidice bis Kalavryta: Widerstand und Besatzungsterror* (Berlin, 1999).

376 CHRISTIAN GERLACH

designated places, that leave aside starvation policies and the hardships for refugees, that underestimate the consequences of aerial attacks, or that look for 'genocide', tend to understate the full effects of modern anti-guerrilla warfare. Often it was precisely these 'softer' factors that caused most victims.

The Ethnic Factor

Ethnic aspects were of obvious importance where colonial governments or foreign occupants tried to prevent nationalist movements from succeeding. But they played a big part in other cases as well. For the combating of Kurdish resistance in Turkey and the repression of Mayas in the highlands of Guatemala, the case is equally clear.[32] The same could be said about the Aymara in Peru or the Makonde in Mozambique. Foreign or national rulers played on existing differences in race, ethnicity, religion, language, or culture. Target populations were often portrayed in ethnic terms in order to discredit the insurgents with their mostly leftist agenda and divert attention from the social or land question. In a wider sense, such ethnization is unsurprising and went beyond mere government manipulation. Conflicts took place in marginal rural areas where regional identities were strong, yet metropolitan elites planned to develop these areas and integrate them into the national economy and polity, to which regional particularism appeared as an obstacle.

Resettlement in British Kenya targeted ethnic Kikuyu. In Malaya, ethnic Chinese squatters were removed from jungle areas, together with the native Orang Asli people and sedentary Chinese agriculturalists. Of 573,000 'resettled', 86 per cent were classified as Chinese and 9 per cent as Malay; and of another 650,000 'regrouped', 42 per cent were considered Indian, 38 per cent Chinese, and only 16 per cent Malay. In 1951, 2,409 of 2,578 alleged Communists killed were Chinese, while of 38,466 men in the Special Constabulary, only 1,860 were Chinese. Malays opposed the proposal that land for 'new villages' for the Chinese

---

[32] The Catholic Church's initiative for the recovery of historical memory, REMHI, found that three-quarters of the acts of violence documented in 55,021 testimonies had been committed against Mayas: Linda Green, *Fear as a Way of Life: Mayan Widows in Rural Guatemala* (New York, 1999), 186 n. 6; Valentino, *Final Solutions*, 211–12, 299 n. 78, offers an alternative view.

Sustainable Violence

was to be given out of Malay reserve land.[33] The first resettlement villages in northern Angola, and in all of Portuguese Africa, were created in 1962–3 for members of the Kongo ethnicity who had fled to Congo.[34] In Thailand, Communist insurgents were dubbed as belonging either to the ethnic Chinese, Lao, or Hmong minorities.[35]

Even in the Greek civil war there was an ethnic aspect because evacuations affected the north of the country and there primarily Macedonians from territories acquired by Greece in 1912. Along with students, tobacco workers, and seamen they were portrayed as 'sociologically unrepresentative' of the Greek population.[36] (Fragmentary statistical data about exiles and political prisoners suggest that these were actually heterogeneous groups, among them 50 to 60 per cent peasants.[37]) Especially in the later years of the insurgency, anti-Communist propaganda played on the 'Slav connection' and called partisans foreign agents, 'wolves from the Bulgarian jungle', asserting a link between the Communists and Macedonian separatists who sided with Bulgarians and Germans in the Second World War.[38]

While ethnically based liberation movements struggled to overcome this limitation, colonial governments on the other side attempted to prevent the spread to other population groups in order to remove the chance of a national independence movement emerging.[39] The Mau Mau movement was portrayed by the British as based on the Kikuyu tribe, even though it also involved Embu, Meru, and people of mixed Massai–Kikuyu heritage.[40] Not necessarily in order to 'wreak havoc and fuel the flames of ethnic passions as a matter of course', but as a means of maintaining the empire in times of crisis, British colonial authorities helped

---

[33] Clutterbuck, *Conflict and Violence in Singapore and Malaysia 1945–1983*, 177; John A. Nagl, *Counterinsurgency Lessons from Malaya and Vietnam: Learning to Eat Soup with a Knife* (Westport, Conn., 2002), 77; Anthony Short, 'Communism, Race and Politics in Malaysia', *Asian Survey*, 10/12 (1970), 1084.

[34] Davidson, 'Angola in the Tenth Year', 47.

[35] Joes, *Resisting Rebellion*, 212.

[36] Id., *America and Guerrilla Warfare*, 174.

[37] Voglis, 'Becoming Communist', 147.

[38] Basil C. Gonneris, 'Social Dimensions of Anticommunism in Northern Greece, 1945–50', in Carabott and Sfikas (eds.), *The Greek Civil War*, 177; Nachmani, *International Intervention in the Greek Civil War*, 116; Woodhouse, *The Struggle for Greece*, 66, 188–9.

[39] Townshend, *Britain's Civil Wars*, 155 (for Malaya).

[40] Ibid. 199–202.

to create and strengthen ethnic identities, heterogeneity, and communalism, while denying that there was a common national identity, as Frank Furedi has argued. Popular anti-colonial forces were seen as illegitimate while Britain favoured 'moderate' middle-class or intelligentsia-based nationalists who held out the promise of maintaining something as close as possible to the existing social order.[41] In the final analysis, such policies weakened the emerging nation-states.

Post-colonial states also tried to exploit ethnic divisions, but by ascribing cultural identities to populations suspected of supporting an insurgency and labelling them as traitors of the nation, or as backward, or a combination of both. They insisted on unconditional national unity instead of confronting socio-economic issues that were at the root of the uprising, whether in Greece, Turkey, Peru, or Guatemala.

Such attempts to instrumentalize ethnic cleavages did not always succeed. Among the independence fighters of the Algerian FLN, the many Kabylians whom the colonial regime had courted as allies over decades were disproportionately represented.[42] In another regard Furedi's analysis falls short of explaining the complexities of late colonial policies. Apart from isolating the Chinese in Malaya and the Kikuyu in Kenya, British authorities successfully attempted to divide these ethnicities among themselves. Given that about 40 per cent of the inhabitants of Malaya counted as Chinese, they had no other choice. By supporting and mobilizing the Malay Chinese Association and by introducing Chinese Home Guards to the 'new villages', they favoured pro-capitalist elite-building or consolidation. This also implies that the British authorities were forced to encourage political organization and participation at a higher than local level. By nurturing the Kikuyu opposed to the Mau Mau insurgency and arming Kikuyu supporters in militias or police units, they strengthened the role of elders and traditionalists where gender, age, and family relations had been challenged by the uprising.[43] In Laos, the US military and the CIA tried to make use of the Hmong people (270,000 of

[41] Frank Furedi, 'Britain's Colonial Wars: Playing the Ethnic Card', *Journal of Commonwealth and Comparative Politics*, 26/1 (1989), 80, 85; id., 'Britain's Colonial Emergencies and the Invisible Nationalists', 247–50, 261.

[42] Gillespie, *Algeria*, 78, 200–1.

[43] Daniel Branch, 'Loyalism during the Mau Mau Rebellion in Kenya, 1952–1960' (Ph.D thesis, University of Oxford, 2005); Furedi, 'Britain's Colonial Wars', 80.

Sustainable Violence

whom now live in the USA), as the French had tried before in North Vietnam. In 1975, about 100,000 Hmong were evacuated to Thailand. Ironically, the Hmong minority in Thailand was divided between supporters of the Thai Communist guerrillas and their opponents who resettled from the northern border in 1969, and they became entrenched in deadly fights against each other.[44]

By contrast, as a supportive measure, other groups were used as a reliable base in different ways. This applied not only to the ethnic Malay and Greek majority populations, but also, for example, to Chinese in East Timor as an unlikely ally of the Indonesians (unlikely given the decade-long persecution of ethnic Chinese in the archipelago nation). Such intensified racial, ethnic, and religious divisions were a powerful means of undermining an emerging national unity in countries on the way to decolonization. Local involvement ensured by economic incentives added to the depth of the conflicts. This also applied to many African tribes; yet none of the imperial post-1945 attempts succeeded because overwhelming white racism in offices and on the ground prevented any intelligent plans for a fundamentally better treatment from being carried out.

Rulers also tried to stabilize their control by exploiting divisions other than ethnic ones. Of all the powers, it was Catholic Portugal that attempted to instrumentalize Islam. Apart from turning supporters of Guinese independence against the main anti-colonial movement (PAIGC), which wanted to achieve national liberation for Cape Verde at the same time as for Guinea, the Portuguese in Guinea Bissau tried to gain the support of the Muslim Fulah people, pitting them and the animists against each other by spreading rumours that the guerrillas wanted to enforce the drinking of alcohol or Islamization respectively.[45] In Algeria the French army's Psychological Action and Information Service came to the conclusion that efforts to spread pro-French, capitalist-modern ideas should concentrate

---

[44] Aranya Siriphon, 'Local Knowledge, Dynamism and the Politics of Struggle: A Case Study of the Hmong in Northern Thailand', *Journal of Southeast Asian Studies*, 37/1 (2006), 68–9; Eric Wakin, *Anthropology Goes to War: Professional Ethics and Counterinsurgency in Thailand* (Madison, 1992), 141.

[45] Gérard Chaliand, 'With the Guerrillas in "Portuguese" Guinea', in id. (ed.), *Guerrilla Strategies*, 194, 209; Joes, *Resisting Rebellion*, 127; Dhada, 'The Liberation War in Guinea Bissau Reconsidered', 586, 589.

on army veterans, women, and young people, while the religious brotherhood and some professions would also have been considered useful for creating divisions in a liberation movement that was perceived as socialist.[46] Nor is 'ethnic cleansing' exclusively ethnic: 'Isolating the mainly non-Malay working class from the Malay peasantry has always been an important undercurrent of British colonial policy.'[47] Resettlement during the Emergency helped to deepen divisions between Malay sedentary farmers, Chinese mining workers, and Tamil rubber estate toilers.

The Transformation of Society

The enforced modernization which accompanied the resettlement programmes involved restructuring the countryside. Economically planned strategic villages such as in Malaya meant land consolidation, clearing out marginal agriculture, and eliminating dispersed settlements; it spelled standardized small farms, villages, social services, and often housing facilities. Less equality-oriented effects included a rise in social status for those emerging elites who seized opportunities in administration, militias, or were successful in commerce.

This led to all the more profound social change, as most affected areas were remote regions, characterized by marginal agriculture, low market integration, weak infrastructure, and often by illiteracy.[48] As Robert Thompson, a British counter-insurgency specialist active during the Malayan insurgency and adviser to the South Vietnamese government from 1961 to 1964, put it, strategic villages were intended to put traditionalist, isolated, and individualistic farmers into contact with the world: 'This attitude is no longer in keeping with the times nor with the general aspiration for progress and advancement.'[49]

Access to resources channelled into resettlement areas or

[46] McCuen, *The Art of Counter-Revolutionary Warfare*, 99.

[47] Furedi, 'Britain's Colonial Wars', 72.

[48] In 1948, 9% of Muslim men and 2.1% of Muslim women in Algeria could write. In Guatemala, 73% of all men and 91% of women were still illiterates in the mid 1990s; in 1992, 3% of Guatemalans read newspapers, 16% had a radio, and only 6% a TV set, according to a UNDP study. By the late 1960s, three-quarters of the population of the Kurdish provinces in Turkey did not speak Turkish. Gillespie, *Algeria*, 35; Green, *Fear as a Way of Life*, 26; Gellert, 'Migration and the Displaced', 114; Kendal, 'Kurdistan in Turkey', 75.

[49] Thompson, *Defeating Communist Insurgency*, 124–5.

Sustainable Violence

earmarked for those evacuated was not equal. In Greece, individuals, groups, and associations tried to outdo each other in anti-Communist rhetoric in order to tap relief funds. The most promising patronage networks that emerged involved deputies, administration officials, army and gendarmerie officers, veterans, and leaders of local militias.[50] The inability of regimes related to the interests of large landowners put limits on equality. For example, the land question in Guatemala remained unresolved, and in South Vietnam, land reform in part served to redistribute land back to former owners who had previously been dispossessed by the Viet Minh.[51]

But social differentiation was also intensified by transforming dislocated agriculturalists into a labour pool for industry or plantations. Enforced concentration in resettlement areas provided estate workers in northern Angola and farm and industrial labourers for white businesses in Rhodesia; the shantytowns around towns or cities in Greece provided hundreds of thousands of workers, further undermining wages in a country gripped by inflation and economic crisis. In Malaya, the measures taken during the Emergency of 1948 can be said to have directly served capitalist business interests: at the outset, plantation-owners and tin-miners had complained about a lack of casual labour and attacked the rights of organized labour. The resettlements and 'relocations' created one of Asia's most urbanized societies. More specifically, squatters were removed from plantation land, better control of the workers was facilitated by concentration of their settlements on estates and near mines, and many squatters and farmers (each represented about half of the close to 600,000 resettled) were turned from agriculturalists into workers in mines and on plantations, timely given the rubber and tin booms during the Korean War. (Similar observations were made for resettlers in the Algerian civil war, although nearly half of them remained unemployed.) However, this favoured bigger enterprises, whereas not a few smaller, mostly Asian-owned, mines and estates were disadvantaged as their workers were relocated to other sites.[52] The very name of the Malayan Emergency was

[50] Gonneris, 'Social Dimensions of Anticommunism in Northern Greece', 175–86.

[51] John Ellis, *From the Barrel of a Gun: A History of Guerrilla, Revolutionary and Counter-Insurgency Warfare, from the Romans to the Present* (London, 1995), 224–5.

[52] See esp. the material in Kernial Singh Sandhu, 'The Saga of the "Squatter" in Malaya: A Preliminary Study of the Causes, Characteristics and Consequences of the

382 CHRISTIAN GERLACH

selected with capital interests in mind; otherwise the insurance contracts of British estates would not have been valid and many plantations would have been given up by their owners.[53]

Similar practices can be observed earlier: US forced resettlements in the Philippines around 1900 helped create a labour army for the plantations of US corporations, and the depopulation of entire areas in north China and the resettlement of 5 million or so in 'Manchukuo' to a large degree served to provide cheap labour for the Japanese industrialization of Manchuria.[54]

For Guatemala, it has been argued that the emergence of plans for a capitalist penetration of the north-central development belt in the 1970s, including oil drilling and hydroelectric and highway projects, caused the military's drive for control of the highlands.[55] But the effects of counter-insurgency were mixed. They reduced the volume of seasonal migration from the Maya highlands to the coastal plantation areas in the south as highland dwellers tried to avoid the trip because of insecurity, traffic disruption, increased travel costs, and a loss of population. Simultaneously, labour demand for coffee, cotton, and sugar estates dropped as a result of depressed world market prices, while less labour-intensive products such as soybeans, sorghum, and beef were expanded, though in other regions of the country. The nation's industry slumped and Guatemala City lost its capacity to absorb labour. Some former seasonal migrants tried to settle permanently near the estates.[56] In fact, some military

Resettlement of Rural Dwellers during the Emergency between 1948 and 1960', *Journal of Southeast Asian History*, 5 (1964), 143–77. The percentage of agriculturalists in the New Villages dropped from 60 to 27 between 1950 and 1952, while the wage-earners in the tin and rubber industries increased equally (ibid. 169). For Algeria, see Pierre Bourdieu, *The Algerians* (Boston, 1962), 174: only 25% of heads of families in resettlement areas stated they were still farmers or farm labourers, while 44% said they were unemployed, and the rest owned some kind of business.

[53] Cf. Phillip Deary, 'The Terminology of Terrorism: Malaya, 1948–1952', *Journal of Southeast Asian Studies*, 34/3 (2003), 231–47, at 237.

[54] See David Tucker, 'Labor Policy and the Construction Industry in Manchukuo: Systems of Recruitment, Management, and Control', and Ju Zhifen, 'Northern Chinese Laborers and Manchukuo', both in Paul Kratoska (ed.), *Asian Labor in the Wartime Japanese Empire* (Armonk, NY, 2005), 25–57 and 61–78.

[55] Terrance W. Kading, 'The Guatemalan Military and the Economics of La Violencia', *Canadian Journal of Latin American and Caribbean Studies*, 24/47 (1999), 57–91.

[56] Green, *Fear as a Way of Life*, 34; Gisela Gellert, 'Migration and the Displaced: Guatemala City in the Context of a Flawed National Transformation', in North and Simmons (eds.), *Journeys of Fear*, 112–29, esp. 118, 122–6 (though with contradictory figures).

Sustainable Violence

commissioners, mayors, and chiefs of civil patrols in the highlands were also contractors or financers of the recruitment of workers for coffee and cotton plantations, creating a short cut between local violence and the labour supply for other regions.[57] Migration patterns could also be reversed in other ways, as in Kenya, where colonial authorities depicted the deportation of half of Nairobi's Kikuyu as an economic opportunity for other ethnicities (mainly Nyanza and Kamba), cultivating the rise of non-Kikuyu politicians and trade unionists.[58]

The building of dams could also become strategic in insurgency areas, by facilitating industrialization through the provision of electricity and incentives for construction industries, and by making intensive agriculture possible by way of large-scale irrigation. It usually also spelled the partial substitution of local ethnicities. In south-eastern Turkey, twenty-two large dams were planned, of which at least twelve have been completed, dislocating 350,000 locals, most of them Kurds, but attracting ethnic Turks as well as some of the displaced with new jobs. For the Ilisu dam alone 184 villages had to be destroyed, 85 of which were already 'supposedly empty' as a result of counter-insurgency measures.[59] If we accept the figure of 4 million Kurds forced from their homes during the suppression of the insurgency of the 1980s and 1990s, close to 9 per cent of these had to move for dam projects. In the Tete province of Mozambique, the huge Cabora Bassa dam was supposed to allow for one million new white settlers, while 25,000 Africans had to leave their homes. Half a million Portuguese were to settle around the Cunene dam project in southern Angola. In both cases, African locals were resettled into strategic villages in order to have them available as a labour reserve for construction works.[60] Plans for huge hydroelectric projects also emerged in the Franja Transversal del Norte, the envisioned north-central 'development' belt of Guatemala, between 1972 and 1974, in the very

---

[57] Matilde Gonzalez, 'The Man Who Brought the Danger to the Village: Representations of the Armed Conflict in Guatemala from a Local Perspective', *Journal of Southern African Studies*, 26 (June 2000), 320.

[58] Furedi, 'Britain's Colonial Wars', 76; cf. Anderson, *Histories of the Hanged*, 352.

[59] Behrooz Morvaridi, 'Resettlement, Rights to Development and the Ilisu Dam, Turkey', *Development and Change*, 35/4 (2004), 719–41, esp. 722–3.

[60] See Bernard Rivers, 'Angola: Massacre and Oppression', *Africa Today*, 21/1 (1974), 51, 54; Martin Stähli et al. (eds.), *Cabora Bassa: Modellfall westlicher Entwicklungspolitik* (Berne, 1971).

384   CHRISTIAN GERLACH

area that soon became embattled. Independent groups say that some massacres near the Pueblo Viejo dam in the north-west of the country were committed in order to get peasants who refused to leave it off their land.[61] Not only there, dam construction sites thus became military and political battlegrounds over different visions of the future of society.

No less an analyst than Pierre Bourdieu has attempted, in his study of Algerian society, to describe the consequences of enforced mass resettlement during anti-guerrilla warfare.[62] The French military gave priority to clearing those secluded areas of the country that so far had been least affected by the colonial enterprise. Border and mountain regions lost population that fled abroad, to France, to the cities, or was taken to resettlement areas designed among other things to 'ensure the emancipation of the Moslem masses'. Adult men often became separated from their families, and women were drawn into the workplace, and the public and political sphere. The displacement—and this is the central point of Bourdieu's analysis—led to the breaking up of old forms of behaviour and customs, of extended families, clans, and village communities. The 200,000 nomads of the country underwent the most radical transformation by being forced into settlements behind barbed wire whose daily rhythm was governed by a curfew. As a result of separation from their own land, peasants were morally broken and lost their urge to work, undergoing 'deruralization' and 'bidonvillisation', the conversion into shantytown dwellers and clients of social welfare institutions. According to Bourdieu, agriculturalists were transformed into 'a sub-proletariat who had lost all memory of their former ideals of honor and dignity and who wavered between attitudes of meek resignation and ineffectual revolt', nurturing resentment against the colonialists.[63]

Bourdieu did notice that some Algerians jumped at what modernization had to offer, as well as the 'appearance of a class of profiteers who were often supported by the army by reason of their "loyalty" and who held a majority of administrative responsibilities'.[64] Without the benefit of hindsight, he may have underestimated both the processes of social differentiation and

---

[61] Kading, 'The Guatemalan Military and the Economics of La Violencia', 66, 84.
[62] Bourdieu, *The Algerians*, esp. 141–3, 163–86.
[63] Quotations ibid. 166, 172, 178, 179.   [64] Ibid. 178 n. 15.

Sustainable Violence

the resilience of old social structures, customs, and values among the locals. He overstated demoralization and passivity. The overthrow of the political order in Algeria allowed many to return to their land (far from all did) but swept away the new civil war elites loyal to the French.

Nevertheless, forced relocation had a long-term impact on settlement patterns. In Malaya the bulk of the 'new villages' and their residents remained in place after independence; anti-guerrilla war created lasting new social structures.[65] Despite all the contempt for the regroupment centres and efforts by the Algerian and even the late French colonial authorities to bring people back, a clear majority stayed on. A similar long-term effect was observed in Tete province, Mozambique.[66] With villages destroyed, families torn apart, land changing hands, and urban centres growing, resettlement during anti-guerrilla warfare changed social structures even where people made strong efforts to rebuild their old homesteads and communities, as in Guatemala. El Salvador was transformed in different ways, as about one million emigrants stayed outside the country and the economy became dependent on their remissions.

Prohibitive Costs of Socio-Economic Modernization

Yet the power of rulers to manipulate the rural population by modernizing the countryside in a way compatible with the capitalist system was far from total. Organized resettlement is expensive. For example, the colonial authorities in Kenya had to make do with Kenya's financial and human resources to defeat the Mau Mau uprising.[67] The services provided to resettlers often concentrated on quite traditional functions of a nineteenth-century-style penetration of the countryside, namely, medical and educational

---

[65] Sandhu, 'The Saga of the "Squatter" in Malaya', esp. 172–3; Robert Jackson, *The Malayan Emergency: The Commonwealth's Wars 1948–1966* (London, 1991), 20; Thompson, *Defeating Communist Insurgency*, 125.

[66] Keith Sutton, 'Population Resettlement—Traumatic Upheavals and the Algerian Experience', *Journal of Modern African Studies*, 15/2 (1977), 289–94; Joao Paulo Coelho, 'State Resettlement Policies in Post-Colonial Rural Mozambique: The Impact of the Communal Village Programme on Tete Province, 1977–1982', *Journal of Southern African Studies*, 24/1 (1998), 61–91, esp. 62–8, 91 n. 89.

[67] Markel, 'Draining the Swamp', 41.

386   CHRISTIAN GERLACH

facilities: 'Winning the population can tritely be summed up as good government in all its aspects. From the point of view of the immediate impact, there are many minor social benefits which can easily and fairly inexpensively be provided, such as improved health measures and clinics . . .; new schools . . .; and improved livelihood and standard of living', such as improved seeds, livestock, and advice on producing cash crops.[68] As in other affected countries, resettlers in Malaya had to build their new homesteads with their own hands.

The Korean War boom supposedly facilitated financing the suppression of the Malayan Communist resurrection. Even before, Malaya had been the British Empire's prime dollar earner; between 1946 and 1950 (largely before Korea), the USA imported US$700 million worth of rubber from Malaya. The British government directly provided £520 million of the about £700 million that the Emergency cost, but this was financed by export-related state revenues, that is, indirectly from international sources.[69] By comparison, the total means provided for the resettlement of about 573,000 Malayans accounted for about Malayan $100 million (£12.5 million).[70] Much of the profit from the Korean War boom actually ended up in the pockets of the predominantly white business community in Malaya, which spurred the readiness of British managers to stay on the rubber plantations despite heightened vulnerability to guerrilla attacks; and part of it indirectly helped the insurgents, as mine and plantation workers were awash with money but did not know how to spend it, sometimes donating it to the Communists instead.[71]

The practice of settlement tended to reflect a racist hierarchy: to settle a single white family in Portugal's African colonies

[68] Thompson, *Defeating Communist Insurgency*, 112–13.

[69] Joes, *Resisting Rebellion*, 110; Phillip Deery, 'Malaya, 1948: Britain's "Asian Cold War"?', Working Paper no. 3, *The Cold War as Global Conflict, International Center for Advanced Studies, New York University*, <http://www.nyu.edu/gsas/dept/icas/PhillipDeery.pdf>, accessed 29 Apr. 2008, 5, 10–11 (in 1947 the USA received 371,000 of 727,000 tons of Malayan rubber and 155,000 of 158,000 tons of Malayan tin exports). Total revenue from duties and taxes on Malayan export goods was around £55 million in 1951 and £92 million in 1952, which compared to the costs of the 'Emergency' US$51.15 million and 69.3 million respectively (calculated on the basis of Malayan $8 being the equivalent of one pound: Leary, *Violence and the Dream People*, 116).

[70] Jackson, *Malayan Emergency*, 20.

[71] See Thomas Mockaitis, 'The Origins of British Counter-Insurgency', *Small Wars and Insurgencies*, 1/3 (Dec. 1990), 210; C. C. Chin and Karl Hack (eds.), *Dialogues with Chin Peng: New Light on the Malayan Communist Party* (Singapore, 2005), 162.

Sustainable Violence

required 300,000 escudos.[72] Only a small fraction of this sum was provided for black involuntary resettlers. In Malaya, the British authorities financed the relocation of about 573,000 mainly Chinese rural dwellers in 'new villages' to the tune of about Malayan $100 million (about $180 per person), but allocated just $810,000 for the relocation of the Indigenous Orang Asli people in 1949–51 ($32 per person, the bulk of which was spent on the salaries of administrators, propaganda material, office furniture, and books). Under these circumstances, the consequent mass deaths of the Orang Asli come even less as a surprise.[73]

While providing large populations with the means for settling in a new location is a luxury many states cannot afford, militias are comparatively cheap. The territorial forces in the villages of South Vietnam received only 2–4 per cent of the war budget; however, they sustained 30 per cent of the deaths of Communist and government forces combined, so that a Vietnamese analyst called them 'the most cost-efficient military forces employed on the allied side'. A similar effect was recorded for the Philippine Constabulary in the insurgency of the early 1900s.[74]

Conversely, employing large numbers of troops or keeping them in an overseas territory tended to overstretch the financial resources of rulers. The case of US troops in the Vietnam War is obvious, but for the Portuguese to have more than 50,000 soldiers in Angola or for the French to have 400,000 in Algeria financially exhausted these countries too. France had kept 52 per cent of its regular army in Indo-China in 1953. The Algerian War cost France £250 million in 1960 alone.[75] Attempts by the Guatemalan military to finance the war against the guerrillas and welfare measures to pacify the highland population by raising taxes repeatedly resulted in major conflicts with business elites in the 1980s.[76]

[72] Rivers, 'Angola: Massacre and Oppression', 54.

[73] Leary, *Violence and the Dream People*, 43, 54–5 (based on the assumption that the total number of Orang Asli was 50,000 and that half of them were resettled).

[74] Joes, *America and Guerrilla Warfare*, 227; McCuen, *The Art of Counter-Revolutionary War*, 211–13. For the role of militia membership and leaders in perpetuating inequality and violence, see Gerlach, *Extremely Violent Societies*.

[75] Davidson, 'Angola in the Tenth Year', 49; Ellis, *From the Barrel of a Gun*, 212; McCuen, *The Art of Counter-Revolutionary Warfare*, 259.

[76] Susanne Jonas, *The Battle for Guatemala: Rebels, Death Squads, and U.S. Power* (Boulder, Colo., 1991), 168–9; Kading, 'The Guatemalan Military and the Economics of La Violencia', 76, 83.

388 CHRISTIAN GERLACH

Anti-Communist governments and colonial regimes covered part of their costs from foreign sources, for the most part from the USA. Between 1951 and 1954 Washington provided the regime of its former colony, the Philippines, with $95 million in non-military aid, in part to fund social improvements during the Huk rebellion. In Greece the US government spent $10,000 to 'eliminate one guerrilla'.[77] Most US aid to Greece from 1947 was channelled to the military, and a large part of a downsized reconstruction budget was used for airport and road construction. Essentially, American financial support served to cover budget and balance of payment deficits.[78] According to the commander of the Greek counter-insurgency forces, 'thanks to American aid the size of the Army was notably enlarged' in 1948; the same applied to local militias.[79] The Indo-China War cost France US$1 billion per year, which was partly recovered through the Marshall Plan. In addition, the US government bore one-third of the French costs by 1950 and poured $1 billion annually into this proxy war in 1953–4.[80] From 1980 to 1988 Guatemala received US$575 million in military and economic aid, and El Salvador received ten times as much.[81] Little of this money actually reached the people; instead, much was wasted on 'white elephants'—oversized development projects—or appropriated by way of corruption, as was most of US 'development aid' for South Vietnam.[82]

Another part of the costs of 'development' projects initiated by the Guatemalan military to cover the basic needs of the population was financed by UN agencies and international non-governmental organizations. Similarly, international development agencies funded economic projects at 'strategic sites' for relocated Hmong people in northern Thailand, including an effort to

[77] Joes, *America and Guerrilla Warfare*, 165, 206.

[78] Jon V. Kofas, *Intervention and Underdevelopment: Greece during the Cold War* (University Park, Pa., 1989), 22, 123, 130; Eudes, *The Kapetanios*, 299; Woodhouse, *The Struggle for Greece*, 203, 247. From 1945 to 1947, the USA had provided three-quarters of $416 million of UNRRA funds (more than half of this contribution in food).

[79] Papagos, 'Guerrilla Warfare', 238.

[80] McCuen, *The Art of Counter-Revolutionary War*, 260.

[81] Jenny Pearce, 'From Civil War to "Civil Society": Has the End of the Cold War Brought Peace to Central America?', *International Affairs*, 74/3 (1998), 594–5; Byrne, *El Salvador's Civil War*, esp. 146–8, 189.

[82] Rolf Steininger, 'Grossbritannien und der Vietnamkrieg 1964/65', *Vierteljahrshefte für Zeitgeschichte*, 45 (1997), 593.

Sustainable Violence

dissuade them from cultivating poppy seeds and persuade them to turn to alternative cash crops. Earlier, a representative of the US Agency for International Development stated before the US Congress that three-quarters of USAID money was concentrated on 'counterinsurgency activities', including Thai police forces.[83]

Because purely military operations were given priority and the old elites objected to massive redistribution of property, large schemes for the capitalist modernization of the countryside often failed as a result of a lack of resources. This is very obvious in the Portuguese colonies, namely eastern Angola,[84] in Guatemala and other post-colonial countries, and in South Vietnam, where 8,000 strategic hamlets were hastily established in 1961–3 but villagers received hardly any financial support. What happened instead was a transformation through the emergence of new elites, who rose in a chaotic struggle by virtue of their function in militias or administrations, by establishing businesses, and accumulating land.

Long-Term Consequences

On 2 December 1989 newspapers reported that the East German parliament had deleted the leading role of the Socialist Unity Party of Germany (SED) from the constitution of the German Democratic Republic on the previous day. On that same day, the chairman of the Malaysian Communist Party, Chin Peng, signed a peace agreement with the government of Malaysia. A total of 1,188 registered guerrillas surrendered, forty-one years after the start of the Malayan Emergency.[85] Although Malaysia is considered a relatively peaceful society, the Malay–Chinese tensions heightened in the Malayan Emergency contributed to the split into Malaysia and Singapore in 1965, to race riots in both countries in the late 1960s, and to the New Economic Policy favouring 'indigenous' (that is, Malay) citizens in Malaysia's public service that was adopted in 1969 and is still in effect.

---

[83] Siriphon, 'Local Knowledge, Dynamism and the Politics of Struggle', 70; Wakin, *Anthropology Goes to War*, 117, 120–1.

[84] See Gerald J. Bender, 'The Limits of Counterinsurgency: An African Case', *Comparative Politics*, 4/3 (1972), esp. 340–6.

[85] Of those who surrendered 494 were born in Malaysia, and 694 in Thailand. Deery, 'Malaya, 1948'; Peter Taaffe, 'End of Empire: Memoirs of a Malaysian Communist Guerrilla Leader', *Socialism Today*, 91 (Apr. 2005), <http://www.socialismtoday.org/91/malaya.html>, accessed 29 Apr. 2008.

390 CHRISTIAN GERLACH

In many countries the long-term fallout from enforced civil involvement in anti-guerrilla warfare is much more obvious. Strategic resettlement was intended to quell certain types of violence. But the application of large-scale counter-violence, and the involvement of large local groups in this, created or widened fault-lines that would remain. The most obvious fallout was the retaliatory and often long-term repression of former 'loyalists' of defeated regimes by informal killings, imprisonment and re-education, trials and executions, economic disadvantages, and exile—from Vietnam to Algeria, from East Timor to the former Portuguese colonies. Estimates of Muslims killed because of their previous support of French rule in Algeria range between 30,000 and 150,000.[86]

Many former 'loyalists' felt compelled to emigrate, including hundreds of thousands of supporters of the South Vietnamese and Cambodian regimes (who left for the USA), many Hmong from Laos and Vietnam who were scattered all over the world, and several thousand Belorussian peasants from 'armed villages' or local police who left their country with the Germans in 1944. The same goes for tens of thousands of former *harkis* from Algeria who, ironically, today have to struggle for their place in French society against, above all, the Front National, a political party representing, among others, former European settlers in Algeria and their descendants, in spite of the fact that these often do not feel quite at home in France.[87]

In other cases, such as Vietnam, former opponents of the liberation movement were held in re-education camps for years, or civil wars ensued, some lasting for decades, as in Cambodia, Angola, and Mozambique. Recent scholarship on Mozambique has stressed the domestic origins of conflict between the government and the notorious Renamo.[88] Insurgencies along class, religious, or ethnic lines have flared up periodically in the Philippines; armed fighting in East Timor and Kurdish resistance as well as its oppression continue. Algeria was shaken by a bloody civil war in the 1990s, with massacres committed by Islamist

---

[86] A number of French historians think that 70,000 is a realistic figure: Maurice Faivre, 'L'Histoire des Harkis', *Guerres mondiales et conflits contemporains*, 202–3 (2002), 59.

[87] For the last point, see the essay by Andrea Smith in this volume.

[88] See Alex Vines, *Renamo: From Terrorism to Democracy in Mozambique?* (2nd rev. edn., London, 1996), esp. 73–119; from a pro-Renamo point of view see David Hoile, *Mozambique, Resistance and Freedom* (London, 1994).

Sustainable Violence 391

insurgents as well as government forces. In Greece, the military dictatorship from 1967 to 1974 drew upon policies of the civil war which lasted from 1945 to 1949 and many unconstitutional practices since 1950; applicants for a position in the public service needed a police certificate, approved by a board of the prefecture, testifying to their 'healthy beliefs' for a quarter of a century after the defeat of the Communist insurgency; and only 10,000 of the 28,000 children evacuated abroad by the guerrillas in 1948–9 had returned to their home country by the 1970s.[89]

Ongoing political violence and intimidation in Guatemala after the peace accord and criminal lawlessness resulted in 6,229 killings in the first eleven months of 1997, while 1,231 people had been kidnapped or disappeared.[90] Violence had become a way of life, primarily in the central highlands but intrinsic also to the nation's capital, where South Americans passing through on their way from the airport to Mexico and further to the USA were frequently assaulted.[91] Even after the Civil Patrols had been dissolved, deep divisions remained embedded within the Maya village communities. Widows maintained that they knew which neighbours had denounced their murdered husbands. They would not take a new partner because of an atmosphere of fear, alcoholism, and worsened machismo after a dozen years of intimidation.[92] In such an environment, the 'reweaving' of old social ties was a major challenge to those returning from exile or domestic displacement—if they were admitted back to their home village, or the charred remnants of it, at all. Often the divisions between old (returning) and new settlers were demonstrated by variations in their readiness to serve in the Civil Patrols.[93] In El Salvador there were 8,000 to 9,000 violent deaths each year from 1994 to 1996, more than during an average civil war year. Even in 2006 almost 4,000 people were murdered.[94]

[89] Gonneris, 'Social Dimensions of Anticommunism in Northern Greece', 183; Woodhouse, *The Struggle for Greece*, 209.

[90] Pearce, 'From Civil War to "Civil Society"', 590; Green, *Fear as a Way of Life*, 55–79, ch. 'Living in a State of Fear'; North and Simmons, 'Fear and Hope', 22 and 24.

[91] Manuel Angel Castillo, 'Exodus and Return with a Changing Migration System', in North and Simmons (eds.), *Journeys of Fear*, 135.

[92] Green, *Fear as a Way of Life*, 31–2, 83–4, 168.

[93] Clark Taylor, *Return of Guatemala's Refugees: Reweaving the Torn* (Philadelphia, 1998), esp. 25, 32–6, 93–6, 149; Gonzalez, 'The Man Who Brought the Danger to the Village', 328–35.

[94] Pearce, 'From Civil War to "Civil Society"', 590; 'Ex-Generalstaatsanwalt ermordet', *Spiegel online*, 12 Oct. 2007.

392   CHRISTIAN GERLACH

Several authors have emphasized that mass rapes during anti-guerrilla operations served to sever ties between women and the rest of society, and to humiliate surviving men, whose male role of protecting their family had been put into question. This could also be accomplished by beating men up in front of their families, as occurred in Algeria. Fear, shame, self-degradation, and loosening family cohesion were among the consequences.[95] This symbolizes how resettlement, militia-building, and enforced modernization carried enduring conflicts into the most intimate environments, into families, villages, and clans.

Conclusion

Large-scale removal of populations did not happen only in a distant racial century before 1950, and such practices have not been restricted to so-called 'failed' states—unless one wants to define, say, the British Empire as a failed state. Nor was the practice only 'ethnic' in nature. The events sketched here had some ethnic origins but also dimensions drawn from politics, class, social change, or religion. Therefore violence became deeply rooted, or, rather, it had many roots.

Ultimately, maintaining a racist colonial order and providing substantial benefits for a significant number of locals were irreconcilable. In the longer run, illusions about military 'victories' such as in Algeria, Malaya, Kenya, South Vietnam, or East Timor gave way to defeat in the political arena, and decolonization or the overthrow of the old regime became inevitable. Within established borders, post-colonial regimes were, at least superficially, much more successful in terms of oppression, yet as a rule without overcoming backwardness and poverty in the region concerned (Greece, Turkey, Guatemala, and Peru). Their social engineering largely failed, and the economic upheaval that often caused the civil wars got out of hand and was exacerbated. Designed to quell one form of strife, the type of participatory violence discussed here, whether developed by late or new colonialists or by young national states, mainly by arming rural dwellers in various forms, led to increasing social differentiation

[95] Green, *Fear as a Way of Life*, 31–2, 176 n. 12; Gonzalez, 'The Man Who Brought the Danger to the Village', 327–8; Bourdieu, *The Algerians*, 185.

and long-term structural or manifest conflicts by nurturing new elites. Enforced socio-economic modernization, welcomed by many locals as an opportunity, while restricted by a lack of resources, also helped to make violence endemic and sustainable.

16

Coerced or Free?
Considering Post-Colonial Returns

ANDREA SMITH

Introduction

Forced removals were an integral feature of colonial rule. This was certainly the case in the USA, a country that developed in tandem with the eviction of Native Americans from their homelands. Autochthonous residents of French Algeria similarly found their lands labelled 'sterile' by outsiders and confiscated. These areas were parcelled out as settler village lots while the evicted Algerians became an impoverished subject proletariat. Removals on such a scale required a concerted effort involving the backing of a state power and its legal apparatuses buttressed by considerable military threat. Evictions were often chaotic and violent. Incoming forces destroyed important symbolic sites and other evidence of the area's departing residents, and seized houses, lands, crops, and livestock. The evicted people were sometimes imprisoned, as in the case of the Navajo, or translocated to more distant territories designated for them, as in the case of the repeated removals of Native American tribes to the other side of an ever-migrating western frontier. They often found themselves stateless or a subject population with considerably fewer rights than the people now inhabiting their former territories. We could cite here hundreds of examples of eviction, displacement, and replacement associated with settler and other colonial conquests worldwide.

Not all mass population transfers associated with colonialism involved subject or colonized populations, however. Less obvious are the migrations of 'colonials' that followed the collapse of colonial rule. As independence movements swept the globe in the mid twentieth century, people who were affiliated with the former colonial powers fled *en masse*. These departures were principally to Europe, to such countries as the Netherlands, Great

396   ANDREA SMITH

Britain, France, Spain, Italy, Belgium, and Portugal, as well as to Japan from its spheres of influence across Asia. The migrations at issue here involved millions of people, and were sufficiently significant in scale to transform many European countries after the Second World War from sites of net population exportation to countries of immigration. Should we view these population transfers as migrations or removals? Were they free or coerced? In this essay I outline how these population transfers compare with other cases of forced removals, emphasizing departures from European settler colonies.

Pieds Noirs *and Other 'Repatriates'*

The elderly former settlers of French Algeria (*pieds noirs*) that I interviewed in southern France in the mid 1990s talked about their time in France as a period of exile, and themselves as *exilés*, a people forced from their home by events outside their control. They often felt at sea in their new land. A woman in her mid seventies, Louise, explained to me her feelings about France: 'France is our *patrie* [fatherland, nation], but it isn't our *pays* [country],' she told me.

The most beautiful country in the world is the one in which you are born. You see, I am not completely integrated, a part of France . . . to the extent that I don't feel *chez moi* [at home]. When I go to California, it's as if, as if . . . I were in France. . . . You see, in France, nothing reminds me of my country [*pays*]. I can go from the north to the south . . . and I don't find the . . . plains, the, the mountains, the . . . the same landscapes [*paysages*], the same smells . . . the same colors, like *chez nous*. So, I get the feeling that I'm always *en voyage* in France. I'm floating . . .[1]

Louise's country (*pays*), her homeland, is Algeria, a place she still misses intensely after leaving it in 1962. While she would certainly bristle at any challenge to her loyalty to France, she has an ambivalent relationship to her new home. Like many other *pieds noirs* I interviewed, Louise talked about her departure as forced upon her, and certainly not her choice. And like her

---

[1] 'Louise' is a pseudonym. Ethnographic fieldwork was conducted from Jan. 1995 to June 1996, followed by month-long visits in 1998, 2001, and 2004. Research methodology and findings are summarized in Andrea Smith, *Colonial Memory and Postcolonial Europe: Maltese Settlers in Algeria and France* (Bloomington, Ind., 2006).

compatriots, she complained about the former settlers' official appellation as 'repatriates', asking how a people could be 'repatriated' to a country they had never seen. French Algeria, not France, is her *pays*.

The experience of these elderly former settlers since their departure from the colony at the end of the Algerian War has many features of a diasporic population. Their identity as *pied noir* revolves around their peculiar exodus from the colony. French Algeria is the focus for many *pied noir* social clubs and, for decades now, groups of former settlers have been reuniting across France around their former colonial home towns, high schools, or workplaces. Like reunions of other people who live in exile, conversations at these gatherings revolve around the 'homeland'. *Pied noir* clubs collect the material detritus of this lost world: not only novels and memoirs, but also colonial-era newspapers, Michelin guides, and street maps. To what degree does this continued attachment to the colony reflect the experiences of former settlers in general? Should we take seriously the *pied noir* claim to be a people living in exile, and view them as another instance of a people forcibly removed? In what follows, I will first consider the *pied noir* example in relation to other notable instances of former colonials displaced at the end of colonial rule. I then turn to the question of coercion, and ask whether or not we should consider these reverse migrations of decolonization to be yet another example of forced removal.

Migrations of Decolonization

Over several decades following the Second World War, millions of people affiliated with former colonial powers fled the newly or soon-to-be independent nations, often settling in Europe. Because of the highly divergent colonial histories and independence trajectories involved, these migrations defy easy generalization. In the most general terms, the people involved included administrators and settler families, usually citizens of the departing power who were often, but not always, former residents of the colonizing power; Europeans of other nationalities, sometimes naturalized citizens; and other outsiders who may have held reduced social or political standing in the colony, such as traders or imported labour, who were viewed locally as affiliated with the colonial power (East African Asians are a case in point). Colonial auxiliaries who served in colonial police and military units, such as the *harkis* of French Algeria or the Hmong of Indo-China, were often evacuated as well, as were people of mixed ancestry and local elites with a strong affinity to the core cultural group, similarly at risk under the new regime.[2]

The unprecedented nature of these population 'refluxes',[3] and the fact that statistically invisible citizens were usually involved, makes it quite difficult to gain exact figures to demonstrate the scale of these population transfers.[4] They were not, at least initially, orchestrated by state agencies, so we can rely on their records for only a fraction of the migrations. Britain is a case in point. Clearly former officers and settled families left India, Kenya, and other colonies for Britain sometime after the Second World War, but we may never know the specifics of this migration pattern. Ceri Peach, extrapolating from the 1991 census, identifies 328,080 'whites' in Britain who had been born in the New Commonwealth (former colonial territories). He suggests that since many of these people were probably children of British-born parents, who themselves would not appear in these statistics, 'the return from former colonies is likely to have been much larger than this'.[5]

Despite statistical uncertainties, we do know that sizeable populations were involved. Working from the numbers of people recorded in the colony before independence, scholars have determined that after the Second World War, approximately 5.4 to 8.5 million people migrated to the European continent over a forty-year period; some 6.2 million Japanese departed Asian territories over the same period.[6] Even larger numbers are involved if we

[2] Dirk Hoerder, *Cultures in Contact: World Migrations in the Second Millennium* (Durham, NC, 2002), 500.

[3] These migrations have yielded a diverse nomenclature. Hoerder refers to them as 'reverse' migrations, while Peach calls them 'refluxes'. See Hoerder, *Cultures in Contact*, 499 and Ceri Peach, 'Postwar Migration to Europe: Reflux, Influx, Refuge', *Social Science Quarterly*, 78/2 (1997), 269–83. Here I refer to them as 'reverse migrations of decolonization'.

[4] Andrea Smith (ed.), *Europe's Invisible Migrants* (Amsterdam, 2003), 10–13. See also Jean-Louis Miège and Colette Dubois (eds.), *L'Europe retrouvée: les migrations de la décolonisation* (Paris, 1994), 17–20.

[5] Peach, 'Postwar Migration to Europe', 271.

[6] B. Etemad, 'Europe and Migration after Decolonisation', *Journal of European Economic History*, 27 (1998), 457–70, at 468.

Coerced or Free? 399

include post-war expellees/returnees to Germany,[7] or the migrations that ensued following the collapse of the Ottoman Empire, which included the compulsory population exchanges of 1.5 million people between Turkey and Greece mandated by the 1923 Treaty of Lausanne.[8]

The pace and scale of the population transfers were highly variable. Some were ongoing affairs that lasted decades, as in the case of the Italians who began leaving Libya in the 1940s, or the British departures from India, Kenya, and Rhodesia/Zimbabwe, which have been ongoing since 1945, the 1950s, and the 1970s, respectively. Migrations in such instances occurred in phases, with the earliest departures composed of people with shallow ties to the colony, such as those recently appointed for service there. People leaving later were often descendants of early migrants, families with long-standing histories in the colony, people with fewer resources, and, in general, people who had more to lose by leaving. Finally, people leaving the colony at independence did not always travel to European destinations at first, such as Belgians who left central for South Africa.[9] Attenuated departures can be associated with a comparatively less violent or intensive colonial heritage, and a less contentious release of metropolitan control. Such departures also suggest a comparatively less hostile attitude toward these human reminders of the former regime. They often followed the collapse of colonial forms characterized by few colonists and administrators, or a more indirect style of colonial rule.

In contrast, some departures were massive, sudden affairs, as in the dismantling of colonies with large settler populations, such as French Algeria, Portuguese West Africa, and the Dutch Indies. Some 300,000 migrants left the Dutch Indies between 1945 and

---

[7] Peach, 'Postwar Migration to Europe', 271.

[8] Renée Hirschon, '"Unmixing Peoples" in the Aegean Region', in ead. (ed.), *Crossing the Aegean: An Appraisal of the 1923 Compulsory Population Exchange between Greece and Turkey* (New York, 2003), 3–12, at 5–6, 3. While Hirschon writes that this was 'in no sense a repatriation for either the Muslims of Greece or the Ottoman Christians', the 1.2 million 'Asia Minor Greeks' received citizenship rights upon arrival and were labelled by Greek state agencies as 'repatriates' or 'returnees', even though they called themselves 'refugees'. See Eftihia Voutira, 'When Greeks Meet Other Greeks: Settlement Policy Issues in the Contemporary Greek Context', in Hirschon (ed.), *Crossing the Aegean*, 145–59, at 148.

[9] Pierre Salman, 'Les Retours en Belgique induits par la décolonisation', in Miège and Dubois (eds.), *L'Europe retrouvée*, 181–212, at 198.

400   ANDREA SMITH

1963, nearly a million settlers of Algeria fled to France during the
weeks leading up to and following Algerian Independence in
1962, and 800,000 *retornados* fled for Portugal between 1974 and
1976. Because of their scale, and the perception among the evacuees of a decided lack of choice, I emphasize these cases here.

Reverse Settler Migrations: Points in Common

The waning years of settler colonies were typically quite disor-
dered. Colonial powers worked hardest at maintaining their
colonies with the largest settler population, and thus migrations
from such territories usually occurred after violent and
protracted wars of independence, such as the Algerian War of
Independence (1954–62), the conflicts in Portuguese West Africa
which started in 1961 and continued for nearly fifteen years, or
the Dutch Indies conflict (1945–9). Citizenship regulations and
international law often allowed the migrants only one possible
destination, at least at first: the metropole. For many people, the
end of the colony was not at all predicted, and the decision to
leave was made at a terrible moment, during the final throes of a
particularly violent sort of civil war. Leaving was often considered to be essential for survival, if not dictated outright by the
departing or incoming governments. Often the migrants left
behind most of their possessions, and certainly their land, homes,
and social ties. This departure was often experienced as the loss
of a whole way of life. During the first decades back 'home',
many 'returnees' lived in a state of shock, trying to accomplish
day-to-day tasks, and unable to plan their future course.

Dutch Indies

The case of the Indies Dutch illustrates many of these general
patterns. When their government capitulated to the Japanese in
1942, Dutch Indies women and children were interned, and men
became slave labourers.[10] Two days after the Japanese surrendered in August 1945, Indonesian Independence was proclaimed,

[10] Hans van Amserfoort and Mies van Niekerk, 'Immigration as a Colonial
Inheritance: Post-Colonial Immigrants in the Netherlands, 1945–2002', *Journal of Ethnic
and Migration Studies*, 32 (2006), 323–46, at 325.

Coerced or Free? 401

and residents endured the violence and chaos of the war of Independence until Indonesian sovereignty at the end of 1949.[11] Many Dutch began leaving for the Netherlands immediately after the Second World War, long before Independence, however, to recuperate from the horrors of the war years. Between 1945 and 1949, some 45,000 moved there even while approximately 125,000 Dutch were leaving the Netherlands for the Indies to carry out their military service in defence of the colony. At Independence, military officers and administrators returned to the Netherlands as mandated by the state. Through negotiations with the new government, Europeans who had lived in Indonesia for at least six months were able to choose Indonesian nationality; approximately 14,000 heads of households (or 36,000 people), mostly Eurasians, selected this opportunity. Migrations to the Netherlands continued between 1952 and 1957, despite the Dutch government's efforts to slow this process; however, approximately 10,000 people migrated to New Guinea instead. It was only in 1957 that the remaining Dutch were granted no other options. Their belongings were confiscated, and some 50,000 Dutch were expelled, followed by the 12,000 Dutch then living in New Guinea when that territory was transferred to Indonesian sovereignty.[12] After fifteen years 'virtually the entire Dutch population left Indonesia',[13] some of whom had been established there for generations.

Most of the migrants who arrived in the Netherlands had never been there before.[14] Their fate upon arrival, according to Wim Willems, depended on the timing of their arrival, the length of their stay in the Indies, and whether or not they still had family ties in the Netherlands. The earliest to arrive faced a Netherlands that had just suffered years of German occupation, crushing unemployment, and housing and food shortages. According to Willems, people who were born and raised in the Netherlands, but who had spent their working years and the war in the Indies, were most incensed about their purported mistreatment by the

[11] Elsbeth Locher-Scholten, 'From Urn to Monument: Dutch Memories of World War II in the Pacific, 1945–1995', in Smith (ed.), *Europe's Invisible Migrants*, 105–28, at 107.

[12] Herman Obdeijn, 'Vers les bords de la Mer du Nord: les retours aux Pays-Bas induits par la décolonisation', in Miège and Dubois (eds.), *L'Europe retrouvée*, 49–71, at 53–4.

[13] van Amserfoort and van Niekerk, 'Immigration as a Colonial Inheritance', 325.

[14] Wim Willems, 'No Sheltering Sky: Migrant Identities of Dutch Nationals from Indonesia', in Smith (ed.), *Europe's Invisible Migrants*, 33–59, at 39.

402   ANDREA SMITH

government upon their return, while people born in the Indies
were more eager to profit from the new opportunities that they
found in their new home.[15]

French Algeria

It is difficult to exaggerate the chaos of the departures of the
French from Algeria. The Algerian War was infamous for the
violence, internecine warfare, and overall disruption it caused on
both sides of the Mediterranean. France came close to civil war
as a series of metropolitan governments collapsed. During the
weeks leading up to the Evian accords of 18 March 1962, which
marked the conclusion of the Algerian War of Independence, the
French government not only did not predict mass emigration of
the colony's million settlers, but it actually tried to prevent departures by limiting ferry services across the Mediterranean.[16]
Military officers and their families were ordered back home not
long before Independence. For the vast majority of the settlers,
however, leaving was only ostensibly a choice. The Evian
accords established Algeria and France as two territories with
distinct nationalities and citizenship. They promised the protection of the settlers, a continued respect of property and civil
rights, dual nationality for three years with an option for
Algerian nationality, and no expropriation of property without
compensation.[17] However, violence increased after the accords,
in part instigated by an unconstitutional referendum on the
accords held exclusively in metropolitan France,[18] which
enflamed the pro-colony settler guerrilla movement, the Secret
Army Organization (OAS). The OAS carried out a scorched-
earth campaign that fuelled reprisals from the armed Algerian
forces, the National Liberation Front (FLN). As the country

[15] Ibid. 43.

[16] French officials asked trans-Mediterranean ferry companies to reduce their weekly
France–Algerian crossings to sixteen, and then to seven in March, and to three by April
1962. Approximately 68,000 settlers left Algeria between Jan. and Apr. 1962. In response
to the ever increasing demand, the companies decided to intensify their crossings on 16
May and emigration increased dramatically: over 500,000 people crossed the
Mediterranean from May to Aug. 1962. Jean-Jacques Jordi, *De l'exode à l'exil: rapatriés et
pieds-noirs en France. L'exemple marseillais* (Paris, 1993), 66.

[17] Anthony Clayton, *The Wars of French Decolonization* (London, 1994), 173.

[18] Todd Shepard, *The Invention of Decolonization: The Algerian War and the Remaking of
France* (Ithaca, NY, 2006), 111–19.

Coerced or Free?

devolved into chaos, settler departures escalated rapidly. Because of the French state's decision to engage in a long and difficult war involving a systematic use of torture, as well as the harsh treatment of the autochthonous population, in which settlers or their ancestors either actively took part or tacitly approved for 130 years, it would have been quite difficult for most French settlers to remain. They realized this, and fled, losing nearly everything in the process

The migrants faced further disruption upon their arrival in France because state and local officials were completely unprepared. In fact, in many parts of France, officials continued to refer to the migrants as *vacanciers*, vacationers, people taking their summer vacations in France, even though it was clear that few planned on returning to Algeria.[19] The end of empire was so unprecedented that officials, the settlers, and the French public alike had not prepared for the mass flight across the Mediterranean. The fortunate few who were able to send their belongings on container ships often found their crates empty at the docks in France.

Portuguese West Africa

Departures from Portugal's African colonies were similarly precipitous and chaotic. The political decolonization of Portugal's African colonies occurred within a span of three months after the 25 April 1974 revolution as the government promised sovereignty to anti-colonial movements in Angola, Mozambique, and Guinea Bissau. Portuguese troops began departing. After failed settler uprisings, most residents of European descent lost their rights. This was followed by the confiscation of European property, and mass panic. Residents and people affiliated with the colonial administration fled. Between May and July 1975, 1,000 people were leaving Angola daily.[20] Over 505,000 arrived in Portugal from late 1974 to early 1976, representing a 5 per cent increase in the population of that small country.[21] These migrants were akin

---

[19] Jean-Jacques Jordi, *1962: l'arrivée des pieds-noirs* (Paris, 1995), 69.

[20] Colette Dubois, 'L'épineux dossier des retornados', in Miège and Dubois, *L'Europe retrouvée*, 213–46, at 228.

[21] Stephen C. Lubkemann, 'Race, Class, and Kin in the Negotiation of "Internal Strangerhood" among Portuguese Retornados, 1975–2000', in Smith (ed.), *Europe's Invisible Migrants*, 75–93, at 78.

404 ANDREA SMITH

to refugees. Thousands arrived in Portugal destitute, without identification, money, and some owning 'absolutely nothing but their clothes'.[22] People often left everything behind, and children were frequently separated from the rest of their family members during the transit period.

Settler Integration back 'Home'

On the surface, these three migrations share many features in common: they were largely unplanned, mass events that followed in the wake of particularly violent colonial wars, the migrants often left behind the majority of their possessions, and they had many difficulties adapting to a foreign land, which was their purported 'home'. However, we also find some striking contrasts that stem from the length of time the settlers were established in the colony, the composition of the settler population, the generation involved, and the amount of time that has passed since their 'return'. Scholars working with objective statistical data often report a complete integration of the returnees, and often link this to the fact that the migrants were usually granted citizenship upon arrival. Ethnographers working with the communities themselves, in contrast, often report a continued sentiment of separateness from wider society.

French of Algeria: Decolonization Diaspora?

The integration of the *pieds noirs* is often heralded as a success story, for soon after their arrival, they were able to remake themselves, achieving not merely a modicum of upward mobility. According to some scholars, the second generation is invisible in contemporary France today.[23] Yet many of the people I interviewed, still members of the arriving generation, lived out the rest of their years lost, disconnected from their new 'home', a place they had been taught to revere in the colony, but which most had never seen. The shock between the France that they imagined and

---

[22] Maria Rocha-Trindade, 'The Repatriation of Portuguese from Africa', in Robin Cohen (ed.), *The Cambridge Survey of World Migration* (Cambridge, 1995), 337–41, at 338.

[23] Richard Alba and Roxane Silberman, 'Decolonisation Immigrations and the Social Origins of the Second Generation: The Case of the North Africans in France', *International Migration Review*, 36 (2002), 1169–93.

Coerced or Free?

the one they experienced was sometimes dramatic. Alienation from this new France was compounded by the fact that for more than half of the *pieds noirs*, this country was that of their nationality, but not of their ethnic origins. Over half of the French settlers of Algeria were from Spain, Italy, or Malta. Their ancestors had been naturalized as French citizens in the colony before the First World War, and thus the generation who arrived in France in 1962 were often French citizens at birth. And yet everything they learned about the metropole was second-hand; many were arriving to a 'homeland' they and their ancestors had never seen. We might refer to the *pied noir* migration as a *diaspora of decolonization*.

Indies Dutch

The Indies Dutch arrived nearly a generation ahead of the *pieds noirs* and two ahead of the *retornados*, and thus offer an important example of the legacy of a reverse decolonization migration nearly half a century after it occurred. Despite the trauma of the migration, the fact that many families had been installed in the Indies for generations, the presence among this population of large numbers of descendants of mixed unions, and the fact that the government at first had no policies devised to handle this novel situation, by most accounts their access to citizenship rights led to a rapid integration into Dutch society. Because the Indies Dutch were citizens, 'a policy was put into practice to absorb them into society as quickly as possible'.[24] This involved contracting private boarding houses, setting apart 5 per cent of newly constructed homes in the social sector for repatriates, the installation of repatriate officers at employment agencies, and special schooling. These measures are credited with the successful absorption of the Indies Dutch by 1973.[25]

Portuguese Retornados

The integration of the *retornados* is also viewed as an unmitigated success, in this case largely because of the migrants' comparatively

---

[24] van Amserfoort and van Niekerk, 'Immigration as a Colonial Inheritance', 326.

[25] Ibid. 328. Of course, generation may be key here. Amersfoort and Niekerk note that some Indies Dutch migrated on to California, and the older generation had relatively more difficulty adjusting to Dutch society (ibid. 328–9).

406 ANDREA SMITH

shorter stays in the colony. In contrast to France and the Netherlands, Portuguese migration to the African colonies was a recent phenomenon, with migrations to empire accelerating, not declining, in the decades after 1950. As a result, the majority of the *retornados* were born in Portugal (including an astounding 85 per cent of those aged 40 and older).[26] Lubkemann has concluded that race, class, and family ties in Portugal were key factors in determining individual migrants' integration experiences, with approximately one-third of the *retornados* settling in the districts in which they had been born. The *retornados* of mixed descent and others without clear family ties, on the other hand, usually moved to urban areas. Phenotype certainly played a role in shaping their reception by Portuguese society, with offspring of mixed or predominantly African ancestry finding themselves classified by fellow Portuguese as immigrants, rather than the fellow citizens that they were.[27] But because of their rapid integration into the workplace and their greater educational and other cultural capital than the average Portuguese upon arrival, they experienced such rapid social integration that, according to Lubkemann, there is no publicly recognized *retornado* ethnicity today.[28]

Comparing Reverse Migrations and Forced Removals

The decolonization migrations outlined here can be distinguished from forced removals in several important ways. Whether mandated in an orchestrated fashion from above, as in the 'peacemaking' population transfers that accompanied the end of world wars, or instigated by individual actors, as in the case of maverick sheriffs in US territories, most of the removals discussed in this volume were carried out with the explicit or tacit backing of one or more states. This was certainly the case when we consider removals associated with the establishment of colonial regimes, which involved the dual force of metropolitan bureaucratic and military apparatuses. In contrast, the early reverse migrations of former settlers were spontaneous affairs that occurred, at least at first, with little or no official planning. Some governments actually tried to prevent the returns at first, as

---

[26] Lubkemann, 'Race, Class, and Kin', 79–80.   [27] Ibid. 89.   [28] Ibid. 90.

we have seen in the cases of the French *pieds noirs*, and the Indies Dutch.

Another noteworthy distinction between decolonization migrants and people forcibly removed from their homes is the social and political status the former enjoyed after leaving the colony. In contrast to the indigenous peoples they or their ancestors had helped displace several decades before, and in contrast to many other examples of forced removals discussed in this volume, decolonization migrants were usually offered some kind of preferential treatment at their final destination, which was construed, at least by representatives of dominant institutions, as their rightful 'home'. On many levels, they had a privileged migration experience, one that was considerably more favourable than even that of labour or economic migrants, as a result of their preferential educational opportunities, remittances, hiring policies, loans, and housing opportunities, as well as the intangible but real psychological boost they received knowing that at least some portion of the metropole felt that they belonged. State officials often tried to foster this view among the general public, arguing that their integration was a national moral duty. In this sense, they resemble the reflux of ethnic Germans who also received special treatment upon arrival because of their purported membership in the nation-state. However, not all decolonization migrants were afforded such favourable treatment, as we shall see. When we consider the question of race, we find that colonial-era racial ideologies played a pivotal role in determining the balance of agency and coercion faced by the reverse migrants of decolonization.

Race and the Post-Colonial

Until now I have avoided the issue of racial difference and instead emphasized the returns of diverse peoples unproblematically conflated as 'repatriates'. However, these reverse migration streams were comprised of highly diverse populations. As I have detailed, class, occupation, mobility, and access to liquid resources often shaped the degree of agency experienced by colonials contemplating departure. But race and related notions of national identity played decisive roles in this process as well. For even while newly independent nations were emerging and

408   ANDREA SMITH

challenging colonial-era mindsets, colonial-era social categories
and racial hierarchies persisted in the metropole and would help
dictate how the migrants from the former colonies would be
treated back in Europe. Options granted to Dutch citizens varied
according to race or degree of Dutchness, as we have seen. At
Indonesian Independence in 1949, not all Dutch citizens were
granted permission to go to the Netherlands; at first, those of
mixed European and Indonesian descent were encouraged to
remain in the new Indonesian republic.[29] Some Indies Dutch
opted to do so and chose Indonesian citizenship, but after experiencing discrimination, many decided to leave. Yet the mixed-
descent among them were encouraged to move on to New
Guinea, not Holland.[30] It was only in 1955 that the Dutch
government allowed them to enter the Netherlands.

Ethnic Dutch, on the other hand, were not only granted preferential treatment in the Netherlands, but could choose additional destinations as well. Many migrated to the USA (some
30,000 by 1962) or Australia (9,000).[31] Again, race was their principal advantage. Willems discusses in detail the negotiations
required before the USA would allow Indies Dutch into the
country under the Refugee Relief Act following the bursting of
dykes in the Netherlands. Even once Sukarno evicted the
remaining Indies Dutch in 1957, the USA would allow only 10
per cent of the refugees admitted to be 'half-caste'.[32]

A similar sorting of peoples occurred in Britain in the early
decades of the decline of empire. The June 1948 British
Nationality Act offered all residents of the British Empire and
Commonwealth the status of British subjects with equal rights and
privileges, an act which Kathleen Paul describes as a 'last stand
against encroaching colonial independence and imperial disintegration'.[33] However, underlying this general policy were different
categories of Britishness. Paul compares the treatment of four
different populations, the residents of the United Kingdom who

[29] Willems, 'No Sheltering Sky', 35.

[30] In fact, Dutch government officials rationalized their continued presence in New
Guinea as resulting from their need for a place for Eurasians who wanted to leave the
Republic of Indonesia. See R. F. Holland, *European Decolonization 1918–1981: An Introductory
Survey* (New York, 1985), 92.

[31] Willems, 'No Sheltering Sky', 46, 36.

[32] Ibid. 46.

[33] Kathleen Paul, 'Communities of Britishness: Migration in the Last Gasp of Empire',
in Stuart Ward (ed.), *British Culture and the End of Empire* (Manchester, 2001), 180–99, at 183.

were encouraged to migrate to the Dominions, continental European refugees brought to Britain to work, Irish citizens, and residents of the former colonies. Underlying factors helped determine which of these peoples would be encouraged to migrate and where. As Paul notes, 'the treatment received by each group . . . clearly reveals that the policy-making elite believed that each group could be categorized according to a hierarchical understanding of the world's population, an understanding based on a racialized conception of humanity.'[34] While white skin was a prerequisite for imperial migration, it also emerged as one of the unstated preferences for state-sponsored migration to Australia, New Zealand, South Rhodesia, and Canada. European aliens in Britain, moreover, were not described as foreign but as European, and their assimilation into British society was fostered by extensive public relations campaigns.[35] Approximately 50,000 to 60,000 Irish nationals were granted the privileges of British subjecthood without that official status. However, when a small group of black British subjects from the West Indies tried to arrive in 1948, an uproar ensued despite the fact that such a migration was well within their rights.[36] Not only were they not welcomed, but non-white migrants were not offered the preferential treatment described above. As arrivals from former colonial territories accelerated, British officials generated new entry restrictions that were implicitly or explicitly about race. These regulations culminated in the 1971 Immigration Act, which reclassified former British subjects into 'patrial' and 'nonpatrial' categories, giving rights of entry to an overwhelmingly white population.[37]

French Algerians encountered a similar sorting of peoples according to colonial-era ideologies at Algerian Independence. In the face of the threat of nationalist movements, there was a generous shift in France's relationship to its colonies that was analogous to the 1948 British Nationality Act. The colonies were renamed 'Overseas France', the French empire became the 'French Union', and French Union citizenship was extended to all French citizens and colonial subjects.[38] While in theory this included Algerian Muslims, a series of measures was established for this population that eventually led to the creation of a category of 'français musulmans d'Algérie' (Muslim French citizens

[34] Ibid. 184.   [35] Ibid. 186.   [36] Ibid. 188.   [37] Ibid. 196.
[38] Shepard, *The Invention of Decolonization*, 40.

from Algeria).[39] The unexpected exodus of the settlers at the end of the Algerian War put a damper on France's liberal stance, and by April 1962 the government began to prevent the entry of Muslim French citizens from Algeria.[40] This had terrible consequences for Muslim auxiliaries in particular, sometimes glossed as the *harkis*, who were singled out for refused entry in a Top Secret note emanating from de Gaulle's office in late May 1962.[41] Unable to leave, thousands of *harkis* were killed in Algeria at the war's end. Approximately 40,000 *harkis* and their families managed to reach the metropole, however, where they were not only not granted the subventions and other benefits offered the *pieds noirs*, but where they were housed in makeshift camps in remote rural areas isolated from wider French society. The legacy of this fiasco lingers on, with the second generation continuing to mobilize for compensation and recognition.[42] Although colonial categories may have been banished in the newly independent states, they held firm in the metropole in the aftermath of colonialism, helping to shape the migration and integration experiences of 'post'-colonial migrants.

As we have seen in the case of the *harkis*, the race factor was especially apparent in the treatment by metropolitan governments of colonial auxiliaries. In their comparative analysis of postcolonial immigrants to the Netherlands, van Amersfoorst and van Niekerk find striking contrasts in the trajectories of Dutch auxiliaries. The Royal Dutch Indian Army (KNIL) of the Dutch East Indies included many local soldiers, recruited especially from the Ambonese Islands, half of whom were Calvinists and viewed as 'absolutely loyal to the Dutch Crown'.[43] However, this purported loyalty would cause problems upon Independence. Soldiers of the KNIL were allowed to choose where they would be discharged. When ex-KNIL soldiers proclaimed an independent state of South Moluccans, many retiring soldiers wanted to be discharged there. This led to considerable resistance from the Indonesian

---

[39] Ibid. 49.   [40] Ibid. 230.   [41] Ibid.

[42] See Christine Font, 'De Nemours à Largentière, une solidarité: le réseau des officiers de la DBFM', in Jean-Jacques Jordi and Emile Temime (eds.), *Marseille et le choc des décolonisations: les rapatriements, 1954–1964* (Aix-en-Provence, 1996), 92–102, at 96–7; Mohand Hamoumou, 'L'Histoire des harkis et Français musulmans: la fin d'un tabou?', in Mohammed Harbi and Benjamin Stora (eds.), *La Guerre d'Algérie, 1954–2004: la fin de l'amnésie* (Paris, 2004).

[43] Ibid. 329.

government, and finally the veterans were sent to the Netherlands. Because this move was viewed as a temporary one, they were not granted citizenship status and the government did not work to facilitate their integration. Instead, a separate agency was developed to monitor their situation. Like the *harkis*, the 'Moluccan' auxiliaries and their families were housed in camps in remote or rural areas. Segregation, not integration, was fostered as the migrants attended separate schools and experienced restricted access to the labour market. Although by the late 1960s it was clear that the Moluccans would probably never be able to return 'home' safely and were thus in the Netherlands forever, 80 per cent still did not have Dutch citizenship in 1968.[44] This situation reached public attention with terrorist attacks in 1970, 1975, and 1977 after which time the government made a concerted effort to assist them. Most now have citizenship rights, and scholars find the experiences of the second generation are much improved.[45]

In his work on Puerto Rico, Grosfuguel questions the 'myth of decolonization' and the related assumption that 'modernity is somehow a more advanced stage disconnected from colonialism and coloniality'.[46] Considering the treatment of Puerto Ricans in the contemporary USA, he argues that 'racial/colonial ideologies' have not been eradicated from metropolitan centres, 'which remain in grave need of a sociocultural decolonization'.[47] Instead, we are living in a world in which 'global coloniality' is the dominant form of core–periphery relationships. This coloniality is in part the result of lasting power relationships stemming from the colonial era. As Grosfoguel writes, 'the entanglement of a global division of labor of core–periphery relationships and a global racial/ethnic hierarchy of Western and non-Western people . . . was not significantly transformed with the end of colonialism and the formation of nation-states in the periphery'.[48]

The differential treatment of the populations affiliated with colonial powers illustrates the persistence of colonial-era ideologies. Racial and ethnic hierarchies forged in colonial times circulated

[44] Ibid. 331.   [45] Ibid. 332–3.
[46] Ramón Grosfoguel, *Colonial Subjects: Puerto Ricans in a Global Perspective* (Berkeley, 2003), 7.
[47] Ibid. 2.   [48] Ibid. 6.

between core and colony and were inscribed in both colonial and metropolitan law. They persisted in the metropole even after decolonization, as the differential treatment of migrants from the former colonies demonstrates. In fact, in both Britain and France, we find that policies became more restrictive, more 'colonial-esque' as the colonial era faded into the distance. It is for this reason that members of the colonizing powers circulated so easily around the globe: thousands of Belgians left the Congo, Rwanda, and Burundi for South Africa,[49] and 'white' British subjects moved freely within the former British Empire: from India to Kenya to Rhodesia/Zimbabwe, as well as Australia, New Zealand, and Canada. Ongoing settler colonies such as the USA and Canada attracted many *pieds noirs* dissatisfied with life in France, while Algerian *harkis* faced an uncertain future housed in camps set apart from French society.

Coerced or Free?

Can we classify the population transfers associated with the decolonization of settler and other colonies as forced removals? As might be expected, the highly diverse reverse migrations of decolonization varied in the degree of coercion involved. In Dirk Hoerder's typology, migrations may be voluntary, coerced, or forced, with the latter two categories characterized by 'particularly pronounced unequal power relationships'. In his view, migrations are free 'only within both the macrolevel constraints in the society of origin and the legal limitations of receiving countries, and given the ability to defray the "opportunity cost" of the move'. Coerced migrations offer less choice upon departure, 'but permit some decision-making upon arrival'.[50] Here Hoerder cites the example of refugees who are sometimes able to decide where to ultimately settle. Forced migrations, in his view, involve little to no migrant agency;[51] an example is the transatlantic migrations of enslaved Africans.

Because they involved such a wide array of peoples and circumstances, we can find all three categories—free, coerced,

---

[49] There were 8,000 Belgians in South Africa in 1965, and 14,000 by 1974. Salman, 'Les Retours', 198.

[50] Hoerder, *Cultures in Contact*, 15.   [51] Ibid.

Coerced or Free?

and forced—among the reverse migrations of decolonization, with race playing a pivotal role in determining for any given individual the balance between coercion and agency. Some short-term (white) residents such as merchants simply moved when they decided that their time in the colony was coming to an end, either travelling to a new colonial setting, or returning home with few lasting consequences. People with multi-generational ties to the colony had less choice, as we have seen, but some could still choose when to depart and/or their final destination, depending on their available resources, geo-political circumstances, and their phenotype. White settlers thus fall more into Hoerder's 'coerced' category because of this ability to engage in some level of decision-making, if not regarding whether or when to leave, then at least where to go. Colonial administrators and members of the military, on the other hand, faced additional restrictions, and many were ordered home by official directive. While we might categorize these returns as 'forced' removals, it should be pointed out that this situation was not unusual for people in such a career. It was not unlike the restricted options faced by their counterparts in the metropole, or their own situation before decolonization commenced. However, the people considered phenotypically distinct or racially linked to the former colonial subject populations, such as the mixed Indies Dutch or colonial auxiliaries, were given little to no choice. They were either relegated to the newly independent state despite any risks they would incur there, or, if evacuated, often found themselves in a legal no man's land, such as the Moluccan auxiliaries. While former settlers such as Louise may have encountered a dramatic loss of agency at decolonization, and may today consider their departures as forced and certainly not their choice, they enjoyed far more freedom of movement in the aftermath of colonialism than most of the other 'colonials' composing this highly diverse migration stream.

Conclusion

The end of European imperialism brought with it a radical reshaping of polities and peoples, and included important mass population transfers. Despite the subjective experience by many of the migrants of a decided lack of agency, however, we cannot categorize reverse migrations of decolonization en bloc as forced removals. These movements were highly diverse in terms of the types of colonies involved, their timing, pacing, scale, and the degree of violence involved. They defy facile generalization. Yet there is one striking commonality that can be found across the cases considered here: colonials in the colony had strikingly different fates at decolonization depending on phenotype. Regardless of their citizenship status, occupation, or former position in the colony, the degree of agency afforded individuals was usually related to their placement in the colonial-era racial hierarchies that continued to shape their treatment in the metropole well after the demise of colonial rule.

PART V
Concluding Thoughts

17

Comparing Forced Removals

Joanna de Groot

The material in this book explores forced migrations of peoples on six continents over a period of some 150 years (from the movements of Cherokee in American Georgia and of Africans within and beyond Africa in the early nineteenth century to the relocation of Vietnamese villagers and white settlers from Algeria in the later twentieth century). This range of instances, experiences, and analyses can provide a useful, almost encyclopedic, survey of the modes and meanings of different forced migrations, but also offers the possibility of comparative discussion. Such a discussion is a matter not just of identifying similarities or common issues, but of pursuing themes or concepts relevant to different instances in such a way as to clarify the specificity of each instance as well as any comparable features. Beyond that, a comparative approach is an *analytical* strategy for deepening understanding of the category/categories of 'forced migration', rather than a means to argue the sameness of the situations under discussion. It enables a thematic and structured appreciation of diversity rather than denying that diversity. In this essay I focus on some key analytical categories that, I argue, can enrich the understanding of specific removals. In a very real sense I am the small bird riding on the wings of eagles to get an overview, in that I draw explicitly and primarily on work by the authors of other essays in this book, and on presentations and discussions at the conference from which those texts originated.[1] My contribution is thus the response of a non-specialist to ideas and information provided by those working in the field.

One issue which drew attention in those discussions was the force, or lack thereof, of the category 'modern' as a tool for analysing the removals examined by the various authors. What, if anything, distinguishes the cases under discussion from the

[1] This conference, entitled 'Removing Peoples: Forced Migration in the Modern World', was held at the University of York in April 2006.

relocation of peoples by rulers in the Ottoman Empire and Iran in the sixteenth and seventeenth centuries, forced settlement in the Roman or Hellenistic empires, or European slave-trading, or deportations of those labelled 'Jews' or 'Moors' in the medieval and early modern periods? This is less an issue of chronology than of historians' varied and contested understandings of the notion of 'modernity'. As Frederick Cooper argues, there are serious intellectual difficulties involved in using this category in a monolithic fashion opposed to a binary Other ('tradition'? 'backwardness'?).[2] However, it does indicate an important range of issues to do with social, technological, and governmental organization that are relevant to the discussion of forced migrations in the nineteenth and twentieth centuries. Such removals drew on 'modern' apparatuses of administration, communication, and coercion, ranging from the use of modern judicial, policing, and bureaucratic controls (identity documents, registers, censuses) in nineteenth-century Georgia or twentieth-century Poland to the role of print propaganda and railway transport in nineteenth-century Australia or twentieth-century India.

These techniques and institutions were arguably distinctive features of 'modern' governmental and social practice, although there may have been analogues in the earlier practices of, for example, imperial Chinese administration, or medieval anti-Jewish preaching. From at least the eighteenth century onward they became articulated with new patterns of commodified production, of nation-state competition, of personal, ethnic, class, and 'national' identity formation, and of more intense and significant global exchanges for everyday purposes (material, cultural, or political). Ideas of what constituted a 'people', and their relation to law, land rights, parentage, or the cultural practices of language, custom, and religion, were re-formed in the material and political context of expanding global and colonial relationships, and the impact of migrations, print cultures, and new forms of political participation. Forced migrations were shaped by new forms of practical authority (the policing of boundaries and official identities, colonial administration, state-sponsored settlement), and by new forms of cultural and ideological power (popular and/or vested interests in ethno-national

[2] See Frederick Cooper, *Colonialism in Question: Theory, Knowledge, History* (Berkeley, 2005), ch. 5.

Comparing Forced Removals

identity, belief in missions of progress, or in the use of law to engineer social change).

Such practical and cultural tools might be wielded most obviously by governments and elites, but might also be used by dissident, subaltern, or subordinated groups. Removals of Native Americans involved contests between American or Canadian governments and European settler attempts to constitute them as 'tribes', 'natives', or 'savages', and their own attempts to constitute themselves as 'nations'.[3] This was a matter not only of political rhetoric, but of appeals to legal processes and precedents, and to treaty provisions. As Bain Attwood has suggested in a comparative discussion of removals of Indigenous peoples in British settler colonies in Australasia, there were clear links between varied modes of colonial settlement (state-led in Australia, non-governmental in New Zealand), the changing extent and forms of involvement with Indigenous people, and the presence or absence of discourses of their legal rights to land, collective recognition, or individual personhood.[4] Greek subjects of Ottoman rule and the Slav subjects of Hapsburgs or Ottomans, like Poles, Israelis, and Czechs after the Second World War, might shape projects of people removal in the name of oppressed/marginalized nationalities and ethno-national purification. The removals associated with Partition in India, or the resettlement of European colonial groups following decolonization in Indonesia and Algeria, like those of Palestinians after 1948, used 'modern' technologies of state power, and ideologies of expulsion, nation-state formation, and collective identities or 'rights' (another construction of 'modern' thought), deployed by colonial authorities, nationalist activists, and settler groups.[5]

However, situating the analysis of forced migration within debates about 'modernity' may not be the most fruitful way to develop comparative explorations of this phenomenon. As already suggested, power relations and inequities are at the core of these experiences, whether they concern rulers and subjects, incoming settlers and indigenous communities, or rivals for land, autonomy, or authority. The discussion in this essay now takes

---

[3] See the essays by Garrison and Haake in this volume.
[4] Bain Attwood, 'Land and Removal in British Settler Societies', paper given at the 'Removing Peoples' conference.
[5] See the essays by Brandes, Morris, Pandey, and Smith in this volume.

420   JOANNA DE GROOT

the perspective of power relations to explore three themes which
are seen as central to an analysis of the varied events and experiences of what are termed here 'forced migrations' (which interestingly combines clear references to coercion, suggestions of
long-term change, and a consciously unemotional tone, as
compared to a term such as 'expulsion').[6] First it will look at the
exercise of *power over and through bodies* in situations of forced migration, as a means to appreciate its physical and material reality and
impact for those involved. Secondly, it will consider the possibly
over-privileged positioning of *state power* as a key agent of forced
migration, and examine its varying significance. Thirdly, it will
explore the *workings of cultural power* in the making, memory,
discourse, and narration of forced migrations in order to emphasize its constitutive functions, and to link the work of historians of
this phenomenon to the experiences they relate and interpret.

Any visual depiction of an episode of forced migration, from
eighteenth-century abolitionist diagrams of slave ships to photographs of 'ethnic Germans' leaving Poland after 1945, or nineteenth-century paintings of Native Americans being 'relocated',
focuses on bodies. In the memories of the victims/survivors,
physical suffering and coercion frequently appear as key features,
whether in Yaqui or African narratives of enslavement and
forced labour, or Palestinian and Sudeten German accounts of
expulsion and violence. Bodily experiences of enforced travel,
incarceration in camps, or on North American reservations and
Australian mission stations, injury, starvation, and, for some,
death, constituted both the lived events and key signifiers of
enforced removal. Bodies moved, bodies sold or imprisoned,
bodies damaged or destroyed, and the bodily presence and
aggression of enforcers, whether the 'communal' violence of
Partition in India and Greek/Turkish/Armenian 'exchanges' or
'expulsions' in Anatolia, or the 'official' control and violence of
Ottoman armies, Australian police, or Bolshevik commissars, are
central to both experience and narrative.

While arguing that the bodily power relations involved in any
forced migration have necessarily been constitutive, it is worth
unpacking the 'body histories' of people removal further, and
acknowledging specificities and contradictions. Thus the material

---

[6] This observation is made by Lüdtke in his contribution to this volume.

Comparing Forced Removals   421

value of the bodies of removed people for forced labour or chattel slavery functioned in tension with the use of bodily control, cruelty, and coercion as part of the removal process. This particular tension would not develop in situations where such material concerns were not involved, as with North American removals driven by land rather than human labour issues, the politically driven 'ethnic' removals of Armenians and Sudeten Germans, or the land and communal interests at stake in the forced migrations of Dalit and other groups after Indian Partition. Symbolic and representational meanings of violence as a controlling manifestation of bodily power relations are entwined in complex ways with its physical impact on living bodies. 'Exemplary' public punishment or killing of a few Native Americans, or forced expulsion from a few Arab or Punjabi villages, exerted bodily power over those involved, and simultaneously served to intimidate, control, or modify the behaviour of other Cherokees, Palestinians, or Punjabis. This interactive duality is comparable to the links between 'spontaneous'/ popular and planned/official expressions of physical power discussed in relation to the Terek Cossacks, the Armenians of the Ottoman Empire, and land seizures from Indigenous peoples in Georgia and New Zealand.[7]

Similar complexities underpin the slippages along, or management of, a spectrum of bodily interventions extending from control of bodies (forcing them to move/stay where directed) to coercion, punishment, and damage or destruction. Compulsory containment on a reservation or mission station, like 'relocation' supervised by officials or police, may be backed up by the selective, intermittent, casual, or demonstrative use of bodily violence (as with the American, central European, and Australian removals discussed in this volume), but are distinguishable from forced removals involving wholesale destruction and killing (as in the Jewish and Armenian 'genocides'). The removals associated with Indian Partition, or the trafficking of enslaved Africans, have their own complex blends of generalized and contained, casual and planned, bodily violence. The making of these distinctions is not intended either to dissolve the argument about the centrality of body power relations to forced migration/removal

---

[7] See the essays by Garrison, O'Rourke, and Suny in this volume.

in a welter of empirical detail, or to create some moral calculus or hierarchy of more or less 'violent'/'evil' episodes or experiences. On the contrary, it can be argued that the range of forms and meanings taken by the exercise of power on and through bodies in the processes of forced migration is testimony to the central importance of such power in all its varied manifestations.

Bodily power relations in situations of forced migration have had important gendered and sexual dimensions. The differential physical treatment of males and females by Sokoto slavers, by Bolsheviks among Terek Cossacks, and by the Mexican government removing Yaquis, indicates that their approaches to forced removal were shaped by assumptions about gender, and that the making and narration of forced removals can be understood as a gendered process. As Canning has argued, the study of bodies in the nineteenth and twentieth centuries can usefully locate them in the discourses and practices of gendered nation-making and ethno-racial ideas.[8]

At an obviously bodily level the appropriation of women's reproductive and sexual capacities in transatlantic and trans-African removals of chattel slaves is an instance of gendered body power in the process of forced migration. As in other situations of conflict, sexual assault on women demonstrated the working of power relations through the assertion of the capacity to control female bodies, and to bring shame on individuals and families through rape and abuse. The latter relies on the culturally specific power of beliefs in the significance of women's sexual status, and in 'ownership'/control of the 'honour' associated with that status by fathers, husbands, brothers, or families rather than women themselves, thus designating unequal power relations not just between abused and abusers, but also between women and family members. Women who had been raped and abducted during the Partition conflicts in India in 1947–8 were often mistreated by their families and communities after forced 'repatriation'.[9]

It is crucial to emphasize that these exercises of body power

[8] K. Canning 'The Body as Method: Reflections on the Place of the Body in Gender History', *Gender and History* (1999), 499–513, esp. 504–5; see also the essays by Lovejoy and O'Rourke in this volume.

[9] See the essay by Talbot in this volume; there is a range of comparable discussion of communal responses to raped women in former Yugoslavia and central Africa in the 1990s.

Comparing Forced Removals

concern and construct *men and masculinities* through the capacity to control, protect, or damage 'their' women and/or families as much as they construct women and femininities. More generally, the force of gendered body power should be explored and analysed not just through the trope of the victimized woman or categories of 'female' identity and experience. Men and masculinities were clearly at stake in the making and telling of forced removals. Like the gendered Indian Partition episodes, discourses of Australian Aboriginal male 'laziness' and 'indiscipline', distinguished from Aboriginal female 'promiscuity' by those who controlled and exploited their bodies and labour, are paralleled by the gender-specific treatment of Terek Cossack men and women in the removals of 1920.[10]

These highly explicit gender practices need to be juxtaposed to instances of forced migration where such practices do not feature in the same way. This was notable where questions of racial or national ethnicity, purity, and identity were dominant, and where clashes over rights and land posed communal collective claims by subordinated groups (Native Americans, Maori, or Australians) against legal, settler, commercial, and governmental claims. However, the gendering of spokesperson and leadership roles as masculine in some cultural settings, like the association of men with headship of households and kin groups, or with armed resistance, in others, often embedded gender distinctions in the resistance, negotiation, and survival strategies of the subordinate. So, too, did women's familial role as transmitters of ancestral customs, language, and memory. Nor can historians ignore how the politics of ethnic purity and communal solidarity, whether among dominant or subject groups, was crucially articulated through gendered and bodily codes of marriage, sexual contact, and pure birth/lineage as makers and breakers of those solidarities and purities. 'Pure-bred', as opposed to 'mixed race', *meti*, hybrid, or 'half-caste', were embodied gender-sexual categories which could be crucial both for those designating potential victims for forced migration, and for those surviving, resisting, and commemorating migration.

The ability to impose such designations may involve power relations within particular groups but, as shown by studies in this

---

[10] See the essays by Pandey, Copland, and O'Rourke in this volume.

volume and elsewhere, also involved institutions, of which many of the most important have been associated with state power. In many instances the enhanced organizing, legislating, and controlling or coercive powers of states, from at least the eighteenth century, have successfully encroached on other holders and forms of power, and been manifest in the removal of peoples. The early strength of English or Spanish monarchies had, of course, been manifest in the expulsion of Jews or Moors from their domains before that period. However, newer practices and structures of legal rationality, colonial governance, and organized and trained administrative or military efficiency marked the ability of European states and their colonial agents to control, and where chosen, remove, peoples in newly effective ways. The use of law courts, bureaucracies, treaty and border diplomacy, and organized policing or state violence reshaped older practices. 'Modern' warfare among competing 'nation-states', and colonial expansion or confrontation, were particular sites for the making of forced migrations involving state power in Europe as well as in the Americas, the Indian subcontinent, and Australasia. Intersecting discourses of 'people', 'state', and 'nation', and of 'reform' or 'progress' in the nineteenth and twentieth centuries, informed the practices and institutions of politics and government, as ruling groups responded variously to new demands for representation or modernization, and new relationships to economic activity or social policy.

This is the context for a discussion of the roles of state institutions and projects in forced migrations. The aim here is not to reiterate statements about the importance of state power, nor to propose an elaborate typology of the different roles it might play, but rather to relate the relative pervasiveness of that power to its *diversity and conditionality*. Thus states have participated in, or initiated, removals of peoples as part of varied, and even incompatible, projects. Rather than being assertions of state power *tout court*, state involvement in such removals developed within complex circumstances and for multiple purposes. While state power takes its own particular forms, and has its own underpinning rationales, it has never operated in isolation from other elements in society, as is evident from the studies of forced migrations presented here. From colonial governments' dealings with settler demands or indigenous societies, to the role of international and popular

Comparing Forced Removals

pressures, as well as material constraints and opportunities in the formation of state policies, a whole matrix of agendas and interests would be in play in any particular removal/expulsion/relocation.

The role of state power in forced migration can be understood and described in terms of the goals or projects to which they might contribute. Thus removals of Indigenous peoples in the Americas and Australia played constitutive roles in the formation of new societies and polities. We can compare the role of the removals in the formation of a federal, racialized, United States, founded on expanding European settlement and entrepreneurship, the development of Canada as a dominion of the British empire grounded in the management of its competing European and Indigenous communities, and the evolution of post-colonial Mexico. In Canada and the United States the high profile of state institutions (treaties, federal legislation, government departments) and official rhetorics of progress, legality, and protection entwined with the politics and economics of European settlement to shape 'Indian' removals. Contests over state boundaries and territorial claims in the USA, and over international boundaries and responsibilities between the USA and Mexico or Canada, linked the containment and removal of Indigenous peoples to the formation and maintenance of these states. This can be compared with the different institutional and political uncertainties and limitations of the post-colonial Mexican state, which was concerned with control of Native labour as well as land issues, and adopted a piecemeal rather than 'national' approach to Indigenous peoples.[11]

In the Australian case the management and removal of Aboriginal peoples involved several levels of state power, from colonial administration in different Australian settlements, and the development of 'dominion'/all-Australian government by the twentieth century, to interventions and decisions by the British government. Examination of the former reveals interactions between white settlers and governmental institutions, with police *and* local vigilantes attacking Aboriginal houses during removal processes in 1870s Queensland, or administrative tolerance of settler-led expulsions in 1830s Victoria/New South Wales.[12] The

---

[11] See essays by Garrison and Haake in this volume.

[12] See Attwood, 'Land and Removal', and the essay by Copland in this volume.

colonial legal and administrative framework tying governance in the colonies to institutions and politics in Britain can be analysed as a set of contending military and legal practices (wars, treaty-making, policing, law-making and enforcement) and rhetorics of colonial authority and responsibility for settlers, local administrators, and Indigenous communities. It can also be situated in a British colonial network of institutions, administrative careers, print cultures, and political campaigns, moving across imperial space to shape the practice and language of forced migration. That network was materially and discursively sustained by the transmission of imperial aims and practices as imperial personnel moved between the United Kingdom and its various colonies, by the movement of ideas and issues across the empire by press or missionaries, and the activism of bodies such as the Aboriginal Protection Society in the colonies and the UK.[13] The material enactment and cultural framework of forced migrations was shaped by these various agencies interacting with the cultures and actions of Indigenous societies.

It should also be noted that removals in colonial settings shaped forms and techniques of governmental and social control (recording/registering, use of health and law and order policies) to be used subsequently or simultaneously in the United Kingdom, contributing to the mutual constitution of state power in colonies and metropolis.[14] Discourses of imperial missions to civilize, create order, and protect imperial subjects through state power, sometimes by relocating them against their will, crossed imperial spaces in both directions, and built notions of 'Britishness' in relation to those of savagery or backwardness. Since, as suggested above, they emerged from specific accommodations among different locations and interests, they were never monolithic. Repudiation of a 'treaty-based' approach to Indigenous peoples in Australia, like its use in South Africa, Canada, or New Zealand,

---

[13] See as examples Zoë Laidlaw, *Colonial Connections 1815–45: Patronage, the Information Revolution and Colonial Government* (Manchester, 2005); David Lambert and Alan Lester (eds.), *Colonial Lives across the British Empire: Imperial Careering in the Long Nineteenth Century* (Cambridge, 2006); Richard Phillips, *Sex, Politics and Empire: A Postcolonial Geography* (Manchester, 2006).

[14] See Catherine Hall and Sonya O. Rose (eds.), *At Home with the Empire: Metropolitan Culture and the Imperial World* (Cambridge, 2006); Laidlaw, *Colonial Connections*; John Marriott, *The Other Empire: Metropolis, India and Progress in the Colonial Imagination* (Manchester, 2003); Diane Robinson-Dunn, *The Harem, Slavery, and British Imperial Culture: Anglo-Muslim Relations in the Late Nineteenth Century* (Manchester, 2006).

Comparing Forced Removals

expressed the particularities which coexisted in the common colonial framework, as did the varying partnerships, or lack of them, between government and missionaries, or employers, in the policing and management of removed peoples.[15]

State power underpinned forced migration in other settings too. The functioning of the Sokoto regime during the nineteenth century was bound up with its involvement in trading enslaved West Africans across and beyond Africa, whose material role was augmented by the ideological legitimization of advancing the Islamic ideals underpinning the Sokoto Caliphate. Enforced exchanges /'cleansings' of populations in the context of the Balkan Wars of 1911–13, the settlement of European boundaries in 1918 and 1945, or Partitions in the Indian subcontinent and Israel/Palestine in 1947–8, asserted claims to 'national' sovereignty and identity through the invention of supposedly 'ethnically' homogeneous polities within particular state boundaries. The removal of millions of European settlers from Indonesia, French Indo-China, and Africa in the 1950s and 1960s was likewise a feature in the construction of new post-colonial states.[16] These twentieth-century processes were the legacy of a century and a half of nationalistic thought and politics linking state-building to ethnic and racialized (rather than civic and constitutional) images of 'nation' and 'people' which had shaped the politics of dominant states and ruling groups, and of dissident, subaltern, or anti-colonial movements.

One question which might give shape to what might otherwise seem like a shapeless list of examples concerns the relationship of forced removals to particular crises in state power. Thus the 'crises of decolonization' faced in different ways by the French, British, and Dutch states after 1945 might be invoked as the context for the forced migrations of various Indian communities, Palestinians, European settlers in Algeria and Indonesia, or Alexandrian Greeks and Iraqi Jews. Similarly the crises of the Ottoman and Hapsburg empires could be linked to the removals and destruction of Armenian, Greek, European Muslim, and Macedonian communities. Here the difficulties of multi-communal and colonial state projects confronted the emergent nationalistic and anti-colonial projects of subject groups. In a different

---

[15] See Copland in this volume.
[16] See the essays by Lovejoy, Smith, Brandes, and Bloxham in this volume.

428 JOANNA DE GROOT

way, forced removals in the Soviet Union were likewise an expression of the clashing aspirations of the emergent Russian Bolshevik regime and those of the 'ethnic' groupings of the former tsarist empire.

A third element in contests over state power and the removal of peoples in the twentieth century was the emergence of international regulation through treaty or supranational bodies. The workings of the Versailles and Potsdam settlements, and the role of the United Nations, or groups of great powers as managers of conflict, brought the use of international sanctions for, or against, forced migrations into play, whether through plebiscites, refugee agencies, or the drawing and policing of boundaries. On the one hand this established forums where the aggrieved might make their case or seek to mitigate the effects of expulsion; on the other it provided arenas where major powers could present and justify self-interested policies as those of the 'international community', legitimized by international institutions and agreements. State power to coerce movements of people has been both undermined and reinforced on the terrain of international institutions, where notions of universal human rights, of ethnic cleansing, and of genocide are contested, and where the interests of particular states or groups of states shape or constrain the power of international bodies.

However, an exclusive focus on the power of material interests or state institutions and their agents would obscure one of the most significant forms of power which has shaped modern forced migrations, the power to conceive, legitimize, and narrate them. The last section of this discussion considers the power of language, image, and discourse through which removals of people have been enacted and understood both at the time and subsequently. From the terms on passports, treaties, birth certificates, and censuses, to the effects of press propaganda, missionary writing, or learned discourses on identity, ethnicity, and nationality, *words* have had a constitutive role in making removals meaningful and acceptable. They have likewise been used by those at the receiving end of forced migration to construct *their* narratives and interpretations of such events and experiences, whether in moments of contemporary resistance, or of retrospective commemoration and condemnation. The unequal power relations implicit in forced migration have been articulated in contests over naming and

Comparing Forced Removals

interpretation, such as over the 'genocide'/'resettlement'/ 'Holocaust'/'final solution'/'Shoah' undergone by European Jews in the 1940s, or its Armenian analogue of 1915. The politics of terminology and narrative have been central to the perpetrators and victims of removal at the time, to their successors seeking to commemorate, justify, or redress past injuries, and to historians constructing their accounts and analyses.

Agents and supporters of forced migrations have drawn on a number of discourses to narrate and normalize them. Terms such as 'exchange', 'transfer', 'relocation', or, indeed, 'removal', are concepts which objectify and neutralize the violent irrationality and coercive power involved in these events through the cool language of reasonable policy-making, or use of purely spatial terminology. Legal, administrative, and physical force imposed on unwilling persons and communities was made invisible by this discourse of practicality or 'common sense'. This discourse is often reinforced by a discourse of 'scientific' social policy, as when the removal of Australian Aborigines was linked to health concerns and 'laziness' or unreliability, Indian Dalits were labelled 'criminal', or Native Americans were termed 'unproductive'.[17] The language describing the treatment of those being forced to relocate is comparable to, and overlapped with, disciplinary languages used by those seeking to define and manage the poor, the sick, or other subordinated groups. As such, it connected forced removals to the broader discourses of efficient administration, market forces, and rational policy-making, which have been dominant, if far from universal, elements in 'modern' thought. This suggests that historians might usefully consider the cultural as well as the practical dynamics of removals as processes which helped to *constitute* 'modernity', rather than as its effects.

Beyond their practical efficacy, discourses of protection, progress, and benevolence added idealistic and ethical elements to accounts justifying forced migration. The rhetoric of virtuous concern to safeguard vulnerable 'natives' from predatory incomers, or to provide them with opportunities to improve their lot by learning how to be better farmers, workers, or citizens, gave moral as well as practical force to narratives of the benefits of removal. They can be traced from American debates on the relocation of

---

[17] See Copland, Garrison, and Pandey in this volume.

the Cherokees to arguments mounted in Australia, South Africa, and New Zealand about the beneficial effects of dispossession and forced migration on 'natives'. The zeal of Bolshevik cadres to control Cossacks through deportation and resettlement expressed not only the authoritarian aspirations of the Soviet state to control all its subjects, but idealistic, 'millenarian' visions of the materially productive, rationally organized, and socially progressive society which they planned to create. Similarly, the enslavement of Africans was also presented by slave-traders and plantation owners as an opportunity to introduce them to more 'civilized' patterns of life and work.[18]

The rhetoric of protection and of improvement was intimately linked to languages of civilization and savagery, or progress and backwardness, which developed through Enlightenment narratives of the 'stages' of human social and political development, and related debates about the nature of human diversity. The former generated materialist and 'improving' discourses, which categorized particular peoples or practices as 'primitive', but saw possibilities for their 'advancement' under the right social, moral, or governmental influences. The latter racialized discussions of difference by emphasis on inherent and inherited human characteristics or potential, rather than doing so by the role of circumstance and social learning in shaping them.[19] In the context of forced removals the depiction of Native 'difference' could deploy elements of both discourses. They distanced Indigenous peoples from white settlers as inherently Other, exoticizing and infantilizing them as having fragile, outmoded, if romantically appealing, modes of life, needing protection from hostile influences, or controlling guidance towards improvement and progress. They racialized them by emphasizing the insuperability of their inherent laziness, violence, immorality, or stupidity and their unsuitability for equal treatment as subjects, employees, or legal persons. Depictions of Maori or Native American warriors and

[18] See O'Rourke and Garrison in this volume.

[19] See e.g. Ivan Hannaford, *Race: The History of an Idea in the West* (Washington, 1996), chs. 7–9; Roxann Wheeler, *The Complexion of Race: Categories of Difference in Eighteenth-Century British Culture* (Philadelphia, 2000); Sankar Muthu, *Enlightenment against Empire* (Princeton, 2003); Tzvetan Todorov, *On Human Diversity: Nationalism, Racism, and Exoticism in French Thought*, trans. Catherine Porter (Cambridge, Mass., 1993); N. Hudson, 'From "Nation" to "Race": The Origin of Racial Classification in Eighteenth-Century Thought', *Eighteenth Century Studies* (1996); Peter Hulme and Ludmilla Jordanova (eds.), *The Enlightenment and its Shadows* (London, 1990).

chiefs, of heathen Natives needing Christianization in Australia or North America, of the oppression of Native women, or of resistance to 'proper' forms of work, education, or family life, only to be overcome by state or settler intervention, used some or all of these discourses.

The role of ethnic and racial discourses in forced migrations within colonial settings is paralleled in European settings. The constitution of ethnic diversity as an 'obstacle' or 'problem' for the formation or protection of nation-states is, of course, a discursive and epistemological move rather than recording empirical or material reality, although those who deployed those moves could mobilize the kind of popular attacks on ethnically defined groups which then created such realities. The ideology involved making ideological links between concepts of inherent or inherited common attributes (customs, personal qualities, religion, history, language) which define a 'people', and demands for specific polit-ical entities (nation-states) as the best, or only, guarantors of the interests, identity, and well-being of such 'peoples'. Ethnic defini-tions of nationality *produced* ethnic diversity as a 'problem' and led to associated demands for 'ethnic purity', and hence for removals of peoples. Sudeten Germans, Greek residents in western Anatolia, Armenians under Ottoman rule, or Poles in East Prussia all became targets of such demands, as propaganda and unofficial violence fuelled the case for state or international intervention and management of forced migrations.

Paradoxically, demands for forced removal to achieve ethnic purity might also be on the agendas of both dominant *and* subordi-nate groups. If Nazi policy deployed the discourse of 'ethnic Germans' against subordinate Poles or Czechs, as Ottoman/ Young Turk regimes moved against Armenians and Greeks, anti-Hapsburg and anti-Ottoman nationalists in central and south-eastern Europe deployed similar discourses against dominant states. The forced removals of the 1920s and 1940s in Europe were not only material responses to the crises of old and new states, as already noted, but signified the power of ethnic nationalisms in various public discourses outside the frame of state institutions to influence the decisions and rhetoric of those institutions. So, too, the politics of anti-colonial nationalism in India drew on, and were undercut by, communal-religious politics, so that the Partition of 1947 was shaped both by the struggle to end colonial rule, and by the contest over different versions (multi-community? communal-religious?) of the post-colonial nation/state and the associated forced migrations. Pandey's account of the Dalit experiences of that Partition shows how the distinctive story of these ex-Untouchable groups was submerged and concealed within the dominant discourses of Hindu or Muslim communalized nationalism, just as Dalits who wanted to stay in Pakistan actually had to convert and rename themselves as Muslims. Discourses of homogeneity and purity with associated medical/coercive notions of 'cleansing' shaped the politics of national emancipation or renewal in Israel, central Europe, or India as well as the politics of 'national' defence and control in Nazi Germany, Soviet Russia, or Anatolia under Young Turk rule.

As with languages of ethnic identity, so languages linking peoples to the land were contested between those enforcing migration and those coerced into it. The cultural power of associating land rights, land use, or simply residence on particular areas of land, with the identity and interests of settlers, tribes, nations, or communities, is a theme in many of the episodes of removal discussed in this book. In parts of North America and in Australia contrasts between the forms of land 'ownership', land 'use', or land 'rights' practised by Indigenous peoples and those imported by incoming European settlers and governments shaped discourses of Native 'backwardness', or denial of legal identity and rights which legitimized dispossession and expulsion.[20] While material questions of competition between settlers and Indigenous peoples for access to land for their specific purposes (hunting, gathering, or cyclical cultivation as opposed to sheep-rearing and commercial agriculture) were core issues, so too were the *cultural and political meanings* of access to, and presence on, the land. The paradoxes to which associations of land and identity might give rise can be glimpsed in the assertion by former European settlers in Algeria, relocated to France after 1962, that France was their *patrie* but not their *pays*.[21] The conflicting aims of the Mexican government and the Yaquis, of Jews and Arabs in Palestine/Israel, or white Australian settlers and Aboriginal groups, like those of Muslim, Hindu, and Dalit landlords and cultivators in India, involved questions of material

[20] See the essays by Garrison, Haake, and Copland in this volume.
[21] See Smith's contribution in this volume.

Comparing Forced Removals

interest, even survival, but also associations between use of and rights to land and the viability and identity of the community/group/tribe/nation. These associations might connect such identities with sacred places and rituals, with forms of social and productive activity on the land, or with histories of continuous presence on ancestral territories. In any of these discourses, forced removal would be recounted by those removed, and descendants as narratives of collective cultural as well as material dispossession and rupture.

The cultural politics of forced removal is very much a politics of memory/commemoration as well as of narratives made at the time of removal. Just as the Delaware, Cherokee, or Cree contested the label of 'tribe' at the time of removal, opposing it with their own uses of the term 'nation', so their later narratives maintain the concept of nation as part of the recent resistance and revival of Native American/First Nation self-assertion by Indigenous North American people. Similarly, Armenian narratives of expulsion and massacre as genocide, like Yaqui narratives of dispossession and removal as enslavement, have been used by succeeding generations as well as by those directly involved. Such narratives challenge other accounts which minimize forced migrations, or present them as painful necessities, as unintended if regrettable errors, as the product of harsh uncontrollable circumstances, or as too complex and messy to allow judgement. This is relevant to narratives of the relocation of *pieds noirs* from Algeria, of ethnic Germans from post-1945 Poland and Czechoslovakia, or of Palestinian Arabs in the *naqba*, as well as to colonial situations.[22] The Indian Partition narrative of expulsions and killings defined in communal-religious terms does not recount the experience of Dalits, just as the official narrative of the formation of the Turkish state cannot yet incorporate the expulsion and massacres of the Armenians. The assertion of Aboriginal dispossession still struggles for inclusion in the national narrative of Australia, just as Aboriginal claims for entitlement to land remain unmet. While the moral meanings of accounts of forced migration constructed by historians will be discussed in their own right, it is worth noting at this point that the contests over narrative considered here, and elsewhere in this

---

[22] See the essays by Smith, Brandes, Talbot, Suny, and Morris in this volume.

volume,[23] do suggest that the culture of politics and the politics of culture should be read through the lens of unequal power relations.

This cultural politics has its own forms of violence, associated with silencing, renaming, and forgetting, and with the obscuring or falsification of records, and the retelling or denial of narratives which exclude persons or events. Lüdtke notes that the concept of 'forced migration' found in the *Encyclopaedia Britannica* of the 1970s was absent in editions produced a decade earlier. The contests referred to in the previous paragraph are in part about denial, and the resistance to denial, of particular experiences, whether the creation of lost generations of Aboriginal Australians, the experiences of Dalits during Partition in India, or of displaced persons in Europe in 1945. Memories and evidence of sexual assaults on women during forced removals might be suppressed by both perpetrators and sufferers in denial of the sex/gender aspects of removal in favour of communal, rights-based, or ethnic narratives. Denials of genocides in the Armenian, Jewish, or Gypsy cases are, of course, well known. The ethno-nationalist rhetoric of pure descent and 'eternal' characteristics entails its own denial of the real complexity of populations and their identities. The overturning of court or treaty provisions with Indigenous peoples in Australasia or North America denied both the agreements or decisions involved, and the legal personhood or status of the parties deprived by such acts of repudiation.

The passions associated with nationalist aspirations, with memories of violence and dispossession, or with projects of state-building and moral or material improvement, as well as the contests between and among dominant and subaltern voices, are all present in the oral or written records on which historians' narratives rely. Palestinian and Israeli contests over the events and experiences of 1948 or 1967, like those of Armenians and Turks over those in Anatolia in 1915, are especially dramatic instances of 'passion in the archives' which can also be traced in the memoirs of displaced colonial settlers, of repatriated ethnic Germans, or of Native Americans relocated to cities.[24] It is significant that these

[23] See the essays by Lüdtke, Suny, and Pandey in this volume.

[24] See the essays by Suny, Morris, and Fixico in this volume; I have also learned from and drawn on narratives by a German woman, originally from East Prussia, recounting girlhood experiences there during the Second World War and in the Berlin area in 1945–6, told to me personally.

Comparing Forced Removals

are not only contests over scholarly evidence and interpretation, but battles for identity, and for public judgement or acknowledgement of the coercive, exploitative use of force on subaltern groups. These latter struggles link disputed versions of the past to the politics of responsibility and reparation. Aboriginal peoples in Australia offer narratives of lost generations and unrecognized rights as corrections to dominant accounts which also sustain claims for due recognition of the unjust character of those experiences, for open acknowledgement of the responsibility of colonial settlers, officials, or missionaries, and for restorative compensation. Discourses of African enslavement, of the *naqba* in Israel/Palestine, or of the 'Trail of Tears' in North America have similarly been linked to political movements for redress, public recognition, and recompense for the descendants or survivors of victimized groups, paralleling the role of Jewish Holocaust narratives.

As with other accounts of the past (narratives of colonial expansion, of people-trafficking, or of the Inquisition) this raises questions about the moral status or intent of the scholarly contributions and evaluations made by historians. Their investigation and presentation of the complex influences and variety of actors at work in the making of any particular forced migration can enrich understanding of the range and impact of different power relations in that particular context within a narrative of dominance and coercion. Thus an analysis of Native American removals in Georgia, Alabama, and Mississippi in the 1830s in terms of the intersecting interests and ideas of landowners, state governments, judges, and public propaganda converging on the Native peoples in those areas allows a fuller appreciation of the varied and combined power of law, administration, ideology, and material concerns in those removals. Similarly, the dispossession and destruction of Armenians in Anatolia in the early twentieth century is more fully comprehended within a rich narrative of Young Turk policy, the shifting activities of Armenian political movements, the impact of war with Russia, communal rivalries, and the ideologies of nationalism and reform espoused by various players. These instances can be compared with the importance of considering the interplay of Aboriginal, settler, governmental, and colonial roles in Australian forced migrations, of communal-religious nationalisms, local conflicts of interest, and imperial decline in the Partition of India, or of victorious allies, emergent

436   JOANNA DE GROOT

'national' governments, and local or international politics in the removals in post-1945 Europe.[25]

Whether seen in terms of different roles (perpetrator, bystander, critic, supporter, victim, observer), or of different forms and levels of involvement (local, national, international, legal, ideological, communal, propagandistic, materially self-interested), a grasp of the shifting, interactive, and many layered features of forced migration can be illuminating. Gerlach's critique of over-monolithic accounts of genocide for neglecting multiple levels of involvement and motivation, for over-privileging state apparatuses and top-down power, and for homogenizing the victims, could be extended to studies of other forms of forced migration.[26] However, this trend towards favouring complexity also poses significant ethical and conceptual questions for those who produce narratives of complexity and multiple causation. In exploring and explaining the involvement of many players with complex motives, do such narratives dissipate the attribution of responsibility to any of those players, thus disempowering survivors, or descendants, of those who suffered forced removal and seek acknowledgement that there were, indeed, responsible perpetrators? In fragmenting stories of forced migration by emphasizing the varied and inconsistent details of a complex process, do historical accounts become denials that the term can be used at all, denials with *political* as well as academic force and significance? In using neutral and dispassionate terms and rational analysis, do these accounts suppress or misrepresent the elements of suffering, coercion, emotion, violence, and trauma which, as the source material indicates, were present in episodes of forced removal? Legitimate critiques of modern 'blame cultures', where people refuse to accept that it is not always reasonable or justifiable to place responsibility for painful events on particular individuals or organizations, should not be used to support arguments that it is *never* appropriate to use notions of responsibility or of perpetrators in cases of forced migrations. At least it should be recognized that in removing those terms from their discourse, historians make choices with serious political and ethical implications.

Just as the importance of the politics of forced removals to

---

[25] See the essays in this volume by Garrison, Suny, Copland, Pandey, and Brandes.
[26] See Gerlach's essay in this volume.

Comparing Forced Removals

both sufferers and perpetrators needs to be incorporated in the analyses of historians, so too does the interplay between practical, rational, and psychological, emotive, or ethical aspects of removal. Rather than opposing rational explanation to the strong feelings, personal experiences, or moral responsibilities involved in these episodes, it is more helpful for historians to explore their interactions and interdependence. The commitment of colonial officials to the rhetoric of order, legality, or modernization, of Indigenous peoples and poor cultivators to the relationship of land and identity, or of political leaders and electorates to ideals of nation and state, can be understood as powerful emotional attachments as well as rationales, or intellectual arguments. The passion behind ideologies of 'cleansing' an area of ethnic Others, of the rule of law, of 'primitive' peoples as 'obstacles' to civilizing and productive progress, or of revenge for past wrongs, was a significant element in the political climate which made forced removals practicable and acceptable. Poles, Czechs, and Germans, or Arabs and Israelis in the 1940s, like white Georgians and Australians in the 1830s, or Turks, Greeks, Slavs, and Armenians in the early twentieth century, acted out their experiences of such conjoined passions and practicalities. For those who suffered forced migration the passions and practicalities associated with material loss, bodily and psychological violence, and the fracturing of established communities similarly shaped experience, memory, and the search for redress and recognition. The making of legal, moral, reforming, nationalistic, governmental, commemorative, or resistance narratives by both perpetrators and sufferers met both psychic and practical needs as each group has sought survival, justification, and meaning after removal.

By weaving these different but connected threads into their narratives, historians can begin to do justice, both ethically and intellectually, to the multiple meanings of any particular forced migration. Appreciation of the many-stranded but nonetheless patterned character of specific instances also gives the comparative discussion of forced migration three important perspectives. It allows historians to combine the examination of material and cultural elements in these events and experiences rather than expending unhelpful effort on counterposing them. It does not privilege physical and material experience over discursive and narrative approaches to histories of removals, or vice versa. It enables historians to explore and explain the workings of power relations in forced migrations while recognizing the agency of subordinate as well as dominant groups or institutions. Such perspectives are helpful for comparative study as well as for the exploration of specific instances, moving away from the creation of models or taxonomies to the comparative evaluation of themes and problems They support qualitative reflections which can illumine the painful and important subject of people removals, respecting both the claims of scholarly analysis and the human significance of forced migration.

Notes on Contributors

RICHARD BESSEL has been Professor of Twentieth-Century History at the University of York since 1998. His publications include *Germany after the First World War* (1993); ed., *Fascist Italy and Nazi Germany: Comparisons and Contrasts* (1996); ed. with Ralph Jessen, *Die Grenzen der Diktatur: Staat und Gesellschaft in der DDR* (1996); ed. with Dirk Schumann, *Life after Death: Approaches to a Social and Cultural History of Europe during the 1940s and 1950s* (2003); *Nazism and War* (2004); and *Germany 1945: From War to Peace* (2009).

DONALD BLOXHAM is Professor of Modern History at Edinburgh University. He is author of *Genocide on Trial: War Crimes Trials and the Formation of Holocaust History and Memory* (2001); *The Great Game of Genocide: Imperialism, Nationalism, and the Destruction of the Ottoman Armenians* (2005); and with Tony Kushner, *The Holocaust: Critical Historical Approaches* (2005). With Mark Levene he is editor of the forthcoming Oxford University Press monograph series Zones of Violence.

DETLEF BRANDES holds a Ph.D. from the University of Munich and did his *Habilitation* in Berlin in East European and Russian history. He has held research and teaching positions at several institutes in Germany, including the Free University of Berlin. He was guest professor at the European University Institute in Florence (Italy), Columbia (New York), Stanford, and State University in Sapporo (Japan). Since 1991 he has been Professor of the Culture and History of the Germans in Eastern Europe at the Heinrich Heine University in Düsseldorf. He holds an honorary doctorate from the Charles University in Prague (2001) and the Palacky medal from the Czech Academy of Science (2003). His publications include *Die Tschechen unter deutschem Protektorat 1939–1945*, 2 vols. (1969, 1975); *Großbritannien und seine osteuropäischen Alliierten 1939–1943: Die Regierungen Polens, der Tschechoslowakei und Jugoslawiens im Londoner Exil vom Kriegsausbruch bis zur Konferenz von Teheran* (1988); and *Der Weg zur Vertreibung*

440   **Notes on Contributors**

1938–1945: Entscheidungen und Pläne zum 'Transfer' der Deutschen aus der Tschechoslowakei und aus Polen (1939–1945) (2001, 2005)—all also published in Czech. He is also the author of *Von den Zaren adoptiert: Die deutschen Kolonisten und die Balkansiedler in Neurussland und Bessarabien 1751–1914* (1993); with Andrej Savin, *Die Sibiriendeutschen im Sowjetstaat 1919–1938* (2001); and *Die Sudetendeutschen im Krisenjahr 1938* (2008).

MARK COPLAND received his Ph.D. from Griffith University. This research involved a project arising out of the recommendations from the *Bringing Them Home* report. One of these recommendations was that archival institutions make efforts to link Indigenous Australians with records relating to the breaking apart of their families. As part of this recommendation a project was initiated by Griffith University and the Queensland Government Department of Aboriginal and Torres Strait Islander Policy (DATSIP). Copland was the principal researcher for this project and used materials from the Queensland State Archives to produce a computer database. This database makes it possible for descendants of Aboriginal people to identify where their ancestors were removed from, removed to, and to locate archival references to these removals. He has since become involved in the creation of Tiwi College on Melville Island.

DONALD L. FIXICO is Distinguished Foundation Professor of History at Arizona State University and a Native scholar who is Shawnee, Sac & Fox, Muscogee Creek, and Seminole. He has been on faculty and a visiting professor at ten universities, including teaching at the John F. Kennedy Center of the Free University in Berlin (Germany) and at the University of Nottingham (UK). He has worked on more than a dozen documentaries about American Indians and has published ten books which include *Treaties with American Indians* (2007); an edited three-volume encyclopedia; and *American Indians in a Modern World* (2008).

TIM ALAN GARRISON is the Director of Native American Studies and Professor of History at Portland State University. He is the author of *The Legal Ideology of Removal: The Southern Judiciary and the Sovereignty of Native American Nations* (2002) and several articles and

Notes on Contributors

441

chapters on the history of the Indian Removal Crisis. He is also co-editor with Paul Finkelman of *The Encyclopedia of United States Indian Policy and Law* (2008).

CHRISTIAN GERLACH is Professor of History at the University of Berne, Switzerland. His major publications include *Krieg, Ernährung, Völkermord: Forschungen zur deutschen Vernichtungspolitik im Zweiten Weltkrieg* (1998); *Kalkulierte Morde: Die deutsche Wirtschafts- und Vernichtungspolitik in Weißrußland 1941–1944* (1999); and with Götz Aly, *Das letzte Kapitel: Realpolitik, Ideologie und der Mord an den ungarischen Juden 1944/45* (2002).

JOANNA DE GROOT works at the University of York, where she is a member of the History Department, the Centre for Women's Studies, and the Centre for Eighteenth-Century Studies. Her main scholarly interests are in the history of Iran since 1800, gender and women's histories since 1700, and colonial and imperial histories in the same period. Her publications include *Religion, Culture and Politics in Iran: From the Qajars to Khomeini* (2007) and numerous articles in journals and edited collections. Dr de Groot is currently working on a book-length study of the impact of colonial connections on history-writing in the United Kingdom since the middle of the eighteenth century.

CLAUDIA B. HAAKE is a Lecturer in History at La Trobe University, Melbourne, and was formerly a lecturer at the University of York. She is the author of *The State, Removal and Indigenous Peoples in the United States and Mexico, 1620–2000* (2007), and of a number of articles on Native American history in the United States and in Mexico. Her current research focuses on land and land loss during the era of Indian removal in the United States.

PAUL E. LOVEJOY is Distinguished Research Professor, Department of History, York University (Ontario, Canada), and holds the Canada Research Chair in African Diaspora History. He is a Fellow of the Royal Society of Canada, Director of the Harriet Tubman Institute for Research on the Global Migrations of African Peoples, and holds an appointment as Research Professor, Wilberforce Institute for the Study of Slavery and

442   **Notes on Contributors**

Emancipation (WISE), University of Hull. His recent publications include *Slavery, Commerce and Production in West Africa: Slave Society in the Sokoto Caliphate* (2005); and *Ecology and Ethnography of Muslim Trade in West Africa* (2005).

ALF LÜDTKE is Professor of Historical Anthropology at the University of Erfurt. Recent publications include co-ed. with Karin Hartewig, *Die DDR im Bild: Der Gebrauch der Fotografie im anderen deutschen Staat* (2004); co-ed. with Stefan Mörchen, *Die Farbe weiß*, a special issue of the journal *WerkstattGeschichte* (2005); co-ed. with Philipp Müller, *Medien-Aneignungen*, a special issue of the journal *Sozialwissenschaftliche Informationen SOWI* (2005); co-ed. with Bernd Weisbrod and contributor to *The No Man's Land of Violence: Extreme Wars in the Twentieth Century* (2006); and co-ed. with Michael Wildt and contributor to *Staats-Gewalt: Ausnahmezustand und Sicherheitsregimes* (2008).

BENNY MORRIS is Professor of History in the Middle East Studies Department at Ben-Gurion University (Israel). His publications include *Righteous Victims: A History of the Zionist–Arab Conflict, 1881–1999* (1999); *The Birth of the Palestinian Refugee Problem Revisited* (2004); and *1948: A History of the First Arab–Israeli War* (2008).

SHANE O'ROURKE is a Senior Lecturer in Russian History at the University of York. He is the author of *Warriors and Peasants: The Don Cossacks in Late Imperial Russia* (1999/2000); and *The Cossacks* (2007). He has also published numerous articles on the Cossacks and related topics.

GYANENDRA PANDEY is Arts and Sciences Distinguished Professor of History at Emory University, Atlanta. Earlier, he taught at the University of Delhi and at the Johns Hopkins University (Baltimore). A founding member of the Subaltern Studies project, he is the author of *The Construction of Communalism in Colonial North India* (1990); *Remembering Partition: Violence, Nationalism and History in India* (2001); *Routine Violence: Nations, Fragments, Histories* (2006); and numerous other single-authored and collaborative books and articles. He is currently working towards a history of the making of the Dalit and the African-American middle classes.

Notes on Contributors

ANDREA SMITH is Associate Professor of Anthropology at Lafayette College. Her research interests include collective memory, silencing, and place; settler societies; French colonialism in North Africa; and identity politics in contemporary Europe. Along with several articles, her publications include an edited volume, *Europe's Invisible Migrants* (2003); and *Colonial Memory and Postcolonial Europe: Maltese Settlers in Algeria and France* (2006). She has commenced a new project on settler ideologies and commemorative practices in the US south-west.

RONALD GRIGOR SUNY is the Charles Tilly Collegiate Professor of Social and Political History at the University of Michigan and Emeritus Professor of Political Science and History at the University of Chicago. He is the author of *The Revenge of the Past: Nationalism, Revolution, and the Collapse of the Soviet Union* (1993); *Looking Toward Ararat: Armenia in Modern History* (1993); *The Making of the Georgian Nation* (1988); and *The Soviet Experiment: Russia, the USSR, and the Successor States* (1998). He is currently involved in a project bringing Armenian and Turkish scholars together in a dialogue on the genocide of 1915.

IAN TALBOT is Director of the Centre for Imperial and Post-Colonial Studies at the University of Southampton. He was awarded his BA and Ph.D. at the University of London and his MA at the University of Oxford. Professor Talbot has researched and written extensively on the creation of Pakistan and its political history. He has published numerous articles in such journals as *Modern Asian Studies, Asian Survey*, and *Journal of Imperial and Commonwealth History*. In addition he has written five monographs and edited four volumes. His recent publications include *Pakistan: A Modern History* (2005); *Divided Cities: Partition and its Aftermath in Lahore and Amritsar 1947–1957* (2006); and *The Deadly Embrace: Religion, Politics and Violence in India and Pakistan 1947–2002* (2007). He is a series editor for Oxford University Press and a founding editor of the *Journal for Punjab Studies*. Talbot has been a consultant for numerous documentaries on south Asia and has advised both the Bertelsmann Transformation Index and Oxford Analytica on issues of democratization and risk assessment in Pakistan.

Index

Abdul Hamid II 212, 214, 226, 228, 230–1, 233, 244, 246
Abdullah (King of Jordan) 350
Aberdeen, South Dakota 113
Aboriginal people (Australia) 9, 11, 131–47, 423, 425, 429, 432–5
Aboriginal Protection and Restriction of the Sale of Opium Act 136
Aboriginal Protection Society 426
Abourezk, James 126
Adana killings 213, 241
Adamawa 160
Adair, Judge 75
Adler, H. G. 13
adultery 59
Advisory Committee on Problems on Foreign Relations (US) 291
Aegean 184
Aflong 338
Africa 28, 149, 159, 161, 164, 417, 427
  see also: North Africa, West Africa
Africans 23, 374, 379, 383, 412, 417, 421, 430
African Americans 120, 126
agriculture 90, 101
Ahdut Ha'avoda 351
Ahmad, Feroz 241
Ahmad, Shahid 324
Aidin province 204
Akhundov, Mirza Fethali 234
Akcura, Yusuf 237
Alabama 36, 435
Albania 241
Albanians 182, 216
Albuquerque 123
Alcatraz, takeover by native Americans 122–3
alcoholism 115, 391
  see also: drunkenness
Alexander II 180, 259
Algeria 5, 8, 362, 366, 368, 372, 375, 379, 384–5, 387, 390, 392, 395–400, 402–3, 405, 409–10, 417, 419, 432–3

European settlers in 427
Algerian Independence 400, 402, 409
Algerian War 372, 380, 387, 397, 400, 402, 410
Algerian *harkis* 412
Algerians 367, 384, 395, 409
alienation, of Native Americans in cities 114
al-Jaylani, Muhammad 157
al-Kanemi, Sheik 163
Allies, in First World War 244
Allies, in Second World War 203, 292
Allotment Act 81
Alvarado, Salvador 100n.
Ambala 332, 336
Ambagaon (interception camp) 335
Ambedkar, Bhimrai Ramji 313
Ambonese Islands 410
American Board of Commissioners for Foreign Missions 40
American Indians, *see:* Native Americans
American Indian Center (Chicago) 118
American Indian Movement (AIM) 115–16, 122–4
van Amersfoorst, Hans 410
Amman 356
Amritsar 323, 327, 343
Anadarko, Oklahoma 113
Anatolia 7–8, 181, 183–4, 197, 204–6, 209, 212–14, 217–18, 220–22, 226–27, 229–30, 233–34, 236–7, 239, 241, 243, 246, 249, 251, 296, 420, 432, 434–5
  Greek residents in, 431
Anglo-Americans 126
Angola 362, 366, 377, 381, 383, 387, 389–90, 403
Angolans 367, 372
Ankara 206
Ansari, Sarah 325
Anschluss 282–3
anti-guerilla warfare, anti-partisan warfare 361, 364–66, 370–1, 374–5, 384–5, 390

Index

antisemitism 27n., 182, 186, 188, 191–4, 350, 355, 418
Apostolic Church 223, 228
Aquash, Anna Mae 123
Arab Higher Committee (AHC) 354, 357
Arab League 350, 356
Arab Liberation Army 350
Arab Women's Organization 357
Arabic 160
Arabs 7, 182, 214, 218, 238–9, 349–57, 432–3, 437
see also: Palestinians
Arendt, Hannah 14
Arizona 112–13, 117
Arkansas 56–7, 60
Arkansas River 64
Arkhangelsk 264
Armenia 183, 204–5, 222, 245
Armenian Apostolic Church, *see:* Apostolic Church
Armenian genocide 168, 187, 209–10, 216–18, 220, 232, 251–2, 421
Armenian Patriarchate 227, 242, 246
Armenian Question 230, 242
Armenian Revolutionary Federation 240
see also: Dashnaktsutium
Armenians 7, 9, 11, 21, 168, 172, 179–82, 184, 187–8, 201, 205, 209–13, 216–33, 235–53, 267, 420–1, 427, 429, 431, 433–5, 437
emigrants to America and Europe, 227
army
Australian 141
French 379
Mexican 91
Ottoman Turkish 212, 242–3, 420
Polish 289, 294
Royal Dutch Indian Army 410
Russian 199
Soviet 185, 365
US 39, 44, 59, 123, 387
see also: soldiers
Arora caste 324
Arya Samaj reform movement 305n.
'Aryanization' 192
Asian Americans 120
Assam 329, 333, 335, 341–2, 346

Assinovskaia 272–3, 275
Assyrians 182
Assyrian Christians in Iraq, massacred by Muslims 355
Athens, Tennessee 42
Atlantic Monthly 110
Atlantic world 4
Attwood, Bain 419
Aurukun mission 134
Auschwitz 198, 293
Australia 9, 131–5, 141, 408–9, 412, 418–20, 423, 425–6, 430–2, 435
Australians 423, 437
see also: Aboriginal people
Austria 281–2
Austro-Hungarian Empire, Austria-Hungary 19, 172, 179, 241
Awami League 340
Axis 192
Aymara 376
Azerbaijan 183
Azeris 184
al-Azhar University 356–7

Bābā, Ahmad 161
Badr-i-Alam 306
Bagmari (Calcutta) 334
Bahawalpur 301
Bailey, Garrick 121
Baku 234, 263
Balkan Wars 169, 180–1, 199, 241, 250, 427
Balkans 175, 178–9, 198, 202, 225, 227
Baltic Germans 286
Baltic states 174, 283, 285, 296
Bangladesh 346, 363
Banks, Dennis 115, 123
bar culture 115
Barars 317
Barisal district 334, 341
Batavia District, Queensland 144
Batavia goldfields 144
Batavia river 134, 145, 147
Battle of Britain 284
Baurias 317
Bay area 120, 124, 127
Bazigars 302–4
Bear, Leonard 110
Bear, Little Light 110
Behala 336

Index

Belarus 362, 364–5, 367, 374–5
Belgium 396
Belgians 399, 412
Beliaghatu (Calcutta) 334
Bell, John A. 63–4
Bellecourt, Clyde 115, 123
Bellecourt, Vernon 116
Bello, Muhammad 157–8, 163
Belorussians 190, 390
  see also: Belarus
Benai, Eddie Benton 115
Beneš, Edvard 184, 202, 284–8, 292–3, 295
Bengal 298n., 300, 322, 329–34, 337, 344–7
  see also: East Bengal, West Bengal
Ben-Gurion, David 184, 351
Berlin 18, 226, 356, 434n.
Bernard, Claude 235
Bessarabia 283
Bethlehem 353
Bettiah 341
Bey, Bedri 243
Bey, Halil 248
Bey, Huseynizade Ali 234
Bey, Reşid 250
Bhangalis 317
Bhargava, Gopichand 315–16
Bhasin, Kamala 321
Bhave, Vinoba 314, 316n.
Big Bear, Tony 110
Big Bear, Martha 110
Bihar 323–4, 330, 341, 346
Bijoygarh 336
Bikaner State (India) 314
Billings, Montana 113
Bismarck, Otto von 173
Bitlis 229, 246
Black Hills 129
Black Sea 242, 262
Blackfeet 115
Bleakley, J. W. 145
Bloxham, Donald 4
Blunt, James 86n., 88
Blythe's Ferry, Tennessee 65
Bober, see: Lausitzer Neisse
Boeing 112
Boer War 369
Bogra district (East Bengal) 338
Bohemia 281–3, 291

Bolshevik ideology 258, 278
Bolshevik regime 174, 420, 422, 428, 430
Bolshevik revolution 188
Bolshevism 205, 273, 276
Bombay 323
Bongaon 335
Bonaparte, Napoleon 172
Borno 153, 161, 163
Bosnia 178
Bosnia-Herzegovina 241
Bosnians 178, 182, 193
Boston 40–1, 69, 115
Boudinot, Elias 38, 63
Bourdieu, Pierre 384
Brainerd 40–1, 49, 60, 62–3
Brandes, Detlev 5, 8
Brass, Paul 321
Brazil 23, 156, 162
Breitman, Leighman 123
Brenning, Erick 131–2
Breslau 290
Brisbane 135
Britain 30, 151, 159, 178, 183, 198, 203, 205–6, 227, 244, 282, 284, 290, 353, 362, 378, 395–6, 398, 408–9, 412, 426–7
British
  abandon resettlement of the Orang Asli 373
  acquiesce to Oder–Neisse line 291
  advocacy of population transfer during Second World War 184
  ambassador in Constantipole 201
  ambassador in Prague 287
  Armenians make overtures to 226
  at Yalta and Potsdam 290
  attacks on Ottoman Empire 221, 243
  backed Greek forces 205
  expeditionary force in Causasus 183
  coerced by Arabs in Palestine 352
  colonial governments in North America 37
  concentration camps in South Africa 369
  consuls in eastern Anatolia 230
  curtail Jewish immigration to Palestine 353
  departures from India, Kenya, and Rhodesia/Zimbabwe 399

448 **Index**

British (*cont.*):
  endorse the emergence of an Arab-
    majority state in Palestine 353
  experience of the two world wars 170
  imperial designs on Anatolia 205
  in Caucasus 262
  in Kenya 374–8
  in Malaya 366, 380–2, 386–7
  leave India, Kenya, and
    Rhodesia/Zimbabwe 399
  policy towards Czechoslovakia 287
  policy towards nationality questions
    in east-central Europe 285
  regional aspirations in the Balkans
    204
  seek to prevent Jewish immigration
    into Palestine 355
  settler colonies in Australasia 419
  support for Ottoman Empire 177
British Commonwealth 408
British Empire 386, 392, 408, 412, 425
British government 286, 290–2, 386,
  425
British Immigration Act (1971) 409
British India, *see*: India
British Mandate (Palestine) 352–3
British Nationality Act (1948) 408–9
British nationalities policy 285, 408
British Overseas Airways Corporation
  326
British Proclamation of 1767 81
Britishness 408, 426
Brno 293
Brother Vail (missionary) 54
Browning, Christopher 14n., 197
Brubaker, Rogers 179
Buchner 235
Buffalo, John 88n.
Bulgaria 182, 184, 191–2, 196, 201, 241
Bulgarians, Bulgs 178, 192, 216, 243,
  377
Bureau of Indian Affairs (BIA) 102n.,
  108–12, 121
Burkino Faso 151
Burnett, John G. 48n., 49n.
Burswan district 344
Burundi 412
Bushyhead, Isaac 57, 67
Butalia, Urvashi 299, 321
Butler, Elizur 63

Butrick, Daniel Sabin 36, 39–78
  anger at policy towards Cherokees
    72–3
  becomes ill 68
  missionary work after the march 77
  opposes removal of the Cherokees 41

Cabora Bassa dam 383
Cadogan, Alexander 287
Cairns, Queensland 132, 139
Cairo 356
Calcutta 326–36, 339–40, 343, 346–7
  Great Calcutta Killings of August
    1946 323, 330–1
Calhoun, Tennessee 52, 64
California 111–13, 117, 123, 396
California State University at
  Northridge 117
Calvinists 410
Campbellpore 311
Cambodia (Kampuchea) 21, 362, 366,
  390
Cameroon 151
Canada 409, 412, 419, 425–6
Canal Colony (West Punjab) 340
Candy's Creek 50
Canning, Kathleen 422
Carpatho-Ukraine 187
Cape Girardeau, Missouri 65, 74
Cape Verde 379
Cape York, Queensland 131, 141–2,
  144, 147
Caribbean 23
Carmel 40
Carter, Jimmy 122
Cassville, Georgia 47
castration 154
Catholics (Armenian) 223
Caucasian Buro of the Bolshevik Party,
  see: Kavbiuro
Caucasians 365
Caucasus 169, 173, 175, 178, 181, 197,
  201, 209, 211, 218, 220, 227, 237,
  242–3, 246, 255, 258–9, 261–2, 267,
  270–1, 276, 296
Central African Republic 151
Central Asia 173–4, 181
Central Intelligence Agency (CIA) 378
Chaldeans 223
Champaran district (Bihar) 341

Index

449

Charabarti, Prafulla 343
Charleston, Tennessee 62
Chattanooga 40, 42
Chechens 8–9, 175, 187–8, 256, 259–61, 264, 266, 270–1, 276–7, 295
Cherkas 227
see also: Circassians
Cherokees, Cherokee Nation 7–9, 35–78, 82, 84–8, 99, 100n., 101–2, 106, 109, 417, 421, 430, 433
  adopt a written constitution in 1827 37
  attempts to convert 40
  enter into agreement with Delawares 84–5, 99, 101n.
  recover after the march 77
Cherokee Agency 42, 52, 64
Cherokee Christians 69
Cherokee–Delaware Agreement 84–6, 88
Cherokee Lighthorse Guard 66
Cherokee Nation v. *Georgia* 38
Cherokee National Council 37–8
Cherokee Phoenix 63
Chetniks 193
Chicago 109, 112, 118, 120, 124, 128
Chief Protector of Aborigines (CPA), *see*: Department of Native Affairs
Chichawatni Sub Tehsil 303
children
  Aboriginal
    removed from their families 134–6, 146
    removed for education 142
    removed by police 144
    taken to England 135
  abducted during Indian Partition 301
  Armenian, forced to leave their homes 209
  born into slavery 154, 160
  of concubines 156
  Cherokee
    born on forced march 47, 70
    die in stockade 52
    die on forced march 68–9, 76
    herded together 44
    removed from families 48–9
    separated from parents 43n.
    sent by boat to Indian Territory 55

Cossack
  deported by Bolsheviks 264
  die in Piatigorsk district 270
  killed by Whites in Russian Civil War 262
  interned by Japanese in Dutch East Indies 400
  native American, removed from parents 126
  targeted for removal in West Africa, 154
Chin Peng 389
China 362, 370, 382, 418
Chinese
  deported by tsarist regime 181
  ethnic Chinese in Thailand 377
  in East Timor 379
  immigrants into the United States 108
  in Malaya, 374, 376, 378, 380, 387
  persecution of in Indonesia 379
Chinese Home Guards (Malaya) 378
Chippewa 115, 127
Chittagong 338
Chittagong Mail (train) 334
Choctaws 88
Christian missionaries, *see:* missionaries
Christian Science Monitor 109
Christianization 431
Christianity 222, 245, 303, 309
Christians 189, 201, 204, 214, 225–6, 228, 230, 232, 240, 243–4, 251–2
  Assyrian Christians in Iraq, massacred by Muslims 355
  attrocities against 178
  Dalit converts 303–4
  in India 299n., 301n., 303, 308
  refugees after First World War 180
  see also: Orthodox Christians
Chuhras (of Lahore) 299
Chumtara 311
Church of England 141
Churchill, Winston 184, 202, 290
Cilento, Raphael 139–40
Cilicia 227, 241
Circassians 201, 214, 227, 250
circumcision 299n.
citizenship 10, 85, 108, 400, 414
  Algerian and French 402
  Dutch 411

Index

citizenship (*cont.*):
French 409
granted to 'returnees' 404–5
Greek 399n.
Indonesian 408
for minority communities in India
and Pakistan 335
Ottoman 218
Palestinian 354
status of Jews 191
Civil and Military Gazette 334
Civil Patrols (Guatamala) 391
Civil War, American 86, 89
Civil war, Greek 170
Civil war, Russian 174, 183, 199, 260–2,
278
Civil war, Spanish 170
class
differences, among Armenians 222,
326, 328
distinctions, in India 305
'enemies', Soviet assault on 174
class-based internationalism 196
Cleveland 112
Coen, Queensland 131, 133, 144–5
Cold War 169
collective farms 365
Colorado 112
commemoration 10
commercial agriculture 90
Commissioner of Indian Affairs 85–6
Committee of Union and Progress
(CUP) 181–2, 196, 209, 213,
217–18, 238–41, 243–4, 252–3
Commonwealth Health Department
139
Communication Protection Villages
(China) 370
Communism 167, 295
Communist Party of India 337
Communists 171, 373–4, 376
in Czechslovakia 288
in Greece 377, 391
in Malaya 386
insurgents in Thailand 377, 379
forces in Vietnam 387
concentration camps 16, 27, 176, 284,
293, 369
concubines 154, 156, 158
Congo 367, 377, 412

Congress (US) 38–9, 108, 114
Congress of the Peoples of the East 263
conscription, *see:* draft
Constantinople 201, 232
see also: Istanbul
consumption (disease) 52
Cookstown, Queensland 132
Cooper, Frederick 418
Cooperstown Academy 40
Copland, Mark 9
Copts 223
Cossacks 8–9, 262, 269, 274, 430
fighting for Germans during Second
World War 365
fighting for Soviet armies 274
see also: Don Cossaks, Terek Cossacks
cotton agriculture 36
Council of Energy Resource Tribes 129
Council of Ministers, Soviet 273
counselling centres, for native
Americans 114
Cree 433
Cretans 180
Crete 241
Crimea 175, 234
Crimean Tartars 175–6, 295
Crimean War 179, 201, 258
'criminal tribes' (Dalit castes) 317–18
Criminal Tribes Act (India) 318
Croats 180, 183, 188, 193
Crossen 289
Cuba 81n., 156, 162–3, 369
Cubillas, Alberto 93n.
Cunene dam (Angola) 383
Curzon line 285, 290
Czech Communists 171
Czechs 185, 281–3, 285, 293, 419, 431,
437
Czechoslovak government 281, 285,
288, 291–3
Czechoslovakia 8, 17–18, 183, 187, 191,
201–2, 281–8, 291–6, 433

Dacca 334, 338–40
Dadrian, Vahakn 215
Dalits (untouchables) 297–319, 328,
341, 346, 421, 429, 432–4
allotted land in East Punjab 315
migrate from West to East Punjab
300, 302, 308

Index

451

refugees from East Bengal, resettled
in West Begal 341
rename themselves as Muslims in
Pakistan 432
Dallas 112, 114, 123–4
Dalmatia 185, 295
Daly City, California 120
Dandakaranya 341
Danzig 203, 284, 289
Dardanelles 243–4, 247
Darwin, Charles 235
Darwinism, *see:* social Darwinism
Dashnaks 235, 240, 242
Dashnaktsutiun (Armenian Revolutionary
Federation) 232, 240, 242
Datta, V. N. 342
Daulatram, Jairamdas 316n.
Dawes Act, *see:* Allotment Act
Dawn (Muslim newspaper in India) 327
'dead zones' (in Belarus) 365
decolonization 4, 10, 379, 392, 397,
403–7, 411–14, 419, 427
de Gaulle, Charles 167, 410
de Groot, Joanna 11
Delhi 298–301, 306, 308, 310–11,
323–4, 327–8, 343–4
Dehli Cloth Mills 307n.
Deloria, Vine 79
Delaware river 82
Delawares 7, 79–90, 98–9, 100n.,
101–2, 105–6, 433
enter into agreement with Cherokees
84–6, 99, 101n.
denunciation, of Yaquis 92
Denver 111–12, 123, 128
Department of Aboriginal and Torres
Strait Islander Policy, Queensland
(DATSIP) 134
Department of the Interior (US) 102n.
Department of Native Affairs (Australia)
136–7, 142, 144
Department of Relief and
Rehabilitation (India) 300
Dera Ghazi Khan 304
Dergachev, M. V. 266, 272
de-Stalinization 175
Detroit 109
dialects 20
'diaspora peoples' 174
Diarbekir 250

Diaz, Porfirio 91
Diaz government 90, 98n., 103
Dinanagar (Batala) 299
displaced persons 434
Dobruja 192
Dominions 409
Don, fighting in 269
Don Cossacks 174, 268
Donbass 264
draft 240
Dreyfus, Alfred 193
drunkenness 46–7, 59–61, 65–6, 71, 110,
114, 116
Dutch 10, 401, 405, 407–8
migrate to USA and Australia 408
Dutch Indies 399–402, 405, 410
Dutch state 427
see also: Netherlands
dysentery 45, 52

East African Asians 398
East Bengal 324, 326–31, 333–41,
343–5, 347
East Germany 17
East Pakistan, *see:* East Bengal
East Prussia 282, 284, 286, 288–9, 292,
431, 434n.
East Punjab 300–2, 308–9, 311, 313–16,
325, 331, 337, 341–3
Hindu and Sikh refugees in 340
East Punjab Liaison Agency 302–3
East Timor 363, 366–8, 372–3, 379,
390, 392
'eastern crisis' of 1875–8 178–9
Eastern Neisse 290
see also: Glatzer Neisse
eastern Silesia, *see:* Upper Silesia
Easy, Jacob 88n.
Eden, Anthony 285–7, 290, 292
Egypt 350
Eichmann, Adolf 14
Einsatzgruppen 197
Eisenhower, Dwight 111, 113
Ekadzhiev 261
El Salvador 363, 368, 385, 388, 391
El Salvadoreans 367
Eltis, David 4
Embu 377
Emmons, Glenn 111
enclosure (in Britain) 159

Index

Encyclopaedia Britannica 16, 434
England 24
Enlightenment 430
enslavement, *see:* slaves, slavery
Entente 196, 201, 221, 243–4
Ermolovskaia 263
Erzeroum 246
Ethiopia, 363, 366
Ethiopians 223
'ethnic cleansing' 4–5, 19–20, 167–9,
    175, 179, 181, 185–6, 194, 252–3,
    296, 323, 330–1, 361, 380, 428, 437
'ethnic Germans' 17, 170–2, 180, 184–7,
    189, 190, 201–2, 206, 283, 407, 420,
    431, 433–4
European Advisory Commission 285
Evian accords 402

Fall Leaf (Captain) 85, 86n.
famine
    in Greece 375n.
    in USSR 173–4
famine relief, in Northern China 370
Faridabad 336
Faridkot 331n.
Faringdon, Missouri 65
Farmington, Missouri 75
fascism 167
fascists, Italian 185
Fayetteville, Arkansas 65
Federal Government (US), *see:* United
    States government
Federal Government (Mexico), *see:*
    Mexican government
Fel'marshal'skaia 261
filariasis 139
Filipinos 369, 375
'final solution' 168–9, 429
    see also: Holocaust
Finns 174, 185
First Congress of the Ottoman
    Opposition 236–7
First World War 143–4, 169, 173, 177,
    179–81, 183, 190, 192, 196, 198–202,
    206, 209, 220, 227, 239, 241–2, 251,
    257, 292, 405
Five Civilized Tribes 89
Fixico, Donald 5
Fiume 185
forced labour 176, 264, 283

Foreign Office (British) 203, 284,
    286–7, 290–2
Foreign Office (German) 283
Foreign Press and Research Office
    (German) 283
Foreign Research and Press Office
    (British) 286, 291
Foreman, Stephen 59
Fort Gibson 59, 76
Fort Worth 114
'fortified villages' (in Belarus) 365
Foucault, Michel 19
Four Corners 111, 129
France 20–1, 151, 191, 193–4, 198, 244,
    282, 284, 362, 367, 384, 387–8,
    390, 396–7, 400, 402–3, 406, 409,
    410–12, 432
    integration of *pied noirs* in 404
    alienation of *pied noirs* in 405
Franco-Prussian War 198
Franja Transversal del Norte 383
Fraser Island 135
French 225, 366, 374, 385
    arrive in France from Algeria 405
    depart from Algeria 402
    forces in Algeria 387
    in Vietnam 379
French empire 409
French government/state 285, 427
French, Patrick 323
French Revolution 177, 189, 218
'French Union' 409
Front National (France) 390
Fulah people 379
Fulani 158, 160
Fulfukde (language) 160
Furedi, Frank 378

Galata 224
Galilee 353
Gallipoli 197, 243–4
Gallup, New Mexico 113, 127
gambling 59, 61
Gandhi, Mohandas Karamchand 298,
    307–8, 311, 332
    martyrdom of 314
Ganganagar colony 314
Ganges–Brahmaputra Delta 331
Garrison, Tim 8
Gasprinskii, Ismail 234

Index

453

Genç Kalemler 237
General Government (Poland) 283
General Zionist Party 351
Generalplan Ost 189
genocide 4–5, 13–14, 19, 21, 77, 167–9,
181, 186–7, 194, 197, 204–5, 209–11,
213–14, 216–17, 219–21, 230, 244,
251–3, 268, 331, 371, 376, 421,
428–9, 433–6
Genocide Convention (United Nations
Convention on the Prevention and
Punishment of Genocide, 1948)
21n., 168, 174
Georgia (Caucasus) 273, 277
Georgia (US) 36–8, 41, 45, 71, 417–18,
421, 435
Georgians (US) 437
Georgian Muslims 182
Gerlach, Christian 8, 436
German Democratic Republic 389
German military forces 364–5, 375
Germans 5, 8, 16–18, 28, 170–2, 174,
180, 186, 190, 202, 244, 252, 281,
284–5, 293–5, 377, 407, 437
Baltic 286
as colonizers in Poland 190
deported by tsarist regime 181
ethnic Germans in USSR 175
evacuated by Nazi authorities 291
expelled from east-central Europe,
170–1, 184–8, 190, 202, 206, 288–9,
291–6
expelled from Yugoslavia 295
minority in Czechoslovakia 183, 201,
284, 287–8
minority in Poland, 190, 201, 281
migration of to Germany after
1918 281
see also: 'ethnic Germans', 'Volga
Germans'
Germany 16–17, 19–20, 151, 168, 172,
177, 186, 190–4, 196, 198, 201–4,
206, 281–2, 285–7, 290, 362, 399
Soviet Occupation Zone of 295
US Occupation Zone of 295
see also: Nazi regime
Glatzer Neisse 289
Gobirawa 157
Gokalp, Ziya 237, 239
Golconda, Illinois 65

Goolpara (Calcutta) 334
Gottwald, Klement 294–5
Graham, Nancy 133
Great Arab Revolt 352–3, 355
Greco-Turkish Exchange 206
Greco-Turkish War of 1921–2 169, 184,
198–9, 205
Greece 170, 184, 204, 219, 241, 362,
366–8, 374–5, 377–8, 381, 388,
391–2, 399
Greek civil war 170, 366, 372–3, 377, 391
Greek counter-insurgency forces 388
Greeks 184–5, 200, 203–6, 216, 218,
224–5, 227, 231n., 238, 244, 296,
367, 375n., 377, 379, 419–20, 427,
431, 437
Green Revolution 341
Griffith University 134
Grosfuguel, Ramón 411
Gross, Jan T. 191
Grozny 262, 276
Guatamala 8, 363, 366–8, 372–3,
376–7, 380n., 381–3, 385, 387–9,
391–2
Guatamala City 367, 382
Guatamalans 367
Guendji 229
guerrilla warfare, by Yaquis 90
guilt 10
Guinea Bissau 363, 366, 379, 403
Guineabés 367
Gujranwala 304, 309, 310
Gujrat 303, 309–10
Guntersville, Alabama 42
Gunter's Landing, Alabama 42
Gwari 160
'Gypsies' 13, 182, 434

Haake, Claudia 5, 9
Haganah 357
Haikey, Jack 121
Hailakandi 335
Hall, Gus 115
Hamid, Abdul 235
Hamidian massacres 213
Hamidian regime 241
Hamidiye 212, 230
Hamilton, Tommy 133
Hanioglu, Şukru 235
Hansen, Anders 321

454 Index

Hapsburg Empire 177, 180, 199, 427
  see also: Austro-Hungarian Empire
Hapsburgs 172, 419, 431
Harijans, see: Dalits
harkis 390, 398, 410–12
Harris, Ben 54
Hashomer Hatza'ir 351
hatred 18, 220, 252, 284
Hausa 160, 162
Haweis 62
Hayden, Robert M. 186
Hebron 352
Hegel, Georg Wilhelm Friedrich 195
Hellenistic Empire 418
Hempel/Nagel model 15
Henlein, Konrad 281–2
Herzegovina 178
Herzl, Theodor 350
Hesse 19
Heydrich, Reinhard 283–4, 286
Hicks, George 70–1
Hightower 40
Hilberg, Raul 13–4
Hindu temples, desecration of 334
Hinduism 311
Hindus 297–8, 300, 303, 305–11, 319,
    324–5, 432
  as victims of violence 299, 332, 334
  driven by Muslims from East Bengal
    331
  elite in West Punjab 346
  in Delhi 324, 344
  influx into West Bengal 329–30, 335
  left in East Bengal after Partition 333
  migrate from West to East Punjab
    300, 312, 324, 333
  nationalism, in India 432
  properties taken over by Muslims in
    Dacca 340
  take over proerties of Muslims in
    West Bengal 346
  refugees from East Bengal 343
  refugees in West Bengal 339
  vacate land in Pakistan 340
Hinton, Alexander 20–2
Hitler, Adolf 13, 186, 188, 191, 202, 281,
    286, 293, 296
Hmong 377–90, 398
Hnchaks, Hnchak party 240, 242
Hoerder, Dirk 4, 412–13

Höss, Rudolf 293
Holocaust 13, 14, 149, 186, 188–89, 199,
    353, 356–7, 429, 435
Hooghly river 336
Hopi 111, 117
Horsman, Reginald 104
Horthy, Miklos 187
House Concurrent Resolution 108
Hu-DeHart 93
Hughenden, Queensland 135
Huk rebellion 388
human rights 428
Humann, Hans 248
Humayan's Tomb (refugee camp) 323
Hungarian Communists 171
Hungarians, see: Magyars
Hungary 187, 191–2, 291, 295–6
Husain, Intizar 345n.
al-Husseini, Haj Muhammad Amin
    354–6
  makes overtures to Nazi regime
    355–6
Hutus 188
Hyderabad 326

Ilisu dam 383
Ilinden Uprising 199
Illinois 70–1
Ilznskaia 261
Ilorin 161–2
'imagined community' 10
immigrants, European into United
    States 108
'immorality', among Aboriginal people
    139, 143, 430
Imperial Ottoman Bank 231
imperialism 27n., 171, 187, 197, 218,
    225, 413
Independence (of India and Pakistan)
    306, 318, 321, 323, 327, 339, 346–7
India 7, 184, 297, 300, 303, 305–6, 309,
    319, 321–2, 324–6, 328, 333, 337,
    347, 398, 412, 418, 422, 431–2
  British leave 399
  Government of 336, 342
Indian Constitution 313
Indian Employment Assistance
    programme 114
Indian Health Service (US) 121
Indian middle class 125

Index

455

Indian Military Evacuation
Organization 332
agrees Joint Evacuation Plan with
Pakistan Military Evacuation
Organization 332
Indian National Airways 327
Indian Partition, see: Partition of India
Indian Patrol 116
Indian Removal Act 37–8, 79–80, 82,
88, 107
Indian Territory 36, 38–9, 51, 55, 56n.,
59–60, 62, 65, 77, 82, 84, 87–8, 101,
128
Indian Vocational Training Act 114
Indiana 82
Indies Dutch 10, 401, 405, 407–8, 413
Indo-China 387, 398, 427
Indo-China War 388
Indonesia, 363, 367, 400–1, 410–11, 419,
427
European settlers in 427
Indonesian Independence 400–1, 408,
410
Indonesians 379
industrial revolution (Britain) 177
influenza 52
Ingush 8–9, 175, 187, 256, 259–61, 266,
269–70, 272, 276–7, 295
Innisfail, Queensland 139
Inquisition 435
Interdepartmental Committee on the
Transfer of German Populations
(British) 292
Internal Security Police (in North China,
under Japanese occuption) 370
internationalism 196
internment camps
for Cherokees 43n.
intestinal diseases 57
Iran 418
Iraq 206, 350, 355, 374, 427
Irish 409
Irish, immigrants into the United States
108, 115
Islam 157, 163, 214–16, 234, 238n., 245,
250, 309–10, 356, 379, 427
conversion to 310
see also: Muslims
Islamist insurgents in Algeria 390–1
Islamic law 161–3

Islamization 379
Israel 7, 185, 349–51, 427, 432, 435
Provisional Government of 357
Israel Defence Forces (IDF) 357
Israelis 419, 434, 437
Istanbul 178, 209, 212, 224–5, 229, 241,
243, 245
see also: Constantinople
Istria 185, 286, 295
Italy 19, 192, 241, 282, 291, 296, 396, 405
Italians 185
leave Libya 399
leave Yugoslavia 295
Izábal, Rafael 91, 94–5
Izmir 204

Jaksch, Wenzel 287, 295
Jackson, Andrew 37–8, 80
Jain, A. P. 343
Jaipur State 317
Jalpaiguri 334
Jama Masjid (refugee camp) 324
Japan 362, 369, 396
Japanese 141, 400
Dutch East Indies capitulate to 400
leave Asian territories after Second
World War 398
Japanese authorities in China 370
Japanese-Americans 111
Jat peasants (Punjabi) 342
Javedpur 336
Jerusalem 226, 353
Jessore 338
Jewish Agency Executive 357
Jewish immigration to Palestine 351–3
'Jewish question' 194–5
Jews 7, 13–14, 16, 18, 172, 180, 182, 188,
191–2, 194, 218, 250–1, 285, 418,
424, 429, 432
deportation of from Hungary 187
deported by tsarist regime 181
emigration of from Nazi Germany 168
in Palestine 352–7
killed in Hebron in 1929 352
in Iraq 427
murder of, genocide 186, 190–3, 197,
199, 283, 375n., 421, 434
see also: Holocaust
tsarist atrocities against 199
used as slave labour 176

456 **Index**

Jezreel Valley 351
Jhang 304
jihad 151, 153, 155–17, 162–4, 214, 356–7
Jinnah Awami League 340
Jind 331
Jones, Evan 48n., 50n.
Jonesborough 75
Jordan 350
  see also: Transjordan
Jos plateau 160
Joshi, Subhadra 308

Kabylians 378
Kaduna river 160
Kahour 311
Kalinovskaia *stanitsa* 263–4
Kalmyks 175, 295
Kamba 383
Kampuchea, *see:* Cambodia
Kano 154–5, 158, 160
Kansas 82, 85, 87
Kansas City 109
Kansas-Nebraska Act 82
Karabagh 183
Karabulakskaia 272
Karachai 175
Karachi 325–6
Karaurthala 331n.
Karelia 185
Karimgunj 335
Karindaye 157
Kars 242
Katsina 160
Kaur, Ravinder 328
Kavbiuro (Caucasian Buro of the Bolshevik Party) 262, 269–70
Kavfront 263
Kavtrudarmy 264–6
Kazakhstan 255
Kebbawa 157
Kellas, Betsy 117
Kemal, Ismail 236
Kemal, Mustafa 182, 184, 203, 205
Kemalists 215, 235
Kentucky 36, 67, 70
Kenya 3, 8, 362, 366, 368, 372, 374–6, 378, 383, 385, 392, 398, 412
  British leave 399
Kenyans 373, 375

Khakhanovskaia 261
Khan, N. M. 338
Khan, Raja Ghazanfar Ali 310–11
Khatri caste 324
Khmer Rouge 21
Khokropar 326
Khosla, G. D. 298, 311, 323
Khrimian, Mkrtich 226
Khuhro, Muhammad Ayub 325
Khulna district 341
Kirkbride, Alec 356
Kikuyu 374–8, 383
Kirov, Sergei 265, 273
Klamath Reservations 129
Kolberg 289
Kongo people 377
Korea 111
Korean War 381, 386
Koreans 296
  deported by tsarist regime 181
Kosior, Stanislav 265–6, 272–3
Kot Khalsa 318
Kuban 62
Kuch-Bandhs 317
kulaks 173
Kun, Bela 263
Kurdistan 204, 363, 366–7, 369
Kurds 182, 206, 212, 214, 218–19, 229–30, 239, 242, 244, 251, 367, 369, 380n., 383
Kurdish resistance 376, 390
Kurmitola 338
Kvirikeliia 265–6, 273

labour (of deportees) 9
Labour Party 289
Lahore 299, 304, 305n., 323, 327–8, 343–4
Lamington, Lord 135
Land Office (Polish) 292
Lajpat Nagar 301
Lao 377
Laos 378, 390
Last, Murray 157
Latvians, deported by tsarist regime 181
Laura, Queensland 132–3, 145
Lausanne Peace Treaty, Lausanne exchange 184–5, 203, 205–6
Lausiter Neisse 289

Index

Le Bon, Gustave 235
League of Nations 201
Lebanon 349
Lebanon, Missouri 65
Lenape, *see:* Delawares
Lenin, Vladimir Ilych 177, 262, 271, 273
León, Miguel 92
Lewis, Bernard 216–17
Liaquat Ali Khan 335
liberal democracy 167
liberalism 225
Libya 241, 399
Lidice 284, 293
Lincoln, Nebraska 114
Lincoln Indian Center 114
Lithuania 285
Lithuanians 181, 190
Little Rock, Arkansas 57, 64n.
Locke, Pat 127
Lockhart River Mission 144–5
Lodz 14
London 135, 288, 290, 331, 352
looting 9, 249–51, 266, 294, 325, 335
Loris-Melikov, Mikhail Tarielovich 259–60, 271
Los Angeles 110–12, 115, 117, 119–21, 123
Los Angeles Indian Center 121
Lovejoy, Paul 7
Lubkemann, Stephen 406
Lublin Committee 290, 292
Lüdtke, Alf 5, 9, 433
Lyallpur 304, 307n., 339

Maasai 3
McKernan, Michael 141
McMinnville, Tennessee 65
McNickle, d'Arcy 100
Macedonia 192, 199
Macedonians 170, 180, 185, 231n., 377, 427
Madagascar 190
Madhya Pradesh 341
Madras 223
Magaria 157
Magra 336
Magyars 295
Mahisya 336
Maiskii, Ivan 352
Makonde 376

malaria 139
malnutrition 57
Malay Chinese Association 378
Malaya 362, 366–8, 372, 374, 376, 378, 380–1, 385–7, 392
Malayans, Malays 367, 376, 379–80, 386, 389
Malayan Emergency 381, 389
Malaysia 389
Malaysian Communist Party 389
Malaysian government 389
Malinovskaia 263
Malta 405
'Manchukuo', *see:* Manchuria
Manchuria 369, 382
Mankiller, Wilma 109, 120
Mapai 351
Marines 111
Mao Tse-tung 364
Maori 423, 430
Mapoon, Queensland 132
Marion, Kentucky 65
Markel, Wade 374
Marrakesh 161
Marshall, John 38
Marshall Plan 388
Marx, Anthony 171
Maschmann, Melita 16
Massachusetts 40
Massai-Kikuyu 377
May, Dawn 143
Maya 81, 391
Maya highlands 382
Mau Mau 373, 375, 377–8, 385
Mayas 367, 376
Maytoreno, José Maria 98n.
Mazatlan 98n.
Means, Russell 111–12, 119
measles 52
Mediterranean coast 216
Mediterranean Sea 198, 202, 353, 402–3
    crossings between Algeria and France 402n.
Meenas 317
Mekhitarists 223
Memel 289
memory 10
Menominee tribe 108, 124
Menominee Reservations 129

458 **Index**

Menon, Ritu 321
mental health, of Aboriginal people 142
Meru 377
Meskhetian Turks 175–6
Mexico 5, 7, 9, 79, 81, 94, 98, 103–6,
 367, 391, 425
Mexican Americans 120, 126
Mexican government 89–91, 93–97,
 104, 422
Mexican Revolution 80, 96–7, 100–1
Mexicans 90
Meyer, Dillon S. 111
Mianwali 304
Mid-America Indian Center 114
Mikołajczyk, Stanislaw 290
Mikoian, Anastas Ivanovich 263, 270,
 273
Military Evacuation Organization
 (Punjab) 302
militias 364–6, 368–70, 380, 387, 389,
 392
 Arab militias in Palestine 350
 in Greece 381, 388
 Kikuyu militias in Kenya 378
 see also: state militias (US)
millet i-sadika, millet system, millets 211,
 215–16, 218, 222–4, 232, 234, 237,
 240, 251
millenarianism (of Bolshevism) 273, 278
Milwaukee 124
mines, mining 90, 92, 129
Ministry of Agriculture (Soviet) 268
Ministry of Conference Works (Polish)
 291
Ministry of Foreign Affairs
 (Czechoslovak) 291
 see also: Foreign Office
Minneapolis 113–15, 124
 see also: twin cities
Minneapolis Native American Center
 114
Minnesota 126
Minsk 374
Mintz, Sidney 23–4
Mirpur colony (Dacca) 339
Miskito 363n.
missionaries 40–1, 54, 59, 63, 145, 211,
 427, 435
 in India 299n.
 see also: Daniel Butrick

Mississippi 6, 435
Mississippi river 36, 65, 72, 74–5, 80,
 128–9
Missouri 66, 82
Mitchell, George 115
mixed marriages, of native Americans
 126
modernity 417–19, 424, 429
modernization 371, 384, 389, 392, 424
Mohawk iron workers 128
Moldavia 174
Molotov, Vyacheslav 189, 288
Moluccans 410–11, 413
Montana 113, 115, 126
Montenegro 178
Montgomery District 303–4
Moon, Penderel 323
Mooney, James 44n., 72
Moors 418, 424
Moravia 282–3
Moreton, Queensland 144
Morgenthau, Henry 243–9, 252
Morocco 161, 367
Morris, Benny 11
Moscow 276, 285, 288, 290
Motzkin 351
Mountain Republic 256, 260, 266–7,
 270, 272, 275–8
Mountbatten, Louis 332
Mozambique 363, 366–76, 383, 385,
 390, 403
Mughannam, Matiel 357
Muhajir League 340
Mukherjee, Shyama Prasad 333
Muladi (East Bengal) 334
Multan Division 302, 304, 318
Mumbai, see: Bombay
Munich Agreement 201, 203, 282, 286–7
murgu 150, 159
Murphy, Thomas 86n., 88
Muscogee Creek, Oklahoma 110
Mush 226
Muskogee, Oklahoma 113
Muslim regions of West Africa 149–51,
 153, 155–6, 164
Muslim society, Muslims 153–4,
 157–64, 178–9, 181, 184, 192–3, 201,
 204–6, 211–12, 214–15, 219, 223,
 227, 229–32, 241, 244, 247, 249–52,
 259, 300, 302, 310, 319, 357, 432

Index

459

Algerian 409–10
in Algeria, discussed by Pierre
  Bordieu 384
killed because of previous support of
  French rule, in Algeria 390
literacy among in Algeria 380n.
as victims of violence 178, 180, 193
  in India 298–9, 306–7, 310–11,
  323–4, 330–1, 334
as refugees in India 300, 307–8, 310,
  314
communities destroyed 427
in Assam 333–5
in Dehli 298, 306, 324
drive Hindus from East Bengal 331
refugees in East Bengal 338–9
migrants to East Bengal/Bangladesh
  346
evacuees from West Bengal 330
who remained in West Bengal 346
flee East Punjab 312–13
forced to leaves homes in Calcutta
  334
forced conversion of 310
nationalism, in India 432
in Guinea Bissau 379
kill Jews in Hebron in 1929 352
left in West Bengal after Partition
  333
massacre Assyrian Christians in Iraq
  355
participate in genocide 214
in Punjab 297
moved from West Punjab from East
  Punjab 325, 332
position of women in 158
recuited for the *Wehrmacht* 356
refugees from the Caucasus and the
  Balkans 227
refugees flood into Karachi 325
refugees in West Punjab 340
religious authorities 356
slavery in 158–62
suspicious of Dalits 303
take over properties of Hindus in
  Dacca 340
deported by tsarist regime 181
Muttahida Qaumi Movement (MQM)
  323
Muzaffargarh 304

Nadia district 329, 344, 346
NAES College, *see:* Native American
  Education Services, Inc.
Nairobi 374, 383
Namasudras 298, 299n., 300, 336
Napoleon, *see:* Bonaparte, Napoleon
Nashville, Tennessee 65, 66n., 69
(popular and) national sovereignty 3, 6,
  37–8, 41
National Liberation Front (FLN)
  (Algeria) 372, 378, 402
National Party (Poland) 289
National Socialism, *see:* Nazism
nationalism, nationalists 6, 171, 177,
  181–2, 187–8, 190, 192–4, 196, 203,
  205–7, 216–21, 223–5, 229, 231,
  235, 295, 431
anti-colonial in India 431
anti-Hapsburg 431
Turkish 217, 219, 234, 236–9, 241,
  431
nationalities policy, Soviet 175
Native Americans 5–7, 79, 81, 107–15,
  118, 120–8, 368, 395, 419–21, 423,
  429–30, 433–5
emergence of Indian middle class
  125
population increase of 128
return to reservations 117
see also: Blackfeet, Cherokees,
  Chippewa, Choctaws, Delawares,
  Hopi, Menominee, Navajo,
  Ojibwa, Oneida, Potawatomi,
  Shawnees
Native American Education Services,
  Inc. 124
Nats 317
Navajo 111, 127, 395
Navajo Reservation 129
Nawab, Rab 311
Nazi imperialism 187, 285
Nazi military tactics 364–5
Nazi population policy 189, 191
Nazi regime 168, 171, 176, 185, 187–8,
  196, 199, 355, 431–2
colludes with USSR 285
Nazi–Soviet Pact 192
Nazis 168, 187, 189–90, 193, 250
Nazism 28, 172, 189, 194, 282, 293
Nehru, Jawaharlal 307–8, 311, 327, 335

460 Index

Nehru, Rameshwari 314, 316n., 317–18
Neisse 289–90
Nesterovskaia 272
Netherlands 395, 401, 405–6, 408,
    410–11
  German occupation of 401
Nevskii, Vladimir Ivanovich 267,
    269–70, 275–6
New Commonwealth 398
New Echota 38, 42, 45
  see also: Treaty of New Echota
New Economic Policy (Malaysia) 389
New Guinea 401, 408
New Mexico 111–13
New South Wales 425
New York City 109
New York (state) 40
New Zealand 409, 412, 419, 421, 426,
    430
Newel, Harriet 49
Nicaragua 363n.
Niger 151
Nigeria 149, 151, 164
van Niekerk, Mies 410
Ningi hills 160
NKVD 277, 290
Noakhali 331–2, 334
Nolte, Ernst 167
nomads 158
North Africa 156, 162–3
North Carolina 36
North China Railway Company 370
North West Frontier Province 324
Northern Territory 143
Northridge, California 117
Nupe 160
Nuremberg trials 293
Nyanza 383

Oads 303
Oaxaca 94n.
October Revolution 257, 260, 268
  see also: Bolshevik revolution
Oder 286, 289, 290
Oder–Neisse line 291
Ohio 82, 111
Ohio river 67, 72, 74
Okara 303
Oklahoma 36, 56, 82, 88, 101, 109–14,
    123

urban Indians in 121
Oklahoma City 112, 114–15, 120
  see also: Indian Territory
Ojibwa 115, 124
Oman 363n.
Oneida 124
Operation Anvil (in Nairobi) 374
Operation Magic Flute (in Belarus)
    374
opium 137
Orang Asli 373, 376, 387
Ordzhonikidze, Sergo 255–6, 261–5,
    268–9, 271–5, 277–8
Oregon 129
Organization of Ukrainian Nationalists
    193
Orissa 341
orphans 328
Orthodox Christians 184
O'Rourke, Shane 8
Ossetians 266, 277
Ottoman Empire, Ottoman state 7, 8,
    156, 169, 172, 177–81, 189, 192,
    196–7, 199, 201, 204–5, 209–12,
    215–22, 225–8, 231–5, 237–8, 240,
    244, 248, 251–3, 259, 369, 399,
    418–19, 421, 427, 431
Ottoman Palestine 354
Ottoman–Russian War 179
Ottomanism 217, 219, 225, 228, 234,
    237–41
'Overseas France' 409
Oversight Hearing on the Welfare of
    Indian Children 126
Oyo 161–3
Oyo Empire 160

'pacification' 11
Padilla, Raquel 97
Pakpattan 303
Pakistan 184, 297–301, 306, 308–10,
    318–19, 321, 323, 326–8, 333,
    337–40, 345, 347, 432
Pakistan Military Evacuation
    Organization 325, 332
  agrees Joint Evacuation Plan with
    Indian Military Evacuation
    Organization 332
Palestine 7, 185, 349–57, 427, 432, 435
Palestine Royal Commission 353–5

Index

461

Palestinians 3, 11, 349, 352, 356–7, 419–21, 427, 433–4
see also: Arabs
Palm Island, Queensland 131, 134, 139–40, 142–6
Pandey, Gyanendra 7, 20, 323, 432
pan-Germanism 285
pan-Islamism 217, 238–9, 241–2
pan-Turanism 217, 238–9, 241–2
paranoia 181, 195
Parganas district 344
Paris 236
Paris Peace Conference 282
see also: Versailles peace settlement
Paris Peace Treaty 201
Parker, Ely S. 86n.
Partido Africano da Independência da Guiné e Cabo Verde (PAIGC), 379
Partition of India 7, 9, 20, 297–301, 305, 311, 318–19, 321–2, 324–9, 332–3, 337, 343, 345–7, 419–23, 427, 431–5
partition plan for Palestine (UN General Assembly Resolution 181) 356
Pasha, Azzam 356
Pasha, Damad Mahmud 235
Pasha, Enver 218, 241–5, 247–8, 252
Pasha, Jemal 239n., 241
Pasha, Midhat 235
Pasha, Mustafa Fazil 235
Pasha, Mustafa Reshid 235
Pasha, Talaat 241, 243–9, 252
Pasrur 299n.
Patiala 331
Patterson, Orlando 153
Paul, Kathleen, 408
Pavelić, Ante 296
Pawar, Ishwar Das 301–2, 304, 316–17
Peach, Ceri 398
Peasant Party (Poland) 289
Peel Commission, *see:* Palesine Royal Commission
Peel, Lord 353, 356
People's Administration (Palestine) 357
Persia 197, 231
Peru 8, 363, 366, 376–7, 392
Peshawar 327
Philippine Constabulary, 369, 387

Philippines 363n., 369, 375, 382, 388
Phoenix, Arizona 113, 123
phrenology 235
Piatigorsk district 269
pied noirs 5, 10, 396–7, 404–5, 410, 433
Pikesville, Tennessee 65
Pilgrim's Progress 60
Piłsudski, Jósef 289
pleurisy 52
pogroms 350
Poinsett, Joel 51
Poland 8, 15, 17–18, 174, 183, 189–91, 197, 200, 202–3, 262, 281–6, 289–96, 418, 420, 433
Poles 16, 174–5, 185, 188, 190–1, 193, 259, 281–3, 286, 290, 293, 296, 419, 431, 437
deported by Soviet regime 189, 295
deported by tsarist regime 181
expelled by Germans from western Poland 189
immigrants into the United States 108
police 18, 116, 123, 131–4, 136–7, 143, 145, 307–8, 311, 318, 334–5, 365, 375, 390, 420, 427
in Nairobi 374
involved in violence in Bengal and Punjab 347
in North China under Japanese occupation 370
Special Constabulary in Malaya 376
unreliability of in Punjab 331
in Thailand 389
police brutality
against native Americans 115–16
against Aboriginal people in Australia 131–3, 144
against Dalits in Jaipur 317
Polish Communists 171
Polish corridor 203, 289
Polish Foreign Minister 284
Polish government 284, 289–92
Polish Supreme Command 294
Polish Underground army 294
Politburo 262, 270, 276–7
'Pomaks' 192
Pomerania 289
Portugal 362, 379, 396, 400, 403–4, 406

462 Index

Portuguese 10, 366, 383
  in Guinea Bissau 379
  migration to the African colonies
    406
  retaliation for 1961 Angolan uprising
    372
  soldiers in Angola 387
Portuguese colonies 368, 377, 386–7,
  389–90, 399–400, 403, 406
  see also: Angola, Mozambique,
    Guinea Bissau
Portukalian, Mkrtich 226
Potawatomi 124
Potsdam conference 178, 185, 290–1,
  295, 428
Prague 295
Prasad, Rajendra 314–15
Pratt, John 88n.
Preston, Paul 170
priests 19
prisoners of war (POWs) 375
Progressive Party (Palestine) 351
promiscuity 139, 423
prostitutes 109
Protectorate of Bohemia and Moravia
  282–3, 286
Protestants (Armenian) 223
Prussia 281
Psychological Action and Information
  Service (French Army in Algeria)
  379
Pueblo Viejo dam 384
Puerto Ricans 411
Puerto Rico 411
Punjab 297–8, 301, 305–6, 311, 314,
  316, 319, 321–3, 325–7, 329–34,
  336, 342, 344–7, 421
  see also: East Punjab, West Punjab
Punjab Alienation of Land Act 313
Punjab Boundary Force 323
Punjab Criminal Tribes Act 317
Punjab Judicial Service 301
Purana Qila (refugee camp) 324
purges, in USSR 173

al-Qawuqji, Fawzi 350
Qidwai, Anees 300, 306, 307n., 308
Queensland 9, 131–5, 137, 139–47, 425
Queensland goverment 134

race thinking/racial discourses 3, 6, 10,
  13, 143, 182, 189, 191, 196, 250,
  407–12, 423, 431
'racial homogenization' 186
racism 113, 118, 120, 124, 176–7, 202,
  379, 392
railways 15, 18, 89–90, 92, 265, 268,
  306, 334–5, 342, 418
  attacked by Cossacks 263
  see also: North China Railway
    Company
Rajpura 336
Rajputs 303
Ram, Chaudhri Chotu 313
Ram, Jagjivan 316n.
Lord Rama 341
Ramayana 341
Ramkavar party 240
Randhawa, Mohinder Singh 312, 340,
  342
Rangpur 338
ransoming 162
rape 134, 392, 422
Rassenschande 15
Rattlesnake Springs, Tennessee 62
Rawalpindi 327
Rawalpindi Division 302
Rawalpindi Massacres of 1947 323, 331
Reagan, Ronald 122
Red Army 261–3, 269, 274, 278, 290
Reece, Jonathan 63
Reed, John 263
Reformation 20
Refugee Businessmen's Rehabilitation
  Board 344
Refugee Relief Act (US) 408
refugees 20, 149, 180, 184, 206, 227,
  299–303, 305–8, 310–16, 318,
  323–30, 332–3, 335–47, 349, 357,
  368, 373, 375–6, 404, 408–9, 412
Rehgarpura 301
religious belief 10, 20
Renamo 390
reparations 291
reservations, lack of employment in 119
retribution 10
retornados 405–6
revenge 8, 10, 18, 187, 193, 196, 246–7,
  252, 266, 293, 331, 437
Revisionist Movement (Palestine) 351

Index

Revolutionary Council of the Kavfront 263
Revolutionary War (American) 37
Rhodesia 363, 366, 368, 372, 381, 409, 412
British leave 399
ribat 155, 157
Richmond, New York 40
Ridge, John 38
Ridge, Major 38
'right of return' 357
Ringelblum archive 16
Riza, Ahmed 234, 236
Rolla, Missouri 65
Roman Empire 418
Romania 178, 180, 183, 191–2, 201
Romanian Communists 171
Romanians 192
Romanov Empire, *see:* Russia, Russian Empire
Romanovs 173
Romanovskaia 263
Roosevelt, Franklin Delano 288–9, 292
Ross, John 38-9, 59, 75
Ross, Lewis 65
Ross, Quattie 64n.
Ross's Landing, Tennessee 52, 62, 64–5
Rostov-na-Donu 275–6
Roy, Bidhan Chandra 337
Royal Dutch Indian Army 410
Ruppin, Artur 351
Russian army, *see:* Army (Russian)
Russian culture 175
Russian diplomats 211
Russia, Russian Empire 19, 172, 177, 179–80, 183, 197, 199, 202, 204, 212, 218–21, 226–8, 231, 233, 242–8, 250, 252, 258, 350–1, 435
see also: Union of Soviet Socialist Republics (USSR)
Russians, fighting for Germans during Second World War 365
Russo-Turkish War of 1877–8 226
Rwanda 20–2, 412

Sabah 363n.
Sabahaddin 237
Sadgops 336

Saint Louis 112
St Paul, Minnesota 123
see also: twin cities
Sahara 156, 161
Salt Lake City 111
Samair 338
Samoans 115
San Francisco 109, 112, 123–4, 127
see also: Bay area
San Stefano 226
Sanacja 289
Sansis 317
Santhals 346
Sarawak 363n.
Sareyan, Martiros 226
Sargodha 304
Sarikamish 197, 242–3
Sassun 229
scarification 159–60
Schermerhorn, Revd John F. 62
schools 20, 118, 120, 123, 155, 157, 224, 229, 238, 344, 365, 386, 397, 411
native Americans establish own, 124–5
Scott, George 114
Scott, Winfield 42, 43n., 45, 50–1, 59, 77
SD (*Sicherheitsdienst*) 197
Seattle 115, 120, 123
Second World War 8, 107, 111, 128, 137, 139–41, 169–71, 174–6, 184–9, 193, 200, 202–3, 295, 336, 377, 396–8, 401, 419, 434n.
Secondine, James 86n.
Secretary of the Interior (US) 86
Secret Army Organization (OAS) 402
Semelin, Jaques 22
Sen, Salil 434
Senate (US) 39
Senegal 367
Sequoyah 41
Serbia 178, 183, 199
Serbs 172, 188, 193, 216
Sèvres peace settlement 203
sexuality 328
Shango (god of thunder) 162
Shawnee, Oklahoma 112
Shawnees 100n.
Shehu Uthman dan Fodio 157
Sheikhupura 304

Index

Shoah 429
see also: 'final solution', Holocaust
Sialkot 299n.
Siberia 173–4, 296
Sikhs 297, 299–300, 302–3, 305–9, 311, 319, 325, 331, 340
    migrate from West to East Punjab 300, 312, 324, 333
    vacate land in Pakistan 340
Sikorski, Władysław 289
Silesia, *see:* Upper Silesia
Sinclair, Upton 109
Sindh 301, 310, 324–7, 345
Singapore 389
Singh, Bhagwan 331
Singh, Bir Davinder 331
Singh, Gurharpal 322
Singh, Partap 315
Sioux 118, 127
Sioux Falls, South Dakota 114
slave market 150–1, 162
slave trade 149, 151
slaves, slavery 23–4, 94, 149–55, 158–9, 161–4, 418, 420, 422, 427, 430, 435
Sleptovskaia 271
Slovakia 291
Slovaks 180, 187, 191, 285, 295
    in Czechoslovakia 183
Slovenes 180
Smith, Andrea 5
Smithsonian Institution 44n.
Smyrna 204
social Darwinism 182–3, 235
Socialist Unity Party of Germany (SED) 389
Sokoto Caliphate 7, 149–63, 421, 427
Sokoto Province, population of towns in 155n.
soldiers
    American 43–5, 49, 51, 54, 76, 141
        in the Phillipines 369
        steal Cherokees' belongings 49
    Australian 141
    Mexican, guard Yaquis captives 94
Sonepat subdivision (Punjab) 316
Songhay Empire 161
Sonora 89–90, 92–7, 98n., 99, 100, 105
South Africa 399, 412, 430
South Carolina 36
South Dakota 126

South Moluccans, *see:* Moluccans
South Sea Islanders 139
South Tyrol 186
South Tyroleans 295
South Vietnam, *see:* Vietnam
sovereignty 3, 6, 37–8, 41
Soviet Council of Ministers 261
Soviet nationalities policy, *see:* nationalities policy, Soviet
Soviet–Polish War 274
Soviet Russia, *see:* Russia, Union of Soviet Socialist Republics (USSR)
Soviet Union, *see:* Union of Soviet Socialist Republics (USSR)
Spain 19, 396, 405
Spanish 369
Spanish civil war 170
Springfield, Missouri 65
SS 18, 197, 365, 375
    see also: Waffen-SS
Stalin, Joseph 170, 174, 256, 262, 270–8, 285–6, 291–2, 296
starvation 19, 43n., 57, 81n., 145, 376, 420
    see also: famine
Stavropol' 255
State Department (US) 287, 292
state militias (US) 39, 42
states' rights (US) 8
Statesman (Calcutta) 336
Stettin 289–90
Stone's River 66
'strategic hamlets' 8, 366–7
Sudan 151, 158, 162–4
Sudeten German Party 281–2, 284–5
Sudeten Germans 281, 284–6, 288, 295, 420–1, 431
Sudetenland 183, 282, 286, 292
suicide (among Cherokees) 53
suicide, attempted by native Americans in cities 115, 126
Sunderbans district (West Bengal) 341
Suny, Ronald 7, 172
Sunzha 263
Sunzhenskaia line 259, 261n., 263, 270
Sunzhenskoe line 268, 274
Supreme Court (US) 38, 41
Swabia 19
Swimmer, Ross 101n.
Syhlet district 334, 338

Index

465

Sykes, Thomas 82n.
Syria 209, 349–50
Syriacs 182
Syrian Jacobites 223
Syrians 244

Talbot, Ian 7, 321
Talking Leaf 121
Talori 229
Taman peninsula 262
Tambov province 255
Tamils, in Malaya 380
Tangale hills 160
Tanwar, Raghuvendra 337, 343
Tanzimat reform movement 212, 218, 225, 228, 235, 239, 251
Tarskaia 269
Tartars, *see:* Crimean Tartars
Taylor, Richard 59–60, 76
Taylor detachment 65, 67, 70, 72, 76
Tehran conference 288, 292
Tehsil Khanewal 318
Tenderloin, district of San Francisco 109
Tenipara (Calcutta) 334
Tennessee 36, 42, 66, 71
Tennessee river 64–5, 68, 74
Terek Cossacks 174, 255–75, 277–9, 421–3
  expulsion of from Western Caucasus in 1863–4 258
Terek, River 272
Terek Voisko 259–60, 273
terror 189
Tete province (Mozambique) 383, 385
Thailand 363, 366, 377, 379, 388
Thantam Hmong 379
Thies, Alex 131, 133
Thomson, Donald 131n., 134
Thompson, Robert 380
Thrace 181, 204
Tiflis 268
Tihar 306–8, 310–11
Tik-i-kiski 43
Timbuktu 161
Tippera district 332, 334
Tirth, Swami Satyanand 330
Tito, Josip Broz 295
Tollygunj 336
Tórin 95
Torres, Luis 95

Torres Strait Islanders 134
torture
  of Yaquis 92
  of Algerians 403
'total war' 167, 198
totalitarianism 371
Townsville, Queensland 132
Transcaucasia 183, 205, 228, 234
Transjordan 349, 353
Transylvania 288
Traverso, Enzo 167
Treaty of Berlin 178, 236
Treaty of Hopewell 37
Treaty of Lausanne 399
Treaty of New Echota 38, 42, 57, 58n., 59, 62–3
Treaty of Versailles, *see:* Versailles peace settlement
Treaty Party (Cherokee) 38
tribal languages 124
Tripura 346
Troitskaia 272
Truman, Harry 111
Truth Commission (East Timor) 373
Tsar 242
Tsar Alexander II, *see:* Alexander II
tsarist government 170, 242, 257–8, 260, 277, 350
Tuareg 157–8
Tula 160
Tulsa, Oklahoma 112, 114
  University of 121
Tunisia 162, 367
Turan 234, 237
Turan (poem) 237
Turkey 7, 184, 192, 204–6, 213, 215–16, 225, 227, 242, 244, 247–8, 253, 363, 367–8, 376–7, 380n., 383, 392, 399, 433
  see also: Ottoman Empire
Türk Dernegi 237
Türk Ocagi 237
Türk Yurdu 237
Turkic language 234, 237–8
Turkification 213, 238–9
Turkmenistan 255
Turks 21, 178–9, 181, 184, 200, 202, 205–6, 210, 212–19, 221, 227–8, 234, 236–9, 241–2, 244–7, 250–2, 295, 383, 420, 434, 437

466   Index

Turks (cont.):
see also: Meskhetian Turks, Young
Turks
Turner, Milton S. 100n.
Tutsis 188
twin cities (Minnesota) 115–16

Ukraine 187, 190, 193, 296
Ukrainians 188, 190–1, 290, 295
Uluberia 336
Union of Soviet Socialist Republics
(USSR) 169–71, 174–5, 187–9, 192,
197, 203, 255–7, 260, 266–7, 288–9,
295–6, 364, 370n., 375, 428, 430,
432
postwar planning of 292
United Kingdom (UK) 171, 408, 426
see also: Britain, England
United Nations 291, 350, 356–7, 388, 428
UN General Assembly Resolution
181 356
UN General Assembly Resolution
194 357
United States of America 5–9, 36–8,
42, 57–8, 61, 79, 81–2, 90, 97–8,
102–7, 121, 124, 129, 156, 171, 287,
289, 292, 362, 366–7, 379, 386,
388, 390–1, 395, 408, 411, 424
forced resettlements in the Phillipines
382
United States Army, see: army
United States Government 8, 36–8,
57–8, 59n., 85–7, 102, 108, 111, 114,
123, 129, 291, 388, 419
see also: Bureau of Indian Affairs
United States Marines, see: Marines
United States military in Laos 378
United States Supreme Court, see:
Supreme Court
US Agency for International
Development (USAID) 389
'untouchables', see: Dalits
Upper Silesia 190, 203, 282, 284, 289,
291–2
Uptown (Chicago) 124
Urals 173–4
Urban Indian Center (Los Angeles) 117
Urdu-speakers 326
Ustashe 193, 296
Utah 112

Uthman dan Fodio 151
Uttar Pradesh (UP) 323–4, 326, 345–6

Van (Turkey) 209, 226, 245–8, 250
Varabedian, Nerses 226
Vaspurakan 226
venereal disease 139–42
Venezia Giulia 286
Venice 223
Venizelos, Eleftheros 204
Versailles peace settlement 173, 177,
183, 186, 189, 192, 201–2, 281, 428
'Vertreibung' 17
Vichy government 193
victimhood 17–18
Victoria (Australia) 425
Victoria Jute Mills (Calcutta) 334
Viet Minh 381
Vietnam 8, 114, 362, 366–8, 374,
379–81, 387–90, 392
Vietnam War 111, 372, 375, 387
Vietnamese 367, 417
vigilante violence 132
Virginia 36
Vladikavkaz, 255, 271, 276
'Volga Germans' 175–6, 188
Volhynian Poles 191
Vrachev, Ivan 264–7, 271, 273–4

Waffen-SS 193
Walker, John 118
War Club 68
War Cabinet (British) 286–7, 292
War Department (US) 42
War of 1812 37
War Relocation Authority (US) 111
Warjawa 160
Warren County, Tennessee 66
Warrior, Clyde 123
Warsaw 14, 191, 283, 290
Washington, DC 388
Washington State 126
Waterloo, Alabama 56
Warthegau 16
Weimar Republic 281
Weizmann, Chaim 351–2
Welles, Sumner 289
West Africa 149, 150, 153–6, 159, 427
West Bengal 324–5, 329–30, 333–7,
339–42, 344–6

Index 467

West Bengal Refugee Rehabilitation
  Committee 329
West Germany 17
West Indies 409
West Pakistan 309, 324, 343–4
West Prussia 203
West Punjab 300, 301n., 302–4, 308,
  312, 315–16, 324–5, 327, 333, 337,
  339–40, 343, 346
  Muslim refugees in 340
  rehabilitation schemes in 339
Western Australia 143
Western Interstate Commission for
  Higher Education 127
Western Neisse 290
  see also: Lausitzer Neisse
White Russians 290, 295
Whites (in Russian civil war) 262
whooping cough 52
Wichita, Kansas 112, 114
Willems, Wim 401, 408
Willstown 40
Wilson, Mary Jane 115
Wilson, Woodrow 204–5
Windsor, Massachusetts 40
Wisconsin 126
women
  abducted during Indian Partition
    301
  in American Indian Movement 116,
    123
  controlled by men 423
  demand for, in Muslim societies 158
  Hindu refugees from East Bengal
    326
  interned by Japanese in Dutch East
    Indies 400
  new roles during Indian Partition
    326
  literacy among in Algeria 380n.
  mass rapes of 392
  oppression of Native women 431
  rapes of during Indian Partition 422
  sexual assault on 422
  sexually mistreated in East Bengal
    334
  shifted to 'safe' areas in advance of
    Partition 327
  targeted for removal in West Africa
    154

as transmitters of customs, language,
  and memory 423
treatment as refugees in India 328
treatment by Sokoto slavers 422
Aboriginal
  alleged promiscuity among 423
  examined for venereal disease 141
  forced to march from home 132–3
  removed from their families 146
Armenian, forced to leave their
  homes 209
Cherokee
  attacked by whites 46–7
  die on march 68–9
  dragged from their homes 43
  herded together 44
  give birth on forced march 47
  maltreated 48, 54
  raped 54, 63
  sent by boat to Indian Territory
    55
  separated from their children 49
  succumb to disease 52
Cossack
  deported by Bolsheviks 264
  killed by Whites in Russian Civil
    War 262
  murdered in Piatigorsk district 270
Worcester v. *Georgia* 38, 41
Worcester, Samuel A. 63
World Zionist Organization 351
Wrangel, Pyotr Nikolayevich 262
Wulf, Joseph 14
Wurno 157–8

xenophobia 174, 232

Yaquis 5, 7, 79–81, 89–101, 103–6, 420,
  422, 433
  sold to employers 96
  work on plantations 97
Yaquis river 97
Yalta conference 290
Yarraden Station, Queensland 133
Yishuv (Jewish community in Palestine)
  351, 354–7
Yoeme, see: Yaquis
Yoruba 160, 162
Young Turk revolution of 1908 213,
  216, 227, 237, 240

468 Index

Young Turkey 46
Young Turks 209–21, 231–2, 234–5,
 237–45, 248, 250–3, 431–2, 435
Yucátan 89–90, 92–7, 99–100, 103, 105
Yugoslavia 3, 20–1, 168–9, 183, 193,
 286, 295–6, 375
Yugoslavian Communists 171

Zakan-Iurtskaia 263
Zambia 367

Zamfara 157
Zangwill, Israel 351
Zaria 154
Zeitoun 245
Zimbabwe, *see:* Rhodesia
Zionism 180, 350–1, 353, 356
Zionist Congress 351
Zionist movement 350–1, 355
Zionist propaganda 349
Zionists 350–2, 355